THE ESSENTIAL ARTICLES SERIES

Bernard N. Schilling
University of Rochester
General Editor

Essential Articles

for the study of Edmund Spenser

Edited by **A. C. Hamilton**
Queen's University
Ontario

Archon Books   **Hamden, Connecticut**   **1972**

Library of Congress Cataloging in Publication Data

Hamilton, A   C   comp.
    Essential articles for the study of Edmund Spenser.

    (The essential articles series)
    1. Spenser, Edmund, 1552?-1599. Faerie queene.
I. Title.
PR2358.H277   821'.3   75-179578
ISBN 0-208-01211-7

CONTENTS

CONTENTS

CONTENTS

FOREWORD

Immense resources are now available for literary study in England and America. The contributions to scholarship and criticism are so numerous and often so valuable that the student preparing himself for a career in literary teaching and study may be embarrassed, not to say overwhelmed. Yet from this mass of commentary certain titles have emerged which seem to compel attention. If one offers a seminar in one of the standard areas or periods of English literature, the syllabus will show year after year some items which cannot be omitted, some pieces every serious student should know. And with each new offering of the course, one must face the task of compiling a list of these selections for the seminar's reserve shelf, of searching out and culling the library's holdings, and reserving space for the twenty or thirty or forty volumes the list may demand. As if this were not enough, one must also attempt to repair or replace the volumes whose popularity has had the unfortunate side effects of frequent circulation and the concomitant wear, abuse, and general deterioration.

We propose an alternative to this procedure. We propose to select from the many learned journals, scholarly studies, and critical books the best selections available, the selections which consistently reappear on graduate seminar shelves and on undergraduate honors program reading lists. Let us choose from those articles which time has sanctioned, those too from the best of more recent performances, and let us draw them into a single volume of convenient size. This offers a clear gain in simplicity and usefulness. The articles chosen make up a body of knowledge that cannot fail to be valuable, and they act as models of the kind of contributions to learning which we are training our students to make themselves. And if we can have ready to hand a concentration of such articles for each of the standard areas, and several individual authors, we may conduct the study of these subjects with greater confidence, knowing more fully the extent and kind of reading we can take for granted. And, while we benefit our classes and students, we can also allow the library to keep the original editions of the articles on its shelves and so fulfill its proper and usual function.

FOREWORD

We must add, finally, that each book in the series, and therefore the whole series, is the result of unselfish help from contributors and editors from all of Great Britain and the United States. We wish to acknowledge their help and the help of the Bowdoin College Research Fund in rendering this useful service.

B. N. S.   Rochester, N.Y.
D. G. A.   Pittsburgh, Pa.
H. G. R.   Atlanta, Ga.

PREFACE

In the Preface to his recent study, Source and Meaning in Spenser's Allegory, J. E. Hankins writes that "the 1960s will be remembered as a great period of Spenser scholarship." It is fitting that one section of his book, first published as an article in 1945, should be included in the present volume. It links modern criticism to the great period of the Variorum scholarship and now takes its place in the criticism of the 1970s. The present critical interest in Spenser shows no signs of abating. That three separate studies of Book V—one of the least critically rewarding of the books—should have appeared within a recent four-year period shows how much may be done for the other books, groups of books, and studies of the whole poem. In selecting the articles for the present collection, one chief pleasure for me has been a growing awareness of a developing critical tradition in Spenser studies. While critics differ radically in their critical premises, approaches and concerns, they are building constructively upon the work of earlier critics, both absorbing and going beyond them, so that a common body of criticism is developing that makes Spenser's poetry more fully available to his readers. Yet one should expect no less from critics of a poem whose climactic virtue is courtesy and whose final enemy is the Blatant Beast. The amount of good modern criticism has made selection difficult: what I offer should best be entitled "Selected Essential Articles on Spenser." Late in the planning of this edition, the rising costs of permission to reprint required that excerpts from books be omitted. Hence the otherwise surprising omission of such critics as Jane Aptekar, Donald Cheney, T. K. Dunseath, Maurice Evans, Angus Fletcher, Graham Hough, and A. Williams. In particular, I regret the omission of an excerpt from Donald Cheney's Spenser's Image of Nature: Wild Man and Shepherd in "The Faerie Queene" (New Haven 1966), which was designed to introduce Paul J. Alpers' review and allow his answer to it. Don Cameron Allen is also omitted; yet, as our Dean of Spenser studies, he is continually present as will be evident in the number of articles reprinted from ELH which appeared while he was editor. I have made one exception: I include an excerpt from C. S. Lewis' Allegory of Love because of its seminal influence on modern Spenser criticism.

PREFACE

I wish to thank Mrs. Sherril Barr for her very great help in typing correspondence, and, as always, my wife, Mary E. Hamilton for general editing and the demanding labours of proof-reading.

A. C. Hamilton

<u>Queen's University, Canada</u>

The articles are reprinted without editorial changes; although obvious typographical errors found in the original articles have been corrected, no attempt has been made to enforce a consistent editorial style throughout this whole volume. Unless otherwise specified all page references in the text and notes are to the original publication.

THE FAERIE QUEENE

THE FAERIE QUEENE

C. S. Lewis

In considering The Faerie Queene as a consciously allegorical poem I shall neglect entirely its political allegory. My qualifications as an historian are not such as would enable me to unravel it; and my critical principles hardly encourage me even to make the attempt. By his political allegory Spenser doubtless intended to give to his poem a certain topical attraction. Time never forgives such concessions to 'the glistering of this present,' and what acted as a bait to unpoetic readers for some decades has become a stumbling-block to poetic readers ever since. The comtemporary allusions in The Faerie Queene are now of interest to the critic chiefly in so far as they explain how some bad passages came to be bad; but since this does not make them good—since to explain by causes is not to justify by reasons—we shall not lose very much by ignoring the matter. My concern is with the moral or philosophical allegory.

In approaching this latter, the modern reader needs a little encouragement. He has been told that the significacio of The Faerie Queene is not worth looking for. Critics have talked as if there were a fatal discrepancy between Spenser's spiritual pretensions and the actual content of his poetry. He has been represented as a man who preached Protestantism while his imagination remained on the side of Rome; or again, as a poet entirely dominated by the senses who believed himself to be an austere moralist. These are profound misunderstandings.

The first—that of unconscious or involuntary Roman Catholicism—may be answered pretty shortly. It is quite true that Una is dressed (in her exile) like a nun, that the House of Holinesse is like a conventual house, that Penaunce dwells there with a whip, and that Contemplation, like the hermit of Book Six,[1] resembles a Catholic recluse. It is equally true that we can find similarly Catholic imagery in Bunyan; and I know a man in our own time who wrote what he intended to be a general apologetic allegory

Reprinted from The Allegory of Love by C. S. Lewis (1936), pp. 321–333, by permission of The Clarendon Press, Oxford.

for 'all who profess and call themselves Christians,' and was surprised to find it both praised and blamed as a defence of Rome. It would appear that all allegories whatever are likely to seem Catholic to the general reader, and this phenomenon is worth investigation. In part, no doubt, it is to be explained by the fact that the visible and tangible aspects of Catholicism are medieval, and therefore steeped in literary suggestion. But is this all? Do Protestant allegorists continue as in a dream to use imagery so likely to mislead their readers without noticing the danger or without better motive than laziness for incurring it? By no means. The truth is not that allegory is Catholic, but that Catholicism is allegorical. Allegory consists in giving an imagined body to the immaterial; but if, in each case, Catholicism claims already to have given it a material body, then the allegorist's symbol will naturally resemble that material body. The whip of Penaunce is an excellent example. No Christian ever doubted that repentance involved 'penaunce' and 'whips' on the spiritual plane: it is when you come to material whips—to Tartuffe's discipline in his closet—that the controversy begins. It is the same with the 'House' of Holinesse. No Christian doubts that those who have offered themselves to God are cut off as if by a wall from the World, are placed under a regula vitae, and 'laid in easy bed' by 'meek Obedience'; but when the wall becomes one of real bricks and mortar, and the Rule one in real ink, superintended by disciplinary officials and reinforced (at times) by the power of the State, then we have reached that sort of actuality which Catholics aim at and Protestants deliberately avoid. Indeed, this difference is the root out of which all other differences between the two religions grow. The one suspects that all spiritual gifts are falsely claimed if they cannot be embodied in bricks and mortar, or official positions, or institutions: the other, that nothing retains its spirituality if incarnation is pushed to that degree and in that way. The difference about Papal infallibility is simply a form of this. The proper corruptions of each Church tell the same tale. When Catholicism goes bad it becomes the world-old, world-wide religio of amulets and holy places and priestcraft: Protestantism, in its corresponding decay, becomes a vague mist of ethical platitudes. Catholicism is accused of being much too like all the other religions; Protestantism of being insufficiently like a religion at all. Hence Plato, with his transcendent Forms, is the doctor of Protestants; Aristotle, with his immanent Forms, the doctor of Catholics. Now allegory exists, so to speak, in that region of the mind where the bifurcation has not yet occurred; for it occurs only when we

reach the material world. In the world of matter, Catholics and
Protestants disagree as to the kind and degree of incarnation or
embodiment which we can safely try to give to the spiritual; but in
the world of imagination, where allegory exists, unlimited embodiment is equally approved by both. Imagined buildings and institutions which have a strong resemblance to the actual buildings and
institutions of the Church of Rome, will therefore appear, and ought
to appear, in any Protestant allegory. If the allegorist knows his
business their prevalence will rather mean that the allegory is not
Catholic than that it is. For allegory is idem in alio. Only a
bungler, like Deguileville, would introduce a monastery into his
poem if he were really writing about monasticism. When Spenser
writes about Protestant sanctity he gives us something like a convent: when he is really talking about the conventual life he gives
us Abessa and Corceca. If I might, without irreverence, twist the
words of an important (and very relevant) Protestant article, I
would say that a Catholic interpretation of The Faerie Queene,
'overthroweth the nature of an allegory.' Certainly, a Catholic
reader anxious to do justice to this great Protestant poem, would
be very ill advised to read it in that way. Here, as in more important matters, frontier courtesies do not help; it is at their fiery
cores that the two faiths are most nearly in sympathy.

The charge of actual sensuality and theoretical austerity cannot
be answered so briefly. The spear-head of this attack is usually
directed against the Bower of Bliss, and it is sometimes strengthened by the statement that the Garden of Adonis is not sufficiently
distinguished from it; and an analysis of these two places is as
good a method as any other of beginning a study of Spenser's allegory. The home of Acrasia is first shown to us in the fifth canto
of Book Two, when Atin finds Cymochles there asleep. The very
first words of the description are

And over him art, striving to compare
With nature, did an Arber greene dispred.[2]

This explicit statement that Acrasia's garden is art not nature can
be paralleled in Tasso, and would be unimportant if it stood alone.
But the interesting thing is that when the Bower of Bliss reappears
seven cantos later, there again the very first stanza of description
tells us that it was

goodly beautifide
With all the ornaments of Floraes pride,

5

Wherewith her mother Art, as halfe in scorne
Of niggard Nature, like a pompous bride
Did decke her, and too lavishly adorne.[3]

In order to be perfectly fair to Spenser's hostile critics, I am prepared to assume that this repetition of the antithesis between art and nature is accidental. But I think the hardest sceptic will hesitate when he reads, eight stanzas further,

And that which all faire workes doth most aggrace,
The art which all that wrought appeared in no place.[4]

And if this does not satisfy him let him read on to the sixty-first stanza where we find the imitation ivy in metal which adorns Acrasia's bathing-pool. Whether those who think that Spenser is secretly on Acrasia's side, themselves approve of metal vegetation as a garden ornament, or whether they regard this passage as a proof of Spenser's abominable bad taste, I do not know; but this is how the poet describes it,

And over all of purest gold was spred
A trayle of yvie in his native hew;
For the rich metall was so coloured
That wight who did not well avis'd it vew
Would surely deeme it to bee yvie trew. [5]

Is it possible now to resist the conviction that Spenser's hostile critics are precisely such wights who have viewed the Bower 'not well avis'd' and therefore erroneously deemed it to be true? Let us suppose, however, that the reader is still unconvinced: let us even help him by pointing out stanza 59 where the antithesis is blurred. But we have still to deal with the garden of Adonis; and surely all suspicion that the insistence on Acrasia's artificiality is accidental must disappear if we find throughout the description of the garden of Adonis an equal insistence on its natural spontaneity. And this is just what we do find. Here, as in the description of the Bower, the very first stanza gives us the key-note: the garden of Adonis is

So faire a place as Nature can devize.[6]

A few stanzas later, in lines which I have already quoted, we are told that it needs no Gardiner because all its plants grow 'of their owne accord' in virtue of the divine word that works within them.

It even needs no water, because these plants have eternall moisture 'in themselves,'[7] Like the Bower, the Garden has an arbour, but it is an arbour

> not by art
> But of the trees owne inclination made.[8]

and the ivy in this arbour is living ivy not painted metal. Finally, the Bower has the story of a false love depicted by art on its gate,[9] and the Garden has faithful lovers growing as live flowers out of its soil.[10] When these facts have once been pointed out, only prejudice can continue to deny the deliberate differentiation between the Bower and the Garden. The one is artifice, sterility, death: the other, nature, fecundity, life. The similarity between them is just that similarity which exists between the two gardens in Jean de Meun;[11] the similarity of the real to the pretended and of the archetype to the imitation. Diabolus simius Dei.

Before continuing our analysis of the Garden and the Bower we must digress for a little to notice an important corollary which has already emerged. Spenser, as I have shown, distinguishes the good and evil paradises by a skilful contrast between nature and art; and this at once throws a flood of light upon his poetic use of the arts in general. It has often been noticed that he is fond of describing pictures or tapestries; but it has not been equally noticed that he usually puts such artefacts in places which he thinks evil. It would be rash to infer from this that the poet disliked pictures: his practice is probably a calculated symbolic device and not a mere slavish obedience to temperament. But the fact is incontestable. There is, so far as I have noticed, only one exception, and it is very easily explained. In the House of Alma, the cells of the brain are internally decorated with pictures because this is the obvious, perhaps the only, way of allegorizing the fact that the external world enters as image into the human mind.[12] Everywhere else Spenser uses art to suggest the artificial in its bad sense—the sham or imitation. Thus he uses pictures to suggest luxurious corruption in the house of Malecasta;[13] and it is deliciously characteristic of our poet (thrifty Spenser) that St. George and Britomart at first sight of the place should wonder uneasily (like the sober English soldier and gentlewoman they are) who is paying for it all, and how.[14] So, again, he uses pictures to build up an unbearable silent splendour in the House of Busirane.[15] In the Temple of Venus, on the other hand, a place 'wall'd by nature gainst invaders wrong,'[16] we have no pictures of lovers, but the living lovers themselves[17] as against the pictured Cupid of Busirane we have 'a flocke of little loves,' all alive and fluttering about the neck and shoulders of Venus, as birds, in another mythology, fly about the head of Aengus.[18] The gardener's art which had been excluded from the home of Adonis is indeed admitted into the Temple of Venus, for a reason which will appear later; but it is allowed only to supplement Nature,[19] not to deceive or sophisticate as it does in the Bower of Bliss. The abiding impression is that of a place 'lavishly enricht with Natures threasure,' 'by nature made.'[20] Thus, again, Pride has a palace, Belphoebe a pavilion in the woods, and the hill where the Graces dance is adorned only 'by natures skill.'[21]

Truth is an unruly subject and, once admitted, comes crowding in on us faster than we wish. I had intended only a short digression to show the deliberate contrast between nature and art (or reality and imitation) in all Spenser's good and bad places, but I find that I have stumbled on another of those great antitheses which run through his whole poem. Like Life and Death, or Light and Darkness, the opposition of natural and artificial, naive and sophisticated, genuine and spurious, meets us at every turn. He had learned from Seneca and the Stoics about the life according to Nature; and he had learned from Plato to see good and evil as the real and the apparent. Both doctrines were congenial to the rustic and humble piety of his temper—that fine flower of Anglican sanctity which meets us again in Herbert or Walton. He is not at home in the artificialities of the court, and if, as a man, he was sometimes seduced, as a poet he never was. The rotting captives in Pride's dungeon are those who 'fell from high Princes court' after long wasting their 'thriftlesse howres.'[22] Guyon, like a true Stoic, rejects Mammon's offers of wealth in favour of 'untroubled Nature,' because 'at the well head the purest streames arise.'[23] Philotime's beauty is not 'her owne native hew, but wrought by art,' and the description of her court ('some thought to raise themselves to high degree' &c.) is so vivid that an officer of my acquaintance thought of presenting a framed and illuminated text of that stanza to the Head Quarters Mess of the ——.[24] The whole conception of the false Florimel, not to mention Braggadochio, expresses the same feeling; and at her making, Nature ' grudg'd to see the counterfet should shame the thing it selfe.'[25] True love is praised because it is 'naturall affection faultlesse,'[26] whereas the false love of Paridell is an 'art' which he 'learned had of yore,' and he himself 'the learned lover' equipped with 'Bransles, ballads, virelayes and verses vaine.'[27] The pictures in the House of Busirane have already been mentioned; but perhaps the simile with which they are introduced gives us more of the depth of Spenser's mind on these matters than the whole description that follows.

> Woven with gold and silke, so close and nere
> That the rich metall lurked privily
> As faining to be hid from envious eye;
> Yet here, and there, and every where, unwares
> It shewd it selfe and shone unwillingly;
> Like a discoloured Snake, whose hidden snares
> Through the greene gras his long bright burnisht back declares.[28]

Any moralist may disapprove luxury and artifice; but Spenser alone can turn the platitude into imagery of such sinister suggestion. It is thought completely converted into immediate sensation. Even the innocent trappings of the courtly life do not attract him, and he dismisses the externals of a tournament as contemptuously as Milton himself: to describe them, he says,

> Were worke fit for an Herauld, not for me.[29]

Clothes and jewellery interest him only when they adorn his 'shining ones,' and become, as a modern critic has well pointed out, the symbol of a spiritual radiance.[30] Everywhere else the pomps and vanities of the 'World' are for him illusions

> Fashion'd to please the eies of them that pas
> Which see not perfect things but in a glas,

and easily rejected by those who compare them with 'plaine Antiquitie.'[31] The Noble Savage, long before Dryden gives him that name, has played his part in the Sixth Book of The Faerie Queene. Una's face is fairest unveiled. 'Naturals'—lions and satyrs—come to her aid. True courtesy dwells among shepherds who alone have never seen the Blatant Beast.[32]

All this is quite compatible with Spenser's horror of something else which is also commonly called 'nature.' As we had to remind ourselves in an earlier chapter, Nature may be opposed not only to the artificial or the spurious, but also to the spiritual or the civil. There is a nature of Hobbes' painting as well as of Rousseau's. Of nature in this second sense, nature as the brutal, the unimproved, the inchoate, Spenser has given us notice enough in his cannibals, brigands, and the like; and, more philosophically, in the 'hatefull darknes' and 'deepe horrore' of the chaos whence all the fair shapes in the garden of Adonis have taken their 'substance.'[33] This is what moderns tend to mean by Nature—the primitive, or original, and Spenser knows what it is like. But most commonly he understands Nature as Aristotle did—the 'nature' of anything being its unimpeded growth from within to perfection, neither checked by accident nor sophisticated by art. To this 'nature' his allegiance never falters, save perhaps in some regrettable compliments to the Queen which accord ill with his general feeling about the court: and when Nature personified enters his poem she turns out to be the greatest of his shining ones. In some respects, indeed, she symbolizes God Himself.[34]

The reader may well be excused if he has, by this, forgotten that the whole subject of nature and art arose out of our analysis of the Bower of Bliss and the Garden of Adonis. But the Bower and the Garden (the very names, I trust, have now become significant) are so important that we have still not exhausted them. We have dealt only with their contrast of nature and art. It still remains to consider the equally careful, and even more important, contrast between the explicitly erotic imagery of the one and the other. We here approach a subject on which Spenser has been much misunderstood. He is full of pictures of virtuous and vicious love, and they are, in fact, exquisitely contrasted. Most readers seem to approach him with the vulgar expectation that his distinction between them is going to be a quantitative one; that the vicious loves are going to be warmly painted and the virtuous tepidly—the sacred draped and the profane nude. It must be stated at once that in so far as Spenser's distinction is quantitative at all, the quantities are the other way round. He is at the opposite pole from the scholastic philosophers. For him, intensity of passion purifies: cold pleasure, such as the scholastics seem to approve, is corruption. But in reality the distinction has very little to do with degree or quantity.

The reader who wishes to understand Spenser in this matter may begin with one of his most elementary contrasts—that between the naked damsels in Acrasia's fountain and the equally naked (in fact rather more naked) damsels who dance round Colin Clout.[35] Here, I presume, no one can be confused. Acrasia's two young women (their names are obviously Cissie and Flossie) are ducking and giggling in a bathing-pool for the benefit of a passerby: a man does not need to go to fairie land to meet them. The Graces are engaged in doing something worth doing,—namely, dancing in a ring 'in order excellent.' They are, at first, much too busy to notice Calidore's arrival, and when they do notice him they vanish. The contrast here is almost too simple to be worth mentioning; and it is only marginal to our immediate subject, for the Graces symbolize no sexual experience at all. Let us proceed to something a little less obvious and more relevant: let us compare the pictured Venus and Adonis in the house of Malecasta with the real Venus and Adonis in

the Garden. We find at once that the latter (the good and real) are
a picture of actual fruition. Venus, in defiance of the forces of
death, the Stygian gods,

Possesseth him and of his sweetnesse takes her fill.[36]

Nothing could be franker; a dainty reader might even object that
the phrase 'takes her fill' brings us too close to other and more
prosaic appetites. But daintiness will be rebuked (as Spenser is
always ready to rebuke it) if any one tries to prefer the pictured
Venus on Malecasta's wall. For she is not in the arms of Adonis:
she is merely looking at him,

And whilst he bath'd, with her two crafty spyes
She secretly would search each daintie lim.[37]

The words 'crafty', 'spies', and 'secretly' warn us sufficiently well
where we have arrived. The good Venus is a picture of fruition:
the bad Venus is a picture not of 'lust in action' but of lust suspended—lust turning into what would now be called skeptophilia. The
contrast is just as clear as that in the previous example, and incal-
culably more important. Thus armed, we may now return to the
Bower. The very first person we meet there is Cymochles. He
has come there for pleasure and he is surrounded by a flock of wanton nymphs. But the wretched creature does not approach one of
them: instead, he lies in the grass ('like an Adder lurking in the
weedes') and

Sometimes he falsely faines himselfe to sleepe
Whiles through their lids his wanton eies do peepe.[38]

The word 'peepe' is the danger signal, and once again we know where
we are. If we turn to the Garden of Adonis we shall find a very different state of affairs. There 'all plenty and all pleasure flowes':
the garden is full of lovers and 'Franckly each Paramor his leman
knowes'.[39] And when we have noticed this it ought to dawn upon us
that the Bower of Bliss is not a place even of healthy animalism, or
indeed of activity of any kind. Acrasia herself does nothing: she is
merely 'discovered', posed on a sofa beside a sleeping young man,
in suitably semi-transparent raiment. It is hardly necessary to add
that her breast is 'bare to ready spoyle of hungry eies;'[40] for eyes,
greedy eyes ('which n'ote therewith be fild') are the tyrants of that
whole region. The Bower of Bliss is not a picture of lawless, that

is, unwedded, love as opposed to lawful love. It is a picture, one of the most powerful ever painted, of the whole sexual nature in disease. There is not a kiss or an embrace in the island: only male prurience and female provocation. Against it we should set not only the Garden of Adonis, but the rapturous reunion of Scudamour with Amoret,[41] or the singularly fresh and frank account of Arthur's meeting with Gloriana.[42] It is not to be supposed of course that Spenser wrote as a scientific 'sexologist' or consciously designed his Bower of Bliss as a picture of sexual perversion. Acrasia indeed does not represent sexual vice in particular, but vicious pleasure in general.[43] Spenser's conscious intention, no doubt, was merely to produce a picture which should do justice both to the pleasantness and to the vice. He has done this in the only way possible—namely, by filling his Bower of Bliss with sweetness showered upon sweetness and yet contriving that there should be something subtly wrong throughout. But perhaps 'contriving' is a bad word. When he wishes to paint disease, the exquisite health of his own imagination shows him what images to exclude.

C. S. LEWIS AND SPENSER: NATURE, ART AND
THE BOWER OF BLISS

N. S. Brooke

The Allegory of Love by C. S. Lewis is that rare thing, a work of criticism which is also a work of art. There are few books on the student's shelves which command more admiration and respect; and therefore all the greater must be the impertinence of him who sets out to disagree with it. My only defence can be that the greater a critical work is, the more worthwhile it is to examine its judgments; and that a part is worth correcting only where the whole is most admired. I have chosen to approach an interpretation of the bower of bliss through an examination of Mr. Lewis's account of it because, firstly, that analysis was a considerable advance on previous criticism; and secondly, persuasive as it was, it has gained such wide currency that it is necessary to give good reason for any divergence from it; and thirdly, since my point of view is not so much a divergence as a contradiction, it may prove helpful to take Mr. Lewis's points and, in contradicting them, establish my own position the more clearly.

Mr. Lewis asserts that Spenser's distinction between the bower of bliss and the garden of Adonis is a distinction between nature and art; from that he develops a theory of Spenser's feeling about nature and art in general; and finally he interprets the bower of bliss as 'a picture, one of the most powerful ever painted, of the whole sexual nature in disease' [12].* In support of his first point, the distinction in the two gardens of nature and art, Mr. Lewis brings a wealth of evidence which as he rightly says is incontestible. The bower of bliss is

goodly beautifide

With all the ornaments of Floraes pride,
Wherewith her mother Art, as halfe in scorne
Of niggard Nature, like a pompous bride
Did decke her, and too lavishly adorne.   (II. xii. 50)

*Numbers in square brackets refer to pages in this volume.

Reprinted from Cambridge Journal, Vol. 2 (1949), pp. 420–434, published by Bowes & Bowes, London, by permission of the author and the publisher.

Whereas the garden of Adonis is

> So faire a place as Nature can devize.   (III. vi. 29)

This statement is somewhat ambiguous: Mr. Lewis takes it to mean that the garden is a place so fair as nature alone can devise; whereas it is equally possible that Spenser meant it was the best that Nature could do. In which case, it would at once be clear why the garden outside the Temple of Venus is later described as seeming to Scudamore

> The only pleasant and delightful place
> That ever troden was of footings trace:
> For all that nature by her mother-wit
> Could frame in earth, and forme of substance base,
> Was there; and all that nature did omit,
> Art, playing second natures part, supplyed it.   (IV. x. 21)

This stanza is very important in a consideration of Spenser's attitude to the relative functions of nature and art: for here they are the same, only the one more advanced than the other. The raw material is earth and substance base out of which nature with her mother-wit frames and forms what she can, art taking on where nature leaves off. So that the difference of composition between this garden and the previous one of Adonis is simply the addition of art. Mr. Lewis does in fact admit that the gardener's art finds a place in the garden of Venus, but comments only that the reason for it will appear later; he returns to the subject on page 343 where he calls the temple 'Amoret's school or university,' whilst the garden of Adonis had been her nursery (this comparison seems apt enough). It is a region, he says, 'neither purely natural, like the Garden, nor artificial in the bad sense, like the Bower of Bliss.' This is perfectly true; but if it is not artificial in the bad sense, it must presumably be so in a good one (or at worst neutral, which would be pointless), and Mr. Lewis has not previously admitted the possibility of such a thing; in fact he asserts [8] that in Spenser the opposition between the natural and the artificial is on a par with the opposition between Life and Death, or Light and Darkness, and is derived from Plato's identification of good and evil with real and apparent.

I have already quoted from the garden of Venus to show that Spenser does not equate the gardener's art with Plato's 'apparent, which is evil,' and I have suggested an alternative interpretation of

the line Mr. Lewis quotes from the garden of Adonis: 'So faire a
place as Nature can devize.' These gardens suggest another Platonic
conception: in the Symposium Socrates discusses man's desire for
immortality, and finds that the humblest means of achieving it
(which man shares with the animals) is the procreation of children;
whereas the highest means is fame—the fame of the statesman or
the poet achieved through their respective arts. The physical immortality achieved in the birth of a child is good, but it is not best.
Evidently Spenser's view of physical generation is higher than
Socrates', but he still represents it as shared by man with the animals, birds and fishes:

> And every sort is in a sondry bed
> Sett by itselfe, and ranckt in comely rew:
> Some fitt for reasonable sowles t'indew;
> Some made for beasts, some made for birds to weare;
> And all the fruitfull spawne of fishes hew
> In endlesse rancks along enraunged were,
> That seemd the ocean could not containe them there.
>
> (III. vi. 35)

—all becoming through Adonis 'eterne' only in 'mutabilitie.' In the
garden of Venus is something higher still, possessed by man alone;
and the difference is achieved precisely by the gardener's art:

> and all that nature did omit,
> Art, playing second natures part, supplyed it.

Spenser in his quest for truth was not an isolated figure among
his contemporaries; he was an innovator, but a conservative one,
standing in relation to the poetry of his age much as Brahms stood
in relation to the music of his. The view of nature which he expressed would be likely to be that of his contemporaries, unless he
went out of his way to show that it was not. In her recent book on
Elizabethan and Metaphysical imagery, Miss Rosemond Tuve shows
that the typical Elizabethan view of nature was not of a finished
article unsusceptible of improvement so much as an half-ordering
of chaos whose potentiality for good is seldom realized without the
additional ordering influence of art. An excellent example of many
such which Miss Tuve quotes is Quintilian's maxim, 'that is most
greatly natural, which nature suffers to be done best' (37—verum id
est maxime naturale, quod fieri natura optime patitur). The relation
of art to nature is bound up with significacio, with illumination in the

sense of abstract truth rather than of natural description. Nature as she is seen has little 'meaning': a tree by itself is just a tree, whereas several trees in a row acquire form, the significance of a straight line. In The Elizabethan World Picture (13) Dr. Tillyard remarks on Spenser's fondness for rows, and comments that 'the arrangement is comely not just because it is pretty and seemly but because it harmonizes with a universal order.' It is true that nature sometimes suffers trees to be done as well as this, but more frequently the line will be broken, or will end in a meaningless confusion. To achieve the best results it is highly desirable to dig up the trees and rearrange them so that the breaks are mended and the confusion resolved. This is the function of the gardener's art in the garden of Venus, ordering the

> walkes and alleyes dight
> With divers trees enrang'd in even ranks. (IV. x. 25)

If I am right then, Mr. Lewis's distinction between art and nature in the gardens as between evil and good turns out to be unfounded: that there is a distinction (as I have already agreed) is quite clear; what it is will appear later. With the disappearance of this distinction must disappear also Mr. Lewis's definition of what Spenser meant by nature, and so it is necessary to examine that definition more closely. On page [9] of The Allegory of Love, after expanding the concept of nature as opposed to the Artificial, he says:

> All this is quite compatible with Spenser's horror of something else which is commonly called 'nature'. . . Nature may be opposed not only to the artificial or the spurious, but also to the spiritual or the civil . . . Of nature in this second sense, nature as the brutal, the unimproved, the inchoate, Spenser has given us notice enough in his cannibals, brigands and the like; and, more philosophically, in the 'hatefull darkness' and 'deepe horrore' of the chaos whence all the fair shapes in the garden of Adonis have taken their 'substance'. . . But most commonly he understands Nature as Aristotle did—the 'nature' of anything being its unimpeded growth from within to perfection.

This is not very clear, but what is clear is that Mr. Lewis conceives nature as definable only by negatives: 'Nature may be opposed not only to the artificial or the spurious, but also to the spiritual or the civil.' Almost the same words are used to develop Mr. Lewis's own philosophy in The Abolition of Man (Riddell Memorial lectures, University of Durham, 1943, p. 34):

16

C. S. LEWIS AND SPENSER

Nature is a word of varying meanings, which can best be understood if we consider its various opposites. The Natural is the
opposite of the Artificial, the Civil, the Human, the Spiritual, and
the Supernatural.

The Human and the Supernatural are not, of course, in the list for
Spenser: the other 'opposites' are the same. No single power could
be opposed to so many different ones unless its unity lay in a vague
and all-embracing conception for which the nineteenth rather than
the sixteenth century was responsible. So that Mr. Lewis would seem
to be accusing Spenser either of using one word in two or more contradictory senses, or else of subscribing to an essentially modern
point of view.

I have already shown that Spenser did not define Nature as opposed to the artificial, at least in the sense of the gardener's art;
and Mr. Lewis's evidence for an opposition to the civil or spiritual
seems to be equally unsatisfactory. In the garden outside the Temple of Venus, quoted above, Spenser speaks of Nature 'forming' out
of 'substance base.' That substance is not nature, but is the raw
material on which nature works. And the same is true of the substances in hatefull darkness and deepe horrore of which Mr. Lewis
speaks: they are the 'substaunces of natures fruitful progenyes'
(III. vi. 36), they too are not nature, and indeed from them

> Infinite shapes of creatures there are bred,
> And uncouth formes, which none yet ever knew.   (ibid. 35)

So that nature, doing the breeding, forms all sorts—both fair things
and the foul beasts (cannibals, brigands and the like) equally. It is
a point which is commonly overlooked that what Mr. Lewis calls the
'fair shapes' in the garden of Adonis were in fact 'infinite shapes'
and 'uncouth formes.' The Nature of these passages not only does
not fulfil either of Mr. Lewis's definitions, it does not seem to require negative definition at all: it is a forming or ordering force,
responsible for the coherence of all phenomena, but not for their
perfection—and it is in this respect that the personified Nature of
the Mutabilitie cantos symbolizes, as Mr. Lewis says, God Himself.
She appears with her sergeant Order, in Dr. Spen's words
(Spenser's Faerie Queene, 44) as 'a personification of the laws of
existence'; in fact of the Law of Nature which, according to Hooker,
is enjoined on all living creatures equally, and on man in 'that
which we work naturally, as when we breathe, sleep, move . . . as
natural agents do' (Eccl. Pol. I. xvi. 5). We must therefore firmly
contradict Mr. Lewis's assertion that Spenser most commonly

17

'understands Nature as Aristotle did—the "nature" of anything being its unimpeded growth from within to perfection': Spenser, not most commonly but always (at least in the parts of his work considered here) understands Nature as a force from without, forming out of substance base (earth and water) what may be formed out of it; for perfection man must turn to his kinship with the angels, and to Divine Revelation.

> With nature [says Hooker, I. iii. 3] it cometh sometimes to pass as with art. Let Phidias have rude and obstinate stuff to carve, though his art do that it should, his work will lack that beauty which otherwise in fitter matter it might have had . . . In the matter whereof things natural consist, that of Theophrastus taketh place . . . 'Much of it is oftentimes such as will by no means yield to receive that impression which were best and most perfect.'

The 'true original cause' of this 'defect in the matter of things natural' is 'divine malediction.' We may now see a more profound significance, at least for Elizabethan readers, in the lines quoted above from Quintilian:

> That is most greatly natural, which nature suffers to be done best.

and from the garden of Venus:

> For all that nature by her mother-wit
> Could frame in earth, and forme of substance base
> Was there; and all that nature did omit,
> Art, playing second natures part, supplyed it.

If the gardener's art was akin to nature in further forming and enranging what nature had already formed and enranged out of substances, there is another art which is more than this: the art of 'imitation,' of painting or of poetry, and both Mr. Lewis and Miss Tuve have much to say about it. Mr. Lewis claims [7] that 'Everywhere else [i.e. except in the house of Alma] Spenser uses art to suggest the artificial in its bad sense—the sham or imitation.' It is unfortunate that in this context Mr. Lewis should use the word 'imitation' in a derogatory sense, for the Elizabethans did, of course, apply the platonic term to art, in a very different way. Miss Tuve (41) quotes Fracastoro defining imitation as 'imitating not the particular [that is, 'the object exactly as it is'] but the simple idea

clothed in its own beauties, which Aristotle calls the universal.'
And again (56) 'Peacham, treating of the "exornation" of persons,
says that like the cunning painter one so manages proportion and
colour that he "compoundeth as it were complexion [i.e. tempera-
ment] with substance and life with countenance"; thus the persons
represented not only make a show of lifelikeness "but also by outward countenance of the inward spirite and affection." ' So art is
an imitation, but an imitation of the intelligible rather than the
visible; artists 'please only by virtue of the habit (in both writer
and reader) of seeing the intelligible in the visible—a habit shared
by most of the arts in an era like the Renaissance, and of which the
extreme example is the emblem' (Tuve, 53). The important thing
in painting then is not its representation but its 'significacio,' and
it is from this aspect that Spenser describes his paintings; as for
instance the tapestry of Venus and Adonis in Castle Joyous:

> First did it shew the bitter balefull stowre,
> Which her essayd with many a fervent fit,
> When first her tender hart was with his beautie smit.
>
> Then with what sleights and sweet allurements she
> Entyst the Boy, as well that art she knew,
> And wooed him her Paramoure to bee;   (III. i. 34—5)

There is not a word here about the physical appearance of the work,
only its meaning is described; and the few naturalistic touches such
as the 'girlonds of each flowre that grew' are added in to accentuate
this meaning. This applies, of course, as much to Spenser's descriptions of nature as of paintings: he never invokes a complete
visual image, but adds in details solely for their emblematic significance. It is by this technique, which is common to Sidney (in the
Arcadia), to Lyly and to the majority of Elizabethans, that the so-
called dream effect (beloved of romantic critics) is imparted: I am
unable to believe that any such effect was intended, or indeed felt by
readers until a later century. Sidney emphasizes this point in the
Apology, in his description of the painting of Lucrecia, wherein the
artist 'painted not Lucrecia, whom he never sawe, but painteth the
outward beauty of such a vertue.' Poetry imitated in the same way,
but with the additional advantages that the poet was less tied to
physical appearance than the painter, and that he could always illuminate his meaning by use of direct statements intermingled with
his images. It is scarcely necessary to quote further to show that
this was Spenser's view of art, both painting and poetry; and that

19

being so it would be surprising if he deliberately used painting, as Mr. Lewis suggests, to symbolize the sham, for in so doing he would be performing a feat like that of the modern detective novelist who causes his characters to abuse the scandalous production of detective novels. Spenser in categorizing art as sham, would be declaring himself a fraud; and that is scarcely compatible with his and other Elizabethan claims for the stature of a poet. In any case, Mr. Lewis's contention [7] that the paintings in the house of Alma are a justifiable exception to a general rule that 'he usually puts such artefacts in places which he thinks evil' is not at all convincing. It is safer to suppose that Spenser described pictures when it suited his allegory to do so, and drew in them the significance required by the circumstances. He clearly used the image of a house as a link in the chain of correspondances between the body politic and the microcosm to represent the domain of its allegorical owner (Mercilla, Fidessa, Alma, and so on) and found pictures on the walls a convenient (and conventional) way of expanding the allegory whilst observing the rules of decorum.

If the raw material of nature was 'substance base,' and of the gardener's art was 'natures progenyes,' that of the imitator's art was Truth; this is not sham, nor can it possibly be equated with evil: but it is susceptible of one obvious perversion—when its subject is not truth but untruth. Perhaps the best example of this in the <u>Faerie Queene</u> is the bower of bliss at the end of book II. It used to be supposed that this was a magnificently irrelevant piece of word-painting which tended to destroy the moral intention which Spenser had set himself; Dr. Janet Spens remarked that it was almost impossible to distinguish it from the gardens of Adonis, 'and the gardens of Adonis are at least not evil' (20–21). The assumption here must be that Spenser was carried away by his physical description, and forgot entirely his moral purpose. But against this must be set Miss Tuve's remark (59) that 'no greater violence to the <u>poetry</u> of Spenser could be done than, by separating the two (generalized abstraction from pictorial imagination), to turn the poem into one vast picture gallery. I do not find this separation possible, nor valid, nor intended, even in Spenser's most vividly sensuous "paintings".' If Miss Tuve is right, then it follows that Miss Spens has misunderstood the passage. The bower of bliss is clearly set as one image, but that does not mean that it has not therefore an allegorical significance which determines the nature of that image. Miss Tuve defines an admirable poetic imitation of nature as one in which 'the images achieve excellence on each of three levels, if we may so schematize it, of poetic intention. The qualities of "artificiality," decorous selec-

tivity, and relative sensuous imprecision are in fact the very qualities which mark Renaissance images as functioning towards Imitation
as Renaissance writers conceived it' (24–5). The surface level, the
formal excellence of the bower of bliss has never been called in question, and so need not be discussed here; the second level, the decorous selection or ordering of nature to give coherence to the artist's
interpretation I shall discuss later. It is the third level, the 'truth-
telling,' the statement of abstract ideas which must be considered
first: for it is on this level that the bower has been supposed wanting.
Spenser's normal method of indicating his moral ideas is by allegory;
most critics assert that he sometimes strayed into pure drama, or
sensual description but, with the exception of the bower of bliss, they
seldom agree as to which are the purely dramatic incidents. In this
connection it is usual to quote from the letter to Raleigh:

> But by occasion hereof many other adventures are intermedled
> but rather as accidents then intendments: As the love of Brito-
> mart, the overthrow of Marinell, the misery of Florimell, the
> vertuousnes of Belphoebe, the lasciviousnes of Hellenora, and
> many the like.

This, however, cannot be taken to imply that these incidents are not
allegorical, for at least several of them are acknowledged to be so.
They are only accidents in so far as they are not essential to the
'continued allegory.' Whether or not there are any purely dramatic
incidents in the Faerie Queene cannot be discussed here, but it is at
least wise to keep an open mind on the subject, and to allow that
there might be none. That many incidents are straight translations
from supposedly non-allegorical sources proves nothing; for at
least some of these passages (such as Britomart's story from Brada-
mante's in Ariosto) are certainly adapted to Spenser's allegory. So
that Dr. Spens's statement (22) that canto xii of book II is 'an almost
literal translation from Tasso's description in the Jerusalem Delivered of the island of Armida' need not, I hope, be a deterrent from
searching for an allegorical meaning in the bower. On the other
hand, for encouragement, there is Miss Tuve's remark (46) that
'Modern readers are more likely to mistake the author's meaning
by forgetting that there may be a controlling didactic aim than by
hunting for one.'

It is necessary to begin the hunt rather earlier in book II, with the
introduction to the house of Alma. Here is one of those 'overt statements' of whose necessity Miss Tuve remarks (58) that Spenser's
judgment is 'extremely subtle':

Of all Gods workes which doe this worlde adorne,
There is no one more faire and excellent
Than is mans body, both for powre and forme,
Whiles it is kept in sober government;
But none then it more fowle and indecent,
Distempred through misrule and passions bace;
It grows a Monster, and incontinent
Doth loose his dignity and native grace:
Behold, who list, both one and other in this place.　　(II. ix. 1)

It is the last line which is important here: 'Behold, who list, both one and other in this place.' The one, the human body in sober government, is of course allegorized in the house of Alma. But the other, the Monster with a capital 'M' is nowhere to be seen. Canto ix is entirely devoted to the house of Alma; canto x is a chronicle of the line of Brute; canto xi shows the cruel warre and sore siege

　　　　which strong affections doe apply
Against the forte of reason evermore,
To bring the sowle into captivity.　　(II. xi. 1)

This war is fought by the five attackers of the senses, the seven deadly sins and their captain Maleger against the house of Alma

But in a body which doth freely yeeld
His partes to reasons rule obedient,
And letteth her that ought the scepter weeld,
All happy peace and goodly government
Is setled there in sure establishment.　　(ibid. 2)

and so the attack fails. The allegory here is in terms of a human battle and so the captain must be a human being; he is in fact allegorized as a composite picture made up of four parts: the tiger (equals animal passion) with on either side the two hags Impatience and Impotence and in the centre the resolution of these three, the burnt-out skeleton Maleger, or evil-eagerness:

As pale and wan as ashes was his looke,
His body leane and meagre as a rake,
And skin all withered like a dryed rooke;　　(ibid. 22)

This is an allegorical study of desire in the abstract (as far as such a thing is possible) represented as a man; not a study of disordered

Man—any more than the seven bands of 'men' that make up the seven deadly sins can be construed as individual men. In fact, it is scarcely going too far to say that in this sort of allegory the last symbol likely to represent 'Man' is a man. In the third stanza of this canto Guyon and the Palmer are shown preparing for their 'purposed journey' and 'adventure hard'; then they are left while the attack of the affections on the body which doth freely yeeld his partes to reasons rule takes place; so that we have still to wait for the reverse, the attack by reason on the body which does not freely yield.

Canto xii opens with Guyon and the Palmer sailing between all the excesses which threaten temperance, passing in review all that has gone before in the book (Mirth, the wailing woman, and so on). Then they come to

> The sacred soil where all our perills grow

and thereon are placed the gardens of Acrasia. Now Acrasia has been throughout the book the arch-witch responsible for all the vices of intemperance; and here her island is 'where all our perills grow.' So it is reasonable to suppose that her dwelling is not the seat of one vice, of sensuality, but of the wider, more general sense of the word incontinence. Mr. Lewis remarks that, as Cupid is not present, we should know that we are not dealing with love; this may or may not be a valid observation, but I would suggest that a better reason for knowing that we are not dealing with love is that book II is not about love, but temperance; so that the climax towards which Guyon's quest has been directed might be expected to show an attack, not on unchaste love alone, but on all the intemperate vices. If we combine this expectation with that other one, that Spenser would show us the human body distempered through misrule and passions bace, we shall expect to find, not another house turned upside down, but another allegory of the body characteristically divided into the three domains of the Liver, the Heart and the Brain.

Once past the porter and well inside the gardens, Guyon and the Palmer encounter three set scenes: the arbour of excess, the fountain, and the bower of bliss; they are not connected with each other, but are taken as three separate images in order. The first is occupied by a comely dame 'clad in fayre weeds but fowle disordered,' this by itself may not mean very much, but her activity is more significant: she is engaged in making wine, just as the cook Concoction makes food in the kitchens of Alma's house; and this concocter is called Excess, whilst the other's companion, Digestion, is nowhere to be seen—for obvious reasons. The liquid which she made,

Guyon upset and it 'stained all the lond' (II. xii. 57); now if this is a
straight-forward piece of description it is remarkably inadequate,
for we are not told what colour it stained the land, nor by what
species of magic one small cupfull can stain so wide an area. But
if the land is the human body, then the liquid will be poison, spread
by the veins throughout the body, and the stain will of course be
coulourless.

Guyon passes on, and comes to another set piece, the central one:

And in the midst of all a fountaine stood,
Of richest substance that on earth might bee
So pure and shiny that the silver flood
Through every channell running one might see;
Most goodly it with curious ymageree
Was overwrought, and shapes of naked boyes,
Of which some seemd with lively jollitee
To fly about, playing their wanton toyes,
Whylest others did them selves embay in liquid joyes.

(II. xii. 60)

This fountain, like everything else in the garden (and, as I have already remarked, in the Faerie Queene as a whole) is described by
the poet not with his eye on a physical object—we are not made to
'see' the place—but with his mind on the meaning: all the points
mentioned are fitted on as emblematic devices. Thus the fountain's
silver flood runs through 'every channel' and this is the first and
last time we hear of the existence of any channels at all: so, if we
remember that it is set in 'the midst of all' it surely becomes obvious that this fountain represents the heart pumping blood through
all the arteries and veins. And for its further sensual significance
there are the naked boyes and the two damzells in the pool whom
C. S. Lewis so aptly calls Cissie and Flossie. It is worth noticing
that here and here only in the garden of Acrasia is Guyon tempted:
excess in the belly and distemper in the brain cannot attract him,
but sensuality in the heart can, and does.

The next, and last, place mentioned in the garden is the bower of
bliss itself: if I have followed the allegory correctly, this should be
the brain, the ratiocinative part. But there is a catch; for this is a
body distempered by disorder: in correct order the brain is in
charge of the body, here it must not be so. And here, in place of
brain we find Acrasia, the witch of incontinence, with her lover and
attendants. One of these attendants sings a short song of the rose,
the familiar symbol of the courtly love tradition. This song recom-

24

mends that as the rose is transitory it should be plucked hastily—
that in other words the appetite should take charge of the will: and
that (if the bower is the brain) amounts to a voluntary abdication by
the brain of its ruling function, in favour of a complete surrender
to the passions. When that has happened, the body will of course
become disordered and the result will be as Spenser said at the
beginning of canto ix:

> It growes a Monster, and incontinent
> Doth loose his dignity and native grace.

It is to this image that Spenser returns to explain the bower at the
end of the book, and he treats it at some length. As soon as Guyon
and the Palmer have destroyed the bower and captured Acrasia,
they return to the beasts whom they had encountered before:

> Then Guyon askt, what meant these beasts which there did ly?
> Sayd he; 'These seeming beasts are men indeed
> Whom this Enchauntress hath transformed thus;
> Whylome her lovers, which her lustes did feed,
> Now turned into figures hideous,
> According to their minds like monstruous.'   (II. xii. 84–5)

This is a general reiteration of the earlier overt statement; but
Spenser evidently felt that more was needed, as he proceeds to turn
one of the beasts back into a man, and to reveal that he has so far
lost 'his dignity and native grace' as to wish to remain a hog:

> Saide Guyon: 'see the mind of beastly man,
> That hath so soon forgot the excellence
> Of his creation, when he life began,
> That now he chooseth with vile difference
> To be a beast and lacke intelligence.'   (II. xii. 87)

This choosing to lack intelligence is precisely the choice recom-
mended by the young man of Acrasia's court in his song of the rose.

The third level of meaning of the bower of bliss, then, is a monstrous 'untruth,' an allegorical study of the disordered human body;
the decorousness of imagery is an involved subject, but it is perfectly clear that in this case it will be correct to emphasize in all
aspects of the picture the upsetting of order. The particular image,
however, must be determined by the general picture which must
also have its significance. In the bower the 'subject' is the allegory,

the 'picture' a garden of sensual delight: the reason for this choice
is obvious, for the conflict between Guyon and Acrasia is represented
as between will and appetite, and consequently the distempered body
is best portrayed in terms of sensuous appeal, the cause of appetite's
victory. Similarly it is decorous to describe generation in the garden of Adonis in terms of sensuous appeal, and so it is necessary to
discover the difference between the two. Mr. Lewis approaches the
problem once again with an assumption which seems to me essentially modern—that sexual activity, unsophisticated and unhindered
by 'accident,' is in itself positively good. He therefore concludes
that the bower is a 'picture, one of the most powerful ever painted,
of the whole sexual nature in disease. There is not a kiss or an
embrace in the island: only male prurience and female provocation.'
But in fact there is a kiss: Acrasia is discovered with her sleeping
lover

> And oft inclining downe, with kisses light
> For feare of waking him, his lips bedewd. (II. xii. 73)

and more than this:

> There she had him now laid aslombering
> In secret shade after long wanton joyes. (ibid. 72)

Unless the allegory is to be taken as a purely static picture whose
significance is not affected by what had happened in the past (which
is not Spenser's habit, and in which case there would be no object
in mentioning the past) this cannot be understood as 'only male
prurience and female provocation.' The sexual nature, functioning
normally, is as much a part of the bower of bliss as of the garden
of Adonis. To appreciate the distinction which Spenser made, it is
necessary to turn to another of those descriptions of virtuous and
vicious love of which, as Mr. Lewis says, he is full. Describing
Malecasta at the beginning of book III, he says:

> Emongst the Roses grew some wicked weeds:
> For this was not to love, but lust, inclind;
> For love does alwaies bring forth bounteous deeds,
> And in each gentle hart desire of honor breeds.

> Nought so of love this looser Dame did skill,
> But as a cole to kindle fleshly flame,
> Giving the bridle to her wanton will,

And treading under foote her honest name:
Such love is hate, and such desire is shame.   (III. i. 49–50)

It is certainly not Malecasta's sexual nature which is at fault: what
is wrong is that she gives the bridle to her wanton will, so that instead of the heart feeding the brain with desire of honour, the brain
is merely used as a tool in the pursuit of desire. In the garden of
Adonis, Venus arranges animal growth without interfering with the
functions of the other gods: the brain is not involved at all in this
proper function of the law of nature, and due order is therefore not
disturbed. But in the bower of bliss it is otherwise: the brain is
subjugated as Malecasta's is, and the sexual nature turns from love
to lust without having undergone any fundamental change whatever.

It is now clear why the imagery of the bower is concerned not
with a perversion of sex, but with a perversion of order. The porter
Genius is contrasted with his fellow porter on the gate of Adonis's
garden (this is the only overt statement of the difference between the
two) and whereas the latter is

> that celestiall powre, to whom the care
> Of life, and generation of all
> That lives, perteines in charge particulare.   (II. xii. 47)

Acrasia's porter is 'the foe of life, that good envyes to all' (ibid. 48).
And instead of art perfecting natures progenyes, the landscape is

> goodly beautifide
> With all the ornaments of Floraes pride,
> Wherewith her mother Art, as halfe in scorne
> Of niggard Nature, like a pompous bride
> Did decke her.   (II. xii. 50)

and, even more explicit:

> One would have thought, (so cunningly the rude
> And scorned parts were mingled with the fine)
> That nature had for wantonesse ensude
> Art, and that Art at nature did repine;
> So striving each th'other to undermine,
> Each did the others worke more beautify;   (ibid. 59)

The image has changed slightly, but the idea of warring elements
producing 'guilefull semblants' is powerfully presented. Perhaps

the most striking image of this perverted order is to be found in the description of the fountain, which Mr. Lewis quotes:

> And over all of purest gold was spred
> A trayle of yvie in his native hew;
> For the rich metal was so coloured,
> That wight who did not well avis'd it vew
> Would surely deeme it to be yvie trew. (ibid. 61)

Gold, the highest substance bearing with it all Dr. Tillyard's chain of correspondences, is disguised as ivy the symbol of incontinence, and once again the difficulty of distinguishing between lust and love is emphasized, with a telling irony: 'wight who did not well avis'd it vew Would surely deeme it to be yvie trew.'

The main subject of the bower of bliss is disorder in the human body, the general image or picture is of the cause of that disorder, the imagery used in painting this picture is all of disorder, and the laws of decorum are satisfied. The art which Spenser uses himself is the art of illumination of Truth; that which he describes in the garden of Acrasia is perverted to the illumination of untruth; and whereas art in the gardens of Venus perfects nature, in the bower it wars with nature. If this observation is correct, Spenser's views on the relations of nature and art in general, and of the three gardens in particular, are very different from Mr. Lewis's exposition of it. But the best argument against Mr. Lewis is to be found, I think, in his own words (333):

> If the reader has some familiarity with the allegorical method in general and an ordinary measure both of sensibility and adult experience, then he may be assured that any significacio which does not seem natural to him after a second reading of the poem, is erroneous.

The intrusion of too much of our own 'adult experience' is one of the greatest dangers to criticism; nevertheless, this is a wise saying and formulates a test by which, I am well aware, my own construction of Spenser's meaning must stand or fall.

SPENSER'S "BOWER OF BLISS" AND A KEY METAPHOR FROM RENAISSANCE POETIC

R. Nevo

Professor C. S. Lewis, in The Allegory of Love,[1] interprets Spenser's symbolism in terms of the great Renaissance polarity, Nature-Art. Acrasia's Bower, he says, represents Art in the sense of artifice, appearance, imitation, deception and therefore sterility, as against the parallel Garden of Adonis where "nature, fecundity, life" are the keynotes.

That in the two passages something we may call "sterility" is opposed, in the final effect, to the idea of "generation" is not to be denied. In addition to the emphasis in the Garden on words like seminarie, progenie, fruits lode, wombe, stocke, replenish; the living loves instead of the painted ones; and the explicit statements of the theme of generation, two striking key passages provide, in terms of a single metaphor, the contrast. Acrasia is seen with her lover "greedily depasturing delight" (II. xii. 73), whereas Venus, in the Garden, was wont "to reap sweet pleasure" of the wanton Adonis (III. vi. 46). From the point of view of the action referred to, it would no doubt have made little difference had Spenser used the more normal expression, "greedily pasturing upon delight." It is the profoundly negative effect of the coinage "depasturing" which rivets the attention of the reader upon that turning back upon itself of erotic pleasure which is the very meaning of the Bower. Yet it should be remembered that reaping, though indicative of natural increase, is an art too, in so far as agriculture is not nature; while in point of fact "depasturing" is a highly natural activity. The Art-Nature dichotomy is not here co-extensive with the theme.

Again, consider the passage describing the suspended animation of the natural seasons in the Bower:

Thereto the Heauens alwayes Iouiall,
Lookt on them louely, still in stedfast state,
Ne suffred storme nor frost on them to fall,

Reprinted from Studies in Western Literature, Vol. 10, ed. D. A. Fineman, Jerusalem 1962, pp. 20–31, by permission of the author and The Magnes Press.

Their tender buds or leaues to violate,
Nor scorching heat, nor cold intemperate
T'afflict the creatures, which therein did dwell,
But the milde aire with season moderate
Gently attempred, and disposd so well,
That still it breathed forth sweet spirit and holesome smell.

(II. xii. 51)

This, at first-sight Eden-like, takes on a similar sterility-productivity significance by comparison with the "continuall spring, and harvest continuall, both meeting at one time" of the Garden (III. vi. 42). The static, moderate season, its elements so equally mixed as to preclude death, no doubt, but equally life, is compared, looking back from the later passage, with the concentrated fruition of spring and harvest fused in one generative process. Here, too, Art versus Nature seems to be a formula which cannot quite account for the "stedfast state" of the Bower.

There are several points indeed at which Lewis's interpretation can be shown to be not quite adequate, or not operative at every turn of the thought, or not fully revealing of Spenser's conception. He himself willingly draws attention to stanza 59 of Book II, Canto xii, where, he says, "the antithesis between art and nature is blurred." It will be my contention that Spenser does not blur the matter—one of central importance, as Lewis demonstrates, and innumerable Renaissance writers testify. The antithesis is not blurred, but it must be understood, not in terms of a simple contrast between Art and Nature, illuminating though this is, nor in terms of a basic contention that Acrasia's Bower is Art and not Nature, but in terms of a complex metaphor of the relationship between Art and Nature.

For it cannot be denied that Nature, untouched and untrammelled by Art, appears in the Bower of Bliss, and that it is good. The storm and frost, which the jovial heavens do not suffer to afflict the tender buds, are seen as "violations"; this Bower is Nature without such violations. Tender, milde, moderate, gently attempred, well disposd, sweet and holesome—the battery of terms is incontrovertible in its effect, and startlingly attuned moreover to the kind of values or sensibility to be associated with Temperance itself. Lewis has pointed out the technical problem the writer is faced with here—the problem of making the Bower sufficiently tempting to Guyon while at the same time revealing its evil, its "subtle wrongness." Certainly so far as the Bower's natural beauty seems here to be an image of his own desired self-realization as Temperance, it must have been supremely tempting. Nothing could have appealed to him more, save the later,

30

climactic, and, for the Renaissance mind, even more deeply grounded attraction of a positively heavenly harmony (II. xii. 70).

It is true, as Lewis notes, that the Musick seemed to be heard from the place where the witch was, so that Acrasia is not necessarily the source of the consort of delightful sounds, tempered one to another in exquisite harmony. Nevertheless, the consort exists, and in her Bower. It is this problem which Lewis solves by suggesting that the seductive beauty is apparent only and not real, and that this notion is conveyed by the deliberate use of the Art-Nature contrasts. But if we examine the relevant passages closely in their context we encounter several difficulties which are not settled by this means. The music is, for example, clearly praiseworthy for its combination or collaboration of Nature (winds, waters, etc.) with Art (voices, instruments, etc.), the result being a consort "in one harmonee [of] all that pleasing is to living eare" (II. xii. 70).

It is from the insistence that there is something special here about this very collaboration that we can most fruitfully pursue the enquiry further. Spenser refers to

> a most melodious sound
> Of all that mote delight a daintie eare,
> Such as attonce might not on liuing ground,
> Saue in this Paradise, be heard elsewhere.   (II. xii. 70)[2]

What is the nature of this Paradise?

> A place pickt out by choice of best aliue
> That natures worke by art can imitate.   (II. xii. 42)

> Ye might have seene the frothy billowes fry
> Vnder the ship, as thorough them she went,
> That seemd the waues were into yuory
> Or yuory into the waues were sent.   (II. xxi. 45)

> [The Genius] doth vs procure to fall,
> Through guilefull semblaunts, which he makes vs see.
>   (II. xii. 48)

So far certainly, the doctrine Professor Lewis quotes, of Diabolus simius Dei. But stanza 50 is less simple.

> A large and spacious plaine, on euery side
> Strowed with pleasauns, whose faire grassy ground

31

Mantled with greene, and goodly beautifide
With all the ornaments of <u>Floraes</u> pride,
Wherewith her mother Art, as halfe in scorne
Of niggard Nature, like a pompous bride
Did decke her, and too lauishly adorne.

Here it is interesting to note that the ornaments of Flora's pride
are exactly parallel to the fresh colors which deck the wanton Prime
in the Garden, in the suggestion both of display or decoration, and of
natural frailties. Moreover the descriptions in the Garden show that
the lavish in itself is not to be regarded as meriting criticism. The
pejorative suggestion of excess here is the result of a scorn for
Nature, on the part of Art, which has upset the proper balance between display—finery—and she who is thus displayed—the bride. It
is the result, in other words, of a faulty relationship between Art
and Nature.

There follows the unambiguous praise of stanza 52:

More sweet and holesome, then the plesaunt hill
Of <u>Rhodope</u> . . .

—praise that is unambiguous in all but the closing qualifications,
"Or Eden selfe, if ought with Eden mote compare"; whose function,
in the light of the succeeding stanza where Guyon braces himself to
resist, is most probably to remind us of the absolute <u>a priori</u> distinction between the perfection of creation before the fall and the
post-lapsarian state, the corruptibility of which is an attribute of
both Art and Nature.

To the bridling of Guyon's will and the mastering of his might,
the Bower responds, as it were, with the intensified wreathings and
claspings of the boughs and branches round the Porch. And it is at
this point, while the embracing vine offers its heavy branches freely
and enticingly into the visitor's hands, that the Art-Nature theme is
taken up again, but with, I suggest, an important additional discrimination.

And them amongst, some were of burnisht gold,
So made by art, to beautifie the rest,
Which did themselues emongst the leaues enfold,
As lurking from the uew of couetous guest,
That the weake bowes, with so rich load opprest,
Did bow adowne, as over-burdened.   (II. xii. 55)

SPENSER'S "BOWER OF BLISS"

It would seem that there is here a relationship other than that of simply the false to the true. The grapes were themselves richly enticing, by virtue of their luscious wine, first of all. They are real edible grapes. (The "seemed" to entice of st. 54 must be a reference to the postulated personified life of the vine, and not a doubt cast upon the reality of the enticement.) The gold artificial grapes appear in order to beautify the rest, already very beautiful in their purple, ruby and emerald green. Still, gold is hierarchically superior even to rubies and emeralds, so that their presence, we can be expected to feel, would naturally bring the scale of beauty to its height. But this process encounters an obstacle. We can see why, being gold, inedible, but precious for other reasons, they lurked "from the uew of couetous guest," but we are then troubled by an evident frustration of their object—to beautify the rest—an object which cannot be attained if we do not see them.[3] The result of this curiously ambiguous situation is an overloading of the weak bowes with so rich load oppressed; and the ambiguity is concentrated in the word <u>rich</u>. For in the Garden too, the trees labor under their rich burden of fruit—a joyous and productive labor—while here they·bow down under the unnatural weight of gold grapes which, perfect gold circles, are neither edible nor fully visible. In the previous stanza, moreover, the hanging down of the branches was ascribed to a free and enticing offer of the rich clusters to the passerby.

Nature and Art, it seems, vie with each other to produce, to multiply delicious appearance; but here they do so to their mutual frustration, since either the natural grapes or the artificial grapes must suffer by the comparison—the former better to eat, the latter better to look at. We are left with a dilemma of taste, and this dilemma is reflected in the dilemma of the gold grapes—whether to show themselves and risk covetous hands, or to hide and so lose the full glory of their appearance.

A similar dilemma is, significantly enough and with a significantly similar use of the word lurk, referred to elsewhere. In the description of the House of Busyrane we find that

> round about, the wals yclothed were
> With goodly arras of great maiesty,
> Wouen with gold and silke so close and nere,
> As faining to be hid from enuious eye;
> That the rich metall lurked priuily,
> Yet here, and there, and euery where vnwares
> It shewd it selfe and shone vnwillingly

Like a discolourd Snake, whose hidden snares
Through the greene gras his long bright burnisht backe declares.

(III. xi. 28)

Professor Lewis sees in the lurking snake passage support for
his contention that "gold" and the "cunning of art" occur in Spenser
as pointers to the presence of deception and artificiality. But both
the Temple of Isis (V. vii. 5–6) and Mercillae's palace (V. xi. 27),
as well as Thames' robe (IV. xi. 27) are adorned by gold and artifice,
where no adverse criticism is intended. On the contrary. Once
more, we must seek beyond the simple opposition Art-Nature if we
wish to account for these apparent contradictions.

It is worth noting at this point that the pleasant arbor in the Garden of Adonis, made, not by art, but by the trees' own "inclination,"
with "rancke braunches [knitted] part to part, with wanton yuie
twyne entrayld athwart" (III. vi. 44), has a specifically defined and
useful purpose—to protect from sun and wind. And when we turn to
the Pallace of Pride:

Whose wals were high, but nothing strong, nor thick,
And golden foile all over them displaid,
That purest skye with brightnesse they dismaid,   (I. iv. 4)

we find the direction now given to our thought confirmed by the
definite reference to the purpose of walls: the gold foil covers walls
too weak for support with brightness which dismays the sky—the
proper source of brightness. Why "dismays"? Both, I suggest, by
reason of the brilliant blaze of competition the sky thus encounters,
and by reason of a sense of confusion engendered by all this brightness in the wrong place—on walls, which are meant for sturdy support, and not for illumination.

Returning then, to the Bower, we remember that Atin had found
"art striving to compaire with nature" in its spreading over Cymochles an Arber greene (III. v. 29). We have, then, not Art versus
Nature as a minus versus a plus, but a corruption of the proper ends
of both by an improper rivalry between them. And if this relationship is perceived, the next reference to Nature and Art leaps into
perspective.

As

the most dainty Paradise on ground
It selfe doth offer to his sober eye . . .

> One would haue thought, (so cunningly, the rude,
> And scorned parts were mingled with the fine,)
> That nature had for wantonesse ensude
> Art, and that Art at nature did repine;
> So striking each th'other to vndermine,
> Each did the others worke more beautifie;
> So diff'ring both in willes, agreed in fine:
> So all agreed through sweete diuersitie,
> This Gardin to adorne with all varietie.   (II. xii. 58–59)

One must not miss the irony in Spenser's conception of this un-holy alliance made, as it were, in the name of the Adversary against Temperance; nor in the lines:

> And that, which all faire workes doth most aggrace,
> The art, which all that wrought, appeared in no place.
>   (II. xii. 58)

Both Art and Nature, in other words, are equally responsible, or rather culpable, in the light of the general motive of seduction, which is the "fine" their differing "willes" agree upon; and this idea is firmly realized through the bathing maidens, whose natural charms are revealed and concealed by the techniques of the art of seduction. It is not, again, that Art is deceptive while Nature is true. Postlapsarian Nature, as we have already been reminded, shares the general tendency to corruption. It too is beset by impurities, perversities and wantonness. It is thus as a result of an illegitimate relationship between them that, not at once, but by stages, perfect deception arises:

> And ouer all, of purest gold was spred,
> A trayle of yuie in his natiue hew;
> For the rich mettall was so coloured,
> That wight, who did not well auis'd it vew,
> Would surely deeme it to be yuie trew.   (II. xii. 61)

The well-avised wight can bring no better aid to the illumination of Spenser's thought than a passage from a well-known contemporary rhetorician, which analyzes the several possible relationships between Art and Nature.

George Puttenham's Arte of English Poesie appeared the year before The Faerie Queene and had been in the process of composition and revision for a period of twenty years.[4] There can be little doubt that Spenser knew the book, but it is sufficient for my purpose to suppose that he shared sufficiently the interests and orientations

35

of contemporary critics for such a line of thought to have been in
his mind.

Of rhetoric Puttenham says:

> What else is language and utterance, and discourse of persuasion,
> and argument in man, then the vertues of a well-constituted bodie
> and minde little lesse natural than his very sensuall actions,
> saving that the one is perfited by nature at once, the other not
> without exercise and iteratian? . . . there bee artes and methods
> both to speake and to persuade . . . by which the naturall is in
> some sort relieved, as the eye by his spectacle . . . in his im-
> perfection . . . in which respect I call those artes of grammer,
> logicke and rhetoricke not bare imitations, as the painters or
> kervers craft and worke in a forraine subject viz. a lively por-
> traite in his table or wood, but by long and studious observation
> rather a repetition or reminiscence naturall, reduced into per-
> fection, and made prompt by use and exercise.[5]

And to complete a description which could well apply to Acrasia's
"rhetoric," comes his account of figures and figurative speeches,
which, he says, are

> Instruments of ornament but also in a sort abuses or trespasses
> passing ordinary limits of utterance and occupied with intent to
> deceive the minde, drawing it to a certaine doubleness . . . seek-
> ing to inveigle and appassionate the minde . . . by a lively and
> good grace set upon words and sentences . . . by alterations in
> shape, sounde and sense, by way of surplusage, defect, disorder,
> mutation, and putting into our speaches more pithe and substaunce,
> subtilitie, quicknesse, efficacie, moderation, in this or that sort
> tuning and tempering them by amplification, abridgement, opening,
> closing, enforcing, meekening, etc.[6]

So far the Rhetorician, Puttenham on the Poet, the Maker as "(by
way of resemblance and reverently) God: who without any travell to
his divine imagination, made all the world of thought," provides us
with a complex definition of the greatest relevance to Spenser's
Bower.

> Our Maker or Poet is to play many parts and not one alone, as
> first to devise his plot or subject, then to fashion his poeme,
> thirdly to use his metricall proportions, and last of all to utter
> with pleasure and delight, which restes in his maner of language
> and stile . . . whereof the many moodes and strange phrases are

called figures, it is not altogether with him as with the craftsman, for in that he uses his metricall proportions by appointed
and harmonicall measures and distances, he is like the Carpenter or Joyner, for borrowing their tymber and stuffe of nature
they appoint and order it by art otherwise then nature would
doe, and work effects in appearance contrary to hers. Also in
that which the Poet speaks or reports of another mans tale or
doings, as Homer of Priamus or Ulisses, he is as the painter or
Kerver that worke by imitation and representation in a forrain
subject, in that he speakes figuratively, or argues subtillie, or
perswades copiously and vehemently, as doth the cunning gardener that using nature as coadjutor, furders her conclusions
and many times maketh her effects more absolute and strange.
But for that in our Maker or Poet, which restes onely in devise
and issues from an excellente sharpe and quick invention, holpen
by a clear and bright phantasie and imagination, he is not as the
painter to counterfeit the naturall by the like effects and not the
same, nor as the gardiner aiding nature to worke both the same
and the like, nor as the Carpenter to worke effects utterly unlike,
but even as nature herselfe, working by her owne peculiar vertue
and proper instinct.[7]

We may now discern more clearly the operation of Spenser's key
metaphor in the Bower of Bliss. It is this metaphor, derived from
such a contemporary analysis of "Art," rather than a simple nega-
tive-positive contrast between Art and Nature, which fully carries,
and carries the full implications of, a relationship to sexual pleasure
which is illegitimate and eventually frustrating. The pleasures of
the senses, nature and art are all in themselves good, and all, in
this sublunary world, subject to "surplusage, defect, disorder."
Acrasia's Bower inveigles Temperance into an improper relationship to the senses, one which subtly shifts the balance of the mind,
making those pleasures ends in themselves, vying one with another,
outdoing each other in delectability and losing the name of action,
as has the Genius of the place, with his loose garment falling to the
ground about his heels, "not fit for speedy pace, or manly exercise"
(II. xii. 46); losing too, while the Rose fades and falls away, their
culmination and consummation—"progenie," the "pleasant and lovely
cause"[8] for which rhetoric, if it is to avoid sophistication, should
plead.

As the improper alliance between Art and Nature, an alliance
which neither represents Nature, nor uses her raw materials for
objects of use, nor furthers her effects by such techniques as graft-

ing and pruning, nor penetrates beyond accident and adjunct to conceive and embody Idea, but in which each partner usurps the other's function in a sterile rivalry, each strives to produce delightful phenomena which are unreplenishable and spend themselves; so the breeding of pleasure upon pleasure ends neither in fruit nor form, but in self-consumption, the greedy depasturing of delight.

It is significant that the "natural" gardening mode of the Art-Nature relationship, mentioned by Puttenham, is referred to by Spenser both in the Garden of Adonis and in the Temple of Venus. In the Garden, the fruitful "seminarie of kindes," wherefrom all plenty and all pleasure flows,

> Ne needs there Gardiner to set, or sow,
> To plant or prune: for of their owne accord
> All things, as they created were, doe grow,
> And yet remember well the mightie word,
> Which first was spoken by th'Almightie lord,
> That bad them to increase and multiply.   (III. vi. 34)

But the Temple of Venus, where Amoret's natural womanhood is brought to civil perfection, lacked no tree, no flower, no pleasure of the senses, and no "queint device"; it is

> The onely pleasant and delightfull place,
> That ever troden was of footings trace.
> For all that nature by her mother wit
> Could frame in earth, and forme of substance base,
> Was there, and all that nature did omit,
> Art playing second natures part, supplyed it.   (IV. x. 21)

In this "luxurious plentie of all pleasure," there are lawns, springs, brooks, mounts, dales, walks, alleys, banks and arbours:

> Delightfull bowres, to solace louers trew;
> False Labyrinthes, fond runners eyes to daze;
> All which by nature made did nature selfe amaze.   (IV. x. 24)

Polixenes' application of the gardening metaphor in Shakespeare's Winter's Tale (IV. iv. 88ff) is in line with Puttenham's and Spenser's, save for a perhaps greater insistence upon, and a more "humane" acceptance of, the ultimately beneficient, natural origin of Art itself. In reply to Perdita's youthful, and properly pastoral, distrust of the adulterations of Art—Gillyvors are called Nature's bastards because

> There is an art which in their piedness, shares
> With great creating nature—

Polixenes argues:

> Say there be;
> Yet nature is made better by no mean,
> But nature makes that mean; so o'er that art
> Which you say adds to nature, is an art
> That nature makes. You see, sweet maid, we marry
> A gentler scion to the wildest stock,
> And make conceive a bark of baser kind
> By bud of nobler race. This is an art
> Which does mend nature, change it rather; but
> The art itself is nature.

It was easier for Shakespeare's Polixenes to be at home with the creativities of Nature and of Art. In Spenser's thought, despite its sanguine Renaissance balance, is implicit the puritan suspicion of the works of Nature equally with the best man can produce as Art. Both must be tamed. Una teaches truth to Satyrane's good "salvage people." The Puritan's central antinomy will be Nature-Grace, and it is this element in the Spenserian synthesis which lives again in Comus. Similarly, the Puritan rhetoricians following Ramus, with their distrust of the pleasures of ornament, will shift the centre of gravity entirely from the gorgeousness of display to the truth displayed by naked argument. John Hoskins, one of the most eloquent of the Ramists, says:

> The order of God's creatures in themselves is not only admirable and glorious, but eloquent; then he that could apprehend the consequences of things in their truth and utter his apprehensions as truly were a right orator.[9]

This brings the wheel full circle with what is almost an epitaph for that Renaissance poetic which was to bow, in the next century, before the onslaughts of the Royal Society:

> So that we may see, that Art is the wisdom of God but yet as it is energetick in the thing, so it is called Ars, so that mark this, that Art is the Law of God, whereunto he created things, whereby he governeth them, and whereunto they yield obedience; for by their obedience we come to see the frame; therefore the Art is Gods wisdom as it is resplendent in things . . . Mark this well, for the Schooles run into many absurdities, whilst they have thought that Art is in a man's head, and not in the thing.[10]

SPENSER AND THE REVELATION OF ST. JOHN

John E. Hankins

It has long been recognized that Spenser made numerous borrowings from the Revelation of St. John in Book I of the Faerie Queene. The Variorum edition conveniently lists those observed by Upton and other commentators. In a recent study, Mrs. Josephine Waters Bennett has suggested that the Revelation not only furnished Spenser with particular passages but largely determined the structure of Book I.[1] Her important contribution is not the discovery of new borrowings, though she observes several, but her exposition of the Revelation from the Protestant point of view. From several English commentaries and from glosses in the Geneva Bible, she shows that the latter half of the Revelation was interpreted in the sixteenth century as an allegory of the Protestant conflict with the Roman church, and concludes that this fact has an important bearing on Book I, which is now generally believed to involve a similar allegory.

To be convincing, Mrs. Bennett's suggestion needs the support of more numerous and impressive parallels than have yet been adduced. Also, the pattern or plan of Spenser's borrowings is left rather vague. In considering these, we should remember that the Revelation itself borrows very extensively from the Old Testament and that commentators regularly noted the relationship of various texts in different parts of the Bible.[2] It is not enough, then, to consider the Revelation alone in studying Spenser's imagery; one must examine other biblical passages to which he would have been referred. In addition to doing this, I have examined the Latin commentaries of a number of the church fathers with a view to discovering any significant interpretations which may throw light upon Spenser's allegory.[3] While it is quite likely that Spenser had read some of these—they are frequently mentioned by his contemporaries—the interpretations which I have noted in the following pages all have the earmarks of theological commonplaces, for which it is not necessary to assign a particular source. Some of them shed new light on the allegory, while others confirm suggestions already tentatively advanced.

Reprinted by permission of the author and the Modern Language Association of America from PMLA, Vol. 60 (1945), pp. 364–381. A revised version of this article appears in the author's Source and Meaning in Spenser's Allegory: A Study of "The Faerie Queene," The Clarendon Press, Oxford, 1971.

The latter half of the Revelation, from chapter 12 on, presents a conflict between the forces of evil and the forces of good in connection with events preceding the Last Judgment. The forces of evil are represented by the Great Dragon, the Beast from the Sea, the False Prophet, and the Babylonian harlot; the forces of good by the Woman clothed with the Sun, the Archangel Michael—usually interpreted as Christ—the Bride of the Lamb, and Christ himself. There is a further contrast between the cities of Babylon and Jerusalem, signifying the congregations of the wicked and of the good, respectively. As I shall demonstrate, all of these find parallels in Spenser's allegory and exercise a controlling influence upon it. Though he has changed his characters and situations to accord with the conventions of medieval romance, they are clearly traceable to their biblical prototypes as interpreted in the commentaries. Besides the political allegory of the conflict between the Roman and the reformed churches, he has used the moral allegory of the restoration to Eden as the symbol of man's spiritual regeneration.

To begin with an admitted parallel, we know that Spenser patterned Duessa after the Babylonian harlot or "great whore" of Rev. 17. Duessa is called a "scarlot whore" (viii. 29); like the harlot, she bears a golden cup in her hand (viii. 14, 25) and rides upon a seven-headed beast. The stripping of Duessa after her champion Orgoglio is killed is traced by Upton to the statement in Rev. 17:16 that the harlot shall be made desolate and naked; and Mrs. Bennett thinks Spenser's details derive from Ariosto.[4] For another significant parallel, however, we may turn to the denunciation of Babylon in Isaiah 47, where we find not only the stripping but also the sorceries and enchantments which Spenser attributes to Duessa:

> Come down, and sit in the dust, O virgin daughter of Babylon; sit on the ground: there is no throne, O daughter of the Chaldeans: for thou shalt no more be called tender and delicate.
> . . . Uncover thy locks, make bare the leg, uncover the thigh, pass over the rivers.
> Thy nakedness shall be uncovered, yea, thy shame shall be seen . . .
> But these two things shall come to thee in a moment in one day, the loss of children, and widowhood: they shall come upon thee in their perfection for the multitude of thy sorceries, and for the great abundance of thine enchantments . . .
> Stand now with thine enchantments, and with the multitude of thy sorceries, wherein thou hast laboured from thy youth.
>
> (vv. 1–3, 9, 12)

The unpleasant details of Duessa's appearance (viii. 46–48) are in part drawn from a similar passage in Isaiah 3, where the prophet declares that God will strip away the finery of the daughters of Jerusalem because of their pride and wantonness:

> Therefore the Lord will smite with a scab the crown of the head of the daughters of Zion, and the Lord will discover their secret parts . . .
> And it shall come to pass, that instead of sweet smell there shall be stink; and instead of a girdle a rent; and instead of well set hair baldness; and instead of a stomacher a girding of sackcloth; and burning instead of beauty. (vv. 17, 24)

Spenser has expanded the description; but the scabby head, baldness, and foul smell appear to be definite reminiscences from this passage.

The figure of Babylon seems also to have been Spenser's major source for the character of Lucifera, who dwells in the House of Pride. As I have shown elsewhere, her name and some hints for her character are drawn from Natalis Comes;[5] but her character is elaborated far beyond these hints. As the primary source for Duessa is the Babylonian harlot, the type of lust, so the primary source for Lucifera is the "daughter of Babylon," the type of pride. For each of his two characters Spenser draws details from both images of Babylon, but in one case his emphasis is upon lust, while in the other it is upon pride.

The word Lucifera is obviously the feminine form of Lucifer, a name which occurs only once in the Scriptures, where it is applied to Nebuchadnezzar, the king of Babylon (Isa. 14:12). Considering Lucifer as a name applied to the king of Babylon, it is logical that Lucifera, the feminine form of his name, should be applied to the feminine personification of his city, so widely known as an example of pride. Spenser must have known the usual identification of Lucifer with Satan;[6] but, granting this identification, it was still appropriate that Babylon should be personified as Lucifera, Satan's feminine counterpart. In the medieval commentaries, just as Jerusalem symbolizes the church, the bride of Christ, so Babylon symbolizes the congregation of the wicked, the spouse of the devil.[7] It is therefore quite fitting that Satan should be Lucifera's companion as she rides forth in her chariot (iv. 36).

We may first observe how the figure of Babylon determines the imagery of Lucifera seated upon her throne, with a dragon beneath her feet. In Rev. 12, the Great Dragon is expelled from heaven, dragging a third part of the stars with him. Since he is referred to in verse 9 as "that old serpent, called the Devil, and Satan," his fall is assumed to be the same as those of Satan (Luke 10:18) and Lucifer. Further identification of Lucifer with the Great Dragon is suggested by Jeremiah 51:34, "Nebuchadrezzar the king of Babylon hath devoured me, . . . he hath swallowed me up like a dragon." I suggest that Lucifera's dragon is one of several incarnations in which the devil appears in the Faerie Queene, and that this comes about through the identification of Lucifer with the king of Babylon and with the Great Dragon, or Satan. Lucifera seated above her dragon is basically the same image as Duessa seated upon her beast, both stemming from the Babylonian harlot and the beast of Rev. 17. Bishop Haymo explains of this beast that it is really the devil, while the harlot represents all sinners, and that just as the church is founded upon Christ, so the congregation of the wicked is founded upon the devil; hence Babylon is presented as mounted upon the beast.[8] Spenser identifies this beast with the Great Dragon by drawing from the latter descriptive details for Duessa's beast (vii. 18). Lucifera's beast is also a "dreadfull dragon," and Lucifera herself represents "all the multitude of the proud," as Augustine interprets the Babylonian harlot.[9] Her personal appearance is imitated from the harlot. She is adorned "with royall robes and gorgeous array . . . In glistring gold and perelesse pretious stone" (iv. 8), while the harlot is "arrayed in purple and scarlet colour, and decked with gold and precious stones and pearls" (Rev. 17:4). Since purple and scarlet are traditional colors of royal robes, the resemblance is apparent. However, Spenser calls her a "mayden queene" in imitation of the "virgin daughter of Babylon" in Isaiah 47:1, and her throne may be a reminiscence of the same verse.

The figure of the Babylonian harlot undergoes another transformation in Spenser's procession of the seven deadly sins (iv. 16–38), where Lucifera, herself representing pride, rides forth in a chariot drawn by six beasts, whose riders are the six other deadly sins. We have just seen that Spenser identifies the harlot's beast with the seven-headed Dragon of Rev. 12; and concerning the Dragon several commentators advance a moral interpretation. Richard of St. Victor identifies the Dragon's seven heads with the seven deadly sins, and the ten horns with the "Decalogue of the impious," the reverse of the Ten Commandments.[10] St. Bruno gives the following account:

> For the great red dragon is the devil, who in the shape of a serpent first deceived man and who now appears red because of the blood of the martyrs, which he ceases not to shed. Here, however, he is said to have seven heads; namely, the seven capital sins, which are born from Mother Pride, and from which as from

beginnings all other sins are born. For these [seven] are vainglory, envy, wrath, sloth, avarice, gluttony, and lust. The ten horns are indeed all other sins, which are derived from these heads and which, since they are many, he seeks to express by that number in which all numbers are contained. For number does not progress beyond ten, but that number revolved upon itself includes all other numbers.[11]

The fact that Lucifera's appearance is drawn from the Babylonian harlot suggests that her advisers and their beasts may in some way be indebted to the beastly heads which represent the deadly sins. For the grotesque details of his procession, Spenser has used other sources,[12] but the inception of his idea of connecting the harlot with the deadly sins may well have come from the commentaries, where the connection was already made. Perhaps he may also have recalled Dante's transformation of the harlot's beast in canto 32 of the Purgatorio, where the chariot which represents the church puts forth seven beastly heads, usually interpreted to mean the seven deadly sins. Upon the chariot seat appears a shameless harlot, and beside her a giant who exchanges lustful kisses with her.

Forgetting Dante's political allegory, we may note his remarkable transformation of the imagery of Rev. 17. The harlot is the same, but her beast is the monstrous perversion of a chariot. It is still a chariot, but from it grow the seven heads of the biblical beast, representing the seven deadly sins. We can see how this image may have suggested a chariot for Lucifera, drawn by the other deadly sins.

If Spenser used Dante's imagery as a source for Lucifera, he may also have used it as a source for Duessa, since both are imitated from the Babylonian harlot. Duessa's beast is taken directly from the biblical images, but her companion Orgoglio may well have been suggested by the giant in Dante. The exchange of lustful kisses suggests the amour of Duessa and Orgoglio, to which there is no specific biblical parallel, the harlot of Rev. 17 not having a masculine companion.

Besides drawing details from the harlot's beast and the Great Dragon, Spenser has used the Beast from the Sea in Rev. 13 as a source for the wounding of Duessa's beast by Prince Arthur.[14] The Beast from the Sea was regularly identified by the commentators as Antichrist, the false Christ who should appear in the last days to persecute Christians and draw them from the true faith (Mat. 24:24, I John 2:18). Augustine thinks he represents the pagan rulers who formerly persecuted the church but in later times represents the heretics within the church.[15] Richard of St. Victor identifies him with the "cruel princes of the pagans."[16] These are perhaps sufficient hints to equal him with the "Paynim king" against whom the Faerie Queene is to fight a great battle near the end of Spenser's epic (xi. 7). Sixteenth century Protestants interpreted Antichrist as the Pope of Rome and the wounded head of the Beast from the Sea as the effect of the Protestant Reformation. The Beast received his authority from the Great Dragon, or the devil (Rev. 13:2), and his demand that all peoples should worship him was taken to mean the claim of papal supremacy.[17]

In Rev. 13, following the Beast from the Sea there emerges the Beast from the Land, having two horns in imitation of a lamb. This beast is later identified as the False Prophet (19:20), whom I take to be the original of Archimago. That enchanter's name may be interpreted either as Arch-magician or Arch-image. In both interpretations it is applicable to the False Prophet, who causes people to worship the Beast from the Sea by drawing down fire from heaven and performing other strange enchantments. He fashions an image of the Beast and insists that all must worship it; those who refuse are persecuted and killed. He causes the image to speak as though alive and works many other miracles to seduce men from the true faith. His very appearance is a hypocritical disguise, imitating the appearance of the Lamb of God and of the true apostles who were sent forth "as lambs among wolves" (Luke 10:3). He is the fulfillment of Christ's warning against "false prophets, which come to you in sheep's clothing, but inwardly they are ravening wolves" (Mat. 7:15) and of St. Paul's caution against "false apostles, deceitful workers, transforming themselves into the apostles of Christ" (II Cor. 11:13).

In explaining the political allegory, students of Spenser have found difficulty in attaching Archimago's activities to any one person and have generally concluded that he represents the subversive activities of the Catholic party in general. This multiple interpretation coincides closely with that usually given of the False Prophet. St. Martin identifies him with "the multitude of the disciples of Antichrist,"[18] Richard of St. Victor with "the chorus of false teachers";[19] and others give similar explanations. Van Der Noot declares that he represents "all manner of false prophets and ungodly teachers," and that in the sixteenth century these are the friars, monks, canons, and priests of the Roman church.[20] In using Archimago to represent all this group, Spenser is imitating the Revelation, where one False Prophet is used to personify the many "false prophets" who are foretold in earlier books of the Bible.[21]

Certain of Archimago's activities are suggested by those of the False Prophet. Both fashion false images as a means of deception, the False Prophet deceiving mankind with an image of Antichrist, Archimago deceiving Redcross with an image of Una. As the False Prophet puts on the disguise of a lamb in imitation of Christ, so Archimago disguises himself in the armor of Redcross, the true follower of Christ. Archimago's imprisonment in the dungeon (I. xii. 36) and subsequent escape therefrom (II. i. 1) are probably suggested by the False Prophet's imprisonment in the pit and lake of fire and his supposed emergence therefrom with Satan and Antichrist shortly before the second resurrection.[22]

Mrs. Bennett has sought to identify Una with the Woman clothed with the Sun (Rev. 12), pointing out that her flight into the wilderness parallels Una's retreat into the wilds.[23] Since the Woman is persecuted by the Great Dragon, who is finally thrown out of heaven by Michael,[24] we have a close parallel with Una's exile from Eden until Redcross overthrows the dragon who has usurped her place there. The Woman clothed with the Sun is variously identified as the Virgin Mary, the mother of Christ,[25] and as the church, the bride of Christ;[26] some commentators also identify her with the bride in Canticles.[27] It is important to realize that the Woman clothed with the Sun, the bride of the Lamb in Rev. 19, and the bride in Canticles were considered to be the same, for Spenser has drawn details for Una from all three sources. Also, since Una is the antitype to Duessa, the allegory identifies her with the Woman clothed with the Sun. In summarizing the allegory of the Revelation, Richard of St. Victor comments as follows:

> These are two cities, one of the devil, the other of God, dissident from the very beginning, never having peace between themselves. These are two women, of whom we read that one is clothed with the sun and that the other sits upon a scarlet beast. For the total mass of the evildoers and the universal sum of the good are two cities and two women. They are cities because they are enriched by the numerous multitude of their citizens. They are women because, being coupled to their husbands, Babylon to the devil and Jerusalem to Christ, they are made fruitful of a multiple progeny.

The antithesis between the Babylonian harlot and the Woman clothed with the Sun suggests that, as Duessa is copied from the former, Una may be indebted to the latter, who is here definitely identified as the bride of Christ.

When Una appears unveiled for her bridal day (xii. 21–23), Spenser's description draws upon the biblical images. Upton has noticed that the whiteness of her raiment recalls Rev. 19:8, and that the phrase "withouten spot" comes from Cant. 4:7, "Thou art all fair, my love; there is no spot in thee." Una's "blazing brightness"and "sunshyny face" may owe something to the Woman clothed with the Sun. Her earlier adventures show a significant indebtedness to Cant. 5, in which occurs the only reference to the bride's having worn a veil:

> I opened to my beloved; but my beloved had withdrawn himself, and was gone . . . I sought him, but I could not find him; I called him, but he gave me no answer.
> The watchmen that went about the city found me, they smote me, they wounded me; the keepers of the walls took away my veil from me. (vv. 6–7)

Here I believe may be an important suggestion for Spenser's plot. The bride awakes after dreaming that she hears the lover's voice and opens the door, but she finds that he is gone, upon which she goes out to seek him and inquire for him. This affords a parallel to Redcross' desertion of Una while she slept, her sad awakening, and her journey in search of him (ii. 6–8). The bride's encounter with the watchmen suggests an incident of Una's journey, Sansloy's attempt upon her chastity, when he uses force upon her and snatches away her veil (vi. 4–6).

We have now demonstrated Una's indebtedness to the bride of Christ, who figuratively represents the church. This coincides with the usual interpretation of Una as the Church of England, as opposed to the false Church of Rome; more particularly, Una represents Elizabeth in her capacity as head of the church. Furthermore, the bride is identified with the Virgin Mary, who also represents the church, a fact which accounts for the stress laid upon Una's virginity and which fits in well with England's love for the Virgin Queen. The use of Una to represent the church may also explain her identification with Truth, since Paul tells us that the church is "the pillar and ground of the truth" (I Tim. 3:15).

Only one major character remains to be interpreted, the Redcross Knight, who, if Spenser has followed consistently the pattern borrowed from the Revelation, should correspond to the figure of Christ. The picture of Christ in Rev. 19 is that of a knight, mounted upon a white charger, attacking and overcoming in turn the Babylonian harlot, Antichrist, the False Prophet, and the Great Dragon. Spenser's identification of his knight is made in the second stanza of the first canto. The knight wears upon his breast a "bloodie crosse," suggested by the biblical knight "clothed with a vesture dipped in blood" (v. 13). Spenser says of his knight, "Right <u>faithfull true</u> he was in deede and word." In the Revelation, the knight "was called Faithful and True, and in righteousness doth he make war" (v. 11). Also, this biblical knight "had a name written, that no man knew, but he himself" (v. 12). Following this lead, Spenser withholds from the reader for a time the name of the Redcross Knight.

As Spenser tells us in his letter to Raleigh, the arms of Redcross are the "whole armor of God" mentioned in Ephesians 6. In this account the shield is the shield of faith. Elsewhere Spenser refers to it as a "sunnebright shield" (xi. 40). This phrase recalls Prince Arthur's shield of diamond, which is so bright as to dazzle Orgoglio and which is called a "sunshiny shield" (viii. 19–20). Dodge suggests the indebtedness of this shield to the magical shield in the Orlando Furioso (xxii. 81–86), because they similarly dazzle opposing fighters;[29] but Ariosto's shield is not of diamond. For this feature, Spenser is probably indebted to the diamond shield in Tasso,[30] who identifies it in his explanation of the allegory as "the special safeguard of the Lord God." It is likely that both Spenser and Tasso had in mind Psalms 84:11, "For the Lord God is a sun and shield," and that Spenser recalls the biblical image in both the silver shield of Redcross and the diamond shield of Arthur.

In studying the pattern of Spenser's allegory as adapted from the Revelation, we should remember that the victories of the knight on the white horse over the harlot, Antichrist, the False Prophet, and the Great Dragon, as well as the subsequent marriage of the Lamb, all accompany the first resurrection, which is to be followed by the millennium. It is important to bear this fact in mind in order to grasp Spenser's meaning. For the general disposition of the medieval church was to follow St. Augustine in denying the existence of the millennium as a period of corporal delights at some time in the future. Rather it refers to the present happiness of those who have been baptized into Christ's church. Augustine interprets Christ's words in John 5:24–25 and 5:28–29 as referring to the two resurrections; the statement that "the hour is coming, and now is" indicates that the first resurrection has already begun and must therefore be a rising from spiritual death through belief in Christ. Augustine is uncertain whether the second resurrection, in which bodies as well as souls shall rise, would actually occur in 1000 A. D., or whether the millennial figure is used as a round number, the solid quadrate or cube of 10, signifying eternity.[31] Commentators after 1000 A. D. naturally adopted the second explanation.

It thus follows that Christ's victory as described in the Revelation is an allegorical portrayal of his earthly ministry. Now, while

SPENSER AND THE REVELATION OF ST. JOHN

Spenser's basic moral allegory in Book I is that of a Christian's
progress through the spiritual perils of this life, he uses the familiar idea of Christ's ministry as the pattern of the Christian's career. And, as in the Revelation, this pattern is symbolically presented in the form of a knightly quest. The parallel is developed in
Redcross' final battle with the dragon in Eden, a battle which corresponds to the victory of Christ over the Great Dragon as described
in the Revelation. But if this is true, Professor Courthope declares,
Spenser has been guilty of careless workmanship, for he has given
us no clue to his meaning in his description of the dragon.[32] The
details of his dragon are found in the medieval romances concerning
St. George but not in the Revelation; his dragon is neither red nor
seven-headed, as is the biblical one.

To discover a clue, we must observe that Spenser's method is
copied from the Bible. That his dragon Error, Lucifera's dragon,
Duessa's beast, and the dragon in Eden represent the devil, or Evil
Principle, in various forms. Similarly, the Bible presents several
beasts who are interpreted to represent the devil. Besides the
Great Dragon of Rev. 12 and the harlot's beast of Rev. 19, there are
the ten-horned beast of Daniel 7 and the Leviathan of Job 41, as well
as several others. Having used the seven-headed beasts of the Revelation as a pattern for Duessa's beast, Spenser models his dragon
in Eden after the more terrifying descriptions in Daniel and Job.
The iron teeth of his dragon are found in Daniel (7:7, 19). The burning eyes, smoking mouth and nostrils, close-fitting scales, invulnerability to wounds, enormous size, and overwhelming power are
reminiscent of the Leviathan.[33] The commentators leave no doubt
that this "king over all the children of pride" is the same as the
Great Dragon.[34] In rendering this passage, Origen translates
"Leviathan" as "the apostate dragon."[35] Isaiah declares that "in
that day the Lord . . . shall punish Leviathan and . . . slay the dragon that is in the sea" (27:1), an apparent prophecy of Christ's victory over the Great Dragon and the Beast from the Sea. Since the
Leviathan and the beast in Daniel are definitely identified with the
Great Dragon, Spenser was free to use their descriptions for his
dragon; and since these descriptions are so like the dragon of the
romances, he was able to give a recognizable picture of the devil
within the framework of the St. George story.

Admitting that Redcross' victory over the dragon in Eden corresponds to the defeat of the Great Dragon in the Revelation, we have
still to interpret it in terms of Christ's earthly ministry. I judge
that the particular significance of Redcross' triumph is the victory
over death. As Christ began his ministry with victory over sin and

ended it with victory over death, so Redcross begins his quest by defeating the dragon Error and ends it by conquering the dragon in Eden. Spenser identifies this dragon with death in xi. 49, where the "ever damned beast" cannot approach the Tree of Life because "he was deadly made." It was the dragon who brought death into Eden (st. 47), exiling mankind thence, and only by his overthrow can man be restored to the joys of Eden, equivalent of the millennial reign and the happiness of those spiritually reborn in Christ.

It should be observed that the three-day period of Redcross' fight with the dragon resembles the period of Christ's victory over death. Christ began his struggle with death on Good Friday and arose from the dead early in the morning of the third day. Redcross struggles with the dragon for two days and achieves victory early in the morning of the third day. The analogy between Christ's victory over physical death and the Christian's victory over spiritual death is too well known to require elaboration. In Redcross' triumph, Christ's victory symbolizes the Christian's deliverance from original sin, "from the body of this death," in the words of St. Paul (Rom. 7:24).

During the period of Christ's entombment, he not only conquered death in his own person but visited the lower world to deliver the souls of the just who had died before his first advent. The Gospel of Nicodemus[36] is the major source of this "harrowing of hell" tradition, later popularized by the medieval miracle plays. According to this gospel, after Christ's entrance into the grave, he descended to hell, burst asunder its brazen doors, overcame and bound Satan, and brought forth the souls of the patriarchs and other good men of former times. He led them to the paradise of Eden, where they shall rest until the second resurrection, after which they shall ascend in the flesh to the holy city of God. Spenser evidently has this imagery in mind. After the dragon's death, Una's parents emerge with their retinue from the brazen doors of their castle and return to their former home in Eden. They represent Adam, Eve, and the patriarchs, symbolizing the human race, delivered by Christ from hell and the jaws of death, and returning to the paradise of Eden, which represents the spiritual bliss of those who abide in Christ.

For his own purposes Spenser has slightly altered the details of the Gospel of Nicodemus. The battle takes place, not in hell, but in Eden itself. He was able to make this change because the scriptural account in Genesis 3 does not specifically say that the Serpent was expelled from Eden along with Adam and Eve. Spenser's authority is probably Rev. 12:9, where Michael expels the Great Dragon from heaven. This is interpreted to mean Christ's expulsion of Satan from the hearts of the faithful, and also his expulsion of the wicked

from the midst of his church. Heaven here represents the church.[37]
The Garden of Eden and its companion garden in Canticles were also
sometimes interpreted to mean the church;[38] politically, Spenser
uses Eden to represent England.[39] By placing the battle in Eden,
Spenser is able to symbolize at the same time Christ's victory over
death for the salvation of all believers and the restoration of Truth
(Una) to the church by the overthrow of false doctrine. The political
allegory is usually taken to mean the restoration of royal supremacy
in the English church to Queen Elizabeth, after it had been surren-
dered to the papacy by Philip and Mary.[40]

There may also seem to be a difficulty in that the brazen tower of
Una's parents does not represent hell, since they enter it for protection against the dragon, not for service to him. The tower represents
the Limbo of the Fathers, in which the souls of the patriarchs were
preserved until Christ's earthly incarnation. Dante follows Aquinas
in making this Limbo the topmost circle in the cavern of hell.[41] Its
inhabitants are subject to the death of the unbaptized but not to the
torments of the wicked. They are thus part of Satan's kingdom of
death but are protected against his persecutions. Since one must
pass through Limbo to reach the lower regions of hell, the doors of
hell and the doors of Limbo are the same. It is these brazen doors
which Christ burst asunder to deliver mankind from death. It is
these same brazen doors from which Una's parents emerge to return to Eden.

Christ's victory over death involves his victory over hell. The
gates of hell are interpreted to mean the gates of death.[42] The
"jaws of death" and the "mouth of hell" are equivalent terms, made
so because "the grave" and "hell" are frequently equivalent in the
Old Testament, both being used to translate "Sheol."[43] In the Revelation the fourth horseman, Death, is accompanied by Hell (6:8); at
the final judgment Death and Hell give up their dead and are cast
together into the lake of fire (20:13−14).

Spenser clearly intends to use this association. In describing the
dragon's head, he writes:

> for his deepe devouring jawes
> Wyde gaped, like the griesly mouth of hell,
> Through which into his darke abysse all ravin fell.   (xi. 12)

"Abyss" is the word used in the Vulgate for the "bottomless pit" of
hell (Rev. 20:1, 3). Spenser's words are borrowed from Isaiah 5:14,
"Therefore gapeth hell, and openeth her mouth marvelous wide."
This is the reading of all sixteenth century versions except the

Genevan but was not adopted in the Authorised Version, with the result that a highly popular Elizabethan phrase is not clear to modern readers. I have suggested elsewhere that this verse from Isaiah is the source of the "hell-mouth" portrayals in medieval miracle plays and in pictorial art of the Renaissance.[44] Hell-mouth is usually represented as a monstrous beastly head with its jaws stretched wide; in a number of pictures it is a brazen head in imitation of the brazen gates of hell.[45]

Spenser thus makes the dragon's mouth resemble the mouth of hell. This gives significance to the final combat when the dragon attempts to swallow up the knight but receives his death wound instead; even so hell and death sought to swallow up Christ but were overcome by him instead. In the Vulgate's description of the Leviathan occurs the reading, "Quis revelabit faciem indumenti eius? et in medium oris eius quis intrabit?"[46] This reading may have determined Spenser's handling of the scene. For it is Christ who dared to enter into the jaws of death and the mouth of hell, and to conquer them for the salvation of the human race as the climax of his earthly ministry; so must the Christian be willing to dare who would conquer sin and death. Spenser has thus given to the battle of St. George and the dragon a profound symbolic meaning.

We have already observed Spenser's use of Babylon the harlot as a source for his imagery but have not discussed his use of Babylon the city. His introduction of the New Jerusalem in the tenth canto suggests that he may employ its opposite, Babylon, the fall of which is pictured in Rev. 18. These two cities play a prominent part in the Bible and among the commentators, who generally agree that one represents the followers of Christ and the other the followers of Satan, wherever they may be found. Allegorically, the names do not designate particular cities in particular places, but rather the congregations of the good and of the evil throughout the whole earth. Augustine explains that Jerusalem means "vision of peace," while Babylon means "confusion."[47] Jerusalem is the City of God (Psalms 46:4); Babylon is the City of Destruction (Isa. 19:18). There are two Jerusalems. The "beloved city" of Rev. 20:9 is the church of Christ on earth, while the New Jerusalem of Rev. 21 is the church of Christ in heaven. Sometimes the two are not clearly distinguished, since one obviously provides the entrance to the other.

Spenser has introduced Babylon, or the assembly of the wicked, in the castles of Lucifera and Orgoglio, while the earthly Jerusalem is represented by the house of Coelia, whose name signifies "heavenly." The key to his plan is found in the Sermon on the Mount. His name for the heavenly city, "the City of the Great King," is taken from Matthew 5:35, where it is applied to Jerusalem and is in turn borrowed from Psalms 48:2. His contrast between the two cities is based on Matthew 7:13–14:

> Enter ye in at the strait gate: for wide is the gate, and broad is the way, that leadeth to destruction, and many there be which go in thereat:
> Because strait is the gate and narrow is the way, which leadeth unto life, and few there be that find it.

Here destruction suggests the City of Destruction, the assembly of the wicked who travel the way to hell, while life represents the eternal life of the heavenly city. The explanation is made more definite by Van Der Noot's comment:

> Here you may see and iudge of God, and the deuil, Christ, and Antechrist, the kyngdome of God, and of Sathan, the Churche of Christe, and the synagoge of Rome, or the assemblie of the reprobate, the broade waye, and the straite gate, heauen and hell, eternall lyfe and euerlastying death. [48]

The approach to Lucifera's House of Pride is "a broad high way" kept bare of vegetation by the multitudes of feet that travel it (iv. 2). This is of course the "broad way" which leads to destruction. Also, in Matthew 7:26 occurs the parable of the House built upon the Sand. Spenser identifies this house with Lucifera's palace, which is built "on a sandie hill" (iv. 5). According to Bishop Haymo, the House built upon the Sand is an image of Babylon: "There are two cities of this world, Jerusalem and Babylon, whose kings are Christ and the devil; one is founded upon the firm rock, the other upon the sand."[49]

The resemblance of Orgoglio's castle to Babylon is found in viii. 35–36. The rich array, royal arras, gold, and great store of all commodities are suggested by the riches of Babylon in Rev. 18:11–16. The blood of the innocents and martyrs comes from 17:6, in which the harlot Babylon is drunken with the blood of the martyrs. The altar from beneath which the spirits of the martyrs cry for vengeance is taken from Rev. 6:9–11. In the Revelation this is the altar before the throne of God, but it is mentioned again in 14:18, when an angel appears from it to cry out for the "harvest of the world" involving the destruction of Babylon.

In the approaches to Coelia's house and to the heavenly city, the "strait gate" and the "narrow way" are stressed repeatedly. In x. 5, one must stoop low to enter the door, which is a "streight and narrow way." Stanza 10 is little more than a paraphrase of the two biblical verses already quoted from Matthew, contrasting the "narrow path" and the "broad high way." Redcross proceeds by a "narrow way" to Mercy's hospital (st. 35), by a "painfull way" to the hermit's chapel (st. 46), and then sees "a little path, that was both steepe and long" which leads on to the heavenly city (st. 55). The entrance to Coelia's house is "warely watched night and day, For fear of many foes" (st. 5). This derives from Nehemiah 4:9, where the author states that when numerous foes conspired to fight Jerusalem and halt its rebuilding, "Nevertheless we made our prayer unto our God, and set a watch against them day and night, because of them." The parallel further identifies Coelia's house as the earthly Jerusalem, or the church of Christ on earth.

In Redcross' journey from Coelia's house to the hermitage of Heavenly Contemplation, he leaves behind Una, or Truth, and receives Mercy as his guide. This arrangement was probably suggested by Proverbs 16:6, "By mercy and truth iniquity is purged," by Psalms 25:10, "All the paths of the Lord are mercy and truth," and by the numerous other instances in which the two words occur together. Mercy and Truth share the task of bringing the sinful soul to repentance and guiding his feet into the right path.

The tenth canto contains several other biblical echoes not usually observed. Una's kiss (st. 29) is the holy kiss of greeting in the early church.[50] The phrase "thou man of earth" addressed to Redcross (st. 52) comes from Paul's sentence, "The first man is of the earth, earthy" (I Cor. 15:47). Since Paul is differentiating between natural bodies of flesh and spiritual bodies which will exist after the resurrection, Spenser's phrase simply means that Redcross will see heaven while still in his fleshly body. The injunction to "fast and pray" (st. 52) is distinctly biblical. The "highest mount" which he then ascends (st. 53) is of course the mount to which the angel carried John to show him the new Jerusalem (Rev. 21:10). It is the mount of vision; St. Bruno calls it "that ecstasy and excess of mind into which we can ascend on no other than spiritual feet."[51] Redcross' wish to remain on the mount or else to begin at once his journey to the heavenly city (st. 63) is recalled from two wishes expressed by Peter. The first was expressed on the Mount of Transfiguration when he exclaimed, "It is good to be here," and wished that he might remain (Mat. 17:4). The second was expressed at the Last Supper when Peter wished to die with Christ and accompany him to paradise but was told, "Whither I go thou canst not follow me now; but thou shalt follow me afterwards" (John 13:36). The terms of the refusal are much the same as those given to Redcross.

John's vision of the New Jerusalem also furnishes two details for Spenser's description of Eden, the Well of Life and the Tree of Life (Rev. 22:1-2). The Tree is the heavenly counterpart of the Tree that flourished in Eden, while the River of the Water of Life is the same as the well of living water offered to the woman of Samaria (John 4:14), the fountain[52] of water which sprang up in Eden (Gen. 2:6), and the river which flowed from the fountain (2:10).

Spenser's reference to Redcross' "baptized hands" (xi. 36) suggests that the Well of Life represents the holy water of baptism. Most of the commentators give this interpretation of the "water of life" in the Revelation;[53] Augustine calls it the baptismal font in the midst of the church.[54] Further proof is afforded by the comparison of Redcross' emergence from the Well to an eagle's renewing its youth in the sea (st. 34). The biblical references to the eagle's rejuvenation are Psalms 103:5 and Isaiah 40:31. Bishop Haymo comments significantly on both of these passages. Of the first he says:

> The nature of the eagle is such that in old age its beak and claws grow so large that it is unable to refresh itself with food. And indeed it then ascends toward the sun, until its feathers are burned away by the heat, and thence it falls into living water. Emerging therefrom, it pares down its beak and claws on a rock and, afterward taking food, renews its youth. So we, filled with many sins, when we are held in the old age of Adam [original sin], draw near to Christ, who is the true sun, by whose warmth and infusion of grace our sins are burned away. And thereafter we are laved with the waters of baptism, whereupon we break and dash to pieces our curved beak, that is our evil habit of mind, on the rock, that is Christ; conforming ourselves to him, we throw off that old age and renew our youth.[55]

This is an account similar to that observed by Professor Padelford in the medieval Physiologus.[56] In his comment on Isaiah 40:31, Bishop Haymo gives a different significance to the eagle's rejuvenation:

> And thus its hair, its feathers, and its whole body are renewed. So the redeemed, who have here experienced attrition by mortifying themselves, are renewed through incorruption, contemplating Christ the sun of justice, just as the eagle gazes at the sun with unwavering eyes.[57]

The phrase concerning attrition, "se attriverunt mortificando seipsos," has reference to the expiations of penance, which subdue the lusts of the body and strengthen the contemplative powers of the mind. By such a contemning of the body, Spenser's seer Heavenly Contemplation has gained powers of spiritual vision "as eagles eie, that can behold the sunne" and looks directly upon the brightness of God (x. 47).

Spenser's Tree of Life is indebted to the Tree in Rev. 22:2, which bears both fruit and "leaves . . . for the healing of the nations." This double function of fruit-bearing and healing is evident in Spenser's Tree. Spenser's fruit is red, the color of Christ's blood, and accordingly represents the Eucharist, the body and blood of Christ in the sacrament of the Lord's Supper. This accords with the commentators, who represent the Tree either as Christ or as the Cross on which Christ's body was broken and his blood was shed.[58] The Tree in the Revelation grows on both sides of the river; on the near side it represents the body and blood of Christ given for our refreshment in this life, but on the far side it represents the direct contemplation of Christ which we shall enjoy in paradise.[59]

The healing balm which flows from Spenser's Tree suggests the sacrament of Extreme Unction, administered to those in peril of death. In this sacrament the limbs are anointed with a healing oil both to strengthen the body and to heal the wounds of the mind. We have reason to believe that it was used in the English church of Spenser's day. Without naming it, Richard Hooker recommends it for those at point of death:

> God forbid we should think that the Church doth sin in permitting the wounds of such to be supplied with that oil which this gracious Sacrament doth yield, and their bruised minds not only need but beg.[60]

The reference to oil identifies this sacrament as Extreme Unction. Hooker's phrase "gracious Sacrament" reminds us of Spenser's "gracious ointment" which flows from the Tree (st. 48), "gracious" meaning "grace-imparting" in both instances.

The flowing of healing oil or balm from the Tree of Life is not Spenser's invention but derives from the Gospel of Nicodemus. There Adam prompts his son Seth to tell how, when Adam lay near death, Seth visited Eden and begged that Michael, the guardian of the gate, would give him some oil from the Tree of Life in order to heal his father. Michael replied that the request could not be granted and that Adam must die, but that after 5500 years from the creation of the world the Son of God should come into the earth and raise up Adam with oil from the Tree of Life.[61]

This concludes my observations of the biblical influences on Book I. Those influences are pervasive and decisive throughout the book. The Revelation of St. John and related passages in other parts of the Bible provide Spenser's basic pattern and much of his imagery. In addition to using the biblical pattern as a moral allegory of man's spiritual regeneration through Christ, he accepts the political explanation common among Protestants of his time and sets the whole in a framework of chivalric romance. The result is a mosaic of extraordinary richness, of which the religious element is a more important part than has generally been perceived.

NATURE AND GRACE IN THE FAERIE QUEENE

A. S. P. Woodhouse

I am to present for your consideration an hypothesis regarding Spenser's Faerie Queene.

Historical criticism is, I believe, more than a mere corrective. It may have for its object to restore, so far as possible, the conditions essential to a full communication between artist and audience, which include a common understanding of the potentialities and limits of the genre and, for the purpose of the poet's argument, the acceptance of a common frame of reference. Historical criticism, thus conceived, entails the use of hypothesis, which must submit to experimental verification. Besides the obvious tests of covering the principal phenomena and not running counter to any of the known evidence, a critical hypothesis is verified whenever it serves to bring into clearer relief the poem's aesthetic pattern and demonstrate its consistency. This is a criterion which we shall have occasion to apply. It involves, of course, an assumption, frequently rejected as hampering to scholarly ingenuity, that a great poet is a conscientious artist and knows what he is about.

The particular hypothesis which I am to advance turns upon one of the intellectual frames of reference common to Spenser and many other writers of the Renaissance, namely, their recognition of two levels of existence and experience, traditionally known as the order of nature and the order of grace. A few years ago I found that to read Milton's Comus in the light of this frame of reference was to sharpen, and also to modify, one's sense of the poem's pattern and its meaning;[1] and I promised myself that some day I would try the experiment of re-reading the Faerie Queene with this frame of reference, this apportionment of experience to the order of nature and the order of grace, in mind, and would see whether here also it might not serve to sharpen, and perhaps to modify, one's sense of the poem's pattern and its meaning. Let this be my excuse for the present delivery of coals to Newcastle, and for the temerity of a mere

Annual Tudor and Stuart Club Lecture, April 29, 1949.
Reprinted from English Literary History, Vol. 16 (1949), pp. 194–228, ©
The Johns Hopkins Press, by permission of The Johns Hopkins Press.

NATURE AND GRACE IN THE FAERIE QUEENE

Miltonist in lecturing on the Faerie Queene in the home of the great Variorum Spenser.

In Spenser's day, as still in Milton's, the two orders of nature and of grace were universally accepted as a frame of reference, whether they were specifically named or not. Within this frame of of reference[2] there was room for every degree of difference in attitude and emphasis: it was a frame of reference, not a body of doctrine. To the Christian, of course, both orders were subject to the power and providence of God, but exercised in a manner sufficiently different to maintain a clear-cut distinction between the two. In the natural order belonged not only the physical world, what is commonly called the world of nature inanimate and animate, but man himself considered simply as a denizen of that world. The rule of its order was expressed not only in the physical laws of nature, but in natural ethics (in what was significantly called the law of nature), and even in natural as opposed to revealed religion. This order was apprehended in experience and interpreted by reason; and it had its own wisdom, for upon the law of nature had been erected the ethical system of a Plato, an Aristotle or a Cicero. It had its own institutions, of which the highest was the state, but this is an aspect of the order of nature which need not detain us here . . . To the order of grace, on the other hand, belonged man in his character of supernatural being, with all that concerned his salvation, under the old dispensation and the new. The law of its government was the revealed will of God, received and interpreted by faith, and it included a special kind of experience called religious experience. The order of grace had also its appropriate institution, the Church, which, like the state, need not concern us here.

The relation between the order of nature and the order of grace was a problem which admitted of various solutions. One group of answers insisted on the contrast and wide divergence of the two orders, and these answers were returned by individuals and sects of opposite tendencies.

The ascetic and rigorist would emphasize the divergence, in order to depress nature and exalt grace; the naturalist, in order to exalt nature and depress grace, finding the demands of the higher order "unnatural" and denying their validity. Still in the same group were others who insisted on the divergence of nature and grace with the intention of accepting them both, but at the same time of avoiding inferences from the one to the other: such was the fideist, who took the order of grace on authority, but in the order of nature pursued his experimental and sceptical way, the Baconian, with his two philosophies, natural and divine, and (though this lies outside our present scope) the Puritan extremist, reactionary in the realm of grace, progressivist in the realm of nature. All these, though for different ends, apply what I have elsewhere called the principle of segregation.[3]

Opposed to them were all those thinkers who, with many different shades of emphasis and inference, agreed in responding to the profound human instinct for a unified view of life. They insisted that the order of grace was the superstructure whose foundations were securely laid in nature; that there was no interval between the two orders; that grace came to perfect nature, an idea including discipline and a miraculous remedy for man's fall; that well-being must be defined in terms of the two orders simultaneously, and that what was for man's good as a natural being could not be to his detriment as a supernatural, or vice versa.

These, with varying degrees of modification, were the assumptions of Christian humanism, whose dominance in the Renaissance, and whose importance for Spenser, will hardly be questioned. These were the assumptions of that long tradition which was about to receive its most majestic English expression in the first book of Hooker's Laws of Ecclesiastical Polity (1593). But the stormy waters upon which the Church of England was already entering are alone sufficient to warn us not to underestimate the variety and strength of opposing currents of Christian thought released and accelerated by the Protestant Reformation, and specifically by the impressive formulations of Calvin, whose influence upon Spenser Padelford has demonstrated.[4] Underlying the struggle of parties in Church and state were opposing ideals of the Christian life, and supporting these ideals were divergent views of the character and the relation of the order of nature and the order of grace.

The frame of reference is everywhere, explicit or implied; and if we ignore it, we neglect an important part of Spenser's, as of Milton's, intellectual background, and a valuable instrument of critical analysis. Such at least is the contention of this lecture, which asks, and (so far as time permits) will try to answer the following questions: What light does this frame of reference throw upon the Faerie Queene? How does it sharpen and perhaps modify our sense of Spenser's aesthetic pattern (for, whatever be true of some other poets, the aesthetic patterning of Spenser and Milton is based upon ideas, upon conceptual thinking)? Does a recognition of the frame of reference help us at some points to see further into Spenser's allegory? Does it help us to appreciate relations of parallel with contrast (for similarity with dissimilarity, parallel with contrast, are of the essence of an aesthetic pattern)? Does it even serve to

explain more adequately than heretofore the significance, intellectual
and aesthetic, of certain characters and episodes? Does it, finally,
give us any indication of the direction which the poem may have taken
in those last six (or is it five and five-sixth?) books which have not
come down to us? I would ask you to remember that whatever I
assert is tentative, and that the purpose is exploration and the testing
of an hypothesis.

2

Some fifty years after Spenser published the second instalment
of the Faerie Queene, an eloquent contemporary of Milton's, whose
name has not come down to us, wrote:

> Christ Jesus, whose is the kingdom, the power and the glory
> both in nature and in grace, hath given several maps and schemes
> of his dominions . . .: both of his great kingdom, the world, . . .
> and also of his special and peculiar kingdom, the kingdom of grace,
> Which kingdoms, though they differ essentially or formally, yet
> they agree in one common subject-matter, man and societies of
> men, though under a diverse consideration. And not only man in
> society, but every man individually, is an epitome either of one
> only or of both these dominions. Of one only: so every natural
> man (who in a natural consideration is called microcosmus, an
> epitome of the world), in whose conscience God hath his throne,
> ruling him by the light of nature to a civil outward good and end.
> Of both: so every believer who, besides this natural conscience
> and rule, hath an enlightened conscience, carrying a more bright
> and lively stamp of the kingly place and power of the Lord Jesus,
> swaying him by the light of faith or scripture, and such a man may
> be called microchristus, the epitome of Christ mystical.[5]

* I suggest that some such relation between the order of nature and
the order of grace is likewise present in Spenser's mind, and some
such distinction between the motives and sanctions of virtue on the
natural level and on the specifically religious, and that these are
consistently applied in the part of the Faerie Queene which we possess; or, to be quite concrete, that Book I moves (as has been generally recognized) on the religious level, or (as I should prefer to
describe it) with reference to the order of grace, and the remaining
books (as has not been recognized) on the natural level only: that
the Redcross Knight is indeed microchristus, but Guyon, and each of
the other heroes of individual books, microcosmus alone.

This hypothesis runs completely counter to one recently put forward,[6] that each of the knights is, as it were, the heir of his predecessors' victories, and together they form a composite picture of the Christian gentleman, or that Guyon, for example, achieves his virtues of temperance and continence, and is able to discharge his task, because he starts from the vantage point of holiness achieved by the Redcross Knight. Few perhaps will accept this hypothesis, which ignores the obvious fact that while the motivation and sanctions of the Redcross Knight's virtue are specifically religious, those of Guyon's, just as clearly, are not. But there is still a middle course, the refuge of vagueness, which recognizes the religious character of the Redcross Knight, and the impossibility of finding in Aristotle, or in Aristotle read in the light of Plato, any equivalent for holiness, which further recognizes the essentially Aristotelian character of Guyon and his virtues, but which breaks down when it comes to Britomart and, in the effort to account for the evident difference between her and Guyon, decides that she must represent a religious virtue, a specifically Christian conception of chastity and love.[7]

We are concerned with testing my hypothesis, and in the degree to which it is verified it will, of course, disprove the other two. All recognize the necessity of some synthesis between the contentions of the various books, but the other two try to provide for the synthesis piecemeal as the poem moves along, while mine, remembering that we have only the first half of the pattern of the Faerie Queene, is content that synthesis should be prepared for, but held in solution, perhaps even till Book XII. Spenser's preparation for his final synthesis, as it appears to me, consists, first, in sharply differentiating between the two orders; secondly, in presenting the virtues of natural ethics in a form which Christianity can assimilate, and has in fact assimilated, and, thirdly, in indicating the limits of nature and the points at which it requires to be supplemented or corrected by grace. It is the second of these three steps that has led the critics without exception to conclude that all or some of the heroes and their virtues are specifically Christian. But the question is not whether the natural virtues can be ratified by religion before being transcended by it (for all of them can), but whether in the particular instance the motivation and the sanctions of the virtue are from nature or from grace.

In the part of the poem which has come down to us, such is my hypothesis, Spenser is careful to differentiate the two orders of nature and grace. He emphasizes the parallels between them, and the differences which only these parallels can bring into relief, and he builds both into his pattern; for parallel with difference is (as we said) of the essence of aesthetic patterning. No doubt he interprets the virtues of the natural order as a Christian would interpret them; but he scrupulously abstains from assigning to them a religious motive and from invoking in their behalf the supernatural sanctions so freely drawn upon in Book I; nor does he bespeak in their support any infusion of divine grace. The natural order, the level on which the remaining books move, is also, it is true, under the power and providence of God, which may intervene to protect the natural man from external evil; but nowhere save in Book I (as we shall see) does Prince Arthur figure forth the grace that works inwardly upon the heart and will.

3

Though it sometimes seems to raise as many problems as it solves, every re-examination of the Faerie Queene must commence with the Letter to Raleigh. For whatever its relation to the composition of the poem, the Letter is clearly Spenser's introduction to a reading of it. As such the purpose of the Letter is severely limited. It is not to anticipate the whole meaning of the work, that would be an almost impossible task, and so far as it were successfully executed, an error of judgment; it is simply to set the reader's feet on the right path, to make clear that the poem is an allegory, that each book deals with one of the private virtues (holiness in the person of the Redcross Knight, temperance in the person of Guyon, chastity in the person of Britomart), that Prince Arthur represents in the whole poem the sum of the virtues, or (as it is called in the Aristotelian scheme) magnanimity,[8] and in the separate books its application to the particular virtue under discussion, and, finally, to give a very necessary indication of the structure of the poem and the occasion of the various adventures recited. The incompleteness of the Letter is evident from the absence of any allusion to the historical allegory, whose existence, and whose importance to Spenser, no one can doubt. This, and much else, the reader is left the pleasure of discovering for himself. The Letter tells him what he needs to know at starting: it does not tell all he will know when he has finished the twelve or even the three books. Thus Spenser may well have foreseen a function for Book XII, which it would have been premature to disclose. Perhaps, in addition to supplying belated explanations, the twelfth book was to have completed the pattern of the whole and, like the Epilogue in Comus, to have furnished the vantage point from which all that went before might be seen in its true relations and its full significance.

It is not surprising, then, that in the Letter the frame of reference is merely hinted, not set out in detail. The reader is told that the virtue of Book I is holiness, which he would instantly recognize as a specifically Christian virtue, outside nature and belonging to the order of grace; that the armour which the Redcross Knight assumes "is the armour of a Christian man specified by Saint Paul," and that this fact alone marked him off, set him above, all the other knights, for when he had donned the armour, this clownish young man, this son of nature, innocent of any cultivation, "seemed the goodliest man in all that company." The reader is then told of Sir Guyon, the knight of temperance, a virtue which (though it had certainly been adopted, like the other natural virtues, into the Christian scheme) belonged in origin and essence to the order or nature, and was, in fact, with justice and magnanimity, the most characteristic of the Aristotelian virtues. He would observe the absence of any reference to religion, and might be expected to take the hint that Books II and I moved upon different levels, and to be rendered sufficiently alert for the contrast which the two books present, and which is an essential element in the aesthetic pattern of the poem.

4

It need no longer be argued in detail that Book I moves upon the level of grace. Padelford's demonstration is conclusive, that holiness is a purely Christian virtue, and that the Institutes of Calvin furnishes a relevant gloss, while the Ethics of Aristotle does not.[9] The attempt of DeMoss to extract Spenser's holiness from Aristotle, and of Miss Winstanley to extract it from a blend of Aristotle and Plato, patently break down.[10] It will suffice to recall in rapid summary the essential features of Spenser's first book: (i) the emphasis upon the Christian's armour, and especially upon the shield of faith; (ii) the character of the Knight's companion and guide, Una, the single and all-sufficient religious truth, in whose presence alone he is safe; (iii) the whole tenor of the Knight's adventures up to canto canto 10, which are not an education in virtue in any ordinary sense, but an illustration of the bankruptcy of the natural man and of the essentially Christian doctrine that only grace can save; (iv) in conformity with this, the special role assigned in this book to Prince Arthur, who certainly does not represent the Aristotelian magnanimity, but on the contrary the operation of divine grace; (v) the completion of the Redcross Knight's education in the House of Holiness:[11] cleansed by repentance, taught by Faith,[12] healed by Hope, led through the works of Charity to the hill of Contemplation, vouchsafed a vision of the New Jerusalem and his own niche as a saint therein, and returned to the world, prepared at last for active service. When Bunyan read the first Book of the Faerie Queene, and especially this episode of the House of Holiness, he did not mistake their purport, but recognized it as purely evangelical and gathered from Spenser hints for his own allegory of salvation.[13]

Something of the relation between the two orders of nature and grace is already apparent in Book I, whose central episodes all move upon the level of grace. The lion which accompanies Una to the dwelling of Abessa, and there slays Kirkrapine, represents (it has been suggested) the law of nature, and the action symbolizes the agreement between natural ethics (so far as natural ethics can go) and true religion: their joint condemnation of a superstitious asceticism and of the corruptions which inevitably attend it.[14] A different relation appears in the two encounters of the Redcross Knight with pride. Spenser is sometimes criticized for suffering his hero to escape from the palace of Lucifera, who represents pride, only to fall a victim to Orgoglio, who also represents pride.[15] A clearer sense of the two orders would show how idle such criticism is, and how sound and consistent is Spenser's allegory. For Lucifera represents worldly pride which leads alike to vice and to disaster. But the vices, the seven deadly sins, are such as the moral sense is perfectly competent to detect and condemn: they impinge upon religion only as religion adds its prohibitions to whatever is condemned on grounds of natural ethics, just as religion (in Spenser's view) assumes and ratifies all the natural virtues before transcending them. And for the disasters, they are such as the world regards: the loss of position, of possessions and of life. It is significantly the Dwarf, who represents worldly prudence or common sense, and no celestial visitant, that warns the Redcross Knight of his danger and prompts his escape. The pride represented by Orgoglio, however, is of a very different sort. It is spiritual pride, which assails the Knight in his religious character when he has laid aside the armour of a Christian man. From it he is powerless to rescue himself. The keyless prison-house will yield to nothing but the onslaught of Prince Arthur, that is, to the violence of grace.[16]

There are subtler relations between the two orders than the rather obvious examples which I have chosen; and these relations will, I hope, become apparent as we proceed. But to turn now to the comparison of Book II with Book I.

Every reader must recognize the similarities of the second Book to the first, in structure and episode, and must believe, when he contrasts them with Books III and IV, that Spenser intended each group to form one of the larger units in the pattern of the whole.

In each of the first two books, a knight (the Redcross Knight and Guyon) is assigned a task by Gloriana and is accompanied as companion and guide by the person at whose instance the task was assigned (Una in the one case, the Palmer in the other). Each knight passes through a series of adventures which are, in one sort or other, an education in the virtue for which he stands and a preparation for his final task. The adventures involve conflicts with single adversaries (the brothers Sansfoy, Sansloy and Sansjoy in Book I, the brothers Pyrochles and Cymochles in Book II), the temporary separation of the Knight from his companion, the encounter with some analogous temptations (the palace of Lucifera, and the cave of Mammon), the rescue of the hero by Prince Arthur, the completion of his education in a retreat (the House of Holiness in Book I, the Castle of Alma in Book II), which affords the final preparation for his assigned task (the slaying of the Dragon by the Redcross Knight, the overthrow of Acrasia and her Bower of Earthly Bliss by Guyon). These are commonplaces of criticism; for the parallels are so obvious as to be inescapable.

But what of the differences which the parallels should bring into relief, and which should rescue the parallelism from monotony? They likewise (as I believe) are so obvious as to have seemed to Spenser inescapable; but to them less than sufficient attention has been paid, and the reason is not far to seek. All the differences depend upon, and derive their significance from, the fact which has been generally overlooked: that whereas what touches the Redcross Knight bears primarily upon revealed religion, or belongs to the order of grace, whatever touches Guyon bears upon natural ethics, or belongs to the order of nature.[17]

This difference leaves its mark upon the whole character of the education which the two knights receive. Guyon's trials and temptations, for the most part successfully surmounted, have the effect of rendering his virtue habitual. At an early stage, in the episode of Medina and her two sisters,[18] Spenser sets forth the Aristotelian doctrine of the mean—the idea that virtue and well-being lie in a mean between the two extremes of excess and defect—a doctrine applied, indeed, throughout the Faerie Queene, but especially in the treatment of temperance.[19] The episode of Medina has been recognized, however, as having a second significance: it is an allegory of the Platonic doctrine of the soul, with Medina and Guyon standing for the rational soul, and the sisters, with their knights, for the two divisions of the irrational, the irascible and appetitive, or (as we might say) for wrath and desire.[20] Temperance and continence (for Spenser combines the two Aristotelian virtues[21]) can be achieved only by the ascendency of the rational over the irrational soul, and it is this ascendency that becomes habitual. Reason dominates Book II as revealed truth dominates Book I, and these are personified in the companion figures of the Palmer and Una.

The education of the Redcross Knight differs markedly (as we have implied) from Guyon's. It proceeds by trial and error—principally by error: indeed until his entry into the House of Holiness he appears to have learned almost nothing, but to have blundered on, despite his innate nobility, from one error into another. The sum total of his education to this point has been one lesson: the bankruptcy of the natural man and his utter dependence for spiritual virtue upon the grace of God:

> What man is he that boasts of fleshly might
> And vain assurance of mortality,
> Which all so soone as it doth come to fight
> Against spirituall foes, yields by and by,
> Or from the field most cowardly doth fly!
> Ne let the man ascribe it to his skill
> That thorough grace hath gained victory:
> If any strength we have it is to ill,
> But all the good is Gods, both power and eke will.[22]

Only as this conviction is borne home to him is St. George ready for the education of the House of Holiness, the vision of the New Jerusalem, and the fulfilment of his task. There is nothing remotely like it in the experience of Guyon.

Fortified by the practice of temperance and continence, Guyon comes to the Castle of Alma, not for correction, and not to receive a vision of higher things, but simply that he may understand more fully the humanistic ethic which has been his guiding principle from the beginning and which will suffice him to the end:

> Of all Gods workes which do this world adorne,
> There is no one more faire and excellent
> Then is mans body both for powre and forme,
> Whiles it is kept in sober government;

But none then it more fowle and indecent,
Distempred through misrule and passions bace:
It growes a monster and incontinent
Doth loose his dignity and native grace.[23]

One must observe in passing that by Spenser the word <u>grace</u> is used
in different senses, which are always sufficiently clear from the
context: (i) it may refer to the grace of God working inwardly upon
the will and infusing power, as in the stanza quoted above from Book
I, and this sense alone is peculiar to the order of grace; (ii) it may
refer to God's overflowing bounty in bestowing outward benefits or
in intervening as providential care in the natural order; (iii) it may
refer to native endowment or to natural excellence, as in the stanza
last quoted, from Book II; or (iv) it may refer to grace of disposition, bearing, or manner.[24] But to return.

At the same crucial point in each of the two books, the poet pauses
to sum up in a single stanza the purport of all that has gone before,
and thus to prepare for what is to follow, for the orientation afforded
by the Castle of Alma and the House of Holiness respectively: in the
one, virtue achieved by man's own effort, by establishing the rule of
reason over the passions, and thus realizing the potentialities of his
nature; in the other, man's impotence to rise above himself, and
thus his utter dependence upon the grace of God. Our knowledge, or
rather our faith, that for Spenser these two positions were not incapable of final reconciliation must not blind us to their strong opposition until that reconciliation is reached. If it does, feature after
feature of Spenser's pattern will be blurred for us, and we shall fail
to appreciate his art as well as his thought. We shall miss the consistent contrast of Guyon with the Redcross Knight, and the dual or
(as I would suggest) the triple role of Prince Arthur in the poem.
We shall fail to recognize how fully Spenser exploits what I will call
the difference in vertical range between the classical and the Christian scheme of things: in the one, man can rise to the specifically
human or sink (like the followers of Acrasia) to the level of the
beasts; in the other, he can rise (like the Redcross Knight) securely
to heaven or fall irrecoverably, and forever, to the bottomless pit.
We shall fail, furthermore, to understand why in Book I the supporting imagery comes from the romances <u>and the Bible</u>, with scarcely
a single draught on Spenser's large accumulations of classical lore,
and in Book II, from the romances <u>and the classics</u>, with no significant reference to the Bible at all. Finally, we shall misapprehend
the purport of Book II itself. For besides the contrast of nature and
grace established by the first two books, Book II commences to ex-

plore the realm of nature with a new contrast in that realm between nature truly and nature falsely conceived, and this contrast (as we shall presently observe) carries us on from Book II to Book III.

6

We have mentioned the dual role of Prince Arthur, now very generally recognized, and have suggested that in reality he plays not a dual, but a triple role.

In those books of the poem which deal with the classical or natural virtues he stands for magnanimity, but just as clearly he stands in Book I for God's grace in its inward operation upon the heart and will. Here then are two distinct roles. What is the significance of each, and where is the propriety of having them discharged by the same person?

How does magnanimity, the crowing and inclusive virtue in the natural order, parallel heavenly grace in the religious order, which is clearly not man's virtue, but (if we may use the term at all) God's? The point of comparison, and the justification of the parallel, lies in the respective roles played by magnanimity and grace in the two systems. Magnanimity, in its Aristotelian sense, means knowing yourself equal to anything, and being so: knowing yourself worthy of the highest things, and being so. It is of the essence of grace, on the other hand, that, in a terrifyingly literal sense, you know yourself equal to nothing and in yourself utterly without worth. The classical scheme of ethics turns upon self-reliance: there is nothing else to rely upon; but the Christian relies upon God. Thus it is in Spenser's poem.

It might be argued that while the roles of magnanimity and grace in the two contrasting systems justify the emphasis on each and a parallel treatment of the two, this very fact would rather suggest the propriety of assigning them to different persons. But Spenser is, no doubt, preparing for an ultimate synthesis of nature and grace in the person of Prince Arthur. Clearly, Spenser would not have been the first to attempt a reconciliation of nature and grace: a long tradition of Christian humanism had worked out a Christian conception, not only of temperance, justice and the other natural virtues, but of magnanimity itself.[25] This fact is certainly relevant to Spenser's final synthesis, but it can obscure his pattern if too early invoked.

It is not the specifically Christian version of temperance that Guyon represents, nor is it Christian magnanimity that intervenes in his rescue, because in neither case is a religious motive or a

religious sanction introduced. When this fact is clearly established,
it is safe, and necessary, to recognize another. There were features in the hard self-sufficiency of Aristotle's magnanimous man
which were incompatible as well with the chivalric as with the
Christian ideal:[26] at moments one feels that he would have been
more at home with Lord Chesterfield than with either St. Paul or
Sir Lancelot; and these features Spenser wisely alters in his portrait
of Prince Arthur, in whom self-reliance is never arrogant, and who
is always a very perfect gentle knight. But Prince Arthur as magnanimity is not a specifically Christian figure: at most, he is a figure rendered compatible with the ideal of Christian knighthood.
When he intervenes to rescue Sir Guyon from the stealthy attack of
Pyrochles and Cymochles,[27] it is no longer as the symbol of heavenly grace intervening to save from inward evil, but as the symbol
of magnanimity, swift to recognize a kindred spirit and to protect
him from the outward depredation of his foes. For this attack of the
brothers upon the unconscious Guyon has evidently a very different
symbolic value from the attack of Orgoglio upon the Redcross Knight;
and from Guyon's earlier battle with Pyrochles, where that embodiment of irascibility menaces, not Guyon's life, but his integrity,
damaging his shield and inflicting a slight wound.[28] Spenser, it
would seem, was perfectly well aware that the effects of evil are not
confined to the human heart: it stalks abroad with fire and sword to
plunder and slay the innocent.

But though this be true, is it not also true, it may be asked, that
Prince Arthur's intervention is providential in the strictest sense,
so that Spenser has merely exchanged one religious conception for
another? It is indeed true that the intervention is providential; and
this, I submit, is the third role of Prince Arthur, to figure forth the
power and providence of God in the natural order.

Here, as occasionally in the Faerie Queene,[29] Spenser offers in
rapid succession two symbolic presentations of the same truth. For
the angel who stands guard over the unconscious Guyon[30] is likewise,
and even more obviously, the minister of God's providence, of the
overflowing grace which extends its protection even to the natural
man:

> And is there care in heaven? And is there love
> In heavenly spirits to these creatures bace,
> That may compassion of their evills move?
> There is; else much more wretched were the cace
> Of men then beasts. But O! th' exceeding grace
> Of highest God that loves his creatures so,

70

And all his workes with mercy doth embrace,
That blessed Angels he sends to and fro,
To serve to wicked man, to serve his wicked foe.[31]

Such a description would apply only to the natural man, and would
by evangelical standards apply to him equally whether morally
virtuous, like Guyon, or the reverse.[32]

Prince Arthur, it would seem then, represents, in the order of
grace, the grace of God in its fullest extent as it works upon the
will of the converted; in the order of nature he represents the virtue of magnanimity, which is as central in classical ethics as is
grace in the Christian scheme; but, also in the order of nature, he
represents the power and providence of God as they intervene to
protect his creatures from outward evils.

7

Only after the elementary distinction between the two orders of
grace and nature has been accepted will one be prepared to appreciate the complexity and consistency of Spenser's findings respect-
ing the second realm, the order of nature, as these are developed
in the second and subsequent books of the poem.

In Book II there is (as we have remarked) a contrast between
nature truly and nature falsely conceived, and this contrast is carried on in Books III and IV and serves to connect them with Book II.
Acrasia's Bower of Bliss represents nature falsely conceived. For
there nature's provision for the replenishment of life is prostituted
to sensual pleasure and is without issue. The Genius of the Bower
is a lord of misrule, and in truth no Genius at all, no spirit of nature, though falsely so called by Acrasia and her followers;[33] and
the contrast with nature truly conceived is emphasized (as Mr.
C. S. Lewis has shown) by the intrusion into the Bower of a false
art whose aim is to deceive[34] and whose effect is to heighten and
at the same time to misdirect natural impulse. But if one paused
at the end of Book II, one might easily mistake Spenser's meaning.
Whatever part nature really has in the Bower of Bliss is rescued
and rehabilitated in Book III, in Spenser's account of the Garden of
Adonis.[35] There, under the auspices of the true Genius, the verita-
ble spirit of nature, life replenishes itself. It is an allegory of the
principle of generation in all things, and pleasure, rejected when it
usurps the role of end, is frankly admitted in its proper role of
natural accompaniment. The Garden of Adonis thus furnishes the
cosmic setting, not indeed for the ideal of chastity represented by

71

Britomart, but for the view of love and marriage associated with it, which is likewise presented in terms of the order of nature and without reference to grace.

As compared with Guyon (representing temperance and continence) Britomart is positive and dynamic, representing the chastity which is coupled with love, which finds its principal motive in love, and which reaches its goal in marriage. But if this is true, and if it is Spenser's sufficient reason for proceeding from the subject of Book II to that of Book III, it is not because the argument is shifted from the order of nature to the order of grace, but because it is more fully elaborated, and under proper qualifications, on the natural level. Granted that the ideal presented in Britomart can be assimilated by a Christian view of love and marriage, it still remains true that at this stage it is not thus assimilated. In other words, there is no more reason to regard Britomart as an embodiment of a specifically Christian ideal of chastity and love than to regard Belphoebe as the embodiment of a Christian ideal of virginity. For in neither case is there the slightest hint of a religious motivation or sanction.

Since Spenser presents his idea of nature in connection, more or less immediate, with his treatment of love, it is desirable to scrutinize carefully his argument on this subject, which extends from the final canto of Book II through Books III and IV, and includes the journey of Britomart in rescue of her lover Artegall, in Book V, cantos 6 and 7, an episode too seldom related to the argument of the preceding books. In broadest outline, then, there are four representations of chastity in these books, Britomart, Belphoebe, Amoret and Florimell, and each is also a representation of beauty and its evocative power.

Of these representations Belphoebe is the simplest, stemming (as her name implies) from the Diana of classic myth, and embodying, like Diana, all the beauty, all the free activity and all the positive human development that the ideal of chastity conceived as virginity, and moving on the natural level, without motivation and direction from religion, will permit. The situation is, if you will, artificially narrowed: the response to it is not artificial, but natural; and Belphoebe, certainly, is no starved and thwarted personality. She and her twin sister Amoret are (as the story of their birth is intended to symbolize) children of nature;[36] but Belphoebe is adopted by Diana and brought up among her nymphs, while Amoret is placed by Venus in the Garden of Adonis, there to be brought up by Psyche with her daughter Pleasure "In all the lore of love and goodly womanhead."[37]

If Belphoebe and Amoret are contrasted in their fortunes, each is again contrasted with Britomart, the central figure of the whole argument. Britomart is as positive and dynamic as Belphoebe, but over a far wider range of experience: as perfectly adjusted but to a far more complex situation. For she is as chaste as Belphoebe, by including in theory and action the principle of generation and its human expression, wedded love, and not by excluding them. From the first Britomart is dedicated to the love of Artegall,[38] and like a Shavian heroine (or, for that matter, Shakespeare's Helena) she sets out to get him, obedient to a principle at work through all nature and symbolized for Spenser by the myth of Venus and Adonis and, on the human level, by the myth of Cupid and Psyche. Like other central figures in the <u>Faerie Queene</u>, Britomart has her companion, old Glauce, who certainly does not symbolize any religious directive,[39] as does Una, but moves, like the Palmer, on the natural level, though with a significant difference. For Glauce does not represent reason or any principle of control, but rather yields to the motive force of love which drives Britomart forward, and from which nothing but Britomart's own spirit, passionate but pure, can derive a principle of control and direction. It is sufficient; and Britomart not only passes scatheless through every danger, and unassailed by any temptation, but wherever she goes brings rebuke to the unchaste and aid to the imcomplete or insecure in virtue. The crowning instance (as Padelford has shown) is her rescue of Amoret from the wicked enchanter Busyrane.[40]

Amoret is as deeply in love with Scudamour as Britomart with Artegall. By nature she is as chaste as Britomart, or as the twin sister Belphoebe. But here education in the Garden of Adonis, while true to nature, has yet been incomplete: it has not contained all the elements requisite for love true and chaste <u>at the human level</u>. There is some failure in integration. She cannot securely transcend the merely physical in her passion for Scudamour; hence her imprisonment by Busyrane. Her natural chastity insists that she must do so; hence her tortured resistance to the enchanter. Assigned the task of her rescue, her lover is powerless to effect it. Perforce he resigns the task to Britomart, who thus in Book III assumes the function of Prince Arthur, or something more, but in his role of magnanimity, not of heavenly grace, and with this role his pursuit of glory:

> Ah! gentlest knight alive (sayd Scudamour)
> What huge heroicke magnanimity
> Dwells in thy bounteous brest! . . .
> Life is not lost (said she) for which is bought
> Endlesse renown, that, more then death, is to be sought.[41]

Britomart is able to effect the rescue because she has by nature the attitude which Amoret must struggle to attain. In Amoret what is required is transcendence, but transcendence on the way to unification. Essentially, it is this unification that Britomart represents.

Britomart is the ideal embodiment of love as well as of chastity, and not, like Belphoebe, of chastity alone. She is the Spenserian equivalent of Milton's 'Hail, wedded love.' In this ideal whatever is natural, so far from being rejected, is ratified and comprehended. There is room in it for all the raptures of Spenser's own Epithala-mion. Part of the significance of Britomart's vision in the Temple of Isis (that wonderful piece of dream psychology and symbolic art) is to show how securely grounded in nature is the ideal structure of Britomart's life and love.[42] They comprehend, and give appropriate human expression to, a principle of generation at work through the whole range of nature. That is why the Garden of Adonis may be said to furnish the cosmic background of the human ideal represente by Britomart.

But that the ideal and its expression are specifically human is of the first importance. There are different levels in the order of nature, and a principle of ascent. The highest level within the natural order is the specifically human level; and (again within the terms of this order) success in living means the secure achievement of the specifically human. It means (to borrow Arnold's phrase) the devel-opment of our humanity proper as distinct from our animality. Nature, said Renan, knows nothing of chastity. And of nature on her sub-human level, this statement (as Spenser would agree) is perfectly true. She knows no more of chastity than she does of temper-ance and continence, of friendship, of justice, of courtesy or constancy or magnanimity. She does not know them because she does not need them, having her own sure law, adequate to each level of existence. But this does not mean that the human virtues are unnatural. On the contrary, they are natural in a double sense: because they belong to the nature of man, and because nature, adequately conceived, is seen to furnish their base and to lend them her sanction. Nowhere does this fact appear more strikingly than in Spenser's conception of love and chastity as represented by Britomart. Here the principle of generation common to the whole natural order reaches its appropriate human expression in wedded love, and here it meets and is harmoniously united with the specifically human virtue of chastity.

The cause of Amoret's predicament, from which only Britomart can rescue her, is not that her education in the Garden of Adonis has run counter to nature, as it would have done, for example, had it been carried on in the garden of Acrasia. The cause is that it has failed sufficiently to distinguish the different levels in the natural order. Her education has failed to unite the human virtue of chastity to the natural principle of generation because it has failed to recognize that on the human level the virtue is as natural as the principle: that the virtue is as natural is attested by Amoret's instinctive and tenacious hold upon it, as well as by the triumphant naturalness of Britomart.

The fourth and final character, Florimell, is dedicated, like Britomart and unlike Belphoebe, to love as well as chastity. But she altogether lacks the magnanimity (in Aristotle's and Spenser's sense of the word) which distinguishes these two heroic figures: she is always in flight from danger and always in danger, real or imagined. Florimell has, however, a second role in the poem. In special degree she represents beauty and its evocative power, so that everyone whose path she crosses is drawn after her, impelled by love in some one of its forms, impure or pure, base or exalted, according to his own nature: the witch's son, the boatman, old Proteus, Sir Guyon, even Prince Arthur, who believes or hopes that she is (or at least is like) the Gloriana of his dreams, and at last the resistance of Marinell himself is broken down. Beauty, as Spenser sings in the first two of his Fowre Hymnes, is the universal principle which evokes the universal passion, love. In the Faerie Queene it is Florimell pre-eminently who illustrates this principle and its evocative power.

All these ideas, and more, Spenser develops in his treatment of love and chastity on the natural level, and one result is to give us our principal insight into the poet's reading of the order of nature.

8

Under the term nature is comprehended the whole range of existence from formed but still inanimate matter up to and including man, save as man in his religious character belongs also to the order of grace. Nature, thus conceived, is an ascending scale, at whose successive levels are added, first, life, then consciousness, then rationality and a moral sense, and finally religious feeling, which last marks the transition to the order of grace. At every level nature connotes a principle of dynamism, a law and a norm; and on the human level the law and the norm are recognized as rational and moral. Thus, as Hooker was soon to argue, the law of nature holds sway over the whole natural order, though its rational character can be apprehended, and its dictates consciously consulted, only at the highest level, that is, by man. Everything seeks its appropriate perfection, and man finally can achieve his, only by a

reference on to the order of grace; but so far as it goes nature is
a sure guide and her law part of the divine law. These assumptions,
made familiar to us by Hooker, Spenser in some measure shares.
They underlie his antithesis between the natural and unnatural, and
between nature adequately and nature inadequately conceived.
Everywhere in the Faerie Queene the unnatural is condemned as
absurdity, as defiance of fact or as perversion of the appointed order of things; and, avowedly or by implication, the natural is accepted and approved.[43]

Acceptance, however, and approval are not unqualified. There
is in Spenser a much sharper line of demarcation between nature
and grace than any that can be discovered in Hooker: there is a
Calvinistic sense of the bankruptcy of the natural man, and a conception of grace as entailing not so much a perfecting of nature as
a new start. Even in his treatment of the natural order, there is
more than a suspicion that nature may on occasion prove for man
a delusive guide. In the garden of Acrasia the antithesis between
nature and the unnatural as represented by an art intended to deceive, is crossed by another idea: up to a point nature herself
seems willing to second Acrasia and her art.

> The joyous birdes, shrouded in chearfull shade,
> Their notes unto the voice attrempred sweet . . .
> The silver sounding instruments did meet
> With the base murmure of the waters fall . . .
> The gentle warbling wind low answered to all.

Such is the accompaniment furnished by nature to the singer of the
Rose Song; and, when he ceased,

> then gan all the choir of birdes
> Their diverse notes t'attune unto his lay,
> As in approvaunce of his pleasing wordes.[44]

And in the Garden of Adonis itself, where nature alone prevails, the
lesson taught, as Amoret proves to her cost, is insufficient for life
on the human level until the ideals peculiar to that level are recognized as likewise natural, and as modifying for humanity the principles common to the whole order of nature.

At certain points, moreover, natural and humanistic ethics require to be rectified by Christian. A striking instance is furnished
in Book V. There Spenser's treatment of justice is strictly Aristotelian, and justice, the justice of natural ethics, is stated to in-

clude equity. But natural ethics, unrectified by the example of Christianity, is incapable of furnishing the principle which must temper justice. By itself human nature cannot rise above the uncertain and unorganized sentiment of pity. Only Christian teaching and example can afford the principle of mercy. Thus in the court of Mercilla there is introduced a specifically Christian note. Mercilla (who represents Elizabeth in her judicial function) administers justice tempered by mercy, and Artegall (who represents natural justice) and Prince Arthur (who represents magnanimity) visit her for instruction. Spenser makes his point by one of his happy adaptations of classic myth. With the daughters of Jove and Themis, Justice, Good Order and Peace, who attended upon Mercilla, he associates the <u>Litae</u>, whose office is to plead the cause of human frailty and to turn aside the wrath of Jove.

> They also doe, by his divine permission
> Upon the thrones of mortall princes tend,
> And often treat for pardon and remission
> To suppliants, through frayltie which offend.[45]

Lest we should miss in this symbolism the Christian reference, Spenser introduces it with an allusion to the angels that encompass the throne and support the canopy of Mercilla, who herself is angel-like.[46] And of mercy indeed he categorically declares that

> in th'Almighties everlasting seat
> She first was bred, and borne of heavenly race,
> From thence pour'd down on men by influence of grace.[47]

Thus Christian teaching must on occasion be called in to rectify natural ethics, just as grace must intervene in rescue of nature. Book II (as we have seen), in contrast to Book I, moves on the natural level: Spenser's treatment of temperance and continence, like his treatment of justice, is strictly Aristotelian. But there is one episode, baffling to the commentators, which becomes, I think, perfectly plain and highly significant if one reads it as symbolizing the limit of man's natural powers and the necessary intervention of grace. In canto 11, Prince Arthur, in his character of magnanimity, is defending the Castle of Alma (that is, the human mind and body) against the assaults of sin and sensuality led by Maleger. It is in this strange and sinister figure that the difficulty of interpretation is met. He bears upon him every mark of disease and death, and is attended by the two hags, Impatience and Impotence; but he is a

swift and resourceful adversary who all but overcomes Prince
Arthur himself. The sword Morddure proves useless, and Arthur,
attacking the fiend with his bare hands, crushes the life from him
and casts the dead body to the ground. But, like the giant Antaeus,
at the touch of earth Maleger leaps to his feet and resumes the
fight. Repeatedly he is slain and as often revives, till at last Arthur
recognizing the cause, bears the body to a standing lake and hurls
it in. Maleger has been variously interpreted:[48] his name (it has
been contended) means evildoer and he represents sensuality or perhaps sin in general or perhaps Satan himself; his name (say others)
means sick unto death, and he represents disease which results from
the sins of the flesh, or again disease, not as the result of sin, but as
a circumstance favourable to it, as lowering resistance to temptation.
But none of these interpretations is satisfactory.

What is required is something that will draw the ideas of disease
and perennial evil into more intimate relation, and will cover all the
details, including Arthur's narrow escape of defeat, the fruitless
effort to destroy Maleger, repeatedly restored by the touch of earth,
and device by which the destruction is finally compassed, with water
standing in symbolic antithesis to earth. I suggest that Maleger is
original sin or human depravity, the result of the fall, and that the
marks of physical disease and death are the symbols of the inherited
taint, the moral and spiritual malady, which man is powerless to remove, and which may betray the strongest and most secure in the
natural virtues. It is in his character of magnanimity (of natural
virtue) that Prince Arthur barely escapes defeat, and then only by
providential intervention. The rescuer stands in need of rescue.
How better could the limits of nature be enforced? But this is not
all. Nothing can destroy Maleger, nothing can finally remove the
inherited taint, but the exercise of grace in its fullest extent. The
manner of his destruction by water is significant. It is intended to
suggest baptismal regeneration, that is to say, it moves in the same
area of symbolism as does the sacrament of baptism. This I am
persuaded is the correct interpretation of the episode of Maleger
and the only one which will cover all the phenomena.[49] The image
of earth is as significant as that of water. Maleger, though momentarily brought under control, revives at the touch of earth. As water
symbolizes grace, earth symbolizes nature; and among the various
ideas shadowed forth in the Faerie Queene is the presence of some
principle of evil in nature itself, and especially in matter, a relic of
the dark forces which ruled in the chaos before it was reduced to
cosmos, and which still struggle to reassert their sway.[50] With
these forces of evil in nature, the evil in fallen man enters into alli-

ance, and in them it finds a support. Hence the necessity of grace to rescue and rectify nature.

Apart, however, from this suggestion of forces of evil in nature, which must not be overemphasized, the two orders of nature and grace are contrasted in another respect: the order of nature is temporal and transient; the order of grace is eternal. In the much debated Cantos of Mutabilitie, which I am inclined to accept as furnishing the cosmic setting for Spenser's treatment of the Aristotelian steadfastness or constancy in the Faerie Queene, three important points about the order of nature are clearly made. First, that mutability holds sway through all the natural order, not even the stars and their courses being exempt from change. Secondly, that change, however, does not connote dissolution merely, but also replenishment. It is true, says Nature,

> that all things steadfastnesse do hate
> And changed be; yet, being rightly wayd,
> They are not changed from their first estate,
> But by their change their being do dilate,
> And turning to themselves at length again,
> Do worke their own perfection so by fate:
> Then over them Change doth not rule and raigne,
> But they rule over Change and do their states maintaine.[51]

If change is the rule of death, it is also in the natural order the rule of life. In Spenser's account of the Garden of Adonis, in Book III, the true Genius presides at once over the two processes of dissolution and replenishment, of death and life.[52] But this is not the end. Man is in nature, but not wholly of nature: man the immortal spirit craves for permanence, and not in vain. For—and this is the third point that is abundantly clear—nature, by her very deficiency, points on to that time when

> all shall changed bee,
> And from thenceforth none no more change shall see.[53]

To this pointing on from time to eternity, from change to permanence, from nature to grace, Spenser instantly responds. He feels, like Shelley, the pathos of change, but he does not conclude that "Nought may endure but Mutability." Like Wordsworth, he hears its rhythm as a "musical but melancholy chime," yet recognizes that amid the ruins "Truth fails not." But the truth to which Spenser has final recourse is the truth of another order:

> Then gin I thinke of that which Nature sayd
> Of that same time when no more change shall be,
> But stedfast rest of all things, firmely stayd
> Upon the pillours of Eternity,
> That is contrayr to Mutabilitie;
> For all that moveth doth in change delight:
> But thenceforth all shall rest eternally
> With him that is the God of Sabaoth hight:
> O that great Sabaoth God, grant me that Sabbaths sight![54]

By accident indeed, not design, these are the last words we have of Spenser's <u>Faerie Queene</u>. And, like the first words, they are about the order of grace.

9

This, like the other facts we have adduced, seems to support our hypothesis that Spenser wrote with the concept of the two orders as a principal frame of reference. Nor is this all. At some points (as we have noticed) a recognition of the frame of reference enables us to see further into Spenser's allegory and, what is more important, to appreciate more fully his aesthetic pattern by understanding its conceptual basis. Not only does it help us to explain, that is, to see more significance in, Maleger and Mercilla, in Britomart as contrasted with Amoret, in the Redcross Knight as contrasted with Guyon and Artegall, in Prince Arthur, and by implication perhaps even in Gloriana herself: it also tends to justify the poet where his art has been called in question. It completely justifies the parallel structure of Books I and II, and the repetition in episodes; for parallel is necessary to bring out the essential difference. Or, to take a single example of the clearing of the aesthetic pattern in Book II considered alone: critics have complained of the division of labour in the final cantos, with Guyon going forward to his destruction of the Bower of Bliss while Prince Arthur is left to defend the Castle of Alma against Maleger and his host.[55] But once we invoke the frame of reference, and understand the meaning of Maleger, we see that the episodes are complementary, and one as necessary as the other. For Guyon, moving upon the natural level, and guided only by reason, can discharge his particular task; but nature and reason have their limits, and when these limits are reached, as by Arthur in his battle with Maleger, only grace can save. And this use of contrast is highly characteristic of Spenser's whole mode of patterning in the <u>Faerie Queene</u>.

80

NATURE, GRACE IN THE FAERIE QUEENE

In broadest outline (as we have observed) Book I moves upon the level of grace and deals with a specifically Christian experience and virtue (call this Spenser's thesis); and the subsequent books which we possess move upon the level of nature and concern themselves with the natural virtues (call this the antithesis). Somehow, before the poem was completed, Spenser must achieve his synthesis, and a synthesis that would, of course, recognize the priority of the order of grace.

No doubt the task was rendered more difficult by Spenser's partial adherence to two different traditions. If, like Hooker, he had been content to emphasize the unity of the whole creation under God, and the steady and relatively unimpeded ascent through nature to grace: if he had simply emphasized one law of perfection operating throughout the whole natural order, as physical law, as biological and, on the human level, as rational and moral: if he had regarded revelation as merely supplementary, as completing this natural law by pointing man on to that fuller perfection which his nature demanded but to which the order of nature could carry him only part of the way: if, unequivocally, Spenser had taken his stand in this tradition, his task would have been easier, though his record of human experience would have been less complete. To this tradition indeed he did respond, and strongly (let there be no mistake about that). But in him it was crossed and partly cancelled by another: by the tradition which we may associate with Calvinism, and which tended to emphasize the insufficiency of nature, and indeed, since the fall, its depravity, and to regard grace as necessary, not merely to complete, but to correct nature and to supply its patent deficiencies. In the one tradition grace could build on the sure foundation of nature. In the other it seemed, rather, to demand a new start. Spenser tries to do justice to the facts of human experience which support these two rival views. And the synthesis at which he aimed in the Faerie Queene, whatever its precise character, must somehow have included them both.

That it did so, we have sufficient indication in the part of the poem we possess. Guyon, Artegall and Britomart achieve their natural virtues of temperance, justice and chastity just as surely as does the Redcross Knight his supernatural virtue of holiness; and just as successfully they fulfil their tasks. In so doing they are supported by nature adequately conceived, that is, by a nature in which human wisdom, deliberate or instinctive, can find a guide; but the manifestations of nature are multifarious, and the guide therein must be sought with discrimination. Once it is found, Spenser emphasizes the harmony of nature with grace so far as nature

goes, and extorts from nature herself a recognition of the higher
order and its claims. Here, plainly, are facts relevant to any attempted synthesis. But there are others. Despite the success of
Guyon and Artegall in achieving temperance and justice as natural
virtues and without recourse to grace, Spenser's sense of the limitations of nature comes out in their books. In Book V, the natural
law of justice includes equity, but has no place for mercy, which
can be learned only from the Gospel. In Book II, the sufficiency of
nature in Guyon is balanced by the necessity of grace for Prince
Arthur's destruction of Maleger.

In Books III and IV, however, this pattern is not maintained. In
Britomart, as in Guyon and Artegall, nature is sufficient, but here
there is no added appeal from nature to grace, either to modify the
ideal of chastity and love or to remove obstacles to its fulfilment:
the whole story moves on the natural level, without reference to
grace. Yet in some ways Britomart seems more readily adoptable
into the Christian scheme than does either Guyon or Artegall, and
the ideal of wedded love which she represents seems to require an
addition merely. In Paradise Lost Milton, adapting to a conception
of Christian marriage the Platonic scale of ascent, sees the possibility that chaste love, such as that of the unfallen Adam and Eve for
each other, may become a ladder leading to the heavenly love. In
Britomart nothing of the sort is suggested. For all we are told,
Spenser might here entertain the opinion strongly suggested by the
last two of the Fowre Hymnes, that heavenly love could not be based
on earthly, but required a new start. Clearly it was a problem for
the poet, as not only the Fowre Hymnes but the hesitations and contradictions of the Amoretti show. But despite the studied silence of
the Britomart-Artegall story on this subject, there is perhaps the
hint of a solution if we bring that story into relation with the very
different one of the Redcross Knight and Una. At the end of Book I,
as a symbol of holiness achieved, and a reward for his task accomplished, the Redcross Knight is betrothed to Una. It is, of course,
a common device in moral allegories, which Spenser has here
adopted; but it clearly presents earthly love as a symbol of heavenly
and so far prepares for, if it does not effect, a synthesis of the two.

This, I believe, illustrates a possible relation of the order of nature to the order of grace, which was essential to Spenser's synthesis. One thing that we miss in his explanation of allegory in the
Letter to Raleigh is any allusion to Dante's four levels of meaning:
possibly because, like other things omitted, it is unnecessary to an
intelligent commencement upon the poem: more probably, because
Spenser did not adopt in its entirety the Dantean scheme. But the

idea that the earthly is a symbol of the heavenly, he clearly does adopt. It is of the very texture of Book I;[56] and, noting the evidence of symmetry in the half of Spenser's pattern which we possess, we should expect this relation to be reasserted in or before Book XII. If there was to be a book devoted to wisdom, with Sophy as hero, where more appropriately could the reassertion occur, since there is a heavenly wisdom as well as an earthly? There is also an earthly and a heavenly glory. The magnanimous man, says Aristotle, desires glory because he alone is worthy of it. Thus Prince Arthur is in search of Gloriana, of whom he has had a vision. But Arthur has his role in the order of grace as well as in the order of nature, and there Gloriana must signify not the undifferentiated glory of the Letter to Raleigh, but that glorification which cannot be achieved by man's worthiness, but only through God's grace. Book XII (as we said) must do more than furnish belated explanations: it must complete Spenser's synthesis, and with it his pattern: like the Epilogue in Comus, it must furnish a vantage point from which everything falls into relation. Among the resources which Spenser had at his disposal was one peculiarly adapted to poetry, the sense that the inferior order stood (as Newman was to phrase it) in a sacramental relation to the higher order: that nature in one aspect might be viewed as "the outward and visible sign of an inward and spiritual grace."[57]

"GOD GUIDE THEE, GUYON": NATURE AND GRACE RECONCILED IN THE FAERIE QUEENE, BOOK II

Robert Hoopes

This paper takes as its point of critical departure Professor
A. S. P. Woodhouse's important article, 'Nature and Grace in The
Faerie Queene,'[1] in which the author made use, for purposes of re-
examination and reinterpretation of Spenser's poem, of the same
intellectual frame of reference which he had brilliantly used eight
years earlier in 'The Argument of Milton's Comus.'[2] Like Milton,
Spenser was shown to have distinguished sharply between the orders
of nature and grace, though he was aware of their parallels as well
as of their differences, and emphasized both aspects of their relationship in building his epic. After quoting a passage from an anonymous contemporary of Milton, which distinguishes between the purely
natural or worldly man, called microcosmus, and the believer, called
microchristus, or 'the epitome of Christ mystical,' Professor Woodhouse writes:

> I suggest that some such relation between the order of nature and
> the order of grace is likewise present in Spenser's mind, and
> some such distinction between the motives and sanctions of virtue
> on the natural level and on the specifically religious, and that
> these are consistently applied in the part of the Faerie Queene
> which we possess: or, to be quite concrete, that Book I moves
> (as has been generally recognized) on the religious level, or (as
> I should prefer to describe it) with reference to the order of
> grace, and the remaining books (as has not been recognized) on
> the natural level only: that the Redcross Knight is indeed micro-
> christus, but Guyon, and each of the other heroes of individual
> books, microcosmus alone. [61]*

From this initial postulate the rest of the analysis derives. Book I,
the book of holiness, moves entirely within the realm of grace; and
in so doing stresses not man's nobility or strength, but his impo-

*Numbers in square brackets refer to pages in this volume.

Reprinted from Review of English Studies, New Series, Vol. 5 (1954), pp.
14–24, by permission of the author and The Clarendon Press, Oxford.

tence, his inability to rise above himself or to improve himself by his own efforts. Its hero, the Redcross Knight, stumbles along his way, is safe only in the presence of Truth, and has to be rescued again and again from his own spectacular failures. In this manner Book I seeks to demonstrate man's utter dependence upon divine grace and thereby outlines an exclusively Christian ideal. In contrast, Book II stresses man's ability to achieve virtue by means of certain capacities inherent in his own nature. From the Palmer Guyon learns the rule of reason over the passions and gradually perfects himself in temperance until, by the end of the book, he is self-sufficient. In emphasizing the potentialities of man's nature, as against Book I, which emphasizes its limitations, Book II may be said to have outlined a classical ideal.

Now Spenser's purpose in all this, according to Professor Woodhouse, is aesthetic contrast and pattern. Although the poet emphasizes the differences between grace and nature, showing on the one hand morally helpless man, utterly dependent upon God, and on the other hand the virtue and perfection which man realizes through his own nature and effort, the two points of view were not incapable of final reconciliation, a reconciliation which, Professor Woodhouse conjectures, Spenser might well have intended for Book XII:

> All [theories of interpretation] recognize the necessity of some synthesis between the contentions of the various books, but [some] try to provide for the synthesis piecemeal as the poem moves along, while mine, remembering that we have only the first half of the pattern of the Faerie Queene, is content that synthesis should be prepared for, but held in solution, perhaps even till Book XII. [p. 62]

In Book II, then (or in the rest of the epic as we have it), the opposition between Christian and classical ideals is not reconciled, such is the implication of Woodhouse's analysis as a whole. As a critical conclusion it has so far gone undisputed. Judah L. Stampfer, following Woodhouse in a recent discussion of the Cantos of Mutability, distinguishes as follows between what he regards as the two dominant attitudes toward 'nature' during the Renaissance:

> According to one, nature is a depraved order with grace as its miraculous corrective; according to the other, nature is a benevolent order, with grace as the crown of its ascending scale of values.[3]

After which he adds, 'These two points of view are never resolved in the Faerie Queene' (p. 149). I do not think that these remarks will bear rigorous scrutiny, though my objections to both Woodhouse and Stampfer are rather to what seems to me to be overstatement than to fundamental misstatement. No one will deny the Renaissance acceptance of the two realms of nature and grace, and few articles have been so genuinely helpful to the teaching of Spenser as Professor Woodhouse's. But in emphasizing the contrast between the two orders as they are depicted in Books I and II, I think he has slighted Spenser's very real effort to show their harmony, especially in Book II. For example:

> . . . while the motivation and sanctions of the Redcross Knight's virtue are specifically religious, those of Guyon's, just as clearly are not. . . No doubt he [Spenser] interprets the virtues of the natural order as a Christian would interpret them; but he scrupulously abstains from assigning to them a religious motive and from invoking in their behalf the supernatural sanctions so freely drawn upon in Book I; nor does he bespeak in their support any infusion of divine grace. (pp. 198–9, 200)

Despite these categorical assertions, Professor Woodhouse himself notes the presence of the angel which stands guard over the unconscious Guyon at the opening of Canto viii, and calls our attention elsewhere in the same study to at least two episodes which imply that both grace and nature are necessary to the life of man. That is: in Canto viii Arthur, presumably in the role of magnanimity, defeats Cymochles and Pyrochles without supernatural aid of any kind; in Canto xi, however, he is permitted to triumph over Maleger (Original Sin) only through the miraculous intervention and efficacy of divine grace, the waters of baptism symbolized by the lake into which Maleger is hurled. Now The Faerie Queene, whatever its attention to classical virtues, takes place after all in a Christian world, and in recognition of this fact Professor Woodhouse proposes Arthur's third role in the epic, as the symbol of the operation of grace within nature. Hence, although he comes as magnanimity to save Guyon from Pyrochles, Arthur's intervention is in the strictest sense of the word a providential one. These observations help somewhat, but they do not answer all the questions. The episodes from Book II cited above certainly suggest the possibility, at least, that the contrast between Books I and II may not be so absolute as Professor Woodhouse's interpretation makes it out to be. If there are two episodes such as these, perhaps there are more; and if close

reading and analysis disclose that there are, what will our interpretation of Spenser's total method and purpose be when we re-examine
Book II in their light? In short, Professor Woodhouse's study itself
suggests that Spenser regarded both grace and nature as necessary
to the life of man, but that in Book II we can only infer the fact, since
Spenser is not explicit on the matter; he does not show clearly how the
the two ideals or orders interact. The purpose of this study is to
show that there is really more interaction than opposition, that the
two ideals are imaginatively, if not philosophically, harmonized
within the narrative action and sequence of Book II, and that Spenser
tried explicitly to reconcile them. To attempt such a demonstration
is not from the outside 'to provide for the synthesis piecemeal'; it
is, I hope, to see and set forth the synthesis that is actually there.
Sir Guyon's immediate motivation from adventure to adventure may
not be specifically religious, as Professor Woodhouse asserts, but
the ultimate sanction of what he does and tries to do is religious.
Spenser did his best—to borrow the language of Comus—to give
'spare Temperance' its 'holy dictates,' and he did his best to make
us see them.

Nothing is really more significant in Book II than the initial
meeting between Guyon and the Redcross Knight. It is, of course,
a commonplace to point out that this incident is Spenser's manner
of linking Books I and II, and incidentally of symbolizing the harmony between the revealed truth of Christianity and the highest
insights of classical wisdom. Given its important position at the
start of the book, however, surely one may reasonably suppose that
it serves other and more specific functions. One thing to remember
is that Book I was, in a sense, the book of conversion; in it the Redcross Knight was incorporated into the faith. The remaining books,
I submit, were intended to record the progress of the soul after conversion, with a different knight as the hero of each book, as Spenser
tells us in the letter to Raleigh, 'for the more variety of the history.'
At any rate, the significant thing about the meeting at the start of
Book II, if I am right, is that before Guyon begins his quest he must
recognize his dependence upon God. It is noteworthy that the Palmer, who represents reason, after commending the Redcross Knight
for having 'wonne' his 'seat . . . with Saints,' laments that 'wretched
we . . . Must now anew begin, like race to runne' (II. i. 32). At this
point, the Palmer turns to his own companion saying:

God guide thee, Guyon, well to end thy warke,
And to the wished hauen bring thy weary barke.

87

We are likely to forget that the Palmer represents Guyon's reason, that he is speaking only as an allegorical figure. This is Guyon speaking to himself, or better, to God. What I am saying, admittedly at the risk of overliteralizing allegory, is that Spenser opens his second book, the book of temperance, with his hero uttering a prayer for God's help. Thus envisaged, Guyon sets out with both supernatural and natural sanction, with the blessing of holiness and the guidance of right reason.

The next important episode for our purpose occurs when Guyon descends to the cave of Mammon. He is alone, the Palmer having been left behind on the shores of the Idle Lake; hence he is without reason. Three days' tour of Mammon's infernal chambers exhausts him, and upon reaching the upper air he is overcome and falls unconscious. But he does not die, for God sends one of his guardian angels to watch over him (a clear indication, as Professor Woodhouse points out, of the operation of God's providence within the natural order). As the Palmer, or reason, returns, Guyon starts to regain consciousness, and at this point the angel departs. Nevertheless, after commending Guyon's 'deare safetie' to the Palmer, he adds:

> Yet will I not forgoe, ne yet forget
> The care thereof my selfe vnto the end,
> But euermore him succour, and defend
> Against his foe and mine.   (II. viii. 8)

At this point, as at the beginning of the book, religion and reason are in joint charge of the knight of temperance.

In his weakened state, however, Guyon is easily attacked by Pyrochles, or fiery wrath, and Cymochles, or sensuality, who represent the irascible and concupiscible instincts of the irrational part of the soul. Arthur intervenes to save him; a providential intervention, to be sure, but I do not agree with Professor Woodhouse that Arthur has already shifted his role from the representative of heavenly grace to the embodiment of magnanimity. In the first place, Arthur is in no way identified as the representative of magnanimity. Instead, when he appears upon the scene, he greets the Palmer, turns, and sees the lifeless body of Guyon upon the ground, 'In whose dead face he red great magnanimity' (II. viii. 23). It is Guyon, not Arthur, who is identified by the Aristotelian virtue. Secondly, the word grace is thrice used in connexion with Prince Arthur during this episode: once to describe him, again to refer to what he has to offer, and finally to confirm his function and significance for the

reader after the battle with the pagan knights. Just as Pyrochles
and Cymochles are about to strip the unconscious Guyon, Spenser
says that they spied the approach of 'An armed knight, of bold and
bounteous grace' (II. viii. 17). And even Archimago goads them into
battle by calling out, a few lines later,

> Yonder comes the prowest knight aliue,
> Prince Arthur flowre of grace and nobilesse.   (II. viii. 18)

If these were the only two places in which the word was used, we
should be justified in taking them to mean 'grace' solely in the
chivalric sense of beauty and dignity of demeanour. Seven stanzas
later, however, the Palmer explains to Arthur what has befallen
Guyon, what the two villainous knights intend doing, and begs him to
'succour [Guyon's] sad plight' because his 'honourable sight / Doth
promise hope of helpe, and timely grace' (II. viii. 25). To this request Arthur replies that perhaps rational dissuasion will suffice to
deflect the wrathful pair from their foul intentions; at least 'Words
well dispost / Have secret powre, t'appease inflamed rage' (II. viii.
26). If they fail to respond to reason, 'leaue vnto me thy knights
last patronage' (ibid.). The two knights, of course, will have nothing
to do with rational dissuasion; and for a while, as so frequently happens in The Faerie Queene, the claims of theological and moral allegory yield to the claims of romance as Spenser allows the battle
to see-saw in familiar fashion until right finally triumphs (even
though, as I am claiming, Arthur here represents grace, and it may
seem a little odd that divine grace should be so put to it in a fight
against two snivelling libertines like Cymochles and Pyrochles).[4]
Cymochles is slain in the fight, but Pyrochles is not, having cast
away the magic sword that will not harm its true owner. At this
point Arthur, as perfect Christian knight and gentleman, offers to
spare the pagan knight if he will repent and become Arthur's follower:

> But full of Princely bounty and great mind,
> The Conquerour noght cared him to slay,
> But casting wrongs and all reuenge behind,
> More glory thought to giue life, then decay,
> And said, Paynim, this is thy dismall day;
> Yet if thou wilt renounce thy miscreaunce,
> And my trew liegeman yield thy selfe for ay,
> Life will I graunt thee for thy valiaunce,
> And all thy wrongs will wipe out of my souenaunce. (II. viii. 51)

The offer may, of course, be interpreted simply as a chivalric refusal to strike an opponent when he is down, but the situation certainly suggests the Catholic and Anglican doctrine of repentance.
Pyrochles is here in the position of a sinner being offered a chance
of salvation, provided he genuinely renounce his past misdeeds and
freely embrace faith in God. He refuses to do so, thereby damning
himself as a lost soul:

> Foole (said the Pagan) I thy gift defye,
> But vse thy fortune, as it doth befall,
> And say, that I not ouercome do dye,
> But in despight of life, for death do call.   (II. viii. 52)

The lines which immediately follow these are, I think, conclusive:

> Wroth was the Prince, and sory yet withall,
> That he so wilfully refused grace.

The interpretation which I have offered thus far may seem to run
counter to, or even to ignore, the fuller analysis of Book II recently
presented by Professor Ernest Sirluck.[5] I have not ignored it, and
I do not think that what I have said conflicts with, so much as (I
hope) it supplements, his view. His fundamental point with respect
to Guyon, namely that in certain episodes he represents Aristotelian
temperance, and in others Aristotelian continence, is, I think, generally sound. When the Palmer is present, Guyon would seem to
represent continence, as in the encounter with Furor, for he requires
the active presence, guidance, and restraint of reason over the strong
appetites and passions which the continent man feels. When the Palmer is absent, Guyon represents temperance, as in the Mammon
episode, for, as Professor Sirluck points out, 'he has no such need;
he does not feel the strong desires which the continent man bridles
by means of his reason; he is, instead, the temperate man who feels
desire only for the right things' (p. 86). According to this view it is
wrong to speak of Guyon's 'struggle' in the Cave of Mammon; there
is no struggle, and he is, in keeping with the concept of virtue as
habitus, invulnerable to temptation. Professor Sirluck might have
added that Spenser himself gives us the clue for this generally convincing view of Guyon in Canto viii, for in the second stanza of
Canto vii we find that 'Guyon hauing lost his trusty guide' continues
on his way,

> of none accompanide;
> And euermore himselfe with comfort feedes,
> Of his owne vertues, and prayse-worthy deedes.

But even if this interpretation be accepted as true, one is forced
to ask why Guyon, presumably self-sufficient in the absence of the
Palmer, is exhausted at the end of his encounter with Mammon. He
may be only 'physically' exhausted, as Professor Sirluck claims,[6]
but he is nevertheless exhausted; and surely Sirluck spoke rashly
in saying that Guyon's separation from the Palmer 'is without ethical significance.'[7] Spenser's allegory will not release us so easily:
when Guyon is separated from the Palmer, he is bereft of reason,
and however fortified he may have been by the habit of temperance,
he might have perished, had it not been for God's love. Otherwise
why did the poet feel compelled to introduce the guardian angel
where he did? I submit that Spenser is showing, as he will show in
another fashion later, the limits of nature. There may be such a
thing as the continent man and there may be such a thing as the temperate man, but there is no such thing as a completely self-sufficient
man, whether continent or temperate. This fact, I think, is confirmed
first of all by the meeting of the Redcross Knight and Guyon at the
opening of Book II; second, by the Palmer's return at the beginning
of Canto viii; third, by Arthur's intervention and the fact that Guyon
does not become fully conscious until after Pyrochles and Cymochles
have been defeated, suggesting that reason has not fully returned
until grace has been accepted. In short, I interpret the whole sequence of episodes to mean that it is itself reasonable for man to
recognize his dependence upon God. But Spenser is not bludgeoning
the point, as I am; he simply assumes it, and in so doing he accommodates his delineation of Aristotelian virtue to a Christian world,
which regards human virtues as themselves gifts of God.

Now, and now only, can Guyon go to the Castle of Alma, and it is
fitting that Arthur accompany him. Spenser has worked things out
to this point to show that religion is an indispensable element of the
virtuous man. Indeed, in a Christian world, the virtues alone and
without supernatural sanction are illusions. Spenser does not deny
the necessity and usefulness of the classical virtues,[8] but he cannot
assert their sufficiency. Book II of The Faerie Queene may be man-
centred, as against Book I, which is God-centred, but the virtues
which Book II outlines are not self-authenticating, and the hero of
the book is neither self-sufficient nor perfectible by his own efforts.

The opening stanza of Canto ix (which looks back as well as forward,
as Spenser's opening stanzas almost always do), emphasizes man's
'native dignity and grace' as well as his perilous position: man is
responsible for preserving himself, lest 'through misrule and passions bace' his nature 'growes a Monster.' But Spenser did not expect us to read Book II (or any other book, for that matter) in isolation, and we are reminded in the opening line of the stanza that man
is first of all 'Gods work':

> Of all Gods workes, which do this world adorne,
> There is no one more faire and excellent,
> Than is mans body both for powre and forme,
> Whiles it is kept in sober gouernment.

In Book II as a whole we are never very long without such remind-
ers.

If one were asked to ascribe more precise theological meanings
to the figures and events which I have been discussing, it might be
argued that the presence of the Redcross Knight at the start of Book
II suggests the concept of prevenient or antecedent grace, that is,
grace which inclines the will to choose the good. Thereafter, we
are given occasional examples, in the person of Arthur, of subsequent or co-operating grace, which assists man to act after the will
has already been inclined to choose the good.[9]

Finally, Arthur's encounter with Maleger in the eleventh canto
is not a new departure, nor is it opposed to earlier events in Book
II, as Professor Woodhouse seems to imply. This episode actually
completes the meaning of the sequence of events as Spenser has
worked it out to this point. Arthur, as magnanimity, cannot overcome Maleger, who represents original sin. Only the waters of
baptism will suffice:

> So greatest and most glorious thing on ground
> May often need the helpe of weaker hand;
> So feeble is mans state, and life vnsound,
> That in assurance it may neuer stand,
> Till it dissolued be from earthly band.
> Proofe be thou Prince, the prowest man aliue,
> And noblest borne of all in Britayne land;
> Yet thee fierce Fortune did so nearly driue,
> That had not grace thee blest, thou shouldest not surviue.
>
> (II. xi. 30)

Arthur has clearly changed function, though after repeated and careful readings I am unable to identify a specific place at which Spenser announces or otherwise makes clear the transition. Whereas Arthur had offered grace to Pyrochles, it is now Arthur himself whom grace has blest. Baptismal deliverance must precede temperance; Arthur must do what he does, Maleger (original sin) must be shown to have been put down before Guyon can do what he does, even though his destruction of Acrasia's bower may, after Arthur's great scene, seem anti-climactic to those who forget the religious basis of Spenser's thought. However artistically unsatisfying, this is the reason why Spenser felt the necessity of the double resolution of the book in the twin victorious exploits of Arthur and Guyon. It also seems to me sufficient proof that Cantos xi and xii were not composed as alternate endings to Book II, as some scholars have suggested, that Spenser specifically intended them to appear in the order in which we have them. The effects of original sin must be overcome before Guyon, the temperate man, can go on and destroy intemperance. To be sure, Acrasia is only bound, not exterminated; but that is simply Christian common sense. At least it is good Anglican and Catholic common sense, and Professor Whitaker has shown beyond a doubt that Spenser did not accept the extreme Calvinistic doctrine of perseverance in grace.[10] Guyon may have achieved greatness through virtue and self-mastery; he may even have been infused with and protected by divine grace; but his greatness, like that of any Christian, remains limited by the Fall. Spenser would regard as preposterous the assumption that the desires and appetites can be completely eliminated from fallen human nature. This is why Guyon can at best represent only continence in the Bower of Bliss, the climactic episode in the book. However successfully some men may learn to control their passions, the result of the Fall is that irrational and unnatural impulses always remain with us.[11] Hence the necessity for reason to be ever on guard and the necessity for the Palmer's presence in the last canto. Even so, one may observe that Guyon, a Christian, does destroy Acrasia's garden, which is more than his pre-Christian predecessors, Odysseus and Aeneas, were able to do: they managed only their own getaways.

We are helped to a fuller understanding of Spenser's total meaning if we look ahead for a moment to the scale of values outlined in Milton's Comus. The distinguishing feature of that scale, as Professor Woodhouse has pointed out, is not renunciation, but 'comprehension and ascent,'[12] and Milton does all he can to keep his argument from seeming austere and repressive. It will be recalled that Comus and the Lady fight to a draw in their central debate until she adds religion to her argument. Her bleak Stoic defence of chastity might alone be construed as pride or mere revulsion from her would-be seducer. A religious sanction for chastity is invoked precisely in order that chastity may become positive, not negative; in order that the Lady's rejection of Comus's argument may not seem mere Stoicism or neurotic revulsion. Sensuality is rejected, but not natural pleasure, which is subordinated to certain higher values in an ascending scale, a scale in which physical pleasure has its place, but is not the end. The Lady's rational objections to intemperance, accordingly, derive their confirmation and real authority from the second part of her speech, wherein the 'Sunclad power of Chastity' is religiously celebrated. The intellectual pattern of Book II of The Faerie Queene is analogous in that Spenser does his best to conduct the action in such a way that Guyon's final destruction of the Bower of Bliss will not seem prudish. And we have to analyse the action of the book closely in order to detect his efforts, remembering that we do not share the assumptions and beliefs about the theocentric universe of Spenser's contemporaries, that men will never again respond instinctively to his world-picture, but that a knowledge of that world-picture is essential to any proper understanding of his poem. If Spenser does not succeed, that is because human beings are what they are; in the twentieth century, to quote from a recent popular song, 'Doin' what comes naturally' no longer means living in accordance with the Law of Nature.

Finally, if Comus seems remote as an analogy, or at best appropriate rather to Book III than to Book II of Spenser's poem, surely Paradise Regained is as valid and striking an analogy as we shall find. Like Guyon, the hero of Milton's short epic is the Aristotelian magnanimous man transmuted and raised to a Christian level.[13] Christ meets Satan's temptations with what appear to be merely human resources, but as Milton makes clear throughout, the most important of these is faith in God.[14] Reason establishes temperance, which enables Christ to refuse Satan; but it is faith in God, the 'Light from above,' that guarantees reason. And when matters are brought to their final issue in Christ's repudiation of the ancients and of all their works, which are the products of natural reason unenlightened by grace, we are shown which has priority. Spenser's hero is not Christ, nor does he give us the final object-lesson found in Paradise Regained, but with Sir Guyon and Prince Arthur he is, as I have tried to show, engaged in precisely the same work of transmutation and elevation. Guyon's reason is not its own authority; it is itself a gift of God. Not only in the background of Book II, but in the foreground, in the action itself, Spenser has done his best to show us that there is something which nourishes and guarantees reason, something which supplies the credentials by which reason operates, something which, to borrow Étienne Gilson's words, makes for a specifically 'Christian exercise of reason,'[15] It is the grace of God.

NATURE AND GRACE IN SPENSER: A REJOINDER

A. S. P. Woodhouse

Mr. Robert Hoopes has been so good as to call my attention to his article, 'God Guide Thee, Guyon' (R.E.S., N.S. V (1954), 14–24)* in which he very courteously takes me to task for misinterpreting The Faerie Queene, Book II. If I felt more certain that those who read Mr. Hoopes had also read my Tudor and Stuart lecture at Johns Hopkins (printed in E.L.H., xvi (1949), 194–228)* and hence were not dependent merely on Mr. Hoope's summary and selection of evidence, I should risk the appearance of letting the question go by default.

In my lecture I advanced and tested the following hypothesis: that, in the part of The Faerie Queene which we possess, Spenser recognized and, for artistic and doctrinal purposes, employed the distinction between the order of nature and the order of grace, then familiar, however strangely it strikes upon the modern and more secular ear; that the primary reference in Book I, with its specifically Christian virtue of holiness and its constant invoking of religious motives and sanctions, is to the order of grace, and the primary reference in the remaining books, until we come to the last pronouncement in the 'Cantos of Mutabilitie,' is to the order of nature; but that Spenser must have envisaged as the culmination of his poem a final synthesis of the two orders and their values, a synthesis for which indeed he is preparing from the first, both by indicating on occasion the limits of natural reason and natural virtue and by the introduction of imagery suggesting a parallel between the two orders.

If I understand Mr. Hoopes aright, he sets out to prove that all this is mistaken, that in Book II Spenser does not prepare for a synthesis of the two orders but effects it, or rather, perhaps, does not require to synthetize since he has never distinguished at all between them, and that he invokes for Guyon's attainment of temperance and continence precisely the same religious motives and sanctions as for for the Redcross Knight's attainment of holiness.

Now, the only evidence which Mr. Hoopes adduces for such moti-

*Reprinted pp. 84–95 and 58–83 respectively.

Reprinted from Review of English Studies, New Series Vol. 6 (1955), pp. 284–288, by permission of The Clarendon Press, Oxford.

vation and sanction is drawn from Guyon's initial encounter with the Redcross Knight (II. i. 26–34), and is susceptible of quite different interpretation. The literary purpose of this episode is to link the second to the first book (cf. a similar linking in III. i. 5 ff.), and its doctrinal significance resides in the ready acknowledgement, prompted by reason, of the superiority of grace to nature, which depends of course on the prior recognition of a clear distinction between them. If the Palmer's statement that Guyon 'Must now anew begin like race to runne' means that Guyon must win a seat among the saints and not simply, as the Redcross Knight had also done, win through to his appropriate virtue and the fulfilment of his task, why is there no hint, in the remaining eleven cantos, of religious motive and sanction or of Guyon's having attained or even progressed towards a seat among the saints? Why are the patent parallels between Guyon's adventures and those of the Redcross Knight always exploited so as to bring out the contrast between them; or why (to take a specific example, does Guyon prepare himself for his final task in the humanistic Castle of Alma instead of in some religious retreat like the House of Holiness? And since when were the Aristotelian temperance and continence specifically Christian virtues (i.e. virtues attainable only by the Christian and on religious grounds) as holiness clearly is? And why is Guyon referred to (II. viii. 1) in terms appropriate to the natural man, but to the convert utterly inappropriate? These and a good many other questions Mr. Hoopes studiously ignores, presumably because he has no answers for them.

He makes much of the fact that God's aid is invoked (II. i. 32), and it is vouchsafed (II. viii). But why should it not be? For the natural order is also God's, and over it God's power and providence preside. In his definitions of both nature and grace (as in definition in general) Mr. Hoopes is at his weakest. Through most of his article he thinks of nature too restrictedly and of grace too loosely. Thus [p. 86] he attributes to me the assertion that (in II. viii) Arthur represents 'the operation of grace <u>within</u> nature.' I said nothing of the kind, for the good reason that the phrase would be meaningless unless (like Mr. Hoopes) one were using <u>grace</u> merely as a synonym for God's bounty to all His creatures, manifested as providential intervention in the natural order, a sense in reality quite distinct from that in which Arthur in Book I represents the working of divine grace upon the heart of the believer. Of the ambivalence of the word <u>grace</u> Spenser was perfectly conscious, and probably designed to turn it to account in the final synthesis for which he was preparing; but ambivalence in Spenser too often becomes confusion in his critics.

It is always possible to determine from the context the primary sense in which the word <u>grace</u> is being used (as I illustrated in my article by distinguishing some of its principal meanings; see [p. 68], n. 24), and it is necessary to do so if one is to follow Spenser's argument and appreciate at their true value the secondary suggestions conveyed. But this necessary, indeed elementary, step in criticism Mr. Hoopes's argument will not permit him to take. Thus in commenting on II. viii. 51–52 [p. 90] he speaks of Arthur's offer to Pyrochles of Christian forgiveness upon repentance and points triumphantly to the words, 'Wroth was the Prince, and sory yet withall/ That he so wilfully refused grace.' But the primary meaning of <u>grace</u> here is rendered unmistakable by the context: it is not heavenly grace that is meant but, in Spenser's own words, Arthur's 'princely bounty and great mind' (i.e. magnanimity) which prompt him to spare a vanquished foe for his 'valiaunce.' If there is a secondary suggestion—if this is as it were a faint image on the natural level—of God's offer of grace to sinners on their repentance, it is one more example of Spenser's, not effecting, but preparing for, his final synthesis. And if Arthur in Book II represents divine grace (as Mr. Hoopes seems to maintain), why does he himself in the encounter with Maleger (II. xi) come so near to defeat, have to be in effect rescued by providential intervention, using weak things (i.e. Timias) as its instrument (30–31), and appeal from nature to grace (symbolized by water) for the destruction of Maleger (46)? In this connexion, I may perhaps be allowed to remind Mr. Hoopes that my interpretation of Spenser's meaning and purpose led me to offer for the first time an explanation of Maleger which accounted for <u>all</u> his attributes, namely, that he stood for Original Sin, an explanation which Mr. Hoopes treats as if it were a critical commonplace, but which his interpretation could not have originated and can, I think, barely tolerate. Indeed, on his interpretation Spenser's sense of the limits of natural virtue is obscured and loses most, if not quite all, of its significance. Thus he passes over in silence the striking and unexpected parallel, in V. ix. 29–32, read in the light of V. x. 1, where, having learned justice and equity as natural virtues, Arthur and Artegall must learn the principle of mercy (as distinct from the unorganized sentiment of pity) from a Christian source. And finally his interpretation precludes his adopting my justification (the only one, I believe, ever offered) of Spenser's artistry in the double ending of Book II with an heroic exploit by Guyon and another by Arthur.

Mr. Hoopes summarizes my argument in such terms as he feels himself capable of dealing with and silently omits all the evidence which his own interpretation is unable to explain. Some of the questions which he must answer, if he is to establish a prima-facie case, I have rapidly suggested above; but I hope that the few readers interested may perhaps do me the justice of reading my original article. Mr. Hoopes seeks a tactical advantage in bracketing me with the late Professor F. M. Padelford (a great Spenserian, with whom in reality it is too much honour to be named) in regarding Spenser as a Calvinist instead of as an Elizabethan Anglican. The antithesis is, of course, no antithesis at all, as any one who had read Archbishop Whitgift might have told Mr. Hoopes. I did not mention, let alone call in question, Spenser's loyalty to the Elizabethan Settlement or the Thirty-nine Articles; but evidently Mr. Hoopes's notions about Calvinism are not more exact than his definitions of nature and grace. What I emphasized was some hesitation in Spenser's attitude towards nature between views which might be conveniently associated with Calvinism and others which suggested rather the tradition to which Hooker was about to give its most eloquent expression (for it was I, and not Mr. Hoopes, who first brought Hooker into the discussion); and of this hesitation there is evidence in other works—for example, in the Fowre Hymnes (as appears in Padelford's exposition of them).

Nothing in Mr. Hoopes's argument is more unconvincing than his final effort to level Guyon and the Christ of Paradise Regained, which entails an excursion into the misinterpretation of Milton, and in effect a lowering of Christ to meet the levitated Guyon half-way. Granted that Christ is tested in the temptation as man; yet we are never allowed to forget that he is at once the Son of God and the 'second Adam,' who by his obedience is regaining all that the first Adam by disobedience lost, or that his motivation is purely and simply religious, namely, loving submission and obedience to the Father, and that it is as a result of this religious motivation that Christ becomes 'this perfect man,' the great exemplar of magnanimity, of temperance, and of every other virtue which natural reason could conceive. But to return to Spenser: we do him wrong if, by impetuously hurrying him on to his final synthesis, we obscure all his preliminary distinctions, not to mention the finer points of his artistry, and attribute to him at every stage of the journey meanings which we are unable to support by a single reliable reference in his text.

I would not, however, end on a note of complaint. One very valuable contribution Mr. Hoopes tucks away in a footnote ([p. 91], n. 8): it is the quotation from Wither's preface to the translation of Nemesius on the Nature of Man, and I thank him for reminding me of it. For, though it is not specially relevant to Book II, it is to the final synthesis for which Spenser seems to be preparing, a synthesis which (as I insisted) could be achieved only by the subordination of nature to grace, and for which (as I tried to show) he prepares first by distinguishing the two orders, then by adumbrating in his imagery and in other ways a parallel between them. Indeed, I would be willing to compromise with Mr. Hoopes by accepting as an epigraph, not for Book II, but for The Faerie Queene as a whole, the two quotations, mine from The Ancient Bounds and his from George Wither.

THE THEOLOGICAL STRUCTURE OF THE FAERIE QUEENE, BOOK I

Virgil K. Whitaker

Theology is a subject which the student of English literature is likely to view from afar, with indifference if not actual hostility. Yet no subject was better known, at least in its fundamentals, to Elizabethan writers. In petty school they learned to read from a primer that consisted merely of selections from the Book of Common Prayer, and they memorized the Catechism from the prayer book as well as sentences from the Scriptures. In grammar school they studied the same catechism in Latin and Greek versions and also, before 1570, the elaborate Latin catechisms of Calvin or Erasmus. After 1570 they mastered the catechism of Alexander Nowell, which has appended to it an elaborate glossary that indicates and demands an advanced knowledge of theological concepts. They seem also to have been questioned on the Thirty-Nine Articles.[1] For all but the incorrigibly irreligious, therefore, moral problems inevitably involved theological problems. Most Elizabethans thought of the connection between their daily sins and Adam's original sin as automatically as we associate turning on the light with electricity, and they were far better grounded in religious doctrine than most of us are in modern physics. This paper is primarily an attempt to show that the moral allegory of Book I of the Faerie Queene is theological in its structure and is based upon the arrangement of points customary in Renaissance confessionals. But I hope that it will also present further evidence of the part that fundamental theological ideas can play in the understanding of Renaissance literature.

Since Book I, the legend of the Redcross knight of holiness, is presented as a biography, the inference that it is a spiritual biography of the typical Christian in search of holiness readily follows and seems to have been accepted, tacitly at least, by most students of Spenser. Yet the moral allegory cannot possibly be

Reprinted from English Literary History, Vol. 19 (1952), pp. 151–164, © The Johns Hopkins Press, by permission of the author and The Johns Hopkins Press.

biographical or chronological, even to the extent of being an idealized account of the struggles of the soul in quest of holiness. Red Cross's victory over Error in Canto i precedes the instruction of Fidelia in Canto x. Canto x, in turn, represents an entire progress through the disciplines of the church and the ultimate mystical experience to which a Christian might aspire; yet baptism does not appear until Red Cross falls into the Well of Life in Canto xi, from which he emerges "a new-borne knight" (xi, 34) with "baptized hands" (xi, 36). Even in the early church, in which baptism followed conversion and religious instruction, baptism would have been an indispensable preliminary for most of the experiences of Canto x; like religious instruction, it would have been needed for the complete victory over error in Canto i.

These, and many other difficulties, are solved if we assume that Book I, like Book II, is organized in terms of concepts. No points in the whole cannon of Spenser criticism are better established than that Book I and Book II show an elaborate and detailed parallelism in the sequence of episodes and that, because of their similarity, they constitute a kind of subgroup within the poem as a whole.[2] It is also well known that the temptations to which Guyon is subjected in Book II are arranged, according to the division going back to Plato, into those related to wrath and lust—the irascible in Cantos i to vi and the concupiscible in Cantos vii to xii.[3] That is, the structure of the moral allegory of Book II is based upon a scheme of classification rather than upon a biographically probable sequence of emotional experiences. It is certainly likely that Spenser would have extended the parallelism between the two books from surface episodes to fundamental structure and that the moral allegory of Book I would also be based upon a well-recognized arrangement of ideas. That probability this paper will attempt to establish as fact by showing that the moral allegory of Book I is organized according to the arrangement of Christian doctrines customary in Renaissance theological treatises and confessionals.

A few examples will establish this pattern. In Calvin's Institutes, for example, Book I considers the nature of God and the authority of the Scriptures and then turns to the state of man before his fall. Books II and III discuss Adam's fall, original sin, Christ's rôle as mediator, the operation of grace, justification by faith, good works, and predestination. Book IV is devoted to the church and the sacraments. The Thirty-Nine Articles of the Church of England begin with discussions of both God and Christ and define the authority of both Scriptures and creeds; from then on they parallel the Institutes closely: original sin, free will (and grace), justification, good works, sin after baptism, predestination; then the church, its authority and ministry, the sacraments, and miscellaneous points. A similar organization is apparent in the proceedings of the Council of Trent.[4] And Fidelia clearly begins to follow the same pattern when she instructs Red Cross "Of God, of grace, of iustice, of free will" (x, 19).

Spenser followed roughly this same pattern as the basis of his moral allegory, omitting for obvious reasons the opening sections on God, the Bible, and Adam's state before the fall. Book I treats first of original sin, of justification, and of problems logically and traditionally associated with justification, such as the nature of sin itself, the hotly debated question of sins after justification, and predestination and election; then of the church and its functions; and finally of the sacraments. Sometimes Spenser employs ideas that were part of the theological heritage of Western Christendom; sometimes he parallels the Thirty-Nine Articles closely. Nowhere, as I have elsewhere argued at length,[5] does he present doctrines peculiar to Calvinism. This structure means, of course, that the sequence of events has no relationship to their probable occurrence in human life but may have logical meaning in the way that one point follows another in philosophic exposition.

I certainly do not intend to imply that Book I of the Faerie Queene is a theological treatise or that every episode can be given a precise theological implication. For one thing, romance had to be attended to. For another, moral and historical allegory intermingle, and the claims of one must yield to the claims of the other. Spenser's method is not a rigorous and unyielding allegory but rather a compromise among conflicting elements.[6] Finally, the allegory often seems to move on more than two levels. Duessa is sometimes falsehood as the opposite of truth, sometimes false religion, sometimes Roman Catholicism, sometimes Mary Queen of Scots; sometimes, apparently, she is all of them at once. But an analysis of the moral allegory of Book I seems to show that the theological scheme of organization outlined above fits the key episodes in Book I and further illuminates them. Such an analysis will now be attempted, in so far as it is feasible in a paper of this length.

In following the traditional theological structure, Spenser would obviously skip the initial matter on God, the Bible and Creeds, and Adam's state before the fall. For him, as for his contemporaries, the logical starting point for a discussion of the path to salvation or holiness would be original sin and justification, doctrines about which centered the fundamental theological controversies of the Reformation. And it seems very likely that these are indicated by the Letter to Raleigh and Canto I. The contrast between original sin and Christian righteousness is first indicated by the transformation in Red Cross when he puts on the Christian armor, and then the process of justification is allegorized. Justification is, of course, the process by which the individual is cleared of his guilt of original sin and God's justice is satisfied for that sin by the merits of Christ's atonement upon the cross.

We first see Red Cross in the Letter to Raleigh as "a tall clownishe young man, who . . . rested him on the floore, vnfitte through his rusticity for a better place."[7] Una appeared, and Red Cross desired the adventure. Understandably reluctant, she finally agreed to accept him as a champion if he could wear the armour which she brought—that is, "the armour of a Christian man specified by Saint Paul v. Ephes . . . which being forthwith put vpon him with dewe furnitures thereunto, he seemed the goodliest man in al that company." The armor of Ephesians includes a breastplate of righteousness and a shield of faith, and these Spenser singles out for mention and places on each of them a cross, as everyone knows. "We are accounted righteous before God," says Article XI of the Thirty-Nine Articles, "only for the merit of our Lord and Saviour Jesus Christ by Faith, and not for our own works or deservings"—that is, our righteousness derives from his cross, which we embrace by faith.

As the narrative begins, Red Cross and Una enter the wandering wood and there encounter Error, half serpent and half woman. This combination is remarkably like that which proved too much for poor Adam in the Garden of Eden and is doubtless intended to suggest Red Cross's liability to error as a son of Adam. Red Cross enters into combat with Error, who leaps upon his shield and wraps her train about his body. "Add faith vnto your force," cries Una (i, 19). Red Cross then grips Error and she vomits forth a poisonous mess full of books and papers. He relaxes his grip, and she pours forth her "cursed spawne of serpents small" (i, 22), which "him encombred sore but could not hurt at all." Finally Red Cross strikes Error "with more than manly force" (i, 24) and cuts off her head; the little "sinlets" drink her blood and die of it; and Red Cross and Una ride on "with God to frend" (i, 28).

In calling upon Red Cross to add faith unto his force, Una was telling him to take the only initiative available under Anglican doctrine to a man in need of salvation: "that we are justified by Faith only is a most wholesome Doctrine, and very full of comfort," says Article XI. But, in recapitulating the process of justification, Spenser commits the absurdity, from the viewpoint of a spiritual biography, of showing Red Cross fully equipped with the armor of righteousness and faith before his first combat with Error—and then having Una admonish him during that combat to add faith unto his force! The poisonous vomit full of books and papers has been conjectured to be religious controversy,[8] but a more definite identification is perhaps possible. In narrating his conversion in the Confessions, St. Augustine distinguishes two steps. First, there came a rejection of false philosophies and an acceptance of Christian doctrine as true. But the lusts of the flesh still held him back. His conversion was complete, therefore, only after he had overcome not only the poison of false doctrine but the lusts of the flesh as well.[9] St. Thomas reflects the same tradition when he speaks of four things as necessary for justification, of which two, an infusion of grace and a remission of sins, are God's gifts, and two, a free choice of God by faith and a free choice against sin, must be man's contribution.[10]

Spenser's allegory involves a somewhat illogical adaptation of these notions to Anglican teaching, which was coming to combine the Protestant doctrine of justification by faith with the traditional concepts of right reason and free will, as in Hooker. The vomit full of books and papers represents false doctrines that must be overcome by faith, which Red Cross provides on his own responsibility at the urging of Una or Truth. The "spawne of serpents small" is the lusts of the flesh that still hinder and must also be overcome; they derive their being and their nourishment from original sin, and in her death they die. But their inability to harm Red Cross, which is artistically ineffective and at first sight puzzles the reader, is in accord with the Protestant emphasis upon faith rather than works. Red Cross's "more than manly force" is due to God's grace, and he departs "well worthy . . . of that Armorie" and "with God to frend" because his guilt has been remitted and he is accompanied by God's grace. All four of St. Thomas's requirements for justification are therefore present.

But Red Cross's troubles are not over. Though the guilt of original sin, as well as of actual sins already committed, has been pardoned,[11] the proneness to sin remains. The ninth of the Thirty-Nine Articles summarizes the view universally accepted:

And this infection of nature doth remain, yea in them that are regenerated; whereby the lust of the flesh . . . is not subject to the Law of God.

Spenser goes on to show how this weakness or lust of the flesh operates in Red Cross. In doing so, he relies upon the traditional concepts of sin derived from Augustine, elaborated by Aquinas, and restated during Spenser's own lifetime by Richard Hooker. He employs, in other words, the same set of ideas which form the basis of <u>Macbeth</u>, as Professor Curry has shown,[12] and which Milton used to explain the fall of Adam and Eve.[13]

In this tradition, as you will recall, sin is always the false choice of a lesser or apparent good instead of a greater or real good. Since sin involves a false choice, it is impossible in the presence of truth, and Red Cross must be separated from Una before he can fall into sin, just as Guyon in Book II must be separated from the Palmer or right reason before he can be tempted by Phaedria or weakened almost to death by Mammon. Man is liable to choose falsely because his reason has been weakened and his will made inordinate by Adam's fall. The false choice itself may have one of three internal causes: ignorance; the soliciting of the will by the appetite, which prevails over reason; and a habit of sin built up by repeated false choices.[14] Both Satan and other men may be external causes of sin, not directly, but only by stimulating the imagination or arousing the appetite, so that the internal causes of sin operate.[15] Pride or inordinate self-love was the original cause of sin both in Satan and in man, and pride and concupiscence, as manifested in the appetite, remain the fundamental internal causes of sin in man.[16] Beginning with Canto ii, Spenser shows how the lust of the flesh, taken as a type to indicate appetite or concupiscence, separates Red Cross from Truth and makes possible and inevitable further false judgments. Pride, the original cause of all sin, seems to serve almost as a symbol of sin itself.

As Una and Red Cross proceed, they encounter Archimago, the arch-enchanter. Many of his characteristics are obviously determined by the historical allegory. But the reference to "his diuelish arts" (ii, 9) surely implies that in the moral allegory he is Satan himself, the father of lies, as the external cause of sin. If so, Spenser is showing the external forces of sin cooperating with man's internal appetite to produce sin, just as Shakespeare shows the witches, who are instruments of Satan, stimulating the evil desires already present in Macbeth.[17] If Archimago is Satan, he sets about separating Red Cross from Una quite orthodoxly by working on imagination and appetite. First, he stimulates lustful reverie in Red Cross, making

> him dreame of loues and lustfull play,
> That nigh his manly hart did melt away,
> Bathed in wanton blis and wicked ioy.　　　　　(i, 47)

> In this great passion of vnwanted lust,
> Or wanted feare of doing ought amis,
> He started vp, (i, 49)

and encountered a false image of Una, who tried to seduce him. But Red Cross, sorely disturbed by Una's apparent falseness, "lay . . . musing at her mood" (i, 55), and by that musing Archimago was for the time being foiled. But Archimago's second assault, the spectacle of the false Una in the embraces of a lusty squire, was too much for Red Cross, whose reason succumbed to his passion. "The eye of reason was with rage yblent" (ii, 5), and he fled from Una, "pricked with wrath and fiery fierce disdain" (ii, 8). He was now separated from truth and a prey to his lower nature; "will was his guide, and griefe led him astray" (ii, 12).

The separation of Red Cross from truth is, of course, an indispensable preliminary to sin if sin involves a false choice. The following episodes seem to indicate, not a plausible sequence of experiences through which the Christian novice might go, but rather the various kinds of experiences to which a soul astray from the truth and ruled by appetite and falsehood may be subject. They investigate the possible consequences of that "infection of nature" which remains even in the regenerated.

The encounter with Sans Foy suggests loss of faith. Fradubio has made Duessa his dame and has been changed by her into a tree, a state from which he can escape only by being bathed in a living well (ii, 43). In other words, he has become so habituated to sin that he has lost the reason which made him man, reason being for Spenser, as for St. Thomas and Hooker, the power to make value judgments or moral choice. He can be saved only by baptism or a similar gift of God's grace, which, as Spenser tells us later, will "guilt of sinfull crimes cleane wash away" and "aged long decay renew" (xi, 30). The visit of Red Cross and Duessa to the Castle of Lucifera involves a presentation of the seven deadly sins. The meaning of Red Cross's escape from the Castle of Pride after the Dwarf has seen the dungeon full of captives seems to be that man, even when deprived of the full light of truth, can escape the more obvious sins by exercising prudence of a lower order. That this kind of narrow and uncertain escape, with no basis in knowledge of truth, brings acute distrust and unhappiness, or Sans Joy, is indicated by the opening stanza of Canto vi, which compares Red Cross to a Marriner who "yet in doubt ne dares to ioy at his foole-happie ouersight."

When Duessa overtakes Red Cross just before the combat with

Orgoglio, he has so yielded to lust for her that he has lost his
power of distinguishing right from wrong, as Spenser indicates
in the opening stanza of Canto vii, which meditates on the inability
of man to distinguish falsehood from truth:

> What man so wise, what earthly wit so ware,
> As to descry the crafty cunning traine,
> By which deceipt doth maske in visour faire,
> And cast her colours dyed deepe in graine,
> To seeme like Truth, whose shape she well can faine.
>
> (vii, 1)

Does this indicate that the Orgoglio episode is merely an elaboration of the point made by the earlier encounter with Fradubio? I
think, rather, that Spenser is passing on to another theological
problem.

Orgoglio's characteristics are obviously determined in large
part by the historical allegory. It has been customary to distinguish him from Duessa by calling him spiritual pride and Duessa
carnal pride, or vice versa,[18] but the text will not support such
a distinction. The introductory stanza of Canto viii, again an exposition of the moral allegory, plainly identifies Arthur as the
grace of God, Una as truth, and Orgoglio as Red Cross's "owne
foolish pride" which makes him thrall to the bonds of sin:

> Ay me, how many perils doe enfold
> The righteous man, to make him daily fall?
> Were not, that heauenly grace doth him vphold,
> And steadfast truth acquite him out of all.
> Her loue is firme, her care continuall,
> So oft as he through his owne foolish pride,
> Or weaknesse is to sinfull bands made thrall:
> Else should this <u>Redcrosse</u> knight in bands haue dyde,
> For whose deliuerance she this Prince doth thither guide.
>
> (viii, 1)

Orgoglio is therefore simply another personification of pride as
the first cause of sin and the symbol of man's liability to sin. The
distinction between him and Lucifera is required by the historical,
not the moral allegory.

The explanation of this episode is probably to be found in a
major theological controversy of Spenser's day. Article XVI of
the Thirty-Nine Articles will clarify the issue and show its im-

portance, although it is possible that Spenser was not thinking
directly of the article. The Thirty-Nine Articles as a whole involve a studious attempt at compromise among conflicting religious positions, and only two of them contain outright condemna-
tions of Calvinist doctrines, Article XXXVII, which speaks out
clearly for royal supremacy over the church, and this one. Its
importance is indicated by its unique intransigence. After con-
demning the Anabaptist doctrine that any sin after baptism is
unpardonable, it continues: "After we have received the Holy
Ghost, we may depart from grace given, and fall into sin, and
by the grace of God we may arise again, and amend our lives."
This statement is directed against the Calvinist doctrine of
perseverance in grace, the belief that "a true liuely iustifying
faith, and the sanctifying spirit of God, is not extinguished nor
vanisheth away in the regenerate, either finally or totally."[19]
The issue focused the conflict between the humanist concept of
free will, which Spenser surely accepted and wrote into the
Faerie Queene, and the Calvinist view of man's total depravity.
For if man has no part in his salvation but must depend wholly
upon God's irresistible grace, any argument that he may fall
after receiving grace involves the logically untenable supposition that God's grace is imperfect in its operation.

Red Cross was caught by Orgoglio when he was without the
Christian armor and engaged in an act of lust. In using lust to
show how man's appetite will lead him to sin, Spenser was following a tradition going back to the New Testament. Milton was
later to use the same device when he first showed the effect of
the fall upon Adam and Eve by making them indulge in carnal
intercourse. Surely Red Cross had departed from grace given
and fallen into sin. But the grace of God protected him. Of
Orgoglio's first blow Spenser says:

> And were not heauenly grace, that him did blesse,
> He had been pouldred all, as thin as flowre.   (vii, 12)

And Arthur, who rescued Red Cross, is identified by many signs
as the grace of God. Except for him "Else should this Redcrosse
knight in bands haue dyde." The death is, of course, spiritual
death in the bands of sin. But, thanks to Arthur or heavenly grace,
Red Cross arose again and amended his life.

Red Cross's next encounter is with Despair. The same combination of ideas is to be found in much literature of the Middle
Ages and Renaissance. Witness Marlowe's handling of the theme

of spiritual despair in <u>Faustus</u>, where, in his opening soliloquy, the scholar states and accepts exactly the same fallacious arguments that Despair urges upon Red Cross. But in Spenser the association of ideas once again parallels the Thirty-Nine Articles, this time "XVII. Of Predestination and Election," the penultimate article in the section on salvation. After summarizing the doctrine of predestination, Article XVII goes on to say:

> As the godly consideration of Predestination, and our Election in Christ, is full of sweet, pleasant, and unspeakable comfort to godly persons . . . So, for curious and carnal persons, lacking the Spirit of Christ, to have continually before their eyes the sentence of God's Predestination, is a most dangerous downfall, whereby the Devil doth thrust them either into desperation, or into wretchedness of most unclean living, no less perilous than desperation.

Despair's arguments turn on God's justice and his inexorable decree:

> Is not he iust, that all this doth behold
> From highest heauen, and beares an equall eye?
> Shall he thy sins vp in his knowledge fold,
> And guiltie be of thine impietie?
> Is not his law, Let euery sinner die:
> Die shall all flesh? (ix, 47)

After snatching the knife from Red Cross's hand, Una replies by assuring Red Cross that he is one of the elect:

> In heauenly mercies has thou not a part?
> Why shouldst thou then despeire, that chosen art?
> Where iustice growes, there grows eke greater grace,
> The which doth quench the brond of hellish smart,
> And that accurst hand-writing doth deface. (ix, 53)

In short, Spenser has combined references to predestination and election with a portrayal of that despair which Article XVII envisions and a statement of its contrary principle that the elect should rejoice in God's mercy.

Space prevents a discussion of Una's wanderings during her separation from Red Cross. They seem, in general, to involve the plight of truth when separated from Christian protection and Christian revelation. If so, her rescue by Sir Satyrane seems to suggest that, like Dante, Spenser rejected the relatively liberal Thomistic view that virtuous pagans unacquainted with Christian revelation may find truth adequate for salvation by following the light of nature, for the Satyres hear Una's "trew sacred lore" (vi, 30) but "hauing cannot hold" her (vi, 33). Only Sir Satyrane, who is half "faerie" and has traveled "through all Faery lond" (vi, 29) "learnd her discipline of faith and veritie" (vi, 31). Spenser shared, rather, the doctrine of Article XVIII:

> They also are to be had accursed that presume to say,
> That every man shall be saved by the Law or Sect which
> he professeth, so that he be diligent to frame his life
> according to that Law, and the light of Nature. For holy
> Scripture doth set out unto us only the Name of Jesus
> Christ, whereby men must be saved.

It seems not to have been noticed that the first stanza of Canto x not only interprets the moral allegory but also involves a major transition in the development of Book I:

> What man is he, that boasts of fleshly might,
> And vaine assurance of mortality,
> Which all so soone, as it doth come to fight,
> Against spirituall foes, yeelds by and by,
> Or from the field most cowardly doth fly?
> Ne let the man ascribe it to his skill,
> That thorough grace hath gained victory.
> If any strength we haue, it is to ill,
> But all the good is Gods, both power and eke will.   (x, 1)

Red Cross has "gained victory" over spiritual foes. Yet his greatest struggle is still to come, and the very next stanza describes him as feeble, faint, weak, and raw. Something other than the final victory of life must be meant. The clue is to be found in the allusions to God's justice noticed at the end of Canto ix and in the implication of the last two lines just quoted, which enunciate the crucial point in the Protestant doctrine of justification by faith—that man's will is incapable of performing works that merit salvation, but that justification is God's free gift to those who have faith. Red Cross's victory is therefore final achievement of justification after his previous lapses. Its recognition marks the end of the section of the poem dealing with original sin, justification, and related problems, and leads to the instruction and disciplines of the church.

The parallel between the rest of Book I and the traditional theological structure needs no elaboration. Canto x, the House of Caelia, has long been recognized as depicting the instructions and spiritual disciplines of the church. It should be noted, however, that Spenser's presentation of penance led him to another and awkward repetition, this time of Red Cross's despair. Canto xi recapitulates the Christian struggle with antichrist in terms of the sacramental system, and, as Dodge demonstrated,[20] its treatment of baptism and the holy communion agrees with the Catechism's teaching that the sacraments are "an outward and visible sign of an inward and spiritual grace, and a means whereby we receive the same."

What, in conclusion, is the artistic significance of this view of the structure of Book I? First, it accounts for the repetition which is the gravest fault in the book—Lucifera and Orgoglio, the double encounter with despair, and, above all, Red Cross's combats with Error and the Dragon. On the positive side, if this paper makes its case, the very fact that the theological organization has so long been overlooked indicates the skill with which Spenser has concealed an analytical structure under the narrative of a quest, so that one of Red Cross's adventures seems to lead smoothly to another. In fact, the encounter with Orgoglio leads to the encounter with Despair far more smoothly than the proposition that man may fall and rise again precedes the treatment of predestination. From this point of view the narrative, and therefore the allegory, in Book I is far more effective than that in Book II.

THE BOWER OF BLISS AND ARMIDA'S PALACE

Robert M. Durling

Since Koeppel in 1889 called attention to the fact that the Bower of Bliss (The Faerie Queene, II, xii) owes much to Armida's palace (Gerusalemme liberata, xv—xvi),[1] it has been customary to assume that Spenser merely imitated Tasso in this instance, and not always very skillfully.[2] Ernest de Selincourt remarked in 1912 that, when Spenser borrowed from the Italian poet, "as in his description of the Bower of Bliss . . . he had no need to change the spirit of his model."[3] In 1936 Alberto Castelli went even further; Spenser, he wrote, "seppe copiare il suo modello."[4] Such facile generalizations seem to have had two principal causes. One of the obstacles to a correct understanding of Spenser's methods has been the wide acceptance of the notion that he was at heart of Acrasia's party; one wishes that Mr. C. S. Lewis' admirable discussion of the Bower in the Allegory of Love[5] had laid that ghost. The other source of difficulty has been the fact that no one seems to have undertaken a close analysis of the differences between the Bower and Armida's palace. This paper attempts such an analysis; I shall examine certain salient changes which Spenser introduced into the material he borrowed from Tasso in the Bower of Bliss. My discussion will be concerned with three principal topics— structure, the treatment of the nature of sensuality and of its cure, and the theme of art versus nature.[6]

Even on the obvious level of physical arrangement, it is clear that Spenser did not "imitate" Tasso in the narrow sense of the term. The elements taken from the Italian poet's description are reshuffled, and much new material is added. Tasso describes in detail the various defenses with which Armida's palace is equipped. It stands on a steep mountain; its approach is guarded by wild beasts; in the plain outside the palace itself is placed the "fonte del riso," the taste of which induces fatally uncontrollable laughter; two sirens are stationed in the lake formed by the fountain's waters; Armida's garden is in the center of a labyrinth of heavy

Reprinted from Comparative Literature, Vol. 6 (1954), pp. 335—347, by permission of the author and the publisher, The University of Oregon.

walls. The Bower of Bliss, on the other hand, is almost defense-less.[6a] It is apparently situated at sea level; the walls that en-close it are "but weak and thin . . . Rather for pleasure than for battery or fight" (F. Q., II, xii, 43). In making the Bower so easy of entrance, Spenser may have expected his readers to remember that "wide is the gate, and broad is the way, that leadeth to de-struction." Tasso's fountain with its sirens has been placed in-side the Bower itself; the only remnants of the elaborate defenses of Armida's palace are the wild beasts.

Armida's garden is not described as divided into several parts, although it includes a great variety of scenery; Tasso describes it, not as it unfolds itself to the eyes of his knights, but from an omniscient point of view, first (G. L., xvi, 9–11)[7] according to its visual aspects and then (xvi, 12–16) according to its auditory aspects. Then in one stanza (xvi, 17) he conducts the knights through all that he has just described to Armida and Rinaldo. The Bower of Bliss is described almost entirely from the viewpoint of Guyon and the Palmer, and is divided into several distinct parts, each clearly demarcated from the others. The first division is the "faire and spacious plaine" (F. Q., II, xii, 50–53), which cor-responds to the plain outside Armida's palace (G. L., xv, 53). By its green grass, flowers, and serene sky, the plain invites Guyon to linger, but he is unaffected by its beauty, and marching on looks "still forward right" (F. Q., II, xii, 53). Tasso, however, allows his stern warriors, who are tired by the climb up the mountain, to relax a bit in the plain (G. L., xv, 55).

The second division of the Bower corresponds to Armida's gar-den proper; it is "the most daintie Paradise on ground" (F. Q., II, xii, 58–69), which contains not only the picturesque scenery of Armida's garden but the fountain and the sirens. We noted above that Tasso describes first the visual, then the auditory aspects of his garden. Spenser follows this order and separation; but, while in Tasso's account both aspects apply to the garden as a whole, Spenser applies the passages he adapts to different parts of the Bower—the visual description to the second division and the audi-tory to the third, the Bower proper, the approach to which is heralded by a burst of music (F. Q., II, xii, 70–71). Then Spenser adopts for a moment the omniscient eye, and gives us a glimpse of Acrasia and Verdant, and we hear the song of the rose (II, xii, 72–75). Reverting to the viewpoint of Guyon and the Palmer, he describes the approach to the lovers, and gives a culminating description of them as they are discovered (Stanzas 76–80). This complex arrangement leading up to the climactic picture of

Acrasia is quite different from Tasso's rather straightforward progression from one detail to the next.

The fact is, of course, that the Bower is contrived as temptation for anyone who may enter it; and, while Carlo and Ubaldo are immune to temptation, Guyon is accessible to it, and very nearly succumbs. The three divisions of the Bower reflect the progress of successful temptation—that of the soul gradually succumbing to sensuality. In this process the figures of Genius and Excess, which are Spenser's creation, play an important part. At the entrance to the Bower one submits to Genius; since he represents the power of "guileful semblaunts" (Stanza 48), the acceptance of his tutelage may represent an initial willingness or tendency to be governed by the senses (but see p. 341 below). The first stage of sensual pleasure, the plain, is a relatively innocent one; but in its emphatic lavishness it prepares the soul for the acceptance of the wine of Excess (clearly a reference to Ephesians 5:18, as well as to Circe's potion in Od., x), the onset of disproportion and intoxication. While Genius is merely effeminate, Excess is lascivious, and the second division affords, in the bathers, direct sexual provocation. Gratification is shown in the third division, and the condition of the soul in the person of Verdant, who, in contrast to Rinaldo, is not even conscious. Verdant is entirely in Acrasia's power, of course, but the final result of her work is the transformation of men into beasts.

In giving the Bower this tripartite arrangement, Spenser may well have had in mind the famous verse from the first Epistle of St. John, "For all that is in the world, the lust of the flesh, and the lust of the eyes, and the pride of life, is not of the Father, but is of the world" (I John 2:16). It is interesting that the three sinful dispositions mentioned in the verse can be applied to the different divisions of the Bower; the pride of life to the plain, the lust of the eyes to the fountain and its bathers, and the lust of the flesh to Acrasia's grove. Obviously we should not insist heavily upon these distinctions, since all three elements underlie the Bower as a whole.

The final result of the process Spenser describes is quite different from that shown in Armida's palace. Armida, after all, does little more than keep Rinaldo from his duty, whereas Acrasia not only turns men into beasts, but causes their death under shameful circumstances and causes a stigma to be attached to their innocent children (F. Q., II, i, 49–ii, 4).[8] There would seem, then, to be a fundamental difference between the attitudes of the two authors. We have seen how Spenser rearranged Tasso's panorama, and how the changes involved a difference in meaning. The same process can be seen in more detail in the scene at the fountain (which, I may repeat, has an altogether different function in the climactic structure of Spenser's Bower from the one it serves in Tasso's account). The sequence of events as Tasso presents it is as follows (G. L., xv, 58–66):

(1) The two warriors, themselves unnoticed, come upon the girls swimming in the lake, and stop to watch them. (2) One of the girls stands up, still unaware of their presence; her beauty inspires the morning-star and Venus similes. (3) Then she sees the knights, and immediately undoes her hair. (4) Blushing and laughing, she invites them to rest from their toils. (5) The other girl accompanies her words with appropriate looks and gestures. (6) The knights, unaffected, move on.

Spenser gives events in the following order (F. Q., II, xii, 63–69):

(1) Guyon sees the two girls wrestling in the fountain; their beauty evokes the morning-star and Venus similes. (2) Guyon slacks "his earnest pace" and embraces "secret pleasurance." (3) The girls see Guyon. (4) One girl hides herself under the waves, but the other rises "rather higher," and displays herself to Guyon. (5) The other, not to be outdone, stands and undoes her hair, blushing and laughing. (6) Guyon's lust is "kindled," so the bathers increase their "wanton meriments." (7) Guyon is rebuked by the Palmer, and the two move on.

The changes Spenser has made have two principal results. First, they increase considerably the lasciviousness of the bathers. While Tasso calls them "donzellette garrule e lascive," there is nothing particularly lascivious about them except the fact that they are naked; they are merely having a swimming race. Spenser's "damzelles," however, are wrestling—performing actions in which the sexual undertone is obvious. Tasso's girls retain at least a modicum of modesty, but Spenser's from the first are shown to be governed by the opposite of that quality. They

> . . . seemed to contend,
> And wrestle wantonly, ne car'd to hyde,
> Their dainty parts from vew of any, which them eyde.
> (F. Q., II, xii, 63)

When Tasso's bather realizes she is observed, she covers her nudity; Spenser's reveals hers. Where Tasso writes,

Una intanto drizzossi, e le mammelle
e tutto ciò che piú la vista alletti
mostrò dal seno in suso, aperto al cielo,[9]   (G. L., xv, 59)

Spenser has,

But th'other rather higher did arise,
And all, that might his melting hart entire,
To her delights, she vnto him bewrayd.[9]   (F. Q., II, xii, 66)

Tasso's phrase, "ciò che piú la vista alletti," might be translated, "that which most attracts the eye." Attracting the eye and enticing the melting heart are quite dissimilar, and the change is a good index of the difference in intention. There is a placid pictorial beauty about the scene as Tasso presents it, well exemplified by the last line of Stanza 59, "E'l lago a l'altre membra era un bel velo." Spenser changes the line to "The rest hid vnderneath, him more desirous made" (F. Q., II, xii, 66), another good instance of the change in tone. No doubt Tasso's sirens invite the knights to a life of sensuality, but they do so in no lewd or obscene way, as do Spenser's.

The second result of Spenser's changes in this scene is a difference in the responses of the men. Because of the genuine pictorial beauty of the scene, we are not surprised that Tasso's warriors should be moved "alquanto." Their response seems more aesthetic than sensual, and in any case they remain fundamentally unmoved by "tal dolcezza." The emphatic lewdness of Spenser's bathers, however, introduces a note of distortion into their beauty. For this reason, the moral quality of the act by which Guyon embraces "secret pleasaunce" is quite different from that of Tasso's knights when they stop to watch the bathers. Tasso's warriors incur no blame, but Guyon earns a harsh rebuke from the Palmer.

These considerations lead us into the problem of the broader meaning of the two episodes, and the question of how they reflect the more general preoccupations of the two authors. Tasso himself published an allegorical interpretation of his poem, and this "allegoria del poema" was printed with most editions of the poem, beginning with Bonná's (1581). According to the allegory, Armida's enchantments are directed at the appetite, and signify "i fallaci sillogismi che ci mettono innanzi gli agi e i diletti del senso sotto apparenza di bene."[10] In another place Tasso states categorically

that there is no "sceleraggine" in any of his warriors, but only
"incontinenze, o violenze d'incanti."[11] These statements are ample
justification, if any is needed beyond the evidence of the text itself,
for interpreting the episode of Armida's palace in terms of the
Aristotelian concept of incontinence. Both Rinaldo and Armida are
overcome by passion,[12] and the mission of Carlo and Ubaldo represents the reinstatement of reason to control over the appetite, most
probably by means of natural persuasion.[13] Although the episode
seems rather consistently planned in terms of its allegory, Tasso
himself claimed that, as regards the poem as a whole, the allegory
was an afterthought, drawn up after most of it had been written.[14]
Certainly, in the Gerusalemme liberata at least, Tasso did not succeed in reconciling his richly sensuous erotic imagination with his
equally intense moral and religious convictions. Much of the interest of the poem springs from the conflict of these elements; the incompatibility of love and duty is one of its fundamental themes.
The conflict is exemplified in Tasso's entire treatment of the love
of Rinaldo and Armida. He cannot make up his mind whether to
share it or condemn it.[15]

It is hardly necessary to point out the dissimilarity of the attitudes of Tasso and Spenser toward these matters. For Spenser
there is no necessary opposition between earthly love and divine
love, nor between love and duty. For Spenser physical love, rightly
used, is a creative force; through it men and women participate in
the cosmic round of creation. The contrast between Agdistes, the
Genius of the Garden of Adonis, and the Genius of the Bower (F. Q.,
II, xii, 47–48), for example, depends upon this idea. At one point
Spenser writes of the sexual act as "sacrifice diuine" (F. Q., VI,
viii, 42). In short, as Mr. Lewis has so clearly demonstrated, the
lust of the Bower is a perversion of the right kind of love. The love
of Armida and Rinaldo, on the other hand, seems intended to be representative of passionate love in general.

Of the three sinful dispositions in the verse from the first epistle
of St. John quoted above, Spenser gives the lust of the eyes particular emphasis, and some of the most significant changes he made in
adapting Tasso serve to introduce it where it was really absent
from Tasso's treatment. We have already seen the lewdness of
Spenser's bathers, who do not hide themselves "from vew of any,
which them eyde," and the change from the image of the veil to the
note of titillation in Stanza 66. There are other examples. When
Tasso's siren undoes her hair, and the poet writes, "Così da l'acque
e da' capelli ascosa/a lor si volse lieta e vergognosa" (G. L., xv,
61), Spenser adapts as follows: "So hid in lockes and waues from

118

lookers theft,/Nought but her louely face she for his looking left"
(F. Q., II, xii, 67). Tasso writes of Armida in Rinaldo's arms,
"Ella dinanzi al petto ha il vel diviso" (G. L., xvi, 20); Spenser
expands, "Her snowy brest was bare to readie spoyle /Of hungry
eies, which n'ote therewith be fild" (F. Q., II, xii, 78). In the same
stanza Spenser writes of Acrasia's eyes that with them "she thrild/
Fraile harts, yet quenched not."

The note of frustration introduced in these last examples is an
essential part of the lust of the eyes, which is, as Mr. Lewis points
out, presented as if independent of normal sexual activity. The
picture of Cymochles in Canto v is almost an epitome of the lust of
the eyes as Spenser understands it, especially the lines which speak
of Cymochles' steeping his "wandring thought in deep desire," and
stealing snatches of "amorous conceipt" (F. Q., II, v, 34). The lust
of the eyes is a technique of exquisite protraction of desire, and
depends upon the active workings of the "wandring thought." The
mind, in other words, is here actively engaged in corrupting the
appetite. Spenser, then, is clearly portraying the condition of intemperance, in which reason itself is corrupt; incontinence, the
state in which the appetite overcomes the unwilling reason, is
merely the downward pathway to intemperance. The beasts outside
the Bower, then, clearly figure intemperance, and the sleeping Verdant is an example of the transitional state of incontinence.[16]

The distinction between incontinence and intemperance was a
common one in Spenser's time; it occurs, for example, in Castiglione's Courtier.[17] It also occurs, of course, in the writings of the
mediaeval Aristotelians, and originally gained currency through
them. There is nothing improbable in the supposition that Spenser
knew, let us say, Aquinas' discussion of intemperance or one derived from it;[18] and, in fact, certain aspects of the Bower suggest
that he thought of the vice it represents in religious rather than
purely ethical terms. There is probably a reference to original
sin in the staining of Ruddymane's hands (F. Q., II, ii, 2–3), and
Professor A. S. P. Woodhouse has suggested that Maleger's drown-
ing (F. Q., II, xi, 46) represents the action of grace in baptism.[19]
These examples are directly relevant to Canto xii, since it is the
culmination of the entire book. One of the most significant changes
Spenser makes in the material he borrows from Tasso is seen in
the song of the rose. Where Tasso writes, "Cogliam d'amor la
rosa: amiamo or quando /esser si puote riamato amando" (G. L.,
xvi, 15), Spenser writes, "Gather the Rose of Loue, whilest yet is
time, /Whilest louing thou mayst loued be with equall crime" (F. Q.,
II, xii, 75). Spenser might be echoing Aquinas' discussion of intem-

perance, where we read, "The intemperate man rejoices in having sinned, because the sinful act has become connatural to him."[20] The Bower of Bliss, as Mr. Lewis says, shows us "the whole sexual nature in disease."[21] It is not merely man's sexual nature which is diseased in the Bower, of course; it is the entire soul—reason, spirit, and appetite. The corruption which the Bower represents is so serious, especially in comparison with that described by Ariosto and Tasso, that it seems certain that Spenser thought of it in terms of sin.

If this is the case, Spenser must have thought of the cure of intemperance in religious terms as well, rather than in the purely ethical terms in which Ariosto and Tasso seem to have presented it. In his discussion of intemperance, Aquinas (whom I quote merely as a representative of the Aristotelian tradition, not as necessarily the source of Spenser's ideas) points out that the correction of intemperance has two aspects: (1) "the inward assistance of grace which quenches concupiscence," and (2) "the application of the external remedy of admonishment and correction."[22] The second aspect of the cure clearly corresponds to the actions of Guyon and the Palmer when they take Acrasia and Verdant prisoners, not with a magic shield, but with a naturally fashioned net (F. Q., II, xii, 81), when they apply "counsel sage" to Verdant (Stanza 82), and when Guyon destroys by hard physical work the Bower which had been so carefully devised (Stanza 83—in direct contrast to Armida's palace, which, as already pointed out, is destroyed by Armida as instantaneously as it was built). The other aspect of the cure, the action of grace, seems to be what Spenser means to suggest by the magical freeing of the beasts. Guyon himself is unable to free them; he must ask the Christian Palmer to do so (Stanza 85). Whereupon the Palmer strikes the beasts with his "vertuous staffe," and they become "comely men." Aquinas, of course, had pointed out that the cure of intemperance is more difficult than that of incontinence because of the corruption of reason which characterizes intemperance.[23]

Since Spenser explicitly refers to the application of admonishment to Verdant, it is unlikely that the action of the Palmer's staff represents the workings of natural rational persuasion. The enchantments of Acrasia, whereby the men became beasts, and the workings of the Palmer's staff, whereby the beasts are first calmed (Stanza 40) and then returned to human shape, are the only magical events which occur in the Bower of Bliss; Spenser apparently means to insist upon the powerlessness of the soul to free itself from sin without the aid of grace.[24]

THE BOWER OF BLISS AND ARMIDA'S PALACE

Let us examine further the activity of the mind in the Bower of
Bliss. We have already seen its corruption in Cymochles and the
beasts; we shall examine it as it creates the Bower itself. Both
Tasso and Spenser lay stress upon the theme of art versus nature,
but they understand it in ways which are quite dissimilar. The art
of Armida's palace is magic. Writing in the tradition of Boiardo
and Ariosto, Tasso consciously tried to outdo them in his treatment
of the enchantress theme. Part of the novelty of his treatment lay
in his Virgilian picture of the pleading Armida, but he also tried to
outdo them in his enchantress' magical virtuosity. Armida, at first
overcome by her incontinent passion for Rinaldo and later enraged
by his departure, both builds and destroys her palace instantaneously
by means of black magic. We have already noted that Spenser did
not place the Bower on the summit of a snowy mountain, but at sea
level. He changes Armida's magical palace, in fact, into an actual,
physical garden, omitting all such magical details as the enchanted
bird which, in Tasso's garden, sings the song of the rose (G. L.,
xvi, 13); in the Bower it is "some one" who sings the "louely lay"
(F. Q., II, xii, 74).

The art of the Bower of Bliss is not magic. It is true that
Acrasia is a sorceress, but Spenser never refers to her enchantments as "art." By art he understands the artistry or artfulness
of the human intellect. The Bower is situated in "A place picked
out by choice of best aliue / That natures work by art can imitate"
(F. Q., II, xii, 42). In other words, it is an actual place which has
been chosen, as it were, by a committee of experts, as most suited
to their purposes. This interpretation is supported by the fact that
Spenser does not, like Tasso, attribute the climatic conditions of
the Bower to magic (G. L., xvi, 10); instead, he compares them to
those which prevail in other favored spots of the real world (F. Q.,
II, xii, 42) and reserves the magical concomitance of flower and
fruit (G. L., xvi, 11) for the Garden of Adonis (F. Q., III, vi, 42).

While Armida's garden is entirely factitious, the effect of her
magic is to make it seem entirely natural:

> Stimi (sí misto il culto è co'l negletto)
> sol naturali e gli ornamenti e i siti.
> Di natura arte par, che per diletto
> l'imitatrice sua scherzando imiti.   (G. L., xvi, 10)

Nature seems to have grown into the patterns of landscape gardening of her own accord. In the Bower of Bliss, however, the actual
craft of gardening, not magic, is seen working against the actual
forces of nature:

> One would haue thought, (so cunningly, the rude,
> And scorned parts were mingled with the fine,)
> That nature had for wantonesse ensude
> Art, and that Art at nature did repine.
> So striuing each th' other to vndermine,
> Each did the others worke more beautifie;
> So diff'ring both in willes, agreed in fine.   (F. Q., II, xii, 59)

Where Spenser seems to be following Tasso most closely, then, he really gives his lines an altogether different meaning. The fact that Tasso uses the word "scherzando" to characterize nature's apparent role in the garden, while Spenser uses the term "wantonesse," is extremely significant. Except for the elements of display in Armida's garden, such as the magical bird, her magic aims at producing the apparently natural; her palace represents "gli agi e i diletti del senso" in general, the natural pleasures of sense, which to Tasso seem inconsistent with the goals of reason. The art of the Bower, however, seeks to corrupt men by making it seem that nature itself is wanton, although, in Spenser's view, it is not, as is shown by the phrases "striuing each th' other to vndermine" and "diff'ring both in willes." The false conception of nature which the Bower attempts to instill is clearly what Spenser means by the "guileful semblaunts" (F. Q., II, xii, 48) by which the Genius of the Bower induces us "to fall" (i.e., to sin).

One of the aims of the art of the Bower, therefore, is the production of an unnaturally "lauish affluence." Sensual delight is "poured forth with plentifull dispense" (F. Q., II, xii, 42). Like the lewdness of the bathers, the lavishness of the Bower is presented as excessive to the point of destroying nature's true beauty. The plain, for example, is

> . . . goodly beautifide
> With all the ornaments of Floraes pride,
> Wherewith her mother Art, as halfe in scorne
> Of niggard Nature, like a pompous bride
> Did decke her, and too lauishly adorne.   (F. Q., II, xii, 50)

A second and no less important aim of this art is the production of artifacts and artificial arrangements designed to imitate human sexuality. The Porch of Excess is a good example. It is formed of carefully trained trees and vines:

No gate, but like one, being goodly dight
With boughes and braunches, which did broad dilate
Their clasping arms, in wanton wreathings intricate.
(<u>F. Q.</u>, II, xii, 53)

In the next stanza Spenser adapts Tasso's description of the concomitant flowers and fruits in a significant way. Tasso writes,

Lussureggiante serpe alto e germoglia
la torta vite ov'è piú l'orto aprico:
qui l'uva ha in fiori acerba, e qui d'or l'have
e di piropo, e giá di nèttar grave.   (<u>G. L.</u>, xvi, 11)

Spenser omits the flowers, but shows grapes in various stages of
maturation; then he adds,

And them amongst, some were of burnisht gold,
So made by art, to beautifie the rest,
Which did themselves emongst the leaues enfold,
As lurking from the vew of couetous gest.   (<u>F. Q.</u>, II, xii, 55)

These lines epitomize the art of the Bower: the golden grapes are
formed by craftsmanship, not magic; they are arranged in such a
way as to tantalize the cupidity of the guests; they are the instruments of a conscious, calculated, artificial protraction of desire.
Spenser omits the details of Tasso's description which could not
apply to an actual vine. He is not describing like Tasso, and
Ariosto before him, the illusions of beauty by which the senses
overcome the unwilling reason, but rather the way in which the
mind shapes actual objects in order to corrupt the appetite.

These remarks apply a fortiori to Spenser's fountain. Tasso
meant his fountain (<u>G. L.</u>, xv, 55–56) to seem a natural mountain
spring, and to appeal to the thirst developed in climbing the mountain. Spenser's fountain, however, is obviously not meant to seem
natural at all; it is elaborately manufactured. Not only is it made
of precious metals and paved with gems; its function is that of
sexual suggestion conveyed by means of artifacts—the sculptured
"naked boyes" and the false ivy.

The Bower of Bliss, then, depicts in a striking way the corrupt
application of highly developed techniques. One is tempted to say
"of technology," to emphasize the relevance of this poetry to our

own problems. For the art of the Bower has a peculiar similarity to certain aspects of the motion-picture and advertising industries. With this analysis of the $\phi\alpha\nu\tau\alpha\sigma\tau\iota\kappa\acute{\eta}$ [25] of intemperance, in fact, Spenser has given his treatment of the Circe theme a complexity and relevance unmatched by the more conventional Renaissance treatments of the theme, such as Ariosto's and Tasso's, which do not depart from the traditional use of magic to symbolize the power of the senses.

The extent to which Spenser departed from Tasso's description of Armida's palace in the Bower of Bliss is, I hope, clear. Although Tasso's poetry clearly had a powerful effect upon Spenser's imagination, Spenser remained profoundly original. The Bower of Bliss is an independent creation which uses the materials offered by Tasso; and Spenser, knowing his work would not suffer in comparison with Tasso's, no doubt expected his readers would make the comparison. Spenser's independence is clear, as I have tried to show, in the physical structure of the Bower itself, which mirrors an analysis of sensuality different from Tasso's. I have suggested, finally, that Spenser thought of the processes of moral corruption and redemption shown in the Bower in terms of the Christian concepts of sin and grace, and that the art of the Bower is an outstanding example of Spenser's originality and power as both poet and moralist.

THE ORGOGLIO EPISODE IN THE FAERIE QUEENE

S. K. Heninger, Jr.

The modern tendency to dissociate the "historical" and the "moral" allegory in The Faerie Queene can easily lead to a perversion of Spenser's purpose. Any dichotomy between history and morality would have been offensive to Elizabethans, whose very reason for studying the past was the hope of finding some ethical norm. As Richard Harvey flatly stated, "the most morals [is] the best History."[1] Protestants especially stressed this moralistic view of history, and furthermore argued that the future would unfold in strict accord with the prophecies set down in the Revelation of St. John. Therefore future events would also be largely determined by the ethical insight which the Apocalypse provided. Spenser adhered to this prevailing attitude, and in The Faerie Queene he hoped to produce convincing testimony that history and morality are indeed but different statements of the same truth. He is explicit on this point in the Proem to Book I; drawing from "the antique rolles" of England (I. proem. 2. 4), he promises that "fierce warres and faithfull loves shall moralize my song" (I. proem. 1. 9).

At his best, Spenser succeeds in contriving poetry which satisfies the special function of the poet to synthesize history and morality—to provide a "continued Allegory," as Spenser says in his letter to Raleigh. And Spenser is at his best in describing the capture of the Red Crosse Knight by the Giant Orgoglio. Although the meaning is complex, each of the intricate details subsists within the same allegorical continuum. Since this episode is the nadir of Red Crosse's fortunes and the turning-point of Book I, it is a stringent test for the coadunating faculty of Spenser's imagination.

Most readers begin their interpretation of Orgoglio by following the linguistic clue that he must be an embodiment of pride. The name would be most immediately meaningful as the Italian word for "pride, disdaine, haughtines,"[2] closely related to Spanish orgullo and French orgueil. Since the root is common to the Ro-

Reprinted from English Literary History, Vol. 26 (1959), pp. 171–187, ©
The Johns Hopkins Press, by permission of the author and The Johns
Hopkins Press.

mance Languages, the appellation would associate the Giant with Rome and Catholicism. We must note, however, that the Giant is not specifically called "Orgoglio" until after he has overcome Red Crosse. We hear the name only when Duessa approaches him with the proposition that he make Red Crosse his bondslave and take her for his paramour (I. vii. 14. 4–9). Therefore the starting-point for an interpretation of this episode does not lie in the meaning of the name "Orgoglio."

A more fundamental point-of-beginning will be found in the genealogical mythus which Spenser provides for the Giant. Here, as he often does, Spenser first suggests the significance of the character. When Orgoglio interrupts the dalliance of Red Crosse and Duessa beside the magic fountain, Spenser devotes one stanza to physical description of the Giant, and then carefully relates his parentage:

> The greatest Earth his vncouth mother was,
> And blustring Æolus his boasted sire,
> Who with his breath, which through the world doth pas,
> Her hollow womb did secretly inspire,
> And fild her hidden caues with stormie yre,
> That she conceiu'd.   (I. vii. 9. 1–6)

Spenser expressly states that Orgoglio has been generated by a boisterous wind blowing through caves in the earth. By the principles of Renaissance meteorology, this origin identifies him as an earthquake. Gabriel Harvey had cited this scientific theory in a letter to Spenser:

> The Materiall Cause of Earthquakes . . . is no doubt great aboundance of wynde, or stoare of grosse and drye vapors, and spirites, fast shut vp, & as a man would saye, emprysoned in the Caues, and Dungeons of the Earth.[3]

No Elizabethan would have missed the transparent mythologizing, the obvious implication that Orgoglio is the mythical embodiment of an earthquake.

This conclusion is supported by much of Orgoglio's physical description. His entrance is heralded by "a dreadfull sownd":

> Which through the wood loud bellowing, did rebownd,
> That all the earth for terrour seemd to shake,
> And trees did tremble.   (I. vii. 7. 5–7)

And when he walks, "the ground eke groned vnder him for dreed" (I. vii. 8. 6). During the battle with Red Crosse, "the Geaunt strooke so maynly mercilesse, / That could haue ouerthrowne a stony towre" (I. vii. 12. 1–2). In the next canto, when Prince Arthur comes to liberate Red Crosse, the Giant's club misses the Prince and digs into the ground:

> The sad earth wounded with so sore assay,
> Did grone full grieuous vnderneath the blow,
> And trembling with strange feare, did like an earthquake show.
> (I. viii. 8. 7–9)

After a violent battle, Prince Arthur finally slays Orgoglio, whose fall "seemd to shake / The stedfast globe of earth, as it for feare did quake" (I. viii. 23. 8–9).

Since Orgoglio is the personification of an earthquake, what significance would this have for Spenser's audience? The occasion of Gabriel Harvey's long letter to Spenser was the terrifying earthquake of 6 April 1580, and this was an event which few Englishmen forgot. It was so frightening that a special order of prayer was decreed "vpon Wednesdayes and Frydayes, to auert and turne Gods wrath from vs, threatned by the late terrible earthquake, to be vsed in all parish churches."[4] Sermons for a long time thereafter cited the earthquake as an admonition "to amende our euill life, to reforme our wicked conuersation, to be renewed in the spirite of the inwarde man, and to be heauenly minded."[5] Here is a vivid example of moral instruction derived from historical incident.

When Orgoglio is seen as an earthquake, and therefore as a visitation of God's wrath to warn man to repentance, this gives allegorical meaning to the opening stanzas of Canto VII. There the Dwarf has just led Red Crosse from the House of Pride, and the Knight is resting beside a spring when Duessa arrives. Cajoled by her, the Knight relaxes in the physical pleasantness of the glade and indulges his sensual appetites. When he quenches his thirst from the stream, which has magical powers to enervate any man who drinks of it, "mightie strong was turnd to feeble fraile" (I. vii. 6. 5). But the Knight continues his sinful relations with Duessa (I. vii. 7. 1–3); and in this weakened condition, unready in the midst of sensual pleasure, the Knight is attacked by Orgoglio and easily captured.

This spring with its magical properties is a truncated version of the Salmacis story that Ovid had related in the Metamorphoses (IV. 285 ff.). Salmacis was the nymph of a fountain in Caria, a vain and slothful girl who never joined her sister-nymphs in the sylvan activities led by Diana. When youthful Hermaphroditus bathed himself in her waters, Salmacis was so undone by passion that she intertwined her body with his and prayed to the gods "that this same wilfull boy and I may never parted bee."[6] The gods capriciously consented to this unusual request, as Ovidian gods so often do, and their bodies were fused as one. When Hermaphroditus realized that his masculinity had been diluted to half its former strength, he also prayed for a boon:

> That whoso commes within this Well may so bee weakened there,
> That of a man but halfe a man he may fro thence retire.[7]

The gods were again compliant, and thenceforth whoever drank from Salmacis' spring lost his strength.

Spenser has used only so much of Ovid's legend as he needs. He has eliminated Hermaphroditus completely, and attributes the enervating properties of the water solely to the displeasure of Diana when the indolent Salmacis showed indifference to the chase (I. vii. 5. 1–9). Ovid has never had more ardent disciples than the Elizabethans, however, and to Spenser's audience this enchanted spring would inevitably recall Salmacis.

Since myth was a form of history, it also was subject to moral interpretation; and the venerated tradition of moralizing Ovid would bring with Salmacis' story a moralized meaning. As Golding summarized it in the epistle preceding his translation of the _Metamorphoses_:

> Hermaphrodite and Salmacis declare that idlenesse
> Is cheefest nurce and cherisher of all volupteousnesse,
> And that voluptuous lyfe breedes sin: which linking all toogither
> May men too bee effeminate, unweeldy, weake and lither.[8]

The interlude beside the fountain shows Red Crosse being both idle and voluptuous, and Spenser focuses the moral significance of this episode by connecting it with the history of Salmacis. The sinfulness of this dalliance with Duessa makes Red Crosse a proper victim for the Giant, the agent of God's wrath, that inevitably follows. Orgoglio wages battle "as when almightie _Ioue_ in wrathfull mood, / To wreake the guilt of mortall sins is bent" (I. viii. 9. 1–2).

II

The interpretation of an earthquake as a warning to repentance
was of course based on the Holy Scriptures. Often in the Bible the
anger of God descends upon sinful men in the form of an earthquake,
but nowhere more terrifyingly than in the Revelation of St. John.
The Book of Revelation provided many of the central doctrines for
the new militant Protestantism, and recent scholarship has shown
its formative influence on Book I of The Faerie Queene.[9] Therefore
by turning to it we can perhaps fit the Orgoglio episode into the
larger framework of allegory based on the Apocalypse.

In the Book of Revelation earthquakes occur as visitations upon
the wicked most prominently as the climaxes of three separate but
interrelated series of prophecies leading up to the final Day of
Judgment: the opening of the seven seals on the book of God (vi. 1-
viii. 1), the trumpetings of the seven angels (viii. 2-xi. 19), and the
vials poured by seven angels into the air (xvi. 11-xvi. 21). These
key passages agree that the Last Judgment will be heralded by an
earthquake destroying the world. Moreover, Protestant scholiasts
derived their theories of damnation and redemption from the Book
of Revelation. With this gloss, for example, Heinrich Bullinger
amplified the meaning of the seven seals:

> In the opening of the seuen seales, there is seuerally ac-
> compted and reckned vp, what and how greate euils should
> come vpon men from the which not somuch as the faithfull
> liuing in this world, should be free. Wares, slaughters,
> famine, pestilences are recyted, and such other lyke plagues:
> Agayne persecutions, seditions, and (a great deale worse then
> all these) ye seducyng, and distroying of men through corrupt
> doctryne . . .
> . . . In the calamities, troubles, euils, and corruptions de-
> clared hitherto, the Aungel of God is brought in, who marketh
> the elect of God, in theyr foreheades: and all they through the
> goodnes and custodye of God, are saued from perdition.[10]

Doomsday will engulf all men, the righteous with the wicked; but the
elect shall be saved by the Angel of God and brought to Heaven.

The process of Red Crosse's redemption can be easily traced in
the Orgoglio episode. Through his relations with Duessa, the Knight

has been guilty of carnality; and even worse, as Bullinger said, he
has been seduced by "corrupt doctryne." When Orgoglio brings in
Judgment Day, the Knight therefore finds himself helpless in the
dungeon beneath the afflictions of his sins. During the battle with
the Giant, however, we have been told that Red Crosse is blessed
with "heauenly grace" (I. vii. 12. 3); he is one of the elect. So now
that he has felt the wrathful hand of God, the Knight is ready for his
spiritual rebirth. The Squire's magic horn which automatically
opens the gates of Orgoglio's stronghold is a clear-cut analogue to
the archangel's trumpet which will open graves on Doomsday.
Prince Arthur then enters as the Angel of God who has come to
mark the elect and save him from damnation. When the Prince finds
Red Crosse, he is "a ruefull spectacle of death" (I. viii. 40. 9).
Spenser graphically describes him as a long-dead corpse: "His sad
dull eyes [are] deepe sunck in hollow pits"; he has "bare thin
cheekes" and "rawbone armes"; "all his vitall powres /[Are]
Decayd, and all his flesh shronk vp like withered flowers" (I. viii.
41. 1–9). Nevertheless, Arthur retrieves Red Crosse from the
perdition of the dungeon (which had "no flore, / But [was] all a deepe
descent, as darke as hell" [I. viii. 39. 7–8]), and brings the Knight
back to Una.

When we read Orgoglio as the earthquake heralding the Last
Judgment, the significance of the Giant's falling upon Red Crosse
becomes evident. The Knight has succumbed to fleshly temptation,
for which he must be punished. The wages of sin are death, and so
in Orgoglio's tomb-like dungeon the Knight undergoes a literal
mortification of the flesh. There he lies helpless, until Divine grace
lifts the soul and reunites it with Divinity. In Spenser's words,
"This good Prince [Arthur] redeemd the Redcrosse knight from
bands" (I. ix. 1. 9), where "redeemd" should be read with Christian
connotations.

Now the introductory stanza of Canto VIII becomes intelligible
as an explication of the allegory:

> Ay me, how many perils doe enfold
> The righteous man, to make him daily fall?
> Were not, that heauenly grace doth him vphold,
> And stedfast truth acquite him out of all.
> Her loue is firme, her care continuall,
> So oft as he through his owne foolish pride,
> Or weaknesse is to sinfull bands made thrall.
>
> (I. viii. 1. 1–7)

Red Crosse, "the righteous man" before us, has been shown beset
by temptation in the grove of Salmacis, which exemplifies the "many
perils" which daily surround us; and he has "fallen," re-enacting
the drama of Original Sin. He is not lost, however: Red Crosse is
rescued from eternal damnation in the dungeon of Orgoglio by
Prince Arthur, or "heauenly grace," and reunited with Una, or
"stedfast truth." She is constant even though he is led into sin by
"his owne foolish pride, / Or weaknesse." Orgoglio, of course, must
be equated with the "sinful bands" which have enthralled the Knight,
just as "bands" = Orgoglio in I. ix. 1. 9.

Prince Arthur properly interprets Red Crosse's capture as a
warning to reform his sinful ways: Arthur knows that "th'only good,
that growes of passed feare, / Is to be wise, and ware of like again"
(I. viii. 44. 5–6). From this experience he also draws the conclusion "that blisse may not abide in state of mortall men" (I. viii.
44. 9), presumably because all men are touched with Original Sin.
But Red Crosse is now eligible for bliss because he no longer exists
as a "mortal" man. He has undergone the mortification of Orgoglio's
dungeon. This episode is indeed the turning-point of Book I, because
from his experience with Orgoglio the Knight emerges as a soul that
has subordinated the flesh. In consequence, he is no longer tempted
by sins induced by the senses. He still must battle the intellectual
crime of hopelessness, though;[11] so in Canto IX the Knight encounters Despair, a sin of the soul, who almost succeeds in having him
commit self-murder. But Una dramatically stops the suicide, and
then leads Red Crosse to the House of Holiness, where after the
proper instruction and repentance he is shown the New Jerusalem.

In this allegory which outlines the steps to salvation, Orgoglio is
an earthquake serving to chastise Red Crosse for his sinfulness,
epitomized by his idleness and lechery beside the magic spring.
And simultaneously he serves a closely related strand of allegory
by representing the destruction of the world on Judgment Day, when
only the elect of God will be retrieved from perdition.

III

This is but one facet of the Giant's allegorical function, however;
and when Red Crosse first lies vanquished and Duessa calls the
Giant by name, "Orgoglio," a wholly new complex of associations is
brought in. Spenser shifts gears, as it were, changing the emphasis
from religio-moral to religio-political instruction. There is no
discontinuity at this point, because the new phase grows smoothly

out of what has gone before. The Revelation of St. John is still the
basic text. Now, however, an exposé of Catholic corruption becomes
the predominant occupation of the allegory. Protestants had read
the Revelation not only as a guidebook along the narrow path to
Heaven, but also as a prophecy of world-wide misery propagated by
Catholic emperors and prelates. They were the Antichrist. The
afflictions disclosed beneath the seven seals and contained in the
seven vials of plague—the "wares, slaughters, famine, pestilences
. . . persecutions, seditions and . . . distroying of men through
corrupt doctryne"—all this suffering was directly attributable to
the Pope and his viceroys. More precisely, Mary's marriage to
Philip had oppressed England as tyrannously as Orgoglio had imprisoned Red Crosse. So at this point in his narrative Spenser
speaks with the indignant voice of an anti-Catholic propagandist.

Now not only the meaning, but the imagery itself derives from
the Book of Revelation. Duessa is clearly labelled as the Whore
of Babylon, and she triumphantly rides upon the seven-headed Beast.
At this point Orgoglio, as Duessa's consort, does become an embodiment of pride—the pride of Catholic despots, of the Pope, of
Antichrist.[12]

In addition to leading the Christian toward the New Jerusalem,
St. John's Apocalypse was also intended to encourage the faithful in
their resistance to the pagan tyranny of Rome. It therefore had
political implications. A blasphemous government, because of its
efforts to eliminate godliness from the individual heart, was inevitably damned; in view of the promised Armageddon, it was just as
inevitably doomed to destruction. And since the Apocalypse does
not deal with what God in Christ has already done, but with what is
yet to come to insure the establishment of His kingdom, each generation rightly interprets the Revelation according to its own milieu.
To St. John writing in Patmos, Babylon was classical Rome in its
hedonistic power, and the Revelation was a promise of its demolition.
To Spenser and his contemporaries, Babylon was figured in the
Church at Rome, and the Revelation was a promise of the overthrow
of Catholic might. In our own times, the number of the Beast has
been found to fit Hitler.

Certainly in Spenser's day it was common to correlate St. John's
Revelation with current events. When Franciscus Junius' commentary on the apocalypse was printed in English, the titlepage adver-
tised it as "a little treatise, applying the words of S. Iohn to our last
times that are full of spirituall and corporall troubles and divisions
in Christendom." Sir John Napier in his Plaine discouery of the
whole Reuelation of S. Iohn (1593) printed in parallel columns (1)

the text of the Apocalypse, (2) a prose paraphrase of the text, and
(3) historical information that supported his interpretation.

When viewed in the light of contemporary history, the victory of
Prince Arthur over Orgoglio becomes the victory of pious Protestantism over corrupt Catholicism. The Giant is finally overthrown
by the God-given brightness of Arthur's visage and armor (I. viii.
19. 1ff.), the sight of which leaves Orgoglio powerless: "for he has
read his end / In that bright shield" (I. viii. 21. 4–5). God in this
way expresses His incontrovertible will. At this point Duessa
throws aside her golden cup and mitre, and attempts to escape (I.
viii. 25. 1–3)—symbolically announcing the defeat of the Babylonian
Whore, the consort of Antichrist, the personification of the Church
at Rome. She is brought to triumphant Prince Arthur (I. viii. 25. 9),
and in the presence of all, her true vile nature is exposed (I. viii. 46.
1ff.). As a perfect gloss on this action, we may note Bullinger's
explanation of God's purpose in transmitting the Apocalypse:

> Especially he sheweth the iudgement (that is to witte, y^e
> punishement) of the harlot in purple, (I meane of the Pope and
> the beast) to be seene. First he brought foorth an honest &
> noble matrone, to weete, the very spouse of Christ. Now as
> it were by opposition he setteth against her a proude whore,
> that false new start vp Romishe Church, who extolling her
> selfe bragoth more of her outwarde apparence then of inward
> furniture. And he affirmeth y^t she shall perish for her great
> offences.[13]

The intended contrast between Una and Duessa is equally obvious.
One of Spenser's intentions was, therefore, a confident re-statement
of the Apocalypse in his own terms. Orgoglio is the incarnation of
Catholic pride and tyranny, which in the end will be overcome and
completely destroyed by Prince Arthur, the allegorical complex
representing English Protestantism. When Red Crosse succumbs
to the power of Orgoglio, Spenser reveals the incapacity of the individual soul if it succumbs to the sensuality and materialism of
popish Rome.

IV

We must not forget, however, that Spenser's vehicle was Italian
romance. He was not attempting to imitate the Bible nor a polemical pamphlet. And so perhaps by concentrating on Orgoglio's significance we have distorted the Giant's true character—that is, we

have dealt with his meaning to the detriment of his actual appearance in the story. In fact, Spenser has done an admirable job of sublimating the serious argument so that on the level of simple narrative-plot Orgoglio is quite convincing in his role of giant in a fairy-tale. He carries his heavy allegorical burden without impairing the childlike wonder and excitement which attends the adventure.

When creating a fairy-tale villain such as Orgoglio, Spenser of course had a rich tradition to draw upon, a tradition which had flourished in folklore, classical mythology, and romance. Here properly we look for Orgoglio's literary antecedents. Spenser labelled him a "Giant," and this would place him under the onus of numerous myths about Giants and Titans related most prominently by Hesiod[14] and Ovid.[15] These malicious superhumans were the offspring of Uranus (Heaven and Ge (Earth), and they were most infamous for the battles which they had waged against the rightful gods.[16]

As C. W. Lemmi has noted,[17] Orgoglio shows a striking resemblance to the Giants described by Natalis Comes. Springing from the basest Element, Earth, the Giants were not accustomed to the virtues of moderation and justice. Instead, they were partial to sensuality and anger, and they dared attack even Jove himself. Natalis Comes asserts that the Giants were no different from rash men who, driven by a craze for wealth and power, flout all Divinity and attempt to take religion into their own hands. So in the Giants, Spenser happily found an embodiment for the Antichrist which would nonetheless accord with his mise en scène of Italian romance. Orgoglio, by being a Giant, is automatically endowed with the vices that Protestant England attributed to Catholic despots; and yet, on the non-allegorical level he convincingly performs in the romance as the wicked ogre who imprisons the hero.

Spenser could have found a pattern for such syncrasis in the common practice of combining the Giants of Biblical legend with those of classical myth to produce prototypes of the evil-doer. The Bible itself lends credence to this confusion of sources when it states in Genesis, "Gigantes regnant super terram" (vi. 4). In the Scriptural tradition, these Giants were defined as the proud tyrants who in all centuries have been inimical to goodness:

> Fuerunt seculis omnibus viri superbi, cum potestate & honorib[us] virtutis & honestatis inimici: unde etiam apud poetas invaluerunt nomina Titanum seu Gigantum, Cyclopum, Centaurorum, Tyrannorum: qui cum Hebræorum nominibus & factionibus conferri debent.[18]

Poets regularly merged the classical and Hebraic Giants, and saw
both as reprehensible sinners. As a specific example of particular
pertinence here, the Giants' attack on heaven by piling mountain
upon mountain was paralleled by the building of the Tower of Babel;
so the anonymous <u>Ovide moralisé</u>[19] lengthily compared these two
affronts against Deity (I. 1065 ff.) and pointed out that both symbolized mortal pride:

> [Ils] Notent les orgueilleus du monde,
> Ou toute mauvaistiez habonde,
> Tout orgueil, toute felonnie,
> Tout traïson, toute envie,
> Qui par foles presumpcions
> Lievent leur cogitacions
> Contre Dieu, pour lui geurroier.   (I. 1189–1195)

Historiographers added that responsibility for building the Tower
of Babel rested on the Babylonian king Nimrod, whom the Septuagint
identifies with the origin of the Giants (Genesis, x. 8).[20] Spenser,
working within the well-established tradition of fusing mythology
and religious allegory, then saw that Giants had Babylonian connections which make Orgoglio a fit paramour for Duessa in her role as
the Scarlet Whore.

One direct link between the Giants and Antichrist which Spenser
probably knew was the oft-quoted attempt of Irenaeus to fit the name
τειταν to the number of the Beast:

> Omnium nominum quæ apud nos inueniuntur, [τειταν] magis
> fide dignum est. Etenim prædictum numerum habet in se, &
> literarum (est) sex, singulis syllabis ex ternis literis con-
> stantibus & vetus & semotum: neque (enim) eorum regum
> qui secundum nos sunt, aliquis vocatus est Titan.[21]

Irenaeus' demonstration that "Titan" meets the specifications was
cited by most commentators on the Apocalypse—for example, by
John Bale and Sir John Napier.[22] If Spenser knew that τειταν fitted
the Beast's number, then his reason for making Orgoglio a Titan
is obvious. But in any event, the Titans and Giants had an evil reputation which would have added an extra dimension to Orgoglio's
wickedness.

V

In presenting Orgoglio as a Giant, Spenser had ready-at-hand a model: Typhon (or Typhoeus), an offspring of Earth and Tartarus,[23] a spiteful monster who generated earthquakes, volcanoes, and tempests. There is considerable legendary history connected with Typhon, most of which seems to be etiological mythology to explain Mt. Aetna and the frequent earthquakes of the region around it. These myths tell how Typhon re-enacted the capital crime of the Giants: he dared challenge the sovereignty of Zeus, who imprisoned him beneath the island of Sicily for punishment.[24]

In addition to the Greek and Roman myths which designated Typhon as the cause of earthquakes, there was a strong tradition that identified him as the principal villain in the stories about Osiris. The best known account of this Egyptian mythology was Plutarch's treatise Of Isis and Osiris,[25] from which Spenser drew his material for the Isis Church episode in Book V. According to Plutarch, Rhea (Earth) bore several children, among whom were Isis, Osiris, and Typhon. Osiris, after marriage to Isis, succeeded to the throne of Egypt, bringing prosperity to his land and civilization to all the world. Typhon, however, is described as "puffed up and swollen by his ignorance and error, dissipating, defacing, and blotting out the sacred word and doctrine"; and in keeping with his evil nature, Typhon planned to overthrow the beneficent regime of Osiris:

> Typhon complotted a conspiracy against him, having drawn into his confederacy seventy two complices, besides a certeine queene of Aethiopia, who likewise combined with him, and her name was Aso.[26]

A scheming "queene of Aethiopia" is not far from the Whore of Babylon, and "Aso" may suggest "Duessa"; but I shall not press the point. What we cannot fail to see, however, is that the Egyptian Typhon possessed the identical vicious nature that characterizes the classical Giants, Catholic despots, the Antichrist, and Orgoglio. When Spenser read about Typhon in Plutarch, it reinforced his conception of a Giant who could feloniously oppose true religion.

Spenser was thoroughly familiar with the legends about Typhon. He makes direct reference to Typhon's descent from Earth (III. vii. 47. 8), to his uprising against the gods (III. vii. 47. 3-6, VII. vi. 15. 6-8), to his punishment (VII. vi. 29. 6), and to his ability to shake the world with "tempestuous rage" (VI. vi. 11. 8-9). The "loud bellowing" (I. vii. 7. 5) which announces Orgoglio's approach is taken from Hesiod, who had said that Typhon produced "the noise of a bull bellowing aloud in proud ungovernable fury."[27] Also from Hesiod[28] comes Spenser's authority for citing Typhon and Echidna as the parents of Orthus, Geryon's fierce two-headed dog (V. x. 10. 6–8). Hesiod in the same passage had reported that Echidna had borne " "the evil-minded Hydra of Lerna" by Typhon; so Spenser intentionally calls Typhon to mind when he compares the Lernaean Hydra to the seven-headed Beast which Orgoglio gives to Duessa (I. vii. 17. 1–3). The fecund coupling of Typhon and Echidna was blamed for a wide variety of monstrous malefactors—Cerberus, the Chimaera, the Gorgon, Scylla, the Sphinx[29]—and Spenser found in this lustful liaison a genealogical mythus for the Blatant Beast (VI. vi. 9. 7–11. 9). If we identify Orgoglio with Typhon, we then see him properly as the monstrous sire of Duessa's seven-headed Beast, and closely related to the Blatant Beast and to the cruel dog of Geryon.

This connection between Orgoglio and Geryon's ferocious dog strengthens Orgoglio's relationship to Geryoneo and Grantorto, both of whom appear as proud Giants and as personifications of Spanish tyranny. Geryoneo has set up an idol of his father, naming him his god and offering human sacrifice (V. x. 28. 5–8). The inclusion of idolatry among Geryoneo's crimes is of course a Protestant remonstrance against the hated cathedral effigies that purportedly demanded human sacrifice as autor-da-fé (V. xi. 19. 6–9). There can be little question that the martyrs beneath Orgoglio's altar have met death in the same way. But to clinch the association between Orgoglio and the Spanish Giants, Spenser describes a monster that feeds upon the corpses beneath Geryon's image (V. xi. 20. 1–4). And what is the lineage of this beast? She was "borne of the brooding of Echidna base" (V. xi. 23. 5), and hence a daughter of Typhon. Most certainly these Spanish Giants—Geryoneo, Grantorto, and Orgoglio—represent Philip II, an historical personage; but equally explicit is the moral castigation of Philip's actions.

In conclusion, the allegorical significance assigned to Typhon's assault on the gods parallels the meaning we have found in Orgoglio:

> Some relate this fable in order to turn men's minds away
> from Ambition . . . there is no care for religion, for humani-
> tas, nor for justice when the madness of Ambition holds sway.
> . . . Jupiter finally overthrows and suppresses this Typhon
> (or Ambition) no matter where it flees; because although
> cupidity may withstand reason and wisdom for awhile, never-
> theless in the long run it is overcome by these.[30]

Here again we have mythical history explicated in moral terms. Pride (manifested through ambition) is allegorically embodied in a monster, and this is the same sort of pride that has animated Orgoglio and Philip II. A half-century later, it was commonplace to identify Typhon with Satan and the Pope:

> The Devill is the very Typhon, who by his pride opposed God, and was thrust downe to hell. . . . The Pope is another Typhon, the son of earth, for he hath turned Christs heavenly kingdome into an earthly Monarchy. . . . He was sent as a plague to punish the world: but at last shall be overcome by the breath of Gods mouth, as Typhon was by Jupiters thunder.[31]

Jupiter's final victory over Typhon is interpreted as the triumph of wise-rule over insane ambition; and it is easy to see how this parallels Prince Arthur's victory over Orgoglio, the victory of English Protestantism over Catholic intrigue, the victory of Christ over Antichrist.

VI

Spenser has crowded much into this episode. He had looked into three areas of history—into classical mythology, the Book of Revelation, and recent politics—and in each he found the same archetypal pattern of evil predominating for awhile, but finally being overcome by Divine beneficence. Spenser thought (perhaps wishfully) that he had found an ethical norm, and this moral provides the theme for the Orgoglio episode.

Spenser presents his theme by progressively augmenting the initial statement that Orgoglio is an earthquake. He becomes a warning to repentance, the destruction of the world heralding the Last Judgment, physical death preparing for the resurrection, the Antichrist who brings misery to mankind, the embodiment of Catholic tyranny. In the Giants of mythology Spenser found a solvent to fuse all these constituent meanings into a single unified character, so that as the episode proceeds they function simultaneously and consistently. As Spenser controls the conditions, various properties of Orgoglio are activated at different moments—but the total Orgoglio is always present at least latently. Therefore when Prince Arthur releases Red Crosse from Orgoglio's dungeon, the complex of meaning must include the simple fairy-tale rescue of the hero from the villian's den, the religio-moral salvation of the elect on Doomsday, and the religio-political deliverance of mankind from Spanish bigotry. To isolate historical or moral allegory is to decompose Spenser's compound.

138

THE IMAGE OF MORTALITY: THE FAERIE QUEENE, II. i–ii

Alastair Fowler

The tragedy of Mordant and Amavia and the miraculous washing
of Ruddymane's hands are commonly regarded as members in the
series of psychological episodes occupying the first half of The
Faerie Queene, Book II.[1] But in reality they are written to quite a
different scale and have an altogether larger function; for they present hieroglyphs of the human condition, which requires Guyon's
ministration, and of the theological role of moral virtue in the regenerate life. In a passage of such general import it is remarkable
that there is so little impression of abstraction. Spenser has here
impacted his matter into a very few minutely described emblems,
so condensed as to implicate deep areas of feeling in their webs of
association. The associations were traditional enough for some of
the images to have been transparent; others were probably intended
from the beginning as mysteries of poetic theology. But time oc-
cluded the whole passage until quite recently a penetrating critic
explained the indelible stain on Ruddymane's hands as an allegory
of the effects of original sin.[2] In the present paper I hope to develop
this insight and to show that almost the whole of the first two cantos
are concerned with baptismal regeneration and with sanctification.

As so often occurs, the allegorical meaning is reached through
an event for which no natural explanation is provided, namely, Mordant's death. The causation of this striking event is entirely magical and, therefore, invites meditation. Occasioned by the nymph's
pure well, the death fulfills a charm placed by Acrasia on the cup
that was her parting gift (II. i. 55). This "sad verse" was wrought
to "give death to him that death does give"—that is, to Mordant; for
his name, found in the form Mortdant in both quarto editions,[3] means
"death-giving." Now it is true that Mordant might be said to give
death to Amavia literally, in that her grief for him leads her to suicide; yet the charm remains obscure enough to assume oracular
portentousness. To interpret it, we clearly need to know Mordant's
allegorical function. Fortunately we have Amavia's statement that
"he was flesh: (all flesh doth frailtie breed)" (II. i. 52). If we regarded these words as belonging to the allegorical sequence, they

Reprinted from Huntington Library Quarterly, Vol. 24 (1961), pp. 91–110,
by permission of author and publisher.

would specify Mordant's role. He would be, in the exact theological sense, "the flesh." Returning now to Acrasia's curse, we find that part at least is meaningful. That the flesh gives death is a biblical notion. The concept of the flesh as virtual death is, indeed, a central theme throughout the epistles of Paul.

This line of interpretation is encouraged by the emblematic description of the dead Mordant (II. i. 41), a rosy-cheeked, ruddy-lipped corpse,[4] as well as by Guyon's comment on the double traged

> Behold the image of mortalitie,
> And feeble nature cloth'd with fleshly tyre   (II. i. 57)

—a comment which would be platitudinous if he only meant that corpses are pictures of death. It is less of a platitude that Mordant and Amavia together comprise—notice Spenser's singular—one allegorical image of the virtual death of man's nature when it exists "after the flesh." This is not the only place where Mordant and Amavia are spoken of as a single, composite organism. They jointly form the "senselesse truncke" of II. ii. 4,[5] in which they are so intimately associated that poison drunk by Mordant could affect Amavia's blood. Spenser even writes "venim, which they druncke," although it was Mordant alone who took the drugs of intemperance (II. i. 54. 8) and drank from Acrasia's cup (II. i. 55). This apparent inconsistency, treated by Bowers as a careless lapse, in fact points to the allegorical sequence.

By "flesh" (sarx) Paul usually means not a part of man but the whole man seen under one aspect. It is "man in his 'worldliness,' in the solidarity of earthly existence."[6] With this "outward man" living according to the flesh, Paul contrasts the "inward man" living in the spirit (II Cor. iv. 16). If, then, Mordant is flesh, one expects Amavia to correspond to the inward man or conscience. If she bear some such meaning, it is not difficult to see why she masquerades as a palmer to reform Mordant (II. i. 52). The Palmer who accompanies Guyon is true divine wisdom; Amavia—the conscience of fleshly life under the law—is only a weak simulacrum. Mordant's captivity to Acrasia (II. i. 54. 3) recalls the captivity of Rom. vii. 23, the captivity to the "law of sin" that the flesh serves in spite of the inward man.[7] It estranges Mordant from his soul so that at first he fails to recognize her. Then, it almost seems as if the flesh, "recured to a better will" (II. i. 54), will be delivered by individual moral effort; but then Mordant drinks and dies.

To any interpretation of Mordant's death the occasion is crucial, for this is dramatically highlighted by the machinery of the curse.

The tragedy is to happen "So soone as Bacchus with the Nymphe does lincke" (II. i. 55. 6), that is, when the wine Mordant has already drunk mingles with the water of the nymph's well. This water, which is explicitly said to be pure (II. ii. 9), is to be not the cause but the occasion of death. The allegorical continuity here fortunately depends on a familiar Pauline context:

> I knew not what sin meant but by the law . . . I once lived without law. But when the commandment came, sin revived, and I was dead. And the very same commandment which was ordained unto life, was found to be unto me an occasion of death, for sin took occasion by the means of the commandment and so deceived me, and by the self commandment slew me . . . sin by the means of that which is good, had wrought death in me.[8]

Mordant's death is in many ways analogous. He, too, was alive in sin so long as "he knew not . . . his owne ill" (II. i. 54. 5); it was only when he reformed that he died. His death, too, appeared to be caused by something good—the pure well—though in reality it was Acrasia who slew him, taking occasion by the well. As Paul was deceived by sin, so was Mordant: "him parting she deceiv'd" (II. i. 55. 3). Acrasia, elsewhere identified as Pleasure (II. ii. 45. 4), only seems unsuited to the part of sin until we remember that Paul attributes the virtual death of the flesh specifically to guilt at concupiscence: "I knew not sin, but by the Law: for I had not known lust, except the Law had said, Thou shalt not lust. But sin took an occasion by the commandment, and wrought in me all manner of concupiscence" (Rom. vii. 7–8). A comprehensive interpretation of the term "concupiscence" was known in the Renaissance; but the narrower sense, that of sexual lust, was more usual and likely to determine an emblematic representation.[9]

My argument would remain tentative were there no analogues to justify such an allegorization, especially as regards the nymph's well. Flowing water was, however, a very familiar traditional symbol for the divine law.[10] The fons sapientiae of the Old Testament received much elaboration from patristic writers, such as Ambrose (De paradiso, Ch. iii); Augustine, we note, set against it an opposing image of poison: "When are you to desire the fountain of Wisdom, while you are still labouring in the venom of iniquity?"[11] Later the Benedictine allegorist Pierre Bersuire was to write of a spiritual river cooling the heat of concupiscence—a river which, like the nymph's cold fountain in Spenser, flows from rock. And the rock is for Bersuire the rock of the Covenant; the river flows "de medio petrarum, i.e. duorum testamentum."[12]

In the same writer we also find what is probably Spenser's immediate source for Acrasia's charm. This is an allegorization of Solinus' account in <u>Polyhistor</u> of a miraculous river Diana whose waters, if drawn by anyone of unchaste character, will not mix with the wine in his body. Bersuire takes this to signify that the impurity of the drinker would be revealed:

> By water can be understood <u>doctrine</u>; and especially by the water of the <u>Diana</u>, which means "manifest" or "intelligible" (<u>clara</u>). By wine, on the other hand, is meant the human will. For water, doctrine, cools; but the human will burns with desire. Therefore the water of good doctrine is applied to the wine of ardent will, so that appetite is tempered as it should be.[13]

Mordant's mortal guilt is similarly revealed by the water of a pure river coming in contact with the wine in his body. As the Palmer explains (II. ii. 5—10), the nymph's fountain was endowed—by Diana, significantly—with miraculous properties that prevent it from mingling with the filth of Acrasia's wine.

We are led on, however, into further reaches of the fountain symbol by iconographical considerations; for the nymph's fountain springs from the two sources into which her tears were metamorphosed (II. ii. 8. 7). Now the usual emblem of repentance and the <u>gratia lachrymarum</u> was just such a twin fountain. In Herman Hugo's <u>Pia desideria</u>, for instance, Penitence is represented as a seated female figure with streams of tears issuing from eyes and hair (Fig. I).[14] For the improbable abundance of tears, we are referred to Jeremiah's prayer: "Oh, that mine head were full of water and mine eyes a fountain of tears" (Jer. ix. 1). The seated figure—the penitent Anima—faces a petrified nymph from whose head and outstretched hands water flows into a large pool. The accompanying epigram is Anima's prayer to be metamorphosed into a fountain, like Acis, Biblis, and Achelous—all of whom shared the fate of Spenser's nymph.

The outstretched hands of Hugo's nymph allude to yet another symbolic fountain, the Fountain of Life. This was an emblem of regenerating grace in which Christ is often represented as a petrified figure with fountains issuing from his outstretched hands and falling into a laver, the bath of salvation.[15] This very popular motif reflected the late medieval cult of the Precious Blood, but in the

Reformation period it came to be associated with baptism rather than with the Mass.[16] It is based on a familiar piece of typological exegesis (originating from I Cor. x. 2–4) that treats the fountain struck by Moses from a rock in the wilderness as a prefiguration of the water of baptism from the spiritual rock, Christ. The fact that Spenser's fountain is used for a symbolic cleansing suggests that it is to be associated with the Fountain of Life also. Guyon's expectation that the water (described as "pure, as purest snow" at II. ii. 9. 7) will wash the Babe's guilty hands recalls the promise in Isaiah of a new Covenant for the repentant: "Your hands are full of blood. Wash you, make you clean . . . though your sins were as crimson, they shall be made white as snow"[17]—a passage traditionally related to the Christian balnea salutatis.

Thus the deceptively simple fountain to which Mordant came when he repented is, in fact, an extraordinarily complex symbol, infolding the various phases of repentance and regeneration. Perhaps its imaginative fusion of the fountain of repentance and the laver of regeneration is meant to convey the reciprocal character of the relationship of grace and the incorporation of the penitent in Christ at baptism.[18]

Once Spenser's subject is seen to be baptismal regeneration, the early episodes, with their conjoined images of death and life, gain significance; for baptism is essentially a dying into life. "We are buried then with [Christ]," writes Paul, "by baptism into his death . . . our old man is crucified with him, that the body of sin might be destroyed, that henceforth we should not serve sin."[19] What is the burial of Mordant-Amavia but a burial of the "old man"?

Since the death of the old man is the beginning of a new life free from the domination of sin and death, Spenser has set over against the image of mortality an image of rebirth. This is the bloody babe, who is as innocent (II. ii. 1. 7) as the baptized are imputed to be, who plays unharmed amid tragic death, and who is compared with the phoenix, a traditional resurrection symbol: "in dead parents balefull ashes bred" (II. ii. 2. 2).[20] The difficulty noticed by Miss Winstanley—that the phoenix rose from its own ashes, not its parents'[21]—is removed (and our confidence in Spenser's mythologizing restored) if Ruddymane is taken as the new man put on at baptism. The new man is reared out of the mortal ashes of the old, while in some sense retaining the same identity.

Although Ruddymane is a positive image of the fresh, emergent quality of the life of grace into which the regenerate are born again, Spenser has only a conditional hope for his future. The ashes of the old man are "balefull" to the new, so that he will suffer, as Guyon bitterly complains, the woe and misery that is "the state of men" (II. ii. 2. 8).[22] The nature he has inherited remains corruptible flesh, as the filthy blood on his hands emblematically demonstrates. He is "sad witnesse of [his] fathers fall" (II. i. 37. 2) in that his stains testify to the fall of the old Adam: the blood is Amavia's, but the indelible filth goes back to Acrasia's poison. The discovery that baptism will not remove the stain drives Guyon into "diverse doubt" (II. ii. 3): conjectures which are correctly interpreted by Hamilton as a reference to the doctrine of original sin.[23] We can, indeed, go further and distinguish two separate theories about original sin:

> He wist not whether blot of foule offence
> Might not be purgd with water nor with bath;
> Or that high God, in lieu of innocence,
> Imprinted had that token of his wrath,
> To shew how sore bloudguiltinesse[24] he hat'th;
> Or that the charme and venim, which they druncke,
> Their bloud with secret filth infected hath,
> Being diffused through the senselesse truncke,
> That through the great contagion direfull deadly stunck.
>
> (II. ii. 4)

The first conjecture is that the blood taint is a token, imprinted when man lost his innocence, to signify God's wrath at sin, wrath so great that it could only be manifested proportionately by extending the token to Adam's descendants. This reatus theory of original sin rests on a forensic metaphor of guilt[25] and thus renders thematically appropriate the legal diction that features so prominently in the early episodes.[26] The second theory (ll. 6–9), employing a medical not a forensic, metaphor, describes the effect of Adam's fall upon his posterity as a hereditary disease in the human constitution: "the corruption," as Burnet puts it, "has overrun our whole kind, the contagion is spread over all." Thus it is with a "great contagion" that the corrupting venom of iniquity diffuses throughout the joint nature of Mordant-Amavia and infects the blood passed on to Ruddymane.[27] In this vitium theory the very texture of human nature is regarded as damaged: the taint is not merely on, but in, Ruddymane's flesh (II. ii. 10.8).

The doctrine of original sin received special attention during the Reformation because of the new emphasis laid on a baptism of repentance. It became crucially important to explain the persistence of sin in the regenerate believer, and this was done by distinguishing between the guilt and the effects of original sin. The Thirty-nine Articles are representative:

144

> this infection of nature [original sin] doth remain, yea in them
> that are regenerated; whereby the lust of the flesh, called in
> the Greek, phronēma sarkos, which some do expound the wis-
> dom, some sensuality, some the affection, some the desire,
> of the flesh, is not subject to the Law of God. And although
> there is no condemnation for them that believe and are bap-
> tized, yet . . . concupiscence and lust hath of itself the na-
> ture of sin. (Article IX)

Baptism removed the guilt of original sin but not the infection itself,
concupiscence. Thus, after Ruddymane's hands have been washed,
they are no longer referred to as guilty, although the stains persist.

While Hamilton recognizes the significance of Ruddymane's taint,
he interprets the washing episode as an allegory of the purifying
action of temperance. In itself this view is improbable; Spenser
would hardly wish to show the ineffectuality of the virtue he is celebrating. But Hamilton has an insight into Guyon's role that can be
accommodated if Spenser's subject is seen as baptismal regeneration. The ablution is performed by Guyon to portray the intimate
relation between baptism and temperance; for Spenser conceives
temperance theologically as the destruction, by repeated mortifications, of the "body of sin," the relic of the old man buried with
Christ at baptism. Baptism, as it were, makes possible and initiates regeneration; temperance puts it into material effect. Guyon's
shaken faith in baptismal regeneration is restored by the divine reason of the Palmer, who tells him a myth (II. ii. 5–10). This myth of
Faunus and the nymph—which Harry Berger calls irrelevant[28] is, in
fact, quite as etiological as it claims to be, even if its profound content is concealed—after the manner of poetic theology—in the simplest of fables. The fountain, says the Palmer, was wrought through
an "occasion" that befell its nymph (II. ii. 7): pursued by Faunus
and unable to escape him, she prayed to Diana, by whom she was
metamorphosed into flowing tears. A simple story, yet its personae
invite consideration. Faunus, a natural but evil figure, was associated with the satyrs. Now the medieval conception of the satyr as
an embodiment of passion or mental excess had opened the way to
a specific identification of Faunus with concupiscence.[29] This is
the meaning he bears in two remarkable chapters of the Hieroglyphicorum collectanea, which connect him with the Genesis myth of
the Fall. The first, "Faunus anguis" (Bk. XIV, Ch. xxv), explains
how Faunus, to seduce Hecate-Semele, took the form of a serpent,
whose successive coils are "the multiplication of pleasure by supply
of variety." (A not unnecessary digression follows, justifying the
mystical interpretation of such a classical myth.) The second

FOWLER

chapter (xxvi), "Sensus a voluptate, mens a sensu decepta," turns
directly to the serpent that tempted Eve (caro nostra) and overthrew
the primitive purity of mind that Adam enjoyed. Valeriano thus
demythologizes Genesis, since for him the tempter is temptation
itself, concupiscent pleasure. For others, however, Faunus anguis
was Satan; so Satan could even be represented pictorially as a satyr
with goat feet and hairy body.[30]

The nymph, also a natural symbol, is nevertheless opposed to
Faunus, who is her enemy (II. ii. 7. 9). If Faunus symbolizes concupiscence, the disorder of natural desires and appetites that
Augustinian theology regarded as having ruined man's original
righteousness, then the nymph he attacks would appear to be that
righteousness itself. Righteousness and uncorrupted faith, the intact puritas animi quae in Adamo primitius fuit, were traditionally
emblematized by virginity—and her virginity is almost the only
thing we know of the nymph. She is, indeed, closely akin to the
"righteous Virgin" of the "Two Cantos of Mutabilitie," who left the
world when wrong was loved and justice sold (VII. vii. 37).[31]

The nymph's metamorphosis signifies that through concupiscence
man's original, rationally ordered virtue is lost. How long lost, how
ancient the Fall, is expressed by the deep chronological perspective
of the myth's golden-age setting. Since that time natural purity of
mind has been impossible: the nymph is gone from the earth, and
only Faunus is left—or rather, Faunus and the fountain. For, by a
special divine gift from Diana (the goddess of spiritual revelation),
the fountain from the rock—regenerating grace—takes the place of
the nymph. That is to say, the life of grace replaces an original
virtue of rational self-control. Thus the Ovidian tale conceals the
same truth as Paul's myth of the two Adams, namely, that Christ,
the first righteous man since the Fall, supersedes the irrecover-
able, naturally ordered body by establishing a new possibility, that
of the spiritual body. Characteristically, Spenser's myth emphasizes the organic continuity between the nymph and Christ, between
the two Adams, between natural virtue and grace. In this respect
it is interesting to compare Spenser's allegory with that of one of
his models, Trissino's L'Italia liberata da Gotti (Bk. IV, ll. 873 ff.),
in which there takes place a metamorphosis almost, but not quite,
identical. Trissino's Acratia (concupiscence) arranges the death of
Sinesia (sunesis, the rationally ordered mind); but when Sinesia's
sister Areta (arete, virtue) weeps, and God Himself takes pity on
her, it is out of Sinesia's corpse and Areta's tears that He forms
a fountain. From this fountain issues what is explicitly named the

146

water of salvation, l'acqua del sanajo.[32] Trissino's allegory is at
once cruder and more doctrinaire; yet we are half grateful for this
obviousness, in that it confirms our schematic interpretation, at
least, of Spenser's more mysterious poem.

The Faunus myth easily resolves Guyon's mystification, for it
provides a simple explanation why baptism cannot wash out the
stain of concupiscence. This seems to be the point of the Palmer's
distinction between two kinds of virtue in fountains: virtue "indewd /
By great Dame Nature" and virtue "by gift of later grace" (II. ii. 6).
The power of the baptismal well, since it is not of natural endowment (being, indeed, "contrary to nature": Rom. xi. 24), can have
no direct effect on the natural body. As a spiritual, not a material,
purification, it leaves the texture of man's material nature unaltered. The point was an obvious one. In his elementary outline of
Christian doctrine, Ficino used the same argument to account for
the baptized having impure seed and concupiscent children. "Baptism," he writes:

> in virtue of the Holy Spirit and our faith in Christ, does away
> the guilt and the bond of sin in the mind of him who is by bap-
> tism cleansed; but the proclivity to sin, inherent in the natu-
> ral body, it does not extirpate. For the spirit and the spiritual
> mystery [of baptism] are not material, but relate exclusively
> to the spirit and to the will.[33]

When the Palmer had finished, Guyon "hearkned to his reason" and
took up Mordant's blood-defiled armor: "An heavie load himselfe
did lightly reare" (II. ii. 11). As the ambiguity in this line indicates,
Guyon was accepting the burden of his own flesh with its unavoidable
sin and decay; "His double burden," we are told in the next stanza,
"did him sore disease." The sentiment is very much that of Paul:
"We that are in this tabernacle, sigh and are burdened, because we
would not be unclothed, but would be clothed upon, that mortality
might be swallowed up of life."[34] Ignorances, diseases, and sins,
all the fatal imperfections of the old Adam, continue after regeneration, and the "fleshly tyre" is still an oppressive integument encum-
bering the spirit; only this corrupt nature is set in a new relation to
God: it is "clothed upon."

Guyon's response to the image of mortality is, like Paul's, a
groan (II. i. 42); but the hopeful Palmer sees more than tragedy in
man's situation. For him, Ruddymane's taint has a positive significance, both as a sign of his mother's innocence and as a remind-

er that her death is to be revenged. This assurance brings an un-
motivated part of the fable into focus. Amavia bequeathed her blood
as a pledge that she died free "from blemish criminall" (II. i. 37
and II. ii. 10); yet we are not told how a mortal wound can prove innocence nor even of what crime she thought herself guilty. In fact,
the continuity of meaning here belongs exclusively to the allegorical
sequence. If Amavia is the inner man, her guilt is understandably
occasioned by drinking from the Fountain of Wisdom and being confronted by God's commandment. Moreover, since guilt such as this
is not the consequence of any particular crime, but of all mortal
sinfulness, it can only be expiated by a death. Amavia is, in fact,
led to suicide by a moral desperation very like that of the Red Cross
Knight in his temptation by Giant Despair.[35] The suicide image was
conventional. We might compare Georgette de Montenay's _Emblemes
ou devises christiennes_, where Emblem II, "Surge," portrays an
armed man stabbing himself in the side. The epigram in the first
edition reads:

> This living man, how little it takes to kill:
> Now he is dead; but how shall he come to life?
> Adam transgressed, and could not restore himself
> To purity. As he by sin was sullied,
> So we shall be, if Christ delivers us not:
> Children of Adam, stained for ever, slaves
> Of sin by which we die. Outside of Christ
> Is nothing, which cruel death does not bind.[36]

This emblem of the old Adam is appropriately followed by Emblem
III, the Fountain of Life; for it is the healing stream from Christ's
side that cures the wound in Adam's.

But if Amavia's death is the result of Adam's sin, how is she
proved innocent? The theological point here seems to be one which
arose in every Reformation discussion of original sin, namely, the
question of who is responsible for this hereditary weakness. Invariably the innocence of Nature was affirmed.[37] Although man was "of
his own nature inclined to evil" (Article IX), this did not mean his
nature as it was created, but rather as ruined by the Fall. The sinner, therefore, was in no way justified in holding Nature—and thus,
by implication, the Creator—responsible for sin and death.[38] In
this connection theologians often used the metaphor of a wound.
Thus Aquinas names concupiscence as one of the wounds of nature;
and Calvin argues: "It is true that nature has received a mortal
wound; but there is a great difference between a wound inflicted

from without, and one inherent in our first condition."[39] Now
Amavia's wound is not inherent in her first condition. It follows
that Ruddymane's taint, which derives not from Amavia's intact
body but from her wound, is of ambivalent import. It is not merely
evidence of the fallen condition of the flesh ("sad witnesse of thy
fathers fall" [II. i. 37. 2]) but also of the innocence of Amavia until
infected by Mordant. Theologically this is creationism, that is, the
theory that the soul is created separately, being infused in a state
of innocence into the body with its inherited flaws. Aquinas—in a
passage which might almost be used as a summary of Spenser's
allegory—writes that "As the divinely infused soul enters into a
human nature through the body to which it is wedded, so the soul
contracts original sin, that is through a body which is propagated
from Adam" (Quaestiones disputatae, IV: de malo, 1). Later
Augustinian theology attached a similar importance to the first
innocence of the soul. It was a fundamental part of the doctrine of
man that the soul inherited its tendency to evil from the body and
not from Nature in the highest, Neoplatonic sense: that is, from
Nature as the agency of creation. Thus the very fact of a vitium in
human nature absolved Nature herself.

The last of the Palmer's counsels is that Ruddymane's taint
should "minde revengement." This can be assigned some meaning
within the fable, where Guyon's arrest of Acrasia does to some
degree revenge Mordant and Amavia. Again, however, there is a
logical discrepancy. For, when Guyon takes his leave of Medina,
he asks her to train Ruddymane in virtuous lore, so that "so soone
as ryper yeares he raught," he might "avenge his Parents death on
them, that had it wrought" (II. iii. 2). This version of the story,
with Ruddymane as avenger, seems on the face of it inconsistent
with the one adhered to elsewhere throughout the book; and those
who have noticed the discrepancy have treated it as a careless error. Yet the detail makes good allegorical sense.

We should, indeed, have expected that it would be Ruddymane
who would avenge Mordant and Amavia, his parents; or (to translate)
that it would be the new man put on with baptism who would re-
establish justice, the original justice, that is, lost by the old Adam's
fall. As soon as the mission of revenge is formulated in this way,
however, we see that the matter is not so simple. If the flaw in
human nature is as ineradicably structural as Spenser has implied,
can man hope to recover original justice and the truly natural? Almost every theologian in Spenser's time would have answered: No,
never in this life. Even Calvin, with all his hopefulness, warned
that only with death could the final victory over concupiscence be

won. The regenerate believer was left to hope that by constant
effort and mortification of the flesh concupiscence might be reduced
and progress be made toward the new nature—toward the spiritual
body that would be immune from all corruption.[40] The inference is
that, within a human life on earth, Mordant and Amavia can never
be completely revenged. Revenge has to wait until Ruddymane attains to "ryper yeares"—the maturity, that is, of the spiritual body.
And that lies outside the limits of Book II. The inconclusiveness of
Guyon's quest—noticed by Berger[41]—is, therefore, an inevitable
result of the allegorical content. Acrasia cannot in this life be put
to death.

The most that can be done is to restrain the concupiscent tendency in human nature; to annihilate it is impossible. <u>Acrasia</u>,
therefore, can only be <u>arrested</u>. Moreover, even this partial vindi-
cation of justice, such as it is, has to be achieved by Guyon, that is,
by the laborious effort of temperance. It requires the moral odyssey
of a lifetime, with all its struggles and mortifications of the flesh,
before a spiritual maturity can be attained capable of resisting
Acrasia.

It is the process of spiritual growth, the painful assumption of a
new, regenerate nature that forms the subject of Book II. Guyon
arrests Acrasia—though he is still far from immune to her charms—
by virtue of what he has become; and it is no exaggeration to say that
his true mission is his own sanctification. As much is implied by
his vow:

> Such and such evill God on <u>Guyon</u> reare,
> And worse and worse young Orphane be thy paine,
> If I or thou dew vengeance doe forebeare. (II. i. 61)

The words are meant precisely: if Guyon fails to put on a new nature in which concupiscence is arrested, his fate will indeed be just
that of Mordant and Amavia—for the regenerate are not necessarily
predestined to salvation. There is nothing automatic about baptism:
it places the believer in the context of grace, but only a long effort
of mortification and edification can alter his nature.

If the above interpretation of the early cantos is anywhere near
the truth, then a revision of our approach to Book II is called for.
Previously, the tendency has been to describe its subject matter as
purely moral and to contrast it in this respect with the religious
Book I. Harry Berger has even argued that for the first seven cantos Guyon is pagan. But, even if Berger were right in his view that
Guyon is sinfully self-dependent, this would hardly make him pagan.

As we have seen, in the earliest episodes the virtue Guyon represents is related to baptism: his mission is from the very beginning
conceived of in theological terms.

Woodhouse at first plausibly maintains that the distinction between Guyon and the Red Cross Knight "is not between pagan and
Christian but between unconverted (natural) man and converted
(regenerate)."[42] But then he goes even further than Berger, by
denying that Guyon ever comes to rely on grace; he finds it an "obvious fact" about Book II as a whole that "while the motivation and
sanctions of the Red Cross Knight's virtue are specifically religious,
those of Guyon's, just as clearly, are not." The more closely the
allegory of Book II has been approached, however, the more it has
revealed its motivations to be specifically religious. Hamilton's
"A Theological Reading of The Faerie Queene, Book II" shows this;
and so does a timely article by T. M. Gang,[43] which justifiably
queries the whole validity of Woodhouse's distinction between the
order of nature and the order of grace as a basis for interpreting
Spenser. Nor has the present inquiry encouraged us to refer Spenser's division of books to Woodhouse's dualism.

A much more accurate account of the relationship between Guyon
and the Red Cross Knight has been given in another article of Ham-
ilton's: "'Like Race to Runne': the Parallel Structure of The
Faerie Queene, Books I and II," PMLA LXXIII (1958). Hamilton
finds the same pattern of regeneration in both books: the Red Cross
Knight's battle to release Una's parents "becomes the pattern for
Guyon's release of man from imprisonment in the Garden of Eden
. . . Guyon . . . imitates him to become a new Adam, one who in
Milton's phrase 'might see and know, and yet abstain,' one who binds
Eve and destroys the Garden in order that man may pass successfully through the world towards his final restoration" (334). With
much of this we may readily agree, especially with Hamilton's illuminating suggestion that "By destroying the Bower, [Guyon] displays
the power of virtue to release man from enshrouding nature, the
womb which imprisons man upon the level of nature without possibility of rebirth." But Hamilton is still enough influenced by Woodhouse to write that "Book I moves upon the level of grace while
Book II remains upon the level of nature" (332). To be sure, he
adds that the levels are "not exclusive" and that Guyon is not excluded from the Red Cross Knight's regeneration but "enjoys its
counterpart upon the natural level." These qualifications are confusing, however, and lend support to Gang's view that it is time to
abandon Woodhouse's categories altogether. The preceding paper
may suggest a fresh approach. For, if stages of the Christian life

are in question, it would argue that, whereas the Red Cross Knight's struggle is for a saving belief, Guyon's is for sanctification and takes belief for granted; or, if the division is regarded more subjectively, that Book I deals with regeneration in respect of belief and the intellect, Book II in respect of passions and the soul. This does not mean that Guyon is any less "supernatural" than the Red Cross Knight; indeed, his concern with the natural order is to inform it with the lucid waters of doctrine and of grace.[44] But it does mean that Book II concentrates on the texture of psychological life in a way that keeps the theological motivation implicit. This is what has given rise to the error of seeing Guyon as restricted to the natural level. Guyon comes, as Hamilton says, to restore man to "his rightful place upon earth"—but in the sense of translating the Red Cross Knight's vision into such actuality as is possible here on earth. The destruction of the Bower, which I take to be the destruction of the "body of sin,"[45] makes way for the edification of a new nature: that spiritual body with which the flesh of the regenerate is increasingly clothed upon. Thus the architectural imagery that Book II abounds in does not refer merely to the structure of the natural body of flesh but to the building of the new man, of a sanctified nature entirely dependent upon grace. Only if "formerly grounded" on grace, indeed, "On firme foundation of true bountihed," can the "goodly frame of Temperance" rise.[46]

THE STRUCTURE OF IMAGERY IN THE FAERIE QUEENE

Northrop Frye

The Faerie Queene, long as it is, is not nearly as long as the poem that Spenser intended to write, according to his letter to Raleigh and two of the Amoretti sonnets. It therefore at once raises the problem of whether the poem as it now stands is unfinished or merely uncompleted. If merely uncompleted, then it still may be a unity, like a torso in sculpture; if unfinished, then, as in Dickens' Mystery of Edwin Drood, certain essential clues to the total meaning are forever withheld from us.

Many readers tend to assume that Spenser wrote the poem in the same way that they read it, starting at the beginning and keeping on until he collapsed with exhaustion. But while The Faerie Queene probably evolved in a much more complicated way than that, there is no evidence of exhaustion. In the eightieth Amoretti sonnet he sounds winded, but not bored; and of course he is not the kind of poet who depends on anything that a Romantic would call inspiration. He is a professional poet, learned in rhetoric, who approaches his sublime passages with the nonchalance of a car-driver shifting into second gear. All the purple patches in Spenser—the temptations of Despair and Acrasia, the praise of Elizabeth in Colin Clouts Come Home Again, the "Bellona" passage in The Shepheards Calender— are deliberate rhetorical exercises. There may be passages in The Faerie Queene that we find dull, but there are very few in which Spenser's own standards are not met. In some cantos of the fifth book, perhaps, he sounds tired and irritable, as though he were preoccupied with his anxieties instead of his subject, and in these cantos there are lapses into muddled argument, tasteless imagery, and cacophonous doggerel. But on the whole no poem in English of comparable scope is more evenly sustained. Further, Spenser is not, like Coleridge, a poet of fragments. Just as there is a touch of Pope himself in Pope's admiration for "The spider's touch, how exquisite-

Reprinted from University of Toronto Quarterly, Vol. 30 (1961), pp. 109–127, by permission of the author and of the publisher, University of Toronto Press. This article appears also in the author's Fables of Identity: Studies in Poetic Mythology, New York 1963.

ly fine!," so there is a touch of Spenser himself in Spenser's admiration for the honey bee "Working for formal rooms in wexen
frame." He thinks inside regular frameworks—the twelve months,
the nine muses, the seven deadly sins—and he goes on filling up his
frame even when his scheme is mistaken from the beginning, as it
certainly is in The Tears of the Muses.

What can be said is that, as one virtue is likely to involve others,
Spenser's scheme was bound to foreshorten as he went on. In the
historical allegory he still had the Armada to deal with, but in the
moral allegory there is already a good deal of inorganic repetition,
especially in the symbols of evil (for example, the Occasion-Ate-
Sclaunder sequence and the reduplicative foul monsters). In the
first book he uses up so much of the structure of Biblical typology
that he could hardly have written a second book in the area of revelation; and chastity and justice, each of which is described as the
supreme virtue, almost exhaust the sources of plausible compliments to Elizabeth. Spenser may well have ended his sixth book
realizing that he might not write any more of it, and designed its
conclusion for either possibility. He provides himself, of course,
with opportunities for carrying on the story. Apart from Prince
Arthur himself, we have a fresh set of characters; a seventh book
would doubtless have got some clothes on Serena, who is left nude
and shivering at the end of the eighth canto; the poet hints that the
baby rescued by Calepine may grow up to be the hero of a future
legend; he allows the Blatant Beast to escape again. But there are
many such dropped stitches in the plots of the other five books, and
they do not interfere with our sense of their unity. At the same time
the appearance of Spenser's "signature" in Colin Clout and two other
symbols from The Shepheards Calender, the four Graces and the envious beast that barks at poets, make the end of the sixth book also
a summing up and conclusion for the entire poem and for Spenser's
poetic career. There is, at least, nothing in the poem as we now
have it that seems to depend for its meaning on anything unwritten.

I shall assume, as a working hypothesis, that the six books we
have form a unified epic structure, regardless of how much might
have been added that wasn't. There are six books, and Spenser has
a curious fondness for mentioning the number six: there are six
counsellors of Lucifera, six couples in the masque of Cupid, two
groups of six knights fighting Britomart, six judges at Cambell's
tournament, six partisans of Marinell at Florimell's tournament,
six grooms of Care, and so on. In most of these groups there is a
crucial seventh, and perhaps the Mutabilitie Cantos have that function in the total scheme of the epic. We shall probably never know

on what manuscript evidence the publisher of the Folio numbered
the two cantos of this poem six and seven. What we can see is that
the Mutabilitie Cantos are certainly not a fragment: they constitute
a single beautifully shaped poem that could not have had a more
logical beginning, development, and end. It is entirely impossible
that the last two stanzas could have been the opening stanzas of an
eighth unfinished canto, as the rubric suggests. Nor is it possible
that in their present form these cantos could have been the "core"
of a seventh book, unless that book was inconceivably different in
its structure from the existing ones. The poem brings us to the
poet's "Sabbath's sight" after his six great efforts of creation, and
there is nothing which at any point can be properly described as
"unperfite."

To demonstrate a unity in The Faerie Queene, we have to examine
the imagery of the poem rather than its allegory. It is Spenser's
habitual technique, developing as it did out of the emblematic visions
he wrote in his nonage, to start with the image, not the allegorical
translation of it, and when he says at the beginning of the final canto
of Book II:

> Now ginnes this goodly frame of Temperaunce
> Fayrely to rise

one feels that the "frame" is built out of the characters and places
that are clearly announced to be what they are, not out of their moral
or historical shadows. Spenser prefaces the whole poem with sonnets
to possible patrons, telling several of them that they are in the poem
somewhere, not specifying where: the implication is that for such
readers the allegory is to be read more or less ad libitum. Spenser's
own language about allegory, "darke conceit," "clowdily enwrapped,"
emphasizes its deliberate vagueness. We know that Belphoebe refers
to Elizabeth: therefore, when Timias speaks of "her, whom the hevens
doe serve and sew," is there, as one edition suggests, a reference to
the storm that wrecked the Armada? I cite this only as an example
of how subjective an allegorical reading can be. Allegory is not only
often uncertain, however, but in the work of one of our greatest allegorical poets it can even be addled, as it is in Mother Hubberds Tale,
where the fox and the ape argue over which of them is more like a
man, and hence more worthy to wear the skin of a lion. In such episodes as the legal decisions of Artegall, too, we can see that Spenser,
unlike Milton, is a poet of very limited conceptual powers, and is
helpless without some kind of visualization to start him thinking. I
am far from urging that we should "let the allegory go" in reading

Spenser, but it is self-evident that the imagery is prior in importance to it. One cannot begin to discuss the allegory without using
the imagery, but one could work out an exhaustive analysis of the
imagery without ever mentioning the allegory.

Our first step is to find a general structure of imagery in the
poem as a whole, and with so public a poet as Spenser we should
hardly expect to find this in Spenser's private possession, as we
might with Blake or Shelley or Keats. We should be better advised
to look for it in the axioms and assumptions which Spenser and his
public shared, and which form the basis of its imaginative communication.[1] Perhaps the Mutabilitie Cantos, which give us so
many clues to the sense of The Faerie Queene as a whole, will help
us here also.

The action of the Mutabilitie Cantos embraces four distinguishable levels of existence. First is that of Mutability herself, the
level of death, corruption, and dissolution, which would also be, if
this poem were using moral categories, the level of sin. Next
comes the world of ordinary experience, the nature of the four
elements, over which Mutability is also dominant. Its central symbol is the cycle, the round of days, months, and hours which Mutability brings forth as evidence of her supremacy. In the cycle there
are two elements: becoming or change, which is certainly Mutability's, and a principle of order or recurrence within which the change
occurs. Hence Mutability's evidence is not conclusive, but could
just as easily be turned against her. Above our world is upper nature, the stars in their courses, a world still cyclical but immortal
and unchanged in essence. This upper world is all that is now left
of nature as God originally created it, the state described in the
Biblical story of Eden and the Classical myth of the Golden Age. Its
regent is Jove, armed with the power which, in a world struggling
against chaos and evil, is "the right hand of justice truly hight." But
Jove, however he may bluster and threaten, has no authority over
Mutability; that authority belongs to the goddess Nature, whose vice-
roy he is. If Mutability could be cast out of the world of ordinary
experience, lower and upper nature would be reunited, man would
re-enter the Golden Age, and the reign of "Saturn's son" would be
replaced by that of Saturn. Above Nature is the real God, to whom
Mutability appeals when she brushes Jove out of her way, who is
invoked in the last stanza of the poem, and who appears in the reference to the Transfiguration of Christ like a mirage behind the
assembly of lower gods.

Man is born into the third of these worlds, the order of physical
nature which is theologically "fallen" and under the sway of Muta-

bility. But though in this world he is not of it: he really belongs
to the upper nature of which he formed part before his fall. The
order of physical nature, the world of animals and plants, is morally neutral: man is confronted from his birth with a moral dialectic, and must either sink below it into sin or rise above it into
his proper human home. This latter he may reach by the practice
of virtue and through education, which includes law, religion, and
everything the Elizabethans meant by art. The question whether
this "art" included what we mean by art, poetry, painting, and
music, was much debated in Spenser's day, and explains why so
much of the criticism of the period took the form of apologetic. As
a poet, Spenser believed in the moral reality of poetry and in its
effectiveness as an educating agent; as a Puritan, he was sensitive
to the abuse and perversion of art which had raised the question of
its moral value in the first place, and he shows his sense of the
importance of the question in his description of the Bower of Bliss.

Spenser means by "Faerie" primarily the world of realized human nature. It is an "antique" world, extending backward to Eden
and the Golden Age, and its central figure of Prince Arthur
was chosen, Spenser tells us, as "furthest from the daunger of
envy, and suspition of present time." It occupies the same space
as the ordinary physical world, a fact which makes contemporary
allusions possible, but its time sequence is different. It is not
timeless: we hear of months or years passing, but time seems
curiously foreshortened, as though it followed instead of establishing the rhythm of conscious life. Such foreshortening of time suggests a world of dream and wishfulfilment, like the fairylands of
Shakespeare's comedies. But Spenser, with his uneasy political
feeling that the price of authority is eternal vigilance, will hardly
allow his virtuous characters even to sleep, much less dream, and
the drowsy narcotic passages which have so impressed his imita-
tors are associated with spiritual peril. He tells us that sleep is
one of the three divisions of the lowest world, the other two being
death and hell; and Prince Arthur's long tirade against night (III, iv)
would be out of proportion if night, like its seasonal counterpart
winter, did not symbolize a lower world than Faerie. The vision of
Faerie may be the author's dream, as the pilgrimage of Christian
is presented as a dream of Bunyan, but what the poet dreams of is
the strenuous effort, physical, mental, and moral, of waking up to
one's true humanity.

In the ordinary physical world good and evil are inextricably
confused; the use and the abuse of natural energies are hard to distinguish, motives are mixed and behaviour inconsistent. The per-

spective of Faerie, the achieved quest of virtue, clarifies this view.
What we now see is a completed moral dialectic. The mixed-up
physical world separates out into a human moral world and a demonic one. In this perspective heroes and villains are purely and
simply heroic and villainous; characters are either white or black,
for the quest or against it; right always has superior might in the
long run, for we are looking at reality from the perspective of man
as he was originally made in the image of God, unconfused about the
difference between heaven and hell. We can now see that physical
nature is a source of energy, but that this energy can run only in
either of two opposing directions: toward its own fulfilment or
towards its own destruction. Nature says to Mutability: "For thy
decay thou seekst by thy desire," and contrasts her with those who,
struggling out of the natural cycle, "Doe worke their owne perfection so by fate."

Spenser, in Hamlet's language, has no interest in holding the
mirror up to nature unless he can thereby show virtue her own feature and scorn her own image. His evil characters are rarely converted to good, and while there is one virtuous character who comes
to a bad end, Sir Terpine in Book V, this exception proves the rule,
as his fate makes an allegorical point about justice. Sometimes the
fiction writer clashes with the moralist in Spenser, though never
for long. When Malbecco offers to take Hellenore back from the
satyrs, he becomes a figure of some dignity as well as pathos; but
Spenser cannot let his dramatic sympathy with Malbecco evolve.
Complicated behaviour, mixed motives, or the kind of driving energy of character which makes moral considerations seem less important, as it does in all Shakespeare's heroes, and even in Milton's
Satan—none of this could be contained in Spenser's framework.

The Faerie Queene in consequence is necessarily a romance, for
romance is the genre of simplified or black and white characterization. The imagery of this romance is organized on two major principles. One is that of the natural cycle, the progression of days and
seasons. The other is that of the moral dialectic, in which symbols
of virtue are parodied by their vicious or demonic counterparts.
Any symbol may be used ambivalently, and may be virtuous or demonic according to its context, an obvious example being the symbolism of gold. Cyclical symbols are subordinated to dialectical
ones; in other words the upward turn from darkness to dawn or
from winter to spring usually symbolizes the lift in perspective
from physical to human nature. Ordinary experience, the morally
neutral world of physical nature, never appears as such in The
Faerie Queene, but its place in Spenser's scheme is symbolized

by nymphs and other elemental spirits, or by the satyrs, who may
be tamed and awed by the sight of Una or more habitually stimulated
by the sight of Hellenore. Satyrane, as his name indicates, is, with
several puns intended, a good-natured man, and two of the chief
heroes, Redcrosse and Artegall, are explicitly said to be natives of
this world and not, like Guyon, natives of Faerie. What this means
in practice is that their quests include a good deal of historical
allegory.

In the letter to Raleigh Spenser speaks of a possible twenty-four
books, twelve to deal with the private virtues of Prince Arthur and
the other twelve with the public ones manifested after he was
crowned king. But this appalling spectre must have been exorcized
very quickly. If we look at the six virtues he did treat, we can see
that the first three, holiness, temperance, and chastity, are essentially private virtues, and that the next three, friendship, justice,
and courtesy, are public ones. Further, that both sets seem to run
in a sort of Hegelian progression. Of all public virtues, friendship
is the most private and personal; justice the most public and impersonal, and courtesy seems to combine the two, Calidore being
notable for his capacity for friendship and yet able to capture the
Blatant Beast that eluded Artegall. Similarly, of all private virtues,
holiness is most dependent on grace and revelation, hence the imagery of Book I is Biblical and apocalyptic, and introduces the theological virtues. Temperance, in contrast, is a virtue shared by the
enlightened heathen, a prerequisite and somewhat pedestrian virtue
(Guyon loses his horse early in the book and does not get it back
until Book V), hence the imagery of Book II is classical, with much
drawn from the Odyssey and from Platonic and Aristotelian ethics.
Chastity, a virtue described by Spenser as "farre above the rest,"
seems to combine something of both. The encounter of Redcrosse
and Guyon is indecisive, but Britomart, by virtue of her enchanted
spear, is clearly stronger than Guyon, and hardly seems to need
Redcrosse's assistance in Castle Joyeous.

We note that in Spenser, as in Milton's Comus, the supreme private virtue appears to be chastity rather than charity. Charity, in
the sense of Christian love, does not fit the scheme of The Faerie
Queene: for Spenser it would primarily mean, not man's love for
God, but God's love for man, as depicted in the Hymn of Heavenly
Love. Charissa appears in Book I, but her main connexions are
with the kindliness that we associate with "giving to charity"; Agape
appears in Book IV, but is so minor and so dim-witted a character
that one wonders whether Spenser knew the connotations of the
word. Hence, though Book I is the only book that deals explicitly

with Christian imagery, it does not follow that holiness is the supreme virtue. Spenser is not dealing with what God gives to man, but with what man does with his gifts, and Redcrosse's grip on holiness is humanly uncertain.

In one of its aspects The Faerie Queene is an educational treatise, based, like other treatises of its time, on the two essential social facts of the Renaissance, the prince and the courtier. The most important person in Renaissance society to educate was the prince, and the next most important was the courtier, the servant of the prince. Spenser's heroes are courtiers who serve the Faerie Queene and who metaphorically make up the body and mind of Prince Arthur. To demonstrate the moral reality of poetry Spenser had to assume a connexion between the educational treatise and the highest forms of literature. For Spenser, as for most Elizabethan writers, the highest form of poetry would be either epic or tragedy, and the epic for him deals essentially with the actions of the heroic prince or leader. The highest form of prose, similarly, would be either a Utopian vision outlined in a Platonic dialogue or in a romance like Sidney's Arcadia, or a description of an ideal prince's ideal education, for which the classical model was Xenophon's Cyropaedia. Spenser's preference of Xenophon's form to Plato's is explicit in the letter to Raleigh. This high view of education is inseparable from Spenser's view of the relation between nature and art. For Spenser, as for Burke centuries later, art is man's nature. Art is nature on the human plane, or what Sidney calls a second nature, a "golden" world, to use another phrase of Sidney's, because essentially the same world as that of the Golden Age, and in contrast to the "brazen" world of physical nature. Hence art is no less natural than physical nature—the art itself is nature, as Polixenes says in The Winter's Tale—but it is the civilized nature appropriate to human life.

Private and public education, then, are the central themes of The Faerie Queene. If we had to find a single word for the virtue underlying all private education, the best word would perhaps be fidelity: that unswerving loyalty to an ideal which is virtue, to a single lady which is love, and to the demands of one's calling which is courage. Fidelity on the specifically human plane of endeavour is faith, the vision of holiness by which one lives; on the natural plane it is temperance, or the ability to live humanely in the physical world. The corresponding term for the virtue of public education is, perhaps, concord or harmony. On the physical plane concord is friendship, again the ability to achieve a human community in ordinary life; on the specifically human plane it is justice and equity, the foundation of society.

In the first two books the symbolism comes to a climax in what we may call a "house of recognition," the House of Holiness in Book I and the House of Alma in Book II. In the third the climax is the vision of the order of nature in the Gardens of Adonis. The second part repeats the same scheme: we have houses of recognition in the Temple of Venus in Book IV and the Palace of Mercilla in Book V, and a second <u>locus amoenus</u> vision in the Mount Acidale canto of Book VI, where the poet himself appears with the Graces. The sequence runs roughly as follows: fidelity in the context of human nature; fidelity in the context of physical nature; fidelity in the context of nature as a whole; concord in the context of physical nature; concord in the context of human nature; concord in the context of nature as a whole. Or, abbreviated: human fidelity, natural fidelity, nature; natural concord, human concord, art. Obviously, such a summary is unacceptable as it stands, but it may give some notion of how the books are related and of how the symbolism flows out of one book into the next one.

The conception of the four levels of existence and the symbols used to represent it come from Spenser's cultural tradition in general and from the Bible in particular. The Bible, as Spenser read it for his purposes, describes how man originally inhabited his own human world, the Garden of Eden, and fell out of it into the present physical world, which fell with him. By his fall he lost the tree and water of life. Below him is hell, represented on earth by the kingdoms of bondage, Egypt, Babylon, and Rome, and symbolized by the serpent of Eden, otherwise Satan, otherwise the huge water-monster called Leviathan or the dragon by the prophets. Man is redeemed by the quest of Christ, who after overcoming the world descended to hell and in three days conquered it too. His descent is usually symbolized in art as walking into the open mouth of a dragon, and when he returns in triumph he carries a banner of a red cross on a white ground, the colours typifying his blood and flesh. At the end of time the dragon of death is finally destroyed, man is restored to Eden, and gets back the water and tree of life. In Christianity these last are symbolized by the two sacraments accepted by the Reformed Church, baptism and the Eucharist.

The quest of the Redcross knight in Book I follows the symbolism of the quest of Christ. He carries the same emblem of a red cross on a white ground; the monster he has to kill is "that old dragon" (quatrain to Canto xi; cf. Rev. xii, 9) who is identical with the Biblical Satan, Leviathan, and serpent of Eden, and the object of killing him is to restore Una's parents, who are Adam and Eve, to their kingdom of Eden, which includes the entire world, now usurped by the dragon. The tyranny of Egypt, Babylon, and the Roman Empire

continues in the tyranny of the Roman Church, and the Book of
Revelation, as Spenser read it, prophesies the future ascendancy
of that church and its ultimate defeat in its vision of the dragon and
Great Whore, the latter identified with his Duessa. St. George
fights the dragon for three days in the garden of Eden, refreshed by
the water and tree of life on the first two days respectively.

But Eden is not heaven: in Spenser, as in Dante, it is rather the
summit of purgatory, which St. George goes through in the House of
Holiness. It is the world of recovered human nature, as it originally
was and still can be when sin is removed. St. George similarly is
not Christ, but only the English people trying to be Christian, and
the dragon, while he may be part of Satan, is considerably less
Satanic than Archimago or Duessa, who survive the book. No monster, however loathsome, can really be evil: for evil there must be
a perversion of intelligence, and Spenser drew his dragon with some
appreciation of the fact mentioned in an essay of Valéry, that in poetry the most frightful creatures always have something rather
childlike about them:

> So dreadfully he towards him did pas,
> Forelifting up aloft his speckled brest,
> And often bounding on the brused gras,
> As for great ioyance of his newcome guest.   (I, xi, 15)

Hence the theatre of operations in the first book is still a human
world. The real heaven appears only in the vision of Jerusalem at
the end of the tenth canto and in a few other traces, like the invisible husband of Charissa and the heavenly music heard in the background of the final betrothal. Eden is within the order of nature
but it is a new earth turned upward, or sacramentally aligned with
a new heaven. The main direction of the imagery is also upward:
this upward movement is the theme of the House of Holiness, of the
final quest, and of various subordinate themes like the worship of
Una by the satyrs.

We have spoken of the principle of symbolic parody, which we
meet in all books of The Faerie Queene. Virtues are contrasted
not only with their vicious opposites, but with vices that have similar names and appearances. Thus the golden mean of temperance
is parodied by the golden means provided by Mammon; "That part
of justice, which is equity" in Book V is parodied by the anarchistic
equality preached by the giant in the second canto, and so on. As
the main theme of Book I is really faith, or spiritual fidelity, the
sharpest parody of this sort is between Fidelia, or true faith, and

Duessa, who calls herself Fidessa. Fidelia holds a golden cup of
wine and water (which in other romance patterns would be the Holy
Grail, though Spenser's one reference to the Grail shows that he
has no interest in it); Duessa holds the golden cup of the Whore of
Babylon. Fidelia's cup also contains a serpent (the redeeming
brazen serpent of Moses typifying the Crucifixion); Duessa sits on
the dragon of the Apocalypse who is metaphorically the same beast
as the serpent of Eden. Fidelia's power to raise the dead is
stressed; Duessa raises Sansjoy from the dead by the power of
Aesculapius, whose emblem is the serpent. Of all such parodies
in the first book the most important for the imagery of the poem as
a whole is the parody of the tree and water of life in Eden. These
symbols have their demonic counterparts in the paralysed trees of
Fradubio and Fraelissa and in the paralysing fountain from which
St. George drinks in the seventh canto.

Thus the first book shows very clearly what we have called the
subordinating of cyclical symbols to dialectical ones: the tree and
water of life, originally symbols of the rebirth of spring, are here
symbols of resurrection, or a permanent change from a life in
physical nature above the animals to life in human nature under
God. The main interest of the second book is also dialectical, but
in the reverse direction, concerned with human life in the ordinary
physical world, and with its separation from the demonic world
below. The Bower of Bliss is a parody of Eden, and just as the
climax of Book I is St. George's three-day battle with the dragon
of death, so the narrative climax of Book II is Guyon's three-day
endurance in the underworld. It is the climax at least as far as
Guyon's heroism is concerned, for it is Arthur who defeats Maleger
and it is really the Palmer who catches Acrasia.

We should expect to find in Book II, therefore, many demonic
parodies of the symbols in Book I, especially of the tree and water
of life and its symbolic relatives. At the beginning we note that
Acrasia, like Duessa, has a golden cup of death, filled, like Fidelia's,
with wine and water ("Bacchus with the nymph"). There follows
Ruddymane, with his bloody hands that cannot be washed. Spenser
speaks of Redcrosse's hands as "baptised" after he falls back into
the well of life, and the Ruddymane incident is partly a reference to
original sin, removable only by baptism or bathing in a "liuing well."
The demonic counterparts of both sacraments appear in the hell
scene in the cave of Mammon, in connexion with Pilate and Tantalus.
Pilate, forever washing his hands in vain, repeats the Ruddymane
image in its demonic context, and Tantalus is the corresponding
parody of the Eucharist. These figures are preceded by the descrip-

tion of the golden appletree in the garden of Proserpina and the river Cocytus. Images of trees and water are considerably expanded in the description of the Bower of Bliss.

The fact that the fountain of Diana's nymph refuses to cleanse Ruddymane's hands indicates the rather subordinate role of Diana in Spenser's symbolism. It is clear, if we compare the description of Venus in Book IV with the description of Nature in the Mutabilitie Cantos, that Venus represents the whole order of nature, in its higher human as well as its lower physical aspect. What Diana stands for is the resistance to corruption, as symbolized by unchastity, which is the beginning, and of course always an essential part, of moral realization. Hence Diana in Spenser is a little like the law in Milton, which can discover sin but not remove it. In the Mutabilitie Cantos the glimpsing of Diana's nakedness by Faunus is parallel, on a small scale, to the rebellion of the lower against the higher nature which is also represented by Mutability's thrusting herself into heaven at the place of Cynthia, who is another form of Diana. Naturally Elizabeth's virginity compelled Spenser to give a high place to Diana and her protégé Belphoebe, but for symbolic as well as political reasons he preferred to make the Faerie Queene a young woman proceeding toward marriage, like Britomart. Meanwhile it is the virginal Faerie Queene whose picture Guyon carries on his shield, Guyon being in his whole moral complex something of a male Diana.

Temperance in Spenser is a rather negative virtue, being the resistance of consciousness to impulsive action which is necessary in order to know whether the action is going up or down in the moral dialectic. Conscious action is real action, Aristotle's proairesis; impulsive action is really pseudo-action, a passion which increasingly becomes passivity. Human life in the physical world has something of the feeling of an army of occupation about it, symbolized by the beleaguered castle of Alma. The House of Alma possesses two things in particular: wealth, in Ruskin's sense of wellbeing, and beauty, in the sense of correct proportion and ordering of parts. Its chief enemies are "Beauty, and money," the minions of Acrasia and Mammon, the external or instrumental possessions which the active mind uses and the passive mind thinks of as ends in themselves. Temperance is also good temperament, or the balancing of humours, and Guyon's enemies are mainly humours in the Elizabethan sense, although the humours are usually symbolized by their corresponding elements, as the choleric Pyrochles is associated with fire and the phlegmatic Cymochles with water. The battleground between the active and the passive mind is the area of sensation, the steady rain of impressions and stimuli coming in from the outer world which the active mind organizes and the passive mind merely yields to. Normally the sanguine humour predominates in the active mind; the passive one becomes a victim of melancholy, with its progressive weakening of will and of the power to distinguish reality from illusion. In Spenser's picture of the mind the fancy (Phantastes) is predisposed to melancholy and the influence of "oblique Saturne"; it is not the seat of the poetic imagination, as it would be in a nineteenth-century Romantic.[2] Maleger, the leader of the assault on Alma, is a spirit of melancholy, and is sprung from the corresponding element of earth.

Having outlined the dialectical extremes of his imagery, Spenser moves on to consider the order of nature on its two main levels in the remaining books. Temperance steers a middle course between care and carelessness, jealousy and wantonness, miserliness and prodigality, Mammon's cave and Acrasia's bower. Acrasia is a kind of sinister Venus, and her victims, Mordant wallowing in his blood, Cymochles, Verdant, have something of a dead, wasted, or frustrated Adonis about them. Mammon is an old man with a daughter, Philotime. Much of the symbolism of the third book is based on these two archetypes. The first half leads up to the description of the Gardens of Adonis in Canto vi by at least three repetitions of the theme of Venus and Adonis. First we have the tapestry in the Castle Joyeous representing the story, with a longish description attached. Then comes the wounding of Marinell on his "precious shore" by Britomart (surely the most irritable heroine known to romance), where the sacrificial imagery, the laments of the nymphs, the strewing of flowers on the bier are all conventional images of Adonis. Next is Timias, discovered by Belphoebe wounded in the thigh with a boar-spear. Both Belphoebe and Marinell's mother Cymoent have pleasant retreats closely analogous to the Gardens of Adonis. In the second half of the book we have three examples of the old man and young woman relationship: Malbecco and Hellenore, Proteus and Florimell, Busirane and Amoret. All these are evil: there is no idealized version of this theme. The reason is that the idealized version would be the counterpart to the vision of charity in the Hymn of Heavenly Love. That is, it would be the vision of the female Sapience sitting in the bosom of the Deity that we meet at the end of the Hymn to Heavenly Beauty, and this would take us outside the scope of The Faerie Queene, or at any rate of its third book.

The central figure in the third book and the fourth is Venus, flanked on either side by Cupid and Adonis, or what a modern poet would call Eros and Thanatos. Cupid and Venus are gods of natural love, and form, not a demonic parody, but a simple analogy of Christian love, an analogy which is the symbolic basis of the Fowre Hymnes. Cupid, like Jesus, is lord of gods and creator of the cosmos, and simultaneously an infant, Venus' relation to him being that of an erotic Madonna, as her relation to Adonis is that of an erotic Pièta. Being androgynous, she brings forth Cupid without male assistance;[3] she loses him and goes in search of him, and he returns in triumph in the great masque at the end as lord of all creation.

The Garden of Adonis, with its Genius and its temperate climate, is so carefully paralleled to the Bower of Bliss that it clearly represents the reality of which the Bower is a mirage. It presents the order of nature as a cyclical process of death and renewal, in itself morally innocent, but still within the realm of Mutability, as the presence of Time shows. Like Eden, it is a paradise: it is nature as nature would be if man could live in his proper human world, the "antique" Golden Age. It is a world where substance is constant but where "Forms are variable and decay"; and hence it is closely connected with the theme of metamorphosis, which is the central symbol of divine love as the pagans conceived it.

Such love naturally has its perverted form, represented by the possessive jealousy of Malbecco, Busirane, and Proteus, all of whom enact variants of the myth of Tithonus and Aurora, the aged lover and the struggling dawn. Hellenore escapes into the world of satyrs, a world too "natural" to be wholly sinful. The torturing of Amoret by Busirane, representing the anguish of jealous love, recurs in various images of bleeding, such as the "long bloody river" in the tapestry of Cupid. Painful or not, it is love that makes the world go round, that keeps the cycle of nature turning, and it is particularly the love of Marinell and Florimell, whose names suggest water and vegetation, that seems linked to the natural cycle. Florimell is imprisoned under the sea during a kind of symbolic winter in which a "snowy" Florimell takes her place. Marinell is not cured of his illness until his mother turns from "watry gods" to the sun, and when he sees Florimell he revives

> As withered weed through cruell winters tine,
> That feels the warmth of sunny beam's reflection
> Lifts up his head, that did before decline
> And gins to spread his leaf before the fair sunshine.
>
> (IV, xii, 34)

Book IV is full of images of natural revival, some in very unlikely places, and it comes to a climax with the symbolism of the tree and water of life in their natural context. At the temple of Venus, we are told, "No tree, that is of count . . . But there was planted," and the next canto is a tremendous outburst of water. The wedding of the Thames and the Medway takes place in Proteus' hall, and Proteus, in the mythological handbooks, is the spirit of metamorphosis, the liquid energy of substance driving through endless varieties of form.

The impulse in sexual love is toward union in one flesh, which is part of the symbolism of Christian marriage. The original conclusion to Book III leaves Scudamour and Amoret locked in an embrace which makes them look like a single hermaphrodite. The reason for this curious epithet becomes clear in Book IV, where we learn that Venus herself is hermaphroditic, and of course all embracing lovers are epiphanies of Venus. Naturally this image lends itself to demonic parody, as in the incestuous birth of Oliphant and Argante. Britomart watches Scudamour and Amoret rather enviously, making a mental resolve to get herself into the same position as soon as she can run her Artegall to earth: for Britomart, though as chaste as Belphoebe, is not vowed to virginity. Perhaps it is her accessibility to human emotions that is symbolized by the bleeding wound she receives from an arrow in the first canto of Book III, an image repeated, with a symmetry unusual even in Spenser, in the last canto.

A slight extension of the same symbol of unity through love takes us into the area of social love, or friendship, the theme of the fourth book. Friendship shows, even more clearly than sexual passion, the power of love as a creative force, separating the elements from chaos by the attraction of like to like. The human counterpart of this ordering of elements is concord or harmony, for which Spenser uses various symbols, notably the golden chain, an image introduced into Book I and parodied by the chain of ambition in the cave of Mammon. We also have the image of two (or three) souls united in one body in the extremely tedious account of Priamond, Diamond, and Triamond. It is rather more interesting that Spenser seems to regard the poetic tradition as a community of friendship of a similar kind. In all six books of The Faerie Queene it is only in the fourth that Spenser refers explicitly to his two great models Chaucer and Ariosto, and his phrase about Chaucer is significant: "thine own spirit, which doth in me survive."

When we move from friendship, an abstract pattern of human community which only noble spirits can form, to justice, in which the base and evil must also be included, we return to historical allegory. Spenser's vision of history (III, ix) focuses on the legend of Troy: the first Troy is recalled by Hellenore and Paridell, and the second, or Rome, by Duessa, who reappears in Books IV and V. The third is of course England itself, which will not collapse in adultery or superstition if her leading poet can prevent it. In the prophecy of this third Troy we meet an image connected with the wedding of the Thames in Book IV:

> It [sc. London] Troynovant is hight, that with the waves
> Of wealthy Thamis washed is along,
> Upon whose stubborn neck, whereat he raves
> With roaring rage, and sore himself does throng,
> That all men fear to tempt his billows strong,
> She fastened hath her foot, which stands so high
> That it a wonder of the world is sung
> In foreign lands, and all which passen by,
> Beholding it from far, do think it threats the sky.

> (III, ix, 45)

I quote this poetically licentious description of the Thames because it is so closely linked with Spenser's conception of justice as the harnessing of physical power to conquer physical nature. In its lower aspects this power is mechanical, symbolized by the "yron man" Talus, who must be one of the earliest "science fiction" or technological symbols in poetry, and who kills without discrimination for the sake of discrimination, like a South African policeman. In its higher aspects where justice becomes equity, or consideration of circumstances, the central image is this one of the virgin guiding the raging monster. We meet this image very early in the adventures of Una and the lion in Book I, and the same symbolic shape reappears in the Gardens of Adonis, where Venus enjoys Adonis with the boar imprisoned in a cave underneath. Next comes the training of Artegall (who begins his career by taming animals) by Astraea, identified with the constellation Virgo. Next is the vision of Isis, where Osiris and the crocodile correspond to Adonis and the boar earlier, but are here explicitly identified. Finally we have Mercilla and the lion under her throne, where Spenser naturally refrains from speculating on the lion's possible identity with a human lover. It may be the link with London on the Thames that lends such prominence in Book V to the image of the river washing away the filth of injustice. At the same time the virgin who dominates the beast is herself the servant of an invisi-

ble male deity, hence the figure of the female rebel is important
in the last two books: Radigund the Amazon in Book V, who rebels
against justice, and Mirabell in Book VI, who rebels against courtesy. Radigund is associated with the moon because she parodies
Isis, and Isis is associated with the moon partly because Queen
Elizabeth is, by virtue of Raleigh's name for her, Cynthia.

Just as Book III deals with the secular and natural counterpart
of love, so Book VI deals with the secular and natural counterpart
of grace. The word grace itself in all its human manifestations is
a thematic word in this book, and when the Graces themselves appear on Mount Acidale we find ourselves in a world that transcends
the world of Venus:

> These three to men all gifts of grace do graunt,
> And all that Venus in herself doth vaunt
> Is borrowed of them.   (VI, x, 15)

The Graces, we are told, were begotten by Jove when he returned
from the wedding of Peleus and Thetis. This wedding is referred
to again in the Mutabilitie Cantos as the most festive occasion the
gods had held before the lawsuit of Mutability. For it was at this
wedding that Jove was originally "confirmed in his imperial see":
the marriage to Peleus removed the threat to Jove's power coming
from the son of Thetis, a threat the secret of which only Prometheus knew, and which Prometheus was crucified on a rock for not
revealing. Thus the wedding also led, though Spenser does not tell
us this, to the reconciling of Jove and Prometheus, and it was
Prometheus, whose name traditionally means forethought or wisdom, who, according to Book II, was the originator of Elves and
Fays—that is, of man's moral and conscious nature. There are
still many demonic symbols in Book VI, especially the attempt to
sacrifice Serena, where the custom of eating the flesh and giving
the blood to the priests has obvious overtones of parody. But the
centre of symbolic gravity, so to speak, in Book VI is a pastoral
Arcadian world, where we seem almost to be entering into the
original home of man where, as in the child's world of Dylan
Thomas's Fern Hill, it was all Adam and maiden. It is no longer
the world of Eros; yet the sixth book is the most erotic, in the
best sense, of all the books in the poem, full of innocent nakedness
and copulation, the surprising of which is so acid a test of courtesy,
and with many symbols of the state of innocence and of possible
regeneration like the Salvage Man and the recognition scene in
which Pastorella is reunited to her parents.

Such a world is a world in which the distinction between art and nature is disappearing because nature is taking on a human form. In the Bower of Bliss the <u>mixing</u> of art and nature is what is stressed: on Mount Acidale the art itself is nature, to quote Polixenes again. Yet art, especially poetry, has a central place in the legend of courtesy. Grace in religion implies revelation by the Word, and human grace depends much on good human words. All through the second part of <u>The Faerie Queene</u>, slander is portrayed as the worst enemy of the human community: we have Ate and Sclaunder herself in Book IV, Malfont with his tongue nailed to a post in Mercilla's court, as an allegory of what ought to be done to <u>other</u> poets; and finally the Blatant Beast, the voice of rumour full of tongues. The dependence of courtesy on reasonable speech is emphasized at every turn, and just as the legend of justice leads us to the figure of the Queen, as set forth in Mercilla, who manifests the order of society, so the legend of courtesy leads us to the figure of the poet himself, who manifests the order of words.

When Calidore commits his one discourteous act and interrupts Colin Clout, all the figures dancing to his pipe vanish. In Elizabethan English a common meaning of art was magic, and Spenser's Colin Clout, like Shakespeare's Prospero, has the magical power of summoning spirits to enact his present fancies, spirits who disappear if anyone speaks and breaks the spell. Nature similarly vanishes mysteriously at the end of the <u>Mutabilitie Cantos</u>, just as the counterpart to Prospero's revels is his subsequent speech on the disappearance of all created things. Colin Clout, understandably annoyed at being suddenly deprived of the company of a hundred and four naked maidens, destroys his pipe, as Prospero drowns his book. Poetry works by suggestion and indirection, and conveys meanings out of all proportion to its words; but in magic the impulse to complete a pattern is very strong. If a spirit is being conjured by the seventy-two names of God as set forth in the <u>Schemhamphoras</u>, it will not do if the magician can remember only seventy-one of them. At the end of the sixth book the magician in Spenser had completed half of his gigantic design, and was ready to start on the other half. But the poet in Spenser was satisfied: he had done his work, and his vision was complete.

NATURE AND ART IN THE FAERIE QUEENE

Millar MacLure

The Faerie Queene is a fragment of a "continued allegory" in the "heroical" genre of Italian romantic epic, designed to celebrate the illustrious lineage and fame of the secular champion of true religion and civility, Elizabeth I of England, by portraying in exemplary figures the virtues which go to make up the res perfecta or "magnificence" embodied in her ideal prince consort, imaged in Prince Arthur; these virtues being severally represented in the Redcrosse knight (the purified British church), Guyon (the exemplar of antique virtue), Artegall (the armed justiciar), Calidore (the mirror of courtesy) and Britomart (the power of "magnificke" chastity). This structure, its outlines altered and re-established by the poet's developing "intendments," its confines expanded by "intermedled accidents," is also a treasury of subsidiary genres: the mask or triumph, the fabliau, the chronicle, the odyssey, the psychomachia, the dream-vision, the pastoral romance, the topographical poem; some of them merely caught in the interstices of the fabric, others woven into the larger design and so transformed. Like all heroic poems, The Faerie Queene is an anthology as well as an artefact; its vast expanse is littered with urfabeln, and it is accordingly an earthly paradise of dainty delights for source-hunters and mythographers. But if we look closely at Spenser's "goodly arras of great majesty" (the tapestry metaphor is inevitable) we discover that his primary working device is the emblem, that his "gallery of pictures" is actually a book of emblems, in which the "essential significance" (significacio) of each picture is set out at large.[1] Most readers would admit this description as applicable to the great icons of the poem, the Temple of Isis for example, or the Gardens of Adonis, but even where the narrative is most diffuse, as in the account of the rescue of Pastorella (VI, xi), we find a composition in chiaroscuro which expresses the "intelligible" aspect of the episode. Consequently an inquiry which, like the present one, is

Reprinted from English Literary History, Vol. 28 (1961), pp. 1–20, © The Johns Hopkins Press, by permission of the author and The Johns Hopkins Press.

concerned at least in part with Spenser's "doctrine," or, more precisely, with his employment of certain ethical and aesthetic assumptions, may well begin with the vocabulary of his icono-graphical comment upon his emblems, specifically with his use in significant contexts of the words "nature" and "art."

I

At the outset we are confronted with more than one difficulty. The words "nature" and "art" were pretty well worn down before Spenser began to use them; granted there is a residual distinction between nature as what is given, the universal order of creation, including human nature, and art as what is made, what man makes, it is also proper to speak of nature as the art or "signature" of God, and of art as the distinguishing quality or evidence of man's nature. A poet, unlike a philosopher, may either use the terms precisely, with an awareness of this paradox, or loosely, as coun-ters of the common speech, and Spenser does both. Secondly, we cannot be sure how carefully Spenser uses his words, or, to put the problem in the terms I have just used, whether all contexts are equally significant. Spenser is no metaphysical poet, and the parts of The Faerie Queene vary greatly in intensity, so that what seems to be a critical word or phrase or image in one place may well be a cliché in another. For example, when Guyon is overthrown by Britomart, Spenser comments on his "hard fortune" in being over-come by a "single damzell" (III, i, 8); "fortune" is a colorless word there, but when Artegall foolishly commits his virtue to the "for-tune" of the bout with Radigund (V, iv, 47; v, 5), or when the de-monic counterfeit of Una babbles to the Redcrosse knight of her "cruell fate" and captivity to "fortune" (I, i, 51–2), the connotations are most vivid and important. On the other hand, the curious and inelegant phrase "graceless chaunce," used of the wound dealt to Cambell by Priamond (IV, ii, 8) is surely empty of the usual signif-icances of its components.

To distinguish between the significant and the casual is not, how-ever, so difficult a task as only to be resolved intuitively. When Spenser employs such terms as "nature" and "art" to make his moral vision explicit and exemplary, we may with modest confi-dence begin by assigning to each a certain set of values or train of associations. Indeed it is in this frame of reference that most of the discussion of this subject has been carried on, especially since C. S. Lewis observed, provocatively and incorrectly, that except in the House of Alma, Spenser always uses "art" (i.e. pictures, arte-facts) "to suggest the artificial in its bad sense."[2]

172

NATURE AND ART IN THE FAERIE QUEENE

I begin, then, with the most obvious consideration, that for Spenser the "natural" is good and the "unnatural" evil. That is good which fulfils the law of its own kind within a universal order, and this order is imaged, in The Faerie Queene, in terms of generation, which distinguishes it from the order of grace.[3] The cosmic dimension of generation, presided over by "that celestial powre" Genius, is shaped by the myth of Venus and Adonis in the Gardens of Adonis, its cyclical aspect represented by the Florimell-Marinell Myth, the marriage of the Thames and the Medway and the pageant of the seasons; its beauty and benignity is expressed in very plesaunce, tree, flower and glade which decks the landscape of fairyland; at the human level, history and national destiny grow out of genealogies into the unions of Arthur and Gloriana, Artegall and Britomart, and the crown of virtue is set upon wedded and fruitful loves, upon that "naturall affection" which "of honor and all vertue is / The roote, and brings forth glorious flowres of fame" (IV, proem, 2). Nature works her revenges upon those who reject her behests, as upon Marinell, who refrained from the "course of nature" and was "loues enimy" (III. iv, 26), or those who "vnxitly" restrain or pervert natural desires, the Malbecco-Hellenore marriage (III, ix) being a persuasive exemplum of this. Spenser's most terrifying images of the "unnatural" are the giant-twins Argante and Ollyphant (III. vii, 37 ff; xi, 4), begotten of incest, themselves incestuous 'gainst natures law," and practising sodomy and bestiality.

Spenser emphasizes what we should now call the nymphomania of Argante, and this, taken with his account of Hellenore's contented indulgence in repeated copulation with the satyr (III, x, 48—51), suggests that he is admitting another sense of "nature." He knew all about the libido. That universal power of Eros which in noble natures like Britomart provokes the elegant passions of love-melancholy is an indifferent power, the moving force of all creation,[4] having the qualities of that "Nature" to whom Shakespeare's Edmund vows his service; unrestrained by civility, that is by "art," it issues in what we call animality. The inevitable emblem of it is, for Spenser, the satyr. The satyrs, when Hellenore comes among them, turn her into a servant, a "housewife" and sex-machine; when they are confronted by Una, they are "astonied" by her beauty and worship her as a "Goddess of the wood" (I, vi, 9—19), seeking unsuccessfully to adapt her to that "natural religion" in which Hellenore happily presides as their "May-lady." In the upper bracket of the ascending scale goat-satyr-man, Sir Satyrane displays the natural virtues of courage and stability, and is capable of learning Una's "discipline of faith and veritie" (I, vi, 31), but he never manages to move easily at the highest levels of civility and virtue.

These are examples of Spenserian anthropology, of which more below; here it is to be observed that Spenser is aware of a primal urge, a chthonic power beneath the veil of nature, creating "infinite shapes of creatures," and "vncouth formes" (III, vi, 35). It is only a step through this mysterious intermediate stage to the imaging of the natural as fallen from that "incorrupted nature" of innocent Eden (I, iv, 47). "Is it possible," asked Hooker, "that Man being not only the noblest creature in the world, but even a very world in himself, his transgressing the Law of his Nature should draw no manner of harm after it?"[5] Indeed it did, "a sickness in the natural powers,"[6] a decay of the world, which Spenser accepts and explains with conventional astronomical evidence in the elegiac proem to Book V; Artegall labors in a degenerate world, for the policing of which he was trained upon wild beasts (V, i, 7–8). But Spenser goes farther than this, and at times seems to take what if he were a theologian we might call a manichean position: "loathly crime" is "ingenerate in fleshly slime" (III, vi, 3); in the "first seminarie of all things that are borne to liue and die" Genius clothes the "naked babes" with "sinfull mire" (III, vi, 32); "all flesh doth frailtie breed" (II, i, 52). Maleger, that nightmare life in death or image of mortal melancholia, revives at the touch of earth his mother (II, xi, 45), that earth whose secrets lie hid in the womb of Night, the "most auncient Grandmother of all" (I, v, 22).

As with nature, so with art. Art also is "good." When nature and art are compared, considered either as opposed or complementary, "nature" has the sense of a forming power, a "mother wit" (IV, x, 21). And although this power may occasionally create perfections beyond the reach of art to express (III, proem, 2; IV, vi, 20), these are not common, and generally art fulfils nature's sometimes inchoate purposes or brings natural forms to perfection.[7] Generally in Spenser's ethical scheme "the arts" are, as Aristotle observed,[8] the voices of reason and framers of civility. The culture-hero Bladud, who "in arts / Exceld at Athens all the learned preace," brought them to Britain and "with sweet science mollifide [the] stubborne harts" of a "salvage nation" (II, x, 7, 25). "Wise words," words "well dispost" have the power which Orphean music has to reduce discord to harmony (IV, ii, i–2), and to assert the rule of reason over the passions; rhetoric has "secret powre t'appease inflamed rage" (II, viii, 26). But the chief images of the glory and goodness of art are those in which art, conceived of either as working upon the "stuffe" of nature, or as bringing nature's forms to perfection, creates a splendid order. There may be some element of bourgeois naiveté, there is certainly something which we recognize as characteristically "Elizabethan" in Spenser's worshipful delineations of the highly decorated and dazzlingly intricate, of precious natures wrought by art into more precious emblems of nobility and virtue.[9] To this order belong the panoply of Prince Arthur at his first appearance (I, vii, 29 ff.), the illuminated New Testament which the Redcrosse knight gives to Arthur (I, ix, 19), Gloriana's House of Fame, "that bright towre built of christall cleene" (I, x, 58), the garments of Belphoebe (II, iii, 26–7). God's "art" is more austere, as in the "faire and excellent" workmanship of the human body, the House of Alma, wherein the "great workmans skill" is displayed in the "goodly diapase" of its sacred proportions (II, ix, 22), and culminates in the "wondrous power" and skill of the brain with its three chambers.

But just as the generative force in nature may be darkly imaged as a libertine and mysterious power, so there is in art a kind of fascination and mystery, producing effects "straunge and miraculous" (to use Puttenham's phrase). Such, in innocent contexts enough, are the "curious slights" in the carving of Arthur's ivory scabbard (I, vii, 30), or the "curiously embost" girdle of Florimell's chastity, which came from Mount Acidale (IV, iv, 15; v, 5); such also is the iron cloak of Mammon:

> A worke of rich entayle and curious mould,
> Wouen with antickes and wild imagery. (III, vii, 4)

With these beauties we enter the ambiguous world of the occult arts, in which it is hard to distinguish good from evil. Arthur's shield was fashioned by Merlin, and Britomart's spear by Bladud, it is true; and, on the other side, the Protean powers and infernal arts of Archimago belong in the black realm with Malengin. But in Merlin's cave Britomart faces the terror which accompanies powers which are beyond good and evil, capable of subverting the order of nature (III, iii, 8–14).

The really sinister aspect of art lies, however, in its power to counterfeit (in our sense, not Sidney's) nature, to deceive by a trompe l'oeil. It is a commonplace, as Miss Tuve has observed,[10] that Elizabethans liked their pictures to be "lifelike"; Spenser praises the "life-resembling pencill" or its equivalent more than once and would subscribe in general to the praise of that art which conceals art. Shakespeare, in praise of Julio Romano, speaks of him as being perfectly Nature's "ape";[11] the idea of art as ape of nature is a commonplace at least from the time of Jean de Meun.[12] But, as no reader of The Faerie Queene (or of C. S. Lewis) can fail to notice, Spenser chooses to present this capacity of art chiefly in its demonic aspect, as a means of deception and temptation, as analogous to diabolus simius dei. The most conspicuous examples of the demonic artificial are the House of Busirane and the Bower of Bliss, but there are others less suggestive and less complex, and I shall begin with them.

The first example in the poem of the forgeries of evil is the lady whom Archimago frames of "liquid ayre" to counterfeit Una,

> So liuely, and so like in all mens sight,
> That weaker sence it could have rauisht quight:
> The maker selfe for all his wondrous witt,
> Was nigh beguiled with so goodly sight.   (I, i, 45)

The implicit reference to the Pygmalion legend is significant; there is something strangely ravishing about the counterfeit, perhaps because it is counterfeit, its whole being directed to one end, to be lifelike. Consider the effect of the false Florimell, framed by the old witch to ease the love-melancholy of her wicked son, "a wondrous worke,"

> Whose like on earth was neuer framed yit,
> That euen Nature selfe enuide the same,
> And grudg'd to see the counterfet should shame
> The thing it selfe.   (III, viii, 5)

The art of her making is compared to that of a "guilefull Goldsmith" who spreads "golden foyle" over some baser metal, and so deceives all eyes, "so forged things do fairest shew" (IV, v, 15). Actually the false Florimell is a robot, a dead carcase activated by a "spright" or fallen angel (III, viii, 6–8), and her components are those employed by the sonneteers to describe their ladies: snow, "vermily," lamps for eyes, golden wire for hair. She (or rather her governing spright) knows all the arts of love, of advance and withdrawal (IV, ii, 9), is "learned" in love like Paridell when he woos Hellenore with his "sleights" and "false engins" (III, x, 6–7). For the art of words may also be perverted, as in the sophistical elegance of Despair's rhetoric, those "inchaunted rimes" which so "enmou'd" the Redcrosse knight (I, ix),

or the art of music, as in the song of Phaedria the party girl, in
which she surpasses the birds' "natiue musicke by her skilfull
art" and perverts the parable of the lilies of the field (II, vi, 15–
17).

Before we turn to the diabolical arts of lust in their most
stately and seductive forms, let us go back to the guileful goldsmith, who was very busy about the palace of Lucifera, that ruin-
ous establishment covered with "golden foile" (I, iv, 4). Again we
notice that distinguishing quality of the demonic artificial: it assaults the senses, has no reserve, holds nothing back—the walls
of the castle "dismay" the heavens with their brightness, the
queen of it "exceeding shone" in "glistering gold" and "blazing
beautie," like a night-club singer uncovered with sequins. (The
house of Pride is very like Las Vegas.) But like Duessa, who
could "forge all colours, saue the trew" (IV, i, 19), and who as
Fidessa protests too much to fool any but the Redcrosse knight
while in him "the eye of reason was with rage yblent" and with
"great passion" smothered (I, ii), Lucifera can be quite easily exposed for what she truly is by prudence and reason. So may Philotime, daughter of Mammon, who sits in "glistering glory,"

> Yet was not that same her owne natiue hew,
> But wrought by art and counterfetted shew.   (II, vii, 45)

Guyon puts off the offer of her hand with sardonic courtesy, nor
does he more than "wonder" at the "garnished" Garden of Pro-
serpine, that sterile product of Mammon's art with its "golden
apples glistering bright." But when with Guyon we come to
Phaedria's island and to Acrasia's realm of bliss, we are on
more dangerous ground.

From examples already cited, it is clear that Spenser thinks
of the diabolic art as aping nature in what is, ethically speaking,
her most dangerous aspect, her abundance and luxuriance, evidence of that wanton dynamism which confronts us in every forest, tide-water and unweeded garden. For Nature, as Spenser
well knew, has her own hothouses, her display pieces, and
Phaedria's island is one of them,

> choisely picked out from all the rest,
> And laid forth for ensample of the best,   (II, vi, 12)

a "chosen plot of fertile land" in which nature hypnotizes the visitor by her profusion: every branch is at home to a singing bird,

every herb and flower is there, blooming madly, overwhelming the
senses and alluring the "fraile mind to careless ease," to what Mr.
Berger calls "lukewarm voluptas."[13] Phaedria does not practice
the arts of Acrasia, she simply takes advantage of nature's tropi-
cal aspect, and in her surroundings the humidity is very high. But
the Bower of Bliss is big magic, and not every reader has passed
through it as masterfully as Guyon, with the palmer holding his
elbow, or Milton, who knew what his sage and serious Spenser was
about. The motif I am in search of is adumbrated in the fifth canto
of the book of Temperance, in the short view of Cymochles at his
luxurious ease in the Bower, where "ouer him, art striving to compaire / With nature," twines the wanton ivy, and it is repeated at the
beginning of the elaborate description of that array of "guilefull
semblaunts" which constitutes the temptation of the flesh:

> A place pickt out by choice of best aliue,
> That natures worke by art can imitate:
> In which what euer in this worldly state
> Is sweet, and pleasing vnto liuing sense,
> Or that may dayntiest fantasie aggrate,
> Was poured forth with plentifull dispence,
> And made there to abound with lauish affluence. (II, xii, 42)

The "nature" that art strives to imitate is herself wanton, the aspect of nature which charms the passions, not that "niggard nature" which eschews superfluity (II, xii, 50), but that power which
"dights" the porch of Excess with boughs and branches "in wanton
wreathings intricate" (xii, 53). In fact this art, this guileful artifice which conceals itself, is in competitive alliance with this
wanton nature:

> One would have thought, (so cunningly, the rude
> And scorned parts were mingled with the fine,)
> That nature had for wantonesse ensude
> Art, and that Art at nature did repine:
> So striuing each th'other to vndermine,
> Each did the others worke more beautifie;
> So diff'ring both in willes, agreed in fine:
> So all agreed through sweete diversitie,
> This Gardin to adorne with all varietie.   (xxi, 59)

This is a summary stanza, and a critical one. Though it is true
that, like the house of Pride, the Bower is insubstantial (xii, 43),

vain, like Excess its portress "clad in faire weedes, but fowle disordered," its attractions wind themselves into the passions through
the senses in the most intimate way because they exist, however
deceitfully, in the middle state where the natural and the artificial
are confused in a common enchantment, which is exactly imaged in
the behavior of those "two naked Damzelles" in the fountain, the
supreme test (it appears) of Guyon's continence, whose action is a
too-elaborate, too nice compound of the bashful (to arouse curiosity) and the careless (to entrap the sight). Together, in their game
of now-you-see-me-now-you-don't, they make up the most complete erotic spectacle in the literature of the English Renaissance;
the sweaty insistence of Shakespeare's Venus and the cool nocturnal loveliness of Marlowe's Hero alike diminish before their
charms. For this is not a burlesque show, merely illusion and
mechanized exhibitionism; this is sexual play, as old as nature, as
new and "artistic" as the diabolic stage-mistress can make it. Nor
is the tableau of Acrasia herself in her bower, relaxed after "her
late sweete toyle," an example only of art's counterfeit powers, except perhaps for the description of her negligée which hides and
reveals at once (xii, 77); within that paradise all is music, in which

> all that pleasing is to liuing eare,
> Was there consorted in one harmonee,
> Birdes, voyces, instruments, winds, waters;

the birds' voices tune their notes in "approuance" of the rose-song,
the lovely dangerous carpe diem lay, with its sentimental evocation
of the great theme of mutability.

The art of the house of Busirane (III, xi–xii), the place of love's
martyrdom, is essentially of a different kind, though its effects,
like those of the Bower, are at once insubstantial (xii, 42) and over-
whelmingly rich and strange. Here is no sinuous and cooperative
"nature"; nature exists here only as the inert "stuff" upon which a
demonic art has exercised its talent for "wilde antickes" and sterile splendor. What this art creates is something "unnatural,"
amour courtois as opposed to wedded love,[14] torture in love instead of joyful fruition, and creates it not by pretending to be what
it is not (as in the Bower of Bliss), but by assaulting the senses
and shutting out the natural world. Like the inner chamber of the
Castle Joyeus, where the scarlet lady Malecasta holds court, surrounded by the wanton tapestry of Venus and Adonis (III, i), the
house of Busirane is an "image of superfluous riotize," but it is
also a prison, a place of suffering. We have to turn to Proust's

brilliant account of the captivity of Albertine within the grotesque and elaborate ritual of Marcel's erotic fantasies to find anything in modern literature comparable to this evocation of the essential paradox of courtly love, that what seems to be the religious adoration of the eidolon of the lady is actually the idolatrous worship of love itself, in which the chief element of the service is the sacrifice of the lady to the god. It should be noticed that the house of Busirane is a mausoleum; not a palace of pleasures but an eerie place of "wastefull emptiness, / And solemne silence" (xi, 53). In the "vtmost roome" hangs the famous tapestry of "Cupids warres," figuring the metamorphoses of the gods under love's power and the disorder he has created in human society,

> the mournefull Tragedyes,
> And spoiles, wherewith he all the ground did strow,

and on the border, "entrayled" a line of broken bows and arrows,

> And a long bloudy riuer through them rayled,
> So liuely and so like, that liuing sence it fayled. (xi, 45–6)

The second room is hung with the broken armor of "conquerors and Captaines strong" who were victims of love's fury, and in the masque of Cupid, which is introduced by Ease in the habit of the Prologue to the "tragique Stage," the "euill ordered traine" ends with the figure of Death. The delicious shudder of fear which accompanies adulterous loves is suggested, but, more than that, the sense of helpless surrender to melodrama, to a "grand passion," which is, in Spenser's terms, idolatrous subjection to an "artificial" situation. The later tenants of the house were the nineteenth-century "decadents," and perhaps it stands empty now.

The distinguishing quality of this artifice is that it "confounds" the senses, not only by its variety and subtlety but by its surpassing richness. The motif is introduced at the beginning, in the description of the gold thread woven in the silk of the tapestry, lurking there "privily," yet showing itself

> Like a discolourd Snake, whose hidden snares
> Through the greene gras his long bright burnisht
> > backe declares.   (xi, 28)

We are perhaps invited to think of the Tempter in Eden, but this subtle glitter is intensified in the monstrous art of the second chamber,

> with pure gold . . . overlayd.
> Wrought with wilde Antickes, which their follies playd,
> In the rich metall, as they liuing were   (xi, 51)

and the "passing brightness" of Cupid's altar dazes the "fraile
sences" of even Britomart. The music of the masque, also, has
such "rare sweetnesse" that it "the feeble senses wholly did confound" (xii, 6). Here the senses, especially the sense of sight,
are "fraile" and "feeble" not because they are faulty in their operation but because more is presented to them than they can naturally
bear. For this is the courtly equivalent of the crazy-house at the
carnival, and like the carnival producer, in which guise he appeared
at Amoret's wedding (IV, i, 3), the enchanter himself is a grubby
"vile" creature, with a knife in his pocket like any travelling tough
(xii, 32). But he can wound Britomart, "albe the wound were nothing
deepe imprest."

II

I have suggested a Spenserian scheme for the relation of art and
nature in the ethical context: two corresponding paradigms of nature (good, indifferent or libertine, fallen) and of art (good, "curious," demonic). But in The Faerie Queene Spenser, without altogether forsaking his professed didactic purpose, succeeds in transcending it by imaging, first, certain anthropological and mythical
ideas of Nature (admittedly conventional and ambiguous) and, con-
genially, an apotheosis of Art. And first, then, of Nature.
The legitimate offspring of the marriage of nature and art is
the state; their pre-marital affair produces a love-child, the pastoral plesaunce. Hence the pastoral life is figured always as an
escape (as it is for Calidore), a retreat either erotic or contemplative, opposed to the life of action, and belonging either to the
freshness of youth or the wisdom of age. The middle-aged do not
belong in the pastoral world: for both the erotic and the contemplative share what the busy man, pursued by the Blatant Beast and
by anxieties about his worldly office, cannot have, carelessness,
so beautifully figured as the life of "careless bird in cage," led by
the aged Hermit who cures Serena and Timias (VI, vi, 4), and
longed for by King Lear. Carelessness does not involve license
but sobriety, "so taught of nature," as Meliboee tells Calidore,
"which doth little need / Of forreine helpes to lifes due nourishment" (VI, ix, 20). This "carelessness," be it noted, is different
from that celebrated in Phaedria's song (II, vi, 15-7), which is an
invitation to idleness and its evil consequences; this is an acceptance of one's fortune and the consequence, which is wisdom—so
Meliboee advises Calidore (ix, 29-30), nor does it exclude the
performance of simple "natural" duties.[15]

For all that, the pastoral life is relaxed, and it has its active
counterpart in the plain heroic life, which like the shepherds' way
despises "superfluities" as non-natural. In "the antique world,"
Guyon asserts in his argument with Mammon, before man began
with "cursed hand" to mine the earth for gold and silver, man
lived in "unreproued truth" (II, vii, 15–7). This is the "plaine
Antiquitie" which was once to be found in princes' courts (and now
only in the "pure minde" of England's Eliza), in which the "high
heroicke spright" contends for honor and not for "worldly mucke."
Belphoebe, who has withdrawn from the "pompe of proud estate,"
sings the praises of this dedicated life:

> Abroad in armes, at home in studious kind
> Who seekes with painfull toile, shall honor soonest find.
> In woods, in waues, in warres she wonts to dwell,
> And will be found with perill and with paine;
> Ne can the man, that moulds in idle cell,
> Vnto her happie mansion attaine:
> Before her gate high God did Sweat ordaine.   (II, iii, 40–1)

Such are the conventions of what Lovejoy calls "hard primitivism,"
and Spenser gives them their usual didactic applications. But
there are no noble savages in Spenser. Instead he takes over from
medieval paintings and heraldic devices, and more directly from
masques, pageants and triumphs, that is from the arts, the figure
variously called the "salvage man," wodehouse, wodewose, wild
man, or homo ferus.[16] The homo ferus was believed to occupy the
place just below true man in the scale of nature; he was a pre-
Darwinian missing link—the term Sir Daniel Wilson applied to
Shakespeare's Caliban, who shares some at least of his qualities
with this conventional figure.[17] It is in this guise that Artegall
first appears, "all his armour . . . like salvage weed, / With woody
mosse bedight," and his motto salvagesse sans finesse, i.e. nature
without nurture (IV, iv, 39). It may be noted also that Artegall even
in his own form as patron of justice has been trained by Astraea "to
make experience / Vpon wyld beasts" (V, i, 7), one of the most
striking of the wild man's traditional powers being his mastery over
the animals, and Hercules, to whom Artegall is conspicuously compared, was also figured as a wild man in some medieval pictures.[18]
The genuine homo ferus, who was conventionally given to lust and
cannibalism, appears first in The Faerie Queene as the grisly ab-
ductor of Amoret (IV, vii): he is "no man," though taller than a
man, "all ouergrowne with haire," with hugh tusks in a hideous
mouth, naked but for a cummerbund of "yuie greene." He first
deflowers his victims and then cruelly devours them.

> But whence he was, or of what wombe ybore,
> Of beasts, or of the earth, I haue not red,

says Spenser (IV, vii, 7). There is a suggestion that he thinks of this creature as one of those uncouth and terrible forms that nature breeds out of the fertile earth; certainly he is lower by a good deal in the scale of nature than the "salvage nation" who take Serena captive (VI, viii, 35–49); they are cannibals and lustful too, but they have a social order, a priesthood of their natural religion, and they are called "damned soules."

Presumably Amoret's savage is uncivilizable, Serena's savages are semi-civilized by a "full wrong divinity," but the "salvage man" who tends the wounded Calepine and guards Serena (VI, iv) is a product of nature without civility, but of a more benign nature; he is, for example, a vegetarian "obeying natures first behest," and, like Sir Satyrane, he despises dread, having a rude natural courage and virtue. But he is a special case, for, as we learn later (v, 2), "he was borne of noble blood," and his nobility shines through even his rude and imperfect elements of social behavior. In fact he provides an example of the "natural" development of civil propriety in better natures abandoned to wild solitude;[19] his passions are developed but not his reason, and hence he speaks the language of the passions:

> For other language had he none nor speach,
> But a soft murmure, and confused sound
> Of senselesse words, which nature did him teach,
> T'expresse his passions, which his reason did empeach.
>
> (iv, 11)

Out of this rather confusing set of "natural men" begins to emerge Spenser's distinction between "the vulgar and the noble seed," and his doctrine of breed, which is conspicuous in the book of Courtesy, so conspicuous in fact that, taking the poem as we have it, we might say that Spenser thinks of nobility in the natural order as corresponding to holiness in the order of grace. There are examples of the base born, of the "base mind," throughout the poem, Braggadochio being perhaps the most remarkable instance, and we learn that Spenser agrees with Lord Herbert of Cherbury that skill in riding the great horse "seemes a science / Proper to gentle bloud" (IV, iv, 1), but these examples accumulate appropriately in the sixth book, in the "vile dunghill mind" of Turpin, and above all in the savage portrait of Mirabella, who, though "a Ladie of great dignitie" is "of meane parentage and kindred base" (vii, 28), and thus is set in careful contrast to the savage whose melior natura is manifest through his rough and wild appearance, as her baseness is exposed through all the refinements of a society lady. Spenser is at one with the Count of Canossa in The Courtier and with Posidonio in Nennio[20] in believing that "some there are borne indeed with such graces, that they seeme not to have been borne, but rather fashioned with the verie hande of some God, and abound in all goodnes both of bodie and minde."[21] Some are "by kind" so "goodly gratious," says Spenser of Calidore, that they win "great liking" in men's eyes by a kind of "enchantment" (ii, 2–3). Tristram is one of these "buds of nobler race" (Polixines' phrase); though he walks in the wood as a green man (ii, 5), Calidore hardly needs to be told that he is "surely borne of some Heroicke seed," so much is he the image of knightly strength and knightly courtesy. True nobility, then, is nature's art"; it is hereditary, and being occult to all save the "gentle" it is the property of the natural elect.

As there is an art that conceals art, so there is, in a manner of speaking, a nature that conceals nature. The open and ubiquitous sign of nature's law is degree, the hierarchy of conditions and existences in macrocosm and microcosm. Order is "Natures Serjeant" (VII, vii, 4), who disposes all the creation on Arlo Hill, and Order is Mercilla's "marshall of the hall" (V, ix, 23). It is in defiance of this principle that the communist giant sets up his scales to reduce all things to equality (V, ii, 30 ff.); Radigund with her monstrous regiment of women has thrown off "wise Natures shamefast bond," which is properly restored by Britomart (V, v, 25; vii, 42); the sad spectacle of Mordant and Amavia moves Guyon to lecture his Palmer on what happens

> When raging passion with fierce tyrannie
> Robs reason of her due regalitie,
> And makes it seruant to her basest part.   (II, i, 57)

These are commonplaces; but if we assume, as I think we must, that there is a philosophical as well as a formal connection between the "Cantos of Mutabilitie" and The Faerie Queene, an intricate paradox confronts us. For Spenser's beautiful Titaness

> the face of earthly things so changed,
> That all which Nature had establisht first
> In good estate, and in meet order ranged,
> She did pervert, and all their statutes burst:

> And all the worlds faire forme (which none yet durst
> Of Gods or men to alter or misguide)
> She alter'd quite, and made them all accurst
> That God had blest.   (VII, vi, 5)

Mutability is in other words the Fall; yet she too is Nature's
"daughter" (vii, 59), her claim (which is purely formal, for she
claims no more than she already has)[22] is accepted, and she is
"put downe and whist" only by invocation of the timeless world
of the heavenly kingdom. Nature's "doom" is actually a definition of her own contingent being: the <u>anima mundi</u> is the presiding deity over a continuous dialectic of substance and form,
movement and stasis, and is herself imaged as a veiled androgynous contradiction,

>   euer yong yet full of eld,
> Still moouing, yet unmoued from her sted;
> Vnseene of any, yet of all beheld,   (vii, 13)

one who reigns but does not rule, and rules but does not reign.
   The corresponding allegory of creation, in the Gardens of
Adonis (III, vi) is also highly ambiguous. The Garden is "the first
seminarie / Of all things, that are borne to liue and die," but like
most earthly paradises it is really an intermediate place, or place
of passage, for the "infinite shapes of creatures" bred there draw
their substances from the deep horror of the womb of Chaos, and,
on the other hand, not all the "naked babes" return "into the
chaungefull world" again, but some are "clad with other hew," that
is they pass into eternity, relieved from the wheel. The Garden,
we are told, is subject to Time, which troubles the happiness of
its fruitful progeny; yet "in the middest of that Paradise" is "a
stately Mount" crowned by a "natural" arbor, in which Venus enjoys her Adonis "in eternall blis," while the wild boar of Chaos
lies forever imprisoned beneath. This Adonis is the oft-trans-
formed "Father of all formes," which is the term applied to the
"God of Nature" to whom Mutability appeals (VII, vi, 35). Adonis,
then, is Nature; but so is the Venus of the fourth book, who, like
Nature in the "Cantos" is veiled and "hath both kinds in one" (IV,
ix, 41).
   The ambiguities of Spenser's "thought," which have troubled
many critics, can after all be resolved by recourse not to definition but to icon, not to argument but to art. Nature (either in III,
vi or the "Cantos") is "eterne in mutabilitie"—an "eternity"

sharply distinguished from the eternity of the order of grace—and
this mystery is imaged by the alchemists' hermetic androgyne,
the figure for the completion of the Great Work, for the transforming principle, the created creator of the elemental order.[23]
The image is sexual and within it nature and art are not at odds
but each blends into the other: the arbor of Venus and Adonis is
made "not by art" (such art as made Acrasia's bower) but by nature playing art's part (III, vi, 44); as Scudamour and Amoret embrace in imitation of the universal creative act, oblivious to time
("nor earthly thing they felt"), they come to resemble "a faire
Hermaphrodite" wrought of white marble; in the garden of Venus
Genetrix, art plays "natures second part," supplying all that "nature by her mother wit" leaves out (IV, x, 21). Furthermore, this
complementary relation between nature and nurture, between generation and civility, is imaged in the implicit correspondences between the Garden of Adonis and Venus' temple. Amoret is fostered
in the first and trained in goodly "womanhood" in the second. The
souls pass out of the wide gates of the Garden, under the direction
of Genius, by "kind"; Scudamour passes a "bridge ybuilt in goodly
wize" (in what, incidentally, is a curious mixture of the gothic and
neo-classical styles), undertakes the conventional romance test of
the shield of love, and its defending knights, and forces his way to
the inner parts of the palace past Doubt and Delay and Daunger,
figures of the artistic ritual of courtly love. As the Garden is a
breeding place of pleasures, so the temple lawns are places of
civilized disport for true friends and noble lovers. The temple
itself, a "goodly frame" of elegant workmanship, corresponds to
the sacred mount in the midst of the Garden: Concord presides
in its porch over her sons Love and Hate, thus repeating in explicitly human and social terms, the terms of art, the double nature of
the myrtle trees on the mount, which make a gloomy garland but
also drop "sweetgum" from their "fruitfull sides," bedewing the
place with "dainty odours, and most sweet delight." Within the
temple, the altar (of quintessential substance) and the "Idole" upon
it correspond to the arbour, the uroboros (IV, x, 40) to the imprisoned boar: the two of nature are fused into the one of art and the
linear thrust of time is turned into the cycle of recurrence.

The predominating note of the Garden is energy, of the Temple
restraint. The perfect image for the harmony of energy and restraint is the dance, and Mount Acidale (VI, x) is a dancing-place.

This dialectic of energy and restraint, outgoing and reserve,
first appears in the "parlour" or heart of Alma, where Arthur and
Guyon consort with Prays-desire and Shamefastness (II, ix), em-

blems appropriate to Arthur's quest and Guyon's virtue; its demonic and unnatural equivalent is the abrupt conjunction of <u>accidia</u> and <u>ira</u> in Cymochles, whose name derives from the uncertain sea (II, v, 37). In erotic terms it seems to be suggested in the figures of Cupid and Psyche, who dwell in the Garden of Adonis; there the emphasis is upon their offspring Pleasure "that doth both gods and men aggrate," companion of Amoret, while among the "beuie of fayre damzels" who sit in graceful attitudes at the feet of Venus' idol (IV, x, 48–52) the emphasis is upon reserve. Amoret sits in the "lap of Womanhood," whom all the rest obey: they are Shamefastness, Cheerfulness, Modesty, Courtesy "that vnto euery person knew her part," Silence and Obedience. The analogy with the Graces, who dance on Mount Acidale, is at once obvious in general and confused in particulars by Spenser's usual happy eclecticism in his use of his sources. His Graces, who dance with "Eliza, Queene of shephardes all," in the April eclogue of <u>The Shepheardes Calender</u>, owe their significance to Seneca, Servius, "Theodontius" and Boccaccio, and stand for "the triple rhythm of generosity, which consists of giving, accepting, and returning." The traditional names of the triad, Aglaia, Euphrosyne and Thalia, are assimilated to this conception by Plutarch (quoting Epicurus), and in Horace, in Botticelli (though in the <u>Primavera</u> the Graces have a significance not wholly equivalent to Spenser's), and in Jonson's <u>Pleasure Reconciled to Virtue</u>, the "characters of passion and restraint" are figured in the "decent" movements of the three.[24] Spenser makes the Graces teachers of "Ciuility" (VI, x, 23), and their dance, within a ring of "an hundred naked maidens lilly white" and about the "country lasse" who is crowned with a "rosie girlond," is the apotheosis of his art. For they dance to Colin's pipe, and the baseless fabric of his vision vanishes when Calidore appears.

The vision of the Acidalian mount, though it completes the pattern of the manifestations of Venus and her powers, inverts or perhaps transcends the assumed heroic values of <u>The Faerie Queene</u>. Its setting is pastoral; it exalts the beauty and virtue of a maiden of low degree, and even the knight beloved over all for his courtesy "mote not see" it—that is, he may spy upon it, coming upon it unawares, but not openly contemplate it, for it does not belong to his world, though he has received the gifts of the Graces, "which decke the bodie and adorne the mynde." If we wish we may explain all this by observing that the episode is Spenser's "signature" in the poem, his private tribute to two of his three Elizabeths, who were celebrated together in <u>Amoretti</u> lxxiv. But we note also that all the visions of the "divine idea" are veiled or withdrawn: in the realm of revelation the Redcrosse knight is granted only a Pisgah sight of the New Jerusalem; in the realm of nature the creative Venus is presented as a veiled "Idol"; Nature is veiled and, her "doom" pronounced, vanishes "whither no man whist." The mount of vision from which the Redcrosse knight perceives with the heavenly eye of contemplation is compared (I, x, 53–4) to Sinai, the mount of the law which governs men subject to death in nature; to the Mount of Olives, where the gospel of the covenant of grace was preached; and to the hill of the Muses, the abode of the arts. His vision of the resurrected body of redeemed man, Eden restored as a city, nature and art in one, dancer and dance indistinguishable, is the ultimate vision which comprehends and transcends the others, the "Sabaoths sight" to which the poet himself looks forward, and of which his own art in its highest reaches is a mysterious type and symbol.

THE CHALLENGE TO CHASTITY: BRITOMART AT THE HOUSE OF BUSYRANE

Thomas P. Roche, Jr.

The final episode of the third book of The Faerie Queene has never received adequate interpretation. By analogy to the final episodes of the other books Busyrane should be the great enemy to chastity, and his defeat should be accomplished through the virtue of chastity. Previous interpretations have not defined the allegorical appropriateness of Busyrane and his mask of Cupid as the climactic testing of Spenser's knight of chastity. The problem for the reader is to see how Britomart's experience at the house of Busyrane solves Amoret's problem and at the same time is the final challenge to her own virtue.

At the beginning of Book IV Spenser tells us the circumstances of Amoret's abduction. We are told that Busyrane brings a mask to the wedding feast, that it is the same mask we have just seen in Canto xii through the eyes of Britomart, and that by its power Amoret has been "conveyed quite away to liuing wight vnknowen." The initial impact of the mask in Canto xii is one of horror and evil, ill-suited for a wedding feast, but we should remember that it was presented at the wedding. This apparent contradiction can be reconciled by examining the mask outside the context of Canto xii. We shall see that its power lies in the essential ambiguity of its figures, an ambiguity that allows three interpretations, that of the wedding guests, that of Amoret, and finally that of Britomart, which is the one we accept as we read the mask in Canto xii.

The mask is presented by Ease, who is followed by six couples: Fancy and Desyre, Doubt and Daunger, Feare and Hope, Dissemblance and Suspect, Grief and Fury, Displeasure and Pleasance. Amoret is led in between Cruelty and Despight, who carry her heart in a silver basin. Riding in triumph, Cupid lifts his blind-

Reprinted by permission of the author and the Modern Language Association of America from PMLA, Vol. 76 (1961), pp. 340–344. A revised version of this article appears in the author's The Kindly Flame: A Study of "The Faerie Queene" III and IV, Princeton 1964. On p. 129 of this book, Professor Roche has a lengthy rejoinder to the reply to his article by A. Kent Hieatt.

fold to behold his latest conquest, and the mask ends with Reproach, Repentance, and Shame, followed by a confused mob of allegorical figures.

We may not immediately be struck by the appropriateness of these figures for a wedding mask, but we should see that Ease is a brother to that charmer Ydelnesse in Chaucer's Romaunt of the Rose,[1] and as presenter of the mask he introduces us to a world we have all seen under a different light—the world of Renaissance love psychology. This is love as mock war, the battlefield of the conventional sonneteer. Ease, the traditional figure of gay and irresponsible love, presents a progressive allegory of a courtship that might have been taken from any sonnet sequence; the twelve figures that follow Ease are sonnet metaphors come to life. Furthermore, Cupid and the first six couples are almost duplicated in a similar wedding mask performed in Beaumont and Fletcher's A Wife for a Moneth.[2] The context of this mask is the bold bawdry of the courtiers and country wenches who have come to see the wedding solemnities. Their knowing and amusing antics remind us that Beaumont and Fletcher's wedding mask is just another manifestation of Cupid the boy archer surveying his latest conquest.

The second half of Spenser's mask, which introduces Amoret between Cruelty and Despight, can also be interpreted in the light of sonnet metaphors. Cruelty is a personification of the metaphor of the cruel mistress or cruel love so common in the sonnets, and similarly Despight is derived from the medieval "despitous" lady. Amoret's main tormentors are those very qualities which have preserved her chastity during her courtship, and she is being punished for her long resistance to the power of love. Amoret, her heart "drawne forth" and "transfixed with a deadly dart," is followed by Cupid, riding on a lion and brandishing his dreadful darts. Behind him come Reproach, Repentance, and Shame, "and lastly Death with infamie" (III.xii.25). Even the bloody details of Amoret's predicament and the figure of Cupid can be viewed as dramatic presentations of common sonnet metaphors. In the context of the wedding feast Cupid is exhibiting not evil but the pride of the conqueror surveying his latest conquest. Reproach, Repentance, and Shame are exactly those qualities which would trouble the lady for her cruel treatment of the lover, and it should be remembered that ignominious death is always the threat to the scornful lady.

The mask that the wedding guests see is the mask of the triumph of love, in which Amoret, the prize, is about to surrender to her victor knight. It is performed in a spirit of jovial festivity, but it presents a view of love that considers only the male's trial in "winning" his lady. This is not the mask that Amoret sees.

Walking among the maskers at the wedding feast, she sees, not the personification of the sonneteer's psychology, but the vengeance of male sexuality on the chastely reticent female. The figures of Cruelty and Despight become for her physical torments of sexual love; the triumphant Cupid is not the allegorical representation of a playful metaphor but a promise of sadism. Her share in this triumph of love can only be reproach, repentance, and shame, the price of her surrender. This means the loss of a fastidious integrity, replaced by strife, sorrow, care, and "lastly Death with infamie." The dreary assortment of ills which follow Cupid corresponds precisely with the Christian interpretation of adulterous love. These are the effects of love outside Christian marriage, which presumably the marriage of Amoret and Scudamour is. Amoret makes no distinction between them; for her there is only the horror and enslavement of physical surrender. Scudamore is not mentioned in the description of the wedding feast, and he does not appear at all in the House of Busyrane except as an abstract masculinity. The mask which takes place at the House of Busyrane is Amoret's interpretation of the wedding mask. The guests see one side of the ambiguity inherent in the mask; Amoret sees the other.

The proof of this reading lies in the ambiguity of Spenser's presentation, which begins in the last line of the description of the wedding feast. Busyrane conveys Amoret "quite away to liuing wight vnknowen" (IV.i.3). This line can be interpreted in two ways. It can mean (1) that Busyrane took Amoret away to a place not known to anyone at the feast, or (2) that Busyrane took her away without being noticed by anyone at the feast. Now the first interpretation is ruled out because Scudamour does know where she is imprisoned. The second interpretation works on two levels. On the narrative level it means that unnoticed Amoret has been carried to the House of Busyrane. On the allegorical level it means that Busyrane has got possession of Amoret's mind. Thus the House of Busyrane—at least on one level—is Amoret's mental attitude toward love and marriage.

If the description of the wedding feast is a clue to the significance of the House of Busyrane as Amoret's attitude toward marriage, the description of the mask itself embodies the double vision of love suggested. The maskers come out in pairs, "enranged orderly." They are dressed and act appropriately for the qualities they represent; Spenser is quite explicit in his description. The picture they present is the joys and pains of love. Then Crueltie and Despight enter with Amoret. We are given a picture of Amoret and the triumphant Cupid, and here the description stops. Of Crueltie, Despight, Repentance, Reproach, Shame, and the other maskers we have no idea. We are told where they come in the mask, but we do not know how they looked. This seems to me purposeful.

The first six couples present the progress of an allegorical courtship in terms of medieval and Renaissance love psychology. The first hint of any ambiguity occurs in Daunger. Instead of the usual defensive figure (IV.x.17) we see an active figure with a net and rusty knife (III.xii.11), whose name, as C. S. Lewis suggests, is probably nearer to our modern word danger.[3] From this point on, Spenser's descriptions are both sonnet conventions and visions of the horrors of love, depending on whether we read them from the man's or woman's point of view. For example, Feare and Hope are the two figures following Daunger. Feare may be either the man protecting himself from his lady's disdain or the lady protecting herself from the figure of Daunger which has preceded. Hope with its holy water sprinkler is to the man his hope of obtaining his lady's "blessing and grace" and to the woman the hope of protection from a Power outside herself. Similarly the other figures, although traditional, betray signs of hypocrisy, jealous voyeurism, masochism, sadism, and finally helplessness in the face of superior power.

At the point of Amoret's entry the description stops. Spenser has set up his ambiguous mask in the description of the first twelve figures, in which the sonnet conventions are predominantly stressed through the use of iconographical details. For the rest of the mask the normal denotations of the names are predominant. The sonnet convention carries over, but we are forced more and more to see these figures as the names they represent in normal usage. The transition is remarkably effective, since by the time Spenser describes Amoret's wounded heart the reader is hardly aware that he has read the same lover's curse in sonnet after sonnet.

This double meaning in the figures of the mask is more than hinted at in the strange way Spenser concludes his account.

> There were full many moe like maladies,
>> Whose names and natures I note readen well;
>> So many moe, as there be phantasies

> In wauering wemens wit, that none can tell;
> Or paines in loue, or punishments in hell;
> All which disguized marcht in masking wise.   (III.xii.26)

Is Spenser not suggesting that the particular tone of terror that these figures present in Canto xii are the fantasies of one wavering woman's wit? But we need only look carefully at their names and attributes to see that the wedding guests could, and did, interpret them differently. The ambiguity of the figures in this allegorical courtship is the charm by which Busyrane gets possession of Amoret's mind. Who then is Busyrane?

A moment's consideration reveals that, although the episode may be clearly remembered, Busyrane cannot be recalled. The reason for this is simply that Spenser does not characterize him as he does almost every other important figure in the poem. He is called the "vile Enchantour" in abducting Amoret, and Scudamour merely names him "Busirane with wicked hand" (III.xii.10) and even when Britomart comes upon him, we are told only,

> And her before the vile Enchantour sate,
>   Figuring straunge characters of his art,
>   With liuing bloud he those characters wrate,
>   Dreadfully dropping from her dying hart,
>   Seeming transfixed with a cruell dart,
>   And all perforce to make her him to loue.
>   (III.xii.31 [Italics mine])

The general assumption that Busyrane represents merely lust is usually accompanied by the tacit assumption that he is trying to possess her, but this need not be the case.[4] First, Busyrane does not appear in the mask, and second, Spenser represents this kind of lust in Book IV, canto vii, where Amoret is rescued from rape by the fortunate appearance of Belphoebe and Timias. Third, the brief passage in which we see Amoret in Busyrane's power does not reflect the nature of lust in action.

Busyrane is trying to transfer Amoret's love for Scudamour to himself by charms, but the conventional romance structure of this episode should not blind us to its real meaning. He is literally trying to kill Amoret. His love is not sexual but destructive—destructive of the will to love within Amoret herself. Amoret is afraid of the physical surrender which her marriage to Scudamour must entail. The wedding mask crystallizes this fear, and she turns from a joyful acceptance to a cold rejection of the claims of

193

the physical. This is why Busyrane is the great enemy to chastity; he represents a negative force of which chastity is the positive ideal. He represents the negation of chastity, and this for Spenser did not mean lust.

Although Spenser gives no iconographical details to identify his Busyrane, we may learn much from the etymology of his name. Warton suggested long ago that Busyrane is derived from Busiris, "the king of Aegypt, famous for his cruelty and inhospitality."[5] Warton, I believe, is correct. Busiris originally was the location of the chief tomb of Osiris, and in later writers Busiris became the king of the place where Osiris was killed. The complicated traditions agree that Busiris is a location or an agent of sacrificial destruction and is associated with the sacrifice of Osiris.[6] The connection may seem remote, but we must recall the identification of Britomart and Arthegall with Isis and Osiris in Book V and remember that Britomart triumphs over Busyrane before she encounters Arthegall. Even more important is Ovid's retelling of the Busiris legend in the first book of the Ars Amatoria. This relates Busiris to the qualities I have been trying to establish as the traits of Busyrane:

> If you are wise, cheat women only, and avoid trouble; keep faith save for this one deceitfulness. Deceive the deceivers; they are mostly an unrighteous sort; let them fall into the snare which they have laid. Egypt is said to have been parched for nine years, when Thrasius approached Busiris, and showed that Jove could be propitiated by the outpoured blood of a stranger. To him said Busiris, "Thou shalt be Jove's first victim, and as a stranger give water unto Egypt." Phalaris too roasted in his fierce bull the limbs of Perillus; its maker first made trial of his ill-omened work. Both were just; for there is no juster law than that contrivers of death should perish by their own contrivances. Therefore, that perjuries may rightly cheat the perjured, let the woman feel the smart of a wound she first inflicted.[7]

Ovid's ironic advice to his hypothetical lover throws a new light on the Busiris legend and brings us back to Warton's suggested etymology. These lines betray an attitude toward love and women; it is the same attitude which underlies the conceit of love as war, and it is of particular interest that the well-known Ovidian treatise should link this attitude with the figure of Busiris. Here, it

would appear, is the nexus between the conventional figure of
Busiris and Spenser's Busyrane; here is the deceit, the sadism,
and the destruction which we associate with Amoret's plight.

But there are further possibilities in Busyrane's name, possibilities that suggest the sixteenth century usage of the word abuse
as imposture, ill-usage, delusion. For example, Sidney's sentence
from the Arcadia quoted in the OED is entirely appropriate: "Was
it not enough for him to have deceived me, and through the deceit
abused me, and after the abuse forsaken me?" or we might use the
obsolete form abusion, which the OED defines as "perversion of
the truth, deceit, deception, imposture," giving as an example
Spenser's lines, "Foolish delights and fond Abusions, / Which do
that sence besiege with light illusions." All of these meanings
are implicit in the etymology of Busyrane—the illusion, the deceit,
the sadism, the destruction.

What then does this make of Busyrane? Is he not the abuse of
marriage just as his house is the objectification of Amoret's fears
of marriage? He is the abuse of marriage, because his mask of
Cupid presents an image of marriage as a sacrifice, just as Busiris
was a place of sacrifice. He is an abuse of marriage because the
mind he possesses cannot distinguish between the act of marriage
and adulterous love. He is an abuse of marriage because the falsity
of his view of love can lead only to lust or death. His power is derived from the abusion of the mind in distorting the image of love.
The meaning he presents to the wedding guests is trivial, at the
most, lust; the meaning he presents to Amoret is the sacrifice of
personal integrity. Lust is the least complex of his perversions;
he is the image of love distorted in the mind, distorted by lascivious anticipation or horrified withdrawal. He becomes the denial
of the unity of body and soul in true love. And in all these respects
he is the chief adversary of Britomart as the knight of chastity.
Britomart's response to the mask and to Busyrane is that of the
intelligent moral reader, who can detect the difference between
true and false love.

This interpretation of Busyrane and his power over Amoret explains why Scudamour cannot rescue her. Amoret's fears are
based on moral and physical grounds. Scudamour can dispel neither. Unwillingly he is the cause of these fears, and any attempt
on his part to dispel them would be self-defeating since it would
mean her eventual surrender, the basis of her fears. Britomart,
on the other hand, can attack these fears on both the moral and
physical grounds. As a woman she understands Amoret's attitude
toward the physical side of love, and as the exemplar of chastity

she is able to make the moral distinction between marriage and
adulterous love. Her entry through the wall of flame gives her an
intimate knowledge of the House of Busyrane, and her understanding finally allows her to release Amoret from her fears.

Britomart's adventure in the House of Busyrane takes her
through three rooms, in each of which she learns something about
the transforming power of love. The first two rooms contain
images of love that represent the psychological suppositions of
Amoret's attitude toward love and lead easily to the more horrible
interpretation of Busyrane's mask.

The first room contains tapestries depicting the transformations of love. The description of these tapestries is one of Spenser's greatest poetic achievements; his mastery of the stanza
never once falters. This passage has been quoted out of context
so often that its function in the House by Busyrane may be overlooked. Its main purpose, however, is its depiction of the gods'
debasing themselves in pursuit of love. Jove appears in all his
animal metamorphoses, ravishing his mortal loves. The pull of
the verse is overwhelming, showing the ease and attraction of sin,
but we should not ignore the fact that it is a picture of love as
bestiality. The description of Apollo's love illustrates another
aspect of debasement. Apollo, the god of light, destroys his mortal loves—Daphne, Hyacinth, and Coronis; they are all transformed
into flowers. And so it is with Neptune and Saturn and Mars and
Venus and even Cupid himself. The love of a god and a mortal
brings debasement for the god and possible destruction for the
mortal. Cupid's victory over the gods is perhaps the original
triumph of love.

> Whiles thus on earth great Ioue these pageaunts playd,
> The winged boy did thrust into his throne,
> And scoffing, thus vnto his mother sayd,
> Lo now the heauens obey to me alone,
> And take me for their Ioue, whiles Ioue to earth is gone.
>
> (III.xi.35)

The second room contains transformations of another sort. The
"monstrous formes" and "wilde Antics" "of mighty Conquerours
and Captaines strong" display their captivity to Cupid in the pure
gold walls. In contrast to the bestial transformation of the first
room these conquerors conquered represent the effects of love
as destruction not only of personal but also of political power.
The scenes, although Spenser does not describe them, probably

196

illustrate the philosophy of "the world well lost." The images of love in both rooms share a common element in depicting love from the male point of view. With the possible exception of Venus all the images are of man transformed and the effect of this transformation on the woman. There are no Medeas or Pasiphaes. Both rooms present a challenge to Britomart.

> The warlike Mayde beholding earnestly
>   The goodly ordinance of this rich place,
>   Did greatly wonder, ne could satisfie
>   Her greedy eyes with gazing a long space,
>   But more she meruaild that no footings trace,
>   Nor wight appear'd but wastefull emptinesse,
>   And solemne silence ouer all that place:
>   Straunge thing it seem'd, that none was to possesse
> So rich purueyance, ne them keepe with carefulnesse.
>
> And as she lookt about, she did behold,
>   How ouer that same dore was likewise writ,
>   Be bold, be bold, and euery where Be bold,
>   That much she muz'd, yet could not construe it
>   By any ridling skill, or commune wit.
>   At last she spyde at that roomes vpper end,
>   Another yron dore, on which was writ,
>   Be not too bold; whereto though she did bend
> Her earnest mind, yet wist not what it might intend.
>
>   (III.xi.53–54)

Britomart is alone and cannot understand either the import of these images of love or their costly art in the absence of any human artificer or owner. The House of Busyrane to Britomart is but "wasteful emptinesse."

As if to tease her to a half-answer the gnomic commands present their own challenge, for these words are nothing more than the ironic commands of Busyrane. The first two rooms image the boldness of love: desire, pursuit, and victory. And yet in every case the victory goes not to the pursuer but to Cupid. Over the entrance to the third room is the contradictory command "Be not too bold," the most ironic of all. It applies to all those who think they understand the mask of Cupid. To those who see it as the wedding guests, it is a warning that the final triumph will be Cupid's. To the true lovers of this world it is a warning that the course of true love never did run smooth—even within the sanctity

of marriage. It stands as a cynical introduction to the plight of
Amoret.

With this preparation Britomart enters the third room. Alone
Britomart is exposed to the terrors of night and "hideous storm"
that precede the mask. After describing the storm and earthquake
Spenser introduces the presenter of his mask with a simile:

> And forth issewd, as on the ready flore
> Of some Theatre, a graue personage,
> That in his hand a branch of laurell bore,
> With comely haueour and count'nance sage,
> Yclad in costly garments, fit for tragicke Stage. (III.xii.3)

This tragic figure is none other than Ease, the traditional figure
of amatory delight. The theatre simile is not only appropriate to
introduce the mask; it also imposes a further unreality on the
action of the mask—the tragic unreality of Amoret's mind. The
ambiguity imposed by the simile is Spenser's way of telling the
reader that Britomart is seeing the mask in a manner different
from the wedding guests and Amoret, and therefore will be able
to resolve the basic ambiguity of the mask itself. This is made
clear by Britomart's reaction at the close of the mask. She runs
up to the door through which it has disappeared, but "it vaine she
thought with rigorous vprore, / For to efforce, when charmes had
closed it afore" (III.xii.27). And we are reassured as she enters
the inner room on the next night that we are seeing "Bold Britomart, . . . Neither of idle shewes, nor of false charmes aghast"
(III.xii.29). Without describing the process by which Britomart
comes to this knowledge Spenser informs us that she has seen the
mask as an idle show, the product of a false charm; and it may be
significant that this resolution comes from "Bold Britomart": the
boldness of love conquered by the boldness of chastity. Only at
this point do we catch a glimpse of the offender Busyrane, when
his charm has been detected. Only at this point can he be defeated. Spenser, perhaps wisely, does not tell us what his charm
was, yet from this encounter Britomart and Amoret learn the
dangers which Busyrane represents, and Britomart can bind him
with the same chain which had imprisoned Amoret. We never
learn what happens to Busyrane as Britomart leads Amoret to
freedom, but there is no need to know. He is no longer of any importance and, like his castle, disappears from the poem and the
consciousness of the reader. As in Petrarch, the triumph of Cupid is succeeded by the triumph of chastity, but Spenser saw that
even this triumph might prove empty and thrusts his heroine into
new situations in the legend of friendship.

SCUDAMOUR'S PRACTICE OF MAISTRYE UPON AMORET

A. Kent Hieatt

Many of us will be in sympathy with some of the views of Thomas P. Roche, Jr., in "Britomart at the House of Busyrane" (PMLA, LXXVI, Sept. 1961, 340–344).* On one important point, however, he is almost certainly wrong. It is not a shortcoming of Amoret, "lessoned / In all the lore of love and goodly woman-head," that she must view her relation to Scudamour in terms of the abusive Masque of Cupid, and that she must confuse her marriage with "adulterous" or "courtly" love. It is Scudamour who forces her into this position by his own practice of an aggressive mastery in the Chaucerian sense. He does not understand the love which depends on mutual freedom of choice and on concord, as in The Franklin's Tale; what he does understand is the imperious force of the love-deity who is imaged, for instance, in The Knight's Tale, in the Masque itself, and on his shield.

The two strongest evidences for this view are in the episode of the Temple of Venus in F.Q. IV.x, where Scudamour relates how he had first won his shield and lady.

The garden and temple, which he there describes himself as entering, belong, of course, to love, but of a particular sort—concordant and harmonious love, the affection characteristic of friendship (this, of course, in the Book of Friendship). Unlike the Garden of Adonis, where nature rules, or the Bower of Bliss, which is supposedly created by a deceptive art, this locus amoenus is formed by the ideal cooperation of nature and art, probably in the sense that natural love is reinforced by the art of friendship and the intelligent molding of free spiritual partnerships between man and woman and man and man. The famous friendships of the past are perpetuated in this garden; Concord, mother of peace and friendship and maintainer of the order of the world against chaos, sits in the porch of the temple and is said to be the one who opens the gate to Venus' grace[1] in the right way. The Venus within is, naturally, the inspirer of joyous love and procreation, but specifically her reconciling power is emphasized: as a planet she pacifies the seas with her smiling look; her feet are encircled by an

*Reprinted pp. 189–198.

Reprinted by permission of the author and the Modern Language Association of America from PMLA, Vol. 77 (1962), pp. 509–510.

emblem of harmony and completeness—a snake with its tail in its mouth; and she symbolizes in herself these qualities in that she is hermaphroditic. At her feet sit the qualities which in women make harmonious, gentle love possible: Womanhood, Shamefastness, Cheerfulness, Modesty, Courtesy, Silence, Obedience. And in Womanhood's lap sits Amoret.

From this allegorical locus of concord and harmony Scudamour forcibly removes her. He is enabled to do so by the image of the imperious, overruling Cupid on his shield, before which the figures of harmony are powerless. The force of amorous passion is stronger than they are, and Amoret is swept away protesting. Scudamour has mastered her (again, in a Chaucerian sense), but, in removing her from the temple and garden of harmonious love, he has rendered her liable to further removal by the Masque of Cupid. Removed she is, at the marriage feast. Scudamour understands only the second half of the couplet:

> Blessed the man that well can use his blis:
> Whose ever be the shield, faire Amoret be his. (IV.x.8.8–9)

The second evidence of Scudamour's culpability is more conclusive than the first. Roche attempts to explain the riddling inscriptions "Be bold," "Be bold," "Be not too bold" in the House of Busyrane by a single reference to "bold Britomart"—"the boldness of love," as he says, "conquered by the boldness of chastity" (p. 344). I believe that this is well said, but a much more convincing and central explanation is at hand in the episode of the Temple of Venus. Scudamour says (my italics):

> I boldly thought (so young mens thoughts are bold)
> That this same brave emprize for me did rest,
> And that both shield and she whom I behold
> Might be my lucky lot; sith all by lot we hold. (IV.x.4.6–9)

And on three further occasions he refers to himself with various forms of bold in this episode; he also contrasts himself with "faintheart fooles" (IV.x.17) and asserts his disdain of sly devices (IV.x. 19). A fourth use of bold, however, seems to me decisive. At the climax of the episode, when Scudamour grasps Amoret by the hand, preparatory to leading her out of the temple, Womanhood "me did blame, and sharpe rebuke, for being over bold" (IV.x.54.1–2; my italics). The coincidence is too startlingly right not to be part of Spenser's pattern: Scudamour has obeyed the injunction in the

SCUDAMOUR'S PRACTICE OF <u>MAISTRYE</u> UPON AMORET

House of Busyrane to be bold and bold; but he has now been "too bold." He has overstepped the bounds of love in asserting a passionate mastery incompatible with what he really wants, which is happy marriage, to be gained in Spenser's estimate only by the superimposition of a freely yielded and mutually willed spiritual friendship upon the equally important facts of Nature. Scudamour is at one with that Cupid who rejoices in having conquered all the other gods; he is following a master who is strikingly similar to the villainess in the Mutability Cantos: Cupid and she desire unique rule over the other powers, not harmonious interplay. Scudamour's boldness is really a kind of youthful brashness, and that <u>Keckheit</u> is to be contrasted with Britomart's temperate (if slightly schoolmarmish) encouragement of him in a moment of despair (III.xi.23–24) and with her informed boldness (III.xii.29. 8–9) at the climactic point, as Roche mentions.

Several Spenserian felicities follow from the interpretation I support here. The final episode of the Book of Chastity parallels the first one, in that both are Britomart's conquests of mastery: in the Malecasta episode Britomart of course quotes (III.i.25.8–9) the relevant couplet from <u>The Franklin's Tale</u>. And the events in and around the House of Busyrane are an elegant transition to the ensuing Book of Friendship, because precisely the element of friendship, in a Renaissance sense, is what Scudamour and Amoret's marriage lacks, and what Britomart allegorically supplies; although Amoret, mistaken like Malecasta on the point of Britomart's gender (but with opposite motives), is not to realize all the facts of the matter for a long time, according to the 1596 edition. In the 1590 quarto she is joined immediately with Scudamour as though "they had been that faire <u>Hermaphrodite.</u>" The fact that Venus is the hermaphrodite in 1596 suggests, by the way, something about how Spenser's imagination worked.

VENUS AND DIANA: SOME USES OF MYTH IN
THE FAERIE QUEENE

Kathleen Williams

The aim of this paper is to suggest and examine some of the ways in which the resources of classical mythology are used by Spenser in the third and fourth books of The Faerie Queene. Any such attempt must be made with some misgiving, for definitions can convey little of the deep responsiveness with which such a poet as Spenser apprehends his myths, and of the richness and fullness of meaning which they have for him. The present study is limited, therefore, to an aspect which I think it is possible to isolate in terms of the main themes of these two books: the relating of material, through myth, so as to outline what Spenser calls the 'general intention.' Even so limited a treatment must distort, by the drastic omission which is necessarily involved, but that organizing function of Spenser's myths which I shall try to isolate is, at least, one which should suffer less than others from the hazard of definition.

In the more recent of the many partial explications of The Faerie Queene, the third and fourth books have been, comparatively, little treated, except as they help to reveal the meaning of other books, as in the now time-honoured association of the Garden of Adonis with Guyon's Bower of Bliss. The most favored books of late have been those of Holiness and Of Temperance, and though many details are still arguable and are likely to remain so we have been made aware of the precision with which these books operate within the framework of their intellectual systems, theological and moral. Whatever the theoretical relationship of these systems, they are present as a scheme which supports a clearly outlined narrative structure: temptations are encountered and a quest achieved. The scheme helps, moreover, to guide our interpretations, including interpretations of the

The Annual Tudor and Stuart Club Lecture, 1960. Reprinted from English Literary History, Vol. 28 (1961), pp. 101–120, © The Johns Hopkins Press by permission of the author and The Johns Hopkins Press. A revised version of this article appeared in the author's Spenser's "Faerie Queene": the World of Glass, London 1966.

meanings contributed by classical myth, both where it is used directly and where it enters in the allusive form of an original adaptation, as in the case of the Circe-like enchantress Acrasia. So, for example, when Guyon encounters Tantalus in the depths of Mammon's cave, we relate him to the moral error which is here under consideration, and recognize that he is present primarily as the moralized Tantalus, signifying that avarice which is the less satisfied the more it acquires. Myth defines meanings but is in its turn defined, as to its central and particular meaning, by the precision of its context. Similarly, in the House of Pride, Lucifera's name alone would be enough to suggest, when she is compared to Phaeton, what the chief point of the comparison is to be. Lucifer, the star who fell, the light-bearer whose light turned to destructive fire, is paralleled by Phaeton who inflamed the sky 'with fire not made to burne, but fairely for to shyne' (I. iv. 9). Phaeton, appearing in connection with pride and with Lucifer who fell through pride, is related to a specific sin. Of course, this guidance is further enforced by the particular and local wording, as well as by the context of the book as a whole; for example by the repetition which makes the transition from Lucifera to Phaeton in terms of excess:

> Yet her bright blazing beautie did assay
> To dim the brightnesse of her glorious throne,
> As envying her selfe, that too exceeding shone.

> Exceeding shone, like <u>Phœbus</u> fairest childe.   (iv. 8–9)

In both these examples, mythological figures are referred to directly and briefly, but the same particularity of relationship is found in the more allusive use of myth and legend, where the original story echoes through the adventure of the knight. Guyon's voyage to Acrasia's Bower is like the voyage of Ulysses because Ulysses was a type of temperate wisdom; both he and Guyon undertook an adventure constantly repeated in the life of moral man, as Red Crosse achieved the unending quest of the Christian soul. The infinite resonance of the ancient and familiar stories is heard of course through Spenser's words: the steadfast toil of Ulysses, the pathos and waste of Phaeton's fall as of Lucifer's, the horror of Tantalus, and this is a great part of their significance. But in each case the point of contact between the myth and Spenser's narrative is exactly placed in relation to the book's central meaning, although that meaning does not comprehend the full significance for him, or the full effect upon us, of the comparison or the allusion.

Thus the first two books have, from the nature of their subjects, a kind of precision which in general it is not too difficult to tabulate. Structure and meaning are interdependent, and illustrative or enriching mythological material can be seen as exact in its primary function, so far as that can be differentiated from the aura of indefinable association which necessarily accompanies and develops it. In the third and fourth books this is, I believe, still true; but the structure, unsupported by a traditional or logical series of temptations and a final victory over dragon or enchantress, is of a different kind, and mythology is used more pervasively and perhaps with more complication. Indeed myth here is itself, in a sense, an element of structure, in that the meanings are in part built up by connections between a few mythological situations and, especially, mythological or legendary personages, who appear in some cases as themselves and also as elements in the characters of Spenser's invention. Thus the characters are inter-related by their relation to a common centre, and the shaping of the material depends to a considerable degree upon this common reference.

In such an arrangement, the myths and legends have to work rather harder, and must often have more than one such central and definable function. One of their tasks approximates to that of the Ulysses story in Book Two. Marinell recalls very clearly certain episodes in the life of Achilles, while Artegall no less clearly recalls both Achilles and Hercules. But even here the use of mythology is less straightforward. As a type of the just hero, using his strength to overthrow injustice and inhumanity, Hercules is relevant to Artegall as was Ulysses to Guyon. But whereas in the second book other aspects of Ulysses's character are not relevant, and we are given no opportunity to consider them—his reputation for craftiness, or for the betrayal of his comrades—in Artegall's case we are led, by the choice of incidents, to remember that Hercules had other characteristics as well as an unusual facility in destroying monsters. His labours as a whole properly represented the exercise of justice, but he was known also for his uncontrolled temper and for his readiness to submit to the feminine tyranny of Omphale, or as Spenser has it of Iole, who showed her power over the hero by making him sit at her spinning wheel. Similarly the fierce and wrathful warrior Achilles possessed a streak of feminine softness which in the centuries after Homer had been more fully treated by the narrators of new versions of the fall of Troy. The moralization of myth here takes second place to the paradoxical elements in the figures of classical story; different aspects are developed which establish meanings through their relation either within one character or between two characters. Spenser's attitude to the myths and legends is, rightly, arbitrary; as Diodorus Siculus advises, he 'takes out of them that which is to the purpose, and is in the form of a similitude.' Arbitrary, but never, I think, unjustifiable. The use he makes of them is always genuinely, if embryonically, present in the myth, is usually traditional, and is pointed to in Spenser's text. And through the deliberate playing of these 'similitudes' against one another, a considerable complexity of meaning is established in perhaps the most economical of all possible ways, that of contrast.

That Spenser makes much use of contrast within likeness has of course long been recognized, and parallelism between two complete books, Holiness and Temperance, has lately been rewardingly explored by Mr. A. C. Hamilton. But in the books which I propose to consider, the method is especially marked and works in a particular way. The figures of myth constitute a firm centre of reference, and the paradoxical quality suggested by a character such as Achilles can then be developed through similarities within difference, and differences within similarity, in a series of related persons. The structure and the meaning which is inseparable from structure here depend chiefly upon such relationships and not upon a progressive narrative. The contrasts, moreover, are now arranged so as to establish the meaning of characters rather than of events. Both, of course, are still important; but whereas in the preceding books one main figure has to encounter a number of different situations, here several more or less main figures have to encounter rather similar situations, and the most important point of differentiation is in their varying reactions. In the first and second books, it is important to know as exactly as we can what the cave of Mammon or the dungeons of Orgoglio are. In the third and fourth, it is at least as important to differentiate between the main figures themselves, within the context suggested by their relation to Achilles, Diana, and the rest, as it is to differentiate between the hyaenas, giants, wild men or foul fosters who throng their paths. Certain places, indeed, are in themselves important, as are the houses of Malecasta and Busyrane, the Temple of Venus, or Isis Church, which though it occurs in the fifth book has relevance to preceding stories. But even these contribute to the system of parallel and contrast between persons: implicit in them is an unavoidable comparison in behavior.

The stories of the chief invented characters, therefore, have a certain rough similarity. Of Amoret, Florimell, and Britomart, each is separated from or searching for a particular knight, but in every case the behavior of the characters is different. Arthur, seeking Gloriana, is another parallel with a difference, and he here serves to bring out further aspects of the theme. Belphoebe, as twin sister of Amoret, is an important part of the whole system of comparison. But Britomart, being both a knight and a woman in search of a knight, is related by likeness and difference to most of the others. They are the faulty attempts at solving the problems set by the figures of myth: she is the complete success. In this sense Britomart dominates the third book as fully as Red Crosse and Guyon do theirs. In Book Four she takes part, and powerfully, in the action, but there is here no one dominant knight. Instead we have, appropriately to the theme, a dominant group of knights, Cambel and the three sons of Agape, set in symmetrical relationship and forming, in themselves, a unity; a unity which is emphasised by another tournament which stands over against theirs, the tournament for Florimell's girdle, a scene of pointless and chaotic strife. As Britomart presents the theme of Book Three in its aspect of success and of completeness, so does this close-knit group present the theme of Book Four. But the themes are two aspects of the same thing, and to speak of the books as one is usual and, I think, legitimate. Technically entitled the Legends of Chastity and of Friendship, they examine the same subject, love, with slightly differing emphasis; love is a kind of friendship, friendship a kind of love. For this reason, the troubled adventures of Amoret and Scudamour, Florimell and Marinell, Britomart and Artegall, are continued in the book Of Friendship and indeed beyond that book.

The series of relationships which builds up both books is repeated in little, and in much more schematic form, within the dominant group of Book Four. First, the three sons of Agape unfold, it has been said, the nature of Agape itself. The differences between the three warrior brothers are real, but complementary, and contribute to a common unity:

> Like three faire branches budding farre and wide,
> That from one roote deriv'd their vitall sap.   (IV. ii. 43)

When two brothers are killed by Cambel, the third, Triamond, possesses both their souls, and all is knit together by a marriage between the two pairs of brother and sister. Thus the group presents an example of the workings of strife and friendship, and of love as an aspect of friendship; an example of concord, schematically shown through the relations not only of two warriors but of the two warriors and the ladies who restrain and accord them, the wedding of force with gentleness, enmity with love. This is a dominant theme of both books; both might be called the Legend of Concord, for the idea of concord in its Renaissance signification underlies the whole structure of likeness and difference, of inadequacy overcome by the conjunction of opposites which, when alone, are useless or even harmful. The subjects of chastity and of friendship are both developed in relation to true and false <u>concordia</u>.

The most precise and particular statement of the nature of concord is that given in Scudamour's description of the Temple of Venus. Outside the Temple stand two young men,

> Both strongly arm'd, as fearing one another;
> Yet were they brethren both of halfe the blood,
> Begotten by two fathers of one mother,
> Though of contrarie natures each to other:
> The one of them hight Love, the other Hate. (IV. x. 32)

Between them stands Concord, tempering them so well that she forces them to join hands, just as she keeps the world steady by holding 'with her blessed hands' air and fire, lands and waters. Concord involves opposition accorded, an equilibrium of opposing principles expressed, in another familiar version of the same conception, by the birth of Harmonia from the union of Mars and Venus. This Renaissance commonplace possessed both profundity and adaptability, and could be applied cosmically, politically, or socially; to friendships and loves, or to the completion of the individual human personality. By taking such a conception as the central idea of his books on love Spenser is able to include a very great deal, for relationships and cross-relationships like those suggested in the true concord of Cambel, Triamond, Canacee and Cambina, or in the imperfect concord of Venus and Diana, can be economically suggested. The idea of discords tempered was not only familiar to Spenser—it could not have failed to be that—but seems far more than an accepted commonplace. It is present elsewhere in <u>The Faerie Queene</u> and elsewhere in the poems. In cosmic terms, <u>An Hymne of Love</u> tells how love at the creation of the world set the elements in order,

> tempering goodly well
> Their contrary dislikes with loved meanes,

while in the human terms of the Amoretti the warring lovers are bound at last in a league that no discord can spill. It is through divine or human love that concord was most readily presented.

So in the two central books of The Faerie Queene the discords, discords incompletely or falsely resolved, and discords properly tempered in concord, are displayed through the behavior of different characters in similar situations, the characters being elucidated by their common reference to figures of classical myth; and these figures are themselves capable of considerable manipulation, since their attributes or their stories had already been seen as giving them a certain ambiguity of meaning. The two on whom I propose to concentrate by way of example, Venus and Diana, make an appearance in the poem in their own persons. Together, they form one point of reference for several of the characters: the problem of relationship, of concord, which they pose is developed in a series of variations.

Venus and Diana make their very spirited joint personal appearance in the third book, and are closely connected there with their respective wards, Amoret and Belphoebe. They are introduced, indeed, by way of explaining the nature of Belphoebe and, later, of Amoret. Their encounter takes place because Venus, searching for her lost child Cupid, enlists Diana's aid in finding him, and their conversation on the subject strikes a rather curious note. It has been described as a debat through which the two unfriendly goddesses reach a reconciliation, but one might more accurately term it a rather suspect alliance in which the two opposing principles are ready surreptitiously to borrow each others' functions, a false imitation of concord. Each is spiteful and jealous, but it is Venus who comes off best in the encounter with her suggestion that Diana's train of nymphs may not be quite what it seems. Here, she hints, is precisely the place for her to start looking for Cupid. The nymphs may well be hiding him; he may even now be present, disguised as one of them. The quarrel is smoothed over, but the suggestion that a hidden relationship exists between Diana's followers and Cupid is firmly established. It emerges into the next stage of the story, where the goddesses, searching for Cupid, instead find and adopt the twin children born without inherited sin,

> Pure and unspotted from all loathly crime,
> That is ingenerate in fleshly slime. (III. vi. 3)

VENUS AND DIANA

Why these two, who never know each other during the course of
the existing poem, are presented as twin sisters, has often been
considered. One modern scholar dismisses the relationship as
a caprice on Spenser's part, but more usually it is suggested that
their virtues are of equal value, or are complementary. It is also
possible that the sisters, offspring of a single birth, are complementary in the sense that they should not have been parted, and
that their relationship underlines, or is underlined by, that of Venus and Diana, who stand opposed to each other and yet have a
devious and hidden kind of kinship.

The kinship had been hinted at often enough, in art and in literature, and it could have various meanings, serious or frivolous,
sound or suspect, according as emphasis was placed. It survived
vigorously until the early eighteenth century, when that understanding Spenserian Matthew Prior used it in his Cloe Hunting,
and it occurs in a stanza, translated from Marot, which was
printed following the Amoretti:

> As Diane hunted on a day,
> She chaunst to come where Cupid lay,
>   his quiver by his head:
> One of his shafts she stole away,
> And one of hers did close convay,
>   into the others stead:
>   With that love wounded my loves hart,
>   but Diane beasts with Cupids dart.

Cupid shoots with the arrows of Diana, Diana with the arrows of
Cupid; a kind of complicated interchange is set up in which chastity becomes a weapon of love, or uses love as a weapon. That
arrows were used by both Cupid and Diana made an appropriate
hinge on which such relationships could turn. And Diana's ward
Belphoebe the huntress grows up to wound Timias

> Through an unwary dart, which did rebound
> From her faire eyes and gracious countenance   (III. v. 42)

even as she tries to cure the wound he has already received from
the cruel shaft of the foster. Indeed there is in the remote and
radiant figure of Belphoebe something of the strangeness of the
Venus/Diana exchanges. In the course of her pursuit of a wounded
beast she is led straight to the wounded Timias, one quarry re-

placing another. So in Book Two, where she first and briefly appears, the same pursuit leads her to Trompart and the hidden Braggadocchio, whom she almost shoots in mistake for her rightful quarry, the wounded hind.

In that earlier appearance Belphoebe is, of course, modelled on the appearance of Venus, in the guise of a huntress nymph, to Aeneas in Virgil's first book. Spenser's is an intricately beautiful passage in which both the Venus aspect and the Diana aspect suggested by the Virgilian parallel are emphasized and enriched. The long description is full of the sensuous imagery of the Canticles, while Belphoebe's clothes are an elaborately decorative and gorgeous version of the simple robe and buskin of the huntress. The analogy with Venus/Diana here is usually seen as relating to the allegorical meanings which were attributed to Virgil's Venus by neoplatonic commentators, Venus Urania manifesting herself in active life, 'the beauty of moral ideals.' Some such meaning is certainly applicable to the Belphoebe of Book Two, and indeed remains applicable to her appearance in Book Three, for throughout there is attached to her a splendour, a suggestion of the rarefied and ideal. But in the third book, where she takes a much greater part in the action, this does not quite account for her. She is here not only the embodiment of an ideal, momentarily revealed; she is rather a person seen as, and behaving as, an ideal. Her remote and not quite human aspiration is seen in relation to another theme, her innocence is considered in its effects upon ordinary fallen humanity. When Timias wakes from his faint to see her, we are referred back to Book Two by his speech,

> Angell, or Goddesse do I call thee right?
> What service may I do unto thee meete,   (III. v. 35)

which echoes the speech of Trompart and, with differences, that of Aeneas before him. We are still to remember Belphoebe as Venus/Diana, and still to appreciate her fineness. But the reminder is straightway followed, here, by the débat of the two goddesses, suggesting that in this book a further aspect of the Venus/Diana connection is to be explored, though without negating the first. Belphoebe acts out her story with Timias, and in doing so she shows her self from another point of view, that of human relationships. She accepts the love of Timias as the adoration due to her, and as requiring no return. As Diana's huntress, she can be loved, but the love must be manifested as worship; yet it is not clearly distinguished from Timias's tenderness to the wounded

Amoret, her unknown complement and twin, which is regarded as
a breach of faith. 'Is this the faith, she said, and said no more.'
And Timias is returned to her grace through the agency of a dove,
bird of Venus as well as of peace, with her present to him tied
around its neck, a jewel like a bleeding heart. But in or out of
favour the situation is at no point presented as a true good for
Timias, for by it he is not inspired to greatness but is kept from
his proper task, the quest, as Arthur's squire, for glory. Refusing to make himself known to Arthur, who is wasting time in
looking for him, he lives uselessly and ignobly, 'all mindlesse of
his owne deare Lord.' His devotion, it seems, should be to something else.

Spenser is here showing us, I think, not the result of worship
of an ideal, but the result of worship of the lady as an ideal, and
he regards it with sympathy and with scepticism. What Belphoebe
demands, and Timias attempts, is shown in action as a very uneasy thing. Her excellence remains, but it is too simple and one-
sided an excellence for a complicated world. Genuine in itself, it
yet produces a confusion of effects it never intends, when Belphoebe emerges from her own isolated 'earthly paradise' in the
midst of the forest of the passions. In the real world, the arrows
of Diana can have an effect hard to be distinguished from that of
the arrows of Cupid; the chase of honor can turn, however unin-
tentionally, into the chase of love. Belphoebe, set apart by her
innocent birth and by Diana's training, and at home in her own
paradise, seems never fully to comprehend the people she meets;
her behavior is not quite adapted to a fallen and a complex state.
The non-human nobleness which is a tribute to a queen operates
a little differently in the moral world of the poem as a whole.

Like Belphoebe, Amoret is brought up in a highly specialized
environment, and again like her sister she demonstrates the
problems raised, in the real world, by the simplifications which
are in place in an earthly paradise. But where Belphoebe is
martial and fiercely aspiring, Amoret is wholly submissive, for
she is reared by Venus in 'true feminitee,' 'In all the lore of love,
and goodly womanhead.' As a child she is brought up in the Garden of Adonis, for which in a sense her innocent birth fits her.
The Garden, one knows, is a complicated place, but so far as it
concerns Amoret it is simple enough, Venus's joyous earthly
paradise,

> the first seminarie
> Of all things, that are borne to live and die,
> According to their kindes.   (III. vi. 30)

211

There

ᵒ

> of their owne accord
> All things, as they created were, doe grow,
> And yet remember well the mightie word,
> Which first was spoken by th'Almightie lord,
> That bad them to increase and multiply.   (III. vi. 34)

As a place of natural generation, it is like the Golden Age—'There
is continuall spring, and harvest there / Continuall'—or more precisely the paradisal images suggest that it is a kind of Eden, where
sensuality is spontaneous, frank, and blameless as in the prelapsarian garden. An etymological connection was of course made.
The Garden is walled, protected, but threatened: time the destroyer is already within the wall, Adonis's boar is imprisoned but alive.
Here as in Eden is potential disaster, and the innocent joy of the
Garden is as precarious as Amoret's is soon seen to be. It exists
only by the rigorous exclusion of whatever may bring harshness
and pain. The Cupid who is allowed to enter is not the annoying
child or the hostile tyrant, but the benevolent husband of Psyche
and father of Pleasure. He must lay his sad darts aside and leave
the 'spoiles and cruelty' with which he has ransacked the 'world,'
the real and painful and fallen world, and here Psyche, her troubles over, brings up Amoret with the child Pleasure. In this aspect, the Garden is essentially the same as Love's heaven or paradise in An Hymne of Love, the dream of the miserable lover in the
real world, a place free from 'the gnawing envie, the hart-fretting
feare.' This paradise, like the Garden, is the home of Pleasure,
and she dwells there without pain and without blame. A similar
distance from painful reality is suggested in the reference to the
Garden of Adonis in Book Two, where it occurs as the equivalent
of Eden in the Elfin History, the place where the first Elfe, newly
created by Prometheus, finds the first Fay. Again the parallel is
with innocence, with love and indeed with life itself as natural,
simple, and protected, lacking all fierceness or self-assertion.
To attain concord, here, is made unnecessary, for the discord
which it should surmount is not allowed to intrude. Instead of
Mars, Adonis, an Adonis who hunts no longer; and even Cupid's
weapons must be left outside the walls.

   From this protected happiness Amoret has to go into the 'world'
of 'spoiles and cruelty,' of strife and inherited sin, where even
love is also war; into Venus's other domain, denoted by her Temple,
guarded as it is by Hate and Love, their hands forcibly linked by

Concord. In the 'world,' the meaning of Amoret's mythological background as Venus's ward is developed and defined by its relation to the tradition of courtly love. This is itself used metaphorically to express a certain attitude to human relationships which has its classical and its modern, as well as its medieval, forms, and which owes its enduring power to its expression (though its distorted expression) of a truth: that in personal relationships, and in love as the most intense and so most representative of such relationships, there is always an element of hostility. The truth as realistically and maturely interpreted can be found in the Amoretti, which are built up partly through variations on this theme. The lady is warrior, tyrant, even traitor, the lover is huntsman, and both fear the prison of love, the loss of liberty to the other. Yet at the close of the sequence the hostility is resolved, the prisoned birds sing, the spider and the bee live in eternal peace. But there are other handlings of the theme in which love stops eternally short of concord, in which the warfare and the chase are perpetual and mutual, in which each feels and inflicts pain, and endless revenge is disguised as affection. And of course the distortion is itself equally true to human life, and is portrayed by Spenser with equal insight.

It is this which the submissive and feminine Amoret, reared in a place from which all hostility is barred, and wholly lacking in the aggressive self-reliance which characterizes her huntress sister, has now to face. All assertion of self she sees as menacing and terrible, and what to Scudamour is a mere convention of behavior becomes to her an obsessive reality. Scudamour fights twenty knights, enters the Temple of Venus, and terrifies Amoret's guardians with his shield, on which, since he is 'Cupid's man,' the sincere but conventional courtly lover, is emblazoned the cruel Cupid excluded from the Garden of Adonis, 'Cupid with his killing bow / And cruell shafts.' He then leads out the protesting Amoret as the prize of his prowess, while the statue of Venus, with the doubtful quality she possesses in the human world, laughs her approval of the desecration of her Temple. Cupid may be shut out of the Temple, replaced by his small and harmless brothers; yet Scudamour his representative is, as he himself suggests, drawn in to that same Temple by its appurtenances, the danger, the parade of modesty, the white-robed virgin priestesses, the exclusive femininity. Venus, the great natural creative power of the universe, is ready to depend for the fulfillment of her purpose in the human world upon hostility, the weapons of Diana and the spoils of Cupid, upon exclusiveness set as a snare for violence. Human happiness, after all, is no part of her concern.

213

This, at least, is how Amoret comes to see her situation, when she has been taken from the Temple as Eurydice was taken from the underworld. The comparison is Scudamour's, proud of an enterprise as dangerous as that of Orpheus; the irony is Spenser's, for as Eurydice was lost again from the threshold of the living world, so is Amoret, on the day of her wedding, lost to the death-like enchantments of Busyrane, and imprisoned in her own obsession. The shadowy Maske of Cupid which conveys her away contains some of the conventional denizens of the Temple of Venus and of the courtly tradition, Danger, and Doubt; but now their traditional function is changed, and from the lady's devices against the lover they have become the torturers of the lady herself. Of them there are as many

> as there be phantasies
> In wavering wemens wit, that none can tell,
> Of paines in love, or punishments in hell.   (III. xii. 26)

Busyrane, who sacrifices Amoret to the destructive Cupid, is presumably named from Busiris, who made human sacrifices to his own god in Egypt. He appears in the mythological commentators and in Diodorus and Apollodorus, but most relevantly in the Ars Amatoria,[1] where he is directly related to the Ovidian (and in part courtly) conception of love as hostility and deceit, a perpetual strife in which concordia is seen as no more than the momentary defeat on one cruelty by another. Ovid's Busiris is an illustration of the theme that love is the result of deceit, which should be avenged by deceit. 'Let them fall into the snares they have set.' The victim is equally the hunter and should, as victim, suffer, so Amoret's Doubt and Danger are turned in more terrible form against her. Busyrane's house is decorated everywhere with the predatory and treacherous loves of the gods: gods as bulls or serpents, love which kills as Semele and Daphne were killed.

> Yet was thy love her death, and her death was thy smart.
> (III. xi. 36)

Everywhere is portrayed the mutual horror of a situation in which each punishes and is punished, 'all Cupids warres they did repeate.' Amoret is freed by Britomart, through whom she unthinks her obsession as Busyrane is made to unread his spells, but she is still not free from the cause of the obsession, the fear of assertion as necessarily destructive. Still 'His will she feard.' Her lack is

explained or typified in her past history, and she will not be free
until her own soft submissiveness is joined with its opposing
principle, gentleness with self-assertive 'will' or, in one of Spenser's figures in Book Four, the dove with the falcon. The incompleteness and consequent distortion suggested by the separation
of the sisters must be overcome, as it is, in the first version of
the poem, in the union of Amoret and Scudamour. The hermaphrodite image there used is a symbol of marriage, but of marriage
as itself a symbol of the necessary concord of opposites on which
the world depends, and individual human welfare also.

In the second version of the poem, this union is displayed not
in Amoret's story but in Britomart's. Britomart stands between
the separated sisters as an example of completed and integrated
human nature, 'aimable grace and manly terror' both, the great
champion who can help knights and ladies alike because in her
are united the masculine and the feminine, the self-sufficient and
the dependent, passion and chastity. In her Venus and Diana, Venus and Mars, are in true and unsurreptitious relation. She is
accepted on her own terms as knight and as lady, neither potential
destroyer nor potential victim; and, herself an example of concord, she achieves a further concord in her connection with Artegall.

How Britomart has become the invincible knight, strong because loving, loving because strong, we are shown after her first
appearance in the poem, in the account of her love for Artegall.
She has seen him first, and uncomprehendingly, in the magic
mirror, and her immediate response has something of Amoret's
confused horror. She hints of it to her old nurse Glauce as if it
were a brutal and destructive visitation, love for a shadow, unnatural and leading to death. The passage is based on the Virgilian Ciris, but it echoes also the talk of Ovid's Myrrha and her
nurse in the Metamorphoses, and it is related to Scylla, Biblis,
Pasiphae, and the whole Ovidian context of perversity and pain.
But through the commonsense wisdom represented by Glauce, and
through the sense of personal responsibility represented by Merlin, Britomart learns that human affections are guided by divine
purpose, that her eyes were led to the mirror by a higher power
than Venus, and that her vision of Artegall will lead to the fulfilling
of heavenly destiny for centuries to come. The looking-glass has
shown her not a shadow, an illusion, but a fuller truth than she could
otherwise see, for it is a little image of the world, a glass globe

Like to the world it selfe, and seem'd a world of glas.

(III. ii. 19)

Its virtue is to 'shew in perfect sight, / What ever thing was in the world contaynd,' 'What ever foe had wrought, or frend had faynd.' For Britomart love is a mirror of truth, a means to fulfillment through the concord of necessary opposites in herself, in her union with Artegall, and in the history of her race. For Merlin's account of the future history of Britain, where she and Artegall and their descendants are to rule, is more than a compliment worked in for the benefit of Elizabeth Tudor. It serves to convince Britomart that no personal situation is merely personal, but may have results that go far beyond ourselves. For her love becomes an instrument of divine providence, and she accepts completely the responsibility of the fully human being for its fellows. Her part, Merlin tells her, is to fit herself to cooperate actively with a creative and purposeful destiny:

> Therefore submit thy wayes unto his will,
> And do by all dew meanes thy destiny fulfill.   (III. iii. 24)

Merlin's prophecy is throughout in terms of the divine, and just, will, which deals with the Britons as did Jehovah with the Hebrews, supporting, checking, punishing; and in this process the union of Artegall with Britomart, of impulsive force with restraining wisdom, of justice with equity, is to play an essential part, culminating in the reconciliation of Briton and Saxon under the house of Tudor, mingling the blood and the attributes of each. In Britomart's story, the theme of concord is taken beyond the realm of the personal; what the others cannot attain is for her only a first step. Throughout, her sense of destiny and responsibility keeps her on her quest where the others, even Arthur, can be distracted, and always what is stressed is her constancy, courage, and perfect balance of qualities. She is, in the phrase of the moralizers of the myths, the true Venus/Diana, or Venus armata, as even her name may suggest: Britomartis, the nymph whose apotheosis as the moon-goddess Diana Dictynna is told in the Ciris. Later, in the prophetic dream of Book Five, Britomart becomes Isis the Queen, the power in whom, as Plutarch and Apuleius would show, all the goddesses are made one, Cybele, Minerva, Venus, Diana Dictynna. In the union of Isis with Osiris is the true justice which sustains the universe.

Complementary to the theme developed through Amoret and Venus, Belphoebe and Diana, is the related one more briefly hinted at in the figures of Artegall and Marinall, again in relation to Britomart, who both represents success and helps them, in their degree,

to achieve it. Here it is Achilles who is the point of classical
reference, himself a sorry failure in the achieving of personal
balance and presenting, in his single figure, an uneasy see-sawing
of opposites, extremes of aggression and passive submission.
Artegall owns Achilles' armour and emulates his wrathfulness,
and he re-enacts also some of the labours of Hercules. Whether
or not Spenser was acquainted with accounts of the ancient rites
and statues which accentuate this ambiguity in both heroes, the
common classical and medieval treatment would have provided
ample material. For Hercules, the subjection to Omphale, re-
enacted by Artegall, and death through Deianeira; for Achilles,
the disguise among women to escape the danger feared by his
mother Thetis, devotion to the Amazon Penthesilea, who thus conquers him even as he kills her (this too lies behind Artegall's defeat by Radigund), and a shameful death at the hands of the effeminate Paris through subjection to Polyxena. These episodes had
become, in Comes, Statius, Ovid's Metamorphoses and Ars
Amatoria, and the non-Homeric versions of the siege of Troy, as
important as the wrath of Achilles, and their shadowy presence in
the adventures of Artegall and Marinell suggests how a nature
which cultivates one aspect of itself to the exclusion of its opposite may be overthrown and enthralled by that opposite. Both are
exaggeratedly masculine characters; Artegall is first known not
as the champion of justice but as the wrathful, wilful knight of
salvagesse sans finesse, the 'tyrant' of the woods where he was
reared and the 'tyrant' of the tournament of Book Four. He is
conquered by the beauty of Britomart, his sword falling from his
hand, but in the same way he is conquered by Radigund, submitting
as totally to the wrong female warrior as to the right. Scudamour's
taunt to him at the earlier defeat, that he is

> now become to live a Ladies thrall,
> That whylome in your minde wont to despise them all
>
> (IV. vi. 28)

turns to literal truth in his degrading subjection to Radigund.
Artegall lives as the warrior who must either subjugate or be
subjugated, who is either all pride or all 'humblesse meek.' The
vision in Isis Church shows what the final harmony is to be. The
fierce and at first inimical beast Osiris/Artegall, now tyrannically
wrathful and now fawning, is to become with Britomart complete
justice, the union of opposed principles operating as the instrument of destiny.

217

The investigation of true and false concord which I have suggested as one function of the main characters is further emphasised in the story of Marinell and Florimell. As creatures of
sea and of meadows, wave and flower, these two provide a version
of the theme which underlines its cosmic scope; here one is aware
of concord as a universal law. But the story, interlinked with and
carefully related to those of Amoret, Britomart, and the rest, suggests also what I must now emphasise, that the mythological connections with which this paper has been concerned form only a
part of the complex organization of these books. Adonis, the dead
yet living god, and the hunt of death and of love with which he is
connected, form another organizing centre of meaning, and from
it stem the events of the forest, into which character after character plunges, among the 'Beares, Lions, and Buls, which romed
them around,' and the events, also, just outside the forest, in the
house of Malecasta. But the subject of the Renaissance Adonis
and his hunt is too vast, and its role in The Faerie Queene too
complex, to be more than touched on here, and it is enough perhaps to suggest that it is linked with that of Venus and Diana as
another, yet related, point of reference. Through it, love as
destruction or as creation, and death as an end or as a beginning,
are shown as part of that structure which is the concord of the
world. The flight and pursuit of Florimell, who is imprisoned
under the sea for the traditional seven months of darkness, contribute to this theme, but she contributes also to the meaning to
which this paper is limited, concord within human nature and
between human beings. In this aspect she too is a type of human
incompleteness, relating to Amoret, Britomart and Belphoebe in
terms of concord and of course of chastity, for each of them portrays one kind of chastity and one kind of love.

Florimell's search for the knight Marinell proves to be very
different from Britomart's steady search for Artegall. From the
beginning it is in effect a mindless flight, dispersing and distracting the knights from their quests. Only Britomart, apparently
rightly, refuses to follow 'beauty's chase.' A chase, a hunt, is
indeed what it soon proves to be, and one of peculiarly futile nature; a flight which, like that of the eternally fleeing nymph, initiates and intensifies pursuit and so helps to bring about the very
chase which it is intended to escape. Florimell fears good and
bad without distinction, 'fears every leaf,' and is compared time
and again to a dove, a hind, fleeing without discrimination from
whatever approaches it. When she first flies past with the streaming hair which is in these books the mark of feminine power she is

compared also to a comet, the blazing star 'with flaming lockes dispred' which bodes misfortune. Like it, she has no ill intentions of her own, yet she is a source of confusion, turning even Arthur aside into the forest because she seems, in her momentary appearance, something like Gloriana herself. On the other hand she can also be parodied, to the conviction of most of the characters concerned, by the false spirit which is summoned to imitate and impersonate her and which 'all the wyles of wemens wits knew passing well.' Only when flight is no longer possible for Florimell, and she has been compelled to resist by her own will and resourcefulness the power of Proteus, can she reach Marinell, who has himself been changed by the action of Britomart. Originally a minor Achilles, fiercely acquisitive yet weakly self-protective, Marinell grows after his wounding by Britomart into a being capable of pity. And at last these two, negative and even destructive in isolation for all their beauty, are tempered and absorbed into the creativeness of the sea, now no longer the cruel source of Marinell's riches, cast up from 'the wreckes of many wretches' upon the Precious Shore, but a place of fecundity and life.

Spenser's theme of reconciliation requires more intricacy in the shaping than do the subjects of some other books of The Faerie Queene, for this is a quest in which one cannot expect to meet one's temptations neatly in turn, as in the achieving of temperance. The way to true concordia is shown by presenting also several mistaken ways which yet resemble the true. But Spenser's knowledge of the human mind is as accurate here as elsewhere, and his methods though more intricate are no less planned. Through his interlinked stories he develops his truth that concord is in every sphere a state of equilibrium, not of subjugation and submission, flight and pursuit, that the war of opposites is one which both contenders are, in a sense, to win, for each is necessary to the completion of the other.

COLIN CLOUT'S COURTESY

R. F. Hill

Modern readers and critics of Spenser's Legend of Courtesie easily accept C. S. Lewis's view that 'the shepherd's country and Mount Acidale in the midst of it are the core of the book, and the key to Spenser's whole conception of Courtesy' (Allegory of Love, 1936, p. 350). The feeling remains even when one is puzzled in the attempt to fit the details of the allegory into the scheme of courtesy, for the compactness and the poetic brilliance of the pastoral cantos raise them far above the rest of Book VI. Besides, only these cantos, especially Colin Clout's vision in canto x, can parallel in allegorical significance those various instructive 'Houses' in the other books which embody the allegorical core of those books. Furthermore, confirmatory evidence of the high significance of the Colin Clout episode in Spenser's conception of courtesy may be inferred from structure; it occurs in canto x, just before the dénouement and capture of the Blatant Beast, the position reserved in four of the five remaining full-length books for incidents climactic to the particular virtue treated, or providing an epitome of its salient features: Book I, canto x, the Red Cross knight in the House of Holiness; Book II, cantos ix and x, Sir Guyon and Prince Arthur in the House of Temperance; Book IV, canto x, Sir Scudamour's description of his quest for Amoret in the Temple of Venus; Book V, canto ix, Sir Artegall and Prince Arthur in the Palace of Mercilla.

Thus, the presumptive importance of the pastoral 'truancy' is soon established but divergencies of opinion emerge once the degree of importance is assessed and the allegory is pressed for detailed significance. Colin Clout's vision is especially prone to variant interpretation since its difficulties tend to drive critics into simplifications based upon partial readings. The matter is the more vexing because the different interpretations are not mutually exclusive; we expect complexity of meaning from a poet who is characteristically synthetic in his thought processes.

Reprinted from Modern Language Review, Vol. 57 (1962), pp. 492–503, by permission of the author and The Modern Humanities Research Association.

There is a graceful and perceptive study of Spenser's ideal of courtesy by H. C. Chang, Allegory and Courtesy in Spenser (Edinburgh, 1955). Since I am in agreement with him almost everywhere, differing only in emphasis, detailed reference here is out of the question. Many of his points are inevitably restated in this essay, especially his insistence on true courtesy as the outward expression of inner grace. What more I have to say assumes fundamental agreement with Chang's interpretation which I extend only at Spenser's prompting. Of other opinions on the Colin Clout episode only two are isolated for comment, as indicative of the degree of divergence and as opening the way to an interpretation not exclusive but, I believe, more faithful to all the details of the allegory. C. S. Lewis suggests that Calidore's sojourn in the shepherds' country implies that for Spenser courtesy 'has very little connexion with court' and that courtesy—in its perfect form— is a natural, not an acquired or artificial grace (Allegory of Love, pp. 350–1). Having cited various evidence for this view he confirms it by reference to the allegory of the Graces in Colin's vision. For Lewis, the important thing about the Graces is that they vanish if disturbed,

> For being gone, none can them bring in place,
> But whom they of them selves list so to grace. (VI, x, 20)

That is to say, the graces of conduct which they bestow cannot be acquired by effort. And, continues Lewis, the relation of the Graces to Colin Clout is that of inspiration: 'the fugitive thing . . . that comes and goes in all human activities—and by its coming adds the last unpurchasable beauty—and specially in our social activities.'

Now, Spenser certainly teaches that true courtesy is an inborn gift, not to be confused with that code of polite intercourse best learned and practised in courts, but there most subject to hypocrisy. But this is not to say that courtesy 'has very little connexion with court.' Courtesy, and indeed all high personal gifts, are constantly associated by him with gentle blood—we need only remind ourselves that the Savage Man and Pastorella are of noble birth—and gentle blood denotes courtly affiliation. Spenser does not ultimately contradict one fundamental concept,

> Of Court it seemes, men Courtesie doe call,
> For that it there most useth to abound; (VI, i, 1)

221

but the allegorical core of the book forms in a pastoral setting to effect a temporary dissociation from the showy compliment which might be thought of as the essence of courtesy. Spenser is anxious to teach the courtier that,

> vertues seat is deepe within the mynd,
> And not in outward shows, but inward thoughts defynd.
>
> (VI, _Proem_, 5)

It must be understood that courtesy is essentially a condition of mind. It will express itself through modes of conduct and compliment appropriate to social station; they are variables and inessentials only validated by the impulse behind them.

To describe the relation of the Graces to Colin Clout as that of 'inspiration' is to penetrate deep into the allegory. Having given us the lead, Lewis intentionally stopped short of a neatly tied up interpretation; but the loose ends which remain have a degree and kind of bearing upon this 'inspiration' to warrant some careful tidying. What, for example, is the significance of the Pastorella love idyll? Does it relate in any way to Colin's vision (for both occur in the country about Mount Acidale, and Calidore clips unobtrusively from one into the other)? What about the Lady in the midst of the Graces? Is she of no importance in point of 'inspiration'? What of the hundred naked maidens who encircle the Graces?

Miss Janet Spens provides answers to some of these questions (Spenser's Faerie Queene, 1934, pp. 96–7). The Lady celebrated by the Graces is Colin Clout's (i.e. Spenser's) bride, the source of inspiration to poetic creation, and the hundred maidens are 'a symbol for the poetic experience,' the poetry inspired by his lady. But this interpretation throws no apparent light upon the theme of courtesy which the vision ought above all things to illuminate. Besides, whilst there is no reason absolutely to deny that the maidens represent the poetry inspired by Spenser's bride, there is evidence which suggests that we ought first of all to view them differently. In Sir Scudamour's description of his quest for Amoret in the Temple of Venus (Book IV, canto x) he tells how he found the idol of Venus upon a central altar encircled by a hundred marble pillars and a hundred lesser altars. Each altar was graced by a damsel, these being the hundred priestesses of Venus. Now, the Graces who attend the Lady of Colin's vision are the handmaidens of Venus and they are themselves encircled by a hundred maidens. (The number, one hundred, is also connected with the Graces by E. K. in his gloss to the June Eclogue.) It would seem, therefore, that whatever else these maidens may be thought to symbolize, their primary connexion is with the principle of Love; they are part of a lavish compliment to Spenser's bride, intended to imply an identification of Elizabeth Boyle and Venus.

We are now faced with a dilemma which admits of one obvious resolution. Cantos ix and x, the Calidore-Pastorella episode and Colin's vision, are the heart of Spenser's conception of courtesy; these cantos are primarily concerned with love relationships; to effect a resolution an intimate association of courtesy and love must be traced.

One is encouraged to pursue this line of inquiry because it has a basis in earlier literature of chivalry and courtly love to which The Faerie Queene is variously indebted. In a general commentary on Chrétien de Troyes, C. Muscatine points out that chivalry is the means of winning and deserving love; that love inspires 'the search for the refined, attenuated ideal of conduct that will bring the hero to the highest level of courtly virtue' (Chaucer and the French Tradition, Berkeley and Los Angeles, 1957, p. 13). C. S. Lewis, in his chapter 'Courtly Love,' cites courtesy as an important characteristic of the courtly love traditions of Troubadour poetry. It is love that makes men courteous, and the legacy of this tradition still remains (or did remain before the 'equality of the sexes') in certain requirements of modern western etiquette. Lewis translates from the medieval De Arte Honeste Amandi of Andreas Capellanus: 'It is agreed among all men that there is no good thing in the world, and no courtesy, which is not derived from love as from its fountain.' It is 'the fountain and origin of all good things'; without it 'all usages of courtesy would be unknown to man' (Allegory of Love, p. 34). The point need not be laboured. If an association of prime importance can be traced between love and courtesy in Spenser's ideal, it is what should be expected in a poem belonging to the genre of romance and chivalry; but Spenser's conception of both love and courtesy will far transcend the worldliness of the courts of love.

The restatement here of familiar Spenserian ideas on love must be excused on the grounds of their central relevance to my interpretation of the pastoral cantos. An epitome of these ideas is to be found at the beginning of Canto iii of the Legend of Chastitie:

> Most sacred fire, that burnest mightily
>   In living brests, ykindled first above,
>   Emongst th'eternall spheres and lamping sky,
>   And thence pourd into men, which men call Love;

> Not that same, which doth base affections move
> In brutish minds, and filthy lust inflame,
> But that sweet fit, that doth true beautie love,
> And choseth vertue for his dearest Dame,
> Whence spring all noble deeds and never dying fame.

Love is heaven-born, it is inspired by true beauty—itself identified with virtue—and it excites men to virtuous action. The Platonism of this conception is even more evident in the Hymns of Love and Beauty. There Spenser paraphrases Plato's theory that the soul, falling from the outer heavens, where it had caught glimpses of ultimate forms of truth and beauty, is embodied in man, and thereafter desires to embrace what on earth expresses most nearly the ultimates seen in the former life. This is the attraction of love towards beauty:

> Therefore in choice of love, he doth desyre
> That seemes on earth most heavenly, to embrace,
> That same in Beautie, borne of heavenly race.
> (Hymn of Love, 110–12)

The beauty with which the loving soul desires to unite itself is not mere outward show but the outward manifestation of that degree of heavenly beauty which the beloved soul has retained in its descent from the outer heavens to the human state. And as the soul is more beautiful so the body is proportionately so:

> Therefore where ever that thou doest behold
> A comely corpse, with beautie faire endewed,
> Know this for certaine, that the same doth hold
> A beauteous soule, with faire conditions thewed,
> Fit to receive the seede of vertue strewed.
> (Hymn of Beauty, 134–8)

This doctrine easily lends itself to the Christianizing which we find in the Amoretti, written during the poet's courtship of Elizabeth Boyle. The beloved's beauty is,

> The glorious image of the makers beautie

and she is

> divinely wrought,
> and of the brood of Angels hevenly borne:

224

> and with the crew of blessed Saynts upbrought,
> each of which did her with theyr guifts adorne. (sonnet LXI)

The Christian lover is thus justified in his mortal love since this
shadows an attraction towards the heavenly beauty and goodness
which shine through the beloved. Of yet greater importance is
the inspiration excited in the lover to raise himself to the beloved's
pitch of virtue and beauty,

> the light wherof hath kindled heavenly fyre,
> in my fraile spirit by her from basenesse raysed.
>
> (sonnet III)

The love of true beauty is the root of honour and all virtue,

> and brings forth glorious flowres of fame,
> That crowne true lovers with immortall blis,
> The meed of them that love, and do not live amisse.
>
> (Book IV, Proem, 2)

With this complex of ideas fresh in mind we may now approach
the involvement of love and courtesy in the pastoral cantos of
Book VI. It will be remembered that Sir Calidore, after having
vanished from the narrative in canto iii in pursuit of the Blatant
Beast, re-enters at the beginning of canto ix still in unavailing
pursuit. At this point he comes upon the pastoral idyll, falls in
love with Pastorella, and decides to remain for a while with her
and her supposed father, the aged Meliboeus. Meliboeus tells
Calidore how, as a young man, he left his country birthplace ambitious to achieve fame and fortune at the court of a Prince. Disappointed in hope, he sickened of the vanities, pride, and discon-
tented ambition he found there. He returned to peace and a humble
pastoral life. Calidore listens entranced,

> That twixt his pleasing tongue, and her (Pastorella's) faire
>   hew,
> He lost himselfe, and like one halfe entraunced grew.
>
> (Canto ix, 26)

He bewails the fortune which has placed him in high degree, de-
siring the simple content enjoyed by Meliboeus. But Meliboeus
reproaches him, pointing out that heaven knows what is fittest for
each man, and that one must rest contented with one's lot. And
here is enforced a general reflexion on outward show and inward

truth which will gradually focus on the particular theme of courtesy. Calidore has been wooed by <u>outward</u> appearances in his attraction to the pastoral life, and Meliboeus wisely stresses the <u>inwardness</u> of true happiness—it is a condition of mind:

> each hath his fortune in his brest.
>
> . . . .
> It is the mynd, that maketh good or ill,
>
> . . . .
> For wisdome is most riches.   (Canto ix, 29, 30)

However, Calidore requests that he may be allowed to stay with Meliboeus for a time in order to rest from his toils. His next gesture is received in such a manner as to suggest once again a nature slightly tainted with attention to outward show. For when he offers Meliboeus gold in recompense for hospitality, the generosity of the offer is acknowledged but the 'rich mould' and 'mucky masse' itself is rejected; it symbolizes the dangers, temptations, and false values of the world of the court which Meliboeus has repudiated and which Calidore still shares in. His relationship to this world is immediately afterwards confirmed in his wooing of Pastorella. She is unmoved by his elegant routines, his 'queint usage' and 'courteous guize,'

> But cared more for <u>Colins</u> carolings
> Then all that he could doe, or ever devize:
> His layes, his loves, his lookes she did them all despize.
> (Canto ix, 35)

The reference to Colin, the poet-visionary of love and courtesy in the next canto, confirms the distinction Spenser is here making between courtliness, an artificial show of manners, and true courtesy, which springs from inner grace. It is not suggested that Calidore's generous offer to Meliboeus and his wooing of Pastorella are not sincere impulses—he is, after all, the knight of courtesy—but it must be made quite clear to him and to us that the inner grace of true courtesy must never be confused with, nor subordinated to, the outer shell of courtliness.

Calidore is quickly schooled. Discarding his unprofitable 'queint usage' he adopts the dress and duties of a shepherd, thus demonstrating that in his love for Pastorella he will, like Ferdinand in <u>The Tempest</u>, stoop to any service, however lowly. And this love-born humility quickly displays its spiritual riches in

Calidore's conduct towards Coridon, his rival in love. Coridon's
love for Pastorella we must believe to be imperfect, material,
and self-regarding, for it finds no favour with her, and in the face
of Calidore's rivalry turns to envy, malice, and hatred. But these
vices are met with the virtues of Calidore's unfailing courtesy.
We are told that in whatever way he could Calidore advanced Coridon in Pastorella's favour; he praised the gifts Coridon brought to
her; he set Coridon in his own place at the head of the dance,

> For <u>Coridon</u> could daunce, and trimly trace;

when Pastorella honoured Calidore with her garland he placed it
upon Coridon's head, and courteously declined the 'oaken crowne'
won by him in a wrestling match with Coridon. So conducting
himself, Calidore earned the esteem of the shepherds, even those
who were his rivals. And just as 'courtesie amongst the rudest
breeds Good will and favour,'

> So it surely wrought
> With this faire Mayd, and in her mynde the seeds
> Of perfect love did sow.   (Canto ix, 45)

Thus we see that the full flower of courtesy springs from love—
Calidore's courtesy only reaches fullness under the inspiration of
his love for Pastorella—and that courtesy thus nurtured does itself
sow the seeds of perfect love in the person of the beloved. Further,
the courtesy shown towards Pastorella and Coridon in this canto is
no exercise in elegant manners; Pastorella is not to be won with a
sonnet and a fine suit of armour. Calidore must show the measure
of his love in such service as is useful and meaningful to her. And
when he guards her flock and helps with the milking we learn with
him that true love and courtesy consist in spiritual graces, as here
in humility and duty. Similarly, his conduct towards Coridon goes
beyond the prescriptions of polite custom; it is marked by the deli-
cacy of a compassioning heart. In his wooing of Pastorella he will
take no unfair advantage of Coridon; he does all he can to advance
his suit and ease his wounded feelings. His courtesy here shows
itself as defined by Spenser as a virtue whose seat is 'deepe within
the mynd, And not in outward shows, but inward thoughts defyned';
a virtue compounded of many, as justice, friendship, humility, generosity, compassion, magnanimity.

It would be easy to cheapen the actions of Calidore as those of
the successful lover, one, moreover, who had all the advantages

HILL

over his rival. It would also be quite wrong. Spenser is clearly
distinguishing courtesy and discourtesy in the conduct of the
lovers; by reducing Calidore to the status of a shepherd, and
making as little as possible of his superior beauty and accom-
plishments, Spenser means us to understand that courtesy is the
point of judgment between them. Pastorella is the reward, above
all things, of true courtesy, of the gentle mind known by its gentle deeds—

> So it surely wrought
> With this faire Mayd, and in her mynde the seeds
> Of perfect love did sow.

This canto demonstrates several ordinary aspects of courtesy;
the relationship, for example, of courtesy and gentle birth, and the
proper conduct of a man towards his social inferiors. But there
are deeper levels to be explored—love as the inspiration and reward of courtesy; courtesy as a condition of spiritual grace, a
conception inevitable for a poet whose ethical imagination is constantly governed by the opposition of inward and outward, spiritual
and material, true and false. I have stressed what seems of first
importance.

These lofty concepts are in harmony with the soaring invocation
to the Muses in the _Proem_ to Book VI:

> Revele to me the sacred noursery
> Of vertue, which with you doth there remaine,
> Where it in silver bowre does hidden ly
> From view of men, and wicked worlds disdaine.
> Since it at first was by the Gods with paine
> Planted in earth, being deriv'd at furst
> From heavenly seedes of bounty soveraine,
>
> . . . .
>
> Amongst them all growes not a fayrer flowre,
> Then is the bloosme of comely courtesie,
>
> . . . .
>
> Of which though present age doe plenteous seeme,
> Yet being matcht with plaine Antiquitie,
> Ye will them all but fayned showes esteeme,
> Which carry colours faire, that feeble eies misdeeme.

Courtesy is heaven-born, originally the equal of the other virtues,
but subsequently debased to hypocritical shows of courtesy; it lies

228

hidden with the other virtues in a 'silver bowre' only to be pene-
trated by the inspiration of the Muses. Two things strike me as
remarkable about this passage.

In the first place, if there is no fairer flower among the virtues than courtesy, then it follows that courtesy must be ranked
in spiritual importance with the great cardinal virtues, truth,
temperance, chastity, and so on. These virtues are religious
imperatives; courtesy is a social imperative and, in its usual
connotations, not of prime ethical importance. But Spenser has
given it such importance. In an examination of English and Italian
courtesy books (The Doctrine of the English Gentleman in the
Sixteenth Century, Urbana, 1929) Ruth Kelso observes that little
is said about courtesy by English idealists, perhaps because the
Italians had treated the matter so well, perhaps because the matter was not important in the eyes of serious-minded Englishmen.
Courtesy was required of a gentleman, but it evidently did not
rank with the solid virtues of justice, prudence, liberality, temperance, and fortitude which characterized the gentleman's code.
Thus from the point of view of the Tudor moralist Spenser's
position is individual, and it is clearly required of him to justify
his noble and unusual conception of courtesy.

The second remarkable feature of Spenser's invocation is that
although the nursery of virtue was planted upon earth by the Gods,
it now remains with the Muses, hidden from common, corrupt
sight in a 'silver bowre'; there follows the surprising corollary
that the poet only, under the inspiration of the Muses, has access
to the ultimate forms of the heaven-descended virtues. Now it is
true that this untroubled mingling of pagan and Christian elements
is typical of Spenser's allegory, and it is also true that a practice
so conventional as that of an invocation to the Muses ought not to
be regarded as having special significance. Convention, for example, governs the Proem to the complete poem, with its invocation to the Muse of History, Cupid, Mars, and Queen Elizabeth;
no one is expected to believe that the poet will actually derive
wisdom and inspiration from this exalted band. However, the invocation which opens the Legend of Courtesie is surely of another
order. The Muses are guardians of an arcana of sacred lore.
Just as the Holy Spirit is invoked by Milton in Paradise Lost so
the Muses are sincerely invoked for aid by Spenser:

Such secret comfort, and such heavenly pleasures,
. . . .
Ne none can find, but who was taught them by the Muse.

229

The appeal here is not to the Muses, properly speaking, but to the spirit of poetry, a force of imaginative insight into divine mysteries available only to the poet. This is a large claim to make for the poet, apparently by-passing both priest and philosopher. But Sir Philip Sidney comes close to making it in his Apology for Poetry where the poet is accorded something of the divine breath of his Maker; his 'erected wit' gives him a vision of perfection beyond the reach of human 'infected will.' The claim was easily possible for the more mystical Spenser who could contemplate in loose association poetic, Platonic, and Protestant notions of the ideal.

In canto ix, in the conduct of Calidore towards Coridon, Spenser has already demonstrated his lofty conception of courtesy by showing it to be a virtue compounded of many. Yet he may have felt that this did not answer to the intensity of his vision; that while he had given the breadth of courtesy, it did not sound the depths which he divined. The virtues of truth, temperance, friendship, chastity, and justice came to Spenser with their own dower of spiritual riches, as ordained by religion and deep-rooted in Christian experience; courtesy might be regarded at best as a social grace, and at worst as a continental parvenu with doubtful origins in the Courts of Love. It is in the next canto, the vision of Colin Clout, that Spenser asserts the spiritual depth he claimed for courtesy in the invocation. At the same time he illustrates that other claim; that only the inspired poet has access to the ultimate reality of spiritual truth, hidden from men by 'wicked worlds disdaine.' A momentary glimpse of his divination may bless another mortal in a state of high grace. Calidore is so graced and so blessed.

Calidore, graced by the love of Pastorella, wanders forth alone one day and comes by chance upon the hill called Acidale, sacred to Venus and the Graces. But before Spenser describes Calidore's experience there he reiterates his persistent contrast between inward reality and outward show. Who is to blame Calidore's desire to abandon the vain shadows, painted show, and false bliss of the court in favour of the 'perfect pleasures' of a pastoral life? And the rightness of his instinct is proved in that it is in the midst of a pastoral scene that he catches a glimpse of Colin's vision.

This vision is seen upon mount Acidale, a place of surpassing natural beauty; and as Spenser insists upon its naturalness, its innocence, its fertility, one is reminded of the contrast he makes between the true and false, the natural and artificial, in his treatment of the Garden of Adonis and the Bower of Bliss (cf. Lewis,

Allegory of Love, pp. 324–33).* And as the description continues
one also feels instinctively that Spenser is picturing forth an
image of the 'silver bowre' described in the invocation as 'the
sacred noursery of vertue . . . hidden . . . From view of men,
and wicked worlds disdaine.' For although mount Acidale is
approached from the fields lying about Pastorella's home, it is
blessed like Eden with peculiar natural virtues. The plain from
which it rises is encircled by a high wood whose branches send
forth leaves in both winter and summer, making 'pavilions' in
which the birds can sing perpetually. At the foot of the hill runs
a clear stream guarded by 'Nymphes and Faeries' from defile-
ment by animals and unworthy men. Thus doubly screened from
a world of mortal impurity, mount Acidale enshrines its secret
within yet another screen. For upon its grassy top dances a ring
of a hundred naked maidens surrounding the three Graces who
themselves celebrate in their midst she who excels all in beauty
and virtue. Calidore stares enraptured, but as soon as his presence is detected the spell is broken, the maidens vanish, and
Colin Clout, to whose music they had been dancing, breaks his
bagpipe in anger.

An explanation of the vision is given by the poet in direct commentary, and by Colin Clout himself. The direct commentary is
brief. We are reminded that the three maidens in the centre of the
circle are the Graces and that they, as handmaidens of Venus, are
the source of all her graces (cf. x. 15). Furthermore, it is from
the Graces that mankind in general receives 'all gifts of grace.'
(And since the Graces are so closely associated with Venus we
have further evidence of Spenser's belief that love for man is a
prime excitation to virtue.) We are then told that Colin is piping
not to the Graces but to the maiden in their midst who is simply
'that iolly Shepheards lasse' and yet there advanced to be another
Grace superior to Venus' handmaidens. Since she takes the place
of Venus in the midst of the Graces she seems to be identified with
Love itself. At any rate we may say that in the eyes of the adoring
lover the shepherd lass has the perfections of Venus.

A question of allegory emerges here. Does the poet intend us
to believe that Colin is piping to an actual country girl, or to a
symbolic figure? That is to say, is the pastoral machinery of
shepherd and shepherd lass a means of celebrating the poet's
love for virtue and beauty embodied in a woman, or for an abstract ideal? Is Colin's beloved that made him 'low to lout' the
person of Elizabeth Boyle or does she symbolize the Platonic
forms of virtue and beauty towards which his soul yearns? That

*Reprinted pp. 5–12.

the 'iolly Shepheards lasse' is transfigured into something far greater than her mortal self seems evident from the fact that she is not merely attended by visionary beings but is of their immaterial nature and spirited away with them. Presumably there are two levels of allegory here. At one level Colin's love is Elizabeth Boyle; at another level she is—what exactly?

It is certain that Calidore would never have seen the vision if he had not been shown it through the divination of the poet, Colin Clout. And even for him the vision comes only in a moment of inspiration which, once passed, cannot be achieved again by mere volition,

> For being gone, none can them bring in place,
> But whom they of them selves list so to grace.

If the poet himself is only for a short while graced with the vision it must represent something more than a celebration of his mortal love, for she he may have always before his eyes. And the clue to this 'something more' may be found in Spenser's 'Platonic' view of love. Colin's love is not to be loved for herself alone but for the spiritual beauty of which her mortal beauty gives assurance. And although the spiritual beauty of the beloved may be recognized by the poet as falling short of the ideal, yet it is a testimony to the existence of the ideal, the ultimate form with which the soul desires union. And in the moment of passionate adoration the ideal is glimpsed beyond the real. Moving away from the earth, striving to pierce the veil of mortality, Colin is rewarded with a vision of the unearthly, the 'silver bowre,' 'the sacred noursery of vertue':

> But that fourth Mayd, which there amidst them traced,
> Who can aread, what creature mote she bee,
> Whether a creature, or a goddesse graced
> With heavenly gifts from heven first enraced?
> . . . .
> Yet was she certes but a countrey lasse . . . (Canto x, 25)

She is a woman but she is a manifestation of the divine. The mortal touch comes with intrusion of Calidore and the vision is lost. But for a dazzling moment Calidore does see the vision; because, through his love for Pastorella, he is in a state of emotional refinement and spiritual aspiration which draws him close to Colin's divination in love.

Calidore had earlier learnt in his love for Pastorella that true courtesy is not a matter of elegance but of inward grace which issues in virtuous and unaffected conduct. The reader has seen that love is the source and reward of such courtesy; Calidore's love for Pastorella begets perfect courtesy in him and this is rewarded by her returning love. What more, then, have we and Calidore to learn in the vision? Well, the vision does not so much add to this view of courtesy as deepen our apprehension of its inwardness. We have been shown, as it were, the immortal soul of courtesy, the ideal beauty which lies beyond and transfigures mortal beauty. In our love for another mortal we must be aware of and aspire to the ideal which lies beyond the real, if such love is to manifest itself in more than shows of courtesy reaching only to self-gratification. Such love of the ideal is inspired to attain it, and thus issues in all virtuous action; and all virtuous action is for Spenser that many-sided virtue, perfect courtesy.

It is significant that when Calidore first sees Pastorella she is seated upon a hillock encircled by shepherds and shepherdesses who celebrate her as if she were a goddess. Given Spenser's neo-Platonic view of the relationship of beauty and virtue, it may be assumed that Calidore is moved by her spiritual as well as by her physical beauty. But he may not be aware of the double nature of the attraction, nor may he clearly sense the ideal beyond the real. So he is privileged to glimpse another Lady, also upon a hill, also graced and celebrated by encircling maidens, the object of Colin's worship. The parallelism of setting makes it certain that Spenser intended comparison to be made between the two incidents. It cannot be that the poet intended merely to augment his flattery of his 'country lass' by an implied superiority to Pastorella. Calidore has been shown a Lady who may surpass the perfections of his Pastorella (for the Elizabethan lover was never shy of hyperbole); but the prime significance is Calidore's apprehension of ideal values through the symbol of Colin's love. In a moment of visionary insight a Lady has stepped forth from the 'silver bowre,' herself the embodiment and inspiration of the 'sacred noursery of vertue.' Calidore is rapt away into the poet's ideal world by the vision and Colin's ensuing discourse,

> That thence, he had no will away to fare,
> But wisht, that with that shepheard he mote dwelling share.
> (Canto x, 30)

But no mortal can bear the light of that world for long, and soon the pangs of love for the mortal Pastorella again assail him.

Nonetheless, having once glimpsed that world Calidore could never wholly forget it. The revelation would remain for him in the same special way as Wordsworth's visions and 'fleeting moods Of shadowy exultation' remained for him:

> the soul,
> Remembering how she felt, but what she felt
> Remembering not, retains an obscure sense
> Of possible sublimity, to which,
> With growing faculties she doth aspire . . .
>
> (Prelude, 1805, Book II, 334–8)

Just so, Calidore will retain a sense of possible sublimity; his love for Pastorella will have a new dimension and will thus be a more potent source of inspiration to virtuous action. Courtesy is inspired by love, but unless that love looks beyond the physical and temporal, the courtesy is likely to be a mere observance of forms of conduct with the risk of hypocrisy attendant upon all social conventions,

> Which carry colours faire, that feeble eies misdeeme.

We must fix our gaze upon the ideal forms of love and beauty, which for Spenser are identified with all moral and spiritual ultimates. Our actions will then need little instruction from social codes for they will spring direct, with inevitable grace, from sources of light which such codes reach back to, but with which they may lose vital touch.

It may be thought that this view of the Colin Clout episode is too recondite, and too little based upon solid evidence from the text. It is true that some of Spenser's own comments suggest more matter-of-fact explanations. His ostensible intention in the whole pastoral 'truancy' (Cantos ix–xi) is simple:

> For all that hetherto hath long delayd
> This gentle knight, from sewing his first quest,
> Though out of course, yet hath not bene missayd,
> To shew the courtesie by him profest,
> Even unto the lowest and the least. (Canto xii, 2)

This has obvious relevance for Canto ix, and might even apply to Colin's vision if we think its most important teaching to be that a country lass may be the equal of a high-born lady as regards vir-

tue and beauty, and therefore worthy of equal admiration and
courteous respect. Yet this is only another approach to the argument that love and beauty inspire true courtesy. Besides, any
candid reader would allow that these two cantos go far beyond
the prose of,

> the courtesie by him profest,
> Even unto the lowest and the least.

Spenser has done this, and much more.
   Another possible interpretation may be read from Colin's explanation of his vision:

> These three on men all gracious gifts bestow,
>   Which decke the body or adorne the mynde,
>   To make them lovely or well favoured show,
>   As comely carriage, entertainement kynde,
>   Sweete semblaunt, friendly offices that bynde,
>   And all the complements of curtesie:
>   They teach us, how to each degree and kynde
>   We should our selves demeane, to low, to hie;
> To friends, to foes, which skill men call Civility.
>
> Therefore they alwaies smoothly seeme to smile,
>   That we likewise should mylde and gentle be,
>   And also naked are, that without guile
>   Or false dissemblaunce all them plaine may see,
>   Simple and true from covert malice free:
>   And eeke them selves so in their daunce they bore,
>   That two of them still froward seem'd to bee,
>   But one still towards shew'd her self afore;
> That good should from us goe, then come in greater store.
>   (Canto x, 23 and 24)

Here we have simple allegory. Courtesy is bestowed upon man
by the Graces whose smiling indicates the mildness of this virtue,
and their nakedness its frankness; the manner of their dance
teaches that virtuous conduct begets greater reward—so Calidore's
courtesy is rewarded with Pastorella's love.
   But can we let the matter rest there? What has Spenser really
said about courtesy? In such generalizations as 'comely carriage,
entertainement kynde' he has told us no more than we already
knew about courtesy. And is it sufficient to remark that courtesy

is bestowed by the Graces unless we know how we may become worthy of their gifts? An Elizabethan moralist would not condemn us to talents unimprovable by discipline. I believe that Spenser, in originating courtesy with the handmaidens of Venus, meant us to understand that its refining discipline comes with love; love, that is to say, as the moral and spiritual experience described in the Hymns and elsewhere.

Perhaps the simplest interpretation of the vision is that Spenser is celebrating his ideal of feminine courtesy in the person of his bride:

> Another Grace she well deserves to be,
> In whom so many Graces gathered are,
> Excelling much the meane of her degree;
> Divine resemblaunce, beauty soveraine rare,
> Firme Chastity, that spight ne blemish dare;
> All which she with such courtesie doth grace . . .
>
> (Canto x, 27)

This is acceptable as far as it goes, but other considerations invite one to sound more deeply. Unless one believes that the autobiographical pull is so strong as to result in an uncritical distortion of structure and balance, one must ask why Spenser so 'wrote up' the Colin Clout episode and why he placed it at the heart of the Legend of Courtesie. One must also ask why Calidore was privileged to see the vision. Is Spenser only gratifying his own pleasure, or was it important that Calidore should glimpse the ideal of feminine courtesy? If the latter, how has it helped him?

Simply, one can answer that in future Calidore will recognize ideal feminine courtesy; in his estimate of other women he will have an absolute standard for judging well. But since this ideal of feminine courtesy is given a central place in the book one would imagine that it was intended to do more than teach a man how to recognize a truly courteous woman; that it would bear significantly on courtesy in general, in man as well as in woman.

If this assumption is valid, then this bearing must surely be that a truly courteous woman inspires the like in man. And such inspiration is vital and complete. Vital because fired by love—the Lady is not only Colin's love but also identified with Love itself and so relevant to Calidore's life as to the lives of all men; complete, because the Lady's courtesy is a miraculous dower of physical, moral and spiritual perfections:

> Divine resemblaunce, beauty soveraine rare,
> Firme Chastity, that spight ne blemish dare.

The word miraculous is properly applied to the Lady for she is also, at one level, a visionary manifestation of ultimate virtue and beauty, the very heart of Spenser's 'silver bowre.' With his sight of the ideal beyond the actual, looking directly through the eyes of the poet, Calidore's instruction is fulfilled; it is an instruction in love, virtue and courtesy, for the three are a 'knot intrinsicate' in Spenser's mind.

THE ALLEGORY OF GUYON'S VOYAGE: AN INTERPRETATION

B. Nellist

The voyage of Guyon to the Bower of Bliss appears to present the reader with no special problem of interpretation. As a narrative it is clearly modelled upon Tasso's account of the voyage of Ubaldo to the Isle of Armida in search of the enthralled Rinaldo.[1] Beyond it lie the great and wondrous voyages of ancient literature, Jason's search for the Fleece and Ulysses' long travel home. Like much serious Renaissance narrative however it offers the reader an idealised representation of a truth with universal significance: a hero tested and strengthened by the experience of much difficulty (like Ulysses, like Jason) approaches the final task in which he is to show not only the nature of the virtue he possesses but even more its heroic magnitude. The voyage and the journey through the Bower of Bliss itself reveal not only his temperance but the inflexible fixity of his will. Guyon through his trials has moved towards a resolute sense of purpose and the recognition of his own heroic stature. The difficulties he faces on the voyage to the Island therefore are devised by Acrasia in an effort to corrupt the will and deflect him from that purpose, at the narrative level not only by sensual attractions but even more by physical horror and simple fear.

Governing the thought of the whole episode are fables like that of Hercules at the cross-roads, that Hallett Smith has suggested inspired much Renaissance heroic theory.[2] More precisely here, we find echoes of the Ulysses and Circe myth. We find the same mixture of sorcery, enchanted isles, bestial transformation. Beyond this we find the same sort of moral associations. If virtue is subordinated to mere physical beauty it will fall in to a foul decay. Love of the desirable is the passive, the feminine principle. When it is controlled and dominated by the force of reason and courage however it becomes a source of joy and relaxation to the good man. Circe bears the child of the noble Ulysses, but only after he has conquered her evil purposes. Samuel Daniel in his

Reprinted from English Literary History, Vol. 30 (1963), pp. 89–106, © The Johns Hopkins Press, by permission of The Johns Hopkins Press.

dialogue of Odysseus and the siren suggests that there can be no question of any equality between the two different standards of value: if the lady cannot subdue the hero then she must come to him on his own terms; for she needs him more than ever he desires her.[3] Moreover courage and spirit are in themselves insufficient as heroic virtues since they fall prey to lust. Ulysses to Renaissance writers was a greater hero than Achilles since it is wisdom alone that safeguards right action. It is Rinaldo, the man of spirit, who falls into the snares of Armida, not the reasonable and sage Geoffrey.[4] Just so, Guyon would often go wrong without the guidance of the Palmer.

This sort of moral expression is to a large degree not allegory at all, except possibly in the sense in which the Renaissance reader was inclined to read his Homer. Chapman uses the barbed word[5] largely because of the paucity of the critical vocabulary of his day. He really reads the Odyssey as though it were an idealised history or fable, a continued paroemia, in which the writer, as Sandys says of Ovid, presents things that "are not, as if they were, or rather as they should be . . . juster then either men or Fortune."[6] Spenser is using something of the same method. He is not even using metaphor. Indeed when Alciati used exactly the same mode in some of his emblems he was criticised for making narrative comparisons rather than using genuine metaphors; when he shows Aeneas carrying Ascanius from the flames of Troy for instance in an emblem extolling filial piety, he is condemned by Masenius for not using strict metaphor.[7] The Faerie Queene as a whole can be read as a narrative. If it simplifies the complexities of human experience into a clear pattern of moral action, it yet simplifies in a representional way through narrative rather than in terms of abstract moral theory as allegory does.

But as soon as we come to consider the structure of the work we recognise the insufficiencies of such a view of it. Though this narrative presents us with the general strategy of this episode it does not lead us to understand with any greater clarity the individual details, the reason for the structure for instance of the series of temptations Guyon faces. If we contrast Spenser's account of the voyage with that in the Gerusalemme Liberata, which very broadly we may accept as the chief source, we find a difference that is radical. Time and place are fixed in Tasso's description. The voyage is wondrous but it has no meaning beyond the apparent sense. The context is simply that of heroic endeavour, in which the names of Hercules and Columbus and the house of Este define the area of meaning. Armida's isle has the usual Romance geography, a mountain whose lower slopes are cold with ice and snow but on whose summit lies a fair and temperate paradise. This is the world of magic but not necessarily of allegory. On the other hand, the dangers that Guyon faces are drawn up with deliberate arrangement and lead us from the consideration of social to an awareness of personal evil. At the start of the voyage Guyon is faced with temptations to bad behaviour, to waste and gluttony, to idleness and wantonness. These temptations increase in their personal application, the later ones being directed in particular at Guyon as temperance and as hero. Because of the associations that the Palmer has come to have for us throughout the story, there is a special significance in his assumption of the role of pilot that the enchanted being in Tasso's history does not possess. Spenser's little vessel is not notable for its supernatural powers like Ubaldo's boat[8] but the poet goes out of his way to emphasise the unfailing strength of the boatman for instance, and the relentlessness of its motion. Spenser's account differs so widely from Tasso's because it is inspired by a concern with moral doctrine, rather than simply with a moral narrative. The Faerie Queene is organised on a basis of ethical thought expressed through the elements of idealised narrative. Spenser shows a unique ability to present the reader at once with a concrete representation of heroic morality in action and with an analysis of a body of thought, concerning the relation of nature to grace for instance, and of reason, the will and innate virtue to the peculiar evils that beset Renaissance man.

The difficulty of such total allegory, in which one set of actions darkly suggests another, as had been pointed out by admirers and critics of Spenser alike, is that it continually makes us pause to ask what the poet means at any given point, so that like a stumbling linguist we are perpetually halting to consider the meaning of each difficult word in a glossary. Like such a man we lose sight of the meaning of the whole in our obsession with the detail. If we treat the Faerie Queene in this way we destroy just that narrative continuity and skill in counterpointing different main sections of the complex story (especially in books three and four) in which Spenser so excels. To Spenser's contemporaries however, I would suggest, his meaning presented no such overwhelming difficulty, at least in the case of Guyon's voyage. They would be familiar with the allegorical traditions which Spenser seems to be using here as the basis for his history.

The allegory of Christian convention upon which Spenser drew differs from Renaissance allegorical narrative as noun differs from adverb. It is concerned with the nature and properties of things rather than with the quality of actions. Having chosen some concrete and conventional image as the referent for a doctrine or spiritual principle the medieval allegorist would then analyse his meaning by dividing the object according to its properties or distinct parts. This is the method that Spenser uses openly in the Castle of Alma, for instance, choosing the ancient simile of man as a house, the structure of which is then made to correspond to the structure of the human body. The reader thus perceives in immediate and memorable terms which are the most important parts of the human complex. The writer is able to show through his cypher how dignity and order are maintained throughout, who is mistress in that establishment and how necessary is the obedience of the servant to the superior. The meaning in Renaissance allegory on the other hand often arises from the way in which characters act. It is typical rather than doctrinal, active rather than static, individual rather than universal, synthetic rather than analytic. The Faerie Queene, however, is satisfying because at its greatest moments as here in the voyage of Guyon it manages to be both synthesising and analytic simultaneously. Beyond the immediate associations of the narrative lie the controlled and doctrinal associations of conventional allegory that give depth and discipline to the moral history.

As a contemporary parallel to Spenser's allegory of Guyon's navigation we may quote from a sermon upon the voyage of our Lord and the disciples upon Galilee during the storm, which was preached to a congregation of sailors at Weymouth by Richard Madoxe, a fellow of All Souls and later chaplain to Fenton on his troublesome voyage, in October 1581.

> "This body of ours is lyke unto a Shippe, wherein the reasonable soule, lyke a marriner sayleth: this world is naught else but a sea of wickednesse: and the provokementes of the fleshe are tempestuous windes, which of our selves: wee are not able to assuage: which if they be not in tyme appeased, will bring us in daunger to be eaten up of the Sea, and so to make a myserable shipwracke."[9]

The notion is familiar but instead of static equations that we have in this conventional schema Spenser creates a narrative in which the protagonists react in typical ways to the different situations in which they are placed. The general situation is the sea of this world, or of sin, in which the ship of man sails to some fixed objective past a series of moral dangers that threaten to destroy the ship or prevent the sailor from reaching his port. According to different conventions the ship could represent Christian perfection, or the Church, or the state or of course sinful man, or the worldly, or even the followers of the devil. A song set to music by Byrd, "All as a sea the world no other is" tells how the ship is tossed about by wanton desires and invaded by pirates.[10] Daniel Price on the other hand in a sermon tells us that "as the world so our bodies were the ships, our Consciences the Pilots, our heart the compasses, our faith the sterne . . . our good workes the oares . . . our haven heaven."[11]

This general scheme is of very ancient origin of course. Probably the longest sea allegory by a great medieval writer is Richard of St. Victor's sermon on the Nativity of our Lady, in which the whole ship is analysed even down to the rigging, all within the pattern of the voyage of life through the waters infested with danger.[12] The convention was often used in commentary upon the voyages on Galilee as described in the Gospel, though the simile of the voyage of life is pagan in origin rather than Biblical.[13] There is a typical use of it in a sermon once ascribed to Chrysostom; "Mari similis est haec vita; navigio, humana natura, portans quasi vectores et gubernatorem cogitationes et mentem."[14] The vessel is opposed by the fury of the devil, the waves of desire and the false froth of pleasures stirred up against us. So here in Guyon's case voyaging is representative of life as a whole, in which we have a purpose and are beset by difficulty and temptation.

The Palmer as Temperance is the guiding principle of Sir Guyon and hence a fit pilot for his boat. The usual convention gives this position to reason, as we see in Price and Madoxe, or to the soul. Plato tells us that the mind in the soul is like a pilot.[15] In the Christian allegory of the ship of the Elect, faith often steered the vessel or prudence might hold the rudder. The image of the tiller of the soul has the implicit sense "rege teipsum" of course. "Rege ergo teipsum, quando turbatur animus, mens fluctuat,"[16] wrote the pseudo-Ambrose. As in Spenser the traditional counsel urges self-control. Such restraint is a deliberate exercise, an act of skill that may be learned like navigation or soldiering. The storm reveals the dexterity of the pilot. An ancient proverb says that in calm every man is pilot.[17] In a graphic and important simile Seneca describes how the storm and the fury of the waves only serve to reveal the true mastery of the Rhodian pilot.[18] Just so, Guyon's voyage demands a pilot of heroic capacity and control. Only reason and temperance could preserve Guyon on the course that is to lead to his objective. The ship is therefore in a state of spiritual and psychological grace. It presents a proper subordination. It is very different from the vessel where the hierarchy is reversed. It is this man,

> "Whose wit and wisdome governde is,
>   By his unruly will . . ."[19]

who inevitably tends to ruin. What use is experience and cunning,

> "When hee that steers will have his will,
>   And drive them where he list perforce."[20]

It is the purpose of reason to discern the dangers that face human existence and so to avoid them. If the soul is disturbed however, wreck will follow:—

> "For once when Reason's driven from the Helme,
>   And we twixt Scylla and Charibdis glide,
>   Ther is no hope but one should overwhelme."[21]

On the other hand the position of the man at the oars is that of strenuous activity, will as against reason. Spenser describes him as a brusque man who speaks rather rudely for instance to the Palmer, "Palmer stere aright" and when Guyon himself wishes to approach the Wandering Isles he is roughly told, "That may not be."[22] All this is very different from the courteous relation that exists between the Palmer and Guyon. We may compare the abstract pattern behind Spenser's narrative with that of a sonnet by Henry Lok published in 1593;

> "Against a streame of lust my will would roe
>   To gain the shoare of grace, the port of peace:
>   But floods of foule affections overfloe."[23]

As the man at the tiller is associated with the reflective virtues, with reason, prudence, and temperance, so the boatman is the active principle, the very spirit of perseverance, will, spirit or courage. Thus in the ship of the Christian the oars are wielded by prayer and in the boat of penitence by the works of restitution.[24] In isolation his very boorishness deprives him of heroic stature, just as the physical feebleness of the Palmer diminishes his power. Yet both are necessary to the success of Guyon's epic endeavour.

The sea-scape through which they pass is as familiar as the boat, the pilot and the boatman:

> "I can compare our life to nothing so fitly as to a ship in the midst of the sea. In what danger is the ship and they that be in it! Here are they in danger of the tempests, there of quicksands; on this side of pirates . . . as the men that sail are most glad when they approach to the haven, even so should we be most glad when we approach to the haven, that is death!"[25]

Humphrey Gifford had a complete lyric devoted to a comparison of life to a voyage in which through a good life we hope to reach "the porte of blisse" through the seas of which Satan is chief ruler.[26] In Guyon's voyage however, Acrasia's Bower of Bliss is a hideous parody of our true haven, which indicates that on earth the reward of effort is still the demand for greater effort.

The dangers of this voyage are the dangers of life itself. Temptations are translated into the terms of physical perils. Thus a sermon ascribed once to St. Augustine has a list of social evils;

> "Adulatores vestros tanquam latentes sub undis scopulos observate. Quando enim mare tranquillum est, tunc saxa latentia non videntur: si tribulationis procella consurgit, tunc inter undarum montes verticem tollunt, tunc in eis apparet periculum quod latebat . . . Obtrectatores omnino contemnendi sunt; quia canes marini sunt . . ."[27]

This is the allegory of nouns of course. Life is reduced to an all-inclusive simile, a static equation which is then analysed through a division of the object itself into a series of properties, of separate nouns, that is. As in Spenser so here the dangers recounted are rather social and moral than theological. Many of these list allegories have a distinct resemblance to those found in the voyage of Guyon. Thus a passage in Joannes Climacus found in that popular Renaissance work, the Hieroglyphica of Pierio Valeriano, tells us that life is dangerous,

> "multis ventorum turbinibus et scopulis, vorticibus, piratis, siphonibus, brevibus, seu Syrtibus, monstrisque et fluctibus redundans."[28]

Life is seen as a skill both here and in Guyon's voyage, but if it is danger rather than simply temptation that faces the sailor, yet the skill is only fully to be learnt by those who are protected by God. This character it shared with the Ship of the Church, which was assured in similar terms,

> "Nulla te quaciet procella curarum,
> ventus inanis gloriae non impellet;
> spumans non obruet volumen undarum,
> nec ad interitum vorago compellet
> Caribdis nec Sirtes nec Scilla nocebunt
> blando Sirenes organo non seducent
> monstra maris ingencia non terrebunt,
> nec tremulos cordi tremores adducent."[29]

The real danger here is despair in fact which would lead to a failure to carry through man's supernatural purpose to its proper end.

Spenser transforms this static pattern into active terms. His allegory uses adverbs rather than nouns, in that the meaning springs from the character of the actions in which the characters engage and the quality of their behaviour. Meaning and purpose in the poem arise from the manners of the hero rather than simply from the objects themselves. The Gulfe of Greedinesse with its attendant waterspout and the Rocke of Vile Reproch first affect the voyagers with fear. The perils present the extremes of social and personal evil, worldly greed and lust. Undaunted by the sight the hero presses on, "Forward they passe, and strongly he them rowes."[30] On the one side is the mouth of Hell that we often find awaits the allegorical ships of the sinful. John Norden for instance tells us in a contemporary prayer-book that the ship of Satan "seemeth to be a most secure cradle" but in fact ends in the Gulf of Perpetual Perdition.[31] The rock on which the ship could wreck occurs as frequently in such allegories of course. In the lyric from Byrd's collection mentioned above this is given a psychological reference. He warns us of the danger of wreck, "Our will the rocks, our want of skill the sands."[32] But Spenser describes both objects in concrete and realisable terms, evoking from the reader an immediate response. Thus of the rock he writes:

> "To which nor fish nor fowle did once approch,
> But yelling Meawes, with Seagulls hoarse and bace,
> And Cormorants with birds of ravenous race,"[33]

the usual collection of usurers, money-lenders and coney catchers

that gathered round the rake of Renaissance England. This is sin
regarded from the aspect of social behaviour; it is overcome by
resolution. The ferryman, "with his stiffe oares did brush the sea
so stronge."[34]

This danger avoided, the travellers approach the Wandering
Islands. Spenser is deliberately using Romance motifs that could
also be considered in the light of the Christian tradition. Guyon
had encountered the islands already on Phaedria's sea and, significantly, there without the benefit of the Palmer's company.
Here heroic purpose could be deflected not through fear but simply by surrender of the will to that which without reason wanders
aimlessly. This is temptation which was presented to Guyon on
the Idle Lake. As usual the allegory arises not simply from the
nature of the objects themselves which are in fact green and lovely pieces of land, but from patterns of behaviour. Because the
islands straggle they are not to be trusted. Because also when
Phaedria meets the travellers she "loudly laught" and even more
because subsequently she fains "dalliance and wanton sport" and
uses "lewd words immodestly" she is, like the islands, representative of all purposeless and wasteful laxity.[35] The artistic decorum of the incident arises not from any narrative necessity but
from its place in the pattern of moral ills. Having passed actual
perversion of the will, the travellers have now approached simple
wilfulness, which is in fact only a euphemism for will-lessness.
Quite appropriately it is the resolute boatman who advises Guyon
against this peril.[36] They then go on to right action which lies
like the narrow channel dividing Scylla from Charybdis. But again
all this is interpreted by Spenser in terms of activity, and like an
affirming chorus once more the poet asserts "Whom nought regarding, they kept their gate."[37]

The boat now approaches therefore the twin perils of the ancient
sea. St. Jerome had interpreted Charybdis as avarice and Scylla
as malice and in another place he writes of the "Charybdis luxuriae"
and the Scylla of lust.[38] In general the dreaded pair suggest the
danger of extremes, that in avoiding the one we wreck on the other,
as the ancient proverb has it.[39] Bacon attributes to the myth a
genuine moral intention in preaching the value of moderation.[40]
Natalis Comes quotes the Nicomachean Ethics: "virtutem esse
medium durum extremorum."[41] Petrus Berchorius, the author of
an Ovide Moralisé (who died in 1362) suggests that the twin-peril
might be taken as ambition and amor mundi with the Syrtes as
avarice and Bythalassus as lust.[42] Robert Chamberlain writing
in 1634 may have been thinking of this passage in Spenser when he

speaks of them as extravagance and meanness.[43] He may on the
other hand have been indebted to Petrarch who may in turn have
inspired Spenser:

> "Ita dum debentem pudo, beneficii expertos dolor agitat,
> inter Scillam et Charibdim fertur cymba beneficii, effec-
> tumque ut multos, qui parce, atque illiberaliter tuti vixis-
> sent, liberalitas insignis in discrimen traxerit."[44]

Because Spenser's Charybdis is like a wheel we may also suppose
that he may have been aware of the interpretation of Deguileville
where the hazard is equated with Fortuna, the power of this world.[45]
Like the other dangers of this section of the sea, the assault is external, demanding skill in the pilot and represents a danger of social
behaviour rather than of individual corruption. What is demanded is
heroic determination and fixity of will, and this the people in the
boat possess,

> "But the heedfull Boateman strongly did stretch
> His brawnie armes, and all his body straine . . ."[46]

Hitherto the threats that have confronted Guyon have been general
rather than directed particularly at him. This section culminates
in the great wave that rises before the ship full of strange monsters.
These are like the "montes undarum" of the allegory from the
pseudo-Augustine quoted above, which arise when the winds of
persecution blow upon the sea of this world. Though Acrasia's
wave is not the result of the wind it is the direct result of her
sorcery. Moreover it is associated with, "deformed Monsters
thousand fold" all the grizly inhabitants of the sea. Traditionally
the ocean was the home of the monster, being as here a malevolent
and evil place, the last hiding-place of the enemies of God.[47] For
pagan antiquity, "Nature's power ends on its shores, save for the
fact that the monsters it has created find refuge beneath Ocean's
waves."[48] In the allegorical sea of Christian tradition the creatures would be associated with those of Ps. 104, the "great and
wide sea, wherein are things creeping innumerable, both small
and great beasts. There go the ships: there is that leviathan."[49]
The allegorical associations of the wave, then, were pride,[50]
(Spenser speaks here of the waves "puft up with proud disdain"),
and, as I have suggested, persecution. Augustine in his sermon
on this Psalm thinks of the malformed animals of this psalm as
the wicked and the haters of God's elect.[51] In the allegorical

journey to the true "bower of Bliss" it is these monsters that are a chief impediment, and the waves with which they are involved. John of Howden writing on the sighs of the faithful for the New Jerusalem, says:

"Maris huius reptilia transmeare,
et iube nos undas transire spumantes,
et hiatus transcurrere comminantes,
qui pedibus nostri fluenta calcare."[52]

The danger in this plight is fear and despair and so the surrender of the divine plan. But though these brutes may appal us Augustine says, nevertheless, "Noli timeri, noli terreri; desidera patriam, intellige peregrinationem."[53] The fears arise within us when we contemplate this opposition and persecution, but they must be subdued with reason, Caduceus, the rod that the Palmer wields.[54] So for Spenser in this series of temptations that culminates in the great wave the real danger is not so much in the betrayal of temperance as upon a neglect of the true purpose of the voyage, the daunting of hope and courage through fear and mistrust: "Ne wonder if these did the knight appall."[55] As a work of the pseudo-Augustine says, all the dangers of this word, Scylla, Charybdis, and the rocks undermine only "The heedless, and the wavering in faith," so that they wreck.[56] It falls to the Palmer, to the sanctified reason, who is the sure guide of the human soul, to explain that,

"These same Monsters are not these in deed,
But are into these fearefull shapes disguiz'd
By that same wicked witch, to worke us dread,
And draw from on this journey to proceede."[57]

But again there is the affirmation of purpose resolutely maintained: "forth their course they kept."[58]

It is now the plan of Acrasia to threaten the hero in the particular virtues of which he is the representative. Spenser's analysis of the course of moral assault here is as accurate as ever: temptation may seem to arise from without but the threat really proceeds from within the mind itself. Acrasia's sorcery places in Guyon's path the dolorous maiden, the "Womanish fine forgery," who appeals to the knight's basic chivalrous instincts but in the process weakens the heroic virtue of perseverance. This would in fact subordinate higher to lower virtues, though it seems at

first to offer opportunity for positive action as against the purely
negative mission on which Guyon is bound. But as the Palmer
shows, even had the maid not been part of the witchcraft, it would
still have been wrong to succour individual need in preference to
the eradication of universal ills. Courage would be dulled and the
will deflected by "foolish pitty."

This conflict between different sets of values is a romance
motif. Thus, when Lancelot is following the Grail he witnesses a
contest between a party of knights in white armour and another in
black. The latter are being defeated. "In incresyng of his
shevalry," Lancelot goes to the aid of the weaker side. In the
battle, the knight who has hitherto been undefeated, is made captive
and allowed to wander away in shame. An anchoress eventually
explains his error to him. He has reacted, he is told, in accordance with a pattern of behaviour suitable to a lower mode of life.
Those in search of the Grail should ask the ultimate questions
"Why" and "Who" before they act. The white knights were the
saints of God battling against the weakening forces of the World.[59]
Similarly, Guyon needs the promptings of right reason to prevent
him from straying. The heroic purpose is maintained in terms of
the usual image;

> "   the Boateman strayt
> Held on his course, with stayed stedfastnesse,
> Ne ever shruncke, ne ever sought to bayt
> His tyred armes for toylesome wearinesse,
> But with his oares did sweepe the watry widernesse."[60]

For Guyon alone is not the hero in this episode but rather the activity as a whole, the area of behaviour represented by all the occupants of the boat, is heroic. It is the heroic experience that is
investigated in the allegorical pattern.

The final great temptation is an assault upon Temperance itself.
If the good man is not misled by appeals to a false sentimentality,
he may be caught by flattery and the offer of what is genuinely his
reward. The sirens are not simply representative of lust. They
were the types of artistic activity, striving with the Muses themselves for the mastery.[61] They offered the feminine values, beauty
and ease and peace. They are a variant of sloth. The other assaults on perseverance have been crude compared to this which
offers Guyon the specious attraction of temporary recreation ("a
while") and that harmony which is the keystone of the Spenserian
structure;

"O turne thy rudder hither-ward a while:
Here may thy storme-bet vessell safely ride;
This is the Port of rest from troublous toyle,
The worlds sweet In, from paine and wearisome turmoyle."[62]

When he heard those voices, Ulysses himself, bound to the mast of
his ship, had cried to the sailors to turn back and linger there, for-
getful of his own land. The lusts of the flesh are dangerous for just
this reason, they are powerful enough to make us neglect our graver
purposes; "Nam et voluptatem pestifera dulcedo, patriae nobis
oblivionem facit"[63] wrote Paulinus of Nola. For Dante also their
chief danger was that they invited to sloth.[64] The usual associations were with sexual lust of course, or with prostitutes in particular.[65] But Erasmus and Alciati compared the harlot to the
remora, dangerous because it has power, however intrinsically
slight it is in itself, to stop the progress of the greatest and most
noble ship.[66] Against this threat ordinary men are powerless,
Sandys was later to point out, following Comes in this. Only,
"heroicall spirits in the midst of beseiging delights are invincibly
fortified by their proper vertue."[67] Even to dally with such pleasures, as Guyon is tempted to do is dangerous. The wise man
sees such evils, says Fulgentius, and passes by them.[68]

"—him the Palmer from that vanity
With temperate advice discounselled,
That they it past . . ."[69]

As the first series of physical dangers had ended in the episode
of the monsters, the fears caused by the forces of evil and the
threat of external persecution, so this series ends appropriately
in the episode of the fog and the evil birds. Birds habitually represent the spiritual as against the material principle simply because they are the inhabitants of the upper regions.[70] Through the
fog Acrasia makes her last attempt on the sea to stop the hero from
approaching his objective. In the abstract allegory it is usually a
sign of the obscurity that sin or ignorance brings up the mind.[71]
Ambrose had likened it to the lusts of the flesh that rise from the
lower faculties of man, "ut gubernator sui animus esse non possit
diem et noctem caligine amoris ignorans."[72] But here it is rather
an image of an ignorance that beclouds the mind generally through
fear of superstitious omens represented by the birds. The hero
should have a mind that relies upon God, not upon supposed supernatural evidences. Guyon is faced with the temptations simply to

leave his declared purpose through fear of the unknown and ignorance of the future.

> "Yet stayd they not, but forward did proceed,
> Whiles th'one did row, and the'other strifly steare."[73]

Ahead of them lies the "sacred soile," where social and personal evil is to be encountered in its most virulent form.

The whole voyage is typical of Spenser's method at its best. It progresses with the purpose of allegory but with the form of narrative. The logical inevitability of allegory disciplines what might otherwise have been simply an arbitrary collection of marvels or physical dangers. But on the other hand the reader does not need to translate the language of objects into the dialect of systematic ethics since the behaviour of the various characters offers a representational, an immediate equivalent of the allegorical elements. Moreover Spenser is using a universal conventional pattern which is immediately recognisable as the sea of evil that has to be negotiated by every man in this world. Through familiarity with this material, the contemporary reader had no difficulty in seeing at once why the Palmer sat at the helm or who the oarsman was or why the dangers occurred in the order in which they did, and have so important and peculiar a place in the narrative. Radical allegory inspires the passage without this being blatantly obtrusive.

Moreover since the work has the propriety of narrative we recognise that the allegory need not have the consistency of abstract and patterned allegory throughout. The boatman does not represent steadfastness. He simply acts steadfastly. Hence the reason for calling this adverbial, as against noun, allegory. When he remains behind at the shore[74] we do not therefore think that "Steadfastness" has been rejected by the hero, since the oarsman had that character only in relation to a particular set of circumstances. We realize that at the narrative level he stays by the shore to look after the boat and at that level we are satisfied. Deprived of the narrative and embodied form, we may transform the pattern back into terms of the Christian tradition easily enough. Ralph Aylett, one of Spenser's most ardent seventeenth century disciples in the line of stanzaic moralising, suggests that Moderation is Guyon's guide,

> "By whose sage help, secure and safe we slide,
> By whirl-pools and deep gulfs which gape for us so wide . . .
> For all through this worlds boistrous Sea must passe,

> Before we at our quiet Hav'n arrive, . . .
> Our Steers-man Temperance it right doth drive
> Besides the Rock that threat this Boat to rive,
> Are many Gulfs and Whirl-pools of decay
> Which wait th'Affections and the Senses five
> By force and sweet Allurements to assay."[75]

If this seems drab and slightly absurd it at least serves as some measure of the greatness of Spenser's achievement. He started from the same place, the conventional allegory of equations. Overt moralising within a general pattern in which Guyon was temperance, the boatman the will, the boat the body, the sea the world and so on was what one could have expected from a lesser writer. But Spenser transforms the whole tradition, associates it with dominant themes from ancient mythology, and treats his book as though it were a romance. He reaches out from the allegory of nouns to full adverbial allegory in fact.

SPENSER'S MUTABILITIE

William Blissett

First, an assumption, not subject to proof on the evidence at
our disposal. Edmund Spenser's "Two Cantos of Mutabilitie"[1]
may in fact be, as they appeared to his printer after the poet's
death, "both for Forme and Matter . . . parcell of some following
Booke of the Faerie Queene, under the Legend of Constancie"; or
they may be material left over from an earlier version of The
Faerie Queene; but I regard them as being now most patient of
interpretation as a detached retrospective commentary on the
poem as a whole, forming as they do a satisfactory conclusion to
a foreshortened draft, a stopping place at which, after a seriatim
reading, can be made a pleasing analysis of all. Indeed, from the
high ground of Arlo Hill perhaps more of Spenser's total work can
be held in conspectus than from any other vantage point. He rounds
out his poetical life with a pageant of times and seasons as he had
entered upon it with eclogues proportionable to the twelve months;
in one of their aspects the cantos are "complaints and meditations
of the worlds vanitie; verie graue and profitable"; with the Daphnaida volume they share the figure of Cynthia and a summer day
in Ireland; the relations with The Faerie Queene in everything but
narrative are apparent; and it is only a little too fanciful to see in
the outcome of the story of Faunus and Molanna an account of the
present state of Ireland, cloudily enwrapped in allegorical devices.

Second, a few summary assertions, to be supported in the ensuing pages. "Mutabilitie" has been variously explained[2] by reference to Lucretius, to Empedocles, to Bruno. More convincingly,
it has been proved to derive from certain passages in Ovid's
Metamorphoses, and to be related to the tradition of Boethius. It
has also been linked speculatively with the poet's own life story.
I shall treat the poem as of intrinsic, not just documentary interest; moreover, I shall argue that it is not confused, not lugubrious,

Reprinted from Essays in English Literature from the Renaissance to the
Victorian Age, presented to A. S. P. Woodhouse 1964, Toronto 1964, pp.
26–42, by permission of the author and the publisher, University of
Toronto Press.

not defeatist, not pietistic. Instead, it is the product of an unusually subtle poetic intelligence, handling with great skill and verve combinations of ideas and modulations of feeling ranging from what the Elizabethans called satire, through mythological romance and masque-like pageantry, to end, equally to our surprise and satisfaction, in prayer. So original is it that it may be termed (with what reservations we shall see) that rare phenomenon in Renaissance literature, a poem without analogues. And it is not a mere virtuoso piece, of purely technical interest, for it has at its centre the permanent problem, or paradox, or mystery, of the alienated consciousness, l'homme révolté. Spenser has been said to be no ironist and of all poets to stand furthest from existentialism;[3] it is true—until he makes this final bold foray.

The poem opens in the tone of Elizabethan melancholy: in the same dark voice that Hamlet is to use in considering how a king may go a progress through the guts of a beggar, Spenser promises to tell of Mutabilitie's cruel sports and briefly identifies her (VII, vi, 5–6) as a Titaness, sister of Hecate and Bellona, who now aspires to heavenly honours along with them:

> For, she the face of earthly things so changed,
>   That all which Nature had establisht first
> In good estate, and in meet order ranged,
>   She did pervert, and all their statutes burst:
>   And all the worlds faire frame (which none yet durst
>   Of Gods or men to alter or misguide)
>   She alter'd quite, and made them all accurst
>   That God had blest; and did at first prouide
> In that still happy state for euer to abide.

> Ne shee the lawes of Nature onely brake,
>   But eke of Iustice, and of Policie;
>   And wrong of right, and bad of good did make,
>   And death for life exchanged foolishlie:
>   Since which, all liuing wights haue learn'd to die,
>   And all this world is woxen daily worse.
>   O pittious worke of MVTABILITIE!
>   By which, we all are subiect to that curse,
> And death in stead of life haue sucked from our Nurse.

If satire is made from our quarrel with the present and complaint from our quarrel with time, the poem thus far promises certainly to be a complaint, probably to be a satire.

Here should be supplied the sort of allegorical note—moral, historical or political, and physical—that would spring to mind in Spenser's day. For Dante's particular kind of divine poem the four levels of scriptural exegesis are appropriate; modern allegorical works are related in elaborate and idiosyncratic ways to various psychological, theosophical, and metapolitical systems; but allegorists of the tradition ending with Spenser regularly arranged their interpretations in three rather simple categories— morale, historice, physice.[4]

In moral allegory, as a state of soul, Mutabilitie embodies vain ambition and presumption, restless titanism, the unhappy consciousness. In political allegory, this state of soul, the temper of the malcontent, expresses itself as a force of restless innovation, a Marlovian "overreacher," daring the gods out of heaven and raising the standard of revolt against constituted authority. And in physical allegory, as a state of the world, Mutabilitie embodies destructive change, vicissitudo rerum as a cosmic principle, the "vanity" to which the creature is made subject at the fall, in Pauline phrase. It will be observed that all three allegories[5] conspire to present a dangerous, demonic figure whom any reader of The Faerie Queene will expect to be required to condemn unequivocally, as he has condemned Duessa and Acrasia and other enemies of Gloriana. But we shall soon learn from Mutabilitie's own mistaken haste not to presume too much or to get ahead of ourselves.

From the beginning, this Mutabilitie is a formidable figure: "were he liefe or sory," she passes through the celestial gates guarded by Time—Time the (Aristotelian) measurer of motion, not Time the (Ovidian) devourer of all things, for she herself has taken over that second function. As she sweeps onward, men on earth fear the return of chaos, and Jove calls to mind other cases of presumption in the earth-born, and their punishment.[6] But when she embarks on the stupendous exploit of forcing the gates of heaven and evicting its occupants, the violence and hubris of the Titaness become, surprisingly, not more but less obnoxious. Whatever the ethical judgment may tell us, we cannot help admiring her audacity, her resolution, her virtù; and it is a law of fiction that a reader or spectator always desires to see an action well begun completed—witness our implication in the designs of Tamburlaine and our anxiety lest the murder of Duncan in Macbeth be interrupted.

Storming into the palace of Cynthia, the bold intruder orders the goddess to give up her throne, to the amazement of the witnessing stars. The scene is brisk and violent, especially so for

Spenser, and if the modern reader is stimulated by it, how much
more shocked would be the reader for whom the poet wrote, for
whom the prime and unmistakable reference of Cynthia must be
none other than the Queen-goddess of England at present reigning.
Let us pause a moment to attune our ears to an "Ode of Cynthia"
sung on May Day, 1600, "before her sacred Maiestie at a shew on
horsebacke. . . ."[7]

> Th'Ancient Readers of Heuens Booke,
> Which with curious eyes did looke
>   Into Natures story;
> All things under Cynthia tooke
>   To bee transitory.
>
> This the learned only knew,
> But now all men finde it true,
>   Cynthia is descended;
> With bright beames and heuenly hew,
>   And lesser starres attended.
>
> Landes and Seas shee rules below,
> Where things change, and ebbe and flowe,
>   Spring, waxe olde, and perish;
> Only Time which all doth mowe,
>   Her alone doth cherish.
>
> Times yong howres attend her still,
> And her Eyes and Cheekes do fill
>   With fresh youth and beautie:
> All her louers olde do grow,
> But their heartes, they do not so
>   In their Loue and duty.

   Who is this Titaness that dares grapple with one who "reigns
in everlasting glory" and in the style and metre of The Faerie
Queene lifts her hand against a type of Gloriana herself? No vulgar upstart, surely, but a figure darkly grand, burning with sullen
intelligence: if Dürer's Melancholia, impelled after long immobility by furor melancholicus, were to bestir herself to action,
she would resemble Mutabilitie.[8] Very early (VII, vi, 2) the poet
finds it

> fittest to vnfold
> Her antique race and linage ancient,
> As I haue found it registred of old
> In <u>Faery</u> Land mongst records permanent.

And Mutabilitie herself later on will recount its details. But
where have we heard something like that before, indeed almost
the very phrases? Where but in the proem to the second book, in
which Spenser promises to present to the "fayrest Princesse under sky" the "antique image of [her] great auncestrie." I do not
mean to suggest that Mutabilitie and Gloriana are identical, just
that they are of comparable stature and allegorical weight. The
stanza about Mutabilitie's sisters bears out this interpretation.
Hecate may be said to personify the sinister side of things lunar
and hence to balance Diana—and the Virgin Queen of the lunar
land. Bellona may by the same token be called a sort of violent
step-sister of Britomart—and of her Tudor descendant. This is
in direct line with the conception of the Titans throughout Western literature and thought: [9] they always possess a certain god-
like grandeur, and if in their arrogance they want nothing as a
gift, this is balanced by a sense of justice in demanding their
rights.

Pride and reaching for power are the reverse side of Glory,
and demonic presumption goes with greatness. The balancing of
Gloriana and Mutabilitie is not a simple opposition such as we
find in Una and Duessa or in the true and the false Florimell:
there is nothing of Duessa in Una, and the false Florimell vanishes in the presence of the true. We have been told incidentally
that Argante, the lustful giantess, is a daughter of Titans, but
not a word do we hear of her in the grander context of Mutabilitie.
Indeed, as the poem develops, Mutabilitie is seen to have little to
do with ordinary moral evil, but rather, in moral and political
allegory, to represent the taint of evil, or presumption, in even
the highest natural good, the pursuit of rightful glory; and in the
physical, the subjection to destructive time of all earthly things,
including the woman whom a conspiracy of song had feigned to be
divine and immortal.

Elizabethan poets, and Spenser foremost among them, had in-
vested heavily in Elizabeth's golden and perpetual youth, exempt
from all variableness and shadow of turning. In this connection
a passage from Thomas Dekker is apposite as showing the work-

ing of a lesser imagination, strongly influenced by Spenser. Old Fortunatus was probably played at court in December, 1599—that is, after Spenser's death but before the posthumous publication of the "Cantos of Mutabilitie." In the prologue two old men speak of their Queen, Eliza: "Some call her Pandora: some Gloriana, some Cynthia: some Belphoebe, some Astraea: all by seuerall names to expresse seuerall loues." And one of them sings her conquest of time:

> I weepe for ioy, to see so many heads
> Of prudent Ladies, clothed in the liuerie
> Of siluer-handed age, for seruing you,
> Whilst in your eyes youthes glory doth renue:
> I weepe for ioy to see the Sunne looke old,
> To see the Moone mad at her often change.
> To see the Starres onely by night to shine,
> Whilst you are still bright, still one, still diuine:
> I weepe for ioy to see the world decay,
> Yet see Eliza flourishing like May. . . .[10]

Could he have alluded so confidently to Spenser's many types of Queen Elizabeth if he had known what lay unpublished with the dead man's papers? When Elizabeth Tudor made her first progress through London as Queen, she saw a pageant erected at the Little Conduit in Cheap, in which a young woman, the Word of Truth, was represented as the daughter of Time. "Time?" said the young Queen, "and Time hath brought me hither."[11] But as her reign wore on, it was not the happy moment or process of time but her timelessness that became the theme of poets, the more when the problem of the succession as she declined in years became the unspoken preoccupation of the graver sort. How Spenser and his friends were privately thinking and feeling on the subject is perhaps best illuminated by a phrase used by Sir Walter Ralegh at his trial in 1603, when he referred to his late sovereign mistress as "a lady whom time had surprised."[12] The phrase would apply to the well-known portrait (necessarily posthumous) of Queen Elizabeth with Time and Death.[13] It would likewise apply to his friend Spenser's Mutabilitie in the palace of his own Cynthia.

In the encounter, though Cynthia retains some dignity, the attention and sympathy of the reader are entirely diverted from her. I am suggesting no more, but no less, than that we are jolted when "Time strong, a checklesse Queene"[14] enters her precincts and touches her person, that we feel a secret sympathy with the ag-

258

gressor because she acts while her victim merely possesses, that we undergo with the poet a tacit abandonment of homage to a figure who (like Oriane de Guermantes) had exacted too long a sacrifice.

The irony of the poem becomes patent in the encounter of Mutabilitie with Jove (VII, vi, 23), which follows hot upon the indecisive clash with Cynthia:

> So, forth she rose, and through the purest sky
> To Ioues high Palace straight cast to ascend,
> To prosecute her plot; Good on-set boads good end.

Jove's stern aspect takes her momentarily aback, but she rallies her spirits and boldly claims legitimate rule through Titan, elder brother of Jove's father, Saturn. Against this, Jove can only appeal to right of conquest. A disturbing thought must cross every reader's mind, that Jove is not the Law but merely nine points of the Law. Mutabilitie is quick to draw the perfectly valid conclusion that he is no equal judge in his own cause, and so she appeals to the higher authority of Nature. Jove's grudging allowance of this appeal is a clear admission of moral defeat for him and victory for her.

If Mutabilitie had less dignity than Cynthia, she has more dignity than Jove and her arguments carry more weight than his. A woman orator, impudent, paradoxical, surprisingly cogent in confounding the right-thinking, persistent and imaginative in her claim to universal sway, Mutabilitie now begins to resemble no one so much as the Folly of Erasmus.[15] An Erasmian ironic tone is pervasive, sharpening here into satire, and we enjoy the discomfiture of Mutabilitie's victims as we enjoy the discomfiture of Hamlet's victims, or Malevole's, or even Vindice's. And yet there is something inherently unstable about an alliance of the reader or spectator with the satirist: it can last only while the moral ambiguity of the satirist's own position is obscured by the patent hypocrisy of his opponents. At the moment, however, Mutabilitie shows herself not inconstant but constant in demanding her rights, and Jove is revealed (or stripped and whipped and anatomized) as an embodiment not of constancy but of mere self-satisfaction in moral allegory, the status quo in political, and in physical of a cosmological worldliness that is pleased to regard the outward governance of the universe as ultimate. The argument of the poem and its tone of feeling are themselves proving mutable; our sage and serious poet is also a chameleon poet.

At this point Mutabilitie and Jove occupy a position in our esteem comparable to Satan and God the Father in the more shame-
faced of the Satanists' misreading of Milton. But Milton opens his
poem by presenting Satan at his most heroic and humanly appealing and then contrives to make the figure shrivel, whereas Spenser
presents Mutabilitie initially as menacing and demonic and then
goes on to admit the cogency of her argument and, what is just as
important for him, the beauty of her person. The reader fresh
from The Faerie Queene will recall other women who combine a
natural beauty with an element of the sinister. The beauty of
Duessa and Lucifera, of Philotime and the False Florimell is unnatural, and that of Acrasia merely seductive; leave them aside.
Radegund in the closest parallel, and it is worthy of note that she
disarms her masculine antagonist by her loveliness and can be
vanquished only by a female figure. For the present no woman
except the hapless Cynthia appears within the purview of Mutabilitie, and her appeal is to the "god of Nature," who can only be
presumed another Jove. And at the moment, if Mutabilitie is
abashed by the majesty of Jove, Jove in turn is struck by her
beauty: though they both rapidly recover themselves, the poem
never quite reverts to the grinding grimness of some of the early
stanzas.

To effect a transition Spenser allows himself a mythological
digression, a traditional feature of the epyllion, or little epic, of
which genre the "Cantos of Mutabilitie" may perhaps be regarded
as an example.[16] This is the story of foolish Faunus, who bribes
Diana's attendant, the nymph Molanna, to conceal him while the
goddess is bathing, and then so enjoys his treat that he laughs
aloud, to the alarm and indignation of Diana and her ladies. The
story purports to explain the reason for the present desolation of
Arlo Hill, and so it has a narrative and a thematic connection with
the poem as a whole—narrative as supplying a description of the
place where Mutabilitie and Jove are to plead before Nature,
thematic in being an account of destructive change, a story of
over-reaching and misdemeanour, of punishment not only of the
culprit but of the scene, the world, of the crime. But "crime"
surely is too strong a word. Like Cynthia in the main story,
Diana in the digression loses only a little of her dignity, her
sacrosanctity. Actually, the final effect is one of pleasantness
and delight: in contrast to the rushing dark satire of the earlier
stanzas, the digression dreamily delights in its own narrative,
spreading out to fill the time between the appeal and the hearing
with the true plenitude of romance.

260

Even the outcome of this subordinate action is not too stern. Arlo Hill is spoiled, but Molanna is united with her lover as Faunus promised her, and Faunus himself escapes serious punishment. One of the vindictive virgins advocates gelding him, but this is vetoed on the ground that the woodgods' breed must still endure; and here too the digression moves in the same direction as the poem as a whole: in effect, nature intervenes to limit the consequences of the fall to suffering and discomfort, not annihilation.

After this relaxation of tension, the main action resumes in the presence of Nature; and with the decision to use the feminine pronoun the poet arouses a curious new feeling of expectation, awe, and repose. The figure of Nature in the "Cantos of Mutabilitie"[17] has long been recognized as related to the goddess in Spenser's Garden of Adonis and Temple of Venus, and as belonging to a long literary and philosophical tradition including Chaucer's Parlement of Foules and Alain de Lille's Complaint of Nature, to both of which the poet alludes. Of two points we may remind ourselves. The first, common to Alain, Chaucer, and Spenser, is that Nature is altogether numinous, not at all secular, natura naturans, not natura naturata; and, as sage Heraclitus long before observed (fragment 123), "Nature likes to hide." The second, common to Spenser and his English master, is that Nature herself does not complain but rather embodies a serene and just power to which high and low, the satisfied and the disaffected, may present their case.

As all living things gather round Nature on Arlo Hill, finding their centre in her, we have a sense, as before in the Garden of Adonis, of being at the still point of the turning world.[18] In the palace of Cynthia, Mutabilitie was an intruder, but not here. By this juncture in the development of the poem we recognize in her a creaturely goodness, as her just appeal has proved and her beauty symbolized. Mutabilitie cannot simply represent sin if she humbles herself before Nature and if Nature in turn can call her "daughter." Perhaps this makes too much of a word of kindness; but there is a family resemblance between the two, for Mutabilitie is presented as a restless tomboy—aggressive as a man and passionate as a woman, and Nature is presented as possessing and rising above the limitations of both sexes. An Italian motto (a favourite saying of Queen Elizabeth) applies to both and joins them: per molto variare la natura è bella.

When all is quiet, Mutabilitie begins her case by arguing that the four elements—earth, water, air, and fire—are all subject to her and not to the gods, and then goes on to call the times and seasons of the year in procession so that Nature may either "demand in generall" or "judge her selfe, by verdit of her eye." Nature assents and commands Order to marshal them, and the pageant of Mutabilitie, the procession of the four seasons, the twelve months, Night and Day, Life and Death, files past. It is not a ragged and shambling shuffle such as might have befitted a spectacle of the decay of the world; neither is it the headlong rush that the Titaness in her earlier mood might have devised. Instead, in its festive ease it cancels, or compensates for, all earlier statements of the idea of destructive time in the Complaints or in The Faerie Queene, much as (for instance) the marriage of the Thames and the Medway had righted any imbalance of feeling caused by the presentation of the watery part of the world as teeming with monsters and hostile to life. Mutabilitie herself is a keen competitor, but here in her pageant she presents no agon of winter and summer, no hubris of the year-daemon demanding a reversal of situation:[19] the figures in the pageant, the spectators on Arlo Hill, the poet and the reader from beginning to end accept the totality of the vision and each of the elements comprising it.

If Mutabilitie intended her argument to be a treatise of reformation without tarrying for any, what actually has emerged, in the presence of Nature, is a ritual procession full of decency and order. The rebel has become for the moment Mistress of the Revels.[20] The unruly rout, satiric or comic, strident or grotesque, of the opening of the poem and the digression, has been succeeded by a pageant, an antimasque by a masque, discordia by concors.[21] Spenser does not labour the paradox, but it is unmistakable: the more successfully Mutabilitie pleads her case against Jove, the more she depends on a constant order implicit in the created world. Here she anticipates the experience of alienation characteristic of intellectuals in politics and the arts throughout modern times. What have we to show today for Elizabethan melancholy and Gothic melancholy, for the "spleen" in England and France, for Weltschmerz and mal du siècle, for the lost generation and the beat generation, but the happy works of the unhappy consciousness?[22]

The enthralling pageant comes to an end; while the spell is still upon us, Jove in a single prosy stanza (VII, vii, 48) states his case:

> Right true it is, that these
> And all things else that vnder heauen dwell
> Are chaung'd of Time, who doth them all disseise
> Of being: But, who is it (to me tell)

> That Time himselfe doth moue and still compell
> To keepe his course? Is not that namely wee
> Which poure that vertue from our heauenly cell,
> That moues them all, and makes them changed be?
> So then we gods doe rule, and in them also thee.

But Mutabilitie will have none of this. Spenser does not intend his shrew to be easily tamed. Reverting to her earlier, scolding tone, and breaking the spell of the pageant altogether, she expresses a rough scepticism of things that cannot be seen and of secret influence, and goes on to argue (but not, as in the pageant, to show) that the planets are mutable and their gods of earthly origin like herself.[23] And then in superb self-confidence she calls on Nature—"O thou greatest goddesse trewe!"—for judgment.

The following stanza (VII, vii, 57) is beautifully placed and beautifully modulated:

> So hauing ended, silence long ensewed,
>   Ne Nature to or fro spake for a space,
>   But with firme eyes affixt, the ground still viewed.
>   Meane while, all creatures, looking in her face,
>   Expecting th'end of this so doubtfull case,
>   Did hang in long suspence what would ensew,
>   To whether side should fall the soueraigne place:
>   At length, she looking vp with chearefull view,
> The silence brake, and gaue her doome in speeches few.

A long silence, for an emphasis awful and apocalyptic. A great expectation and doubt, because the gods and creatures at the parley know as well as we that Mutabilitie has made the better case, but all must fear that she would make the worse ruler. And then, so important for the interpretation of the tone of feeling of the poem, Nature looks up cheerfully.[24] Cheerfulness breaks in as never in Alain de Lille, as never in Spenser's own Complaints. The very absence of anxiety and strain is a judgment against Mutabilitie: before she says a word, Nature tells the unhappy consciousness what it most needs and most fears to hear: rejoice. And this cheerfulness if we reflect for a moment should come as no surprise to us or to Mutabilitie, for the impresario must have inwardly rejoiced with all the other spectators at the success of her show. Spenser has a little modified, and greatly deepened, the insight of his friend Gabriel Harvey—"Nature herself is changeable and most of all delighted with vanitye; and art, after a sort her ape, conformeth herself to the like mutabilitye."[25]

This is the long-awaited doom of Nature (VII, vii, 58–59):

> I well consider all that ye haue sayd,
>   And find that all things stedfastnes doe hate
>   And changed be: yet being rightly wayd
>   They are not changed from their first estate;
>   But by their change their being doe dilate:
>   And turning to themselues at length againe,
>   Doe worke their owne perfection so by fate:
>   Then ouer them Change doth not rule and raigne;
> But they raigne ouer change, and doe their states maintaine.

Like all other creatures, Mutabilitie seeks her own perfection. This is promised in the beauty of her person, it is performed in her masque. But her own perfection is not to have absolute sway:

> Cease therefore daughter further to aspire,
>   And thee content thus to be rul'd by me:
>   For thy decay thou seekst by thy desire;
>   But time shall come that all shall changed bee,
>   And from thenceforth, none no more change shall see.

Nature's judgment is perhaps not far different from Jove's plea—with the important difference that it issues from Nature, not from Jove, who if "confirmed in his imperial see," is seen to hold power not in his own right but by Nature's delegation. As for Mutabilitie, we realize now (if we follow out the implications of the argument)[26] that in claiming all the works and manifestations of nature as her own, she has also illogically claimed both to be Nature and to be judged by her—to be judge, that is, in her own cause, the very injustice she would not allow to Jove. La femme révoltée is "quite put down and whist," with many of her arguments allowed provisionally, all disallowed ultimately, and one refuted on the spot—for Mutabilitie, who had appealed to Nature, argued against the power and the very existence of the unseen, and yet, when judgment is delivered, "Natures selfe did vanish, whither no man wist." What we have seen in the "Two Cantos" is Mutabilitie dilating her being, first in strident aggression born of frustration and resentment, then in imaginative order springing from joy of creation, and finally at the word of Nature returning to herself again.

Attached to the two cantos are two stanzas, perhaps as the cantos themselves are attached to The Faerie Queene:

When I bethink me on that speech whyleare,
 Of <u>Mutability</u>, and well it way:
 Me seemes, that though she all vnworthy were
 Of Heav'ns Rule; yet very sooth to say,
 In all things else she beares the greatest sway.
 Which makes me loath this state of life so tickle,
 And loue of things so vaine to cast away;
 Whose flowring pride, so fading and so fickle,
Short <u>Time</u> shall soone cut downe with his consuming sickle.

Then gin I thinke on that which Nature sayd,
 Of that same time when no more <u>Change</u> shall be,
 But stedfast rest of all things firmely stayd
 Vpon the pillours of Eternity,
 That is contrayr to <u>Mutabilitie</u>:
 For, all that moueth, doth in <u>Change</u> delight:
 But thence-forth all shall rest eternally
 With Him that is the God of Sabbaoth hight:
O! that great Sabbaoth God, grant me that Sabaoths sight.

The last line is a full stop, both to the "Cantos" and to <u>The Faerie Queene</u>: to read it is really to be "in at the death of the Blatant Beast"—nothing more can happen. Again, it is a return, in its explicit Christianity, after much dilation in the order of nature, to the order of grace,[27] and so links the end of the poem as we have it with the beginning, the omega with the alpha.

The stanzas have something of the quality of a medieval "retractation"—in glorified Renaissance version.[28] They recall the prayer with which Chaucer brings his long secular poem <u>Troilus and Criseyde</u> to a close; they recall too the direction and goal of Petrarch's <u>Trionfi</u>, in which Chastity triumphs over Love, Death over Chastity, Fame over Death, Time over Fame, and Eternity over Time. "Thou my mind, aspire to higher things," Spenser is in effect saying—"And death once dead, there's no more dying then."

If this is a retractation, what does the poet retract? The presumptuous and demonic in Ann Boleyn's daughter, in Gloriana, in <u>The Faerie Queene</u>. This is done in no fit of pietism or religious melancholia. The "Cantos of Mutabilitie" is not a lugubrious poem: quite apart from the promise of eternity, Nature and the poet's Muse look upon the mutable world itself with calmness and joy. Spenser and his poem and his land of faerie desire ultimately to vanish with Nature, or turn their view as Nature does from the world to God, but this longing, which in another context might be called escapism or a failure of nerve, is expressed—and only expressed—in the last stanza of a poem printed at the end of an immense unfinished epic, a life-work dealing with every conceivable contingency, both private and public, in the secular world. But simply because the epic, with the exception of the Legend of Holiness, is secular, time-ridden, written under the inspiration of Clio, Spenser may, indeed must, round it out by leaving it behind, give significance to the milling crowd of contingencies by asserting the one ultimate:

> These things have served their purpose: let them be.
> So with your own, and pray they be forgiven
>   By others, as I pray you to forgive
>   Both bad and good.—[29]

Both Mutabilitie and Gloriana.

THE FAERIE QUEENE, I AND V

Frank Kermode

To speak of the "world" of a particular poet is to use a figure no one will find unfamiliar. It is a question of the natural uniformity, cohesion and interrelation of a body of work, however various, however divided into continents and elements. It is to assert that in Wordsworth, for example, there is a force universally at work, like gravity. And indeed the study of such worlds has sometimes been held to be analogous to physics. It would seem, on the face of it, that to make such a world (and poets have not scrupled to claim that they imitated God in doing so) is the labour of a major poet. For one thing, there is a requirement of size; a world has bulk before it has this kind of complexity. There is also a requirement of order and continuity, qualities one senses in a Shakespeare as well as in a Dante or a Milton, in the artist who seems to have no explicit philosophical or theological programme as well as in the poet whom we think of as in some way "committed."

Literate persons bring to such worlds certain expectations. These are the product of civilized conversation, of allusions encountered in literary comment. But the first thing that happens when they reach the new world is that these expectations are falsified and have to be dismantled. It is something like the experience Keats describes in his sonnet on Homer. The unaffected reader of Milton has a similar experience; he approaches Eden with certain expectations of severity and is disarmed by pleasure and human beauty, two features often omitted from maps of Milton. This dismantling process tends to be more violent with Spenser than with almost anybody else, partly because his poem is less well known than Paradise Lost or Hamlet, even to people who admire it. It is long, unfinished, and darkly related to the learning and images of an age fundamentally strange to us. It is true that there is an

Reprinted from the Bulletin of The John Rylands Library, Vol. 47 (1965), pp. 123-150, by permission of the author and the publisher. The article was first delivered as a lecture in the Library series of public lectures and has been included in the author's Shakespeare, Spenser, Donne: Renaissance Essays, London 1971.

abundance of scholarly guidance to be had; but in the end that also creates, as guides to public monuments usually do, expectations not always to be exactly realized. Furthermore, the guide one employs will always omit to mention what to the unconditioned eye may seem very striking features, so that there are not only unattained but unexpected experiences.

What I have now to say takes issue with some learned and acute modern guides to Spenser; but I say it not in a spirit of contention, but with proper gratitude for the help I have accepted from them. Spenser is very diverse, and lends support to many generalizations which seem flatly counter to one another. Thus, as everybody knows, The Faerie Queene fluctuates from a philosophical extreme—as in The Garden of Adonis, and the Mutability Cantos— to relatively naïve allegory such as the House of Alma.[1] It contains passages—such as Guyon's stay in the Cave of Mammon, or Britomart's in the Church of Isis—which seem to deal with high matters, but deliberately conceal their full meaning; yet it also contains transparent historical allusions to the trial of Mary Queen of Scots and the campaigns in the Netherlands. Its mood varies from the apocalyptic in Book I to the pastoral in Book VI. Sometimes, as with Florimel, one senses the need to complete Spenser's allegory for him, and sometimes one feels that he has for the time being almost forgotten about it; yet there are other times when one wonders at the density of meanings the fiction is made to bear. Readers of Spenser's own epoch seem to have enjoyed the allusions to great men of the age as well as the moral allegories; but later there was some danger of his sinking under the explanations of scholars, and in recent years there has been a noticeable trend towards simplicity of interpretation.

Obviously, we should not cumber his world with our own planetary ingenuities; but I think this process has gone too far. I shall now briefly characterize some of these simplifications, and then examine some aspects of the poem which seem to me to remain stubbornly what the simplifiers do not wish them to be.

At the beginning of this century it was assumed by all who considered Spenser's more philosophical passages that he knew Plato's dialogues, and that he may have interested himself in Renaissance Neo-Platonism. Later there came a different understanding; philosophical sources were found in Lucretius, in Empedocles, in "old religious cults." And it became a common-place of scholarship that Spenser could be illuminated by reference to the learning of Ficino, Benivieni, or Bruno.[2]

The picture of Spenser as a very learned man is not in itself absurd, since he understood that the heroic poet should be a "curious and universal scholar." But perhaps only an unfamiliarity with the conditions of Renaissance scholarship could have permitted anyone to imagine him to be systematically acquisitive of learning. Also there was prevalent an oversimple view of the Renaissance as a clean new start, which implied a failure to understand the extent to which medieval syntheses—including much Aristotle and Plato which scholars have misguidedly traced back to the original— persisted in the learning of Spenser's time. Thus the Garden of Adonis, which has attracted much speculation, possibly contains little philosophy that would have surprised an educated reader in any age between that of Spenser and that of Boethius. Not surprisingly there has been a reaction, and such influential books as those of W. L. Renwick (1925) and C. S. Lewis (1936) presented a more credible philosopher-poet, Lewis even labelling him, in a famous passage, "homely" and "churchwardenly."[3] Whether or no we accept this provocative formula, it remains true that Spenser used compendia, handbooks of iconography and so on; that he learnt from popular festivals; and that it would have been harder than used to be supposed to catch him working with an ancient classic open before him.

Yet we should not make the mistake of thinking that what seems exotic or far-fetched to us necessarily seemed so to Spenser. It is enough, perhaps, to remind ourselves of the great differences between his map of knowledge and ours—to remember, for instance, the continuing importance of astrology; the over-riding authority of theology; and a view of classical antiquity which seems to us simply fantastic. Spenser's mind was trained in forms of knowledge alien to us, and habituated to large symbolic systems of a kind which, when we read of them in Huizinga's The Waning of the Middle Ages, are likely to strike us as almost absurdly frivolous. Yet he was very serious in his wish to "make it new"—"it" being the sum of knowledge as it appeared to an Englishman at what seemed to be a great crisis of world history. It is hard for us to remember that Spenser served a queen whom he regarded as technically an empress, and whose accession was regularly thought of as the sounding of the seventh trumpet in the Book of Revelation.[4] Spenser saw this world as a vast infolded, mutually relevant structure, as inclusive as the Freudian dream; but he also saw it as disconnected, decaying, mutable, disorderly. We should expect to find his mind, especially when he deals with systematic ideas of order, very strange to us; and we should not easily allow this strangeness to be lost in learned simplifications.

I turn now to a second device for reducing the proportion of relatively inaccessible meaning in The Faerie Queene. This is to minimize the importance of a characteristic which had certainly appealed to Spenser's contemporaries, namely the element of historical allegory. Dryden thought that each of Spenser's knights represented an Elizabethan courtier; even Upton, who in his way knew so much more about The Faerie Queene than we do, stressed the historical allegory and elaborately explained allusions to Elizabethan history. This way of reading Spenser persisted and, perhaps reached its climax in the work of Lilian Winstanley half a century ago. But it was dealt a blow from which it has not recovered at the hands of the great American Spenserian, Edwin Greenlaw, in his book Studies in Spenser's Historical Allegory (1932).

Greenlaw's object is, broadly, to subordinate historical to ethical allegory. Historical allegory, he says, has reference principally to general topics; it refers to specific persons only momentarily and with no high degree of organization. This is now, I think the received opinion, and it certainly makes sense to relieve Spenser of barrenly ingenious commentary relating his poem to obscure forgotten, political intrigues. But if we apply Greenlaw's criteria indiscriminately we are likely to be left with a Spenser drained of that historical urgency which seems to be one of his most remarkable characteristics; it is the adhesive which binds the dream image to immediate reality. And certainly one consequence of the modern simplification of Spenser has been to loosen the bond between his great First Book and an actual world by denying the complexity of his historical allegory.

Finally, there is a third and very sophisticated mode of simplification, and this we can represent by reference to two critics, Mr. A. C. Hamilton in his The Structure of Allegory in the Faerie Queene (1951) and Mr. Graham Hough in his Preface to the Faerie Queene (1962). Mr. Hamilton is an enemy of "hidden allegorical significance," at any rate in Spenser, though of course he knows how much Renaissance critical theory has to say about "dark conceits." He suggests that we have now established "a fatal dichotomy" between poet and thinker, and that the despised old romantic habit of reading the poem for the beauties of its surface was no more harmful than the modern way of looking straight through to the emblematical puzzles beneath. We have, he argues, made the poem a kind of Duessa "whose borrowed beauty disguises her reality." Or, ignoring the fiction, we seek historical allusion, treating Book I, for example, as a concealed history of the English Reformation; or we devise some "moral reading yielding platitudes

which the poet need never have laboured to conceal." Offering
some instances of this, he asks, "Is this the morality which More
found divine? . . . The 'conceit as passing all conceit?' " And he
proposes his "radical reorientation": by concentrating upon the
fiction—the image—he will show that the poem is not like Duessa
but like Una, who "did seem such, as she was." He finds support
for his policy of subordinating all allegorical meanings to the
literal in some remarks of Sidney, and asks us to see the moral
senses not as kernels of which the fiction is the shell, but as the
expanding petals of a multifoliate rose—the meaning "expanding
from a clear centre."[5]

Mr. Hamilton shows much skill and sensibility in developing a
reading along these lines. But the method, attractive as it sounds,
will not serve. We lose too much. Not that I deny the pre-eminence
of the literal meaning, which Aquinas himself would have accepted;
only it does not mean quite what Mr. Hamilton thinks. The praise
of Henry More, for example, which was not in the least extravagant,
depended upon a well established view that images could combine
old truths to make a new one; the whole was greater than its parts,
and if you broke down the "icon" into its original constituents the
parts together would have less meaning than the whole icon. The
pleasure and instruction, you may say, is double: it is the intellectual delight of breaking down the icon and the intuitive benefit of
perceiving its global meaning. In short, although we may welcome
the figure of the multifoliate rose, we still need the idea of the ker-
nel and the shell, or of the fiction as a means of concealment: it
will not, in Spenser, be as perversely opaque as it is in Chapman,
but it may well be as elaborate as the sixth book of Aeneid, as read
by Renaissance mythographers.

What you find under the surface depends upon your learning and
penetration. Behind the Garden of Adonis are philosophic constituents, behind the First Book, constituents of world history; behind
the Fifth Book and especially the elaborate dream of Britomart,
high matters of imperial and national legal theory. I want, so far
as it is possible to have the best of both worlds, to enjoy the fiction
much as Mr. Hamilton does, but also to deny his contention that the
"universal reference prevents our translating events into historical
terms." Thus I am sure that Book V is impoverished if the Church
of Isis passage is treated simply as a figurative rendering of the
love-relationship of Artegall and Britomart; and this is how Mr.
Hamilton, following a note in A. S. P. Woodhouse's famous essay,
would have us read it.[6]

Mr. Hough tries, in his very agreeable book, to satisfy the contestants in this kind of quarrel by arguing that there are intermediate stages in literature between complete "realism" and naïve allegory; Shakespeare is equidistant between these extremes, his magic fully absorbing his theme so that one might speak of an "incarnation." Nobody, I suppose, using Mr. Hough's chart, would care to put Spenser—so far as the epic poem is concerned—anywhere save where he puts him, between Shakespeare and "naïve" allegory, as a maker of "poetic structures with various degrees of allegorical explicitness." And Mr. Hough's insistence that the allegory is "relaxed and intermittent" ought to remind us of the constantly varying "thickness" of Spenser's thematic meanings. But I do not think he serves us so well in asking us to depend in our reading upon our "general sense" of how "mythical poetry" works."[7] The Faerie Queene is an epic and so historical; we simply do not have an instinct which enables us to participate in historical myths relating to the religious, political and dynastic situations of Spenser's day. And our feeling for "mythical poetry" tells us nothing relevant to the juristic imperialism of his Church of Isis.

I have respect for both of these books; each in its way says that Spenser is a great poet who can mean much to modern readers; and I have given only a very partial account of them. But I quarrel with them, as with the others, because they habitually ignore what I think may be the peculiar strength of Spenser. Probably no other English poet has ever achieved so remarkable a summa as his. And it seems to me that we must not modernize him at the cost of forgetting this. "Poetry is the scholar's art." We should be glad to find in The Faerie Queene not only the significances of dream, but that fantastic cobweb of conscious correspondences, running over all the interlinked systems of knowledge, which a scholar-poet and a courtier might be expected to produce. Leaving out of account the philosophical simplification I began with, I intend now to speak of two parts of the poem: the historical allegory of Book I, and the allegory of justice in two parts of Book V. In each case, I myself find that the hidden meanings contribute to the delight of the fiction, because some of this delight arises from recognition of the writer's complex intent. And I do not think it does the dreamlike narrative any harm to include in it elements recognizable by conscious analysis.

The First Book of The Faerie Queene is well known to be apocalyptic, in the sense that it presents a version of world history founded rather closely upon the English Protestant interpretation of the Book of Revelation. I have elsewhere[8] tried to explain how the force of the book—as I see it—stems from a peculiarly subtle and active interplay of actual history with apocalyptic-sibylline prophecy. In its more political aspect, Book I is a celebration of the part of Elizabeth Tudor, the Protestant Empress, in the workings of providence. This a writer sufficiently sympathetic to Spenser—Milton, for example—would take in at a glance; and nothing in Milton is more Spenserian than the apocalyptic exhortations to England in the pamphlets On Reformation and Areopagitica, with their emphasis on God's manner of dealing with the nations, and the special role chosen for his Englishmen in the overthrow of antichrist. The Puritan commentators on Revelation, especially Bullinger and Bale, had long insisted upon the degree to which the text foretold the history of the Church, now reaching a climax; and for the better part of a century English opinion accepted Foxe's reading of ecclesiastical history as prefigured in the flight of the woman clothed with the sun—the true catholic church—into a wilderness from which, after forty-two months, she returns to her own as the Church of England. Discussing elsewhere the profusion of references to Revelation in Spenser's text, I expressed some surprise that the very scholars who, by the citation of patristic and Reformist commentaries, have made these identifications so sure, should, under the inhibition of Greenlaw, have forborne to study them in their obvious historical dimension. The text of The Faerie Queene, Book I is admittedly studded with the prophetic emblems of Revelation; it admittedly suggests that the Elizabethan settlement—the renovatio mundi brought by the Phoenix, the Astraean Elizabeth—fulfils the plan of history laid down in the Bible. Would it not seem likely that the narrative should allude to the history of the Church in the wilderness—that the story of Una and Duessa should, like Foxe's history of the Church, demonstrate the culmination of the divine plan in Elizabeth's accession?

It is clear that the limited series of allusions admitted by most editors to the course of English Reform under Henry VIII and Edward VI would not be enough for the apocalyptic-historical purpose Spenser announces with his imagery from Revelation. If you once identify the English with the primitive Catholic Church, you begin its history, as Jewel said, "after the first creation of the world."[9] After that, Joseph of Arimathaea brought Eastern Christianity to England; later there was a Christian king, Lucius; hence the early splendours and purity of the English Church, and the historic English independence of Rome and the "ten-horned beast" or Latin Empire, impaired only by the treachery of Hilde-

273

brand and his successors.[10]   The imperial claims of Elizabeth, however, defied the papal power and were traced back to Constantine.

Now the celebration in image and allegory of the Foxian version of history is not a remote and learned fancy; just as The Faerie Queene had her "yearly solemne feaste," so had Elizabeth. Her Accession day (17 November) was celebrated with increasing fervour, especially after the Armada, so that the Papists called it blasphemous and a parody of the adoration of the Virgin. Mr. Roy C. Strong has well surveyed the main themes of sermon, tract, ballad and entertainment relating to this feast.[11] Elizabeth is rarissima Phoenix, ultima Astraea, the renewer of the Church and faithful true opponent of antichrist. She has undone the work of the wicked popes who usurped the emperor's power and rights; she inherits both Lucius' recognized position as God's vicar, and the imperial power of Constantine and Justinian. Antichrist, the murderous sorcerers of the see of Rome, stands finally exposed. The queen is the defender of the true Church in an evil world. In a sense she is that Church. When Mr. Strong's preacher speaks of her as the sun shedding beams of religion, he is remembering "the woman clothed with the sun," who turns into the Una of whose sunshiny face Spenser speaks, "glistening euery way about with the light of the euerlasting Gospel."[12] As Mr. Strong observes, "the complexities of eschatological and imperial theory are never far away from the Accession Day themes."[13] Foxe's book, available with the Bible in every church, had become part of the body of patriotic thought, a textbook of English imperialism.

Now "homely Spenser" made, in the First Book of his poem, an epic of these very Accession Day themes, and he too chains up Foxe beside the Bible. An appeal to history was a prerequisite not only of the claims of the Catholic Church of England to antiquity and purity, but also of the queen's claim to possess imperial power over the bishops. The Faerie Queene may be mythical poetry; but its myths are the myths of English polity in the fifteen-eighties and nineties. Greenlaw himself observed that the use of Arthurian legend was for the Elizabethans not a Tennysonian archaism, but an argument from antiquity. The Elizabethans in fact saw Arthur's not as Malory's world, but as a unified Britain, and Arthur himself as king of the whole island, which, under the diadem of Constantine, was an empire according to Leges Anglorum.[14] Greenlaw observed also that it was commonplace in popular pageants to present the queen as True Religion; and that Spenser's poem reflects the view that her greatest service was the

establishment of true religion in England.[15] We are speaking of
an age that venerated Foxe—the age of Archbishop Parker, of
Sandys, of a queen who herself insisted upon her role as head of
a church founded by Joseph of Arimathaea and a State that inherited the powers of the Constantinian Empire. Indeed she had,
the claim ran, reunited the two.[16] Spenser could not avoid allusion to the whole of church history according to Foxe in describing the struggle between Una and antichrist.

Earlier interpretations of this kind—such as those of Scott and
Keightley—have been ignored or coldly dismissed by Spenser's
modern editors.[17] I think Scott and Keightley were wrong in detail, since they did not look at the history of the church through
the medium of Elizabethan propaganda; but they had the right
instinct. Any apologist of the Elizabethan settlement was obliged
to produce historical arguments, and Spenser, as an allegorical
poet, did so by means of hidden meanings in his fiction.

No one is in much doubt about the relationship of Una and
Duessa. Una is pure religion, which came to England direct from
the East: she is descended from "ancient Kings and Queenes, that
had of yore / Their scepters stretcht from East to Westerne
shore" (I. i. 5). Duessa, on the other hand, claims descent only
from an Emperor "that the wide West under his rule has / And
high hath set his throne, where Tiberis doth pas" (I. ii. 22). Her
false description of her father as emperor alludes to papal usurpa-
tions on the imperial power, a constant source of Protestant complaint. As Miss Frances Yates rightly says, Duessa and Una
"symbolize the story of impure papal religion and pure imperial
religion."[18] The success of the Tudors against the papacy is a
restoration of Una, of imperial rights over the sacerdotium. The
emperor, or empress, is, as Jewel says,[19] the Pope's lord and
master; Rome is not directly descended, he adds, from the primitive Eastern church, whereas the reformed Church of England can
make exactly this claim. Duessa is in fact a representative of a
religion not only antichristian but also anti-imperialist, anti-uni-
versalist. Duessa's very name accuses her of schism.

The Red Cross Knight has dealings with both ladies, appearing
first with Una in his capacity of defender of the true faith. It is
part of the dreamshift technique of the poem that he begins thus,
and as miles Christi, to end as the knight fidelis et verax or
Christ himself (whose bride Una is the Church)—after a career of
error typical of the human pilgrimage and also of the history of
England. In confronting him with Error in the opening Canto,
Spenser fulfils a multiple purpose, having in mind not only Christ's

victory over sin in the wilderness, but Una's great enemy, heresy, against which the early English Church protected her. Scott thought Error stood for Arianism; it probably corresponds more generally to that series of heresies which Bale associates with the opening of the second and third apocalyptic seals: Sabellianism, Nestorianism, Manichaeism, as well as Arianism.[20] Modern heresy, for which Jewel firmly places the responsibility on Rome, is the brood of these earlier errors. The locusts of stanza xiv derive, as Upton pointed out, from Revelation ix. 7, and were traditionally associated with heretical teaching—a point made by that herald of reform, Matthew of Paris, whom Foxe quotes approvingly.[21] The association is also remembered by Bale.[22] The enemies of Una had existed as long as there had been a Roman antichrist; Red Cross is her champion, since God had entrusted her, as Milton thought it natural, to "his Englishmen." The victory of Constantine, which made possible the Christian Empire, was ac-achieved, according to Foxe, with the aid of British troops; he thought it represented the end of 294 years since the Passion, and the binding of Satan for a thousand years. Constantine was him-self of course British, born of St. Helena at York.

Archimago, as is generally agreed, corresponds to the false prophet and the beast from the land, and so to antichrist. But it is worth observing that Spenser gives him a name which suggests that he is a magician; and this is a charge incessantly made against popes by Foxe and many others. Marlorat's compendious commen-tary on Revelation, published in 1574, says, on Rev. xiii. 15 (where the dragon seeks by supernatural means to destroy the woman clothed with the sun), that popes were often "nigromancers." He cites Cardinal Buno, who, in a life of Gregory VII, "writeth that many obtained the Popedom by divelish arts," especially Sylvester II, John XVIII, John XX, Benedict VIII, and Benedict IX. Gregory VII himself, "erst called Hildebrand," was a "notable nigromancer, who with the shaking of his sleeues woulde make as it were sparks of fire to flye abroad as often as he liked."[23] Boniface VII and VIII and most of the sixteenth-century popes, are also on the list. Napier the mathematician, in his commentary of 1593, finds allu-sion to popish necromancy in the Sibylline books, and says on the evidence of "Platina, the Popes own secretarie," that there have been twenty-two "Necromantick Popes and . . . eight Atheists."[24]

Sylvester II, who is frequently said to have sold his soul to the devil, was in fact a man of learning, a mathematician, and one who had a good try at reconciling papacy with empire; but doubtless the special odium reserved to him may be accounted for by his having been Pope in A.D.1000, when according to some accounts (not Foxe's) Satan was loosed after a thousand years of bondage. The other Pope most persistently charged with necromancy is Gregory VII, who was specially detested because, having gained authority in England through the Conqueror, he began that interference with English government which disfigured so many subsequent reigns, notably those of Henry II (who claimed judicial authority over the clergy) and John. Foxe singles him out as the Pope who started the encroachment on the rights of the temporal governor "whereby the Pope was brought to his full pride and perfection of power in the fourteenth century."[25] I have little doubt that Spenser was thinking chiefly of Hildebrand when he made Archimago a master of magic arts and described his plots against Red Cross.

We hear of Archimago's arts in xxxvi, and in xlviii he produces a succubus, a false church "most like that virgin true" until her real nature is revealed. She deceives Red Cross with her claim to be una sancta ecclesia, and makes outrageous demands on his body. Spenser may not have been thinking only of the troubles of the eleventh to the fourteenth century; the Synod of Whitby, where, according to Foxe,[26] Wilfrid first led England into the power of Rome, may also have been in his mind. But Gregory VII, who first claimed control of both the swords, ecclesiastical and temporal,[1] and so usurped the power of the emperor (Foxe has a woodcut illustrating the incident of Henry IV waiting Hildebrand's pleasure in the snow), was the greatest papal villain.[27] The powers resigned by Henry IV and later by Barbarossa, upon whose neck Alexander III set his foot, were recovered and refurbished by Spenser's empress, a point upon which Jewel is explicit.[28] So Spenser allows Archimago to conjure up the demonic church which tried to rule the world, and which the British Tudors were to exorcise. But the disgrace of Red Cross, which begins here, represents the long misery of the English Church from the time of Gregory VII until the first stirrings of reformation with Wyclif.

Other crucial events in the Anglican version of church history are reflected in Spenser's narrative. The presumptions of Boniface III coincided with the rise of Islam, and a monk called Sergius gave aid and comfort to these new enemies. The Turks were part of antichrist, said Foxe,[29] taking the contemporary threat from this quarter to be the loosing of the angels of the river Euphrates (Rev. xvi. 12); it reached its present form and strength at the end of the thirteenth century, just when papal power was greatest. Now Spenser has this, or something very like it, in mind when he makes Sansfoy an ally of Archimago. Red Cross first meets Duessa in the company of the infidel Sansfoy (ii. 13). She is adorned with a Persian mitre which, together with the bells and flounces of her "wanton palfry," signify the union of popish flummery and oriental presumption.[30] Sansfoy is the pagan antichrist, defeated by Red Cross as Arthur defeated the pagan Saxons and the crusades the Saracens. I do not say he does not, with his brothers, make a triad opposed to that of the Theological Virtues; the readings are perfectly consistent with one another. Sansloy and Sansjoy are also aspects of antichrist and paganism. It all goes back to Boniface and the Turks—even, perhaps, Duessa's lie about her past when she claims[31] to have been betrothed to a great prince who was murdered, which might be an allusion to the establishment by Boniface III of the puppet emperor Phocas.

There is surely reason to suppose that Spenser would think along these lines. Let me, to avoid tedium, spare analysis of the Fraelissa and Fradubio episode, clearly another allegory of the wrong choice of faith, and pass on to the story of Kirkrapine, Abessa and Corceca. Corceca is obviously blind devotion, Abessa, as Sr. Mary R. Falls established,[32] is not an abbess but absentee-ism, from abesse. The main difficulty is with Kirkrapine. I agree with Sr. Mary Falls that he cannot refer to the evils of monasti-cism; she argues, with some force, that the reference to church-robbing is more likely to apply to the behaviour of English bishops and courtiers after the Reformation. She cites much evidence, and more could be adduced. Sandys, for example (though himself not innocent of the charges he brings against others), asked the queen to end the abuses of the "surveyors"[33] "that trot from one diocese to another, prying into churches. The pretence is reformation; but the practice is deformation. They reform not offences, but for money grant licences to offend." And he asks the queen—"our most mild Moses"—to stay the hand of these "church-robbers." But he also calls this a perpetuation of a characteristic antichristian practice; and this is really our clue. Spenser is not thinking ex-clusively of a topical issue; what he has in mind is the duty of the newly restored church to abolish a practice typical of popery, that of using the goods of the church for personal and temporal pur-poses. Luther gloomily foresaw that church-robbers would not be checked till Armageddon.[34] Long afterwards Milton echoed him in Of Reformation,[35] speaking fiercely of prelates: "How can these men not be corrupt, whose very cause is the bribe of their own pleading, whose mouths cannot open without the strong breath and loud stench of avarice, simony and sacrilege, embezzling the treasury of the church on painted and gilded walls of temples, wherein God hath testified to have no delight, warming their palace kitchens, and from thence their unctuous and epicurean paunches, with the alms of the blind, the lame, the impotent, the aged, the orphan, the widow?" Milton accuses the prelates of theft in several kinds; Jewel specifically calls the Roman hierarchy sacrilegos, which is in the contemporary translation "church-robbers," for refusing the laity the wine at communion. Clearly any act which impoverished the church could be called church-robbing; there were contemporary instances, but Spenser has in mind the long record of antichrist and his misdeeds. In The Shepheardes Calender "September"[36] he is more specifically attacking contemporary misappropriations; but when he speaks of the foxes replacing the wolves in England he is thinking of the clergy as having taken over the role of thieves from the pagans. To compare the antichristian clergy to foxes is an old device stemming from Christ's description of Herod as a fox, and from a gloss on Cant. ii. 14; Sandys uses it[37] and so does Spenser when he gives Duessa, revealed in all her ugliness, a fox's tail (I. vii. 48). What is scandalous is that this ancient wrong should have survived in the reformed church. Kirkrapine, incidentally, lives in concubinage with Abessa. This certainly suggests the unholy relation between simony and absenteeism in Spenser's time, but also suggests that it is a leftover from an earlier period; for Abessa reproaches Una with unchastity, which hints at the Romanist distaste for the married priesthood of the reformed church,[38] and again associates Kirkrapine with the bad religion before reform.

Archimago, disguised as Red Cross and having Una in his charge, represents a bogus English church betraying true religion. That Sansloy should bring Archimago near to death suggests the self-destructive follies of Urban VI (1318–89, Pope from 1378), who seems in fact to have been more or less insane; Wyclif said that he destroyed the authority of the papacy; after him "there is none to be received for the pope, but every man is to live after the manner of the Greeks, under his own law."[39] This lawless folly, and the contemporary inroads of the Turks, probably account for the episode. The rescue of Una from Sansloy by satyrs, as Upton noticed,[40] means the succour of Christianity by primitivist movements such as the Waldensian and Albigensian; some primitives fall into idolatry (hence the follies of some puritan heretics) but the true Reformation line is represented by the well-born primitive Satyrane, who instantly knows the truth and opposes Sansloy.

The subjection of Red Cross to Orgoglio is the popish captivity of England from Gregory VII to Wyclif (about 300 years, the three months of viii. 38). The miles Christi, disarmed, drinks of the enervating fountain of corrupt gospel and submits to Rome. He is rescued by Arthur, doing duty for Elizabeth as Emperor of the Last Days, saviour of the English Church. The viciously acquired wealth of Duessa is confiscated. In ix. 17 Red Cross places Una under the charge of Gloriana, head of the Church. In this warp of allegory the capitulation to Despair must mean the Marian lapse; after that Red Cross is assured of his Englishness, and shown the New Jerusalem, of which Cleopolis or London, capital of the Earthly Paradise,[41] seat of the empress, is the earthly counterpart. Only then does he assume the role of the warrior fidelis et verax and, with the aid of the two sacraments of the true church, enact the slaying of the beast, the harrowing of hell, the restoration of Eden and the binding of Archimago. The English settlement—to which, as Revelation proved, all history tended, is a type of that final pacification at the end of time. Spenser makes it clear that it is only typical; but the boldness with which he conflates history and the archetype in Revelation proves how fully he accepted Foxe's bold formula, "the whole church of Christ, namely . . . the church of England."[42]

I have tried, in making this sketch of the allegory of ecclesiastical history in Book I, not to forget that Spenser's historical view was that of Anglican church historians. This, after all, is rather to be expected than not, in view of the apocalyptic and protestant-imperialist nature of Spenser's poem. What I suggest, in short, is that given the apocalyptic character of Book I—which cannot be denied—allegories of the kind I propose must be present in the poem; consequently the historical allegory is not the flickering limited affair it is sometimes said to be; nor can we pick it up in all its depth by a learnedly ignorant contemplation of the surface of the fiction.

I now turn to a different aspect of Spenser's allegory, the episodes of Mercilla and the Church of Isis in Book V. I take it that the allegory is both juristic and imperialist. Obviously Justitia is here presented as superior to the private virtue treated by Aristotle, and of course also to ius, which is one of its servants. Thus it is in the great fourteenth-century fresco at Siena, and thus it is in the commonplaces of Roman law.

There is no longer any need to prove the existence of Spenser's imperial theme; Miss Yates has clearly established it. Elizabeth claimed imperial status, adapting with the Emperor Charles V and others a view of empire that goes back to the Ghibellines. She was

the world-leader who maintained the imperial peace, and renewed
the time, preparing her people for the coming of Christ. This was
the official role of Spenser's Virgin, the Empress-Astraea.[43] And
this Protestant and nationalist imperialism denies what even Frederick II admitted, that the Pope has a complementary task. In the
empress the potestates distinctae—imperium and sacerdotium—of
medieval law are united.

The opening lines of Book V describe how very far we have got
from the age of gold. Spenser's poem throughout maintains a tension between the ideal and the actual, and he knows that the return
of the Imperial Virgin, first prophesied for Constantine, has occurred only in a figurative and restricted sense. Yet he is prepared to maintain this tension, and to present his Elizabeth as
Iustitia or Astraea.[44]

He speaks thus of Justice:

> Most sacred virtue she of all the rest
> Resembling God in his imperiall might:

And thus of Elizabeth:

> Dread Souerayne Goddesse, that doeth highest sit
> in seate of judgement, in th'Almighties stead . . .

First we hear of the agents of justice, of Arthegall as pupil of
Astraea and disciple of Bacchus and Hercules, dispensing justice
with the aid of Talus. The allegory proceeds simply enough until
Arthegall falls victim, Hercules-like, to Radigund; and although
there is much of political interest in these cantos, and we see
instances of Injustice, we have not yet encountered the formal
Iustitia. This we do when Britomart, at the beginning of Canto vii,
enters the Church of Isis to prepare for the liberation of Arthegall.

We shall understand neither the Church of Isis nor the Court of
Mercilla unless we have some notion of the contemporary connotations of the word "Equity," and its relation to Justice. Spenser,
though in translating Plutarch's "Iseion" he probably borrowed the
expression "Isis Church" from Adlington's Apuleius,[45] obviously
intended in this part of the Fifth Book to make a formal Templum
Justitiae.[46] In doing so he is remembering a tradition at least as
old as Augustus, whom Ovid congratulated on raising a temple to
Justitia. Ulpian called judges the priests of Justice; Justinian
speaks of the "most holy temple of Justice" and of "the temple of
the Roman Justice." Statues were made showing governors, as

Justice embodied, with Dike, Eunomia and Themis beside them.[47]
The twelfth-century glossator Placentinus elaborately describes
an allegorical Temple of Justice: Justitia is a dignified figure
with Ratio over her head, many Virtues about her, and Equity in
her embrace.[48]

This figuration developed along with the Roman law. The Neapolitan lawyer Lucas de Penna held that Iustitia, properly conceived, is identical with equity.[49] Equity is indeed the source of
law, that which makes Justice just; for summa ius, summa iniuria
is an old saying. Penna's jurisprudence was influential in sixteenth-century France,[50] and the allegorical representations of
Justice and Equity were modified accordingly. Thus Delbene
shows Equity controlling Justice with a rod (obtemperatio quasi
virgula).[51] Equity is the mother of law, the mediator between
natural and human law; and this point was given cosmological
significance by the equation between mater and materia in the dicta
of late medieval jurisprudence.[52] In this way the justification of
cosmic inequalities and of human law—perhaps even of human salvation, since the Billigkeit of Luther is related to these conceptions
of equity[53]—are all related, and Spenser's choice of the Plutarchan
myth of Isis begins to have the look of a very rich allegorical invention.

Imagery of this kind formed a part of that juristic myth which,
as Kantorowicz showed, replaced earlier liturgical conceptions of
the emperor after the death of Frederick II.[54] It is therefore intimately associated with the imperial mythology cultivated at the
court of Elizabeth I. The emperor, as a fount of equity, directly
mediates divine law, without the intervention of the Pope. But even
if it is allowed (as it must be) that the Elizabethan propaganda borrowed freely from European imperialist mythology, it is also evident that the imagery so far spoken of is related to Roman law, and
not to English. This calls for a word on the contacts between the
two systems.

The prospect of a Reception of Roman law in England seems to
have existed but briefly during the reign of Henry VIII. More,
Elyot and Starkey admired Roman law, largely because of its
superior equity; the king's cousin Cardinal Pole was its advocate.
The king himself, when he abolished the study of canon law in
England, set up Chairs of Civil Law at Oxford and Cambridge, and
Gentile at Oxford, an Italian refugee, was a learned Roman civilian.
Maitland, who at one time held the view (now disputed) that a Re-
ception came very near to occurring, notes that Roman law "made
pleasant reading for a King who wished to be a monarch in church

as well as state: pleasanter reading than could be found in our
ancient English law-books."[55] But the common lawyers prevailed.
How then could the king's daughter develop her imperial mythology
in terms of the Roman law? Admittedly, the close relationship between English and French courts in the fifteen-eighties, when there
were high hopes of a politique agreement, might alone have ensured
that the French mystique of imperium should affect English practice. Of course it was possible to maintain that even "by the common law of England, a Prince can do no wrong," as Bacon put it to
the Council during the examination of Essex in 1600.[56] And the
Tudors had always founded their rights in the common law. But
they were certainly not unwilling to improve their security by reference to another system (appropriate, after all, to the re-embod-
iment of Augustus and Constantine) in which the Prince was not
merely legibus solutus but also lex animata and a god on earth.

That Elizabethan England was conscious of a double standard
in law is suggested by the contemporary debate on English equity.
Formerly it had been considered an aspect of the common law, and
since 1873 it has returned to the common law; but in the time of
Elizabeth it was the province of the queen. The prerogative courts,
especially those of Chancery and Star Chamber, represented the
queen's justice independent of the common law courts. The Chancellor in Chancery was not bound by common law precedent but by
equity and conscience; Hatton called himself the queen's conscience,
and when Hamlet speaks of "the conscience of the King" he is presumably remembering a familiar expression, "the conscience of
the Queen," which was the motive of Chancery. The positive function of the Court was to remedy injustices that had no remedy in
common law. This might be for many reasons, and not only because the common lawyers were bound by rule and precedent, and
the common law incompetent in certain causes, such as those relating to uses and trusts. The plaintiff might be a poor man, or
the defendant a magnate with power to bribe, threaten or persuade
a jury. (One remembers that the earl of Leicester was surprised
to be told that it was an offence to influence a juryman.)[57] The
increased use of this court brought many protests from Elizabethan
lawyers, who saw in the growing activity of the courts of equity a
usurpation of their authority.[58] Already, in fact, Chancery was
building up the colossal backlog of business and the concern for
precedent that made it, for Dickens, not so much a court of equity
as a death-trap for innocent litigants. But in Spenser's time it
was still the court of the queen's conscience; and inevitably the
judgements of the chancellor, which were unrelated to the common
law, touched the older tradition of the Roman law at many points.

So did the Court of Star Chamber. This court grew out of the Council, and dealt equity in criminal cases, notably those touching the security of the queen. Thus it punished scandals, seditions, riots, and, in this reign, recusancy; for which reason, and because of its brutal examinations and punishments, it was hated by Puritans and abolished when the Long Parliament came to power in 1641. Chancery had its enemies also. Star Chamber was a court in which the monarch was present, either symbolically (as in Elizabeth's reign) or in person, as at least twice in the reign of James I.[59] The association of this court with absolutism was strong in the minds of its enemies, and absolutist doctrine was in turn associated with the Roman law.[60] In 1610 Cowell, a Cambridge law professor, argued that Roman law and absolute monarchy went hand in hand; and Bacon on the other side assured James I that the Court of Chancery was the court of his absolute power, as well as the conscience of the realm.[61] It is hardly surprising, then, that when Parliament triumphed so did the common law; when Star Chamber was put down Chancery narrowly escaped. In the reign of Elizabeth a Roman absolutism would affect not only the imagery of a poet but the speculations of jurists. Raleigh argued that the capacity of Parliament was merely advisory;[62] and later Lord Ellesmere, known as the great enemy of the common law, could declare that the judges had no rights of equity since these belonged to the chancellor in his capacity as the king's conscience.[63]

In the native English conception, law is logically prior to equity, hence the maxim "Equity follows law." In Roman law, as we have seen, equity can be called the source or foundation of law: lex est super aequitate fundata; ius simpliciter sumptum est aequitas.[64] Without equity law has nothing to do with justice: summa ius, summa iniuria. In the England of Elizabeth there was a conflict between the common and the imperial interpretation, and Spenser favours the latter. The fount of imperial equity is the emperor; and the relation of lex scripta to his will is analogous to the relation of Scripture to the will of God.[65] On this view the object of a court of equity is to enable the emperor to justify the law (even when it proceeds like Star Chamber, to do so, by ear-lopping and other mutilation). The theological parallel is intimate. Like her father, Elizabeth, as head of Church and State, must have found comfort in the Roman law; she wielded the two swords, and was charged with all the powers of imperium and sacerdotium.

With all this in mind, let us look at the Church of Isis, Spenser's Templum Iustitiae. He begins with a conventional assertion

of the pre-eminence of Justice over the other virtues, and approves
the ancient custom of establishing temples to Justice (Iustitiam
namque colimus quasi Deam sanctissimam says an old jurist, who
cannot think of Justice as merely a virtue).[66] But what he then
celebrates is not Justice but Equity—"that part of Iustice, which is
Equity"; and in the end he will show it to be the better part. The
choice of Plutarch's myth has all Spenser's subtlety of invention.
Plutarch notices that at Hermopolis Isis was identified with Justice.[67]
She is also associated with Astraea; with the moon, emblem of the
imperium; and with matter.[68] He wants us to remember that Justice
and Equity reflect a vast cosmic process; that Equity is like matter,
and that Justice gives it mutable forms. But he also means that
Osiris is the common law considered in isolation from the equity
courts. The priests of Isis are Ulpian's learned civilians, servants
of the imperial equity (their long hair distinguishing them from the
tonsured canonists) and they practise in such prerogative courts as
Chancery and Star Chamber. (Spenser apparently borrowed the detail of their long hair from an account of the priesthood of Rhea.)[69]
Their slightly feminine appearance may also be appropriate to the
service of an empress, and their asceticism to the intense virginity
cult which attached to this inheritor of the titles vicarius Iustitiae
(from the Empire) and vicarius Christi (from the British King
Lucius). But chiefly their abstinence from wine, the blood of the
rebellious Titans, alludes to their implacable opposition to innovation and recusancy (we recall the earlier association of the giant
with Anabaptism). The foot set on the crocodile and the foot fast
on the ground (vii) reflect the criminal equity of Star Chamber; the
wand, like the one in Delbene which signified the control of Justice
by Equity, stands for the power of Chancery in civil cases. Why
does the crocodile enwreath her waist with his tail? (For I assume
we must emend vi. 9: "That with his wreathed tail . . .") In Plutarch the crocodile is Typhon, an evil force, destroyer of Osiris.
Here the Plutarchan sense is present also; Plutarch speaks of
Typhon as discord and heat. Crocodiles were engendered by the
sun on the mud of the Nile, and were in consequence a product,
like wine, of the earth, and so in Spenser's allegory associated
with rebellion and injustice. Here the crocodile is purely human
law: summa ius, summa iniuria. Its tail suggests an impotent
enmity towards imperial Equity; but the foot of Isis controls it as
firmly as, in the woodcuts, that of Elizabeth controls the papacy.

In her dream, Britomart becomes a priest, but is at once (xiv)
transformed into an empress, robed in imperial purple and crowned
with the sun symbol. In view of what we already know about her as

progenitress of the Tudors, we see that Britomart is now, in a vision, the imperial power of the dynasty. The Typhonic tempest and fire that follow are rebellion against this power, as established by the settlement—rebellion both political and religious, and suppressed by the common laws of England, here represented by the crocodile.[70] The presumption of the crocodile after this can represent the impatience of the common lawyers with absolutist claims, and with the increased use of prerogative courts; and the strange union of Britomart and the crocodile is the full union of justice and equity in the imperial dispositions of the queen. Human law, according to medieval jurisprudence, can attain to natural law only in union with equity; and the source of equity is the empress. According to the priestly interpreter of the dream, the crocodile is Arthegall, who throughout the Book has stood for Justice considered independently of Equity; and from the union springs a lion, symbol of the natural law. Thus the empress, maintaining a proper relation between the common law and equity, is making proper use of her prerogative courts for the purpose of controlling the habitual and inevitable injustice of the law, and the forces tending to rebellion. Spenser, in short, has refashioned the traditional figures of Justice allegories in order to intervene in the current controversy between the courts of law and the courts of equity; and this in its turn implies a defence of the imperial claims of Elizabeth, which necessarily involve the Roman law.

We turn now to the Court of Mercilla. It is often said that Spenser's methods are not truly pictorial; but sometimes The Faerie Queene has the air of a great fresco, where one part should be seen in a simultaneous spatial relation with another, as in Lorenzetti's great allegories for the Palazzo Pubblico in Siena. So it is here. We remember that Britomart, fortified by her might in Isis Church, goes off to overthrow Radigund, the type of female tyranny. This is exactly echoed in Canto ix; for Mercilla is an aspect of Isis. They are related to one another much as are Iustitia and Buon Governo in Lorenzetti.[71] And in Mercilla's presence we are once more in the prerogative courts of England. Overseen by Awe, regulated by Order, the people seek the true justice denied them in the common law, a justice not perverted by "brybes, or threates" (xxiv). A poet punished by the nailing of his tongue to a post has committed slander (he accused the queen of "forged guile," which is a quotation from the Isis Church canto [VII. vii. 3] and there associated with the rebellious Typhon-crocodile). His offence and its punishment remind us of the jurisdiction and also of the penalties of the Court of Star Chamber. The queen's throne, with the lions and fleurs-de-

lys of England and France, recalls the obligatory presence of her
State in that court. Above her is a cloud-like canopy borne up by
angels, perhaps a deliberate reminiscence of the maestà.[72] She
has two swords—the sceptre of peace and clemency and the rusted
sword of justice; the imperium demands clemency,[73] but equity is
not merely a matter of mercy, and the rusted sword is sometimes
used. The presence of two swords can, in addition, hardly fail to
suggest the potestates distinctae of medieval political theory; she
embodies both the imperium and the sacerdotium.[74]

   She is surrounded by the daughters of Jove, the Litae, properly
the horai of Hesiod, whose function is equity. They are Dike (Justice, and sometimes called Astraea), Eunomia, Ius, and Irene (Pax).
With them are Temperance and Reverence. These are imperial
virtues. Long before Elizabeth, the emperor has been enthroned
with Dike and Eunomia; the other virtues echo those represented
in Lorenzetti's Sienese frescoes. The lion at the feet of Mercilla—
and reminding us of the statue at Nonsuch of Henry VIII trampling
a lion—again fulfils Britomart's dream, but is the common law in
bondage to equity.

   The tone of this passage is that of a courtly version of the popular Queen's Day celebrations, wherein Elizabeth was thanked for
delivering the realm from the evil power of the Pope, and for
maintaining the peace and security of the realm. Her accession
day God had ordained as a Holy Day "next to that of his sonne
Christ,"[75] and Spenser, though he thinks of her as Astraea and as
Isis, also thinks of her as the Blessed Virgin. Being herself Justice incarnate as Equity, she proceeds, as Britomart proceeded
to the suppression of Radigund, to the trial of Duessa. Duessa is
frankly Mary Queen of Scots, the most distinguished victim of
Elizabeth's prerogative courts; and the book moves on to an easy
historical allegory of the Netherlands campaign against the Spanish supporters of antichrist. We are reminded of III. iii. 49, and
the prophecy of a universal peace under a royal virgin who "shall
Stretch her white rod over the Belgicke shore"—the rod, we see,
was the rod of Isis-Equity in the seventh canto of the Book of Justice.

   It would seem, then, that the Fifth Book has, at its critical
points, a most elaborate juristic-imperialist allegory. I have not
explained it in full; for my immediate purposes I shall be satisfied
if it appears that scholars are wrong to reduce the Isis Church
episode to a "marriage debate," and explain the vision of the crocodile threatening Britomart as a recapitulation of the rape of
Amoret. Even Woodhouse's elaborate and rather fine interpreta-

tion[76] makes it only a dream allegory of the future union of Britomart and Arthegall. I have tried to put the episode into a context
of juristic allegory, and restore its links with Spenser's dominant
heroic theme, the vision of Empire.

I have said enough, perhaps, in arguing for Protestant-imperialist ecclesiastical history in Book I, and for Protestant-imperialist equity in Book V, to show that I believe in a Spenser more
rather than less historical in his allegory, a Spenser more susceptible than it has lately been fashionable to believe, to historical
analysis. In fact I do not think one can enter fully into his long
dream without the kind of knowledge such analysis has provided,
and should provide. Spenser followed the antique poets heroical
in this: he excluded no learning that would subserve his national
theme, and enable him to show knowledge and history as they are
related to a vision of his country as the heir of Empire and of Eden.

THE FAUNUS EPISODE[1]

Richard N. Ringler

The sudden and irreverent irruption of "Foolish God Faunus"[2] into Spenser's Mutability Cantos has puzzled many critics. Graham Hough finds that the episode "is charming, and it throws light on Spenser's attitude to Ireland . . . but it is not otherwise connected with the Mutability theme."[3] According to Douglas Bush, "Spenser's invented or adapted myths usually have an allegorical purpose, but it is hard to find one here, and the tone of the digression is certainly out of key with the prevailing seriousness of Mutability."[4] I hope to show in the present paper not only that the episode does indeed have an allegorical purpose, and one which contributes usefully to the over-all meaning of the Cantos, but also that its tone is consonant with—even if contrasted to—that of the Cantos as a whole.

Sebastian Evans long ago characterized the episode as a "topographical allegory to account for the presence of thieves and wolves in [Ireland],"[5] and this of course is Spenser's avowed purpose in introducing the story: it is an etiological myth in the right line of Ovid's Metamorphoses. Modern brains, however, have proved more fruitful of interpretation, and two efforts have been made recently to impale the Faunus episode on the horns of historical allegory. The first of these—that of Mary K. Woodworth—claimed the identification of Molanna with Arabella Stuart and of Faunus with "a member of the Hertford family."[6] The second effort—that of Judah K. Stampfer—proposed the following identifications: Faunus equals Tyrone, Cynthia equals Elizabeth, Molanna equals the Irish populace, Arlo Hill equals Munster. Faunus' desire to see Cynthia naked is Tyrone's desire "to see Elizabeth stripped of her power and majesty in Ireland."[7] To accomplish this wish he must first corrupt Molanna, the Irish populace. He promises to unite her with the Fanchin, who is either "national freedom" or "what is more likely, the Roman Catholic Church." Needless to say, the wholesale application of such mechanical allegories hopelessly vulgarizes the poem.

Reprinted from Modern Philology, Vol. 63 1965), pp. 12–19, by permission of the author and the publisher, The University of Chicago Press.

My own interpretation, which is not historical, relates the episode to its context in six ways, some of complement, some of contrast. Thus it satisfies our a priori expectation that an interpolated episode of this sort will pull both toward and away from its context, will complement it fully by being at once reinforcement and relaxation. "Pull away" will be registered in tone and in certain aspects of diction, "pull toward" in underlying significance and other aspects of diction.

1. The first way in which the Faunus episode contrasts and complements the account of Mutability is by supplying what may not unjustly be called "comic relief"—or perhaps "relief" is not quite the word for it, since the preceding part of the Canto had itself contained elements of comedy. In any event, Faunus and his adventures introduce a refreshing change of tone and dramatis personae.

2. The Faunus episode, like the earlier account of Mutability's revolt, describes an assault made upon Cynthia. The earlier attack had been leveled at her planetary identity as ruler of the "kingdome of the Night, and waters"; Faunus assaults her in her pastoral role, "soueraine Queene profest / Of woods and forrests."

3. The attack in both cases is made by a person whose boldness and foolishness are emphasized, but whereas Mutability's story had stressed the boldness of evil ambition, the Faunus episode stresses its foolishness.[8] In this sense both stories have the same subject and support each other by approaching it from different angles.

4. Canto 6 had dealt with Mutability's rebellion, her treason. Here, in the Faunus episode, is another tale of treason (Molanna's)—comical enough, we think, until we realize that it ends with a symbolic death. It represents another aspect of treason—not rebellion this time, but betrayal. "In the earliest days to which we can go back the man who aided the enemies of his own tribe was hanged; probably his death was sacrificial."[9] Again, "to betray one's lord was already in Alfred's day the worst of all crimes; it was the crime of Judas; he betrayed his lord."[10] Molanna also betrays her lord, and at the end of this strange episode she dies for it. Her crime is more reprehensible than that of Faunus and her punishment is correspondingly more severe.

5. Related to all this is the fact that the Faunus episode, like the story that surrounds it, features a trial and introduces several legal ideas along with a certain amount of legal terminology.[11] Naïve Molanna—Spenser calls her "the simple maid"—has made herself an accessory to Faunus' crime by concealing him. Diana,

when she hears Faunus' irreverent laughter, leaps at once from "the guilty brooke": the brook is Molanna herself and therefore "guilty." Running to the source of the laughter, Cynthia "Enclos'd the bush about" and apprehended the malefactor,

> Like darred Larke; not daring vp to looke[12]
> On her whose sight before so much he sought.

Faunus is now within the "baile"[13] of Diana and her nymphs, who mock and scorn him so severely that Spenser suddenly relents and calls him "poore soule." Meanwhile, the nymphs debate his "sentence":

> · Some would haue gelt him, but that same would spill
> The Wood-gods breed, which must for euer liue.

Castration, we may note, was the punishment meted out for rape by William the Conqueror;[14] it has always been regarded as a sexual punishment peculiarly suited to serious sexual offences. But Faunus may not be gelded since he is the progenitor of the "Wood-gods breed."[15] For much the same reason Jove was not able to destroy Mutability with a thunderbolt: "progeny" would thus have been "rooted out." Perhaps we have here another nexus between the Faunus episode and the main story of the Cantos.

In any event, the "sentence" finally decided upon by the nymphs is Faunus

> in Deares skin to clad; and in that plight
> To hunt him with their hounds, him selfe saue how hee might.

But Cynthia, not satisfied to punish only Faunus ("And of her shame to make a gamesome iest") and determined to unearth his accomplice, began to "examine him in straighter sort," which suggests that the poor wood-god was submitted to some sort of inquisition. He, "much affeard," confessed that it was Molanna who "bewraid" her, and immediately they all seize Molanna. Molanna cannot be dealt with until after Faunus is sentenced because of "the rule that the accessory can not be brought to trial until the principal has been convicted."[16] Or as Donne puts it:

> Still before Accessories doe abide
> A triall, must the principall be tride.[17]

I think there is little doubt that the trial of Faunus and Molanna, and the legal terminology that accompanies it, are intended to contrast and complement the more important trial and more extensive use of legal terms in Mutability's story.

6. Finally, and most important, the Faunus episode is Spenser's commentary on protean change and, therefore, it is an essential part of his treatment of mutability. In the seventh Canto he intends to concern himself with two kinds of change (secular and cyclic) and the relationship between them. Here he must dispose of a third alternative, and he does this by denying protean change, that is, change of the metamorphic sort. He accomplishes this by conflating three Ovidian episodes, each of which ends with a metamorphosis. He thereby conjures up a feeling of Ovid's world, where metamorphoses are the normal order of the day. Then he proceeds, in his own story, to deny three times that metamorphosis occurs. The denial is accomplished, not in so many words, but by a subtle reinterpretation of myth. The wealth of Ovidian material in the episode, therefore, is far from accidental: it reinforces the Ovidian tone, the Ovidian feeling, that Spenser deliberately refuses to consummate by permitting any actual metamorphoses to happen. Metamorphosis, Spenser feels, is an impossibility in Nature's universe, and he demonstrates this in an episode that also furnishes a welcome change of tone.

The three Ovidian stories of metamorphosis are those of Calisto (<u>Met.</u> II, 401–495), Alpheus and Arethusa (<u>Met.</u> V, 572–641), and Actaeon (<u>Met.</u> III, 138–252).[18] William P. Cumming says that Spenser's combination of them into one story "is an interesting Ovidian influence,"[19] but the really interesting thing is the degree of freedom with which Spenser handles his three sources, creating in the end a story with many new elements, a story that cannot be said to depend very exclusively on any of the three.

The sources may be summarized very briefly. (1) Calisto, a "soldier" of Phoebe, is raped by Jove. Showing evident signs of guilt, she rejoins Diana and her nymphs on Mount Maenalus. Diana, however, is not suspicious of her until all undress for a swim. Then "nudo patuit cum corpore crimen,"[20] she is banished from Diana's train and subsequently transformed into a bear by Juno. (2) Arethusa tells how she once excited the love of the brook Alpheus, in which she was bathing. She fled, he pursued. She begged Diana's aid and was transformed into a fountain. Alpheus cleverly, "positoque viri, quod sumpserat, ore / vertitur in proprias, ut se mihi misceat, undas." Diana, to confound this stratagem, clove the earth, and thus Arethusa's water runs underground

for part of her course. (3) Actaeon, grandson of Cadmus, accidentally saw Diana bathing while he was hunting. Diana changed him
to a stag and he was pulled down by his own hounds.

Mere hints come from all of these: from the first comes the
idea of a "betrayal" of Diana by one of her nymphs, the punishment
of the nymph, perhaps a hint for the mountain setting; from the
second comes the idea of the love of two rivers, betokened by the
mingling of their waters—although the story is handled quite differently by the two authors; from the last comes the idea of someone watching Diana bathing and later being punished for it.

The Ovidian influence does not stop, however, with these mingled stories of metamorphosis. It supplies Faunus' motive as
well, for if we want a reason why Faunus should have his curious
desire to see Cynthia naked or, conversely, why the idea of seeing
Cynthia naked should suggest the character Faunus to Spenser, we
find it in the _Fasti_ (II, 267-358).[21] Ovid (after assigning the "Fauni
sacra bicornis" to February 15) speaks of the custom of the Luperci
to run naked on that day. Why? First of all because Faunus loves
to run; then because "ipse deus nudus nudos iubet ire ministros."
Ovid says he will explain this:

> sed cur praecipue fugiat velamina Faunus,
> traditur antiqui fabula plena ioci.

Once upon a time Faunus, standing by chance on a high hill, saw
Omphale out walking with her lover Hercules. Faunus "vidit et
incaluit." At midnight, when the pair were asleep in a cave, he
stole inside, full of lecherous plans. "Quid non amor improbus
audet?" Unbeknownst to him, however, Hercules and Omphale
had changed clothes. "Temerarius" Faunus groped to the first
bed, felt Hercules' lion-skin, and withdrew in panic. Soon, however, he touched the "velamina . . . mollia" of the other couch
and, heartened, scrambled up. Hercules woke and shoved the
intruder off the bed. "Fit sonus." Tumult. "Lights there, ho!"
Poor Faunus was revealed and ridiculed:

> ridet et Alcides et qui videre iacentem,
> ridet amatorem Lyda puella suum.

The result, says Ovid, is that Faunus hates clothing:

> veste deus lusus fallentes lumina vestes
> non amat et nudos ad sua sacra vocat.

293

The similarities between all this and Spenser's account are interesting. In the first place, Faunus' mania about seeing Cynthia naked undoubtedly springs from his experience in the Fasti. Then again, both Fauni make an audacious sexual assault, fail, and are ridiculed. Finally, the tone of the two passages is very similar, and both poets introduce their stories with a reference to their lighter character.[22]

If I am correct in detecting the influence of Ovid's unlucky Faunus, then the punishment which Spenser visits on his hero is seen to be peculiarly fitting. Faunus has a mania about being naked himself—"ipse deus nudus"—and desires to see other people naked: clearly the most suitable punishment will be to clothe him. The ignominy of it! Moreover, since he has an equally powerful mania about running ("ipse deus velox discurrere gaudet in altis / montibus et subitas concipit ipse fugas") it will be satisfactorily ironic to "hunt him with [our] hounds." And so exit Faunus,

> With a Deeres-skin . . . couered, and then chast
> With all their hounds that after him did speed.

Luckily Faunus is in practice and easily outdistances his pursuers.

I have digressed considerably from my avowed purpose, which is to show how Spenser in the Faunus episode rejects protean change by establishing a highly Ovidian atmosphere, conflating three stories of metamorphosis, and then denying three times that metamorphosis occurs. Hitherto I have tried to suggest the Ovidian atmosphere; now it is time to turn to the three denials.

The first is in some ways the most illuminating. Spenser tells us that Molanna hid Faunus

> . . . where he close might view
> That neuer any saw, saue onely one;
> Who, for his hire to so foole-hardy dew,
> Was of his hounds devour'd in Hunters hew.

The reference is of course to Actaeon.

In the usual version of the story, Actaeon was transformed to a stag. Spenser not only follows a different version but states definitely that he is doing so; "in Hunters hew" is clearly an assertion that, despite what Ovid may have said about Actaeon in particular and metamorphosis in general,

294

> all creatures do retaine
> Their olde accustomed shape, and in their wonted guise
>   remaine.[23]

The variant version of the myth that Spenser uses is probably, as
H. G. Lotspeich noted,[24] from Natalis Comes (VI. xxiv): "Alij
[dixerunt] Actæonem non versum in ceruum, neq; cerui pelle
tectum fuisse arbitrantur, sed opinionem canibus immissam, vt
feram putarent."[25] The point is not so much that Spenser follows
this suggestion from Comes; it is rather that in a tale clearly intended to recall Ovid, he resists Ovid's conclusion.[26]

In the usual version of the story, Actaeon blunders into Diana's
presence. His crime is therefore accidental and his punishment
surprisingly severe. Even Ovid emphasizes its injustice (Met. III,
141-42):

> at bene si quaeras, Fortunae crimen in illo,
> non scelus invenies; quod enim scelus error habebat?

Spenser, however, calls Actaeon "foole-hardy" and by comparing
him to Faunus suggests that his viewing Diana was not accidental.
But a "foole-hardy" Actaeon is as much of an innovation as an un-
metamorphosized Actaeon. Comes, who interprets the story as a
warning against curiosity, may have suggested this aspect of
Actaeon (and Faunus) to Spenser: "Admonemur præterea per hanc
fabulam, ne simus nimis curiosi in rebus nihil ad nos pertinentib.
quoniam multis perniciosum fuit res arcanas aliorum cognouisse,
aut principium ciuitatum, summorumq́; virorum, aut Deorũ
præcipuè" (VI. xxiv).

Probably, however, Spenser is here following a hint from Statius,
who does in fact characterize Actaeon as a peeping-Tom, like
Faunus. Aletes (Thebaid III, 201-4) says that he will not bemoan
various Theban catastrophes,

> nec quod tibi, Delia, castos prolapsum
> fontes specula temerare profana heu dominum insani nihil
> agnovere Molossi, deflerim magis.

An Actaeon who has just "crept forth from his unholy spying-place
to profane, O Delia, thy chaste fountains,"[27] may have provided
Spenser with any number of suggestions: Spenser's Faunus is

> placed where he close might view
> That neuer any saw, saue onely one;
> Who, for his hire to so foole-hardy dew,
> Was of his hounds devour'd in Hunters hew.

Statius would have suggested "foole-hardinesse" rather than bad
luck as the cause of the incident, the covert where Faunus hides,
and the "profanation" of the brook (the "guilty brooke" in Spenser). This profanation is the reason why Diana abandons Arlo,
and this abandonment is ostensibly the reason for telling the whole
Faunus anecdote. Seen in this way, the Statius passage becomes
very relevant.

Finally, we have in Spenser's brief allusion to Actaeon an excellent narrative analogue to his habit of bringing "into a simile
myth which is, in reality, the source or pattern of the thing he is
comparing. The two parts of the simile are in origin the same."[28]
Lotspeich cites Cambina's "rod of peace" (IV. iii. 42), which is
silently modeled on Mercury's caduceus and then compared directly to it. This technique in simile can also of course be used, as
here, as a technique in narrative. Faunus' story is modeled on
Actaeon's and then the source is pronounced to be an analogue.
This is an interesting technique of reinforcement and here, of
course, it is doubly purposive, since the myth which inspires the
story is itself reinterpreted by the story.

The second rejection of metamorphosis occurs when Faunus is
sentenced. Diana and her nymphs decide

> Him in Deares skin to clad; and in that plight
> To hunt him with their hounds, him selfe saue how hee might.

This punishment was no doubt suggested by the third of Natalis
Comes' versions of the fate of Actaeon: "Alij dixerunt Actæone
cerui pelle à Diana tectum laniatum fuisse à canibus ad eum lacer-
andum incitatis" (VI. xxiv). No one even suggests that Faunus
be metamorphosed—a significant omission.

The third and last rejection of metamorphosis occurs at the execution of Molanna. According to P. W. Joyce, the Molanna (Behanna
river

> . . . is very steep in the first part of its course; and the
> winter torrents have, in the course of ages, rolled down
> vast quantities of large stones and gravel, and deposited
> them in the level part of its bed . . . The poet has figured

this feature of the river bed, under a thin veil, in the passage where he tells us that the nymphs, at the command of Diana, overwhelmed Molanna with stones.[29]

Or as Rudolph B. Gottfried puts it, Spenser's whole etiological myth has been designed to explain topography, that is, the actual physical characteristics of the Behanna—how it "springs out of two marble rocks and why its course is . . . blocked with stones."[30]
Gottfried points out that Spenser, although he calls the river a nymph, treats her throughout as the actual stream—a procedure which makes visualization difficult. For this reason Spenser's treatment of the myth is to be distinguished from Ovid's treatment of Alpheus and Arethusa: "Ovid's myth is pivoted on the transformation of a nymph, or semi-human being, into a stream, a procedure essentially opposed to Spenser's assumption that nymph and stream are one from first to last."[31] Gottfried attributes Spenser's omission of a metamorphosis to the fact that, unlike "his more literal-minded predecessors,"[32] he "feels no compulsion to bring his story into visual consistency with real things."[33] My readers will no doubt already have anticipated the alternative solution that I am about to offer: we have here Spenser's third and final rejection of Ovidian metamorphosis, and at a moment in his story which irresistibly implies that such a metamorphosis should occur.
The Faunus episode was introduced ostensibly to explain

how Arlo through Dianaes spights
(Beeing of old the best and fairest Hill
That was in all this holy-Islands hights)
Was made the most vnpleasant, and most ill.

Spenser concludes by returning to this point of departure and emphasizing Arlo's present unpleasantness. But how many other things he has done en route! He has told a topographical myth about the marriage of two rivers, he has narrated the intrigues of "Foolish God Faunus," he has reinforced everything with four sharp reminiscences of Ovid, and, most important, he has connected the whole episode in different ways to his central narrative, the adventures of Mutability. With the evidence now behind us, we may briefly review the six most important of these nexuses: (1) the episode offers a change in tone, characters, and type of humor; (2) it records another frustrated assault upon Cynthia; (3) it is concerned with the foolishness of boldness, a matter that

Spenser wisely separates from his account of boldness itself; (4) it is a story of betrayal (Molanna), which is another aspect of the rebellion perpetrated by Mutability; (5) it describes, like its context, a trial, and employs legal terminology and legal notions. In all these ways it is a parody of the larger story in which it is embedded: it is a kind of antimasque, a "grotesque interlude between the acts of a masque, to which it serve[s] as a foil, and of which it was at first often a burlesque" (NED). It is a comic inversion of all the more serious matters by which it is surrounded.[34]

Sixth, and finally, it is Spenser's deliberately Ovidian rejection of Ovidian metamorphosis as a possible kind of change.

> For so to interpose a little ease,
> Let our frail thoughts dally with false surmise.

It not only complements but advances the main argument, which is an analysis of the mechanism and scope of mutability. With protean change disposed of, Spenser may go on in Canto 7 to his sobering discussion of Change in her two real and ominous forms, secula (growth and decay) and cyclic (celestial motions).[35]

Finally we may observe with Lotspeich that the "whole episode is in that vein of playful pleasantry, with just a touch of seriousness, which the Elizabethans controlled supremely well."[36] This decorum is maintained throughout. And—above and beyond the six links I have already suggested—the episode complements its context by filling in several of the dark lines in its spectrum: the bright, continuous whole that results suggests the full variety and extent of the creation. Here is God's plenty. Or, as C. S. Lewis puts it, this "intermeddling of the high and low—the poet's eye glancing not only from earth to heaven but from the shapeless, funny gambollings of instinct to the heights of contemplation—is as grave, perhaps even as religious, as the decorum that would, in a different convention, have forbidden it."[37]

A SECULAR READING OF THE FAERIE QUEENE, BOOK II

Lewis H. Miller, Jr.

As Mammon leads Guyon through the golden intricacies of his soot-filled cavern, he turns deliberately to his guest and offers him the world:

> Loe here the worldes blis, loe here the end,
> To which all men do ayme, rich to be made:
> Such grace now to be happy, is before thee laid.
> (Book II, canto vii, stanza 32)[1]

Theological readers of Book II, with the lines of St. Matthew ringing in their ears ("ye cannot serve God and mammon"), might well anticipate the direction of Guyon's reply:

> Certes (said he) I n'ill thine offred grace,
> Ne to be made so happy do intend:
> Another blis before mine eyes I place,
> Another happinesse, another end.
> To them, that list, these base regardes I lend: (vii, 33)

If these were the words of the Red Crosse Knight, there could be little question of his devotion to a heavenly concern. But where an eschatological statement may seem most proper, Guyon qualifies the nature of the "blis" with which he confronts Mammon's golden offer: "But I in armes, and in atchieuements braue / Do rather choose my flitting houres to spend" (vii, 33). In other words, Guyon is firmly rooted in the here and now. This particular passage is Spenser's way of telling us that Guyon's experience in the cave of Mammon is not, as so many critics find, a Christian struggle between flesh and the spirit, the city of this world and the City of God.[2] Such a qualification applies not only to the episode of Mammon's cave but to Book II as a whole; for, as I shall hope to

Reprinted from English Literary History, Vol. 33 (1966), pp. 154–169, © The Johns Hopkins Press, by permission of the author and The Johns Hopkins Press.

show, Spenser's story of the quest for Temperance is peculiarly immune to the theological incursions which make their ways into the fabric of Book I. The fact which critics shirk and which will here be confronted is that Spenser consistently urges his readers not to view the quest for Temperance from a theological perspective.[3]

We shall do well first to examine the incident concerning Amavia, Mordant, and Ruddymane; for it is here, early in Book II, that we (and Guyon) are first informed of the nature of Guyon's quest; it is here that Spenser establishes the humanistic, non-sacramental ethic which is to underlie and control the remainder of the Book. Guyon's fruitless endeavor in canto ii to wash Amavia's blood from the hands of Ruddymane has recently elicited much critical speculation of a theological nature:

> Then soft himselfe inclyning on his knee
> Downe to that well, did in the water weene
> (So loue does loath disdainfull nicitee)
> His guiltie hands from bloudie gore to cleene.
> He washt them oft and oft, yet nought they beene
> For all his washing cleaner. Still he stroue,
> Yet still the litle hands were bloudie seene;
> The which him into great amaz'ment droue,
> And into diuerse doubt his wauering wonder cloue. (II, ii, 3)

In his article, "A Theological Reading of The Faerie Queene, Book II," Mr. A. C. Hamilton finds this episode theologically significant: "The parallel set up with the occasion of Redcross Knight's adventures where the parents imprisoned in the brazen castle by the huge dragon indicates man's spiritual bondage in the fallen world suggests that the bloody-handed Babe stands for mankind which from its infancy has been infected by original sin. (Blood upon the hands being the usual token of man's guilty state.)"[4] And Mr. A. D. S. Fowler extends Hamilton's theology to include the fountain in which Guyon unsuccessfully bathes the child: "In the earliest episodes the virtue Guyon represents is related to baptism: his mission is from the very beginning conceived of in theological terms."[5] Such sacramental readings are relevant to the waters of Book I, but here in Book II they ignore what seems to me Spenser's own explanation for the significance of the fountain and the indelibly bloody hands of Ruddymane. Guyon himself is perplexed by these symbols:

> He wist not whether blot of foule offence
> Might not be purgd with water nor with bath;
> Or that high God, in lieu of innocence,
> Imprinted had that token of his wrath,
> To shew how sore bloudguiltinesse he hat'th;
> Or that the charme and venim, which they druncke,
> Their bloud with secret filth infected hath,
> Being diffused through the senselesse truncke,
> That through the great contagion direfull deadly stunck.
>
> (ii, 4)

Note that Guyon proposes his own theological reading of these allegorical events ("or that high God, . . . bloudguiltinesse he hat'th");[6] Spenser, however, is not content to leave this unqualified. With "goodly reason" Guyon's Palmer immediately dismisses the possible theological explanation proposed by his companion: "Ye bene right hard amated, gratious Lord, / And of your ignorance great maruell make, / Whiles cause not well conceiued ye mistake" (ii, 5). The Palmer follows with a rendering of mythological chemistry which is so important to our argument that I cite it in full:

> Such is this well, wrought by occasion straunge,
> Which to her Nymph befell. Vpon a day,
> As she the woods with bow and shafts did raunge,
> The hartlesse Hind and Robucke to dismay,
> Dan Faunus chaunst to meet her by the way,
> And kindling fire at her faire burning eye,
> Inflamed was to follow beauties pray,
> And chaced her, that fast from him did fly;
> As Hind from her, so she fled her enimy.
>
> At last when fayling breath began to faint,
> And saw no meanes to scape, of shame affrayd,
> She set her downe to weepe for sore constraint,
> And to Diana calling lowd for ayde,
> Her deare besought, to let her dye a mayd.
> The goddesse heard, and suddeine where she sate,
> Welling out streames of teares, and quite dismayd
> With stony feare of that rude rustick mate,
> Transformd her to a stone from stedfast virgins state.

Lo now she is that stone, from whose two heads,
As from two weeping eyes, fresh streames do flow,
Yet cold through fear, and old conceiued dreads;
And yet the stone her semblance seemes to show,
Shapt like a maid, that such ye may her know;
And yet her vertues in her water byde:
For it is chast and pure, as purest snow,
Ne lets her waues with any filth be dyde,
But euer like her selfe vnstained hath been tryde.

From thence it comes, that this babes bloudy hand
May not be clensd with water of this well:
Ne certes Sir striue you it to withstand,
But let them still be bloudy, as befell,
That they his mothers innocence may tell,
As she bequeathd in her last testament;
That as a sacred Symbole it may dwell
In her sonnes flesh, to minde reuengement,
And be for all chast Dames an endlesse moniment.

(II, ii, 7–10)

The Palmer's mythic analysis (a blend of the Daphne and Arethusa tales) replaces any theological notions we or Guyon may have entertained. The indelible blood stains upon the infant's hands do not, Guyon's reason[7] assures us, serve to symbolize man's ingenerate sin but rather to remind us and Guyon of a crime which remains unavenged—the fatal machinations of Acrasia. This is not to assert that Spenser was incapable of veiling theological doctrine under mythological drapery. But here the explicit rejection by the Palmer of an interpretation (such as Guyon's and Hamilton's) which alludes to God's wrath and man's "bloudguiltinesse," followed by the Palmer's literal assertion of the bloody babe's secular significance, precludes the possibility of hidden theological meanings. Mr. Fowler, for example, has searched long and hard for such meanings; but after we have painfully followed him through a Christianization of the Palmer's myth which must account for Mordant's reward of death at the "Fountain of Life," we find ourselves whirling dizzily at several removes from Spenser's text.[8]

We must not forget that Mordant's death is occasioned by Acrasia's curse: "Sad verse, giue death . . . / So soone as Bacchus with the Nymphe does lincke" (i, 55); surely we disregard all that Acrasia suggests if we believe that the lascivious enchantress in her reference to the fountain ("Nymphe"), could possibly be con-

templating divine law, baptism, regeneration. The "Bacchus" of
Acrasia's curse refers, of course, to the wine of Excesse on which
Mordant had surfeited in the Bower of Bliss. As Mordant turns
from the excesses of "lust and lewd desires" (i, 54) to the Nymphe's
fountain, Acrasia's curse is irrevocably fulfilled: "Till comming to
this well, he stoupt to drincke: / The charme fulfild, dead suddenly
he downe did sincke" (i, 55). Moving radically from the excesses of
Acrasia's Bower to the purity of the Nymphe's waters, Mordant
describes a psychological pattern which, as I have suggested elsewhere, underlies Guyon's own struggles to complete his quest.[9]

Under the secular scheme presented to us in Medina's castle
(ii, 13–38)—the Aristotelian ethic in which moral virtue is described as a mean between two vicious extremes—the fountain itself comes to represent an extreme. Without turning to the Church
Fathers, we find that the Palmer's story of Faunus and the Nymphe
is significant in its own right. Desperately fleeing the advances of
Faunus, the Nymphe of the fountain, like Daphne of the myth and
unlike the virgin Belphoebe of canto iii, displays an extreme sense
of fear and shame. While Belphoebe parries Braggadocchio's
crude advances by "fiercely" menacing him with her weapons (he
"gan burne in filthy lust, and leaping light, / Thought in his bastard
armes her to embrace"—iii, 42), the Nymphe of the fountain makes
no attempt to threaten Faunus with her "bow and shafts"; instead
she flees "of shame affrayd," and her "stony feare" is ultimately
responsible for her metamorphosis into a stone from whose two
heads "fresh streames do flow, / Yet cold through feare" (ii, 8 and
9).[10] The Nymphe of the fountain is as chaste and pure, "as purest
snow." One thinks ahead to Books III and IV where Florimell's
irrational flight, her "stony feare," her icy attitudes, are exemplified by Proteus, his rocky sea cave (IV, xii) and by a "false"
Florimell composed of "purest snow" (III, viii, 6). The conception
of these elements in Books III and IV is completely divorced from
the sacrament of baptism; and I suggest that in Book II, ii, Spenser
employs stone, ice, and snow to denote extreme attitudes of deficiency in respect to the physical aspects of love. This is to say
that Mordant having been freed from the enticing web of Acrasia's
excesses, brings death upon himself by swinging to the opposite
extreme, the deficiency represented by the waters of the icy fountain.[11] Far from holding theological significance, the allegorical
events which lead to Mordant's death prepare us for the purely
secular conflicts of soul with which Sir Guyon will have to grapple.[12] Yet if Book II is, as I have suggested, immune to the theological incursions of Book I, how are we to account for the miracu-

lous powers which arrive in canto viii to succour a swooning Guyon and defend him from the machinations of Pyrochles and Cymochles?
Canto viii opens with a gracious recognition of "th'exceeding grace / Of highest God"—

> And is there care in heauen? and is there loue
> In heauenly spirits to thes creatures bace,
> That may compassion of their euils moue?
> There is: else much more wretched were the cace
> Of men, then beasts. But O th'exceeding grace
> Of highest God, that loues his creatures so,
> And all his workes with mercy doth embrace,
> That blessed Angels, he sends to and fro,
> To serue to wicked man, to serue his wicked foe.
>
> How oft do they, their siluer bowers leaue,   (I, viii, 1)

It must be granted that "grace" does enter the natural realm of Book II. Spenser's apostrophe to God's merciful concern for His "creatures bace" and the delightful Cupid-like angel which descends (stanzas 5–6), are invariably pointed to as prime examples of that which was lacking in cantos i through vii, and of that which will sustain our hero and his quest throughout the remainder of the book. As Harry Berger puts it: "The turning point of Book II, the point at which amor manifestly changes Guyon's world, occurs when the guardian angel descends."[13] The amor to which Mr. Berger refers is Divine Love. And it is here that Mr. Berger finds a shift from a classic to a Christian cosmology.[14] A. C. Hamilton points not directly to the ministering angel but to Arthur as a dispenser of grace when he states that "man's spiritual nature which is revealed in Book I is embodied in the second book in the perfection of man's natural body governed by temperance and upheld by divine grace."[15] The assumption underlying both Berger and Hamilton's views is that grace enters Book II at canto viii in order to aid, sustain, and transform in one way or another, the natural virtue which Guyon represents. This we shall see is not the case. Although Mr. Hamilton is always careful to distinguish between the types of events which occur in Book I and in Book II, his view of the grace of God in Book II as a phenomenon very similar to the grace of Book I seems to me to overlook some exceedingly important differences. The opening apostrophe to God in canto viii of Book II has been cited. Let us compare it to its counterpart in Book I:

> Ay me, how many perils doe enfold
> The righteous man, to make him daily fall?
> Were not, that heauenly grace doth him vphold,
> And stedfast truth acquite him out of all.
> Her loue is firme, her care continuall,
> So oft as he through his owne foolish pride,
> Or weaknesse is to sinfull bands made thrall:
> Else should this Redcrosse knight in bands haue dyde,
> For whose deliuerance, she this Prince doth thither guide.
>
> (I, viii, 1)

In Book I, Arthur has been brought by Una to rescue Red Crosse from his desperate position in the dungeon of Orgoglio. Consequently, the "heauenly grace" in line 3 refers to Arthur, while the "righteous man" of line 2 refers to Red Crosse (as well as to Everyman), and "stedfast truth" in line 4 points to Una. The similarities between the two stanzas are obvious and do not warrant examination; the differences, however, are so important to our purposes that they must be emphasized—for in these two presentations of the ways in which grace enters the world as man knows it lie some crucial assumptions which underlie the textures of both books. In Book II, canto viii, stanza 1, Guyon (or Everyman) is <u>not</u> referred to as the "righteous man" who has fallen; he is, instead, one of "these creatures bace"; he is "wicked man." The implication here is that Book II is dealing with a very different realm from that of Book I, not only in cantos i–vii, but in viii–xii as well. Guyon is not the righteous man who falls into error only to be finally redeemed by heavenly grace. Guyon is the natural man who in striving to perfect his internal organization, to achieve a particular psychic harmony called Temperance, has fallen into error or vice ("wicked man") only insofar as he has been irresponsible enough to act without his reason.[16] Although at the close of canto vii we do find a Guyon who is utterly helpless, he is not to be <u>redeemed</u> by the grace of God. Admittedly, Guyon's passive, reasonless position demands help from without; but—and this is very important—once "succour" does arrive from God, it performs its duties efficiently (and we shall examine this) and then departs: in Book II the exceeding grace of highest God invades the natural realm to "<u>serue</u> to wicked man" (II, viii, 1) and <u>not</u> to "him <u>vphold</u>" (I, viii, 1). While in Book I the grace of God upholds, sustains, redeems the righteous man who has fallen, the grace of God in Book II offers what help it can in order to give wicked man (Guyon) a chance to <u>redeem himself</u>. And Spenser has been very careful to make this distinction, not only in the passages we have just examined, but in the peculiar manner in which grace manifests itself in Book II.

The little angel who as God's ambassador loudly and clearly calls "come hither, come hither," does virtually no more than this. It is as if Spenser were emphasizing the point that grace has an extremely limited role in a book which deals with Temperance. It is the Palmer who usurps the role which grace has played in Book I. Persisting in his search for the lost Guyon, the Palmer hears the angel's call and thereby locates his "pupill." Translating this into doctrinal form, we can say that through the grace of God, Guyon's reason is restored. But Spenser has nothing more to do with God's grace in Book II. Once the Palmer has been reunited with Guyon, the angel very deliberately relinquishes his charge: "The charge, which God doth vnto me arret, /Of his deare safetie, I to thee [the Palmer] commend" (II, viii, 8; my emphasis). [17] The Palmer is left alone to deal with the brothers Pyrochles and Cymochles, who pose a very real threat to the slumbering Guyon. With unexpected sophistry, the Palmer is able momentarily to stall the ranting brothers in their desire for vengeance; and at the crucial moment when "both fiercely bent to have him [Guyon] disaraid," Prince Arthur arrives.

There has been a good deal of critical fudging in regard to the Arthur of Book II. The problems inherent in viewing Arthur as grace or the dispenser of grace make themselves manifest in the contradictions into which most critics fall when attending to Arthur; and it should prove illuminating to note some examples of this. A. S. P. Woodhouse, whose discussions of Books I and II in terms of the orders nature and grace have done so much to clarify issues, does not do so well by Arthur: having established that in the order of grace (Book I) Arthur represents "the grace of God in its fullest extent as it works upon the will of the converted," and that Arthur in the order of nature (Book II) "represents the virtue of magnanimity, which is as central in classical ethics as is grace in the Christian scheme," Woodhouse muddles the issue by adding: "but, also, in the order of nature, he represents the power and providence of God as they intervene to protect his creatures from outward evils." [18] Woodhouse seems to feel impelled, in spite of his clear distinctions between nature and grace, to find in the natural Arthur of Book II vestiges of a supernatural order. [19] But it is in the careful and sensitive book of Mr. Hamilton that one becomes even more fully aware of the contradictions which arise from an attempt to find vestiges of grace in the Arthur of Book II. Hamilton begins his discussions of the

Arthur of Book II by viewing him and the Arthur of Book I as Christ figures.[20] He proceeds to equate Arthur of the second book with the grace of God: "The full limitation of natural virtue is seen when Guyon falls and Arthur must come to rescue him. For though the temperate body is strong, . . . it stands only by the power of grace."[21] Yet we are led into confusion from Hamilton's close look at Arthur's encounter with Pyrochles and Cymochles: "The first part of the battle (stanzas 32–38) ends with Arthur helpless, himself standing in need of grace. Grace comes in the Palmer who offers him Guyon's sword, that is, the power of reason."[22] What Mr. Hamilton in this passage means by "grace" is indeed puzzling. Can grace stand in need of itself? Can the Palmer, Guyon's reason, be a dispenser of divine grace? A rather surprising solution to this puzzle occurs when finally we see that Mr. Hamilton would rather not talk of Arthur in terms of grace after all. Referring to the movement of the early stanzas in canto viii, he says: "The bridge is thus complete from God's grace, to the ministering angels, to 'right reason,' to the sum of all virtues which may rescue man."[23] Arthur, in the final analysis, becomes for Hamilton Aristotle's magnanimous man, a down-to-earth individual with nothing supernatural about him. And this, it seems to me, is the only sensible way in which to begin to talk about the Arthur of Book II.

When first we and Una encounter Arthur in Book I, we are dazzled by his light (see I, vii, 29ff.); Arthur's figure (and especially his uncovered shield which darkens Phoebus's face) is the translation into a living form of the Lux est umbra Dei proposition. The shield, whose diamond surface dispels all falsehood and illuminates the way to Truth, is unquestionably imbued with the power of the Almighty:

> No magicke arts hereof had any might,
> Nor bloudie wordes of bold Enchaunters call,
> But all that was not such as seemd in sight,
> Before that shield did fade, and suddeine fall.　　(I, vii, 35)

In Book II, Arthur's attributes conspicuously lack such lustre:

> An armed knight, of bold and bounteous grace,
> Whose squire bore after him an heben launce,
> And couerd shield. Well kend him so farre space
> Th'enchaunter [Archimago] by his armes and amenaunce,
> When vnder him he saw his Lybian steed to praunce.
> 　　　　　　　　　　　　　　　　　　(II, viii, 17)

307

This is obviously pitched in a lower key. In comparison to the
Arthur of Book I, this Arthur is most ordinary; there is not a
glitter of light on or emanating from him. And it is slightly ironical—in the light of Arthur's prowess in Book I to dispel all magic
arts of bold enchanters—that it is the cunning and dangerous enchanter Archimago who first recognizes Arthur, not by glitter and
sheen, but by his horse. Spenser seems deliberately to distinguish
between the Arthurs of the first two books, not only by his descriptions of them, but by the very noticeable failure of Arthur, in Book
II, to unveil his covered shield. It is as if the flashes of grace
which so effectively emanate from the face of Arthur's shield in
Book I are veiled in Book II in order to indicate that the heavenly
concerns in the Legend of Holiness are largely irrelevant to the
more secular realm of the natural virtue Temperance in Book II.

Canto viii affords us one of the most curious allegorical movements in The Faerie Queene. It is here that we witness a reaching
out of the psychic elements of one individual to include and affect
another individual, all performed with an astonishing allegorical
economy. It is surprising that students of Spenser have so often
ignored the very extraordinary conditions under which Arthur's
fight with Pyrochles and Cymochles (the brothers irascibility and
concupiscence) takes place. In no other episode of The Faerie
Queene does such a transference of weapons occur.[24] Archimago,
the evil enchanter, in possession of Prince Arthur's magically
tempered sword, Morddure, is loth to lend it to Pyrochles:

> In vaine therefore, Pyrochles, should I lend
> The same to thee, against his lord to fight,
> For sure it would deceiue thy labour, and thy might.
>
> (II, viii, 21)

But Pyrochles, as we might have guessed from his nature, is not
to be deterred:

> Foolish old man, said then the Pagan wroth,
> That weenest words or charmes may force withstond:
> Soone shalt thou see, and then beleeue for troth,
> That I can carue with this inchaunted brond
> His Lords owne flesh. Therewith out of his hond
> That vertuous steele he rudely snatch away,
> And Guyons shield about his wrest he bond;
> So readie dight, fierce battaile to assay,
> And match his brother proud in battailous array.
>
> (II, viii, 22)

The deliberate seizure by Pyrochles of Arthur's sword and of Guyon's shield, and the concomitant effectiveness of his wielding both (in spite of Morddure's special virtue), points emphatically to the allegorical meaning. In the act of clutching the crucial accoutrements of the two heroes, Pyrochles clutches them—which is to say that Guyon and Arthur are by Pyrochles possessed.[25]

We should now be prepared to examine Arthur's encounter with Pyrochles and Cymochles from the very human perspective which, I believe, Spenser urges upon us. Unassuaged by Arthur's courteous words, Pyrochles lifts Arthur's own "good sword Morddure" and aims for the Prince's head:

> The faithfull steele such treason no'uld endure,
> But swaruing from the marke, his Lords life did assure.
>
> Yet was the force so furious and so fell,
> That horse and man it made to reele aside;
> Nath'lesse the Prince would not forsake his sell:
> For well of yore he learned had to ride,
> But full of anger fiercely to him cride;
> False traitour miscreant, thou broken hast
> The law of armes, to strike foe vndefide.
> But thou thy treasons fruit, I hope, shalt taste
> Right sowre, and feele, the law, the which thou hast defast.
>
> (viii, 30–31)

Although Morddure cannot touch Arthur, Pyrochles's blow is quite effective and provokes the Prince to anger: "full of anger fiercely to him cride." Such a response suggests that Arthur is indeed possessed by the very quality with which he fights. Furthermore, Arthur's angered reaction to Pyrochles's unknightly stroke presents us with a perfect analogue to Pyrochles's own behavior in his encounter with Guyon in canto v. We recall that Guyon inadvertently struck off the head of Pyrochles's horse, an action—had it been intentional—directly opposed to proper knightly behavior (v, 4–5). Like Arthur in canto viii, Pyrochles is unduly angered by this apparent breach of code:

> And all enraged, thus him [Guyon] loudly shent;
> Disleall knight, whose coward courage chose
> To wreake it selfe on beast all innocent,
> . . . .
> So hast thou oft with guile thine honour blent;
>
> (v, 5)

309

The echoes become more persistent as we follow the immediate actions sparked by the anger of Arthur (viii) and Pyrochles (v) respectively. Although Arthur lacks his sword, he does have his spear; and immediately after railing at Pyrochles as we have heard, Arthur wields his weapon in the following manner:

> With that his balefull speare, he fiercely bent
> Against the Pagans brest, and therewith thought
> His cursed life out of her lodge haue rent:
> But ere the point arriued, where it ought,
> That seuen-fold shield which he from Guyon brought
> He cast betwene to ward the bitter stound:
> Through all those foldes the steelehead passage wrought
> And through his shoulder pierst; wherwith to ground
> He groueling fell, all gored in his gushing wound.   (viii, 32)

In canto v, stanza 6, Pyrochles also strikes "fiercely"; and there too, it is Guyon's seven-fold shield which intercepts the force of the blows and literally saves the life of him who possesses it (Guyon). This is to say that in Arthur's encounter with Pyrochles, Spenser presents us with an exact inversion—we might say, per-version—of that earlier encounter, and insists that we view Arthur's behavior in terms of its Pyrochlean elements.[26] For the moment, we watch Arthur play the role of Pyrochles, while Pyrochles assumes the role of Guyon, or Temperance, implying perhaps that next to Arthur's rage, rage itself appears to be temperate, or that the shield of Temperance (disregarding for the moment Pyrochles's possession of it) works to blunt the edge of Arthur's fury. In any case, it is obvious enough that Arthur is pursuing Pyrochles in exactly the wrong manner. Fire cannot be fought with fire, any more than rage can be fought with rage. And from this point in his struggle, Arthur makes little or no advance. He is forced from his horse by Cymochles (33); he is able to wound Cymochles in the thigh, but he breaks his spear (his only weapon) in the process (36); Cymochles recovers quickly and retaliates by inflicting a wide wound in Arthur's right side (38–39);[27] until, finally, on foot, without a sword or spear (he employs the broken shaft to ward off Cymochles), "in huge perplexity, / The Prince now stood" (39). It is at this lull in the combat, when Arthur is virtually helpless, that the Palmer comes to his aid by giving him Guyon's own sword (40). The power of Temperance is entrusted into the hands of Arthur who is finally able to extricate himself from his graceless position. Employing the sword of Temperance

"so wisely as it ought," he makes ready dispatch of Cymochles and
sends his ghost flying to "th'infernall shade" (45). Against his arch-
foe Pyrochles, he displays uncommon restraint and composure; the
inverted roles which Arthur and Pyrochles assumed in stanzas 31–
32 are now turned right-side-up as Pyrochles "at him did flye, /
And strooke, and foynd, and lasht outrageously, / Withouten reason
or regard," while Prince Arthur employs "patience and sufferaunce
sly" (47).[28] He seems at last to have learned that Pyrochles cannot be overcome by rage. Yet we must not forget what Spenser
tells us in no uncertain terms—that Arthur's final success in this
desperate encounter is dependent upon "borrowd blade." Like Sir
Guyon, Prince Arthur displays his own limitations, his own dependence upon a power which he has yet to make his own—the virtue
Temperance.[29] Pyrochles and Cymochles have been subdued, but
not by the grace of God.

Having pointed up the secular nature of those events in Book II
which have hitherto been shrouded in sacramental or religious
drapery, this discussion, it is hoped, will provide a new perspective from which to view the allegorical movement of Book II. Sub-
merged in the holy water of Book I or dazzled by its lights of
grace, readers of Spenser have come to Book II with Augustinian
expectations which they satisfy by acknowledging original sin or
the gracious meddling of the Almighty. Spenser, I feel, did not
intend such a response. As a Christian humanist he could treat
artistically man's ultimate dependence upon God as well as man's
total reliance upon his own powers. While Book I offers its hero
a vision of the New Jerusalem, the City of God, Book II deals
solely with the realm of Cleopolis, the City of Earthly Glory. The
Augustinian view so aptly displayed through the adventures of Red
Crosse, is complemented by the bolder, more humanistic focus of
Guyon's story in which the liberating spirit of a Pico della Mirandola offers man the rare privilege of controlling his own destiny,
of effecting his own destruction or, indeed, his own salvation.
This is not to suggest that Sir Guyon has the capacity to extricate
himself from original sin. The point to be made is that Book II
does not in fact deal with original sin but with one of its consequences—intemperance; and that Spenser within the particular
sphere encompassed by the virtue Temperance grants his hero
the freedom to choose between vice or virtue, to perfect himself
(if he does not choose to undo himself) without direct sustenance
from the Almighty.

From the secular point of view which I have proposed, Sir

Guyon's observations upon Grille's hoggish condition are most
fitting as the final sentiments of Book II:

> Said <u>Guyon</u>, See the mind of beastly man,
> That hath so soone forgot the excellence
> Of his creation, when he life began,
> That now he chooseth, with vile difference,
> To be a beast, and lacke intelligence. (xii, 87)

A. C. Hamilton views this concluding passage in his own way:
"That original sin remains ingenerate in human nature is significantly rendered in the concluding stanza of the book where Guyon
denounces Grill who chooses the life of a beast."[30] Mr. Hamilton
overlooks the crucial significance of the word he himself employs:
Grille does indeed <u>choose</u> to be a beast and lack intelligence. For
far from pointing to the ingenerate nature of man's sin, Spenser
is once more asserting the humanistic ethic which underlies his
story of Temperance: Man, Protean creature that he is, can
choose his own lot, can, in the words of Pico, fashion himself in
what ever shape he shall prefer. "Thou shalt have the power to
degenerate into lower forms of life, which are brutish. Thou
shalt have the power, out of thy soul's judgment, to be reborn into
the higher forms which are divine."[31] Spenser's final stanza
pertinently reminds us that while Grille has chosen his form, Sir
Guyon has also made <u>his</u> choice.

THE SECRET WIT OF SPENSER'S LANGUAGE

Martha Craig

The language of The Faerie Queene to most modern readers seems alien and unaccountable. Spenser seems to have overlooked the expressive possibilities of idiomatic speech revealed so magnificently by Shakespeare and devised an artificial language which, in contrast to the artificialities of Milton's language in Paradise Lost, seems less significant and less forceful than the ordinary language it replaces. Many qualities may seem unfortunate, but perhaps the most vitiating are the archaisms and an apparently purposeless distortion of words. Even after careful study, Spenser's archaism seems superficial and specious, consisting more in odd spellings and grammatical forms than in a genuine rejuvenation of obsolete words that are needed because they are particularly meaningful or expressive. And his liberties with language, the coinages and peculiar forms seem willful and meaningless; alteration of words for the sake of rhyme seems to betray not only lack of resourcefulness but irresponsibility. It is no exaggeration to say that for many readers the language of The Faerie Queene is at best merely curious or quaint, at worst hollow and contorted. And this is especially puzzling because the faults seem not only bad but often utterly gratuitous.

The traditional account of Spenser's language provides no reassurance but instead confirms the reader's suspicions. Spenser's diction is said to be "decorative" and to appeal "through spontaneity and inherent suggestiveness, independent of source or application."[1] If so, this has become not a defense but a condemnation. And any other defense of The Faerie Queene, of the structure or the allegory, for example, seems ineffectual to the modern reader, for according to his expectations, his implicit hierarchy of literary values, in ignoring the language it presupposes what is primary and most in doubt.

Reprinted from Elizabethan Poetry: Modern Essays in Criticism, ed. Paul J. Alpers, pp. 447–472. Copyright © 1967 by Oxford University Press. Reprinted by permission of the author and the publisher. This essay is based on the author's unpublished doctoral dissertation, "Language and Concept in The Faerie Queene," submitted at Yale University, June 1959.

The most influential modern critic of Spenser, C. S. Lewis, suggests that the reader revise these values. Spenser's poetry belongs to an older narrative school in which richness or subtlety of language is not required and would even be inappropriate. It "has in view an audience who have settled down to hear a long story and do not want to savour each line as a separate work of art. Much of The Faerie Queene will therefore seem thin or over-obvious if judged by modern standards. The 'thickness' or 'density' which I have claimed for it does not come from its language."[2] This account will not solve the reader's problem, however, for the language seems to call more than usual attention to itself. The peculiarities of spelling and form, the rare words, and the high degree of formal organization in the Spenserian stanza seem to encourage and even enforce close inspection of the language. If Spenser's language lacks the density of Donne or Shakespeare, it also lacks the seeming transparency of Chaucer. A language merely thin or over-obvious might be more generally acceptable, but to many the language does seem dense, not dense with meaning but slightly muddy or opaque in a way they do not penetrate or understand and yet can not ignore.

Another account offered by W. L. Renwick explains the language in terms of the linguistic goals of the Renaissance. Spenser is said to have been influenced by the program of the Pleiade which urged the poet to revive archaic words, introduce foreign words, and construct new ones out of the existing vocabulary. The purpose was to enrich the language, ultimately the language as a whole but intermediately the language of poetry.[3] Spenser certainly shares the spirit of the Pleiade and their belief in the creative right and creative power of the poet. But their program does not explain his style very exactly nor justify his style to the modern reader, for it does not show how the language has been truly "enriched." The vocabulary of The Faerie Queene is in general rather circumscribed compared to that of Spenser's contemporaries. Most of his archaisms consist not in the revival of obsolete words to enrich the language but simply in the substitution of archaic forms for modern ones. Though Spenser does adopt some foreign words and invent some new ones, the liberties he takes consist primarily in special modifications of current words, and even these are not consistent in the poem.[4] Why, for example, should the text of the proem to Book I read "scryne" instead of "shrine" as it does in the proem to Book III?

The qualities of style that seem puzzling may be accounted for more adequately if, in place of the specific recommendations of the Pleiade, we consult a more fundamental view of language and reality which the recommendations of the Pleiade only in part represent, that is, the Platonic or "Platonistic" view. A useful document to study in this connection is Plato's Cratylus, useful because as an abstract exposition of the fundamental view, it makes the view explicit.

The Cratylus is cited prominently by two of Spenser's mentors in their works on language, and references to the dialogue elsewhere during the Renaissance suggest that Plato's discussion had a certain vogue.[5] Spenser must surely have been aware of it and the view of language it presents. The specific question of influence is not primary to an understanding of his poem, however. The dialogue is important to the modern reader as a rationale to account for Spenser's linguistic impulses and to disclose the attitude toward language which The Faerie Queene presupposes.

In the Cratylus Socrates sets forth the view that words must be not merely conventional and arbitrary, as many believe, but in fact "correct" and "true." For if there is such a thing as reality and knowledge of it, our statements must be about reality, and they must be true to it. And if statements as a whole are to be true, the parts, that is, the words of which they are composed must be true as well. Or, on the analogy of a craft like weaving or cutting, speaking is an action performed for a certain purpose and must be done not according to our own opinion or arbitrary whim but according to nature. We must have the proper instrument correctly suited to the task. In the craft of weaving, the instrument is the shuttle used to separate the web. In the craft of speaking, the instrument is the word.

The instruments of a craft are originally made by someone; so words, too, must have been constructed by an original law-giver or name-maker. An instrument that is good must be constructed according to an ideal. The one who judges whether this has been done successfully, who superintends, is the one who uses the instrument; the carpenter judges the awl. In the case of words the one who judges is the one who knows how to ask and answer questions, who knows how to use words, that is, the dialectician.

What, then, is the principle of "correctness" in words? Socrates says that he does not have the money for a course with the Sophists, so he suggests that the poets be consulted instead. For the modern student of Plato, this advice is tinged with irony, but the Renaissance Platonist, who took at face value the description of poetic inspiration in the Ion, Marsilio Ficino, for example, accepts and even approves of the appeal to the poets.

> After thus carefully inquiring from whom the correctness of
> names, that is, the proper principle by which they are con-
> stituted, is to be learned, he mocks the Sophists, and he leads
> us rather to the poets, not just any of them but the divine
> ones, as if they had received the true names of things from
> the gods, among whom are the true names.[6]

In a similar spirit, the Ramist logic acknowledged no fundamental
distinction between dialectic and poetry.[7] In respect to words as
well as ideas, the poet ideally is a dialectician; he has divinely inspired insight into the truth.

If we consult the poet Homer, we discover that correctness of
words consists in revealing the nature of the things named. Words
reveal reality through their etymologies. The composition of
"Agamemnon," for example, shows that he is admirable (agastos)
for enduring (menein); the derivation of "Atreus" shows that he is
the destructive one (atēros). Words contain within them little self-
explanatory statements. The subject of the statement is the word
itself, the predicate is the elemental word or words from which it
is made, what we would call the morphemes. Words are "true"
because they imply a true statement.

The Ramists on these grounds even introduced etymologizing
into logic. Words are a form of argument because the "notation"
or etymology of the word bears some logical relation to the
"notion" of the thing.[8] "A woman is a woe man because shee
worketh a man woe."[9] As the Ramist discussion reveals, the
"etymology" here is not necessarily the grammatical one, for this
may not furnish a second term: we can not make a significant
statement out of "argument" from "argue." The etymology required is the "logical" one which "explains the cause why this
name is imposed for this thing."[10] That is, the "etymology" or
"true" word is not historically true but philosophically true, and
it is not the function of the grammarian but the dialectician to interpret words. Often philosophically true turns out to be what we
would simply call "fanciful," but neither Plato nor the Renaissance
Platonists had any definite standard for distinguishing the two nor
any desire to do so.

The names of Spenser's characters are clearly philosophic and
true, for they reveal the nature of the one named through the etymology. The heroes' names, like the names of Homer's heroes,
are "composed according to a certain allegorical rationale," as
Ficino would say.[11] Belphoebe is the "beautiful, pure one,"
Artegall is the "art of justice." As a poet-dialectician Spenser

also interprets given words truly and philosophically through etymology. "Magnificence" is not properly conspicuous consumption
but "doing great deeds" as the etymology shows.

When a suitable etymology is not apparent in the current form
of a word, Socrates looks to its archaic form or other archaic
words to see if they are more suggestive, for if language has been
handed down from some original name-maker, words may have
been corrupted in the course of time. If so, the early form should
be the right one (Cratylus 418–19). Through his theory of language
Plato in fact acts out the etymology of "etymology": the true explanation of words is in their origin. The original name-maker in
Plato is really a metaphor for whatever principle of order and
reason there may be in language. The search for older forms is
a search for the true forms that are ideally expressive.

Plato's etymologizing expedient explains the sort of archaizing
Spenser does in The Faerie Queene. Through archaism Spenser
carries out the basic Platonic metaphor of the poem, the metaphor
of the antique world, a time in the past when the world was more
rational and comprehensible, an ideal time, "ideal" not because
there was no evil or difference, but because evil and difference
could be more readily perceived and understood. The purpose of
his archaisms is not primarily to enlarge his vocabulary, the concern of the Pleiade, but to make it more flexible and expressive.
The archaic forms and form words, "-en" endings, "y-" prefixes,
and expressions like "ywis" act as a sort of solvent of language,
dissolving ordinary patterns and the reader's usual expectation.
With archaism established as a mode of diction, Spenser is free to
pick out archaic forms that are more suggestive of philosophic
meaning.

The state of the language in the sixteenth century made such
usage more possible and more likely than it would be now. No
fixed standard of spelling and syntax had been established. There
was less pattern or expectation to overcome, and the writer was
free to choose among many forms available. Spenser simply exercised this freedom more widely than other writers of the time
by reviving forms that were obsolete or obsolescent. Because
there was no fixed standard, the sixteenth century reader always
needed to be more resourceful and interpretive than we. It might
not be obvious or indisputable even what word was before him.
He would always examine word forms more carefully than we and
so would be more apt to see their "etymological" nature, the
meaningful affinities which they suggest.

As the analysis of words in the Cratylus progresses, it soon becomes clear that even the aid of archaism does not yield a perfect language. The given language is clearly deficient; it is not an adequate or reliable source of truth. But for that very reason language should be improved. Words are only approximations, but as such, they can be perfected. Numbers, because they are images simply of quantities can not be; if we change II to III, we do not refer to the same number better, we refer to another number. But if we change "demon" to "daemon," we improve the word and make it more revealing by showing more clearly the identity of spirit and intelligence.[12]

The poet's alterations are an effort to correct language according to his vision or insight so that it reveals reality more adequately. Forms and spellings are improved in order to disclose the etymological rationale of the word. Slight alterations in sound or spelling are admitted so that connections in meaning may be clearer. Rhyme words are spelled the same, not only implying connection in sound but encouraging comparison of meaning. Portmanteau words are devised to cover complex notions.

The lack of "realism," the uncolloquial, unidiomatic character of the language ultimately follows from Spenser's philosophic realism, his belief that truth is not found in the everyday or in immediate surroundings, the "world of appearances," but in a realm of ideas that are only partially and imperfectly reflected in the everyday world. Ordinary language is not adequate to this world of fuller insight. So Spenser's major heroes are not personifications of common terms, like most of the characters in medieval allegory, but of words he has invented. He writes not of "chastity" but of "Belphoebe," a perfected insight into chastity, not of "courtesy" but "Calidore," a concept something like courtesy but refined and redefined.[13] It is the same basic impulse at work which occasions the form "scryne" to suggest that the shrine the poet seeks in his invocation is, according to the Latin root of the word, a scrinium or box of papers where the secret wisdom of the sacred muse may be found.

What the modern reader or the lexicographer sees as a distortion of language is in fact an impulse to perfect it. Like the action as a whole, individual words are allegorical; they contain hidden meaning or implied metaphors. It has frequently been said that Spenser's language suits the poem—a fancy language for a fanciful world. This should at least be supplemented: a more fully significant language for a more fully significant world.

No word even so perfected is ever quite adequate to the idea, however, for words according to Plato are ultimately a kind of image. An image can never be a perfect reproduction, for if it were, it would not be an image at all but the very thing; it would be not the word "horse" but the real horse itself. Such inevitable inadequacy of language might, it seems, lead to despair of ever successfully expressing the truth. In the Seventh Epistle[14] Plato vehemently disavows a pupil precisely for trying to state first principles, ultimate realities, explicitly. Yet truth can be reached. It is reached through indirection, through the use of three separate but mutually complementary instruments: the word, the definition, and the image. Each of these suggests different aspects of the truth. By the continual, energetic comparison of the three, the soul rises to a comprehension of the thing itself. The three are constantly rubbed together, so to speak, and the friction ignites and illuminates the soul.

In poetry the definition is dramatized either literally or symbolically by the action. The meaning of "Agamemnon" in the view of classical and Renaissance commentators, is implicit in the etymology, but it is fully disclosed only in the action of the Iliad. The reader discovers the meaning of the name by analyzing the action of the poem. Homer, with the aid of divine inspiration, originally discovered the proper name, or the true meaning of the given name, by analyzing the conduct of his character in life. Since the heroes of The Faerie Queene are not types but concepts and universals, their proper names must be discovered in the conduct of life as a whole. The author, if a true poet-dialectician, was inspired to direct intuition of the concept, only adumbrated in life. He then invented the proper name, a personification, and a symbolic action through which it is fully revealed.

The action of Spenser's heroes in The Faerie Queene continually unfolds an "etymological" rationale, the secret wit of reality which his language is devised to disclose. Nothing, therefore, could be more misleading than the opinion that Spenser's language is negligible in our reading of the poem. In fact "etymological" associations of language are a constant guide to the implicit meaning of the poem and form the very principle of its organization. From the beginning, the poem evolves according to such a rationale: for example, in the action of Book I, a hero inspired by eros (these terms are explicitly connected in the Cratylus, 398 D and make up a traditional "etymology") rides forth as a knight errant. His first adventure as a knight errant is, naturally, an encounter with Errour: he defeats her but then proceeds to err through eros, the misplaced affections of his "heroicke" heart.[15] So misled, he goes to the house of Pride from which he emerges safely, only to err again in

the arrogance of Orgoglio, the presumptuous spirit, the airs of
man. He is then redeemed from Orgoglio by Arthur, the ardor
and the art or efficacy of grace. Yet again he almost errs in despair before he is led to the house of Holiness by Una where he
is restored to wholeness and the whole of holiness is symbolically
revealed.

The action thus proceeds by a series of etymological puns, yet
their presence is frequently unobtrusive; the wit appears to us as
a secret wit. At the opening of the poem when the knight, his lady,
and the dwarf enter the "covert" to find shelter from the storm,
we enter into their vision of things. The traditional catalogue of
trees becomes a dramatic record of enthrallment, the process of
being "led with delight" and so beguiled. The trees, clad with
summer's "pride," conceal "heavens light" and the guiding star:
what is simply "farre" seems "faire." We are warned by Una that
"This is the wandring wood, this Errours den," and the double
meaning of "knots" and "boughtes" (bouts) anticipates the implication of the knight's encounter with this tortuous beast. Yet the
climactic pun drawing so deeply upon the very wit of the language
itself takes us by surprise: "God helpe the man so wrapt in Errours endlesse traine."

With the killing of Errour the knight's first encounter is complete. He proves that he is not in this sense an errant knight: he
is not subject to a form of error which, as the language re-asserts
again and again, can be made "plaine." He proves worthy of the
"Armorie" which first won his heroic heart.

The action then proceeds to show that the knight is "errant,"
however, in another sense made fully clear when the word is at
last used in Fradubio's speech: he is subject to Duessa or duplicity. "The author then (said he) of all my smarts, / Is one
Duessa a false sorceresse, / That many errant knights hath brought
to wretchednesse" (I. ii. 34. 7–9). "Duessa" is, of course, associated with duo, two, to suggest her doubleness or deceit but also with
Greek dus-, bad, ill and due, misery to suggest the wretchedness
she brings.

The Red Cross Knight is parted from Una, the one truth, by
Archimago, the arch magician, and can be because "Archimago"
in his "Hermitage" is the architect of images, of delusive like-
nesses. Archimago sends to "Morpheus," the former or fashion-
er, for a "diverse" or, etymologically, misleading dream, subtler
and more seductive than the "diverse doubt" of Errour because
the threat then made "plaine" now becomes an ambiguous "plaint."
The "doubtfull words" of the dream-lady make the "redoubted

knight / Suspect her truth." Yet "since no' untruth he knew," he is not seduced but interprets her appeal in an honorable way. Sheer ambiguity can not destroy him because if the evil is truly ambiguous, the interpreter must ascertain or supply it, and the knight as "redoubted," reverent as well as revered, has no such evil in him to supply. Archimago must create a definite false illusion of Una as unfaithful which exploits the knight's virtue, his love of her. Una and the Red Cross are thus divided into "double parts" or separated through duplicity and Una left "wandring," the end of Archimago's "drift," leaving the Red Cross to Duessa's wiles.

The nature of the Red Cross Knight's susceptibility is then further dramatized by the difference between Duessa and Sans Foy. The Red Cross defeats Sans Foy; it is not a complete loss of faith on his part which is leading him astray. But he errs, he falls prey to Duessa as Fidessa, a superficially perfect semblance of faith, through his impulse to love, the "heroicke" character of his stout heart. His love for Duessa is certainly a crude bedazzlement revealed in the way he looks her up and down, and in respect to him she is "Fidessa" or little faith, but it is significant that his faith is not lost primarily but misplaced: he always believes but he may misbelieve.

The analysis of error which began in the "wandring wood" is completed in the encounter with Fradubio, metamorphosed into a tree or an instance of error in its more refined and significant sense. In the symbolic plant the meaning of the action which began with the earlier "plaints" is "plast in open plaines" (I. ii. 32. 9; 33. 6) and made explicit. Fradubio like the Red Cross was overcome not by doubt per se but by guile, the guile to which doubt as an indeterminate state of mind makes him prey. When he tried to judge between his lady and Duessa, "the doubtfull ballaunce" swayed equally; doubt itself determines in no way. So Duessa intervened with an act of misrepresentation, obscuring his lady in a fog. Fradubio suggests dubius, doubting, and reflects its dangers; more specifically, though, he is the victim of "fraud" (I. iv. i. 3), the active evil to which the uncommitted state of doubt makes him vulnerable.

The Red Cross Knight misled by Archimago's Duessa next appears at the house of Pride, implicitly the palace of hypocrisy, as playfully derived from Hyper chrysos, covered over with gold.[16]

A stately Pallace built of squared bricke,
Which cunningly was without morter laid,
Whose wals were high, but nothing strong, nor thick,

And golden foile all over them displaid,
That purest skye with brightnesse they dismaid.   (I. iv. 4)

It is a house, as the Bible suggests, not on the strait but the broad
way and built on sand, but it is "painted cunningly." The porter
"Malvenu," a parody of bienvenu or welcome, greets them, pre-
figuring the evil that will come. Then "Lucifera" appears, the
bringer of light who like Phaeton proudly burns and bedazzles with
light intended "fairely for to shyne" or phaëthōn (I. iv. 9. 9).

In the pageant of the Seven Deadly Sins which follows Spenser's
wit is comically farfetched in keeping with the gaudy cartoon quality
of the parade. The first sin "Idlenesse," dressed like a monk in
"habit blacke, and amis thin," which may by some extravagant
puns suggest the poet's condemnation, carries his "Portesse," but
unfortunately the prayer book is only a "portesse" only carried
and rarely read. Certainly the "wayne" is poorly led with such a
vacuous and inattentive fellow guiding its "way." Idlenesse
"esloynes" himself and challenges "essoyne" "from worldly
cares," (soins in French); the legal terms suggest his Jesuitical
invocation of the letter of the law to free him ironically for "lawlesse riotise."

Gluttony follows with the long fine neck of a crane; "gluttony" in
Latin is derived from glutire, to swallow. He is depicted as Silenus
the satyr (satur, full); his drunken "corse" reflects the course he
leads. Lechery, who appears on the traditional goat, caper, is true
to that depiction, capricious; his "whally" eyes, white or wall eyes,
are the goat's eye or oeil de chèvre in French.[17]

Envy is presented primarily as a vile mouth, stressed by the
rare form "chaw" for jaw to reiterate his endless malicious and
mordant backbiting. His gown of satin as "discolourd say" seems
to pun on the vicious things he says; the snake he carries in his
bosom "implyes" his mortal sting. Envy's gown "ypainted full of
eyes" reflects the root meaning of envy in Latin, invidia, the evil
eye. He eyes all with hatred but particularly looks at his precursor
"Covetyse" or avarice with covet eyes, reflecting their close connection.

Wrath is depicted through associations in English as rash or
rathe; his is a "hasty rage." And when Satan tries to drive this
"laesie teme" of evils, Idleness is called "Slowth," spelled as if
derived from "slow."

The pride of the Red Cross Knight is mettle, spirit and courage
(I. x. 66. 7), zeal, not the pride of this house. As the inhabitants
go forth to sport, he estranges himself from their "joyaunce vaine"
and therefore encounters Sans Joy. By the defeat of Sans Joy he

reveals that it is only vain joy, proud and empty pleasure that he is estranged from, however; though his "cheere" seems initially "too solemne sad," his solemnity is not a puritanical joylessness but reverence.

The Red Cross Knight's Dwarf discovers those who have "mortgaged" (I. v. 46. 4) their lives or literally pledged their lives to death through pride and warns his master who escapes. The Dwarf, who is always the "wary" dwarf, the "carefull" dwarf, seems—in part through association with the archaic term "dwere," meaning doubt or dread—to symbolize not common sense as critics have believed but the fear implicit in the reverence of holiness. His first speech of warning epitomizes his nature: "Fly fly (quoth then / The fearefull Dwarfe:) this is no place for living men." (I. i. 13. 8—9).

The Red Cross escapes the house of Pride only to encounter pride in another form, Orgoglio. According to mythographers pride is derived from heaven and earth, ex aethere et terra, but Spenser corrects this through a series of puns to suggest that pride as symbolized by Orgoglio is not from heaven and earth but merely from earth and air. As a "Geant" Orgoglio is born of Gea, the earth, but his "boasted sire" is "blustring Aeolus" from aella, stormy wind, and aiolos, shifting, changeable. Pride is man's earthliness blown up by the vicissitudes of his mortal circumstance. Aeolus "secretly inspired" the earth with "stormy yre," a form which suggests both ire and air, creating Orgoglio. Orgoglio takes "arrogant delight," again with a suggestion of air, in his "high descent," but such descent suggests not true divinity but rather how far he has fallen. Orgoglio thus suggests Greek orgaein, to swell, to teem, and orgē, temperament, wrath, passion, as well as the Italian orgoglio, pride.

This association of Orgoglio with air apparently alludes to the Prince of the Power of the Air in Ephesians, chapter II, and explains why an encounter with Orgoglio succeeds the Red Cross Knight's rejection of the house of Pride. In Ephesians Paul recalls that all men once followed

> the course of this world, according to the Prince of the Power of the Air, the spirit that now worketh in the children of disobedience: Among whom also we all had our conversation in times past in the lusts of our flesh, fulfilling the desires of the flesh and of the mind; and were by nature the children of wrath, even as others. But God, who is rich in mercy, for his great love wherewith he loved us, even when we were dead in sins, hath quickened us together with Christ. . . . For by grace are ye saved through faith; and that not of

yourselves: It is the gift of God: Not of works, lest any
man should boast. (Authorized Version. The earlier translations contain the same key phrases.)

When he leaves the house of Pride, the Red Cross Knight, wea-
ried by the ordeal, disarms and sits down to rest by a fountain; he
thus puts off the armor of faith, to which Spenser in the prefatory
letter ascribes all his success, and fails to stand, according to the
teaching of Ephesians (chapter VI, verses 10ff.), having done all
in the whole armor of God. Instead, like the natural man or the
child of wrath in Ephesians, he indulges the desires of the flesh
and the mind by bathing in the pleasure of the shade, listening to
the music of the birds, and taking solace with his lady. He drinks
from the fountain, the antithesis of the well of life which is later
to renew him in his battle with the dragon, for this makes all who
drink from it feeble and faint. It comes from a nymph who "tyr'd
with heat of scorching ayre" like the knight sat down in the midst
of her race, making the goddess Diana "wroth." So disarmed, the
knight encounters Orgoglio. The monster, boasting of his high
descent and matchless might, symbolizes the knight's pride and
the divine wrath such pride arouses: the pride of indulging himself in the confidence of his achievement. Duessa intercedes with
Orgoglio begging him not to destroy her knight but to make him an
"eternal bondslave," the thrall of pride in works, especially works
as a sign of "high descent," of election. And he is so enthralled,
erring in the arrogance of the Prince of the Power of the Air, until
he is redeemed by grace.

The Red Cross is redeemed from the wrath of Orgoglio by
Arthur, symbol of the ardor and art of God's grace. Arthur represents not the magnanimity of God, his potentiality or etymologically his great spirit, but his magnificence, his actuality or etymologically his doing great deeds. Arthur's image and genealogy
are resplendent with the glory of such greatness. He appears
with a headpiece like an almond tree on the top of "greene Selinis";
"Selinis" in Greek resembles selinon, the plant from which the
chaplets of victors in the ancient games were made; Virgil calls
it "palmosa Selinus" (Aeneid III. 705).

A comparison of Spenser's image of Arthur with Marlowe's
adaptation in Tamburlaine reveals how carefully Spenser's language maintains the suggestions of the almond tree and transfers
them to his hero.

> Upon the top of all his <u>loftie crest</u>,
> A bunch of haires discolourd diversly,
> With sprincled pearle, and gold full richly drest,
> Did shake, and seem'd to daunce for jollity,
> Like to an Almond tree ymounted hye
> On top of greene <u>Selinis</u> all alone,
> With blossomes brave bedecked daintily;
> Whose tender <u>locks</u> do tremble every one
> At every little <u>breath</u>, that under heaven is <u>blowne</u>.
>   (I. vii. 32)

> I'll ride in golden armour like the sun;
> And in my <u>helm</u> a triple <u>plume</u> shall spring,
> Spangled with diamonds, dancing in the air,
> To note me emperor of the three-fold world;
> Like to an almond tree ymounted high
> Upon the lofty and celestial mount
> Of ever green Selinis, quaintly decked
> With bloom more white than Herycina's brows,
> Whose tender <u>blossoms</u> tremble every one
> At every little breath that thorough heaven is blown.
>   Tam. 4092–4101 (Pt. II, IV, iii, 115–24)

In both passages there is a personification; the hero is compared
to the personified almond tree. But in Marlowe the personification is incidental while in Spenser it is so radical and persistent
that the language seems continuously symbolic of the hero. Instead of "helm" Spenser uses "crest" which suggests not only the
plume on the helmet but an identifying insignia, as if the crest
were Arthur's sign; "crest" also suggests the summit of a mountain, anticipating the comparison and so suggesting that the almond
on Selinis is the sign. Yet because this is merely suggested the
tree on the mountain remains natural, free, and alive.

Applied to the ambivalent "crest," Spenser's "loftie" exercises
more of its ethical implication than in the Marlowe passage when
applied to the more literal "mount." "Haires" in place of "plume"
helps to personify the crest; "drest" applies more readily than
"spangled" to a person in the sense clothed, to hair in the sense
combed, and to the plume in the sense adorned. The line could even
be a description of the person instead of the plume. The phrase
"for jollity" makes sure that "daunce" keeps its literal as well as

its transferred meaning, while in Marlowe's phrase "dancing in the air" the personification is almost dead. Even "daintily" with its association of gentleness seems more human than Marlowe's "quaintly."

The suggestions are further carried out by the term "brave" which in contrast to the phrase "more white than Herycina's brows," suggests the courage as well as the esthetic splendor of the glory implied. "Locks" instead of "blossoms" suggests tufts of hair as well as foliage, maintaining the personification and implying that Arthur himself as the succourer trembles in sympathy at every breath blown. The idea is not clearly controlled in Marlowe's lines; it would certainly be inappropriate for Tamburlaine, yet without it this part of the comparison seems pointless. In Spenser's stanza there is even a slight metaphoric play in the phrase "all alone" between "by itself" and "the only one" which underlines Arthur's pre-eminence and makes an obtrusive explicating phrase like Marlowe's "to note me emperor of the three-fold world" totally unnecessary. We notice, incidentally, that Spenser's Selinis is not "celestial," and his almond tree trembles at every breath blown "under" not "thorough" heaven. Though the almond tree is "ymounted hye" on the mount, it is in this world. Arthur is the highest man and one alone, God's vice-regent, but he is not God.

After his victory Arthur explains to Una and the Red Cross that he was raised by "Timon" or in Greek honor, worth, and he is accompanied by "Timias," his squire, "th'admirer of his might," who is similarly derived. He was raised "Under the foot of Rauran mossy hore, / From whence the river Dee as silver cleene / His tombling billowes rolls with gentle rore" (I. ix. 4. 6 ff). The river Dee suggests his divine origin; this is the explicit etymology of the river in the marriage catalogue of Book IV: "Dee, which Britons long ygone / Did call divine . . ." (IV. xi. 3, 4). (The Rauran seems so named because it is where the Dee gently "rores." Arthur's shield is made of "diamond," suggesting its function of representing God in the world.[18] It was made by the great magician Merlin, the antithesis of Archimago, who created the shield to expose everything false. Merlin, too, seems related to honor and wonder through Latin mirus by virtue of his "admirable deedes." Arthur's sword was made by Merlin from metal mixed with "Medaewart" or meadwort, so spelled suggesting that it wards off cunning and magic, mēdea in Greek: it is so made "that no enchauntment from his dint might save." (II. viii. 20. 6).

When Arthur appears to save the Red Cross Knight, the poet proclaims the "goodly golden chaine" by which the virtues are linked in love, and each hero aids the other. This chain is literally "concord," the cord that ties all things together (cf. III. i. 12. 8) through con and cor, the uniting of the heroes' hearts.

Arthur departs in search of the Faerie Queene whom he discovered in the revelation of a dream, the antithesis of the Red Cross Knight's dream delusion contrived by Archimago in canto one. The Red Cross and Una set off and are soon accosted by a knight fleeing a ghastly sight, the sight, we soon learn, of Despair. The knight Trevisan with his head disarmed and a rope about his neck approaches looking back continually in fear. His steed flies with winged heels "As he had beene a fole of Pegasus his kind."

The myth of Pegasus and Bellerophon, according to mythographers, signifies the importance of neither exulting too much in good fortune, nor sorrowing too much in adversity since God is the governor of all. Bellerophon, over-elated by his success, decided to fly to the sun on his horse, Pegasus, but he was struck down for such pride by Jupiter and so taught the true limits and proper temperament of man. Both "Trevisan" and his companion "Terwin" reflect the topsy-turvy fate and temperament of Bellerophon in his fall. "Trevisan," however, sees (viso) and escapes.

God brought such a disaster upon Bellerophon, according to mythographers, to reveal his true source and sustainer. As the poet asserts in the opening stanza of the next canto, "all the good is Gods, both power and eke will." But God is good, as his name itself implies, and he is merciful to man. The "fole" (I. ix. 21. 9) or foal of Pegasus, and his rider, is also a fool thus in his "foltring" (ix. 24. 9) terror of despair.

Pegasus is traditionally the symbol of poetry; the tradition is germane to the depiction of Despair, for his victim Terwin is a victim of Petrarchan despair in love, so closely associated with poetry, and, more important, Despair's appeal is through the power of rhetoric. The Red Cross Knight is nearly overwhelmed by the poetry of Despair, almost charmed by the "inchaunted" rhyme of the "Miscreant," the unbeliever who miscreates or distorts his argument, evoking doom by the omission of God's grace, insisting that the knight will eternally err: "For he, that once hath missed the right way, / The further he doth goe, the further he doth stray." Even the knight's response is the traditional literary one; he begins to "tremble like a leafe of Aspin greene" (the only use of this figure in the poem.)

Like most of the evils in Book I, Despair is associated with division and doubleness. The main accusation he brings is that

CRAIG

the Red Cross was false to his faith and served "Duessa." The
term first appears in Book I when Una is originally "from her
knight divorced in despaire" (I. iii. 2. 8); she herself remains
faithful, but she is "forsaken, wofull, solitarie" through his error,
his displaced faith. Spenser seems to suggest that despair is the
dis-spirited state which occurs when Una or the one truth of grace
and the Red Cross Knight are divided or dispaired. At any rate it
is Una who now rescues the Red Cross from the rhetoric of Despair, calling him away from vain words and "the accurst hand-
writing" of God's justice to action and grace.

The knight then proceeds to the house of Holiness where the
whole of holiness is symbolized. In this house he is taught repentance and the way to "heavenly blesse," according to the argument of the canto. The spelling distinguishes "blesse" from
"blisse," though the two were often identified in Elizabethan
English and come ultimately from the same etymological source.
The Bower of Bliss thus lies in contrast to the house of Holiness
as the house of Unblessed Bliss, an ironic Eden or garden of
pleasure in Hebrew. The excess of "Acrasia" which we see there
is implicitly contrasted with the abundance of "Charissa." "Acrasia" is presented in Book II as a perversion of charis or true
grace; she "depastures" delight, a term Spenser coined, as the
ironic pastor in her bower who takes life rather than nourishing
it, destroying her worshippers.

In the house of Holiness Saint George at last gains his name and
full identity as his sainthood is foreseen. He learns that he like
Arthur is a changeling. Arthur was taken from his mother and delivered to the faery knight "old Timon" thus, it seems, being taught
by time, as Achilles was taught by Cheiron, son of Chronos. Saint
George, however, was found where a faerie left him in the furrow
of a field.

> Thence she thee brought into this Faerie lond,
> And in an heaped furrow did thee hyde,
> Where thee a Ploughman all unweeting fond,
> As he his toylesome teme that way did guyde,
> And brought thee up in ploughmans state to byde,
> Whereof Georgos he thee gave to name;
> Till prikt with courage, and thy forces pryde,
> To Faery court thou cam'st to seeke for fame,
> And prove thy puissaunt armes, as seemes thee best
> became.

(I. x. 76)

"Georgos" is derived from the Greek term for plowman as "Adam" was derived from the Hebrew term for earth. The etymology suggests their ultimate affinity in the moral allegory. It suggests, too, in retrospect that the earthly giant "Orgoglio" is George himself, inspired or blown up with the air of arrogance to which every man in his weakness may succumb.

The etymology of St. George functions also in a very different way: it presents an allusion to English literary history and the career of "holiness" as a topic for poetry. The truth of holiness was lost but then "fond" or found again as invention, matter for poetry in Piers Plowman, substantiating the traditional name of the English saint as "ploughman" or man of the soil. Spenser eventually returns the topic to the simple, rural world through the career of "grace" in the poem. "Of Court it seemes, men Courtesie doe call" (VI. i. 1), but Spenser eventually corrects this to show that the court is the source of false courtesy, of "courting"; true "courtesy" is a form of "grace" which thrives best not at court but in the pastoral milieu, or pastoral ideal, of Book VI.

Spenser's secret wit suggests not only the moral implication of the action but political and social instances which substantiate and exemplify. A most vivid instance occurs in Guyon's encounter with Phaedria, Book II, canto vi; a series of puns associates her with Italy and the Italian way of life during the Renaissance. Phaedria's boat is called a "little Gondelay" and a "little frigot." Both terms had been introduced into English not long before from the Italian. With his use of them in the Phaedria passage Spenser seems to be punning in Italian: "gondola" suggests the Italian term gongolare, "to laugh till ones heart be sore or shoulders ake, to shuckle and be full of joy, or excessive gladnesse"; "frigot" suggests frigotare, "to shuckle, to shrug, or strut for overjoy." These puns are reinforced by the epithets of her "shallow ship," "painted bote" (false good), and "flit barke," (meaning airy, insubstantial, as well as swift.) The puns become an allusion to Italy through the meaning of "gondola" which Florio defines as "a little boat or whirry used no where but a bout and in Venice."[19]

Other references suggest the allusion. In repudiating war, Phaedria refers to the kind of skirmishes she prefers as "scarmoges." This spelling instead of the usual "skirmish" (IV. ix. 20. 2) associates the term with Italian scaramuccia, the name of Harlequin's companion with his buffoonish battles in the Italian farce. Phaedria locates her world "In this wide Inland sea, that hight by name / The Idle Lake"; "Inland sea" is a translation of "Mediterranean"; the "Idle Lake" is apparently the Adriatic, which

329

Spenser associates with adraneia, inactivity. She lives on an idyllic island suggesting Venice, to the Renaissance Englishman the very land of Venus. The 1590 edition of The Faerie Queene even carried a proverbial allusion to the pope: "Sometimes she sung, as loud as lark in aire, / Sometimes she laught, as merry as Pope Jone." The song she sings is the magnificent perversion of the Biblical "Behold the lilies of the field, they toil not neither do they spin."

Through such puns the Phaedria incident forms an elaborate commentary on the Italian way of life during the Renaissance and a criticism of the young Englishman's practice of sowing his wild oats there and affecting the Italianate style. Spenser finds reflected in Italy the prototype of inane mirth and shallow epicureanism; in the virtual enclosure of the Mediterranean Sea he finds a symbol of stagnation and idleness.

Phaedria entertains her companions with stories like those of the joke-books, the thesauri of merry tales which flourished in the period, many from Italy, offering crude tales without any formal elegance: ". . . And greatly joyed merry tales to faine, / Of which a store-house did with her remaine, / Yet seemed, nothing well they her became; / For all her words she drownd with laughter vaine, / And wanted grace in utt'ring of the same. . . ." (II. vi. 6). Part of Spenser's ambition to "overgo" Ariosto was a desire to prevent the epic from descending to this level.

In the Bower of Bliss Spenser continues such allusions but also turns to the goals of the Elizabethan Merchant Adventurers, the ports they sought in ships like the "Delight," the "Desire," and the "Castle of Comfort" as they sailed for the expected sweet life of the West Indies. The "wandering Islands" recall Cuba and La Dominica, called the wandring islands because they wandered all over the map in Spain and Portugal's dispute over their location and thus ownership. "Verdant" may recall Cape Verde; the Bower of Bliss itself suggests Deseado or Port Desire and more generally Florida. It is "goodly beautifide / With all the ornaments of Floraes pride, / Wherewith her mother Art, as halfe in scorne / Of niggard Nature . . . did decke her." The art that Spenser refers to would include the art of the voyagers in their hyperbolic accounts which "too lavishly adorne" with wealth and fertility the nature they actually encountered.

The journey to the Bower of Bliss reveals the financial disaster which resulted from adventuring in the hope of perfect pleasure. The most vivid depiction is in "The Rocke of vile Reproch," a dramatization of bankruptcy as the bank on which men break. The rock hovers over its potential victims "Threatning it selfe on them to ruinate"; one sees on its "sharpe clifts the ribs of vessels broke" and the "carkasses exanimate / Of such, as having all their substance spent / In wanton joyes, and lustes intemperate, / Did afterwards make shipwracke violent, / Both of their life, and fame for ever fowly blent." The greedy "Cormoyrants" or moneylenders and "birds of ravenous race" wait there for the "spoyle of wretches," that is, their ruin and so the confiscation of their goods "After lost credite and consumed thrift, / At last them driven hath to this despairefull drift." "Credit" had just recently acquired its specifically commercial sense in addition to the more general moral one, and "thrift," too, contains a comparable ambiguity. "The Rocke of vile Reproch" is the counterpart of Homer's Scylla, etymologized to skyleuein, to strip, to spoil. The Gulf of Greediness opposite corresponds to Charybdis (charis hybris) which Cicero, for example, uses as a metaphor for prodigality in attacking Antony (Phillipics II. xxvii. 67).

"The wandring Islands," the counterpart of Homer's Wandering Rocks, in respect to the commercial and social world etymologically suggest the vagabonds and vagrants, travesties of the knight errant, whose devices Robert Greene was soon to expose. Pictured as "wandring Islands" "seeming now and than" like the classical Delos, which Spenser etymologizes traditionally to dēlos, apparent because the islands simply appeared out of nowhere, their seemingly fair and fruitful grounds are seductive but unsure. When Phaedria re-appears on a "wandring Island" with her little boat beside her, the boat is called a "skippet" meaning basket, a nonce usage by Spenser here (N. E. D.), suggesting perhaps the baudy baskets exposed by Greene's precursor Thomas Harman in his A Caveat or Warening for Common Cursetors, Vulgarely Called Vagabones (chapter xvi). The basket was a device of Elizabethan prostitutes who first presented themselves as pedlars of notions before they exposed their baudy purposes. Certainly Phaedria at her reappearance is more crudely and clearly just such a wayside prostitute. Spenser's term "skippet" resembling "skipper" and "skiff" accommodates her very nicely to the maritime setting and resembling "skip" implies the frivolity and the insecurity of her mode of travel, her way of life.

It may even seem as if Spenser in calling Acrasia's victim "Verdant" was alluding to Greene himself whose demise he thereby predicts and attempts to prevent. Greene at any rate gained a witty benefit from his degradation by moralizing on himself with such a pun in the last stanza of his poem of repentance: "My

331

wretched end may warn Greene springing youth / To use delights,
as toyes that will deceive / And scorne the world before the world
them leaves: / For all worlds trust, is ruine without ruth."[20]

But the development which emerges most strongly moves in
the direction of amplifying symbolic implication rather than pursuing social allusions in detail. Like "Mordant" (or "Mortdant"
II. i. 49. 9) his counterpart, "Verdant," the flourishing young man
whose spirit Acrasia "depastures," must receive what he gives,
though in his case the outcome is happily reversed. Acrasia with
her curse enacting "Mortdant" gives "death to him that death does
give,"[21] the Palmer, through his "counsel sage" enacting "Verdant"
gives truth to him that truth does give or instructs the victim in
the true harm of Acrasia which he depicts and so frees him from
her.

The language of the voyage projects a world of the moral imagination above the social scene to which it simply dips in specific
allusion with an occasional detail of incident, image, or term. The
sea-beasts encountered by Guyon and the Palmer are not the conies
and quail of the Elizabethan underworld or their sea counterparts,
nor even sea-lions and sea-foxes but the most fantastic monsters
imaginable. The catalogue begins by literary allusion: a battle
with the "many headed hydra" is Plato's symbol in Book IV of the
Republic (426 e) for the futility of attempting to legislate the end
of fraud instead of converting the spirit of man, since without such
a change of spirit new forms of fraud like the heads of a hydra
will continually spring forth. The scolopendra, it was thought,
"feeling himselfe taken with a hooke, casteth out his bowels, untill
he hath unloosed the hooke, and then swalloweth them up againe,"[22]
which perhaps resembles certain specific devices of the sharper.
But what the chosen epithets depict is images of evil monstrously
general. The hazards of the course are immense and indefinable
except as threat, the "Ziffius" or swordfish, for example, and its
consequence, the morse, which Spenser derives from the Latin
mors to mean death.

This is the advantage of Spenser's secret wit. He may suggest
implications at every possible level of experience without dis-
rupting the symbolic unity and continuity of the moral world. The
operation of his style was perfectly described by Spenser's first
critic, Kenelm Digby, in a letter of appreciation addressed to
Henry May, 1638:

Spencer in what he sayth hath a way of expression peculiar
to himselfe; he bringeth downe the highest and deepest mys-

> teries that are contained in humane learning, to an easie and
> gentle forme of delivery; wch. sheweth he is Master of what
> he treateth of; he can wield it as he pleaseth: And he hath
> done this so cunningly, that if one heede him not wth. great
> attention, rare and wonderful conceptions will unperceived
> slide by him that readeth his workes, and he will thinke he
> hath mett wth. nothing but familiar and easie discourses:
> But lett one dwell a while upon them, and he shall feele a
> strange fulness and roundness in all he sayth.[23]

The Faerie Queene has disappointed the modern reader, for in
an age that admires the difficult and complex it seems "familiar
and easy." But, as Kenelm Digby testifies, it offers "rare and
wonderful conceptions" to the attentive reader who does not let
them slide by. To discover their fullness the reader must heed
the language closely, however. The language must be savored for
the cunning within its gentleness and ease.

HOW TO READ THE FAERIE QUEENE

Paul Alpers

   Despite the recent flood of books on Spenser, the common reader can still find little to help him read The Faerie Queene with
pleasure, or understand how, in its alien mode, it has the complexity and human importance we expect of great poetry. Donald
Cheney's Spenser's Image of Nature: Wild Man and Shepherd in
'The Faerie Queen' (Yale University Press) should provide such
help; the fact that it does not can at least let us see some of our
difficulties with the poem. Cheney's sense of the poem is most
neatly stated in his conclusion:

> The poet's triumph over a recalcitrant reality lies in his
> imitation of its complexity, in his celebration of the endless
> pattern of oppositions by which the worlds of physical nature
> and of man's moral nature are to be conceived. Critics who
> tend to dismiss Spenser's allegory as an incomplete or one-
> sided presentation of reality seem radically insensitive to
> this aspect of the poem. It is the poem's richness, its re-
> fusal to reduce its world to any neat conceptual pattern, or
> to exclude any discordant impulse when it arises, which
> must in the end constitute its chief claim to imaginative
> validity.   (p. 247)

These ideas seem to me true, and they should provide a fruitful
way of reading The Faerie Queene. They put in their true light a
passage like Spenser's commentary on Calidore's stay among the
shepherds (6.10.1-3), in which Spenser—by first blaming, then
excusing, then commending the 'truant' knight—deliberately makes
us see a moral question from all sides, and deliberately avoids the
casuistry which fills the critical and scholarly literature on this
episode. Cheney's frank acceptance of the poem's contradictions
is exactly right for this passage or for the dialogue between the
hermit Contemplation and the Red Cross Knight (1.10.57-67), in

Reprinted from Essays in Criticism, Vol. 18 (1968), pp. 429-443, by permission of the author and the publisher, F. W. Bateson.

which Spenser feels perfectly free to let his characters contradict themselves as he lays forth the conflicting claims of heavenly and earthly glory, and the complexities inherent in a Christian's attitude towards earthly endeavour. And Cheney knows that the continually shifting perspectives of The Faerie Queene are to be found not only in passages of explicit moral dialectic, but in the details and texture of the verse. His arguments are always based on close analysis of individual stanzas, and the book has many felicitous and useful observations—for example, that the description of Arthur's armour 'insists on those details which had earlier seemed to be the indices of evil' (p. 69). Yet for all its real and potential virtues, Spenser's Image of Nature has most of the faults of most books on The Faerie Queene—most importantly, rigid interpretations and the distortion of details in the interest of a previously determined point of view or argument. The book is an exceptionally striking, and therefore instructive, instance of the gaps that can exist between intelligent general statements and particular critical analyses and demonstrations.

Cheney begins at the beginning, when a storm drives the Red Cross Knight and Una into the wandering wood:

> Enforst to seeke some couert nigh at hand,
> A shadie groue not far away they spide,
> That promist ayde the tempest to withstand:
> Whose loftie trees yclad with sommers pride,
> Did spred so broad, that heauens light did hide,
> Not perceable with power of any starre:
> And all within were pathes and alleies wide,
> With footing worne, and leading inward farre:
> Faire harbour that them seemes; so in they entred arre.
>
> And foorth they passe, with pleasure forward led,
> Ioying to heare the birdes sweete harmony,
> Which therein shrouded from the tempest dred,
> Seemd in their song to scorne the cruell sky.
> Much can they prayse the trees so straight and hy,
> The sayling Pine, the Cedar proud and tall,
> The vine-prop Elme, the Poplar neuer dry,
> The builder Oake, sole king of forrests all,
> The Aspine good for staues, the Cypresse funerall.

(1.1.7–8)

This catalogue of trees, which continues for another full stanza, is a great stumbling block for critics of the poem. Students always see perfectly clearly that its point and function are indicated by the first line of the stanza that follows it: 'Led with delight, they thus beguile the way' (1.1.10). The simple pleasures of the verse—an expert performance in which Spenser self-consciously rivals earlier poets—carry us along, until, having also been 'led with delight,' we share the plight in which the knight and lady find themselves:

> When weening to returne, whence they did stray,
> They cannot finde that path, which first was showne,
> But wander too and fro in wayes vnknowne.   (1.1.10)

All this seems a wonderfully appropriate development of the image of the wood of life—the point of which is that it represents the life of man in general, all not some of us—and thoroughly in the nature of allegory, which does not respect individuals, but examines and brings to life universal realities. But Spenserians make heavy weather of the passage because they think that the main point of allegory is to pass moral judgments, and the student who finds that this opening passage is fun to read will be told, for example, that the catalogue of trees shows that the Red Cross Knight is guilty of succumbing to a visual allurement that weakens his rational powers. Now Cheney's view of the poem seems directly intended to prevent this kind of desiccating distortion. He introduces his discussion of this passage by warning us against 'the reductive reading which [Spenser] has too frequently received' (p. 22), and by insisting on finding the poem's meaning by following its sequence—thus warning us against looking ahead to discover that 'This is the wandring wood, this <u>Errours den</u>' (1.1.13). The whole point of postponing Una's announcement (though presumably she knew it all along) is that the 'label' serves us as a moral recognition of what we have undergone, participated in, rather than as a shield, or as wax to plug our ears against the siren song of 'the birdes sweete harmony.' The postponed naming of the wood is a variant of something Cheney points out, also by way of introducing this passage, about the names of characters in <u>The Faerie Queene</u>: Spenser 'repeatedly gives his characters names symbolic of their roles but announces those names only after showing them in action, so that the names themselves become capsule summaries or mottoes' (p. 22).

And now, alas, let us see what Cheney actually says about this passage:

In fleeing the shower, they have abandoned one kind of nature
for another. On the plain they are exposed to the elements
and almost ludicrously unprepared to confront them. To see
how far this is from the 'tempest' of epic or tragedy—in the
sense of the hostile environment which tests man's capacity
to endure—one need only compare this shower with the storm
which confronts Aeneas in Book I of the Aeneid. Spenser
makes no attempt here to develop a theme of divine wrath—
his allusion to 'angry Ioue' seems the shallowest of epithets
for the darkened sky—and the abruptness of the rain is such
that everyone has fled before the question of any possible
resistance to it can arise. If there is any similarity here to
a Virgilian storm, it is more likely to the shower that drives
Dido and Aeneas together, for in Virgil too the absence of
any extended description of that later storm suggests the
instinctive nature of the lovers' flight from it. Redcross
and Una do not hesitate to take cover, and they find themselves in a wood which they seem to know all too well: willfully shrouding themselves from the light as well as the rain,
they praise the trees in a catalogue which reflects man's
confident moral dissection of his universe. In such a context it is ominously appropriate that the foliage of the trees
should be their 'sommers pride,' and that the birds whose
song 'seemd . . . to scorne the cruell sky' provide the background for the human praise of the trees: man seems to
share with the lower creatures this false sense of a security
which ignores the changing seasons.   (pp. 23–24)

Almost every one of these statements seems to me totally without
foundation in the poem. How can it possibly be relevant to say that
Una and the knight are 'almost ludicrously unprepared' to face the
elements, when Spenser says:

And angry Ioue an hideous storme of raine
Did poure into his Lemans lap so fast,
That euery wight to shrowd it did constrain.   (1.1.6)

Cheney is simply inventing reasons for a moral judgment against
the knight and Una: thus the remark about 'angry Ioue' is an attempt to dismiss the fact that this storm is sent by God, or at
least by the powers that rule nature. Although the remarks about
the Aeneid are not the mere fancy footwork they seem in isolation—
Cheney has plausible and interesting ideas about the way allusion

works in <u>The Faerie Queene</u> (cf. pp. 7, 148, 201)—their irrelevance reveals his inability to put his general theories into critical
practice.

It is not that Spenser does not call for moral awareness as we
read these stanzas, but that our awareness does not take the form
that Cheney assumes it must. Like every moralistic interpreter,
he singles out the phrase 'sommers pride' and the following line
about hiding heaven's light. He ignores the fact that 'sommers
pride' can be a valid descriptive epithet for the trees' leaves,[1] and
that 'heauens light did hide' is followed by 'Not perceable with power of any starre,' which suggests immunity from malignant powers.[2]
Cheney has told us to look for ambiguities of exactly the sort found
in 'sommers pride' and for shifts of perspective such as occur in
the two following lines. But he cannot reveal the poem he knows is
there, because he assumes that moral awareness consists of judging characters in action. Thus he accuses Una and the knight of
'willfully [because of "fain" in 1.1.6?] shrouding themselves from
the light as well as the rain,' and later, turning allegorical description into narrative action that simply does not occur, says
'they have abandoned the sunlight as well as the storms of the
plain' (p. 24). But this stanza is an allegory, unfolding, under the
pastoral image of a 'shadie groue,' the attractions and dangers of
the sublunary world. We are to feel the weight of all the words,
not just the last, in the phrase, 'Faire harbour that them seemes.'
The stanza calls not for judgments, choices, or moral actions—
no one person could act coherently on the basis of the multifarious
feelings and awarenesses aroused—but contemplation of human
nature and the human condition. By the same token, the steady
listing of the tree catalogue makes us take in all aspects of man's
life—the noble ('The Laurell, meed of mightie Conquerours'), the
ordinary ('The Birch for shaftes, the Sallow for the mill'), the
frail or corrupt ('the Maple seeldom inward sound'). Moralistic
critics who try to size up the wood by noticing only the last category are telling us, in the first instance, to deny our actual reading experience and ultimately to deny that the human condition is
our own.

Cheney consistently reduces moral issues to judgments of
character—thus going, as Rosemond Tuve has brilliantly shown,
against the nature of allegory as Spenser inherited it and the nature of <u>The Faerie Queene</u> itself. Throughout his chapter on the
Garden of Adonis, he simply assumes that one of his main tasks
is to decide what is 'wrong' with Amoret and her upbringing that
she should be imprisoned and tortured by Busyrane, five cantos

later. But Amoret is an extreme instance of the way Spenser
handles his characters—not as coherent dramatic individuals,
about whom ethical judgments would be appropriate, but as con-
geries of characteristics which he can exploit to reveal fundamental realities of all human personality. Thus his interest in
the House of Busyrane is not the ethical question, 'Why is Amoret
tortured?' but the fact that human love is always painful; his whole
poetic endeavour centres not on Amoret as a personality, but on
the traditional emblem produced by her torture—the heart transfixed with a dart. Even in Book VI, where he is directly concerned
with the type-figures of the wild man and the shepherd, Cheney
cannot conceive that Spenser puts us in possession of truths about
courtesy by any means other than making us prefer one character
to another. The adventures of Calepine, who takes over from
Calidore as the hero of the middle cantos, show, he says, 'the difficulties and perils confronting man in his social role' (p. 202). A
very good way, one would think, of seeing Calepine's first adventure: forced to walk in his armour as he supports his beloved
Serena, who has been wounded by the Blatant Beast, he is cruelly
mocked by a strange knight (later identified as Sir Turpine), who
simply refuses to acknowledge chivalric obligations, either to help
Calepine or to accept his challenge to battle when help is refused
(6.3.27 ff.). All Cheney can do with this well-conceived and sometimes moving episode is to make it show Calepine's moral inferi-
ority to Calidore: 'his difficulties arise from his inability to elicit
courteous responses from others' (p. 204), and his 'inability to defend himself against Turpine demonstrates his failure to appreciate
the full responsibilities of the courtesy which he attempts to practice' (p. 205). (The real reason he cannot defend himself is that he
is on foot and Turpine is on horseback.) And lest we think Calepine's situation shows that 'All flesh is frayle, and full of fickle-
nesse, / Subiect to fortunes chance, still chaunging new' and draw
Calidore's moral, 'Who will not mercie vnto others shew, / How
can he mercy euer hope to haue?' (6.1.41–42), we are told that
'such a man [as Turpine] can menace only those who put their faith
in the appearances of rank' (p. 207).

One is struck not only by Cheney's insistence on moral judgments, but also by the terms in which these judgments are stated.
They are as unreal as they are untraditional, and they show why
Cheney's actual readings and interpretations are so disappointing:
he cannot take The Faerie Queene on its own terms. The catalogue of trees is said to be an image of this world and its limitations not because Spenser gives a full range of human use and

significance to the trees, but because it 'reflects man's confident moral dissection of his universe.' When the Red Cross Knight meets Duessa (Book I, canto 2), Cheney speaks not of lust and infidelity, but says the knight is 'ludicrously unprepared to read images' (p. 35). The Red Cross Knight's aims—'To winne him worship, and her [Gloriana's] grace to haue' and 'To proue his puissance in battell braue' (1.1.3)—are said to be stated in 'transcendent terms,' but 'such transcendence implies a consequent lack of concrete definition' (p. 41). In such formulations, Cheney no doubt seeks to avoid 'obvious' or 'reductive' readings. But in this he reveals an attitude towards moral discourse that is totally foreign to Spenser, who is genuinely interested in moral terms and the truths they contain and does not regard them as naive simplifications of experience. The famous descriptive passage—

> his glistring armor made
> A litle glooming light, much like a shade,
> By which he saw the vgly monster plaine   (1.1.14)

is not merely verbal painting, but a testing of the truth of the Red Cross Knight's confident aphorism, 'Vertue giues her selfe light, through darkenesse for to wade' (1.1.12). To juxtapose the dimming of this light in Error's murky den with its showing her plain both criticises and confirms the aphorism, and thus makes us aware that man's native spiritual strengths are genuine, yet are of the earth, involved in their element. It is 'an ironic comment,' as Cheney says, but it is the true Spenserian irony, that of a poised intelligence seeing all around a spiritual phenomenon, and not the presumed sophistication that presents 'a transition from complacent philosophizing to a frantic search for the appropriate tag-ends of philosophy' (p. 26).

How could a man like Cheney, to whom aphorisms are always 'naive' or 'easy,' even read the stanza in which Spenser renders Una's deception by Archimago disguised as the Red Cross Knight?

> His louely words her seemd due recompence
> Of all her passed paines: one louing howre
> For many yeares of sorrow can dispence:
> A dram of sweet is worth a pound of sowre:
> She has forgot, how many a wofull stowre
> For him she late endur'd; she speakes no more
> Of past: true is, that true loue hath no powre

> To looken backe; his eyes be fixt before.
> Before her stands her knight, for whom she toyld so sore.
>
> (1.3.30)

Where a poet like Ariosto would make Una's deception persuasive by a physical description of Archimago's disguise, Spenser produces 'Before her stands her knight' from the general truth of the preceding line. Aphorism, which at first serves for a knowing, though entirely generous, commentary on Una's willingness to believe, becomes at the end of the stanza the statement of a truth whose force we must acknowledge. As in any great poet, technical mastery manifests itself as moral intelligence: the interlacing of aphorism and narration and the turn on 'before' are the means by which Spenser makes us both see around and participate in Una's deception. It is so frank and lucid that one wonders how anyone could ever fail to admire and enjoy it and the hundreds and hundreds of stanzas like it in The Faerie Queene.

The answer, of course, is that The Faerie Queene is radically undramatic, and that it therefore defeats all the modern reader's expectations about the primacy of dramatic narration, about the relation of moral generalisation to the specific instances and 'evidence' offered, and about the nature of 'concrete' details in the verse: Cheney, for example, continually explains moral and psychological matters in terms of the ontological and epistemological status of physical images. Consider the first description of the Bower of Bliss:

> Thus being entred, they behold around
> A large and spacious plaine, on euery side
> Strowed with pleasauns, whose faire grassy ground
> Mantled with greene, and goodly beautifide
> With all the ornaments of Floraes pride,
> Wherewith her mother Art, as halfe in scorne
> Of niggard Nature, like a pompous bride
> Did decke her, and too lauishly adorne,
> When forth from virgin bowre she comes in th'early morne.
>
> (2.12.50)

The interest in this stanza is neither in concrete description nor in abstract moral judgment, but in unfolding—Cheney well remarks how literally explicable The Faerie Queene is (p. 15)—the conventional locution 'all the ornaments of Floraes pride.' As we come to it, this line expresses the natural attractiveness of a pastoral landscape. But the next line turns the apparently casual personification of Flora into a decisive one; at the same time, the conventional metaphor in 'ornaments' is taken seriously and is made to render a sense of artificial excess. We might argue that these lines make the true meaning of line 5 apparent, were it not for the alexandrine, which again represents 'Floraes pride' as natural and wholesome. All this is clear enough when pointed out, but it is still difficult to get used to the conditions of our perceiving, taking in, and mentally possessing the movement and point of the stanza. Just as the 'description' is incoherent as fictional narration (what is the relation between 'goodly beautifide' and 'too lauishly adorne' or of the last line to the previous description of Flora?), so the narrator of the poem and the reader attending to it do not have a dramatic relation to the verse. The subject and point of the stanza are similar to those of Marvell's 'The Mower against Gardens,' but whereas in Marvell's poem it is essential to catch the precise tone of scorn and wonder in which the mower speaks, here it is positively wrong to specify the tone in which one says, 'With all the ornaments of Floraes pride.' The line includes meanings that would dictate very different tones of voice in a speaker dramatically conceived. The verse obviously requires and rewards attention, yet at the same time we must be passive and selfless. We do not even maintain the control given by syntax. Despite the apparently strong enjambments in lines 6–8, we read them line by line, and it is clear—e.g. from the way line 8 rings so independently, and in the collocation of 'niggard' and 'pompous' to produce a sense of false bounty—that Spenser meant us to read that way.

There are essential difficulties in establishing a right relation to Spenser's verse, and they are best stated by Empson, in chapter 1 of Seven Types of Ambiguity:

> The size, the possible variety, and the fixity of this unit [the Spenserian stanza] give something of the blankness that comes from fixing your eyes on a bright spot; you have to yield yourself to it very completely to take in the variety of its movement, and, at the same time, there is no need to concentrate the elements of the situation into a judgment as if for action. As a result of this, when there are ambiguities of idea, it is whole civilisations rather than details of the moment which are their elements; he can pour into the even dreamwork of his fairyland Christian, classical, and chival-

342

rous materials with an air, not of ignoring their differences, but of holding all their systems of values floating as if at a distance, so as not to interfere with one another, in the prolonged and diffused energies of his mind.

(3rd edn., 1953, p. 34)

The importance of this aside (it was unfortunately no more than that) is that it treats Spenser's and the reader's passivity not as a specialised aesthetic sensuousness, but as the manifestation of a full, humane intelligence. The critic who should have revealed this intelligence to us was Lewis, but his hostility to modern aesthetics and modern morals turned his profound understanding of Spenser from disinterested criticism into proselytising. His celebrated discussion of the Bower of Bliss consists too much of attaching hostile labels, as when he vulgarly names the girls in the fountain (whom Spenser compares to Venus rising from the sea) Cissie and Flossie. He dismisses the following stanza with the remark (Allegory of Love, p. 325),* 'Whether those who think that Spenser is secretly on Acrasia's side, themselves approve of metal vegetation as a garden ornament, or whether they regard this passage as a proof of Spenser's abominable bad taste, I do not know; but this is how the poet describes it':

And ouer all, of purest gold was spred,
A trayle of yuie in his natiue hew:
For the rich mettall was so coloured,
That wight, who did not well auis'd it vew,
Would surely deeme it to be yuie trew:
Low his lasciuious armes adown did creepe,
That themselues dipping in the siluer dew,
Their fleecy flowres they tenderly did steepe,
Which drops of Christall seemd for wantones to weepe.

(2.12.61)

Lewis rightly said that Spenser's descriptions are not poetical gossamer but have a moral feel, but to make his case he had to pretend that the final lines here are simply repugnant. But we apprehend the moral clarity of those lines precisely when we respond to the richness and felicity of the verse, and by empathetic participation understand the self-indulgence and self-dissipation of 'wantones.' However, the really difficult aspect of this stanza lies in lines 4 and 5. The modern reader would treat them as an unsuccessful attempt to ward off, with moralistic terms, the pow-

*Reprinted p. 6.

ALPERS

erful sensuousness of the final lines. But to attribute this kind of
motive, and the resultant confusion, to Spenser is to assume that
his verse should—and would if it could—express a mind that is
concentrated into a judgment as if for action. On the contrary, the
stanza is an exceptionally clear example of the habit of mind Empson describes. What is so hard to grasp and trust is that Spenser
could state these lines so flatly, almost as a warning, and then
confirm the persuasiveness of the 'yuie trew' by the sudden sensuousness of the next line. By the same token, the first three
lines do not make us 'well auis'd' in the sense Lewis wants them
to. They indeed tell us the facts of the case, but they create a
vague assent to the deception simply by the kinds of assent involved in the act of reading. The sensuous appeal of 'purest gold'
and 'rich mettall' gets what we may call moral support from the
plain and strong meaning of 'natiue hew,' and 'trayle' (which is an
architectural term for a metal ornament) acquires its usual meaning from the line in which it appears. These effects keep 'wight' a
truly open term, as it should be in allegory.

Trust the verse—that is what the reader of The Faerie Queene
must learn to do. The last stanza suggests how hard this is for
the modern reader, even though it shows how frankly and gener-
ously Spenser's verse offers itself. One can readily imagine that
Cheney, seeing what was involved in single stanzas, did not trust
the verse, or perhaps did not trust himself, enough to see the
poem through to the end on its own terms. The deepest fault of
his book is that he seeks to interpret and organise what he perceives in the terms that are familiar to him—terms that are
damagingly provincial in time, and perhaps too in place. With a
book so elliptically written that the wild man and the shepherd of
the subtitle are not mentioned until p. 174, one may be excused for
quoting the dust-jacket: '[Mr. Cheney] views allegory as a means
by which the poet embraces a vast array of expanding knowledge
and gives it unity based not upon objective categories but upon a
common involvement in the dialectical processes of the reader.
The result, Mr. Cheney suggests, is a poem of infinite complexity,
offering endless opportunity for explication, a poem which derives
unity and intelligibility from the figure of the poet who strives
through his art to create meaning, an epic of imagination.' This
summarises an aspect of Cheney's thought more clearly than anything in the book. It puts together a number of things one notices
about the book: the lack of substantive content in moral analysis,
the consistent speaking of Spenser's multifariousness in terms of
paired opposites and dialectic, the dwelling on Spenser's 'personal'

344

appearances in the poem. Most important, it explains why this book about an open-ended poem is itself so rigid—in its moral interpretations, in its account of the continuities that exist in the poem, in its notion that Spenser's allusions entitle one to transfer directly the The Faerie Queene points made about Elizabethan history or other poems (e.g. pp. 45, 143–44, 173–74, 225). All this comes from thinking that a poem creates its own meanings—not simply in the broad and truistic sense, but in the sense that poetic usages and processes are uniquely meaningful in a meaningless world. Very similar notions underly the search for structural, ideological, and iconographic keys to The Faerie Queene, even when their proponents rightly insist that Spenser's idea of his poem was totally different from one like Cheney's. For the insistence on Spenser's absolute beliefs bears witness to our own lack of them, and we simply assume that a poet who views the universe as ordered from top to bottom will embody that order in a poem. But this is not necessarily so. It is precisely when a poet trusts that the universe really is ordered and assumes that the source of order is God, not the individual poet, that he can allow his poem to expatiate freely. It is no accident that Lewis, the critic who most deeply understood Spenser's trusting habit of mind, has also most encouraged us to take The Faerie Queene as it comes.

When we do, when we accept the offer of the verse, we unquestionably become different from what we are when we read almost everything else that gives us pleasure and illumination. But to do this is not to learn to 'think like an Elizabethan' in the narrow sense too often urged on us by scholars. Quite the contrary, it is liberating and restorative to enter the mind of a man who could so trust man's traditional wisdom about himself and the ultimate goodness of his world. Consider the following stanza:

> The third [almoner] had of their wardrobe custodie,
> In which were not rich tyres, nor garments gay,
> The plumes of pride, and wings of vanitie,
> But clothes meet to keepe keene could away,
> And naked nature seemely to aray;
> With which bare wretched wights he dayly clad,
> The images of God in earthly clay;
> And if that no spare cloths to giue he had,
> His owne coate he would cut, and it distribute glad.
>
> (1.10.39)

This is really ordinary Spenserian verse, from a canto usually dismissed as the most tediously traditional sort of allegory. But when we consider what happens to these formulas in King Lear, where agony and destruction come from insisting that they be mutually consistent and answerable to experience, we can understand the value of a poet for whom taking them seriously simply meant registering their human point and value in line after line, stanza after stanza. We are all children of Shakespeare, and no one today could write a poem like The Faerie Queene. But in an age so bewilderingly compounded of pleasures, opportunities, and achievements, and at the same time of brutality, tedium, moral horror, and spiritual disaster, it would be tragic to lose so luminous an exemplar of clear-sightedness and acceptance.

THE GOODLY FRAME OF TEMPERANCE: THE METAPHOR
OF COSMOS IN <u>THE FAERIE QUEENE</u>, BOOK II

James Carscallen

For Spenser temperance has various images: it is a golden
rule or square, it is a bridle, it is water tempering wine.[1] It is
also a structure or frame—the frame at once of the individual
man, the commonwealth, and the universe itself; and this is as
we should expect from an age in which La Primaudaye can introduce temperance by praising God's cosmic workmanship:

> The divine excellencie of the order, of the equall and won-
> derfull constancy of the parts of the world, as well in the
> goodly and temperate moderation of the seasons of the
> yeare, as in the mutuall coniunction of the elements, obey-
> ing altogether with a perfect harmony the gracious and
> soueraigne government of their Creator, was the cause that
> <u>Pythagoras</u> first called all the compasse of this universall
> frame by this name of <u>World</u>, which without such an excel-
> lent disposition would bee but disorder and a world of con-
> fusion. For this word World signifieth as much as Orna-
> ment, or a well disposed order of things. Now as a constant
> and temperate order is the foundation thereof, so the ground-
> worke and preservation of mans happy life, for whom all
> things were made, is the vertue of Temperance . . .[2]

The universe, as Elizabethan poets often remember,[3] was made
when a divine authority ended the jarring of the elements, bringing
them into obedience and measure; and these attributes enable us
to say that the universe has temperance, although we can equally
say that it has holiness, chastity, concord, justice, and courtesy.
In man temperance comes about in a similar way, as reason's government is brought to the passions; and in ruling these reason also
rules their objects, the prosperity and adversity brought by an ex-

Reprinted from <u>University of Toronto Quarterly</u>, Vol. 37 (1968), pp. 136–
155, by permission of the author and the publisher, University of Toronto
Press.

ternal world that was itself made for man. Standing firm against any disorder from within or from without, man is tempered as steel is tempered by fire and water, and is thus fitted to make the whole world the castle of his soul. There is nothing unfamiliar in this notion of temperance—or of virtue in general—as a well-governed structure of universal proportions;[4] but I believe it can help us better than any other metaphor to see the order of Spenser's second book—to discover in it a nobility of "structure," in a different sense, for which it has not always received the praise it deserves.

In speaking of temperance as a goodly frame, I shall be adding still another scheme—one based on the four elements—to the schemes that have already been used by scholars to help interpret this book, such as that of the virtues and vices "as Aristotle hath devised" and that of the Seven Deadly Sins.[5] All these schemes are by themselves purely classificatory or expository, in the sense that their order is unrelated to processes in time. If they are to turn into the shape of a story, they must be somehow transformed, for the hero of a story is a being in time who makes choices and is made by them, and if he encounters a series of evils, he will face each new one with a new and more complex constitution of his experience. To serve as a trial for him, these evils will at least have to get harder to deal with as they go on, and they may grow in complexity as well, just as his experience does. If so, they will be like the increasingly subtle guises of a single shape-changing magician, who again and again can say, with Eliot's Tempter, "I am an unexpected visitor."

When we discuss Spenser's use of any expository scheme, then, we may well ask whether he is using the parts only or the whole— the scheme as a scheme, in other words—and, if he is doing the latter, how he has assimilated the scheme to the temporal nature of a story. In The Faerie Queene schemes that have not been assimilated in this way seem to occur mainly on the largest scale, that of the poem as a whole, and on the smallest, that of pageants and other displays shown at some one point in the story when its own development is suspended. Even here, as we can observe in sequences like the Pageant of the Seven Deadly Sins and the Masque of Cupid, the parts tend to appear in an order that suggests psychological development in time; and on the scale of a hero's quest— the scale, normally, of a book—an expository scheme that remained wholly alien to the story as such could only be imposed by something like martial law. Fortunately, schemes can often suit their ways to stories easily enough, and the scheme I am going to consider seems to do this very naturally. In it the elements make a series of structures, and successive structures, like the heroes who encounter them, can take on higher and higher organizations, ranging from La Primaudaye's "world of confusion" toward a perfect cosmos. This, I think, is what happens in the story of Sir Guyon: the demon of chaos puts on more and more subtle forms in an attempt to bring Guyon's temperance to ruin, until conclusively overcome by a virtue whose structure is more whole than any that chaos can assume.

When Guyon sets out on his quest from the House of Medina, his way is blocked by Furor and Occasion, two grotesque emblems of the dangers he must now begin to meet. Furor, although in his present form more dangerous to himself than to Guyon, suggests not only the pitiable distemper of another human being but the raging of the universal elements themselves, with which the words "furor" and "fury" had associations in Spenser's day as in ours.[6] The most plainly furious and destructive of all the elements appears in Furor's "burning eyen," which throw forth "sparkes of fyre" (iv, 15); and his successor Pyrochles, as his name and behaviour show, is altogether a man of fire. He is succeeded in turn by Cymochles, a watery individual whose name seems to come from the Greek kuma or wave. Like Furor, these two brothers cast their shadows on the entire universe, for they are descended from the primordial figures of Phlegeton, Jarre, Herebus, Night, and ultimately Aeternitie (iv. 41).[7] Behind them loom universal catastrophes of fire and flood, well known to the Renaissance from both classical and Biblical traditions,[8] and beyond even these there looms a dark eternity of nothingness—the nothingness that for Spenser always waits to reclaim whatever fabric has succeeded in rising out of it. The remaining elements appear in Phaedria and Mammon, the latter unmistakeably an earth-figure and the former as unmistakeably one of air if we remember how everything about Phaedria is haunted by rustling leaves, birds, flowers, odours, laughter, music—by everything that is delicate or elusive or volatile or invisible. Phaedria's bark skims the water "More swift, then swallow sheres the liquid skie" (vi, 5); her island is "a litle nest" (vi, 12), and she herself sings "as loud as larke in aire" (vi, 3). Earthly paradises in literature, being elusive places haunted by elusive presences, usually have special associations with the element of air; and Phaedria is very much a bird of paradise.

We should also think of these four elemental characters in terms of the other sets of four traditionally linked with the elements, and especially the complexions and the perturbations. This is not to say that we can expect consistent correspondences. The elements in themselves take on different meanings in different contexts throughout the book: water in the Well of the Nymph, for instance, does not play at all the same role as water in the Idle Lake. The relation of the elements to other things, then, cannot be a simple one, and we must also remember that Spenser, in spite of his great reverence for authors and traditions, can be very independent in his quiet way when it comes to picking and choosing among these for his own design. Cymochles' watery nature, to the extent that it means being sensual and capricious, is less like the nature of a phlegmatic man than like that of a slothful man;[9] and Pyrochles and Mammon have obvious links with the sins of wrath and avarice. On the other hand, Cymochles' laziness is phlegmatic enough, and there can be no question of Pyrochles' fiery choler. Phaedria's "immodest Merth" is a typical distemper of the airy sanguine complexion,[10] and Mammon, the dweller in the earth, is like all melancholy men, "crafty, avaricious, despondent, misanthropic, and timid."[11] We must handle the perturbations with the same wariness as the complexions, for they vary widely in literary catalogues, and even the cardinal four of joy, sorrow, hope, and fear will not simply coalesce with the scheme of the four elements.[12] But like the elements they are all aspects of a world in furor, swirling about the hero as he moves; and while Spenser's comments on "stubborne perturbation" (v, 1) seem to refer especially to Atin's incitements to strife, a less obvious form of perturbation is equally at work in the efforts of Phaedria and Mammon to arouse Guyon's desires. If he allows himself to be moved by any of these assailants, he will be as much Furor's victim as Phaedon, and in the Palmer's gnomic warning to Phaedon we find that the perturbations which destroy a lover make an ominous figure of four, linked with at least three of the elements.

> Wrath, gealosie, griefe, love do thus expell:
> Wrath is a fire, and gealosie a weede,
> Griefe is a flood, and love a monster fell;
> The fire of sparkes, the weede of little seede,
> The flood of drops, the Monster filth did breede. [iv, 35][13]

As Guyon's quest continues, we are brought increasingly to see that a fundamental opposition generates all the shifting configurations of furor; and perhaps we can best learn what the elements ultimately mean to Spenser by exploring this opposition. It will fully disclose itself only with the gradual appearance of all Guyon's

enemies, but its presence can be sensed from the beginning, both
in the horrifying story of Mordant and Amavia and in the not very
horrifying story of Medina, where Spenser shows us something
closer to the everyday surface of intemperance. It is with the
latter of these episodes that intemperance begins the growth in
subtlety and power which is to lead to the Bower of Acrasia, and
we will do well to make it our starting-place as it is Spenser's.
We must begin, then, with a castle set on a rock above the furious
sea, and a virtuous lady who tries to bring "governance" to her
two sisters—rightful heirs of their father both, but highly un-
seemly in their behaviour. These images do not point us very
firmly toward Aristotle, or at least not toward the <u>Nicomachean
Ethics</u>: for although Medina's castle is the home of the mean and
the extremes, Aristotle never thinks of the latter as opposite constituents that remain as the very "ingredients of virtue," in Milton's phrase, if they can be governed and reconciled to one another.
Aristotelian or not, Spenser's images are always a good place to
begin, and we may proceed by trying to put some flesh on this relatively abstract notion of the mean and the extremes, which must
somehow fit with the imagery of the three daughters in the castle.
Mean and extremes in what? Is there some more concrete way in
which these sisters show themselves virtuous or unruly? One answer readily suggests itself: in their courtesy.

However else they may fail, Medina's sisters certainly do so in
their "cheare" and "entertainment," for Elissa thinks it base to
show her lover any "solace" or "court" or "dalliance" (ii, 35),
while Perissa is "full of disport" (36) and is matched by the bold
Sansloy, than whom one could not find a "franker franion" (37).
We can feel here all the mediaeval concern with <u>danger</u> and <u>bel
accueil</u>, and if the two extreme sisters could fittingly combine
these they would achieve the courtesy that graces Medina, a courtesy in which due regard for her own dignity unites with regard
for the dignity of others. All three sisters would then make a
gracious order in which each part would at the same time be its
own order, having its own integrity and independence. If Spenser
were Plato, he might have spoken of human beings as something
like raw material for a craftsman's working; but Spenser is a son
of the Middle Ages. For him all order is a matter of due regard,
looking outward and looking inward, on the part of personal beings;
and temperance, as we shall see, is perfected in a gracious relationship between two persons.

If courtesy can act as a metaphor for temperance, we can go on
to ask what metaphors Spenser uses for courtesy; and we may re-

member that Perissa and Elissa are respectively very "forward" and very "froward," as William Nelson has pointed out.[14] This metaphor can be carried to similar pairs of characters throughout The Faerie Queene, and suggests not only the "cheer" that persons show one another but the larger rhythm of ebb and flow that for Spenser pervades the whole temporal world. In Book II "forward" and "froward" seem to be happier terms for all pairs of characters than "concupiscible" and "irascible." These latter may have some relevance to Cymochles and Pyrochles, but they cannot adequately explain, in any of their Renaissance senses, why the two brothers should feel the variety of emotions that we find in them: why Pyrochles has to be warned against love (v, 16), and why Cymochles is in one mood a violent fighter. The terms "forward" and "froward" must themselves be used with care. They must, for instance, be understood in something more than a literal way, as Professor Nelson would no doubt agree, since the froward Pyrochles is not very obviously retreating when he smokes across the plain toward Guyon, and Cymochles is not very obviously advancing when he lies "in secret shadow" (v, 32), peeping at Acrasia's damsels "like an Adder, lurking in the weeds" (34). The two brothers seem to be utterly different in personality both when they advance and when they retire, just as they are utterly different in their ways of feeling both concupiscible and irascible emotions. Roused by Atin, Cymochles is all rage in a moment; Phaedria can appease him "With one sweet drop of sensuall delight" (vi, 8) and then he flies into rage once more when he sees Guyon in her company. But Pyrochles, who burns even in the Idle Lake, would not have changed so easily.

Cymochles, to return to the imagery of the elements and their frame, is one of the many characters in Spenser and other Elizabethan writers who share the looseness and lightness of all easily fluid things. Perissa, "poured out in pleasure and delight" (ii, 36), is another:

> In wine and meats she flowd above the bancke,
> And in excesse exceeded her owne might. [ii, 36]

Her looseness represents one of the two aspects of discourtesy: it bespeaks a character that has no firmness, no frame; one that will not husband its strength or dignity, but squanders itself recklessly in pleasures and favours. The commonest habitat of Spenser's Perissa is near flowing streams or cups, and they should also be looked for on the Rock of Vile Reproach and the Quicksand of Un-

thriftyhed. The economic aspect of lightness occurs unforgettably
in the fabliau of Malbecco, whose wife Hellenore not only tends to
have the wine spilt in her neighbourhood, but in her later entertainment of Paridell shows herself very eager indeed for a quick
sale:

> she her love and hart hath wholy sold
> To him, without regard of gaine or scath,
> Or care of credite.   [III, x, 11]

Paridell himself, whose pain is no pain at all (ix, 30), is a worthy
counterpart of Sansloy; but the miser Malbecco is more like the
froward Sir Huddibras, who watching Sansloy's dalliance

> Did see and grieve at his bold fashion;
> Hardly could he endure his hardiment,
> Yett still he sat, and inly did him selfe torment.   [II, ii, 37]

Huddibras is one of Spenser's morbidly grave characters. He is
always at war, but even if he were to attack as unremittingly and
violently as Pyrochles, it would be as true of him as Guyon knows
it to be of Pyrochles (v, 16) that outer war is only a shadow of
inner war. The froward man is really a figure of weakness, devoured by a resentment and suspicion that explode outward because
they have first drawn defensively inward: for like Malbecco, the
froward man always locks his doors. Such characters in Spenser
have a high suicide rate, and those who remain alive do so by feeding on their own vitals, like Envy in Book V.
     These two types of people have a confusing way of putting on
each other's attributes: characters like Perissa are quite capable
of sulking, while more froward characters may affect a forwardness that is really alien to them. We have the latter of these possibilities when Philotime, deep in the Cave of Mammon, puts on a
"gorgeous gay" appearance (vii, 44), although her court is anything
but a place of lightness or ease, and when Redcrosse seeks solace
in lightness for wounds to his pride that his "solemne sad" nature
(I, i, 2) cannot lightly forget. But what a grave character can never
do is to flit between anger and pleasure at whim, and this is because
he is a slave to everything the Elizabethans meant by "care." The
light man is as he is because he does not know care: he shares the
unconcern of all the "loose livers" in Tudor literature, all the people like Skelton's Fancy:

That was before, I set behind:
Now too courteous, forthwith unkind,
Sometime too sober, sometime too sad,
Sometime too merry, sometime too mad;
Sometime I sit as I were solemn proud,
Sometime I laugh over-loud,
Sometime I weep for a gee gaw,
Sometime I laugh at wagging of a straw;
With a pear my love you may win,
And ye may lose it for a pin.[15]

To fail in courtesy or in thrift or in frame is always to fail in caring, to be in the wrong way either a careless or "careful" man.

Care can be a petty response to petty things, but in its largest implication it is a world-view: the concern of a man facing the whole fallen or temporally divided state of things that he finds within him and without. There is something like an unfallen care too, of which the fallen is a shadow. If we think of Spenser's great places of peace, we find that in them the most "forward" bounty and ease is one with the greatest observance of order and degree. Such is Mount Acidale, which unites the freest pleasure with the "order excellent" (VI, x, 13) of the stars in their courses; and the grace and courtesy of Mount Acidale recall an even higher vision. The very angels of New Jerusalem, who like the graces move to and fro as they link Heaven and Earth, walk "as commonly as frend does with his frend" (I, x, 56) and yet in perfect measure. Poets like Crashaw or Shelley may imagine the beatific state as one of almost pure fluidity, but in Spenser even the "Sabaoths sight" is of a grace that is also a mighty frame,

firmely stayd
Upon the pillours of eternity.   [Mutabilitie, viii, 2]

Here we see the unfallen counterparts of both forwardness and frowardness, of carelessness and care—or we could say of friendship and chastity, courtesy and justice. What marks a fallen world is that these have split apart, and can only be brought together by an unceasing effort "to care and not to care."

Since this is an effort, we must think of man's right state in a fallen world as primarily a careful one—unlike that of Acrasia's rose, who is most carelessly displayed in the middle of her progress. If man neglects his due care, he will fall into the sloth or ease that for Spenser initiates the Pageant of the Deadly Sins and the Masque of Cupid. But he needs a kind of carelessness too, and never more so than when he is deepest in care. The Christian knight must add faith to his force, and faith is not only a weapon for combatting dragons but a careless assurance that the visible world is not the final reality. Acrasia would like us to suppose just the contrary about the visible world, but if we did so any carelessness we might feel would only be a mask for hopelessness, and any combining of carelessness and care we might achieve would be a mere mockery of their true combination. Perhaps Guyon's most desolate moment comes when he first gazes at Acrasia's handiwork: the bodies of Mordant—"him that death does give"—and Amavia—"her that loves to live" (i, 55). Before his encounter with the enchantress, Mordant had been froward in the right way—a true figure of masculine "high courage" (50)— and Amavia had been his true feminine complement. After their separation Acrasia's poison undid the stronger by "infirmitie" and the weaker by "bold furie" (57) leading to self-violence: the forward and froward characters in their fallen sense were born, and could unite only in death.

Acrasia's world begins to come upon Guyon himself when he first sees Furor as a distinct figure, although it is hard to say "world" even metaphorically in relation to this demented and helpless being. Pyrochles is hardly less helpless, but as Guyon moves on, the elemental characters begin to show disturbing signs of awareness and order. True, Cymochles has to be told by Phaedria that they are fellow-servants of Acrasia (vi, 9); and even Phaedria and Mammon, while much more knowing and controlled than their precursors, are themselves victims of their humours, puzzled and offended when Guyon refuses what they consider real goods. But whereas in the House of Medina sister fights sister, and prospective brother-in-law prospective brother-in-law, the Sons of Acrates help one another to the extent that they can organize their forces at all, and are eventually able to attack Guyon in concert. Furor is beginning to take on its own kind of order.

In introducing the elements, Spenser begins with the two that can be most plainly opposite to each other and most plainly fatal to man: Pyrochles rages with fire, and Cymochles can rage like the ocean in storm. In a more unruffled mood Cymochles matches Phaedria in idleness; but when Phaedria rushes between him and Guyon, like Medina on a similar occasion, we see that she is a considerably different being from either of the Sons of Acrates: for Phaedria is less like a raw force. She may be as capricious as Cymochles, but in her inland sea she has a kind of constancy in whim that he does not have:

> Ne swelling <u>Neptune</u>, ne loud thundring <u>Jove</u>
> Can chaunge my cheare, or make me ever mourne. [vi, 10]

When she appeals for an end to all strife except love's wars (34–5), she is trying to create a little cosmos, and her words echo traditions not only of love-making but of cosmogony.[16] Her island, for which Pyrochles and Cymochles have no equivalents, is itself a little world with its own sort of completeness, like the world of Mammon; and like Mammon Phaedria is a kind of <u>genius loci</u>, related to Elizabethan notions about such sprites as the Sons of Acrates are not.[17] Like Mammon again, Phaedria has an intellectual order to match her physical order: for she has a philosophy of her own, and refuses to allow on her island either Guyon's Palmer or Cymochles' Atin, who would certainly speak against it.

Although Spenser never suggests the Platonic tradition of a vertical chain linking the four elements through common qualities, his island of air and cave of earth are more vertically related to one another than his figures of fire and water; and with Phaedria and Mammon lightness and gravity come to imply something like spirit and matter, the upper and the lower, as parts of the natural state. In Phaedria's world the flowers and fields leave all care to the Earth beneath them, which allows them to flourish without any need for labour or inquiry. Phaedria's moral is that we should take no thought, since we can have as much of a good time without it; and while this is not quite the point that the Sermon on the Mount is trying to make, it can lead to a careless contentment like that of faith itself. Mammon is of earthier stuff: he speaks for material being and its need for material sustenance.

Both these characters live from their own to themselves, making whole worlds out of their carelessness and care respectively. But unless spirit and matter can unite, neither can have any real bounty, for it is only as Nature unites her elements that she remains a fruitful mother. Guyon, too, must keep his wholeness if he is to find any strength in himself—and when he is confronted by Phaedria and Mammon he has no other source of strength to draw on. Having seen Mordant and Amavia, he can no longer assume a dependable base of strength underlying human nature. When he came away from that encounter his horse had disappeared, and he will not recover anything like it to bear him until Alma provides him with her boatman. Now he is also without the Palmer's counsel from above. In the strength that is peculiarly his own he must find the counterparts of both his horse and his counsellor, with their qualities of matter and spirit, since no other sustenance is apparent except

what can be had from Mammon and Phaedria. Against Phaedria's
invitation to carelessness he must affirm true care, the self-concern that human dignity cannot live without; and he must then resist Mammon's argument that care itself, if accepted as the whole
of one's world, can finally offer man something like the innocent
bounty he hungers for. This is the temptation of earth, and although,
as Mutabilitie remarks, earth would seem to be the least mutable
(and hence the least furious) of the elements (Mutabilitie, vii, 17),
Mammon's temptation is the most formidable that Guyon has yet
come against.

Mammon is one of Spenser's most vivid pictures of the froward
character: a brooding, uncivil, timorous being who lives deep in
a shady wilderness, and on being disturbed tries to hide his gold—
already obscured with rust and dirt and bearing the marks of obscure and ancient rulers—by pouring it into the Earth. Phaedria
had asked Guyon, "What bootes it all to have, and nothing use?"
(vi, 17) and it is with the same question that he himself confronts
Mammon:

> What art thou man, (if man at all thou art)
> That here in desert hast thine habitaunce,
> And these rich heapes of wealth doest hide apart
> From the worldes eye, and from her right usaunce? [vii, 7]

To be froward is to neglect use, but the Elizabethans were deeply
convinced that the good must come forth, be manifested, act out
its function. Man, into whose hands the good of Nature has come,
must give as freely as Nature herself or Nature's Creator; and at
the same time he must practise the husbandry that keeps Nature
to her real use as "a spouse, for generation, fruit, and comfort."
In the latter of these two obligations Phaedria comes short: her
"use" is no true use at all, since she urges Guyon merely to take
his pleasure with Nature. But Mammon fails in the opposite way,
for he is the very emblem of a fallen world without liberality or
frankness, hiding from the air and the light, and compulsively hug-
ging its own.

When Guyon charges Mammon with his miserliness, Mammon's
reply has a touch of injured pride: he protests that he is a god

> That of my plenty poure out unto all,
> And unto none my graces do envye.   [vii, 8]

If Guyon will serve him, Mammon will offer him ten times what

he now sees, "francke and free" (9). But in its fallen state care
can only seem to give: all we can ultimately receive from it is
the barren gift of care itself. Thus Mammon cannot make kingdoms as he claims. He can only bring "great citties" low and
set up "wrongfull government" (13)—the work not of true law but
of false "policie" (I, iv, 12), as Spenser observes of Lucifera.
Policy, usury, and harlotry all put a price on their gifts, and thus
really reserve them. They can never know the blessedness of
"spiritual usury," the free giving by which alone man can husband
Nature's riches from expense. There were different ways of understanding the nature of usury in Spenser's day, but this was one
that his contemporaries spoke about with special forcefulness.

> Nowe lord god, what a straunge thinge is this, that god suf-
> fering the sunne to shyne upon us freely and the ayre to be
> comon to all, aswell poore as rych, wythout anye gayne
> taking, that we not considering so liberal a goodnes of god,
> should so farre be from charitie that we will sell tyme and
> ayre so deerely, having it of god so freely! Assuredly such
> caterpillers upon earth are accursed of god above, because
> thei have no property of god in them belowe. For god geveth
> power for the sunne to shyne, sendeth rayne in due season,
> appointeth the starres to keep their courses, and al for the
> behoofe and benefit of man; and man onely, I meane the
> usurer, is enemie both to god and man.[18]

Mammon's gold, then, is tainted by the care that puts conditions
on it; and when he objects that, after all, other men than Guyon have
been willing enough to take and keep what he offers, Guyon points
beyond the care of avarice to an untainted world, at once Biblical
and Ovidian, in which men were thankful for sufficiency alone. They
accepted the Earth's gifts without incestuously rifling the womb of
their common mother: for to Spenser and his tradition that is what
men are doing whenever they become greedy and possessive in
taking pleasure, wealth, power, or learning.[19] Man's fall was, as
we have already seen, a split, and in terms appropriate to Mammon, it was the beginning both of a forward luxuriousness and a
froward avarice. It is both of these in the context of the latter—
both as expressions of grasping and hoarding—that Mammon speaks
for. His answer to Guyon's charge is hence a double one: Guyon
would surely not accept "the rudenesse of that antique age"; and if
he would not, then he has no choice but to

wage
Thy workes for wealth, and life for gold engage.   [vii, 18]

But Mammon's most seductive bait is his claim that all this need
not mean tainted gold at all. Phaedria may find a sort of innocence by flitting in the air above a polluted earth; Mammon would
rather accept the earth fully, descend to its depths: for eye hath
not seen the treasure that grows there abundant and unpolluted
precisely because the light and the air have never reached it. And
if what Mammon offers were innocent, Guyon might legitimately
accept it and bring it into good use—this, I feel, is why he is not
doing wrong in going to inspect Mammon's treasury.[20] And so
Guyon passes toward his second false paradise. As he nears the
heart of the Cave, the brooding silence of the storeroom and the
compulsive labour of the furnace-room give way to the splendid,
if feverish, court of Philotime; and this in turn gives way to a
peaceful garden with its own tree of life at the centre, "loaden all
with fruit as thicke as it might bee" (53). Here indeed is the careless bounty that care can provide.

When Guyon looks down into Mammon's counterpart of the river
of life, he sees that its water will not wash Pilate's hands nor allow
Tantalus to drink; and when he returns from the world of earth to
the air he collapses, for he has come among elements which, being
estranged from their common lord, are estranged from one another
as well. Mixture, krasis, is what makes a cosmos, but we have
already seen in the stories of Mordant and Ruddymane that under
the spell of Acrasia even the water of virginal purity cannot temper the wine of licentious pleasure or the blood of suicide, and in
fact is deadly when it meets them. In a less "vertical" context,
Pyrochles' anger cannot be tempered with the water of idleness,
and Cymochles can only veer between untempered sloth and untempered wrath. Now we have found that Phaedria and Mammon
bring man to a similar plight. Although both claim to have their
own worlds, the spirit and body of Phaedria's world are nothing
but air, and those of Mammon's world nothing but earth. Neither
by itself has any nourishment or cleansing, and neither can
survive the touch of its opposite. Exhausted by their incompatibility, man is given over to the simpler destructive forces of fire and
water, which now re-appear to attack him. Through their very
inability to combine, the four elements have in effect combined for
his destruction.

When this great antimasque is dispelled by the manifestation of

359

Arthur and of the House of Alma, Guyon moves beyond the assaults
of the separate elements: such assaults are now to be gathered
within a larger final ordeal, which has been foreshadowed in the
combination of the uncombinable that we have just seen. The earlier kind of ordeal is recapitulated in Guyon's sea-voyage, though
with more rapid and bewildering alternations than ever before;[21]
but his most serious danger is no longer from the successive
threats of the voyage itself. He has survived the tests of Phaedria
and Mammon unaided, and he can now draw on the strength of the
Palmer and the Boatman as well as his own. Phaedria, who reappears briefly like a wraith out of the past, has clearly lost whatever chance she once had to win him. He is moving toward a
deadlier peril when he finds the mermaids and their surroundings
making "a straunge kinde of harmony" (xii, 33), and when, immediately after this, he sees the face of Heaven suddenly covered
with a thick fog, so that

> all things one, and one as nothing was,
> And this great Universe seemd one confused mas.   [34]

Instead of the dove of Creation, birds of ill omen flutter about
the travellers, prophesying their ruin. Then, beyond both the
mermaids' harmony and the confusion of the fog, Guyon arrives
at the lovely island of Acrasia, seemingly a perfect cosmos in the
midst of chaos.

To understand Acrasia in the terms of the present discussion,
we should first turn back to Arthur's antagonist Maleger, who is
more closely related to Acrasia than he seems. Maleger's workings are as chaotic as we finally see the ocean about Acrasia's
island to be: for his followers scatter before Arthur like withered
leaves before the wind, and are themselves like the destructiveness
of wind and hail and snow and flood (xi, 18–19). Nowhere before
in the book have heterogeneous forces mingled as they do in this
wild rout of all the forward and froward things by which the body
can harm and be harmed. But if these somehow combine into an
army, we must be witnessing the very order of disorder, just as
we are witnessing the very power of impotence. Maleger himself
is as uncanny a oneness of contraries as his army: he retreats
and attacks at once; he is both a mighty warrior springing from
the earth and a thing completely loosened and discomposed, riding
the wind like a ghost with unbound grave-clothes. He has nothing
like Mammon's wily arguments to use as a weapon, but there is
something more deeply baffling in his simple malevolence: for in

this adversary Arthur has met the body of death itself, man's own
substance as man's enemy. And while the body of death must continually die, it is also in a spectral way as powerfully tempered
and as enduring as the House of Alma, so that in order to destroy
it Arthur must cast it into something even more alien to man than
the dark earth that is Maleger's mother as well as ours. The
standing lake in which Maleger finally perishes is like the negative
eternity from which the Sons of Acrates take their descent. We
might call it "non-being," the final opposite of any goodly frame
to which even chaos must come in the end.22

As finally as is possible within time, Arthur overcomes the
natural man's sickness unto death; and while he does so Guyon
co-operates with the Palmer to overcome the illusion that this
sickness can be health—that there can be a paradisal island where
there is only chaotic ocean. Maleger presides over an "anti-
world," Acrasia over a counterfeit world, and thus the two complement one another, for each suggests one aspect of a false whole,
whereas Phaedria and Mammon are more suggestive of mere
parts. Hence Maleger and Acrasia must be completely rejected,
whereas Guyon was ready to accept Phaedria's pleasures and
Mammon's commodities within the limit of virtue. It is true that
the two pairs of characters are also significantly similar, in that
each has a froward and a forward member; but just as Maleger's
frowardness is more deeply baffling than Mammon's, so Acrasia's
forwardness is far subtler and more inclusive than Phaedria's.
We may primarily remember only the simplest kind of forwardness in a place where all the pleasures of sense and fancy are

> poured forth with plentifull dispence,
> And made there to abound with lavish affluence;   [42]

but even as its delights grow headier and headier, the Bower of
Bliss is more than uncontained affluence: it apes the perfect
temper which preserves and generates all true affluence and all
true constancy.

> Thereto the heavens always Joviall,
>   Lookt on them lovely, still in stedfast state,
>   Ne suffred storme nor frost on them to fall,
>   Their tender buds or leaves to violate,
>   Nor scorching heat, nor cold intemperate
>   T'afflict the creatures, which therein did dwell,
>   But the mild aire with season moderate

> Gently attempred, and disposed so well,
> That still it breathed forth sweet spirit and holesome smell.
> [51]

This same apparent perfection of temper can be seen in the way the Bower brings art and nature together. It is primarily a place of nature, just as it is primarily a place of forwardness, but the state of nature which is imitated here by false art and debauch is itself one in which art and nature are in perfect concord.[23] On Phaedria's island we find no art: there are no bowers or banquet houses, and lilies neither toil nor spin. In Mammon's cave, on the contrary, everything is art, in the sense that everything springs from the care that can produce only inedible fruit,

> Not such, as earth out of her fruitfull woomb
> Throwes forth to men, sweet and well savoured. [vii, 51]

In the Bower of Bliss nature and art seem to wed, and with the most exquisite results; but while it is usual enough for earthly paradises to make us feel that art has mysteriously become nature, and nature art, the sweet diversity of the Bower of Bliss represents the effort of nature and art to undermine each other, a most unharmonious kind of "concert."[24] The Bower is in reality only a place of equal crime.

The persuasions that the inhabitants of the Bower use to win Guyon over contain a similar, and similarly false, pair of opposites. He is invited to take ease, although his state should primarily be one that does without ease; yet the rose-song is at once caressing and menacing, and in it we can hear something like Mammon's invitation to care mingling potently with something like Phaedria's invitation to carelessness: the motto of the Bower might be, "Take thought, and take pleasure." Persuasions like these are not complex in themselves, nor do Acrasia's servants make the same attempt as Mammon or Phaedria to convince Guyon that what they offer is innocent. No matter how persuasive the girls of the fountain may be with their interweaving of advances and shyness, there is no doubt whatever that they are inviting Guyon to a very illicit form of "immodest mirth"; and he would know this whether he resisted them or not. Moreover, the falsehood underlying the whole enterprise of the Bower is something that Acrasia does not try to keep altogether concealed: for there is a patent lie in a natural place that pretends to have the immutability of perfect temper, and at the same time broadcasts

singing commercials telling us that natural life passes in a day.
Yet if Guyon is infected by the fear that subtly pervades the
Bower, he will cling to the lie all the more pathetically for knowing it to be one. In the simplicity of the rose-song there is something more deeply deceitful than ordinary lying or sophistry. Its
assumption that there is nothing except the temporal world is
quite true from a merely fallen or temporal viewpoint, like so
many of the claims made by Milton's Satan. If Guyon lets himself
take this point of view, the only concord possible for him will be
that offered by Acrasia, however false he may know it to be. And
in spite of its falsehood, this concord appears graced with all the
peace and bounty of a world made whole. As Acrasia smiles on
Verdant, she seems to have a sweetness that custom cannot stale,
and to bring the light of a heavenly world down to reunite with the
calmed waves of the lower elements:

> her faire eyes sweet smyling in delight,
> Moystened their fierie beames, with which she thrild
> Fraile harts, yet quenched not; like starry light
> Which sparckling on the silent waves, does seeme more
> bright. [xii, 78]

Just as Acrasia offers truth in falsehood when she tells us that
there is no time beyond time, so she is being truthful when she
says that we must take the present. It is true, Spenser would
agree, that man must find life and joy in the present, since only
the present is real. The paradise that man lost, and journeys to
regain, is itself an eternal present. But what Acrasia offers is a
present to be exploited out of fear of the future, and hence not a
true present at all. The gracious Lady Pleasure is really someone
Guyon met when he first met Furor, a lame hag with a bald head
and a forelock; and her verdant son and lover, with his

> sweet regard, and amiable grace,
> Mixed with manly sternnesse, [79]

is no better off than Furor himself, or Guyon at the mercy of
Furor's elements. Remembering the close iconographic connection
in the Renaissance of such figures as Occasion, Fortune, Venus,
and Circe,[25] we can now see that Time in a female form, Time inviting to fear and denial, is the witch who has opposed Guyon early
and late. She did not show herself openly in the distempers of the
House of Medina, which were accordingly simpler than any that

were to follow; as the hag with the forelock she only tried to upset Guyon's temper in the ordinary sense of the phrase; and even when Phaedria and Mammon urged him to take the goods of the world, the horror of age and death remained in the background because neither Phaedria nor Mammon could offer any answer to it. It is only at the end of the road that Guyon hears the rose-song, telling him with incomparable persuasiveness to seize occasion.

Occasion of vice is also occasion of virtue, but if Guyon is to see and know and yet abstain in such a temptation he must look beyond Nature altogether: he must see that there is a higher reality to which she owes allegiance, and that in denying this she has forgotten the excellence of her creation. Her failure to regard her Maker means that each of her parts will also fail in its due regard, no matter how delightful the results may be. Thus we can say that her failure, like that of Medina's sisters, is at once distemper and discourtesy. Guyon, on the other hand, does not fail in his allegiance to what is beyond him: he helps the Palmer to throw his net over Acrasia and Verdant—and a palmer is a man who has been to Jerusalem.[26] Through him a higher order of courtesy is realized against which Acrasia cannot succeed. Guyon's own power and dignity lie in what Spenser calls his shamefastness: he would have been ashamed to accept the dishonourable worlds of Phaedria and Mammon, and he reminded the latter how man in the state of innocence would not have offended against the dignity of the Creator or the Earth he created. This was courtesy, and there was the same courtesy when the Creator left Guyon to prove himself alone against the powers of air and earth. But Guyon must also stand against a total perversion of Nature that natural strength by itself cannot conquer, any more than it can conquer Maleger; and the courtesy that regarded the distinctness of Creator and creature now fulfils its great rhythm of withdrawal and advance as it brings them once again into conjunction.[27]

It is to this true conjunction of Heaven and Earth that all conjunctions of forwardness and frowardness, carelessness and care, have finally led. Here is the highest temperance, and within its frame Guyon is able to achieve his true address to the elements of his world. This address is suggested for a last time in the Palmer's final words to Guyon. Phaedria had warned him,

> Who fares on sea, may not commaund his way,
> Ne wind and weather at his pleasure call.   [vi, 23]

Acrasia had contrived to have such command for a time, to be like

a <u>stella maris</u> watching over the sea—and the sea in such contexts
becomes the whole lower world of the elements through which man
must take his course.[28] But it is the wise and holy Palmer who
can truly still the sea-monsters, and the loyal Boatman who can
bear Guyon safely past them. In alliance with these powers above
and below him Guyon is able both to resist the full assault of the
elements' usurpation and to affirm their "right usaunce": both to
bind the witch Acrasia and to set sail again "whilest wether serves
and wind."

BOOK VI AS CONCLUSION TO THE FAERIE QUEENE

Richard Neuse

The case for the unity of The Faerie Queene is similar to that for the unity of the Canterbury Tales urged by Ralph Baldwin and others. Both poems are very much "work in progress," full of loose ends and inconsistencies, so that little is finally fixed and everything seems potentially subject to further vision and revision. That both poems were intended to be even longer than they are is the most obvious reason for their peculiarly mutable character: looking ahead to the unwritten part, the reader is led to speculate how it might affect his understanding of what is actually there on the page, in what new light it would place the whole apparent drift of the poem.[1] Any argument for unity will therefore have to bear in mind the open, almost provisional form (much more obvious, of course, as regards the Canterbury Tales) of the works concerned. But with this proviso we may still accept Northrop Frye's suggestion that the six books of The Faerie Queene "form a unified epic structure, regardless of how much might have been added that wasn't."[2]

What is this structure and what is its principle of unity? Frye suggests that the answer lies in the imagery, but that term will scarcely accommodate the diverse elements of the poem, as witness Frye's own comments on Book VI:

> Spenser may well have ended his sixth book realizing that he might not write any more of it, and designed its conclusion for either possibility. He provides himself, of course, with opportunities for carrying on the story. Apart from Prince Arthur himself, we have a fresh set of characters . . . ; the poet hints that the baby rescued by Calepine may grow up to be the hero of a future legend; he allows the Blatant Beast to escape again. But there are many such dropped stitches in the . . . other five books, and they do

Reprinted from English Literary History, Vol. 35 (1968), pp. 329–353, © The Johns Hopkins Press, by permission of the author and The Johns Hopkins Press.

not interfere with our sense of their unity. At the same time the appearance of Spenser's "signature" in Colin Clout and two other symbols from The Shepheards Calendar, the four Graces and the envious beast that barks at poets, make the end of the sixth book a summing up and conclusion for the entire poem and for Spenser's poetic career.[3]

This passage accurately suggests the variety of heterogeneous elements that make up Spenser's poem. No single hypothesis, surely, will reduce such variety to a unity, and yet any attempt, like the present one, to show the particular kind of conclusion the sixth book represents will involve a conception of The Faerie Queen's total structure that needs to be articulated.

One way of conceiving this structure is that suggested by the Letter to Raleigh and the headings of the various books: as a kind of anatomy of ethics in epic form proceeding (roughly) from the private to the public virtues. Within such a framework, the very subject of Book VI, Courtesy, would seem to represent an ideal conclusion for a poem whose "end," in the author's words, was "to fashion a gentleman or noble person in vertuous and gentle discipline." In light of Renaissance didactic theories of poetry, this gentleman is ultimately the reader himself, who may not have been fashioned in all the virtues, but whose initiation into the mysteries of Courtesy has at the same time, it is suggested, introduced him to the essence of the moral and civilized life. This suggestion comes out most strongly in the famous scene on Mount Acidale. Here the reader is the privileged spectator of a rite which, linked as it is with Colin Clout, gives him the sense that the poet's vision and his own vision momentarily coincide. Meanwhile the scene serves its purpose of showing how piping and courtesy, the conduct of poetry and "the poetry of conduct" (to use C. S. Lewis' brilliant gloss), spring from one root. Both depend upon imaginative attention, vision, and the grace of inspiration which Lewis saw symbolized in the Graces dancing before Colin.[4] All the 'virtues' of The Faerie Queene, starting with holiness, require such grace not only for their perfection but also for their inception. Courtesy, however, combining as it does the profoundly ethical and spiritual with the esthetic (rite, gesture, 'ceremony'), appears as the supreme poetic possibility in human existence, and as such represents the perfect point of transition from (poet's) art to (reader's) life. By introducing his 'autobiographical' persona into his fiction Spenser seems to say to the reader: So far can I, as poet, take you; here begins your own life—and mine.

But this, of course, is not the conclusion of the book, which ends two and a half cantos later on a very different note:

> Ne may this homely verse, of many meanest,
> Hope to escape his [the Blatant Beast's] venemous despite,
> More then my former writs, all were they clearest
> From blamefull blot, and free from all that wite,
> With which some wicked tongues did it backebite,
> And bringe into a mighty Peres displeasure,
> That neuer so deserued to endite.
> Therefore do you my rimes keep better measure,
> And seeke to please, that now is counted wisemens threasure.

These lines convey an impression of finality: the ideal of courtesy does not triumph, because what "now is counted wisemens threasure" in poetry as in life is "to seeke to please." As he ironically counsels his rimes to "keep better measure," the poet acknowledges that his art, far from enhancing and subserving real life, is in fact threatened by it.

We have here no sudden reversal of feeling: the dominant sense of Book VI is one of disillusionment, of the disparity between the poet's ideals and the reality he envisions. And in this respect Book VI seems to complete a development traceable in earlier books, a development that provides a clue to the structure of The Faerie Queene as we now have it. For the failure of courtesy, I believe, dramatizes Spenser's implicit avowal that the potential ideal which his epic was designed to embody has been defeated by a world hopelessly antagonistic to its realization.

The nature of this potential ideal is complex and many-faceted, but if one word can sum it up, conceptually and etymologically, it is Courtesy. The ideal centers on an image and conception of the court. In this poem "doctrinal and exemplary to a nation," the court of Elizabeth was invited to measure and fashion itself by the reflection that the mirror of art held up to it. The proems constantly revert to this theme, and the proem to Book VI, while it plays with the idea of true and false mirrors—the present age having fashioned a "glass so gay, that it can blynd / The wisest sight, to thinke gold that is bras" (5)—also has a great restatement of the ideal nature of Elizabeth's court:

> Then pardon me, most dreaded Soueraine,
> That from your selfe I doe this vertue bring,
> So from the Ocean all riuers spring,
> And tribute backe repay as to their king.[5]

> Right so from you all goodly vertues well
> Into the rest, which round about you ring,
> Faire Lords and Ladies, which about you dwell,
> And doe adorne your Court, where courtesies excell. (7)

Before our eyes the actual Queen and her court turn into the prototypes of Gloriana and her court. The latter remains invisible
offstage throughout The Faerie Queene and never assumes the
position assigned to it in the Letter to Raleigh. Yet it is the focus,
fictively and symbolically, of the entire poem. It is the ultimate
goal of Arthur's quest. Furthermore, the various books of The
Faerie Queene construct an image of society whose center is always the court, all other courts being referable to it. To the
source of his inspiration the poet presents his work—in the stanza
just cited—in a gesture that parallels the action of the courtier-
knights who, infused with the seeds of virtue, set forth to define
and develop their particular virtue and then return to the court.
"So like a wheele around they runne from old to new."

In a general way this seems to me the plan of The Faerie
Queene. Its literary-intellectual presupposition is the familiar
combination of medieval chivalry—a caste of men specially endowed, trained and dedicated to the active life—with the Renaissance courtier whose domain is the court as center of civility and
political power. Its idealism is aristocratic in the fullest sense,
in that nobility is achieved and maintained in action, not just inherited; but it is also 'ideological' in the sense that this action,
to be socially effective and exemplary, is informed by moral and
intellectual theory.

Such a conception of the courtier-knight fits in well with the
humanist "myth of political effectiveness" of which G. K. Hunter
has written.[6] It also obviously involves an element of deliberate
archaism which Spenser indicates when he writes that his fable
is "coloured with an historicall fiction" in the manner of "all the
antique Poets historicall." Thus, the fiction of a historical past
and the sense of a contemporary reality are constantly played off
against each other, most explicitly in the Proems and the 'historical' allegory. The implication is that the past is continuous with
the present and can possess exemplary value for it.

But it might be better to phrase this proposition in the form of
a question: Can a past whose ideals are summed up in the term
"chivalry" validly reflect and give shape to the modern courtier
and polity? I envision the poet of The Faerie Queene as setting
out on his quest armed with some such hypothesis and fairyland
as his testing ground. In the first two books he encounters no in-

superable obstacles: their symmetrical structure expresses a secure framework for the chivalric quest which in both books leads to personal wholeness and thus to further meaningful action in the world. If the first two books are basically comic in that they assert a beneficent world order, the third might be called a problem comedy: its looser structure reflects the wider net the poet is casting as he deals with more broadly social problems, but it also marks the beginning disintegration of the earlier framework. Chivalry is losing its determinate, purposive character, and chastity comes to be defined almost entirely in opposition to the bad faith of society.

Book IV introduces the bitter or dark comedy of the last three books, in which chivalry as a formative force breaks down almost completely. For the courtier chivalry becomes largely a label, a matter of social status, not the test and exercise of a noble nature. Conformity to a code of conduct now is unattended by a corresponding urge to bring the soul into harmony with the spiritual idea the code envisages. In short, chivalry is reduced to empty forms, and Book IV presents a society whose institutions, customs, even concepts, have lost most of their substance. The wedding of the rivers at the end of the book, suggesting a world of renewed vitality and harmony, is in sharp contrast to the human world whose warring atoms an ideal of friendship seems powerless to harmonize.

Book V has the wintry atmosphere of Mother Hubberds Tale where values are known primarily by their inversion. Artegall, the representative of the 'antique' aristocratic ideal, does undergo an education in the manner of the earlier heroes. But the chief recourse in the attempt to establish justice remains violence. This is due, in part, to the kind of problems and antagonists that the agent of justice has to deal with. For in this book there emerges an anarchic social type dominated by impersonal drives and scarcely susceptible to the power of reason. This "revolt of the masses" is made explicit when an actual revolt, led by the Egalitarian Giant, erupts in canto 2 as a sympton of the ailment besetting the society. Artegall's response to it is not really satisfactory,[7] and I take his (at least partial) failure to indicate, early in the book, the insufficiency of violence as an instrument of justice, and, secondly, the perplexities of chivalry faced with the politics of a mass society.

Recalled from his unfinished task, Artegall at the end of Book V stalks through an alien landscape beset by the Hags and the Blatant Beast. His melancholy forbearance in the face of their attacks asserts his aristocratic dignity. But the chivalric ideal as a way of dealing with the problems of ethics and politics now seems like a hopeless dream. And by our initial hypothesis this means the poet's increasing inability to deal with contemporary reality. If it were possible, he would finally exclude this reality from his poem, and in a sense this is what he attempts to do in Book VI.

The 'escapism' so frequently remarked in this last book, the repeated motif of retirement from court to a greener world,[8] thus takes on a clearer significance when viewed against the development of the first five books that I have suggested. It reflects the poet's desire to find solace in a pastoral idyll from the harshness of the historical world. But an intractable reality nonetheless obtrudes itself: its most obvious, I had almost said its most blatant, symbol is the Blatant Beast.

The significance of this Beast has not yet been adequately appreciated; in fact, like Calidore (but for different reasons), critics tend to forget its existence. From its first appearance at the end of Book V, when it harasses Artegall on his return to Gloriana's court, it seems more ominous than the other monsters that course through The Faerie Queene and threaten the noble quest. There is its uncertain genealogy: Calidore and the Hermit give different accounts of it (6.1.8; 6.6.9–12); its elusiveness; the mysterious wounds it inflicts; and its many tongues, varying in number from one hundred to one thousand (5.12.41; 6.1.9; 6.12.27–8). This last detail particularly underlines the social nature of the Beast, its connection with the mob or mass. By the time we get to the last canto of Book VI, with the Beast ubiquitous and raging beyond all control, there can be no doubt of its kinship with the Great Beast of Plato's Republic.[9] This is particularly apparent in the two stanzas on the Beast's tongues, where the Beast is nearly 'demythologized':

> And therein [its mouth] were a thousand tongs empight,
> Of sundry kinds, and sundry quality,
> Some were of dogs, that barked day and night,
> And some of cats, that wrawling still did cry,
> And some of Beares, that groynd continually,
> And some of Tygres, that did seeme to gren,
> And snarl at all, that euer passed by:
> But most of them were tongues of mortall men,
> Which spake reprochfully, not caring where nor when.

371

> And them amongst were mingled here and there,
> The tongues of Serpents with three forked stings,
> That spat out poyson and gore bloudy gere
> At all, that came within his rauenings,
> And spake licentious words, and hatefull things
> Of good and bad alike, of low and hie;
> Ne Kesars spared he a whit, nor Kings,
> But either blotted them with infamie,
> Or bit them with his banefull teeth of iniury.   (6.12.27–8)

The Beast contains a whole bestiary of vicious types and its totally indiscriminate, 'democratic' character in attacking all, "good and bad alike," "low and hie," is repeatedly insisted upon (cf. 6.6.12). Here is a vast extension, multiplication, of Ate, the hag who in Book IV symbolizes the energies of individuals and societies turned destructively in upon themselves. The Beast is thus a symbol of a disease of which the entire society is both the victim and the cause. The poet's particular anguish, as the final stanzas of the book all but state, is that given this condition of society, poetry as he conceives it can have no place in it. Poetry has been ousted by the Blatant Beast.[10]

What of the Beast's hellish origins? For elucidation we may turn again to the Republic and Plato's likening of the soul

> to one of those many fabulous monsters said to have existed long ago, such as the Chimaera or Scylla or Cerberus, which combined the forms of several creatures in one. Imagine to begin with, the figure of a multifarious and many-headed beast, girt round with heads of animals, tame and wild, which it can grow out of itself and transform at will. . . . Now add two other forms, a lion and a man. . . . Then join them in such a way that the three somehow grow together into one.

For justice to prevail, it is necessary

> that all our words and actions should tend towards giving the man within us complete mastery over the whole human creature, and letting him take the many-headed beast under his care and tame his wildness, like the gardener who trains his cherished plants while he checks the growth of weeds.[11]

In a similar spirit Carlyle has written of the "world of internal

372

Madness" out of which man's "world of Wisdom has been creative-
ly built together, and now rests there, as on its dark foundations
does a habitable flowery Earth-rind."[12] This "Demon-Empire"
below the surface of conscious life appears everywhere and in
countless guises in The Faerie Queene.[13] It finds perhaps its fullest expression in the portrait of Ate, particularly her subterranean
dwelling (4.1.19–26) which constitutes a kind of anti-world in which
destruction and barrenness are the paradoxical constitutive principles. That these negative principles have their positive counterpart even in Ate herself is especially apparent from certain of her
characteristics:

> vnequall were her handes twaine,
> That one did reach, the other pusht away,
> That one did make, the other mard againe. . . .   (4.1.29)

These hands express the interrelationship between the constructive and destructive impulses. It is just that for Ate, who since
Homer has symbolized the spiritual blindness that leads to uncontrolled violence, all construction is for the sake of destruction.

Ate was "raised from below" by Duessa, as "most fit to trouble
noble knights, / Which hunt for honor" (4.1.19). Here is the recognition, familiar from Hobbes, that precisely the life of strenuous
aspiration, of the noble pursuit, is exposed to the dangers of a perversion of its energies. Now the problem with chivalry by the time
we get to Book VI is that it is no longer "troubled" by Ate because
it is no longer engaged in significant action and aspiration. The
court, as I see it, has abdicated its (morally) exemplary role:
socially, the knights are no longer concerned to fashion "that gold-
en chaine of concord" (5.1.12; cf. 4.1.30); personally, they no
longer forge for themselves a distinctive style of life but are content to follow courtly fashion. But as courtiers they still preserve
their privileged status, and the result is that they become divorced
from the essential issues of the society, and their role becomes
ornamental, even frivolous.

It is at this point, when the moral governance of the society as
symbolized by the court has disintegrated, that the Blatant Beast
is unleashed. In a sense the Beast takes over the function of moral
arbiter or judge, in the form of many-tongued 'public opinion,'
rumor, gossip, scandal, 'fame.' As such it is or perhaps becomes
the perfect expression of a mass society: impersonal, anonymous,
indiscriminate, and unendingly clamorous. Speaking mythically,
the Beast objectifies or embodies those recalcitrant, chaotic but

373

vital forces with which the courtier no longer struggles, which, in effect, he has refined out of his existence. Consequently it is the failure of the court that gives rise to the Beast's demonic existence, even though the Beast symbolically encompasses the condition of an entire society. Now this failure of the court has already occurred by the time the sixth book opens, as my sketch of the development of The Faerie Queene has suggested. But on the surface the knights of Book VI act as though nothing had happened, and it is only gradually that the basic unreality and hollowness of their situation becomes apparent to the reader. Insofar as they themselves sense this unreality, it would account for the dominant note of escapism—not the poet's but that of the various courtiers, from the Hermit and Calidore to the couples copulating in the woods. For the woods, from being the realm of the unknown and hence the testing ground of knighthood,[14] now serve as another retreat like the pastoral world.

At the same time the forest also maintains its primeval quality, its saluagesse,[15] and it is in the changed relationship between the civilized and the savage, the courtier and the wild man, that Book VI most clearly signals the bankrupt status of the courtly class. For "saluagesse," from being presented largely as a negative, morally inferior, often dangerous condition earlier in The Faerie Queene, in the Savage comes to stand for a humanly incomplete but ultimately more substantial reality than that of the courtiers. The Savage is very nearly an ideal.[16]

How great this change is—and yet how it has been prepared for—we can see if we glance back over the treatment of the wild man motif in the previous books. In Book I, Sir Satyrane, despite his comically precarious control over his instincts,[17] is nonetheless on his way to being civilized under the spell of a noble court and chivalry. By Book III, however, his 'education' seems to have stopped. The spiritual crudeness he brought with him from the woods is now indistinguishable from the moral insensitivity of the Squire of Dames, Paridell, and the others. And if Satyrane still seems to be a bit of an outsider straining to appear as sophisticated as his companions (cf. 3.7.53–61), in Book IV he has moved to center stage at the head of a whole company of knights—the knights of Maidenhead! He has become the representative of the new chivalry, acting by a code he does not understand and motivated by impulses of which he must remain largely ignorant.

Satyrane's tournament for the girdle of Florimell, with all its absurd irrationality, is the symbolic center of the courtly society presented in this book. Its irony—in terms of our theme—is heightened by the sudden appearance of Artegall in wild man's disguise bearing the motto: Saluagesse sans finesse. This is not the place to explore the intricacies of this irony or of the other wild man motifs in Book IV. Suffice it to say that Artegall's disguise foreshadows the role—only partially tempered by Britomart's intervention—thrust upon him by the savage world of Book V.[18] But however ambiguous "saluagesse" has become, it is still felt as a threat to the body politic in Book V, whereas the Savage Man of Book VI stands out as Nature's nobleman over against the courtly reality. It is as though the poet has traveled back in time to a state of humanity stripped of the encrustations of civility to rediscover "the thing itself." The result is encouraging to human nature, but not to the court: morally the Savage proves himself superior to the sophisticates of the book.

The first thing that strikes us when we compare the Savage with the "patron" of courtesy is that the two are antithetical in almost every respect. Whereas Calidore has all the advantages of a noble birth, personal beauty, charm, and courtly training that the courtesy books recommend,[19] the Savage was "both rudely borne and bred, / Ne euer saw faire guize, ne learned good" (6.5.2). Furthermore, he is unprepossessing in appearance: Serena is afraid at the mere sight of him (4.10), Timias at first sight takes him for a "hylding hound" (5.25). Calidore's gift for "gracious speach" (1.2) is repeatedly emphasized (2.3); the Savage, on the other hand, has no language

> But a soft murmure, and confused sound
> Of senseles words, which nature did him teach,
> T'expresse his passions, which his reason did empeach.
>
> (4.11)

In spite of all these handicaps, however, the Savage turns out to be a model of instinctive courtesy. The spontaneous sympathy with the plight of others by which he is actuated appears to be an instinctual counterpart to, or prototype of, the imaginative act that we have seen to be a requisite of true courtesy in the book.

This is shown in his first appearance, the providential rescue of Calepine from the brutal Turpine:

> The saluage man, that neuer till this houre
> Did taste of pittie, neither gentlesse knew,
> Seeing his sharpe assault and cruell stoure
> Was much emmoued at this perils vew,

375

That euen his ruder hart began to rew,
And feele compassion of his euill plight,
Against his foe that did him so pursew. . . .   (6.4.3)

At Serena's signs of fear, the Savage wordlessly conveys his
feelings of sympathy; he

Came to her creeping like a fawning hound,
And by rude tokens made to her appeare
His deepe compassion of her dolefull stound,
Kissing his hands, and crouching to the ground.   (11)

To the wounded Calepine he similarly displays his compassion
and provides first aid in the form of herbs. He then takes the two
to his forest dwelling and continues to treat them with the utmost
care and courtesy (14).

Twice the Savage appears in a providential role, the second
time when he awakens Arthur, whose life is threatened by Turpine
(7.23–24). It would be wrong, nonetheless, to regard him as an
unqualified ideal. Like Talus, he must be restrained from further
slaughter when he and Arthur capture Turpine's castle (6.38 f.).
Instincts however noble are clearly not a sufficient guide to life,
at least life in society. At the same time, however, it is these
noble instincts that are sufficient to throw into question the aristocratic assumption with which The Faerie Queene began. What,
for instance, are we to make of the first two stanzas of canto 5,
beginning "O what an easie thing is to descry / The gentle bloud,
how euer it be wrapt / In sad misfortunes foule deformity"?
Spenser must have been aware of the debate about "gentilesse"
extending from Boethius to his own time; we should therefore be
put on our guard by the excessively relaxed tone of "O what an
easie thing . . . ," and the overly neat syllogism whose major
premise is suspect to say the least: any signs of "gentle mind"
are evidence of "gentle blood"; the Savage's treatment of Serena
was "gentle"; therefore he was born of "gentle blood."

These two stanzas, then, seem to me to maintain the aristocratic fiction at the expense of a great deal of irony. In relation
to the Savage, "gentle" seems to mean rather something like
'human' in the sense in which Boethius speaks of the human race:

The general race of men from a like birth is born.
All things one Father have, Who doth them all adorn, . . .
He souls fetched down from high in bodies did enclose;

>And thus from noble seed [nobile germen] all men did first
> compose.
>Why brag you of your stock? Since none is counted base,
>If you consider God the author of your race,
>But he that with foul vice doth his own birth deface.[20]

The terms are found significantly coupled in Serena's praise of
the Savage:

>In such a saluage wight, of brutish kynd,
>Amongst wilde beastes in desert forrests bred,
>It is most straunge and wonderful to fynd,
>So milde humanity, and perfect gentle mynd.   (5.29)

We find, therefore, the apparent paradox of the savage who is
gentle, 'apparent' because what he represents is a humanity that
has kept the nobility of its origin (nobile germen) uncorrupted by
a courtly civilization.

The Savage does put on (Calepine's) armor (5.8)—and just as
casually doffs it a little later (5.10)—, but it has not the power to
transform him as it does the Redcrosse knight and Satyrane, for
example. Not, presumably, because he is incapable of the virtues
that chivalry ideally demands: his instinctive loyalty and sense of
service is never in doubt (see 5.9, for example). He attaches
himself to Arthur out of love for him and saves him from fairly
certain death. But after this episode he simply vanishes from the
poem. In short, one gets the impression that with the possible
exception of Arthur chivalry has lost its spiritual pull, the mag-
netism that drew Satyrane, another wild man, out of the forest,
and Redcrosse, shepherd-plowman, out of the fields.

What is the position of Calidore in relation to this? Does he
not stand for an ideal of courtoisie that would redeem whatever
lapse court and chivalry had suffered? At first glance it would
certainly seem so. Thus among the "curteous Knights and
Ladies" of Faery court he is "beloued ouer all," because in him

>it seems, that gentlenesse of spright
>And manners mylde were planted naturall;
>To which he adding comely guize withall,
>And gracious speach, did steal mens hearts away.   (6.1.2)

With these prepossessing gifts (dona) the practice of courtesy is
for him a matter of consummate ease:

Ne was there Knight, ne was there Lady found
In Faery court, but him did deare embrace,
For his faire vsage and conditions sound,
The which in all mens liking gayned place,
And with the greatest purchast greatest grace:
Which he could wisely vse, and well apply,
To please the best, and th'euill to embase.
For he loathd leasing, and base flattery,
And loued simple truth and stedfast honesty. (3)

But the language in this stanza—especially "purchast," "vse,"
"apply"—has disturbing connotations. Is Calidore putting his
charming gifts to morally ambiguous uses? Who are "the greatest" and "the best" (lines 5 and 7)? Are these moral categories,
or social and political ones? And is he mainly concerned "to
please" (line 7)?[21] The last two lines, finally, are made most
suspect when we observe Calidore's conduct in canto 3. There
he swears to Priscilla's father that he found her

Most perfect pure, and guiltlesse innocent
Of blame, as he did on his Knighthood sweare,
Since first he saw her, and did free from feare
Of a discourteous Knight, who her had reft
And by outragious force away did beare. (3.18)

Granted the falsehood about the discourteous knight (whose head
he displays) is well-intentioned. But is his hyperbolical near-
perjury really necessary? And is it part of genuine courtesy or
love of "simple truth and stedfast honesty" to go to such lengths
to protect a dubious reputation?

The same scene also suggests Calidore's eagerness to maintain the appearances, and thus his acceptance of the world as it
is. This is brought out again when, next, Calidore stumbles upon
the lovemaking of Calepine and Serena. The situation is apparently seen through Calidore's eyes, including the lady who "was full
faire to see, / And courteous withall, becomming her degree,"
which under the circumstances must be taken as a joke, I think.

To whom Sir Calidore approaching nye,
Ere they were well aware of liuing wight,
Them much abasht, but more him selfe thereby,
That he so rudely did vppon them light,
And troubled had their quiet loues delight.

> Yet since it was his fortune, not his fault,
> Him selfe thereof he labour'd to acquite,
> And pardon crau'd for his so rash default,
> That he gainst courtesie so fowly did default.　　　(3.21)

It is embarrassing, but by what criterion has it anything to do with courtesy?[22] It seems to call for a graceful and fast retreat on the part of the intruder, who, to the contrary, ignores the breach of etiquette in this semi-public love-making and proceeds to apply his charm,

> With which his gentle words and goodly wit
> He soone allayd that Knights conceiu'd displeasure,
> That he besought him downe by him to sit.　　　(3.22)

And so we get the rather ludicrous picture of these two complaisant men engaged in "ciuill conversation" about this and that while Serena is left to wander off by herself. Roused by her shouts when she is seized by the Blatant Beast, the two knights dash to the rescue and at this point Calidore disappears, in pursuit of the Beast, until canto 9.

It has been plausibly suggested that during Calidore's long absence from Book VI Calepine serves as his surrogate or, in Donald Cheney's words, "less gifted substitute." He and Serena, says Cheney, are "relatively tame products of a civilized world," because "their survival is contingent on the tameness of those with whom they come in contact."[23] The contrast with Calidore seems well taken, since he repeatedly shows his fighting ability and courage whereas Calepine's encounters with Turpine end ignominiously with his hiding behind his lady (3.49). But Calepine's perverse failure to recognize Turpine for what he is and his insistence on challenging him to conbat when discretion so obviously would have been the better part of valor (3.31–51), suggest that his chief failing is not so much lack of prowess as of imagination. (In his comic encounter with the bear in the next canto he appears brave enough.) And in this sense, I believe, Calepine and Calidore share a "tameness": both seem examples of a type that has been given a penetrating analysis by John S. White under the heading of "aesthetic man." A lineal descendant of Castiglione's Courtier, this person is in his very essence a social being, tied to his class and to the society which he needs "as a resonance box."[24] His aim in life is to please and to this end he strives to make himself "the object of aesthetic enjoy-

ment by forming his individuality according to the rules of art."
In so doing, White suggests, he "will not avoid effects based on
deceit," because

> the final aim . . . is less the personality than the effect of
> the personality, less "being" than "seeming"; and thus such
> a personality will be somewhat empty, somewhat anemic,
> in spite of its abilities and faculties. What is missing is a
> stable center, a moral marrow.[25]

The relevance of this analysis to Calidore will perhaps already
be evident from our examination of his conduct in the first part of
the book. At any rate, it leads us to the conclusion that, far from
combining the civilized and the natural or instinctive in an ideal
synthesis,[26] Calidore stands at the opposite extreme from the
Savage—as our comparison of the two has already hinted. Between
the "compleat courtier" and "saluagesse" there is simply no contact.

It might be argued that the opening cantos present a Calidore
in the process of learning, and that they deliberately show the in-
adequacies of his virtue and his person so that these may be perfected later. In opposition to this I shall try to show that unlike
some earlier heroes, Guyon, for instance, Calidore does not possess the innocence that allows him to be transformed by experience; that he remains to the end the smooth, self-contained
courtier who, far from redeeming the failure of the court, actually sums it up in his person. Thus, rather than evolving towards
an ideal, Calidore's character seems to me to develop, if at all,
in a reverse direction. His courtesy, to cite the most obvious
example, gradually loses all semblance of the ideal virtue set
out in the Proem. Let us observe his encounter with Meliboe in
canto 9, which is symptomatic of his behavior among the shepherds.

Meliboe concludes the history of his life with an extended
homily on the theme that "It is the mynd, that maketh good or
ill, / That maketh wretch or happie, rich or poore." Calidore
responds by requesting to stay among the shepherds and proceeds
to—offer money! Surely this is an act of discourtesy or worse.
Unless one (charitably) assumes that, with his eyes riveted on
Pastorella, he has not been listening to the old man. For while
Meliboe spoke, Calidore

> was rapt with double rauishment,
> Both of his speach that wrought him great content,
> And also of the obiect of his vew,
> On which his hungry eye was alwayes bent;
> That twixt his pleasing tongue, and her faire hew,
> He lost himselfe, and like one halfe entraunced grew.   (26)

Regardless of which view we take, the irony is still heavily
weighted against Calidore. Even in his trance, it appears, he has
time to devise the role he will play and to engage in the duplicity
that characterizes his conduct among the shepherds:

> Yet to occasion meanes, to worke his mind,
> And to insinuate his harts desire,
> He thus replyde: Now surely syre, I find,
> That all this worlds gay showes, which we admire,
> Be but vaine shadowes to this safe retyre
> Of life, which here in lowlinesse ye lead.   (27)

By such clichés he ingratiates himself with the old man, who can
be relied upon to give the stock responses and delight in the
honeyed voice which earned him his name.

With Pastorella he does not have such immediate success and
therefore decides "To chaunge the manner of his loftie looke"
(36) and dress as a shepherd. This sartorial change, as well as
change in strategy, earns him a simile devastating in its moral
implications:

> That who had seen him then, would haue bethought
> On Phrygian Paris by Plexippus brooke,
> When he the loue of fayre Oenone sought,
> What time the golden apple was vnto him brought.   (36)

One false shepherd illuminates another.

Calidore's conduct towards Coridon manifests a more complex
duplicity. Outwardly, he treats him with punctilious courtesy and
graciousness. But this never appears to be done out of genuine
concern for his rival; instead it always suggests the sly wink of
contempt for the hapless peasant who is being bested in the competition for Pastorella's favor. Thus at the festival for which
Colin does the piping, Coridon pouts when Calidore is selected to

"lead the ring, as hee / That most in Pastorellaes grace did sit."
Thereupon,

> Calidore of courteous inclination
> Tooke Coridon, and set him in his place,
> That he should lead the daunce, and trimly trace.
> And when as Pastorella, him to grace,
> Her flowry garlond tooke from her owne head,
> And plast on his, he did it soone displace,
> And did it put on Coridons in stead:
> Then Coridon woxe frollicke, that erst seemed dead.   (42)

The simple-minded shepherd is taken in by Calidore's gestures.
But are they not rather absurd acts of condescension? There can
be no doubt that this is the case at the wrestling match, in which
Calidore gives Coridon the inevitable drubbing.

> Then was the oaken crowne by Pastorell
> Giuen to Calidore, as his due right;
> But he, that did in courtesies excell,
> Gaue it to Coridon, and said he wonne it well.   (44)

Here we are no longer remotely dealing with courtesy but with an
insulting lie. Yet among the rude unlettered hinds Calidore can
get away with it:

> Thus did the gentle knight himselfe abeare
> Amongst that rusticke rout in all his deeds,
> That euen they, the which his riuals were,
> Could not maligne him, but commend him needs:
> For courtesie amongst the rudest breeds
> Good will and fauour. So it surely wrought
> With this faire Mayd. . . .   (45)

So Calidore continually asserts his virtù, his superiority over the
"base and viler clown," to an invisible audience of his courtly
peers as well as for its effects on the shepherds. But most importantly, his actions are part of his strategy for gaining Pastorella's love,

> Which hauing got, he vsed without crime
> Or blamefull blot, but menaged so well,
> That he of all the rest, which there did dwell,
> Was fauored, and to her grace commended.   (46)

What kind of "management" is this? It sounds almost as though for Calidore love is part of an exercise in 'public relations.' But with that we have arrived at what I conceive to be a central idea of Book VI, namely that love leads to true courtesy, an idea that in Calidore's conduct finds its radical parodistic perversion.

The link between love and courtesy is most clearly expressed in the scene on Mount Acidale of the next canto. But it finds a very curious anticipation in canto 8. There the cannibals' rite around the naked Serena proves, upon reflection, to be an inversion (or perversion) of the authentic courtesy that consists of "doing reverence to Revelation in the Flesh."[27] However incongruous, or by its very incongruity, the Canticles (and sonneteers') imagery applied to Serena focusses attention upon the human body as temple of the spirit. In place of reverence, of course, the cannibals pay it an idolatrous worship, their ogling an index of diseased sexuality and their dietary intent a reprise (perhaps) of the female sex horror touched on in Book III.

Serena's incongruous concern with her nakedness—"Yet fearing death, and next to death the lacke / Of clothes to couer, what they ought by kind" (8.49)—further helps to link the episode with the one in which Colin pipes to "An hundred naked maidens lilly white, / All raunged in a ring, and dauncing in delight" (10.11). In the midst of the ring of Graces there is precisely such a naked maiden to whom Colin does reverence above all (10.25). She is "but a countrey lasse," but Colin's encomium emphasizes the fact that her humble status is irrelevant to her excellence, her inherent worth:

> Another Grace she well deserues to be,
> In whom so many Graces gathered are,
> Excelling much the meane of her degree;
> Diuine resemblance, beauties soueraine rare,
> Firme Chastity, that spight ne blemish dare;
> All which she with such courtesie doth grace,
> That all her peres cannot with her compare,
> But quite are dimmed, when she is in place.
> She made me often pipe and now to pipe apace.   (27)

The juxtaposition of Queen and lowly shepherdess in the following stanza suggests the two distinct yet related poles of the poet's inspiration, the one public and the other private. The Queen is the ideal source of "all goodly vertues" that the poet would celebrate in his poem. But the naked lass at the center of the Graces' dance provides the first impulse to pipe, to

praise,[28] to do reverence. In short, she is the source of courtesy
for him, because the image he has of her, expressive of her essential selfhood and "diuine resemblance," guides his conduct as
it informs his relations to other selves. Such a notion of courtesy
has its roots in the medieval tradition of courtoisie to which The
Faerie Queene always harks back and of which one scholar has
written that it

> comes into being and is needed at that moment when one en-
> counters the "other"; one must behold him, look at him for
> who he is and what he is in himself, without heedlessly re-
> jecting him on the basis of a preconceived opinion or on the
> basis of one's own otherness; and one must acknowledge
> and honor him.[29]

Calidore sees the dancers from a distance and in spite of his
fear that he might break their dance if he were seen (10.11), he
comes closer out of sheer curiosity. This should be Calidore's
moment of truth. But neither the instant disappearance of the
dancers nor Colin's breaking of his pipe in anger at the intrusion,
has any real effect on Calidore. He approaches with a "Haile iolly
shepheard" and an extended question that ignores Colin's discomfiture (19), though it is probably designed to smooth things over. He
maintains his breezy, urbane manner throughout the interview with
Colin and though curious does not really seem interested in Colin's
explanation. Witness his reply to Colin's opening rebuke:

> Not I so happy, answerd then that swaine,
> As thou vnhappy, which them thence didst chace,
> Whom by no meanes thou canst recall againe,
> For being gone, none can them bring in place,
> But whom they of them selues list so to grace,
> Right sory I, (saide then Sir Calidore,)
> That my ill fortune did them hence displace.
> But since things passed none may now restore,
> Tell me, what were they all, whose lack thee grieues so
>   sore.   (20)

And at the end of Colin's exposition he shows that he sees in it no
relevance to himself as he strives to ingratiate himself with the
rural piper:

> Now sure it yrketh mee,
> That to thy blisse I made this luckelesse breach,
> As now the author of thy bale to be,
> Thus to bereaue thy loues deare sight from thee:
> But gentle Shepheard pardon thou my shame,
> Who rashly sought that, which I mote not see,
> Thus did the courteous Knight excuse his blame,
> And to recomfort him, all comely meanes did frame.   (29)

The entire scene suggests Calidore's fundamental inability to
appreciate the ideal on which Spenser's version of courtesy is
founded, and the sequel to it dramatizes the point as the calculated artifice of Calidore's courtesy is again made apparent. Returning to the other shepherds, Calidore makes the courtship of
Pastorella his chief program again:

> Ne any paines ne perill did he shonne,
> By which he might her to his loue allure,
> And liking in her yet vntamed heart procure.   (32)

The peril appears providentially in the form of a tiger while they
are picking wild strawberries. Coridon flees and Calidore kills
it. Pastorella rejects the "cowherd" as fit only for sheep and
grants her full favor (again?) to the hero.

> Yet Calidore did not despise him quight,
> But vsde him friendly for further intent,
> That by his fellowship, he colour might,
> Both his estate, and loue from skill of any wight.
>
> So well he wood her, and so well he wrought her,
> With humble seruice, and with daily sute,
> That at the last vnto his will he brought her;
> Which he so wisely well did prosecute,
> That of his loue he reapt the timely frute,
> And ioyed long in close felicity.   (37, 38)

This sounds like a very deliberately conducted court amour, with
the conventions (like secrecy) almost compulsively observed. It
seems significant, moreover, that we learn nothing further about
their relationship by the time Calidore leaves Pastorella for his

quest in canto 11. It looks as though Calidore, having had his fling, abandons the girl after making sure she is in safe hands.

The scene on Mount Acidale points up, further, the utter disparity between Colin and Calidore, where we would expect a closer rapprochement between the two if Calidore were the true hero of the book, as he is usually taken to be. For the ideal courtier is, unlike Calidore, a cultivator of the muses, as Spenser makes clear in a number of poems like Mother Hubberds Tale.[30] Calidore, on the other hand, lacks (in the words of John White[31]) "the organ for feeling the demonic forces of life," and it is in the struggle with these forces that the poet shapes the fabric of his vision, as I believe is implied by the curious simile applied to the concentric rings of dancers on Mount Acidale:

> Looke how the Crowne, which Ariadne wore
> Vpon the yuory forehead that same day,
> That Theseus her vnto his bridale bore,
> When the bold Centaures made that bloudy fray,
> With the fierce Lapithes, which did them dismay;
> Being now placed in the firmament,
> Through the bright heauen doth her beames display. . . .
>
> (13)

This scene of violent discord at the center of an image of harmony seems to imply that all significant harmony is achieved through conflict. Just as Theseus can consummate his wedding only by participation in conquering the Centaurs,[32] so the poet or any 'culture hero' can create genuine order only by subduing the "saluage" powers within as well as outside the self.

To all this Calidore seems a stranger. He can work up a sweat, and he is not lacking in strength and courage. But his fight with the Blatant Beast occurs almost as an afterthought in the latter part of canto 12 rather than as the climax of a spiritual struggle. From the outset, indeed, Calidore has had trouble finding the Beast even though it is said to be a nearly universal scourge (cf. 5.12.37; 41; 6.1.7–8), and when he finally confronts it, it does not call forth a shudder of recognition in our knight; on the contrary, he feels that it is completely alien to him and his experience:

> Tho when the Beast saw, he mought nought auaile,
> By force, he gan his hundred tongues apply,
> And sharply at him to reuile and raile,

> With bitter termes of shamefull infamy;
> Oft interlacing many a forged lie,
> <u>Whose like he neuer once did speake, nor heare,</u>
> <u>Nor euer thought thing so vnworthily:</u>
> Yet did he nought for all that him forbeare,
> But strained him so streightly, that he chokt him neare.
>
> (12.33)

And is it not characteristic of Calidore that once he has subdued the Beast he leads it around the country in what Harry Berger has aptly called a ticker-tape parade?[33] With this final image of a gaping crowd swarming out of all the towns (12.37) our hero passes from view. It is not altogether surprising that the Blatant Beast has not been definitely subdued and eventually escapes again.

What manner of hero, or man, then, is Calidore? I have tried to suggest that he is radically inadequate to his task. He never penetrates to the essence of courtesy, seems in fact incapable of doing so. And his conquest of the Blatant Beast, if it is not meaningless, fails to have exemplary value because he never comes to an understanding of its nature. He is incapable of dealing with the social evil it represents, being himself one expression or sympton of that very evil.

Not that Calidore is a villain. He is, rather, in the class of the anti-heroes. His courtesy might better be called civility, a matter of "skill" in that you have to know the right things, how to conduct yourself to people of different "degrees," for instance.[34] And Calidore possesses and exercises this skill to a consummate degree. What he lacks, in spite of all his gifts, is the spiritual faculty that would allow him to sense the mystery of courtesy. For "vertues seat is deep within the mynd, / And not in outward shows, but inward thoughts defynd" (6.Pr.5), and at no point in the book does Calidore appear to withdraw into his mind or struggle to define his inward thoughts. Calidore, then, should be included in the poet's condemnation of the present age in the proem to the sixth book (where his name does not appear, however):

> But in the triall of true curtesie,
> Its now so farre from that, which then it was [in "plaine
>   Antiquitie"]
> That it indeed is nought but forgerie,
> Fashion'd to please the eies of them, that pas.   (5)

Between them, Calidore and the Blatant Beast represent major
aspects of a society which, as I have suggested, has no room for
the Spenserian poet or poetry. We are now perhaps in a better
position to see the implications of this point. What is radically
threatened in this particular society that stands under the sign of
the Beast, so to speak, is the element of the personal, the individual, the contemplative-reflective, in a word, the element of
privacy in the fullest sense. Calidore, as we have seen, feels no
need of this element, and the Beast is of course its very antithesis. No wonder it reenacts the dissolution of the monasteries:

> The Elfin Knight,
> Who now no place besides vnsought had left,
> At length into a Monastere did light,
> Where he him found despoyling all with maine and might.
>
> Into their cloysters now he broken had,
> Through which the Monckes he chaced here and there,
> And them pursu'd into their dortours sad,
> And searched all their cels and secrets neare;
> In which what filth and ordure did appeare,
> Were yrkesome to report; yet that foule Beast
> Nought sparing them, the more did tosse and teare,
> And ransacke all their dennes from most to least,
> Regarding nought religion, nor their holy heast.   (12.23—4)

Spenser's view of the actual historical event is of no real account
here; what matters is the 'logic' of the Beast. Anything that is
private, withdrawn from the public eye and ear, must contain
secret filth and therefore has to be overthrown. And this means
that the life of contemplation, the basis of religion but also of
poetry, as of any 'mystery,' is overthrown with it.

By the end of Book VI the Beast is triumphant and even threat-
ens to disengage itself from the fiction. At this point, the poem,
in one of those characteristic Spenserian twists, becomes a spell
to ward off its own destruction. Is this not the poet's final acknowledgment that his quest, though unfinished, has reached the
limits of his epic enterprise?

PLACEMENT "IN THE MIDDEST" IN <u>THE FAERIE QUEENE</u>

Michael Baybak, Paul Delany, and A. Kent Hieatt

It is now a commonplace of criticism that Spenser describes the "stately mount" rising in the middle of the Garden of Adonis (<u>FQ</u> III. vi. 43) in terms which identify it with the anatomical <u>mons Veneris</u>.[1] But most critics have simply noted the correspondence, and passed on. As we shall show, however, Spenser introduced this anatomically central elevation in the arithmetically central stanza of Book III. We maintain that the mount is central both to the thought and to the narrative structure of its Book. Moreover, Spenser used similar narrative devices and settings in the central passages of Books I and II. All three books, as originally published, turn upon passages that are central by both arithmetic and significance.[2] In addition, all three passages are signaled by the phrase "in the middest" or a variant; in two of the passages the phrase occurs in the central stanzas and in the other it immediately precedes.

As Renaissance Platonism valued circles, so it necessarily valued centers. Castiglione reminds us: "Beauty cometh of God, and is like a circle, the goodness whereof is the center."[3] Donne, parodying the commonplace, brought the circles to a different center:

> Although wee see celestiall bodies move
> Above the earth, the earth we till and love:
> So we her ayres contemplate, words and hart
> And vertues; But we love the Centrique part.[4]

He was not alone in fixing man's center at the pudenda; the human body was often shown as circumscribed by a circle which the outstretched hands and feet touched at four points, and whose center was the pubis.[5] The mount in Spenser's garden represents, then, the center of the little world of man as well as the fruitful and generative center of the poem's external world.[6] And Spenser

Reprinted from <u>Papers on Language and Literature</u>, Vol. 5 (1969), pp. 227–234, by permission of the authors and the publisher.

reinforced this position of double centrality by a device which has apparently not been noticed before: Stanza 43 of Canto vi, whose first line is "Right in the middest of that Paradise," occupies, in the 1590 text, the exact midpoint of Book III as the 340th of 679 stanzas.[7]

The mount's central position in Book III is appropriate in many ways. On its "round top" Venus and Adonis create the forms which populate the world outside the garden. One may find it paradoxical that a "Legend of Chastitie" should enact its rich pageant of diverse loves (cf. III. v. 1) around the central and dominant landmark of the mons Veneris; yet such an apotheosis of the generative organs is typical of the peculiar combination of mysticism and forthrightness in Spenser's conception of sexuality. In particular, the timeless union of Venus and Adonis on the mount finds its counterpart, in the historical sphere, in the great end which Book III looks toward: the union of its heroine, Britomart, with Arthegall. This supreme work of the "sacred fire" of Love will bring together a couple whose intercourse will inaugurate Britain's historical mission:

> From whose two loynes thou [Love] afterwards did rayse
> Most famous fruits of matrimoniall bowre,
> Which through the earth haue spred their liuing prayse,
> That fame in trompe of gold eternally displayes.[8]
>
> (III. iii. 3.)

One aspect of the sexuality of the Mount, as well as of the Garden, is thus fertility. Another is sexual pleasure perfected. Venus and Adonis' enjoyment of each other is explicitly anatomical: it occurs within the "pleasant arbour" within the myrtle grove on the summit of the mons. This sensual bliss is an implicit criticism of love's aberrations in the rest of Book III. A. C. Hamilton has drawn attention to the several permutations of the Venus and Adonis myth in Book III;[9] for the present purpose we single out the myth's relevance to what might be called the theme of "enemies of Love." In Spenser's world, these are, especially, the forms of sexuality which are facile, violent, or unnatural, and which sometimes masquerade under the conventions of Courtly Love. In contrast to the central bower, for instance, the bower of Venus and Adonis depicted on the arras of Malecasta's castle (III. i. 34–38) sadly travesties the lovers' relationship. This scene shows love as it exists at the circumference of the circle whose center is the idyllic mount. Here, at

the beginning of the Book, Adonis is destroyed by the malignant
forces which thwart love in the fallen world:

> . . . he lyeth languishing,
> Deadly engored of a great wild Bore,
> And by his side the Goddesse groueling
> Makes for him endlesse mone, and euermore
> With her soft garment wipes away the gore,
> Which staines his snowy skin . . .   (III. i. 38.)

With their elaborate yet base rituals, the abode of Malecasta,
and that of Busirane in Cantos xi, xii, at the other end of the
Book, show how the instinct of sexual love can be perverted.
They serve as foils to the innocent, paradisal naturalism of the
Garden of Adonis. In both castles, and only there, Britomart is
wounded; her hurts are superficial, but it is not until she sees
her own blood that she is roused to use her full strength in over-
powering the guardians of the two dwellings.[10] Since her chastity
includes, potentially at least, the chaste sexuality of married
love, her adventures should aim at an ideal condition in which she
could lay aside her weapons and no longer fear the assaults of
corrupt and worldly love. She does not achieve this state in Book
III, but we do find its symbolic equivalent in the safe and "eternall
blis" enjoyed by Adonis in his central bower:

> Ne feareth he henceforth that foe of his,
> Which with his cruell tuske him deadly cloyd:
> For that wilde Bore, the which him once annoyd,
> She firmely hath emprisoned for ay,
> That her sweet loue his malice mote auoyd, . . .
>
> (III. vi. 48.)

In the cantos furthest away from the center of Book III, then, we
find two powerful visions of sexuality perverted, degraded, or
tortured. Britomart may be imagined as questing through the
area of lust and violence which surrounds the central paradise of
the Book; eventually, by her union with Arthegall, she will reconcile chastity and sexuality and will make her womb the fountain of
a great race of Faerie Kings and Queens who will continue her
battle against the outer anarchy. We therefore suggest that both
the central mount and the idea of a central harmony contrasted
with a peripheral disorder provide a keystone for the structure
of Book III, in contrast to the more linear narrative of the first
two books.[11]

Although Book III may lack the narrative coherence of, say, Robinson Crusoe or Joseph Andrews, it is rich in a kind of form and symmetry of which Spenser is the peculiar master in English literature. The arithmetic symmetry already pointed out we take to be simply Spenser's way of reinforcing the Book's structure. Furthermore, Books I and II provide corroborative evidence for this practice: Spenser appears to have paid particular attention to the midpoints of all the three books of The Faerie Queene that appeared in 1590.[12]

Each of the first two books follows the career of a dominant hero to a decisive outcome. In Book I the Red Cross Knight both kills the Dragon and espouses Una in the last canto, although his progress to this final success has not been smooth and unhampered. As has often been pointed out, it is central to Spenser's schemes that Red Cross should falter halfway through his quest and have to be redeemed by Arthur, an instrument of Grace (I. vii.).[13] In his account of this episode, Spenser draws an implicit parallel with another malingerer, the nymph who lives in the fountain from which Red Cross drinks:

> . . . one day when Phoebe fayre
> With all her band was following the chace,
> This Nymph, quite tyr'd with heat of scorching ayre
> Sat downe to rest in middest of the race.   (I. vii. 5.)

As Robert Kellogg and Oliver Steele note, she "is apparently an invention of Spenser's designed as a mythological emblem of Red Cross's sitting "down to rest in middest of the race" (our italics).[14] Her fane is a locus amoenus, and as such it parallels the settings of the central passages of Books II and III, as we shall note. We hear of a "breathing wind," "trembling leaues," "chereful birds" chanting "sweet musick" (vii. 3), a "bubbling waue" (vii. 4).

This part of the episode, containing the significant phrase "in middest," does not, however, occupy the arithmetical center of Book I; that center, seven stanzas further along, is reserved for the downfall of Red Cross himself, which the Nymph's action prefigures. After drinking from the Nymph's fountain, and while remaining in her fane, he is so weakened that when the giant Orgoglio appears and aims a huge blow at him he cannot resist. He sidesteps the blow itself, but the force of it is so great "That with the wind it did him overthrow, / And all his sences stound, that still he lay full low" (vii. 12). The stanza in which he is thus felled and the following one, containing a simile on his condition, mark the precise midpoint of Book I in the 1590 text.[15] Orgoglio then throws him into a dungeon, where he languishes until released by Arthur. That the downfall of the hero of Book I occurs at precisely this point would seem to be more than mere coincidence.

In Book II, the numerical midpoint in the edition of 1590 falls within the episode of Mammon's final temptation of Guyon in the Garden of Proserpina. This passage exhibits the devices which we have already indicated. The three stanzas (II. vii. 53–55) which describe Proserpina's silver seat and the golden apples growing nearby form this midpoint, and in the first of these stanzas the familiar catch-phrase recurs: "The Garden of Proserpina this hight; / And in the midst thereof a siluer seat" (II. vii. 53).[16] Further, the Garden itself is a locus amoenus in reverse: it is "goodly garnished/With hearbs and fruits" (vii. 51), but of a "Direful deadly blacke, both leafe and bloom"; there is "a thicke Arber" (vii. 53), as in the deeply protected abode of Venus and Adonis; there are "golden apples" (vii. 53); and there is a "blacke flood" (vii. 56) instead of the bubbling wave (I. vii. 4) of the Nymph's retreat where Red Cross met his doom.[17]

The structural centrality of this episode helps to corroborate what others have already maintained concerning the central importance of this temptation to Spenser's concerns in Book II. As Frank Kermode has pointed out, there is considerable agreement that the ordeal in the cave is the crisis of Guyon's quest.[18] Kermode's interpretation, to which we in part subscribe, is that the temptation by Mammon, like that of Christ in the Wilderness, is a nearly total one (excluding concupiscence, the subject of the Bower of Bliss), and that the climactic temptation, that in the Garden of Proserpina, is toward mental intemperance, indulgence in vain learning. Whether or not the aim of the temptation is precisely this, it seems fitting that the Book of Temperance should have at its center golden apples—symbols of both classical and biblical temptations—which the hero in exercising his peculiar virtue refuses to pluck. The apple of Genesis is not explicitly mentioned; but, like Milton, we cannot help contrasting Guyon's abstention with Eve's seduction by the fruit.[19]

At the numerical center of Book I, to conclude, we find a symbolic action—the Red Cross Knight's swoon—and at the numerical centers of Books II and III symbolic objects: the silver seat and golden apples and the mons Veneris. The arithmetical calculation is sufficiently precise to make coincidence very unlikely: the "numerical centers" here are the central stanza of III, the two central stanzas of I, and the three central stanzas of II, in terms of the total number of nine-line <u>Faerie Queene</u>-stanzas in all twelve cantos of each Book of the first edition. Furthermore, the phrase "in [the] middest [midst]," construed by us as a kind of covert signal, occurs in these stanzas in II and III, and seven stanzas earlier in I where an event prefigures the immediately ensuing central one. The locales of all three central events have a certain similarity within differences: in III, a grove of trees making a pleasant central arbor; in I, a grove surrounding an apparently pleasant fountain of covertly malign effect; in II, an arbor sheltering a central seat of which the temptations are obviously malign.

The fact that Spenser disturbed two of these numerical symmetries by changes in the edition of 1596 seems to us of less importance than two other points which we feel have been almost surely demonstrated: his interest in numerical composition was strong enough during the process of original composition for him to have built significant numerical midpoints into all of the Books of the first edition, and the very existence of these midpoints is sufficient evidence that the episodes embodying them are of overriding importance in the Books in which they occur.[20] Analysis of these landmarks can tell much about Spenser's notions of poetic structure and about his general concept of poetic art.

THE FAERIE QUEENE, BOOK III: A GENERAL DESCRIPTION

Harry Berger, Jr.

    The world of Book III is limited in a number of ways. The experience of the important characters is primarily one of inner preparation, and the events of the book for the most part affect essentially isolated or separated creatures. Relationships seem mainly to be those which precede involvement with others at the personal level. The problems of Book III are generic and archetypal—impersonal rather than personal—in the sense that they arise from one's being a masculine or feminine creature rather than a unique individual like Arthur or Britomart. The feminine fears and fantasies which contribute to the power of Busirane are not caused by the particular responses of Amoret or Britomart, but by "wavering wemens wit" in general. They are the products of tendencies inherent in the female psyche and encouraged by the existing climate of custom, institutions, traditions and literature. And finally, the problems posed by the opposition of chastity and eros in III seem to be those which can be resolved by happy sexual union: chastity has little to do with insight and second sight, with knowledge and consideration of the other person (the beloved) as a second self. Chastity no less than eros aims at the moment of embrace exemplified in the rejected first ending of Book III by the hermaphroditic reunion of Amoret and Scudamour, exemplified also by the reconciliation of Cupid and Psyche (male desire and the feminine soul) in the Garden of Adonis "after long troubles and unmeet upbrayes."

    The limited character of this reconciliation is suggested in the fact that the child of Cupid and Psyche is Pleasure, "that doth both gods and men aggrate" by bringing an end to pain. The rewards of chastity for Amoret are the intensity of her relief and the streightness of her fusion with Scudamour, who ran to her

Reprinted from Criticism, Vol. 11 (1969), pp. 234–261, © Wayne State University Press, by permission of the author and the publisher, Wayne State University Press.

> with hasty egernesse,
> Like as a Deare, that greedily embayes
> In the coole soile, after long thirstinesse,
> Which he in chace endured hath, now nigh breathlesse.
>
> Lightly he clipt her twixt his arms twaine,
> And streightly did embrace her body bright,
> Her body, late the prison of sad paine,
> Now the sweet lodge of love and delight:
> But she faire Lady overcommen quight
> Of huge affection, did in pleasure melt,
> No word they spake, nor earthly thing they felt,
> But like two senceles stocks in long embracement dwelt.
>
> (III. xii. 44–45 <u>rej</u>.)

The next stanza, which compares them to a <u>marble statue</u> of the Hermaphrodite, suggests both their desire to freeze eternally into that posture and their urge to melt into unconsciousness. As the goal of a human lover, this happy ending is incomplete and illusory, and it is an example of too violent oscillation: completely separated from and alien to each other in the Busirane experience, they close as if the otherness separating them could be entirely dissolved, and by the mere act of <u>physical</u> embrace. Something like this is implied by the imagery with which Spenser concludes the <u>Hymn of Love</u>. These are Cupid's gifts to chaste and assured lovers:

> There thou them placest in a Paradize
> Of all delight and joyous happie rest,
> Where they doe feede on Nectar heavenly wize,
> With Hercules and Hebe, and the rest
> Of Venus dearlings, through her bountie blest,
> And lie like Gods in yvorie beds arayd,
> With rose and lillies over them displayd.   (280–286)

But the limited nature of this goal is further stressed by the fact that the happy ending of which the stanza is part is forcibly imposed as an artificial conclusion, a false reconciliation following hot on what seems an irreconcileable list of lover's pains:

> The gnawing envie, the hart-fretting feare,
> The vaine surmizes, the distrustfull showes,
> The false reports that flying tales doe beare,

> The doubts, the daungers, the delayes, the woes,
> The fayned friends, the unassured foes,
> With thousands moe than any tongue can tell,
> Doe make a lovers life a wretches hell.
>
> Yet is there one more cursed than they all,
> That cancker worme, that monster Gelosie,
> Which eates the hart, and feedes upon the gall,
> Turning all loves delight to miserie,
> Through feare of loosing his felicitie.
> Ah Gods, that ever ye that monster placed
> In gentle love, that all his joyes defaced.
>
> By these, O Love, thou doest thy entrance make,
> Unto thy heaven, and doest the more endeere,
> Thy pleasures unto those which them partake. . . .
>
> (259–275)

This hate, which in Book III is depicted in the experiences of Malbecco, Scudamour and Busirane, impels the unbalanced psyche too violently in the opposite direction; the triumph of Love over his older half-brother may be too complete unless tempered by Concord.

The general character of Book III is illuminated by C. S. Lewis' insight that Spenser was his predecessor in sketching the history and demise of courtly love. In III, as throughout his poetry, he consciously and conspicuously revises not only a literary and cultural view of love but also a literary and cultural view of woman. The problem he poses for both Britomart and himself is a modified version of the problem confronted by Chaucer's Wife of Bath: how to redress the balance in a culture whose images of woman and love, whose institutions affecting women and love, were products of the male imagination?—

> Here have I cause, in men just blame to find,
>   That in their proper prayse too partiall bee,
>   And not indifferent to woman kind. . . .   (III. ii. 1)
>
> Where is the Antique glory now become,
>   That whilome wont in women to appear?
>   Where be the brave atchievements doen by some?
>   (III. iv. 1)

In his epic as in his minor poetry he sets himself the task of realizing the otherness and complex reality of woman by seeing life from the feminine point of view. The traditional vision of relationship must be transformed into a new and personal vision, and it is entirely in accord with his own conceptions of poetry and love that he displays the act of revision as part of the content of his poem.

The world of Book III is composed of a number of fragmented, partial or elemental landscapes which are not only places in Faerie but also topoi of the collective cultural imagination. As this world reveals only hostile or defective forms of love which must be faced and corrected by Britomart in her search for the real Artegal who will fulfill her visionary (and thus too perfect) image, so the literary traditions available to Spenser offer no forms adequate or suitable to the vision he wishes to actualize in poetry. In redressing the balance, however, he does not simply idealize woman or the feminine viewpoint, for this would amount to the kind of withdrawal from reality which he frequently criticizes. Rather he recognizes that feminine nature has its own inherent limits and tensions, and he therefore acknowledges this by representing feminine defects and excesses. In the Amoretti, for example, he demands active cooperation from his beloved yet this cooperation is slow in forthcoming. If he shows during the sonnet sequence that he stands in need of improvement, and that his lady's reluctance is a means to improvement, he also shows that he cannot do all the work by himself. It is the lady's fault as well as his that plaints, prayers and vows reverberate throughout the first fifty-seven sonnets, and the implication is that her reluctance, protracted beyond reason, comes to be perverse and harmful. The lady must be a lover as well as a beloved. If the poet is to improve his own attitudes and images, she must relent, must share herself, must stamp her true impression on his soul.

The relations and experiences of Book III are those which belong to an early pre-courtship phase. During this period elemental states and figures emerge from a matrix or chaos and move through early confusion toward separation into simple opposites. In this phase eros naturally manifests itself as hate, i.e. martial or erotic aggression—warfare and hostility, the struggle to possess and devour or to break free from possession, the urge to keep one's elemental condition pure and not to mingle or merge with one's opposites except on one's own terms. The natural thrust of the elemental state or figure tends toward a one-sided structure of response which obscures the character of self and world. In this phase it is difficult to acknowledge the right of

others to be different and equal: opposites are not conceived as
genuine others standing over against the self, but as objects which
exist to threaten or gratify the self. The elemental or primitive
consciousness substitutes an image—based on need and desire—
for the real object, and tries then to possess or destroy that object, or to assimilate it by negating its otherness and reducing it
to the desired image. Desire may be indiscriminately aroused by
and directed toward any number of objects as well as different
kinds of objects. The result is often a primitive or regressive
confusion of drives and functions distinct in more developed
stages of experience.

Spenser's frequent references to the antiquity of his story
serve to locate it in the qualitatively "early" or archaic world.
Antiquity is not merely "a long time ago," not merely a way of
defining the imaginary and/or ideal character of the story, but
also a particular primitive phase of psycho-cultural experience.
It is a fictional then which is—or ought to be—different from the
now of poet and reader, even though that "antique" experience
may represent critical aspects of current or universal human
experience. The passages on the antique glory of women quoted
above were presented somewhat misleadingly out of context, for
the contexts suggest that limited opportunities for expression
were then available to women. During the early phase depicted
in III, when eros was manifested primarily as hostility, they were
forced to express themselves on alien grounds and to compete
with men in physical warfare:

> Here have I cause, in men just blame to find,
>> That in their proper prayse too partiall bee,
>> And not indifferent to woman kind,
>> To whom no share in armes and chevalrie
>> They do impart, ne maken memorie
>> Of their brave gestes and prowesse martiall;
>> Scarse do they spare to one or two or three,
>> Rowme in their writs; yet the same writing small
> Does all their deeds deface, and dims their glories all.

> But by record of antique times I find,
>> That women wont in warres to beare most sway,
>> And to all great exploits them selves inclind:
>> Of which they still the girlond bore away,
>> Till envious Men fearing their rules decay,
>> Gan coyne streight lawes to curbe their liberty;

399

> Yet sith they warlike armes have layd away,
>   They have exceld in artes and pollicy,
> That now we foolish men that prayse gin eke t'envy.
>
> Of warlike puissaunce in ages spent,
>   Be thou faire Britomart, whose prayse I write,
> But of all wisedome be thou precedent,
>   O soveraigne Queene, whose prayse I would endite. . . .
>   (ii. 1–3)

As we shall see more fully later, Britomart is not simply the
Ideal Woman; she embodies and is constrained by a certain level
of psycho-cultural organization. Her virtue is not the only virtue
women need: it is fundamental not merely because essential, but
also because rudimentary. Embattled woman, threatened from
within and from the outside, needs this militant virtue if she as
well as her lover is to be fulfilled. But chastity in the service of
love—the chastity of Britomart or Florimell—is presented as an
intuitive rather than an acquired habit; the dangers and frustra-
tions which women face in early experience may intensify this
self-protective response until it becomes irrational, obsessive
and even destructive. By the end of III.iv the problems confronting women have become more oppressive, and the stanzas which
introduce this canto present feminine warfare in a more strident
manner:

> Where is the Antique glory now become,
>   That whilome wont in women to appeare?
> Where be the brave atchievements doen by some?
> Where be the battels, where the shield and speare,
> And all the conquests, which them high did reare,
>   That matter made for famous Poets verse,
>   And boastfull men so oft abasht to heare?
> Bene they all dead, and laid in dolefull herse?
> Or doen they onely sleepe, and shall againe reverse?
>
> If they be dead, then woe is me therefore:
>   But if they sleepe, O let them soone awake:
> For all too long I burne with envy sore,
>   To heare the warlike feates, which Homere spake
> Of bold Penthesilee, which made a lake
> Of Greekish bloud so oft in Troian plaine;
>   But when I read, how stout Debora strake

> Proud Sisera, and how Camill' hath slaine
> The huge Orsilochus, I swell with great disdaine.
>
> Yet these, and all that else had puissaunce,
>   Cannot with noble Britomart compare,
>   As well for glory of great valiaunce,
>   As for pure chastitie and vertue rare,
>   That all her goodly deeds do well declare.
>   Well worthy stock, from which the branches sprong,
>   That in late yeares so faire a blossome bare,
>   As thee, O Queene, the matter of my song,
> Whose lignage from this Lady I derive along.   (iv. 1–3)

The comically exaggerated gestures of the poet, culminating in "I
swell with great disdaine," help define the relation between then
and now: thinking and reading about violent man-killers of old, he
passionately identifies himself with their cause—very much like a
youthful reader of Classic Comics caught up in an outmoded and
outlandish world, taking sides with his stereotyped heroines.
These heroines are immediately passed by in his own revised
version, though Britomart is still an example of that early type.
Insofar as the <u>bold</u> and <u>stout</u> warriors represent chastity it is a
chastity which has nothing to do with love and everything to do
with war—they are at once too masculine in behavior and too misanthropic in feeling. Within the context of Britomart's experience
so excessive a response may be caused by the martial and erotic
aggression of men, or simply by the natural force of her own passion aroused by the image of Artegal. This response appears
as an incipient threat during the early cantos of III, but it does
not become serious until Book V, when it is embodied in its degenerate form as Radegund. Pointedly associated with Artemis
and Belphoebe (see FQ V. v. 2–3 and compare II. iii. 26–27),
Radegund displays the instinctive Belphoeban chastity exacerbated
by frustration (V. iv. 29 ff.) until it has become pathological. Already in Book III Spenser shows how the Perils of Florimell convert her chaste love of Marinell to irrational fear, a fear which
also affects Amoret in Busirane's house, and in the proem to FQ
IV he refers this problem to his virgin Queen:

> To her I sing of love, that loveth best,
> And best is lov'd of all alive I weene:
> To her this song most fitly is addrest,
> The Queene of love, and Prince of peace from heaven blest.

> Which that she may the better deigne to heare,
>   Do thou dred infant, Venus dearling dove,
>   From her high spirit chase imperious feare,
>   And use of awfull Majestie remove:
>   In sted thereof with drops of melting love,
>   Deawd with ambrosiall kisses, by thee gotten
>   From thy sweete smyling mother from above,
>   Sprinckle her heart, and haughtie courage soften,
> That she may hearke to love, and reade this lesson often.
>
> (IV. Pr. 4–5)

The phrasing allows us to read the "use of awfull Majestie" as a defense against love, a defense perhaps prompted by fear which is imperious (and not only by the empress' fear). Though masked in the ceremonial rhetoric demanded by this occasion of address, the context of events preceding the proem in III and following it in IV vaguely associates this fear with chastity as a fixation. Yet as a contemporary figure—"of all wisedome . . . precedent" and not merely "of warlike puissaunce is ages spent"—Elizabeth is exhorted to embody a more evolved and flexible form of psychic organization, to move beyond the "early" structure of habits dominated by chastity toward the complex sophisticated structure dominated by wisdom.

I shall devote the remainder of this essay to a discussion of three leading characteristics displayed by eros in early or primitive psycho-cultural experience: 1) It is a tyrannical and confusing force cutting across such normally distinct forms of affection as those between man and woman, parent and child, friend and friend. 2) It is a pain-giving force felt at first as hate and hostility. 3) It is a regressive force drawing creatures back toward the undifferentiated matrix from which they derive their origins and from which they struggle to emerge.

II

Normal relationships come into focus only gradually, and with difficulty. Thus although Book IV deals with new ("later") levels of organization, new kinds of relations of elements—those involved in personal and social situations—it is not until the opening stanzas of IV. ix that Spenser explicitly voices the sequence of changes with which the poem has been concerned since the beginning of III:

> Hard is the doubt, and difficult to deeme,
>   When all three kinds of love together meet,
>   And doe dispart the hart with powre extreme,
>   Whether shall weigh the balance down; to weet
>   The deare affection unto kindred sweet,
>   Or raging fire of love to woman kind,
>   Or zeale of friends combynd with vertues meet.
>   But of them all the band of vertuous mind
> Me seemes the gentle hart should most assured bind.

> For naturall affection soone doth cesse,
>   And quenched is with Cupids greater flame;
>   But faithfull friendship doth them both suppresse,
>   And them with maystring discipline doth tame,
>   Through thoughts aspyring to eternall fame.

The elemental metaphor (the fire of sexual love quenching the love of kind) separates the first two forms of affection from true friendship, which transcends and redirects them, and which depends on a more mature, a more disciplined, ethical consciousness. A similar movement is implied in the porch of Concord (IV. x. 32–33): Spenser does not name Concord until he has named and characterized Hate and Love. The two half-brothers visualize a more primitive, universal and instinctive pattern of behavior, and they must manifest themselves before Concord can exercise her more strictly human and rational functions of control.

This confusion of drives and functions may be either primitive or regressive, as the following examples will demonstrate: The assault of the woman-eating monster on Florimell, in cantos vii and viii, comprises an unpleasant mixture of the urges to violate, to devour and to destroy. Cymoent's excessive concern for her son Marinell, a concern which effectually cripples him, is more than pure parental affection: it is blurred by overtones of maternal narcissism ("Deare image of my self . . . that is, / The Wretched sonne of wretched mother borne," iv. 36) and also by a vague sense that Cymoent sees in Marinell a surrogate for his father, "the famous Dumarin,"

> who on a day
> Finding the Nymph a sleepe in secret wheare,
> As he by chaunce did wander that same way,
> Was taken with her love, and by her closely lay.

403

> There he this knight of her begot, whom borne
> She of his father Marinell did name,
> And in a rocky cave as wight forlorne,
> Long time she fostred up, till he became
> A mightie man at armes, and mickle fame. . . .
>
> (iv. 19–20)

A similarly blurred situation is hinted at in Spenser's treatment
of Venus and her wanton boy Adonis (i. 34 ff., vi. 46 ff.), and in the
Venus-Cupid relationship which is the paradigm for that between
Cymoent and Marinell (vi. 50); Spenser's associating Cupid with
Adonis (both lost at vi. 28–29 and secure at vi. 49) sharpens our
sense that Venus' possessiveness is not clearly distinguishable
into maternal and erotic affection. When Britomart's nurse,
Glauce, tries to ease her lovelorn charge she displays normal
motherly behavior, yet it is comically qualified by the fact that
we have already seen Britomart in action as a strapping Amazon,
and by two passages of description, in the first of which Spenser
echoes gestures he had attributed to Venus at i, 36:

> And whilst he slept, she over him would spred
> Her mantle, colour'd like the atarry skyes,
> And her soft arme lay underneath his hed,
> And with ambrosiall kisses bathe his eyes. . . .

So Glauce to Britomart, though with somewhat different intentions:

> her twixt her armes twaine
> She straightly straynd, and colled tenderly,
> And every trembling joynt, and every vaine
> She softly felt, and rubbed busily,
> To doe the frosen cold away to fly;
> And her faire deawy eies with kisses deare
> She oft did bath, and oft againe did dry. . . .　　(ii. 34)

> upleaning on her elbow weake,
> Her alablaster brest she soft did kis,
> Which all that while she felt to pant and quake,
> As it an Earth-quake were. . . .　　(ii. 42)

The atmosphere of Book III is saturated with various kinds of
confusion and ambiguity produced by eros in its early or regressive phases. Oceanic and chaotic matrices are ambiguously womb

and tomb, benign and threatening, male and female. Desire is
ambiguously martial and erotic, wounds ambiguously physical and
psychic. At iii. i Spenser distinguishes between noble and base
love, but at the same time, in the cantos surrounding this distinction, he describes Britomart's "sacred fire" for Artegal in terms
which make it identical to the elemental affections "that move / In
brutish minds." The various suitors of the false Florimell are
unwittingly involved in a relation at once auto-erotic and homo-
sexual (viii. 5–8). Proteus' attitude toward Florimell slips from
paternal care to tyrannical lust (viii. 33–42). Malbecco's lust is
directed with equal fervor toward two objects, his gold and his
wife. A final example, which will lead into discussion of the
second aspect of eros: the Squire of Dames and his lady Columbell, whose courtship is turned farcically awry by the double
meaning of service:

> That gentle Lady, whom I love and serve,
> After long suit and weary servicis,
> Did aske me, how I could her love deserve,
> And how she might be sure, that I would never swerve.
>
> I glad by any meanes her grace to gaine,
> Bad her commaund my life to save, or spill.
> Eftsoones she bad me, with incessaunt paine
> To wander through the world abroad at will,
> And every where, where with my power or skill
> I might do service unto gentle Dames,
> That I the same should faithfully fulfill,
> And at the twelve monethes end should bring their names
> And pledges; as the spoiles of my victorious games.
>
> So well I to faire Ladies service did,
> And found such favour in their loving hartes,
> That ere the yeare his course had compassid,
> Three hundred pledges for my good desartes,
> And thrise three hundred thanks for my good partes
> I with me brought, and did to her present:
> Which when she saw, more bent to eke my smartes,
> Then to reward my trusty true intent,
> She gan for me devise a grievous punishment.
>
> To weet, that I my travell should resume,
> And with like labour walke the world around,

Ne ever to her presence should presume,
Till I so many other Dames had found,
The which, for all the suit I could propound,
Would me refuse their pledges to afford,
But did abide for ever chast and sound.   (vii. 53–56)

This presentation is so guarded—on Spenser's part—that it is
impossible to tell whether the Squire misinterpreted his lady's
will, or whether Columbell's charge to him is itself confused by
a morbid and ambivalent set of desires: to test his loyalty ("that
I would never swerve") and his prowess ("how I could her love
deserve"); to protract her own freedom from submission yet tit-
illate her fantasy with vicarious enjoyment of his conquests. We
cannot know whether his "trusty true intent" was fulfilled beyond
or contrary to her expectations or whether his success aroused
anger, jealousy and frustration as the concomitants of her vicarious pleasure. Her name suggests her connection with Venus, and
later, in IV. x, when Spenser has Scudamour describe his conquest
of Amoret, he depicts in greater symbolic detail the virgin's desire to be a priestess of Venus without sacrificing her freedom
or integrity to man's love. Briefly, but densely, Spenser's ambiguous treatment of the Squire's tale reveals the sexes working
at cross-purposes, love as a warfare in which efforts at cooperation and trouthe break down, changing into lust and hate under the
pressures of self-interest.

III

A second leading characteristic of eros in its early phases is
its pain-giving quality. During the initial period of separation or
differentiation, when elements and individuals emerge over against
their environment and each other, when they strive blindly for an
autonomy (or a union) which is absolute, the eros which drives
them is manifested as hate, physical hostility and war. This is the
dominant tonality of the "historical period" in which Britomart
"lived," of the natural and psychic worlds rendered in III, and of
the peculiar sequence of events which gives the book its narrative
shape. I have already suggested the relation of this atmosphere
to the antique image of woman and chastity (p. 236 ff.), and I should
now like to show some of the different ways in which Spenser renders the martial-erotic phase of experience. His basic method is
to ring interesting changes on the manner in which the two sides
of the conventional love-war ambiguity may be related: love as

painful and warlike; the desire to inflict pain and make war as a form of erotic pleasure, either simple or compensatory. This gives point to the stanzas which introduce the third canto:

> Most sacred fire, that burnest mightily
> In living brests, ykindled first above,
> Emongst th' eternall spheres and lamping sky,
> And thence pourd into men, which men call Love;
> Not that same, which doth base affections move
> In brutish minds, and filthy lust inflame,
> But that sweet fit, that doth true beautie love,
> And choseth vertue for his dearest Dame,
> Whence spring all noble deeds and never dying fame:

> Well did Antiquitie a God thee deeme,
> That over mortall minds hast so great might,
> To order them, as best to thee doth seeme,
> And all their actions to direct aright;
> The fatall purpose of divine foresight,
> Thou doest effect in destined descents,
> Through deepe impression of thy secret might,
> And stirredst up th' Heroes high intents,
> Which the late world admyres for wondrous moniments.

> But thy dread darts in none doe triumph more,
> Ne braver proofe in any, of thy powre
> Shew'dst thou, then in this royall Maid of yore,
> Making her seeke an unknowne Paramoure,
> From the worlds end, through many a bitter stowre. . . .

The ambiguity centers not only on the difference between noble and base love, a difference which is not yet discernible and cannot emerge until later and more developed ethical phases of consciousness; it centers also on the relation between loving and fighting. Eros manifests itself in antiquity as high spirit—it is poured into brests and stirs up the high intents of heroes, among whom Britomart is numbered. Its might remains secret until the full dynamic of love is impressed on and partly guided by responsive human consciousness. Then the late world may "look back" on the moniments of early experience, seeing there both monuments of the past and admonitions for the present. The statement that Antiquity named eros a god seems to allude most directly to the Symposium and we may recall that Socrates in that dialogue criticizes the

preceding speakers for misconstruing a state of human consciousness as an objective deity: such a projection permits the soul to
shift responsibility, yet Spenser (like Plato) allows some truth in
the statement since consciousness in its early phases is determined primarily by external influence. The distinction of sources—
what comes from "above" and what from the self—is part of the
secret which cannot be revealed until one arrives at the kind of
retrospective view Spenser is at pains to dramatize in these stanzas. And the fact that "historical retrospect" is itself part of the
fiction is affirmed in the next stanza when he invokes a Clio whose
parents are Memory and Phoebus.

The retrospective view of an ancient warlike environment is
amplified in the treatment of Merlin. Thus Spenser's introductory
account of the conventional Merlin—everybody's Merlin—is amused
and even condescending because it is presented in quotation marks
as an example of the old mythology. We are shown a Merlin produced by the superstitious mind, the popular imagination which
may once have been a fresh and significant cultural force but can
no longer be taken seriously. Glauce and Britomart journey

> To Maridunum, that is now by chaunge
> Of name Cayr-Merdin cald . . .
> There the wise Merlin whylome wont (they say)
> To make his wonne, low underneath the ground,
> In a deepe delve, farre from the vew of day,
> That of no living wight he mote be found,
> Where so he counseld with his sprights encompast round.
>
> (iii. 7)

Spenser could have found the antiquity stressed in Camden who
cites the account given by Giraldus Cambrensis in the twelfth
century, remarking that the original name, Maridunum, was given
by Ptolemy. Here as elsewhere in III the etymological play draws
our attention to the bond between ocean and war, and the sequence
Maridunum—Cayr-Merdin—Merlin allows some of this to rub off
on Merlin; the echoes of dune and care strengthen the ocean-war
reference.

This sophistication is clearly located by Spenser in his own
revised versions of the myth, and separated from the antique
model, which stands beside it in caricature form. As he continues
to parody the tone of the old wives' tale, he adapts the Mage of
early legend more and more to his own themes. The direct address to the reader (the old wife conjuring the child) enforces the

distance between the contemporary folk environment of the speaker and the early world of the story:

> And if thou ever happen that same way
>   To travell, goe to see that dreadful place:
>   It is an hideous hollow cave (they say)
>   Under a rocke that lyes a little space
>   From the swift Barry, tombling downe apace,
>   Emongst the woodie hilles of Dynevowre:
>   But dare thou not, I charge, in any cace,
>   To enter into that same balefull Bowre,
> For fear the cruell Feends should thee unwares devowre.

> But standing high aloft, low lay thine eare,
>   And there such ghastly noise of yron chaines.
>   And brasen Caudrons thou shalt rombling heare,
>   Which thousand sprights with long enduring paines
>   Doe tosse, that it will stonne thy feeble braines,
>   And oftentimes great grones, and grievous stounds,
>   When too huge toile and labour them constraines:
>   And oftentimes loud strokes, and ringing sounds
> From under that deepe Rocke most horribly rebounds.

> The cause some say is this: A little while
>   Before that Merlin dyde, he did intend,
>   A brasen wall in compas to compile
>   About Cairmardin, and did it commend
>   Unto these Sprights, to bring to perfect end.
>   During which worke the Ladie of the Lake,
>   Whom long he lov'd, for him in hast did send,
>   Who thereby forst his workemen to forsake,
> Them bound till his returne, their labour not to slake.

> In the meane time through that false Ladies traine,
>   He was surprisd, and buried under beare,
>   Ne ever to his worke returnd againe:
>   Nath'lesse those feends may not their worke forbeare,
>   So greatly his commaundement they feare,
>   But there doe toyle and travell day and night,
>   Untill that brasen wall they up doe reare:
>   For Merlin had in Magicke more insight,
> Then ever him before or after living wight.

> For he by words could call out of the sky
>> Both Sunne and Moone, and make them him obay:
>> The land to sea, and sea to maineland dry,
>> And darkesome night he eke could turne to day:
>> Huge hostes of men he could alone dismay,
>> And hostes of men of meanest things could frame,
>> When so him list his enimies to fray:
>> That to this day for terror of his fame,
> The feends do quake, when any him to them does name.
>
> (iii. 8—12)

The antics described in the final stanza may, as Todd put it, be "agreeable to the custom of classical magicians" (Var. III. 225), but they also recall the powers Spenser and God gave to Fidelia at I. x. 20, the faith that could command the sun to stop, dismay great hosts of men, walk on water and move mountains to throw themselves into the "raging sea with roaring threat." The point of the echo lies in the difference rather than the similarity of the two passages: the difference between mystical and magical power, between a theological virtue and a legendary Welsh magician, between biblical allusion and what may be a folk distortion or reduction of scripture. The enumeration of Merlin's powers has little to do with his function in Book III, which is limited to prophecy. Rather it seems slanted toward the emphasis on warfare (as its differences from the Fidelia passage suggest) and toward the theme of hostility between sexes: all Merlin's powers were of no avail in his encounter with the Lady of the Lake, for Spenser's Merlin is a victim of the "historical" phase of eros to which he belongs; his fate is not unlike that of other male figures in the first half of III—Adonis, Marinell and Timias.

The same warfare is evident in the genealogy which Spenser has concocted for the present context:

> And sooth, men say that he was not the sonne
>> Of mortall Syre, or other living wight,
>> But wondrously begotten, and begonne
>> By false illusion of a guilefull Spright,
>> On a fare Ladie Nonne, that whilome hight
>> Matilda, daughter to Pubidius,
>> Who was the Lord of Mathravall by right,
>> And coosen unto king Ambrosius:
> Whence he indued was with skill so marvellous.　　(iii. 13)

The names seem to allow translations which are thematically appropriate: War-maiden, daughter of Youth (Puberty), lord of War-Tangle, kin to Immortal. There is again an apparent distorted echo of Christian myth and a direct reference to this phase of eros: the chaste maiden withdrawing from war to the nunnery during a "youthful" period of psycho-history when opposites are at war; the possibility of love only through force or deceit.

Merlin's relation to martial eros had been suggested in the second canto when Spenser introduced the magic mirror through whose agency Britomart fell in love, "as it in bookes hath written bene of old":

> In Deheubarth that now South-Wales is hight,
> What time king Ryence raign'd, and dealed right,
> The great Magitian Merlin had deviz'd,
> By his deepe science, and hell-dreaded might,
> A looking glasse, right wondrously aguiz'd,
> Whose vertues through the wyde world soone were solemniz'd.

> It vertue had, to shew in perfect sight,
> What ever thing was in the world contaynd,
> Betwixt the lowest earth and heavens hight,
> So that it to the looker appertaynd;
> What ever foe had wrought, or frend had faynd,
> Therein discovered was, ne ought mote pas,
> Ne ought in secret from the same remaynd;
> For thy it round and hollow shaped was,
> Like to the world it selfe, and seem'd a world of glas.

> Who wonders not, that reades so wonderous worke?
> But who does wonder, that has red the Towre,
> Wherein th'Ægyptian Phao long did lurke
> From all men's vew, that none might her discoure,
> Yet she might all men vew out of her bowre?
> Great Ptolomæe it for his lemans sake
> Ybuilded all of glasse, by Magicke powre,
> And also it impregnable did make;
> Yet when his love was false, he with a peaze it brake.

> Such was the glassie globe that Merlin made,
> And gave unto king Ryence for his gard,
> That never foes his kingdome might invade,

> But he it knew at home before he hard
> Tydings thereof, and so them still debar'd.   (ii. 18—21)

Again, the battle between the sexes; the one-sided and narcissis-
tic eros of the woman who withdraws like Malecasta's Venus to
feed her fantasy in furtive security (hence the voyeurism, which
keeps its objects at eyebeam distance, and hence the name Phao);
the vain wish-fulfilling attempt at total maistrie through magic
rather than through the more difficult human efforts to sustain
relationship; the reference to "ancient Britain" as wartorn and
treacherous—even friends faynd—and the appeal to magic to cope
with violence or guile.

"Get thee to a nunnery": Hamlet's extremes, whorehouse or
convent, aggressive lust or militant chastity, are feasible alternatives in a world dominated by Mars and mare. Spenser depicts
an atmosphere of elemental strife in which, to use Glauce's
words, "all Britanie doth burne in armes bright" (iii. 52). Uther
is fighting "the Paynim brethren, hight / Octa and Oza," Angela
and her Saxons are fighting the Britons, Christians are in conflict with pagans, native tribes with foreign tribes, women with
men. Glauce warns Britomart that if she is to seek her beloved
in relative security she must become a Matilda and cope with
men as a man:

> That therefore nought our passage may empeach,
>   Let us in feigned armes our selves disguize,
>   And our weake hands (whom need new strength shall teach)
> The dreadfull speare and shield to exercize:
> Ne certes daughter that same warlike wize
> I weene, would you misseeme; for ye bene tall,
> And large of limbe, t'atchieve an hard emprize,
> Ne ought ye want, but skill, which practize small
> Will bring, and shortly make you a mayd Martiall.

> And sooth, it ought your courage much inflame,
>   To heare so often, in that royall hous,
>   From whence to none inferious ye came,
> Bards tell of many women valorous
> Which have full many feats adventurous
> Performd, in paragone of proudest men:
> The bold Bunduca, whose victorious
> Exploits made Rome to quake, stout Guendolen,
> Renowmed Martia, and redoubted Emmilen.   (iii. 53—54)

This accords with the views expressed in the opening stanzas of cantos ii and iv in which women are praised not for feminine virtues but for being killers, conquerors or emulators of men. Glauce urges Britomart to arm for aggression and "greedy hardiment" rather than for love, and at iii. 57 Britomart responds in kind:

> Her harty words so deepe into the mynd
>> Of the young Damzell sunke, that great desire
>> Of warlike armes in her forthwith they tynd,
>> And generous stout courage did inspire,
>> That she resolv'd, unweeting to her Sire,
>> Advent'rous knighthood on her selfe to don,
>> And counseld with her Nourse, her Maides attire
>> To turne into a massy habergeon. . . .

In the ambiguous climate of Book III, this martial motive immediately fuses with Britomart's erotic pain, as her encounter with Marinell reveals:

> Her dolour soone she ceast, and on her dight
> Her Helmet, to her Courser mounting light:
> Her former sorrow into suddein wrath,
> Both coosen passions of distroubled spright,
> Converting, forth she beates the dustie path;
> Love and despight attonce her courage kindled hath.

> As when a foggy mist hath overcast
>> The face of heaven, and the cleare aire engrost,
>> The world in darkenesse dwels, till that at last
>> The watry Southwinde from the seabord cost
>> Upblowing, doth disperse the vapour lo'st,
>> And poures it selfe forth in a stormy showre;
>> So the faire Britomart having disclo'st
>> Her clowdy care into a wrathfull stowre,
> The mist of griefe dissolv'd, did into vengeance powre.
>>> (iv. 12–13)

She protects herself against aggressive male warfare by wearing armor, against aggressive male passion by wearing disguise, and against the assaults of eros within by using the forms of male aggressiveness as an outlet. I think it likely that Spenser means to present Britomart as too fierce and aggressive; here her effort to project her frustration into warfare and get rid of it may possibly be an effort at too violent and quick relief. The episode follows Britomart's allegorical complaint to ocean, and this, together with the simile in stanza 13 above, contributes to the ambiguous climate which characterizes early experience: psyche is scarcely separable from nature, inscape from landscape; since ocean momentarily condenses into the figure of Marinell, it stands indifferently for male and female eros, and this is so because it embodies both human and cosmic eros. The model for Britomart's inner turmoil as for her head-on fight with Marinell is the warfare of elements. Therefore if we are asked to be somewhat critical of Britomart's masculine aggressiveness, we are also given reason to sympathize with her predicament: it is forced on her by the behavior of man in this phase of experience, by the strife of opposites, by the blind thrust of self-enclosed wills seeking to protect or ease themselves in action which is violent, immediate and physical. It is not yet the time for woman to express herself as woman. For the nonce she must abjure feminine behavior and play the game a man's way.

The extreme instance of woman asserting autonomy by playing the man's role occurs significantly at the very beginning of III: in the name Malecasta we hear not only unchastity and an echo of evil castle but also an echo of male castle. This is a man's, not a woman's image of the ideal courtly life for women—i.e., if a man were to envisage the kind of courtly pleasure he should like to have as a woman, this would be it. The figure of the master-woman (mi dons) presiding over her court of love projects the one-sided culture, dominated by male imagination, which Spenser is about to revise. Spenser recalls this culture by having Britomart paraphrase Chaucer's Franklin:

> Ne may love be compeld by maisterie;
> For soone as maisterie comes, sweet love anone
> Taketh his nimble wings, and soone away is gone.   (i. 25)

Woman as master of man is the perverted form of the ideal to be exemplified by Britomart, woman as equal and companion of man. In Malecasta's fantasy world, men have no choice:

> every knight, which doth this way repaire,
> In case he have no Ladie, nor no love,
> Shall doe unto her service never to remove.

414

But if he have a Ladie or a Love,
   Then must he her forgoe with foule defame,
   Or else with us by dint of sword approve,
   That she is fairer, then our fairest Dame,
   As did this knight, before ye hither came.
   Perdie (said Britomart) the choise is hard:
   But what reward had he, that overcame?
   He should advaunced be to high regard,
(Said they) and have our Ladies love for his reward
                                 (i. 26–27)

The first of them by name Gardante hight,
   A jolly person, and of comely vew;
   The second was Parlante, a bold knight,
   And next to him Jocante did ensew;
   Basciante did him selfe most curteous shew;
   But fierce Bacchante seemd too fell and keene;
   And yet in armes Noctante greater grew:
   All were faire knights, and goodly well beseene,
But to faire Britomart they all but shadowes beene.   (i. 44)

These shadows are intended to guarantee the master woman a controlled pattern of ritual foreplay which delays and thus intensifies her pleasure. Her castle is "plaste for pleasure" near a forest "whose hideous horror and sad trembling sound / Full griesly seem'd," and in which no living creatures were found "Save Beares, Lions, and Buls, which romed them around" (i. 14). It is from this forest that Florimell first appears, fleeing in full career from its human embodiment, the "griesly Foster . . . / Breathing out beastly lust" (i. 17). Spenser's transition from the fearful Florimell, helpless in a world of savage male lust, to Malecasta's efforts at mastery, represents a violent swing of the pendulum: the insecurity and hysterical fear of Florimell may be seen as causally related to Malecasta's equally hysterical drive toward control, domination (daunger in the male sense) and total pleasure. The castle is in this sense protective, but it is also a lure and a trap: "faire before the gate a spatious plaine, / Mantled with greene, it selfe did spredden wyde" (i. 20). She wants what Florimell flees from, but domesticated, refined and submissive to her whim. It is between the extremes of Malecasta and Florimell that Britomart, who has a Florimell within, must locate her course.

IV

The third characteristic of eros appears in the backward or downward pull exerted by the matrix or chaos on figures struggling to emerge and break free. We see this most clearly in the relation of Cymoent to Marinell: the mother will not let her son go, and his defeat by Britomart in effect sends him back to the womb for a second chance. A similar influence is exerted by the witch on her son (III. vii–viii) and by Venus. The backward pull may manifest itself as an urge to escape from life's difficulties and limitations, a longing to return to the paradisaic or womb-like situation from which one was ejected. This is represented briefly and at the most general level in the early stanzas describing the Garden of Adonis, where the emphasis is not on departure, but on the return to the ideal mythic place of origins:

> double gates it had, which opened wide,
> By which both in and out men moten pas;
> Th'one faire and fresh, the other old and dride:
> Old Genius the porter of them was,
> Old Genius, the which a double nature has.
>
> He letteth in, he letteth out to wend,
> All that to come into the world desire;
> A thousand thousand naked babes attend
> About him day and night, which doe require,
> That he with fleshly weedes would them attire:
> Such as him list, such as eternall fate
> Ordained hath, he clothes with sinfull mire,
> And sendeth forth to live in mortall state,
> Till they againe returne backe by the hinder gate.
>
> After that they againe returned beene,
> They in that Gardin planted be againe;
> And grow afresh, as they had never seene
> Fleshly corruption, nor mortall paine.
> Some thousand yeares so doen they there remaine;
> And then of him are clad with other hew,
> Or sent into the chaungefull world againe,
> Till thither they returne, where first they grew:
> So like a wheele around they runne from old to new.

> Ne needs there Gardiner to set, or sow,
>   To plant or prune: for of their owne accord
>   All things, as they created were, doe grow. . . .
>
> (vi. 31—34)

A different but related form of this attraction is embodied in
Argante and Ollyphant, the monstrous brother and sister who,
"whiles in their mothers wombe enclosd they were . . . in fleshly lust were mingled":

> So liv'd they ever after in like sin,
>   Gainst natures law, and good behavioure:
>   But greatest shame was to that maiden twin,
>   Who not content so fowly to devoure
>   Her native flesh, and staine her brothers bowre,
>   Did wallow in all other fleshly myre,
>   And suffred beasts her body to deflowre:
>   So whot she burned in that lustfull fyre,
> Yet all that might not slake her sensuall desyre.
>
> But over all the countrey she did raunge,
>   To seeke young men, to quench her flaming thrust,
>   And feed her fancy with delightfull chaunge. . . .
>
> (vii. 48—50)

Thus they pass their lives compulsively repeating, trying to recover and perpetuate their prenatal pleasure. In contrast to this
is the separation and development of another set of twins: The
complex and dialectically articulated structures of response embodied in Belphoebe and Amoret are shown to emerge from a
simpler more incomplete matrix in the golden birth produced by
the juncture of pure opposites—the nymph Chrysogone and the
sun, water and fire, passive and active, the too helpless feminine
and the too potent masculine principles. Chrysogone is the
daughter of an even vaguer figure, only a name—Amphisa, which
means, among other things, undifferentiated (both the same).
That the twins are fostered by Venus and Diana adds another
dimension to the developmental aspect of the myth, especially
since the portraits of Venus and Diana in III. vi represent them as
stock literary figures, the conventionally opposed feminine responses to eros. The traditional view of the feminine psyche

417

based on the Venus-Diana model is simplistic and inadequate, a one-sided masculine caricature. A psyche composed of—or rather divided by—two such exclusive and antipathetic dispositions is not open to the kind of relationship Spenser envisages as married love. His solution is to revise and complicate the traditional male view of woman, and the myth in III. vi is central to this revision. Each twin contains and is partly determined by a differently inflected mixture of Venerean and Artemisian elements. Together with Florimell, the twins are infolded into the more complete image of the feminine psyche of which Britomart is the exemplar in the Faerie Queene. Thus there are two quite different—yet interrelated—lines of development: the development of the feminine psyche from early phases which may be thought of as mythic or archetypal (female rather than feminine), and which are inadequate—too "close to nature"—for the complexities of human experience; and the development of man's image of woman from the traditionally limited views to the Spenserian revision which more fully respects the complexities of human experience. Spenser presupposes not only a matrix of "nature" but also a matrix of convention.

The primal matrix is variously represented in Book III by Ocean, Night, caves, the Chaos under the Garden of Adonis, Chrysogone, Venus as Great Mother, Cymoent and Glauce. The latter, as her name suggests, embodies the ambiguous blue or green or gray of ocean, the undisciplined lore of old wives' experience. Benign but rude, she understands Britomart's predicament and moves her to do something about it, but she does not know how or in what direction to guide her. She simply turns Britomart round and round trying, in a parody of superstitious incantation, "to undoe her daughters love" (ii. 51), and this turning also symbolizes the treadmill repetition of life lived close to its origins in chaos or ocean. To approach the ocean, or return to it, or be driven into it symbolizes a jeopardy which may come from within the self, or from outside it, or both. Britomart, Florimell, Marinell, the old fisherman and Malbecco: in various degrees all come close to dissolution of the complex self; overwhelmed by erotic force (either as hate or as love) all are threatened with submission to a single compulsive urge. This singleness, being primitive, is ambiguous, a blurred mixture of different passions and motives: desire, fear, hate, jealousy, despair.

The pattern of return is schematically suggested in the figure of the earthly peer Dumarin, who fulfills his name by his casual undine encounter with Cymoent in which, as Spenser is careful to

phrase it, he "was taken with her love." Later, the oceanic state
is metaphorically applied to Paridell, whose ancestor Parius
sailed to the isle of Paros,

> which before
> Hight Nausa, there he many yeares did raine,
> And built Nausicle by the Pontick shore,
> The which he dying left next in remaine
> To Paridas his sonne.
> From whom I Paridell by kin descend;
> But for faire Ladies love, and glories gaine,
> My native soil have left, my dayes to spend
> In sewing deeds of armes, my lives and labours end.
>
> (ix. 37)

Like the old fisherman, Paridell is unwittingly out of control, in
effect a floating island (named Ship) spending his days and ending
his life and labor asea. He and his partner Hellenore (Helen-
whore, Helen-over-again) are lesser versions of Paris and Helen.
Effectually tyrannized by their ancient literary prototypes, they
can only repeat over and over again what those lovers did. And
where the original act had tragic and historical consequences,
Paris' idell descendant has withdrawn from history to Faerie, to
the unending repetition of the waves of love and war (love as war
and war as love) which encompass him. Like Florimell, though
without any consciousness of the fact, he dramatically embodies
the condition described by Britomart in her complaint:

> Huge sea of sorrow, and tempestuous grief,
> Wherein my feeble barke is tossed long,
> Far from the hoped haven of reliefe,
> Why do thy cruell billowes beat so strong,
> And thy moyst mountaines each on others throng,
> Threatning to swallow up my fearefull life?
> O do thy cruell wrath and spightfull wrong
> At length allay, and stint thy stormy strife,
> Which in these troubled bowels raignes, and rageth rife.
>
> For else my feeble vessell crazd, and crackt
> Through thy strong buffets and outrageous blowes,
> Cannot endure, but needs it must be wrackt
> On the rough rocks, or on the sandy shallowes,
> The whiles that love it steres, and fortune rowes;

> Love my lewd Pilot hath a restless mind
> And fortune Boteswaine no assuraunce knowes,
> But saile withouten starres gainst tide and wind:
> How can they other do, sith both are bold and blind?
>
> (iv. 8–9)

Paridell and Hellenore represent a psychic and cultural dead end,
a kind of genealogical blind alley, a one-way tendency toward
death and chaos which can never be reversed but can never be
resolved. The simile Spenser applies to him when he is unhorsed
by Britomart (ix. 15) encapsulates his condition:

> Tho hastily remounting to his steed,
> He forth issew'd; like as a boistrous wind,
> Which in th'earthes hollow caves hath long bin hid,
> And shut up fast within her prisons blind,
> Makes the huge element against her kind
> To move, and tremble as it were agast,
> Untill that it an issew forth may find;
> Then forth it breakes, and with his furious blast
> Confounds both land and seas, and skyes doth overcast.

The tyranny of the primordial archetype and its antihistorical
recurrence is manifested in a variety of ways in III. One of the
more obvious manifestations is the salient recurrence of archetypal figures: the wizards, magicians (Merlin, Proteus, Busirane)
and other more pathetic old men (the fishermen, Malbecco); the
mothers; the sacrificial Adonis figures (Marinell, Timias, Adonis);
the virgins, temptresses, monsters, prisoners and lechers.
Though individual archetypal figures differ from each other—often
in significant and contrastive ways—their generic qualities are
primary, and the result is that as we move through Book III we
seem to encounter recurrent examples of a few archetypes varied
by the pressures of new and changing contexts. This effect is
reinforced by a patterned recurrence of symbolic landscapes (in
cantos i–vi, forest-castles-ocean-forest-garden, and in vii–xii,
forest-ocean-castle-forest-ocean-forest-castle), and by an
Ariostan plot treatment which dissipates the force of chronological happening. The sequence of events is displaced by the sequence of cantos, of imagistic and symbolic patterns, and of significant juxtapositions which produce contrast and parallel rather
than straight narrative development. In Cantos ii–iii and vi Spenser flashes back to the geneses of Britomart's love and Chryso-

gone's daughters, while the plot line is further dislocated by the
temporal obscurity of the Britomart-Marinell and Florimell-Marinell stories. Added to the recurrence of archetypal figures are
the repeated narrative motifs (e.g., the rhythmic alternations of
pursuit and flight) and the increasingly frequent return of night
(i. 57, ii. 28, iv. 52, viii. 51, x. 12, x. 46, xi. 55, xii. 29). Most of the
action during cantos ix–xii is nocturnal, and the particular qualities which Spenser rhetorically assigns to night are those which
associate it with chaos and ocean or water (the humid element
whose psychic and organic functions relate to the lower urges—
desire and lust—and basic processes—generation, sleep, death),
e.g.:

> By this th'eternall lampes, wherewith high Jove
> Doth light the lower world, were halfe yspent,
> And the moist daughters of huge Atlas strove
> Into the Ocean deepe to drive their weary drove.   (i. 57)

> Now whenas all the world in silence deepe
> Yshrowded was, and every mortall wight
> Was drowned in the depth of deadly sleepe. . . .   (i. 59)

> All suddenly dim woxe the dampish ayre,
> And griesly shadowes covered heaven bright. . . .(iv. 52)

> Now gan the humid vapour shed the ground
> With perly deaw, and th'Earthes gloomy shade
> Did dim the brightnesse of the welkin round,
> That every bird and beast awarned made,
> To shrowd themselves, whiles sleepe their senses did
>   invade.   (x. 46)

> chearelesse Night ycovered had
> Faire heaven with an universall cloud. . . .   (xii. 1)

Night periodically inundates the world and soul, bringing with it a
threat of the restoration of its ancient domain, strengthening all
those elemental impulses which waking reason must coordinate
and control.

The primacy of night during the last four cantos contributes to
a larger pattern of regression and decline, a pattern in which
Spenser parades before us—in all their ugliness and absurd inadequacy—one after another conventional model of love: the

fabliau triangle in which Malbecco and Hellenore replay January and May while Paridell replays the courtly adulterer; the frustrated and helpless lover wallowing narcissistically in his misery (Scudamour); the Ovidian lovers in Busirane's tapestry and the Petrarchan sonnet figures in his masque. These episodes do more than merely allude to traditional literary genres and cultural institutions; they dramatize and exemplify them. Spenser presents them as flat, artificial and archaic—not only cliché and perverse but also simplistic. They actualize one-sided masculine conceptions of love which Spenser and Britomart encounter and render obsolete. This atmosphere of literary artifice is conflated with a resurgence of elemental and inorganic imagery, one example of which has already been described above (p. 255 ff) in the figure of Paridell. Another is provided by Malbecco, victim of a single obsessive humor and the literary stereotype based on that humor. Still others appear in the outbursts of fire, gold and air which punctuate Britomart's adventure at Busirane's house:

> . . . in the Porch, that did them sore amate,
> A flaming fire, ymixt with smouldry smoke,
> And stinking Sulphure, that with griesly hate
> And dreadfull horrour did all entrance choke. . . . (xi. 21)

> . . . with pure gold it all was overlayd,
> Wrought with wild Antickes, which their follies playd,
> In the rich metall, as they living were:
> A thousand monstrous formes therein were made,
> Such as false love doth oft upon him weare. . . .   (xi. 51)

>   an hideous storme of winde arose,
> With dreadfull thunder and lightning atwixt,
> And an earth-quake, as if it streight would lose
> The worlds foundations from his centre fixt;
> A direfull stench of smoke and sulphure mixt
> Ensewd. . . .   (xii. 2)

As the language of the second passage makes clear, these wild antickes, foolish and archaic, do not emerge from but are imposed on the material; they are the forms created by a mind fundamentally out of control. Erotic uncontrol and esthetic control, chaos and art, primitive ends and over-refined means, converge in Busirane's decadence. Spurred to revenge by pain and jealousy, the attempts at maistrie—the Busy-reign—of the male imagination become frenetic as the feminine will recoils in ever greater panic (Amoret and "wavering wemens wit"), and the orderly masque degenerates into a "rude confused rout / Of persons . . . whose names is hard to read" (xii. 25).

Thus there is a return to a new and more sinister level of chaos as the recently distinguished sets of contraries fail in the mutual task of upholding each other. Obsessively caught in relationships of increasing repulsion, the opposites collapse, reviving or sinking back into polymorphous disorder. The last six cantos of Book III, in its thematic and narrative movements from the failure of the witch's pathetic son and diseased monster to the triumph of False Florimell, from the helplessness of Malbecco to the "power" of Busirane—these cantos trace a single psychic pattern: The first response of the thwarted psyche is violence, rape, intensified fury. When this fails, when the true object is totally beyond attainment, the second attempt at gratification is withdrawal into—or substitution by—magic or art. The emphasis throughout Book III on riches, hoarding, sumptuous interiors and artifacts in connected to this failure. Those who are frustrated in their misguided efforts to gain total power and pleasure are much occupied with wealth and lavish living—Malecasta, Malbecco, Busirane, the creators and lovers of False Florimell. Precious elements may be more easily obtained and shaped to their owner's whim than may women, who are alive and conscious and have wills of their own. Having material possessions is a one-way relation in which the self may fulfill itself with minimal resistance from the objects of desire. As Spenser shows in the instance of Marinell, hoarding has something in common with fighting, in which people are controlled by being reduced to corpses: both are safer than loving insofar as they free the self from the bother of personal relationships. Thus wealth is only ironically a symbol of power; it is actually a symbol of failure in the normal sphere of "adult" and personal relations. It marks a revival of autistic impulses directed toward a world of inorganic objects which may be safely vivified by projection. The False Florimell reveals how attitudes toward women are modelled after the attitudes toward dead Things. She is a magico-mechanical robot made to the specifications of the sonneteer's ideal and operated by an evil spirit (viii. 5–7): the witch "in the stead / Of life, . . . put a Spright to rule the carkasse dead." The operator is a male demon, for men know best what pleases men in feminine behavior. But the creatrix is female, for women collaborate in this perversion which allows men to fulfill the desire to possess women who are basically male, who have no independence or otherness, who are therefore totally controllable machines of stimulation and pleasure. The enemy is everything in feminine nature which makes woman more than this. Book III thus ends with the absolute and mutual aversion of the two contraries—male and female—which have emerged from the matrix of the pre-human, the pre-sexual, the pre-rational. These contraries are centered in the Garden of Adonis and the House of Busirane. Each asserts wholly different claims, each wants to be the whole, yet each betrays its lack of self-sufficiency.

Book III has therefore traced a process of distinction which has become too radical. Book IV will deal with new efforts and problems of getting-together under the aspect of Concord. But the paradox of III is that the mutual hostility and aversion of opposites is a by-product of the mutual urge toward union. Again and again Spenser presents examples of one-sided and premature union, development or fulfillment which must be obstructed or destroyed so that they may be repeated in more adequate form at a later more appropriate phase of relationship: poet and lady in Amoretti / Epithalamion; the recreative shepherds in the Shepherd's Calendar; Clarion in Muiopotmos; Redcross and Una, Britomart and Artegal, Marinell and Florimell, Scudamour and Amoret. This motif is a special case of a more general category in which a first or instinctive form of behavior must be experienced, felt as insufficient, corrected and revised. The second chance occurs at a later time, a more sophisticated or complex phase of a poem, or a career, or a relationship, or a culture. This is the Hegelian dynamic of sublation (aufheben): the new context and usage confer on earlier simpler forms a destiny more inclusive than their own, a more universal and organic function, so that they may transcend themselves in a manner not possible to them in their first isolated thrust toward fulfillment.

THE DRAGON'S SPARK AND STING AND THE STRUCTURE OF RED CROSS'S DRAGON-FIGHT: THE FAERIE QUEENE, I.xi–xii

Carol V. Kaske

The structure of Red Cross's climactic battle with the dragon in The Faerie Queene, I. xi–xii has never, to my knowledge, received any explanation beyond the inevitable association of its three days with those of Christ's death and resurrection—which itself raises several familiar problems. What has been explained in the episode is Red Cross's advances and reinforcements: Red Cross's ultimate victory typifies a temporal victory or victories of Christ over Satan, particularly Christ's Harrowing of Hell; and the succouring Well and Tree symbolize among other things the aid of baptism and Holy Communion in the psychomachia of an Everyman.[1] But even here, the question of how the Christian Red Cross can lack baptism and receive it only after the first day is but the greatest of several problems which this otherwise convincing interpretation leaves unsolved. In addition Red Cross suffers, among several setbacks, two major ones to which no particular meaning has ever been assigned: on the first day, a spark accompanying a cry of frustration from the dragon unluckily finds its way to the knight's beard, burns him both directly and by heating his armor, and finally brings on his slapstick tumble into the Well of Life, thus defeating him for the first round (26–8); on the second day, the dragon impales him on his scorpion-like tail, which Red Cross manages to sever but not extract; in a similar exchange, the dragon then leaves a claw in his shield (37–48). Almost every comment on such setbacks has so far had to admit that they are in one sense or another anticlimactic—perhaps to a fault, in that, if they have no spiritual meaning, they are perfunctory since the battle is long and Red Cross's victory inevitable, but if they represent spiritual backsliding, they are destructive of any progression one might expect to see in Red Cross's character.[2]

Reprinted from Studies in Philology, Vol. 66 (1969), pp. 609–638, with corrections by the author, by permission of the author and the publisher, the University of North Carolina Press.

What defects, of any spiritual import, could remain in a knight who has long possessed "the armour of a Christian man specified by Saint Paul vi. Ephes." (Letter to Ralegh) and who has recently graduated from the House of Holiness? One defect that is ineradicable, according to Christian moralists from St. Paul to Richard Hooker, is "concupiscence" or "lust"—comprising both those involuntary impulses ("first motions") and that general proneness toward sin ("corruption of nature," or the fomes peccati) springing inevitably from the corrupted bodies we all inherit from Adam In itself a small sin or only a temptation, but the beginning of full-fledged willful sins, concupiscence could be symbolized appropriately by a spark or a sting, and indeed we shall find that the fomes underlies them both. The fact that some sin or other remains inevitably in every Christian is explained by Luther in his popular commentary on Galatians in images of fire catching and of a severed serpent: "Albeit then that the Galathians were lightned and did beleve, and had now receaved the holy Ghost by the preaching of faith, notwithstanding this remnant of vice (this foolishness I meane) and the original corruption [Latin fomes] which afterward did easily burst out in to the flame of false doctrine, remained in them still. . . . In deede many things are purged in us, and principally the head of the Serpent, that is to say, infidelitie and ignorance of God is cutte of and brused, but the slime [Latin squamosum corpus] and the relikes of sinne remaine still in us."[3]

Spenser's curious detail of the beard in which the spark catches (I. xi. 26. 4)—not previously traced to any source and possessing in itself no very relevant conventional associations—simply dramatizes tinder, the literal meaning of Latin fomes. The resulting flame would then represent the first motions; Peter Martyr, one of the guiding spirits of the English Reformation, adapts the similar biblical proverb "Can a man take fire in his bosome, and his clothes not be burnt?" to a description of concupiscence. The whole incident of the spark seems to be a development of the universal metaphor of sin as fire. An anonymous Allegoriae (printed c. 1520, c. 1550, and in 1574) employs the images of spark, tinder (fomes), flame, and conflagration for the devil's procedural steps in any temptation (any temptation, be it noted for future reference, except that of Christ, who was free from corruption): "Cum ergo callidus tentator et malignus insidiator intus aliquem scintillulae fomitem signo quolibet deprehendit, . . . paleas undique cogit concupiscentiae quas comperit aptas; quatinus si praevalet de scintilla flammam excutiat, et domum pectoris nostri, de nostro simul et suo, comburat."[4] A beard also of course looks and feels like tinder; moreover, it resembles its theological namesake. The fomes is "the mere ablenes, proanesse, and readie disposition unto ill dooing" (CP 2, 219b) which remains beneath the ebb and flow of concupiscent desires (first motions), just as Red Cross's having something so combustible as a beard about him underlies his getting burned. Regeneration can mitigate or help to control the fomes, but not eradicate it; so a beard can be cut back but not eradicated. As a corruption inherent only since the Fall, the fomes is de nostro yet not precisely of our essence, just as a beard is both natural and yet something of an excrescence. The beard as symbol, then, expresses the origin of the fomes and its precise degree of responsibility for sin; we shall see that the image of the severed serpent, while less precise, dramatizes measures for its control.

Luther portrays the fomes as a cut-off serpent somehow remaining even in a Christian; Spenser attaches the serpent to the Christian by a scorpion-like sting which carries concentric but wider meanings. Peter Martyr compares this proneness toward sin to the sting carried by a scorpion (CP 2, 219b); and stings, especially of a scorpion, are widely associated with concupiscence or lust in its ordinary, sexual sense.[5] The sting evokes two famous biblical passages on concupiscence, by way of the word stimulus, one of its Latin equivalents. Stimulus is the word used for St. Paul's well-known "thorn in the flesh" (stimulus carni meae) in the Vulgate and Tremellius versions of II Cor. 12. 7: Et ne extollerer propter excellentiam revelationum, traditus est mihi stimulus carni meae, angelus Satanae, ut colaphis caederet me, ne extollerer" (Tremellius).[6] This "thorn in the flesh" is often interpreted as concupiscence, perhaps most suggestively for Spenser by the gloss of the Geneva Bible, the ordinary Bible of the Elizabethan layman: "He meaneth concupiscence, that sticketh fast in us, as it were a pricke, in so much as it constrained Paul himselfe being regenerate, to crye out, I doo not that good that I would, etc. [Rom. 7. 19]." The fact that St. Paul is the victim, the gloss says earlier, illustrates that "God will have even his best servants to be vexed of Satan." In this same manner, the dragon's sting "fast . . . stucke, ne would there out be got" (I. xi. 38. 7)[7] in God's good servant Red Cross. For an education in virtue to end by uncovering the fomes, then, either as beard or as sting, is an anticlimax which does not in itself deny previous moral progress in the hero[8] or raise problems for the reader.

A "mortall sting" like that in the tail of a scorpion is interpreted as a metaphor for concupiscence in another Pauline passage. After the famous question, "O death, where is thy sting?" (stimulus), Paul adds, "The sting of death is sinne, and the strength of sinne is the Lawe" (I Cor. 15. 55–6). Augustine compares this sting to that of a scorpion; and he identifies the sin as concupiscence, because according to Rom. 7. 8, concupiscence is aggravated by law.[9] The fact that the sting sticks in the hero instead of being destroyed by him as the sting of death is by Christ, brackets the general correspondences with this passage as ironical but prophetic; Red Cross so far is not Christ, but we are led to anticipate a Christ.

Red Cross's counterattack is paralleled in both Luther and Martyr by the measures whereby a Christian can at least control though not eradicate concupiscence: "Moreover, [in regeneration] the spirit is given, wherewith the strength of concupiscence maie be broken; that although it doo sticke within us, yet that it shall not reigne over us; for to this end Paule exhorteth us, when he saith: 'Let not sinne reigne in your mortall bodies' " (CP 2, 222a, citing Rom. 6. 12; see also 272; Luther, ibid.). Just so, although the sting is "fast stuck," Red Cross, having been "baptized" and regenerated the previous night in the Well of Life (36. 4; 34. 9), manages to break its strength—that is, to sever it from the dragon's tail—by his "sword of the Spirit" (I. xi. 39. 6–9, cf. Ephes. 6, the chapter cited in the Letter to Ralegh, verse 17). He thus prevents it from "reigning over" him (i.e., he does not consent but resists, CP 2, 272b) as it certainly would have if it had kept him impaled on the dragon's tail. As a result, the sting is not so decisive a setback as, for example, the spark was on the day before. In fact, his good recovery belittles his subsequent fall: whereas at the end of the first day, the knight was "overthrowen" (30. 9), here he resists the dragon in all but being "forst . . . to retire / A little backward for his best defence" (45); his eventual fall is compassed only with the co-operation of other, natural factors (45. 7–8). If my interpretation so far is correct, the portentously specific "five joynts" of the dragon's tail left attached to the sting and hence to Red Cross would appropriately represent what indeed they inevitably suggest: man's five senses as the points of his contact with sin, somewhat as they are portrayed in the Castle of Alma (II. xi. 7–13).

The dragon's fixing his claws in the shield immediately after and leaving one of them there, cut off by Red Cross's sword (40. 9–43. 9), I take to be a corresponding attack of concupiscence against "the shield of faith"—that is, an impulse of doubt in the reason, which according to Protestants can also be affected by concupiscence in the form, among others, of doubt.[10] Allegorically, Red Cross's response parallels his response to the sting: with the same "sword of the spirit," some doubts (the first claw) can be refuted (forced to let go); those doubts that inevitably remain as a sort of concupiscence or inherent weakness in the reason (the tenacious claw) can at least be resisted by the same means (i.e., severed from the dragon's body) to the point of not assenting to them. The sword's vigorous double blows sundering the dragon's joints (42. 4; 43. 6–7; see also 39. 9) recall the operation of "the word of God" in Heb. 4. 12: "For the worde of God is lively, and mightie in operation, and sharper than any two edged sword, and entreth through, even unto the dividing asunder of the soule and the spirit, and of the joynts, and the marow,"—thus evoking the additional Pauline identification, "the sworde of the spirite, which is the worde of God" (Ephes. 6. 17). Our anonymous Allegoriae glosses the biblical sundering of joints precisely as I do that in Spenser: it symbolizes the repression of a sin at a stage earlier than consent (p. 590). On the first day of the battle, as we shall see, a divine pronouncement has had just the opposite effect.

According to the Geneva gloss on Rom. 7. 18, concupiscence, while it "hindreth . . . or holdeth . . . back" the regenerate, "doeth wholy possesse" the unregenerate. In view of this, Red Cross's recent baptism, whatever it may mean in itself, invites us to return to the first day for a contrasting representation of concupiscence in the unregenerate. As expected, we find several clear contrasts: Red Cross "overthrowen," as noted above, at the end of the day (30. 9); the sword which when "hardned in that holy water dew" (36. 1–3) will wound the dragon as he has never been wounded before and will sever his sting and claw, unable even to bite (24–5); and the spear biting—inconclusively—only on the third try (16–7; 20). We have concluded that the flame arising from the spark represents a stage of sin beyond the fomes peccati. Still worse, Red Cross's desire to disarm (26. 9) surely recalls in some way the temptation he succumbed to with Duessa at the nadir of his career (I. vii. 2. 8; 8. 1–2; 11. 6; 51. 3). We therefore expect to find the fomes, the motions of concupiscence which it conceives, and also some full-fledged sin and the backsliding to an unregenerate state this was often thought to entail, in the curious and complicated incident of Red Cross's first setback:

> [The dragon] from his wide devouring oven sent
> A flake of fire, that flashing in his beard,
> Him all amazd, and almost made affeard:
> The scorching flame sore swinged all his face,
> And through his armour all his bodie seard,
> That he could not endure so cruell cace,
> But thought his armes to leave, and helmet to unlace.

Red Cross is compared to Hercules wearing the "poysoned garment."

> Faint, wearie, sore emboyled, grieved, brent
> With heat, toyle, wounds, armes, smart, and inward fire
> That never man such mischiefes did torment;
> Death better were, death did he oft desire,
> But death will never come, when needes require.
> Whom so dismayd when that his foe beheld,
> He cast to suffer him no more respire,
> But gan his sturdie sterne about to weld,
> And him so strongly stroke, that to the ground him feld.
>
> (xi. 26–28)

A spark sent by the devil and growing into a fire associated with sin inevitably calls to mind some initial stage of sin such as temptation—as it does, for example, to our allegorizer quoted above and also to Bersuire. Moreover, the breath of Leviathan, the dragon-like monster in Job 40–41 (whose many superficial affinities to Spenser's dragon are listed by Hankins) is allegorized by Gregory the Great—quoted in the sixteenth century by Hieronymus Lauretus—as "perversa daemonis suggestio."[11] Now suggestio for Gregory means the first stage, corresponding to temptation, in his much-quoted analysis of degrees of sin;[12] and perhaps the salient feature of stanza 26 in our episode is the way in which this spark brings on Red Cross's defeat by degrees—from the spark "flashing in his beard" to the scorching flame singeing "all his face" to the flame inside the armor searing "all his bodie," presumably symbolizing ever more culpable, though perhaps not psychologically distinguishable, degrees of sin. A similar figurative progression—a flying object discoloring face or headgear and then wounding, and the devil killing—and the same pattern of increasing depth and gravity, appear in a related analysis of degrees of sin by Bernard of Clairvaux, as paraphrased in the Middle English Ancrene Riwle: "þreo degrez beoð þerinne, as Seint Beornard

430

witneð. Þe uorme is cogitaciun; þe oðer is affectiun; þe þridde
is kunsence. Cogitaciuns, þet beoð fleoinde þouhtes þet ne lesteð
nout; and þeos, ase Seint Beornard seið, ne hurteð nout ðe soule,
auh þauh heo bispeteð hire mid hire blake spotle. . . . Affectiun
is hwon ðe þouht geð inward, and ðe delit kumeð up, and ðe lust
waxeð þeonne. Ase was ðe spotle er uppon ðe hwite hude, þer
waxeð wunde and deopeð into ðe soule, efter ðet þe lust geð, and
to delit þerinne, furðre and furðre . . . Kunsence, ðet is skiles
ȝettunge [reason's acquiescence] . . . þeonne [þe ueond] . . . bit
deaðes bite."[13]

The difficulty of resisting the fire also increases. Under the
spark the knight was "almost affeard"; the rhetoric is belittling.
Under the hot armor he

> . . . could not endure so cruell cace,
> But thought his armes to leave, and helmet to unlace.
> . . . .
> Faint, wearie, sore, emboyled, grieved, brent
> With heat, toyle, wounds, armes, smart, and inward fire
> That never man such mischiefes did torment;
> Death better were, death did he oft desire.

Spenser pulls out all the stops, even adding a long epic simile, to
describe the increased stress of the temptation. Spenser elsewhere explicitly analyzes sin or temptation into two stages, calls
them spark and fire, and describes the spark stage as manage-
able, as the time to "quench" the fire, but the fire stage as seemingly uncontrollable (II. iv. 34–5; the possible limitations of the
speaker—the Palmer—do not affect the truth of his analysis).
Red Cross's desire to disarm is characterized by Spenser as
a stage of mental development. At first he was "all amazd"; then
he "thought his armes to leave, and helmet to unlace." "Amaze"
in Spenser, and in Elizabethan English generally, often expresses
mental confusion, while "thought to," on the contrary, often means
not just "considered whether to" but "intended to" (cf. 25. 8). This
crystallization of an intention out of that confusion which usually
precedes commission of a sin, is exactly what the long tradition
of analyses of degrees of sin is concerned with; Bernard, as cited
above, actually calls the final stage intentio; and Nicolas of Lyra,
a late medieval commentator much abused and used by Luther,
explicitly distinguishes (in a passage cited below) the Gregorian
stages by their increasing engagement of reason and will. Spenser then has literally dramatized two of the traditional stages of

sin to start us on the right track, implying in his imagery a positively scholastic proliferation of further psychological stages and
factors, at least some of which are presumably to be translated
with the help of the tradition.

Just as the dragon sent the spark, so the devil is said to initiate the first stage of any given sin. The spark would be that first
stage—causing confusion of mind ("all amazd") but only slight
temptation ("almost made affeard")—which is usually labelled
suggestio or cogitatio. The spark is felt as a flash—the blinding
reinforces the idea of mental confusion and the suddenness shows
how suggestio escapes the reason, by coming too fast for reason
to act, as Nicolas puts it. The flash represents, in short, that
instinctive response to the stimulus which constitutes the state of
being tempted, like shrinking from pain or salivating from hunger.
Since it obviously cannot be prevented, Nicolas reasons, it is only
a temptation, not a sin; similarly the flash is not portrayed as
injurious. (As I read it, objectively described injury represents
guilt; and psychologically described anguish, as in Stanza 28,
represents the strength of the temptation.)

We have seen, so far, the beard as the susceptibility within
embracing the spark of a tempting situation from without, thus
producing the flash of suggestio. A second stage, called "lingering delectation" by the scholastics and Nicolas, occurs if the suggestio is not definitely resisted as soon as possible but retained
"after it has been felt," even though "without consent."[14] This
corresponds to failure to quench the spark of sin in the Palmer's
sermon referred to above (II. iv. 35). So Red Cross's "face," and
of course later the armor and body, will retain the spark, thus
feeding it into a "scorching flame" which "sore swinged" him,
injuring him, presumably, with guilt for a degree of concupiscence
that could have been avoided. Although the incident generally possesses both an unmistakable allegorical flavor (a vice attacks the
face of a virtue with a torch in Prudentius's Psychomachia, 40 ff.
and in Statius's Thebaid, XI) and the psychological progressions
outlined above, the images of beard, face, and body (like Bernard's
of skin, flesh, and bone) resist specific translation. The face as
the site of the beard or fomes and also of the conjunction of all five
senses (cf. Lauretus, "Facies," p. 321), might be meant to suggest
the sensitive appetite where both suggestio and delectatio occur.
Now Red Cross's face feels the fire only after and because of the
beard. If the face corresponds to the sensitive appetite, then the
classical distrust of the lower faculties is receiving here a typically Christian correction—the fault is not precisely in the sensi-

tive appetite, with which man was after all created, but in the fomes, an excrescence of that appetite evoked by the Fall. However that may be, the flame as the second stage and as merely local burning corresponds to the patristic second stage—delectatio, or resistible concupiscence, as Nicolas defines it above. It is a continuum embracing all those possible odds in the mental or moral struggle intervening between the moment of the involuntary response and the moment of full consent; and an author could therefore picture two or more degrees of it. I believe it is as an intensification of this intermediate stage that Spenser introduces the next stage, the product of an extra factor, the armor.

The treachery of the armor—not protecting its wearer but helping the flame to sear instead of singe his entire body instead of his face, so that he decides to take it off—is the most fully elaborated and at the same time the most puzzling detail of the whole incident:

> The scorching flame sore swinged all his face,
> And through his armour all his bodie seard,
> That he could not endure so cruell cace,
> But thought his armes to leave, and helmet to unlace.
>
> Not that great Champion of the antique world,
> Whom famous Poetes verse so much doth vaunt,
> And hath for twelve huge labours high extold,
> So many furies and sharpe fits did haunt,
> When him the poysoned garment did enchaunt
> With Centaures bloud, and bloudie verses charm'd,
> As did this knight twelve thousand dolours daunt,
> Whom fyrie steele now burnt, that earst him arm'd,
> That erst him goodly arm'd, now most of all him harm'd.
>
> Faint, wearie, sore, emboyled, grieved, brent
> With heat, toyle, wounds, armes, smart, and inward fire
> That never man such mischiefes did torment;
> Death better were, death did he oft desire,
> But death will never come, when needes require.
>
> (xi. 26–28. 5)

Such treacherous armor can hardly represent "the armour of a Christian man" of the Letter to Ralegh, the "armes" extolled above the "man" in the invocation to this canto (xi. 7. 9). That the armor represents something inferior on the first day, is evident from the renewal the sword subsequently undergoes in the baptizing well. Rather it suggests Augustine's paradox alluded to by the Glossa ordinaria and others—"Armis tuis te vicit, armis tuis te interemit"—"With your own arms [sin] conquered you, with your own arms it slew you" (cf. especially xi. 27. 8—9). The statement is a metaphorical summary of the first half of Rom. 7. In this chapter—the main biblical discussion of concupiscence frequently referred to already—a personified sin glossed as the devil employed the very prohibitions of Mosaic law to increase St. Paul's concupiscence;[15] similarly, in our passage, the dragon or Satan sends the spark, and the armor itself augments a flame which I have identified as concupiscence. Again, the new attractiveness a temptation gains from a thou-shalt-not is a feeling of rebelliousness, out of a kind of negative suggestibility in human nature;[16] and rebellion is implied by the curious way in which Spenser pictures the resulting consummation of the sin more as a reaction against the armor than as a consent to the fire, symbol of the original temptation. We may note in passing that the Pauline paradox is one universally recognized in sexual temptations (see, for example, Montaigne, Essays, II. 15 and his references), and that the progression from "face," possibly meaning the visual sense, to "all his bodie," could be meant to recall that of sexual desire in traditional love-psychology. A remarkable similarity also exists between Paul's consequent longing for death, "O wretched man that I am, who shall deliver me from the body of this death?" (Rom. 7. 24) and that of Red Cross, ". . . never man such mischiefes did torment; / Death better were, death did he oft desire" (xi. 28. 3—4).

Why did Spenser introduce the armor or law, and place its intervention within this particular stage of sin, delectatio? Law as described in Rom. 7 is classified by Peter Martyr as an occasion of sin along with the causes of sin here portrayed—the devil, the fomes, and the will.[17] Our incident evidently aims at comprehensiveness not only in analyzing but in assigning responsibility for sin. That it is delectatio in particular which is intensified by a prohibition is stated by Augustine; and Paul's general condition in Rom. 7 is characterized by the moral psychologists as delectatio.[18] To show an ordinary and never entirely transcendable means to virtue such as law only making matters worse is to say that delectatio is well-nigh irresistible; and Spenser does so again in his use of the spark-flame imagery in Book II (iv. 34—5). Free will does play a part in that the whole situation could have been avoided, as Spenser will say through the Palmer, by resistance at the earlier stage of the spark.

Spenser's epic comparison of Red Cross in the hot armor to
Hercules with the shirt of Nessus upon him is apt not only for his
literal plight (e.g., each hero's present torture and future death
are by something described as fire, Met. IX, 202; 229 ff.) but for
the plight of Paul in Rom. 7 which it allegorizes. Most important,
both the shirt (as described, for example, in Met. IX, 152 ff.) and
Red Cross's armor as Mosaic law are garments which were intended for good but worked evil. Moreover, Bersuire, in two of
his several overlapping interpretations of the Hercules story,
moralizes the "poisoned fire" in Hercules's garment just as we
have done the fire in Red Cross's garment, as concupiscence:
"ut sic mediante sensualitate vel carne, [diabolus] possit animum
per concupiscentiam urere et tandem per vicia cremare. . . .
Uritur igitur animus primo veneno temptationum, tandem con-
crematur ignibus infernalium terribilium. . . .Vel dic quod Hercules, qui voluntarie se combussit ut ignem venenosum qui eum
comburebat evaderet, significat viros sanctos, qui ut ignem venenosum scilicet concupiscentiam carnalem . . . evaderent, se in
ignem tribulationum mundalium posuerunt. . . ."[19] A charm composed of "bloody verses" again symbolizes concupiscence as described in Rom. 7 in FQ II. i. 55, as Fowler has shown.

The line "But thought his armes to leave, and helmet to unlace"
marks the stage of consent to the sin. How it is portrayed as deliberate, I have already explained. The feeling of Spenserians
that to disarm, at least, would have been a sin, is borne out by
its parallelism with Red Cross's previous disarming just before
being similarly knocked down by Orgoglio (I. vii. 2. 8; 8. 1–2; 11–2).
Disarming would in Red Cross's present situation be a cessation
of struggle, a surrender to sin; and the final stage of consent,
according to another part of our passage in the Ancrene Riwle, is
when the sinner's heart cries "creaunt"—a chivalric sign of surrender: "þis is hwon þe heorte . . . leið hire sulf aduneward,
and buhð him [ðe ueonde] ase he bit, and ӡeieð, 'creaunt, creaunt!'
ase swowinde" (p. 130). Red Cross is now mature enough to leave
off his plan of disarming short of the outward act, a fourth stage
of sin which is sometimes mentioned; but it is already at consent
that the sin is said to become mortal, whatever outward act it
may afterwards entail, in accord with the highminded principle
enunciated in Mt. 5. 27–8: "Whosoever looketh on a woman [supply
"with the deliberate intention"] to lust after her, hath committed
adulterie with her already in his heart." This judgment seems to
be expressed by Spenser's introduction here of the adjective "dismayd" (28. 6)—a cause for defeat which the Orgoglio episode has

taught us to equate with "disarmd" ("disarmd . . . dismayde," vii. 11. 6; 51. 3). The reminiscences imply that Red Cross has not only sinned, but somehow regressed, albeit under greater temptation, to essentially the same state in which he fell to Orgoglio.

That spiritual death which comes with consent is symbolized, I believe, by the dragon's final blow:

> Whom so dismayd when that his foe beheld,
> He cast to suffer him no more respire,
> But gan his sturdie sterne about to weld,
> And him so strongly stroke, that to the ground him feld.
>
> (28.6—9)

To begin with, the blow resembles some sort of death in that the dragon intends it to finish off a disabled victim (28. 8); it comes as a poetic answer to Red Cross's own desire for death (28. 4–5); and Una fears it has killed him (32). Though not a part of the spark-flame progression, the blow is connected with it as act to motive: "Whom so dismayd when that his foe beheld, / He cast to" finish him off. In this it parallels Red Cross's consent: the flame burned him "[So] that he could not endure so cruell cace, / But thought" to disarm; the dragon's act would seem to be the symbolic equivalent of the knight's decision, as spiritual death is often said to be nothing more than that alienation of the will from God which occurs in consent. The imagery of blows and killing is often employed for the stage of consent or actual sin. Both sin's killing the protagonist of Rom. 7 and the fire that finished off Hercules are sometimes interpreted as the stage of consent.[20] The image of a blow is used by Gregory for consent, as well as for his other stages, as he sees them illustrated in Adam's fall: "By these . . . blows the old Adversary smashed that uprightness of primal man" (Mor. in Job, IV. xxvii. 49, cited above). Similar, too, is the deadly bite employed for consent by the author of the Ancrene Riwle in the passage quoted above, "Kunsence, ðet is skiles ȝettunge . . . þeonne . . . [ðe ueonde] bit deaðes bite" (p. 130).

The fact that Red Cross goes so far as allowing the spark to develop and eventually consenting to it—tantamount to doing again what he did with such disastrous results in the Orgoglio episode— along with the desperation of Spenser's rhetoric, is what places this incident in the role of a moral anticlimax for Red Cross. In this it contrasts with his practical victory over the sting and Spenser's low-key treatment of that setback on the second day. This

contrast of moods reflects accurately Paul's despair over concupiscence in Rom. 7 as against his relative complacency about
the "thorn in the flesh" in II Cor. 12. Such despair could conceivably have afflicted a good Christian: as noted above, Paul in
a few early verses of Rom. 7 even seems, like Red Cross, to have
gone so far as consent or actual sin; and Luther paints a similar
picture of how far a Christian can fall, "especially if he tries to
[resist Satan] with his own strength" (Comm. Gal. 3. 1), but Paul
in Rom. 7. 5 attributes this to his having been "in the flesh," and
hence somehow "out of character," at the time; and commentators
insofar as they take his gloomy confessions at face value tend to
qualify them with the similar observation that consent could have
occurred in the face of such generally good intentions only before
regeneration, either in Paul himself or in mankind in history
whose persona he adopts. They are reasoning from the doctrine,
alluded to in all our contrasts of the second day with the first
(and previously sensed by Spenserians), that the unregenerate
man, while still free in each individual temptation, of necessity
sins sooner or later, whereas a well-intentioned Christian would
have been able to avoid all but concupiscence.[21] Applying this
explanation to the relapse of the equally well-intentioned Red
Cross makes it represent not so much the incorrigibility of his
own or of human nature or Spenser's deficient sense of climax
as the emergence of a different sort of allegory, to be explored
below, in which Red Cross for the moment plays the part of an
unregenerate man.

Finally, the tone of this passage wavers curiously between
that of the heroic and moving comparison to Hercules and the
farcical quality of a dragon assaying the can-can ("he gan his
sturdie sterne about to weld," 28. 8); of the scorching beard; of
the plight of a person with something painful inside his clothes,
analogous to various practical jokes such as the "hot foot"; and
of a knight being slapped backwards into a spring. Influenced by
Ariosto as this farce may be, its effect is not the Ariostan kidding
of the genre itself, for there is nothing but solemnity in the remainder of the battle (unless it be the slight touch in the knight's
slipping in the mire the next evening). On the other hand, there
are grounds on this day for humiliation of the knight; for there
is about a defeat such as this of a morally perfect person by a
weakness of the flesh a certain humor of the wry sort exemplified
in the proverb which recurs in Bergman films: "Whichever way
you turn, your backside is always behind you." And the natural
mode of comedy to express weakness of the flesh would be farce.

This, then, is Spenser's picture of concupiscence and its related stages of sin before regeneration, and of concupiscence and its cure after regeneration, introduced so late in Red Cross's development seemingly to show to what degree sin is inevitable in mankind at its best. Spenser shares the almost universal view that concupiscence is inevitable in any case; and Red Cross's consent could be extenuated as representing the further general inevitability, to an unregenerate man, of actual sin. These two complications of the dragon-fight—the spark and the sting—are certainly not perfunctory, since between themselves they make up a tight psychological progression. To begin with, a person giving every evidence of moral perfection encounters a schematic temptation. The original Tempter casts at his sensitive appetite, made susceptible by the _fomes_ resulting from the Fall, the stimulus of a tempting situation, which inspires in him an involuntary desire to sin and throws him momentarily off balance. Instead of quenching this spark he proceeds to agonize over the temptation—a small but fatal weakness. After this, recollecting a divine prohibition of this particular sin only increases its attractiveness so that the will and reason first hesitate and then consent, thus reducing the person to a state of mortal sin. At this unlikely point, for a reason to be explained below, the person is baptized. After baptism, he again encounters a temptation and again cannot help feeling its attractiveness with his senses; but this time, by the power of the Holy Spirit, he is able to avoid consenting to it. Similarly, the tempter attacks his faith itself; and by the same Spirit as embodied in Scripture, some doubts are altogether refuted; and those which remain are resisted at least to the point of not acting on them. It remains to be seen how these setbacks fit into the larger pattern of the episode.

As I mentioned at the outset, Red Cross's baptism in the course of the battle has been a problem—one recognized, for example, by Professor Whitaker and M. P. Parker—since it could happen only to a non-Christian.[22] While it can be explained away, this initial shock must have been intended by Spenser. Similarly, Red Cross's backsliding into mortal sin on the first day before the combined opposition of concupiscence and the law is possible in Lutheran or Anglican doctrine (cf. Luther, Comm. Gal. 3. 1; 39 Articles, Article XV), but so stupidly repetitious of former falls and rescues and so far beneath his exemplary regenerate self-control on the second day that by itself it seems anticlimactic and out of character. These two anachronisms become credible and poetic if seen as non-mimetic recapitulations of earlier events in Book I. Spenser has Red Cross defeated on the first day by the same antagonist and in the same land as were those he seeks to save (cf. I. vii. 43–4; Letter to Ralegh), thus tying the beginning of his quest in with the ending and highlighting both his kinship with the victims in weakness and the power of the dragon. The temporary failure of his rescue attempt recapitulates also those earlier abortive rescues in Una's life-story (I. vii. 45), apparently for the same purpose. In particular, the presumable inclusion of Red Cross's defeat under the "guilt of sinful crimes" (xi. 30. 2) which the Well of Life washes away shows his defeat to be indeed a spiritual one and links it with that "guilt of sin" (vii. 45. 8) which betrayed his predecessors to the dragon. The decision to disarm, the defeat by a blow, the battle outside a prison-castle suggestive of Hell, the interceding lady, and the monster opponent recall his own and Arthur's encounters with Orgoglio and his Beast. The agency of law in his fall repeats with a significant difference law's agency in his earlier fall to Despaire (ix. 50). Red Cross passively saved by the "living well" (xi. 31. 6) which could "wash" sin, experiences that salvation awaited by the earlier characters Fradubio and Fraelissa—to be "bathed in a living well" (ii. 43. 1). All these reminiscences will become meaningful also in the related themes of the uses of law and the religious history of mankind. What is clear so far is that Red Cross's backsliding is dictated not only by his rather repetitious personal development but by a certain representative role.

The contrast of this first day with the second—though following the neat before-and-after pattern which I noted at the outset—is as nothing, however, beside the change we see on the third day, a change which has never been sufficiently appreciated. Red Cross exhibits not two but three distinct levels of performance, doing better each day than the day before, until on the third day, and only then, his power is absolute.

To begin with, no distinctively Christological details, except those arising from the battle as one victorious whole, appear before the third day. Even the three-day duration of the battle, in order to fulfill its obvious symbolism, requires that the hero be Christ, not on all three days but only on the third day—the day on which the concrete event to be typified, the Harrowing of Hell, actually took place. True, the second day's action has alluded to the famous "O death where is thy sting?"; but only to answer the question in a way that turns the parallel into irony: "It sticketh fast in us." A "sting of death" which "is sinne" would not get "stuck" inextricably in a hero who typified Christ; Red Cross therefore is only trying to imitate Christ the destroyer of sin

and death, and so far not succeeding. Cornelius a Lapide gives
an example of the sort of picture that ought properly to be conjured up by the "O death where is thy sting?" passage; and it is
a picture as unlike Red Cross's first and second days as it is like
his third: The answer is, "It has perished." "Death" means
"Limbo," whither "everyone descended before Christ"; this verse
"began to be fulfilled when Christ arose and led the souls of the
saints back out of Limbo . . . as from a bite [quasi morsu]." In
the words of Jerome, "When you think [Christ] to be a prey in
your avid jaws, your insides are pierced by a hooked tooth [cf.
Job 40. 20–21]" (p. 333 at I Cor. 15. 55). On the second day, in
short, the most that can be said for the knight's achievement is
that he gives as good as he gets; he remains in a state of grace,
as he does not on the first day, but he is still not Christ.

On the third day, however, he neither retains (52. 2) nor incurs
any wounds, and his first and only blow kills the dragon. His
task—to kill once for all a dragon symbolizing Satan, to rescue
the king and queen of Eden from the dragon's brazen prison, and
to restore them to their realm (FQ I. vii. 43. 3–9; xii. 26. 1)—has
been shown to typify the Harrowing of Hell. Further Christological details of the third day—such as the knight's killing the dragon
by stabbing through a mouth opened to devour him (53), figuring
the Harrowing of Hell by way of the defeat of the monster Leviathan (Job 40–41, as in the quotations from Cornelius and Jerome
above)—could be adduced.[23]

One of them, suggested by the foregoing analysis, changes the
meaning of the quest and accounts for other details of the battle,
pointed out by Rosemond Tuve,[24] which do not fit the Harrowing
of Hell. Everything fits together under Christ's liberating us
"from the Lawe, he being dead in whom we were holden" (Rom.
7. 6)—a liberation which was accomplished in the historical event
of Christ's abolition of Mosaic law at the Crucifixion. The first
to be liberated, according to the Harrowing of Hell legend, were
the Old Testament saints in Limbo—the best after-life they could
attain by their inevitably imperfect obedience to the law. The
brazen tower as both a defense and a prison, both keeping out and
keeping in (vii. 44; xii. 4; Letter to Ralegh) corresponds less to
Limbo than to the portrayal of Mosaic law in Gal. 3. 23 and its
commentators: "we were kept under the Lawe, as under a garison
[the verb in Gk. is φρουρέω, in Lat., custodio], shut up [Gk.
συγκλείω, Lat. concludo, comprehendo] unto the faith which should
afterward be reveiled." The tower also resembles Red Cross's
armor of law both in being a container made of metal and in its

ambivalent function. The watchman (xi. 3; xii. 2) on the tower,
looking outward for Christ's coming like the Old Testament
prophets (see n. 23, above), also by his very nature guards those
inside. The tower, then, is a symbol of law; the watchman is a
human personification of it like the garrison (custos in Beza's
Latin gloss) or the schoolmaster of Gal. 3. 23—4. Luther on verse
23 emphasizes the negative aspect of law as a prison and a hell:
true, it "compel[s] us to be outwardly good" and "restraineth and
shutteth uppe the wicked, that they runne not . . . into all kindes
of mischiefe" as Adam and Eve and their people after their fall
are shut up from any further assaults of the Satan-dragon; but to
well-intentioned souls such as they, it "is also a spirituall prison,
and a very hell. For when it revealeth sinne, threateneth death,
and the eternal wrath of God, a man cannot avoide it, nor find any
comfort, For it is not in the power of man."[25] The tower, then,
is above ground unlike Limbo, as Tuve objects, because it represents a hell experienced not only by Old Testament saints after
death but also by everyone in this life—the hell to which law condemns even its best followers (Gal. 3. 22) if they have only this to
justify them.

An unregenerate man under law, a Christian, and Christ—they
have in common their good intentions and a representative human
nature, indicating that Red Cross's continuing role is that of mankind at its best; and they progress not exactly in time but in how
far each kind of human nature is a match for the devil, climaxing
in Christ as "that greater Man." Spenser's progression as I see
it is modeled on the many theological patternings of history or of
various states of human nature, such as Augustine's four status of
sin, law, grace, and glory; Paul's statement (just before "O death,
where is thy sting?") that "as we have borne the image of the
earthly [man, i.e., Adam], so shal we beare the image of the heavenly [man, i.e., Christ]" (I Cor. 15. 49); or the shifting meanings
of Piers in Piers Plowman. It could be abbreviated to "mankind
without grace, mankind under grace, and mankind joined to divinity."

The two anachronisms, and most of the recapitulations whose
presence signals the existence of another level, are historical in
function. Red Cross's recapitulation on the first day of the defeat
of the king and queen of Eden suggests the Fall, though the agency
of the beard or fomes (a result rather than a cause of the Fall) reduces what might have been allegory to a mere archetypal resonance. The further presence of Mosaic law suggests law's period
of dominance in history when "the law entred thereupon" after the
Fall "that sin might abound" (Rom. 5. 20); and if so, Red Cross's

backsliding abetted by this law must typify, as does Paul's un-
characteristic sin in Rom. 7 (according to Augustine, quoted in
n. 21, above), that of well-intentioned mankind in this darker
period of its salvation-history. A generally similar allegory is
seen by Augustine in the famous battle of David and Goliath (I
Sam. 17)—a "figura" of Christ fighting the devil; and both of the
inconvenient suits of armor, that of Goliath and that which David
tried on and rejected, are allegorized as Mosaic Law.[26] Within
the poem, Red Cross's defeat looks back to that of Una's earlier
champions, who "for want of faith, or guilt of sin, / The pitteous
pray of his fierce crueltie have bin" (viii. 45. 8—9). As previously
noted, Red Cross seems to share their "guilt of sinfull crimes"
(x. 30. 2); and the same well that cures this disability in him re-
news his ineffectual sword against the dragon's claw fixed on the
"shield of faith" (xi. 36; 42); it arms him, that is, against "want
of faith," the other disability of the earlier knights. Only with
Christianity was mankind placed, as Milton says, "on even ground
against his mortal foe."

Christ too had unsuccessful predecessors, who might furnish
specific historical counterparts for the knights preceding Red
Cross: according to a contrast of law with gospel in Heb. 7. 27—8,
the priests of the Old Law were trying to save mankind just as
Christ did but were disabled by being guilty of sin themselves.
More generally, armed men going before into the promised land,
according to Lauretus, allegorize the Old Testament saints and
prophets ("Arma," p. 102). The earlier knights, then, and Red
Cross as he imitates them on the first day, probably represent
not only mankind at large under law but specifically the priests
and leaders trying to restore a fallen mankind (the king of Eden
and his people) but failing through their own sin. On the third
day, Red Cross is contrastingly sinless and successful and represents Christ, characterized in Hebrews as the one successful
Priest. Whenever he is fighting, then, Red Cross represents
mankind actively saving itself—something like another figural
concept, the Church Militant.

When he is down, his resemblance on the first night to Fradubio and Fraelissa and on the second night to the position of the
skull of Adam in iconography of the Crucifixion link him to Adam
and Eve in their Limbo tower as mankind passively "wayting" (xi.
3. 7) to be saved. The curiously passive way in which he falls into
the Well and the precinct of the Tree (xi. 29—30; 45. 6—9), whereas
the individual (or his baptismal sponsor) has to seek out the sacraments deliberately, befits mankind at large, to whom the sacra-

ments simply were given. The Well as baptism, then, epitomizes the advent of Christianity, the coming of grace to mankind, pictured in the form in which it first comes to the individual. The progression (examined below) by way of the Tree to the next status of human nature, that of the God-man, is not chronological but qualitative, except insofar as the finality of the victory seems to bring in Christ's victory in the Last Days. Again, in Canto xii, the echoes of the Marriage of the Lamb suggest the Last Days only to jerk us back to the Passion with the warning that this is only a betrothal. One could say that both Advents of Christ have been telescoped into the third day by these two double references, and if so, only the chronological overlapping of the second status with the beginning of the third hinders the progression from being not only qualitative but chronological as well. The last-minute reappearance of Duessa and Archimago—characters also from the Book of Revelation but in this poem carrying only Revelation's polemical significance of Catholic as opposed to Protestant—serves to merge the figural level back into that of the familiar "historical allegory."

The literal and the hardly-distinguishable moral levels, of course, remain the story of an individual Christian, a St. George. Having settled his own problems and tasted the contemplative life (Canto x), Red Cross returns to the active life to perform one of the Seven Corporal Works of Mercy, release of prisoners, commended in the House of Holinesse as analogous to Christ's Harrowing of Hell (x. 40). It is a quest which invites not only a historical but a moral symbolism. Red Cross's presumable figuration of the Old Testament priesthood and of Christ as High Priest crystallizes the associations about it of "saving souls," perhaps through the Reformed priesthood, as the consummate occupation of the individual Christian. In the battle, he encounters a physical dragon; and the first exchanges seem "intermeddled more as accidents than intendments." Three features, however, seem to foreshadow the moral allegory of concupiscence to follow: the horse paradoxically entangling himself the more he tries to escape (xi. 23); the dragon (seemingly reflecting in himself what he is about to do to Red Cross) both getting Red Cross's spear "stucke fast" in him even though he severs the shaft, and trying to fly with one of his wings wounded—a variation of one standard emblem of concupiscence.[27] Red Cross is defeated in the incident of the spark, which is difficult to read as anything but a moral backsliding, and rises again, as Kathleen Williams has suggested, through a meditational reliving of his past baptism[28] first to normal regenerate self-control and finally by a mental crucifixion with Christ to an "imi-

tation of Christ" and a physical if miraculous victory like that of
St. George. Red Cross's figural role on the second day, that of
Every-Christian, is therefore simply his ordinary role elevated
to the universal.

My contention is, first, that Red Cross's failure, recovery, and
ultimate success are exaggerated beyond the mimetic—for example,
by naming the prisoners the king and queen of Eden—in order to
suggest at one extreme a man who has never been baptized and at
the other Christ Himself, and second, that from this tension a
second general and historical level comes into existence beside
the individual and moral one. Such an allegory is characteristic
of that distinctively Biblical and Dantesque mode sometimes con-
fusedly called "typology" or "the allegorical level" in the medieval
four-level scheme, but better designated by Auerbach as figura.[29]
Particularly characteristic, according to A. C. Charity's definition
of figura, is the way in which historical events have a reduplicative
power to be reenacted by individuals in the poem. Besides the obvious example of Red Cross's imitation of Christ, there is the liberation from law experienced in our episode by the purely historical Adam and Eve but experienced earlier by Red Cross as an
individual, when Arthur as Christ-figure harrowed him out of
Orgoglio's hell-like dungeon (viii. 37—41).[30] That law-inspired
suicidal moral despair which is symbolized on the figural level
by the tower as "a spiritual prison and a very hell" and for Red
Cross personally by Orgoglio's hell-like dungeon, is realistically
dramatized, as Torczon has shown, in Red Cross's encounter with
Despaire. As Luther says of liberation from law as described in
Galatians, "This Paule speaketh in respect of the fulness of the
time wherin Christ came. But we must applie it, not only to that
time, but also to the inward man. For that which is done as an
hystorie, and according to the time wherein Christ came, . . . is
always done spiritually in every Christian; in whom is found continually some while the time of the law, and some while the time of
grace" (fol. 160^v—161^r on 3. 23b).

Law is emerging, in the light of recent interpretations, as a
central theme of Book I. Preoccupation with law is a characteristic of early Reformed writers, one which they derive from their
favorite books of the Bible—Romans and Galatians—as well as
from the Epistle to the Hebrews. Spenser, on this issue as on
others, has a foot in both camps, as does Peter Martyr. To Luther, for example, law represented more than just an earlier dispensation (either Mosaic law or Mosaic law plus natural law),
more than legalism; it represented the whole element of code-

observance and the analytic approach to ethics. Against it they set up the passivity of justification by faith, holistic concepts like the old man and the new man, mortification and vivification, and the spontaneity of Christian liberty (see, for example, Luther's scholia on Rom. 7. 1 and 7. 6), thus administering a fatal blow to faculty-psychology and fathering Progressive Education. While law had a limited use in mortification ("penance" in the old ethics), it invited abuses, and all these abuses were thought to have been reincarnated in the Church of Rome.

We have seen that it is the Tree alone and not both reinforcements, as Hamilton assumes, which transforms Red Cross from a Christian into a Christ-figure. Another unappreciated part of the threefold structure is a differentiation of the Well and the Tree in line with their different effects—their transformations, respectively, of a natural man to a regenerate man and of a regenerate man to "that greater Man." While the Well bestows simple "life" (30. 1), the Tree bestows "happie life . . . And life eke everlasting" (46. 5–6) and "life and long health" (48. 6); although they both can raise the dead, the Well specializes in chronic disabilities, "sicknesse" and "aged long decay," (30. 3–4), whereas the Tree specializes in acute disabilities, "deadly woundes" (48. 7)—that is, in original and in actual sin, respectively. Well and Tree cannot, therefore, stand for the same undifferentiated grace, as Tuve implies. My case requires only so much from the Well and Tree, and it contributes only this to their still problematic interpretation—this and further support for the traditional, though by no means unchallenged, characterization of the Tree as Holy Communion. Granting that the Tree is less clearly identified than the Well, and that any sacrament bestows something of Christ on the participant, Holy Communion in Spenser's view bestows specifically Christ's Real Presence (see the first sentence of Article XXVIII and Spenser's poetic echo of the doctrine in HHL 195); and it bestows the Real Presence of Christ crucified, as Spenser has just reminded us through Fidelia's cup of wine and water with the serpent in it (I. x. 13. 4–5, cf. Num. 21. 9 and Jn. 3. 14) and here recalls through the Passion-symbols of fruit-tree and balm. It is the events following the Crucifixion, of course, that Red Cross reenacts when he becomes a Christ-figure. When Red Cross emerges, then, from the precinct of the Tree in a magically complete identification with the risen Christ, he is exhibiting physically and completely what happens to every communicant spiritually and to some extent. Moreover, such a view of Holy Communion gives the Crucifixion a power to reduplicate itself in individual lives like that which A. C. Charity ascribes to an event in <u>figura</u>, and makes it the hinge at which, with only slight exaggeration, the life-story of a Christian could merge with that of Christ.

The three-day structure of the battle, then, is that of a re-enactment of mankind's struggle for deliverance from "That old Dragon," in three states of human nature: it begins on the first day with unregenerate man under law—identified as such by his inconvenient armor, his defeat through unchecked concupiscence, and his subsequent baptism; it progresses through Christian regenerate man, identified by his use and need of both sacraments and his qualified victory over concupiscence; it culminates in Christ the perfect man, showing his swift and final victory over Satan both on his own behalf and that of others. This whole pattern can be appreciated, of course, only on rereading, as is typical of <u>figura</u>, which resembles that which it typifies only by an overall analogy. Red Cross's backsliding on the first day, then, does not so much detract from his personal character as it elevates him to that role of mankind whose "grandeur of generality" makes the dragon-fight as a whole the fitting climax to Book I which Spenser intended it to be.

"NOR MAN IT IS": THE KNIGHT OF JUSTICE IN BOOK V OF SPENSER'S FAERIE QUEENE

Judith H. Anderson

The basic problem in Book V is evident enough: justice is the most inclusive and exalted moral virtue in The Faerie Queene;[1] the Book of Justice is the most comprehensive Book, drawing together the central symbols and concerns of earlier Books;[2] yet Artegall, "the Champion of true Iustice," seems the most disappointing and ineffectual hero in the entire poem. His justice in the early cantos of Book V is simplistic, furious, even vengeful; by the end of the Book, his justice is inconclusive. Upon examination, Artegall's limitations and those of his Legend prove inseparable from the virtue which he champions, for this virtue, taken as an absolute ideal, makes demands which neither human history nor individual human beings can satisfy. If the very subject of justice leads to the dream of a Golden Age, it leads also to the presence of topical, or historical, allegory in Book V, a painful reminder of Elizabethan shortcomings. The logical structure of Book V has a vicious, circular validity, and the figure of Artegall is enmeshed in it.

By definition—Aristotle's or Aquinas's—Artegall's virtue is "distinguished among the virtues by the fact that it governs relations among men."[3] If for the present we except courtesy, justice is without question the most socially oriented of all the moral virtues: "justice, alone of the virtues, is thought to be 'another's good,' because it is related to our neighbour; for it does what is advantageous to another."[4] Given the nature of justice, it is perfectly sensible that Book V should reflect the social and political affairs of the sixteenth century, but it is significant that the poet should have chosen to refer to these affairs so directly and so insistently. To the degree that Book V refers to actual events of the 70's, 80's, and 90's, Spenser absolutely flouts common Renaissance views about the treatment of recent history.[5] Further, departing from his usual practice in earlier Books, he repeatedly

Reprinted by permission of the author and the Modern Language Association of America from PMLA, Vol. 85 (1970), pp. 65–77.

neglects to distance historical allusions. Suddenly, and to a surprising degree, the poet invites us to go outside the poem and to glance at a denoted world. With Irena and Belge, for example, the transparency of name and situation—Irena's island or Belge's seventeen sons—is explicitly and inescapably topical.

Allusions to recent history are all the more obvious because they exist in the Book which again and again recapitulates promises made earlier in the poem and tantalizes us with the possibility of their fulfillment. Surely Book V signals a rebirth in the union of Florimell and Marinell: the return of Persephone to earth, the coming of spring, the fruitful conjunction of water and earth, the point at which the human and the elemental touch, the harmony born of a Mars and Venus, the restoration of beauty to society.[6] Other symbolic centers of meaning, linked by theme and poetic detail to the centers of earlier Books, reinforce these suggestions of a dawning Golden Age. With Isis, Osiris, Florimell, Marinell, Britomart, and Artegall in a single Book, Spenser must really have gone out of his way to avoid a full-blown apocalypse in Book V.[7]

Artegall's experiences reflect both the historical and symbolic poles in Book V; they mirror a strain and a more general duality in the techniques and concerns of this Book. From the beginning of Book V, Artegall is divided against himself. With two exceptions, brief moments of unified identity found in his meetings with Arthur and Britomart, he has always a choice between being Justice, a virtue and an abstraction, and being a Knight, a virtuous man and a human being. The complexities and discords which underlie this choice become particularly blatant when Artegall encounters Burbon and Fleurdelis in canto xi. Artegall sees that Burbon is beset by a "rude rout," not of sins or temptations as in Book II, but simply of peasants. He notices that the peasants "his [Burbon's] shield in peeces battred haue,/And forced him to throw it quite away." Immediately after these lines, which afford a perfectly sensible account of Burbon's action, there follows the comment: "from the day that he thus did it [the shield] leaue,/Amongst all Knights he blotted was with blame." Burbon next explains that he has wrested his love, Fleurdelis, from Grantorto, who has sent the "troupe of villains" to fetch her back. No sooner has Burbon finished his tale than Artegall asks, "But why haue ye . . . forborne/Your owne good shield in daungerous dismay?" Burbon answers that he threw aside the shield in order to "stint all strife" and to obtain his love. After Artegall has told Burbon that necessity is not excuse, he continues, "Knights ought be true, and truth is one in all."[8] In effect he tells Burbon that he is not a true Knight.

Then, of all things, Burbon requests Artegall's aid "of courtesie," and Artegall, overdue already on his own quest, gives it to him, as one Knight to another, when a lady is at stake. By the time that Burbon and Fleurdelis ride into the distance, we cannot help feeling that the whole scene is enormously strained, that we have heard the gears grind as the poem shifted from one level to another. In fact, we have witnessed an alternation between the shield as an instrument of war and its moral signification, between Burbon as a Knight beset and Burbon as an apostate, between Artegall as a Knight and Artegall as a Justice.

Yet before the Burbon incident passes from view, there is an even more pronounced conflict of meanings and, indeed, of worlds. From Burbon's story we know of his love for Fleurdelis, and we also know that Artegall has found, in Burbon's abandoning his shield, evidence of the Knight's untruth. There has been no reference to Fleurdelis's lands or wealth, let alone to Burbon's desire for them. All we know, in fact, is that Fleurdelis herself can be enticed by "golden giftes." Then the poet tells us that Burbon was a good Knight until ambition, the love of power—not the love of Fleurdelis—made him faithless. In the light of the Burbon story, the poet's comment—"Vntill the loue of Lordship and of lands"[9]—a comment which comes with no preparation, is inexplicable. (With some straining, "Lordship" could be given a psychic meaning, but with "lands" such a meaning is ludicrous in context.) Here we are invited to do more than glance at a contemporary and actual world: it becomes necessary to go outside the fable in order to understand the topical reference. In short, the fifth Book tends progressively to point to the contemporary social world and presents us with an image of this world as it actually is:

> Witnesse may Burbon be, whom all the bands,
> Which may a Knight assure, had surely bound,
> Vntill the loue of Lordship and of lands
> Made him become most faithlesse and vnsound   (xii.2)

If we were to compare these lines with another stanza that could conceivably have come from an earlier Book, the problem in Book V might be clarified. The stanza refers to Artegall's succumbing to Radigund:

> Some men, I wote, will deeme in Artegall
> Great weaknesse, and report of him much ill,
> For yeelding so himselfe a wretched thrall,

449

> To th'insolent commaund of womens will;
> That all his former praise doth fowly spill.
> But he the man, that say or doe so dare,
> Be well aduiz'd, that he stand stedfast still:
> For neuer yet was wight so well aware,
> But he at first or last was trapt in womens snare.   (vi.1)

Given that the last line refers to the unhappiness of Artegall's plight, this stanza makes an appeal to experience, to facts psychically true. The poem does not force us to stand outside these lines and to stare impersonally at them: first, they bear a direct and valid relation to Artegall's history; second, they relate Artegall's experiences to our own.

In contrast, the lines about Burbon appeal to what a reader might have read or heard—to what we "figure" rather than feel is true. They employ an analogy which is based on an intellectual abstraction, rather than on a process worked out or realized within the poem. The fable action to which they refer concerns a man's desire for a woman; then, suddenly, the poet transfers this desire to the desire for a kingdom. Nothing is done to abstract Burbon sufficiently from his role as a courtly lover. The poet simply makes an analogy between the two desires. This analogy does not pivot on a type of consciousness, as, for example, in the case of Malbecco, the Jealous Man, jealous of his wife and of his money.[10] Burbon is too specifically presented, at once too externally and too tangibly a person, and then he is used too much as an abstraction. He comes to be treated as if he were a figure named and realized as Greed, Desire, or Cupidity. Yet Burbon is not only a figure whose very name denotes a historical identity, he is also the Knight whom Artegall assists out "of courtesie," even when his delay may cost Irena her life.

The analogy of Burbon's desire for a kingdom with his desire for Fleurdelis does not involve a psychic world such as that implicit in the case of Artegall, cited above. Nor is it between any two aspects of a psychic world, as in the case of Malbecco. It is not between two things of the same kind but between two kinds of desires for two different kinds of things, and in the final analysis, it is between two different kinds of worlds.

II

At least part of the problem in Book V lies in the fact that justice is a social virtue and that it involves not a mean that someone is, but a mean that is: "It is no longer a question, therefore, of someone who keeps himself in the just mean but of keeping the just mean of some thing."[11] In this sense justice is external to the just or virtuous man. This is not generally what we find in earlier Books. There the world is "inly" ours; its focus is centripetal to the psyche, rather than to an external world. Despair or the Mask of Cupid directly involve a personal and affective world: there we are less likely to find the barriers of specificity—time, space, matter—intervening between our responses and those of the poet or of his heroes. In Book V, on the other hand, we cannot say that Lady Munera is "inly" ours in quite the same way. To the degree that she is "inly" ours we tend to pity her; yet our pity is frustrated by her metal hands and feet. On the one hand Lady Munera reminds us just a little too much of an attractive but misguided young woman, led astray by a wicked but indulgent parent (witness Poeana); on the other hand she is a mechanical allegorization of a special form of social corruption (even Poeana lacks metal hands and feet). There is a definite strain in the surface of the poem as we are alternately drawn toward, or pushed away from, Lady Munera.

As long as we concentrate on the landscape of Book V and on the minor figures that people it, we see only the possibility of contrast, incongruity, a lack of direct relation between two worlds: one personal and subjective, one social and objective.[12] In the early cantos of Book V, Artegall belongs entirely to this landscape: Justice as such is external to the virtuous man—rather like the relation of Talus to Artegall—and its externality seems to be coincident with its inhumanity. Talus, the iron man, whose name means "heel" and suggests the giant Talos,[13] is said to "doe what euer thing he [Artegall] did intend" (i.12). In that case, though Artegall himself rues Munera's plight, Artegallian justice runs the following course:

> Yet for no pitty would he change the course
>   Of Iustice, which in Talus hand did lye;
>   Who rudely hayled her forth without remorse,
>   Still holding vp her suppliant hands on hye,
>   And kneeling at his feete submissiuely. . . .
> Her selfe then tooke he by the sclender wast
>   In vaine loud crying, and into the flood
>   Ouer the Castle wall adowne her cast,
>   And there her drowned in the durty mud:
>   But the streame washt away her guilty blood.   (ii.26–27)

The last line, in its echo of purgation by water, reflects with quiet irony on Talus's actions. In these same stanzas, however, we also find that reference to Munera's "hands of gold" and "feete of siluer trye," and it has been suggested that such a reference exonerates Artegall.[14] Yet these hands and feet cannot <u>cancel</u> the dominant tone of the passage, even though they fail to <u>harmonize</u> with it. Throughout the description of Munera's "seemelesse plight," there is a distinct strain between narrative tone and allegorical significa-cation, again, as in the case of Fleurdelis, a strain between the woman and the thing.

The portrayal of Lady Munera carries a doubly pejorative thrust. To the degree that Lady Munera is a personal figure, a woman, she exposes the inhumanity of Artegall's justice. To the degree that she is an impersonal figure, a thing, for Artegall or for us, she does not even belong to a really objective world; she belongs instead to a world merely of objects. The abrupt and un-even pacing of the early episodes in Book V, especially in the first two cantos, enforces suggestions of a perfunctory, robotistic, and inhuman element in Artegall's justice. In the early cantos of Book V, Artegall's justice has essentially two flaws: while it is unre-lated and insensitive to an inner and personal world, it does not even refer to a truly objective world. On two counts, then, Arte-gall is not dealing justly with reality.

When we are first introduced to Artegall, we are led to expect the hero who will institute a reign of righteousness. Throughout the early cantos, the poet inflates his hero, mythologizing him and making a virtuous example of him: "Such first was <u>Bacchus</u>," "Next <u>Hercules</u>,"

> And such was he, of whom I haue to tell,
> The Champion of true Iustice <u>Artegall</u> . . . (i.2–3)

> Whilome those great Heroes got thereby
> Their greatest glory, for their rightfull deedes,
> And place deserued with the Gods on hy.
> Herein the noblesse of this knight exceedes,
> Who now to perils great for iustice sake proceedes. (ii.1)

> Whereof no brauer president this day
> Remaines on earth, preseru'd from yron rust
> Of rude obliuion, and long times decay,
> Then this of <u>Artegall</u>, which here we haue to say. (iv.2)

THE KNIGHT OF JUSTICE IN THE FAERIE QUEENE

In context, such inflation is ambiguous and comes to be increasingly ironic: the disparate aspects of reality keep reasserting themselves. Until the Radigund episode, nearly every time Artegall's image is blown up it is similarly questioned and often deflated. For example, when Artegall encounters Pollente ("With bright Chrysaor in his cruell hand"), it is "As when a Dolphin and a Sele are met" . . .

> The maysterdome of each by force to gaine,
> And dreadfull battaile twixt them do darraine:
> They snuf, they snort, they bounce, they rage, they rore . . .
> (ii.15)

When Artegall forces Pollente from his horse and into the water, a faintly mock-heroic quality again stems from the pressure of details too practical, too mundane, too "realistic" for the Knight praised hyperbolically just a few stanzas before:

> . . . then no ods at all in him he fownd:
> For Artegall in swimming skilfull was,
> And durst the depth of any water sownd.
> So ought each Knight, that vse of perill has,
> In swimming be expert through waters force to pas. . . .
> But Artegall was better breath'd beside . . .   (ii.16–17)

These details mirror ironically Artegall's naive and excessive reliance on an external world, on proof and talismanic signs, on force and physical prowess. Like the virtue of justice, Artegall's quest should be committed to an actual and objective world, but not to a world which is factitiously simple or fictively ideal. Artegall is always preferable to his opponents in these early cantos, but his path is justly dogged by tonal dislocations and by the distant threat of parody.

Even Artegall's sword, Chrysaor, the very symbol of his quest, has a dubious history. After all, it is odd that the sword of Justice should have been stolen by Astraea from Jove:

> Which steely brand, to make him dreaded more,
> She gaue vnto him, gotten by her slight
> And earnest search, where it was kept in store
> In Ioues eternall house, vnwist of wight . . .   (i.9)

ANDERSON

Prior to the Radigund episode, Artegall is portrayed as if he were
in fact an avenging deity. In a society of sinners, there is no place
for such a figure, for justice unmitigated by mercy. As in the case
of Munera, this kind of justice "Oft spilles the principall, to saue
the part" (x.2).

III

In canto xii, some of the railings of Detraction and Envy against
Artegall are calumnious; some have an element of truth in them.
The hags claim that Artegall has abused his honor and has stained
the sword of Justice "with reprochful crueltie" (xii.40). Artegall
is at once vulnerable to the hags and apparently unable to destroy
them. Yet by canto xii, we find the hags' slanders unfair. Between
the beginning and end of Book V, Artegall has obviously changed,
and unmistakable evidence of this change can be found in canto v,
where Artegall, Radigund, and Clarinda are all involved in a typical romance situation. As in Book III, there is considerable realization (characterization) of figures, considerable dialogue, and, in
general, an evenly mixed romance style—all very much in contrast
to the uneven extremes of tone and portrayal which disrupt earlier
portions of the Book. In canto v Talus is notably absent from these
romance scenes, and both Radigund and Artegall are presented as
persons—as Lady and Knight, rather than as a Vice and a Virtue,
or as Tyrant and Justicer.[15]
Artegall's change from a principle to a person takes place in
his battle with Radigund. When he battles with her, he is compared to a blacksmith who subdues stubborn metal: "Soone as he
feeles it mollifide with heat, / With his great yron sledge doth
strongly on it beat." Here is all the fury and the impersonality
of Artegall, as we have seen it earlier: "So did Sir Artegall vpon
her lay, / As if she had an yron anduile beene."[16] In the course
of battle, Artegall finally knocks Radigund to the ground, "In
sencelesse swoune." As soon as Artegall sees her down, he leaps
to her, unlaces her helmet, and intends to cut off head and helmet
in a single blow:

> But when as he discouered had her face,
>   He saw his senses straunge astonishment,
>   A miracle of natures goodly grace,
>   In her faire visage voide of ornament,
>   But bath'd in bloud and sweat together ment;
>   Which in the rudenesse of that euill plight,
>   Bewrayd the signes of feature excellent . . .

454

> At sight thereof his cruell minded hart
> Empierced was with pittifull regard,
> That his sharpe sword he threw from him apart,
> Cursing his hand that had that visage mard:
> No hand so cruell, nor no hart so hard,
> But ruth of beautie will it mollifie. (v.12–13)

We could reduce this passage simply to the fact that the vice corresponding to mercy is pity—hence Artegall has fallen into sin. But the vice corresponding to justice is cruelty, and we would then be hard pressed to explain Artegall's "cruell minded hart."[17]

The passage actually recounts Artegall's fall into a human context, a human condition.[18] There is not the least possibility that Radigund has hands of gold or feet of silver; "natures goodly grace" is embodied in a woman, and it is as a man and a Knight that Artegall reacts. Once Artegall sees a human reality outside himself, he becomes aware of his own feelings and, at least to this degree, of himself. He realizes "his senses straunge astonishment" because he sees Radigund. He does not simply "feel" his "senses" astonishment; he becomes aware or conscious of it. Such astonishment is "straunge" or new to him. Artegall has no choice; he is caught between cruelty and pity, between the inhumanity of a static principle compulsively enforced and the too-much, too-human, humanity of a fallen world. The issue is not between principles but between human beings, and it is no longer external to the just man. Artegall moves from one extreme to the other, from cruelty to pity, and he throws away his sword. He retreats from a world of actions and things external to himself, into a world of selves and psychic experiences. As Radigund puts it: "not my valour, but his own braue mind / Subiected . . . [him] to my vnequall might" (v.32).

Once Artegall enters a psychic world, the world of Books III and IV, reference is made to Britomart for the first time in Book V: Artegall remains a prisoner in Radegone and is beloved by both Radigund and Clarinda, "but litle frended; / Vntill his owne true loue his freedome gayned" (v.57). Artegall needs both his own love and the object of his love, Britomart, to rescue him. Britomart embodies a force external to his oath as a prisoner and, therefore, not bound by it.[19] More important, she embodies the inner mean relevant to a psychic world. In Radegone Artegall is trapped between two extremes, sensuous pity and insensitive cruelty, and only another habit of mind, an expression of love such as mercy or clemency, can free him. He awaits the inner mean between emotions, which corresponds to the outer mean between things, namely, justice.

Throughout Artegall's imprisonment, one point is stressed in his favor: "To his owne loue his loialtie he saued," and had he not, "such blot his honour blemish should" (vi.2). In allegorical terms, Britomart is not love as such, but she is Artegall's love; love brings her to him, and love keeps him faithful to her. In short, love is the principle that results in his rescue and enables him to return to his quest in the external world of things and of society.

In terms of the story, however, Britomart's rescue of Artegall is far from a panacea. After the rescue, Artegall separates from Britomart once again, and with this separation, the fissure reappears between his abstract and personal identities. When Artegall leaves Britomart, the poet tells us that the "fetters of a golden tresse" can mollify with pleasure men's "hardned hearts, enur'd to bloud and cruelty." He continues, "Such wondrous powre hath wemens faire aspect, / To captiue men, and make them all the world reiect" (viii.1–2). But not Artegall. He does not reject the world external to him:

> But left his loue, albe her strong request,
> Faire Britomart in languor and vnrest,
> And rode him selfe vppon his first intent . . .
> Ne wight but onely Talus with him went,
> The true guide of his way and vertuous gouernment. (viii.3)

Artegall has to leave the world of inner and personal concerns; he is the Champion of Justice, and justice as such is external to the just or virtuous man. Artegall cannot simply revert to being an inhuman principle, however; love never leaves a figure in The Faerie Queene as it finds him. He has been humanized, he has become a man in the Radigund episode, and this fact cannot be cancelled so simply. It is as if Spenser were trying to say that a Justicer can, or at least should be, a human being; but when Artegall returns to his quest, his "first intent," this suggestion seems to be pushed aside. Britomart gives way to Talus, and Artegall is supposed to turn into a Justicer, not a man but a mean between things, an animate principle. Thus an attempt is made to reduce Artegall's humanity as a Knight—a change in what he has become as a person—to its signification in an allegory of Justice, which has no respect of person.

As a result of the Radigund episode, Artegall has more firmly

than ever before a seemingly double identity. His position has
only been complicated, as we saw in his "wauering mind" when
called to assist Burbon. We see a similar complication in his
explaining to Sergis the reasons for the delay of his quest. The
delay is traced to his imprisonment in Radegone:

> But witnesse vnto me, ye heauens, that know
> How cleare I am from blame of this vpbraide:
> For ye into like thraldome me did throw,
> And kept from complishing the faith, which I did owe.
>
> (xi.41)

We see Artegall leave the world of Radegone, supposedly accepting only its import for the humanizing of his principle, rather
than of himself as a person—a man, a Knight, Britomart's lover.
Yet only recognition of the validity of Artegall's plight in Radegone will justify his explanation to Sergis or allow us to refrain
from joining wholeheartedly in Detraction's slanders: "Most
shamefull, most vnrighteous, most vntrew."

IV

Book V stresses the difference between existence in Faerie,
in a type of dreamworld, and existence in the actual world.[20]
Books III and IV do just the opposite; they stress the similarity.
From one perspective or another, these earlier Books have
dealt with love, with the forces of harmony, or if we speak in
terms of heroes, with an inclusiveness, a wholeness of persons.
This is certainly not to disclaim wholeness of persons as a part
of Book V; in fact, a concern with persons constitutes a major
reason why V fails to be an image of abstract Justice, but fulfills,
I believe, its intention as a poem.

To be sure, episodes such as Artegall's disguise—first as a
Knight and then as a woman—are psychic and involve various degrees of self-recognition. Yet in both cases his disguise associates him with falsehood and deceit or is representative of falsehood (Braggadochio's armor; no armor in Radegone). Whenever
Artegall acts as a man or a Knight, he turns out to be false to his
role as the Champion of Justice. In both cases his disguising
actually furthers the cause of injustice.

Artegall's disguising himself as a Knight at Marinell's wedding
and his subsequent entrance into a chivalric world constitute the
chief preparation we are given for the Radigund episode. Guyon's

touching Artegall with temperance during the wedding feast similarly involves a type of self-recognition for the Justicer, one in
which the necessity of interiorizing justice becomes obvious. Yet
these earlier recognitions simply prepare for, and lead to, the
Radigund episode. The significance of these episodes may enrich
the character of Artegall, but there is no real way to channel them
into a fable of justice as such. They are not directly relevant to it.

Britomart's role affords a paradigm of the fate of psychic experiences in Book V. One of the many paired figures in V (Munera,
Pollente; Florimell, Marinell; Adicia, the Suldan; Isis, Osiris),
Britomart embodies the inner principle that complements the outer
and at her first appearance in V, she, like Artegall, also embodies
a lopsided emphasis on a single aspect of reality. When Britomart
hears from Talus that Artegall has been vanquished "Not by that
Tyrant, his intended foe; / But by a Tyrannesse," her response is
childish, unreasonable, and rather unfair. She rages "as a way-
ward childe," and her rage centers on the fact that Artegall has
fallen prey to another woman. She immediately loses sight of
forces which are not strictly personal, and she certainly lacks all
sense of Artegall's signification in an allegory of Justice. Flying
to her room, Britomart paces, she chafes, she throws herself on
the bed, and laments,

> Like as a wayward childe, whose sounder sleepe
>   Is broken with some fearefull dreames affright,
>   With froward will doth set him selfe to weepe;
>   Ne can be stild for all his nurses might,
>   But kicks, and squals, and shriekes for fell despight:
>   Now scratching her, and her loose locks misusing;
>   Now seeking darkenesse, and now seeking light;
>   Then crauing sucke, and then the sucke refusing.
> Such was this Ladies fit, in her loues fond accusing. (vi.14)

Britomart's responses are portrayed so realistically in themselves, so directed to earth, so couched in mimetic verse, simply
so insistent in their own right, that they cannot readily be translated to another sphere, context, or level. Such frenzy and such
uncontrolled passion neither could be nor should be expended in
a lamentation for Justice, a Virtue.[21]

After her outburst at the news about Artegall's imprisonment,
Britomart sets out with Talus to revenge herself on Radigund. As
she rides "melancholicke," she says nothing, looks to neither side,
but with her eyes on the ground, chaws "the cud of griefe and in-

ward paine" (vi.18–19). In this frame of mind, she meets Dolon
and enters his castle. Once within and in the dead of night, Britomart gives voice to her inward pain:

> Ye guilty eyes (sayd she) the which with guyle
>   My heart at first betrayd, will ye betray
>   My life now to, for which a little whyle
>   Ye will not watch? false watches, wellaway,
>   I wote when ye did watch both night and day
>   Vnto your losse: and now needes will ye sleepe?   (vi.25)

Then, just before Dolon springs his trap, it is

> What time the natiue Belman of the night,
>   The bird, that warned Peter of his fall,
>   First rings his siluer Bell t'each sleepy wight   (vi.27)

As yet we know little of Dolon's plan, only that he has some sort
of "purpose," not even specified as an evil one. Britomart knows
absolutely nothing of Dolon's plan and has no particular reason to
suspect his "kindnesse." Yet we hear these Biblical echoes of
betrayal, treachery, lack of faith. The tone is threatening, treacherous. We nearly expect to see a recurrence of the maskers—
Reproach, Repentance, Shame. At the very least, Britomart is
experiencing something—inward pain, a fall, betrayal, lack of
faith.[22]
   But it turns out that the fall is only the letting down of a trick
bed. The betrayal is all external, and her "waylfull plaints" in
the "weary night" are used chiefly to create atmosphere. When
we question the significance of Britomart's experiences, our
questions are put off in an unusual aside—"Now mote ye know
(that which to Britomart / Vnknowen was) whence all this did proceede" (vi.31). The poet rationalizes her experiences. Dolon and
his sons think that Britomart is Artegall, and when they accuse
her in Artegall's name, "Strange were the words in Britomartis
eare" (vi.38). Britomart has entered a strange world. She does
not, so to speak, realize that this is a world external to her; these
forces of injustice are outside her. Betrayal is not in her "guilty
eyes," and bad faith is not personally relevant to her. She does
not realize that she is Mercy, bent on the virtual redemption of
Justice. As suggested before, she has Artegall in mind.
   Britomart's experiences in the Temple of Isis clarify what is
happening to her as both person and figure. In the Temple, as in

459

ANDERSON

Dolon's house, her experiences are predominantly psychic. This time, the priest makes sense of all the fear and force and fury in his rationalization of Britomart's dream.[23] The rationalization suggests only meanings relevant to a Book of order and justice and overlooks the very qualities in the dream which raise "troublous passion" in Britomart's "pensiue mind" (vii.19). As the priest tells her,

> . . . that same Crocodile doth represent
> The righteous Knight, that is thy faithfull louer,
> Like to Osyris in all iust endeuer.
> For that same Crocodile Osyris is,
> That vnder Isis feete doth sleepe for euer:
> To shew that clemence oft in things amis,
> Restraines those sterne behests, and cruell doomes of his.
>
> (vii.22)

Britomart, the too-human woman whom we first see in Book V, is gradually being rationalized right out of her own individual existence. As she moves through Book V she takes on an increasingly mythic and abstract identity—here Isis and clemency.

The need to balance, to complete, and to perfect in Book V is always in danger of generating the substitution of one kind of reality for another, the mere replacement of an old distortion by a new one: passion by reason or the subjective by the objective or an immoderate woman by a myth. Britomart's progress through Book V involves a type of education, and when she finally finds Artegall, she is more fully aware of forces beyond her own will and desires (vii.40–44). She becomes a more reasonable person, but her route to Radegone leaves us asking precisely what this reason has cost and what it has meant; indeed, whether it has spilled the principal or merely the part. Her route strangely resembles a process of sublimation or transference. Even if we were to call this process "transcendence" (a term which the tone and concerns of Book V and especially Britomart's portrayal resist) the problem remains that Britomart herself has eventually to be transcended. If she improves as a person, she becomes irrelevant as one.

It is only for a few stanzas at the end of canto vii that Britomart is presented as a person simply (vii.38–44). No matter how she reaches these stanzas or what happens after them, here she does not have to exist in terms of one aspect of her identity, to the virtual exclusion of the other. She suddenly finds true what before her jealousy had untruly feared: "And then too well beleeu'd, that which tofore / Iealous suspect as true vntruely drad." Her realization complements Artegall's in his battle with Radigund. Unlike Artegall, however, she is astonished not to discover the power and validity of her passions, but the limitations and deceptions of them. In discovering the relation between Artegall's quest in an external world and his honor, she also becomes conscious of a relation between an impersonal and a personal world. Thus Britomart deals "true Iustice"; she reforms Radegone, moderates her own smart, and tempers her passion. In short she embodies the inner mean, and she becomes truly like Isis. Yet even in these stanzas, we do not find an all-inclusive Eden, only the world of inner order to which Britomart belongs. Artegall is strangely passive and strangely silent at the end of canto vii. His presence is itself a qualification. At the end of vii, Artegall has no specific role, for his quest properly belongs to another kind of world.

Once Britomart has rescued Artegall, the Knight's psychic experiences at Radegone are thrown away, or channeled by the poet simply into the fact that Artegall is now free to return to his quest, free to follow his principle of Justice. When Artegall leaves Radegone, Britomart presumably goes back to her castle; her import as a humanizer of Justice has been fulfilled. Her rescue remains significant for the development of the just man, Artegall, but she becomes primarily an instrument, a means or device, for freeing Artegall. She is used; she becomes unimportant in her own right. The demands of the fable require that she should really become Isis: "That all they as a Goddesse her adoring, / Her wisedome" might admire and hearken "to her loring" (vii.42).

V

Unlike Book V, Books II to IV deal with personal virtues, and if these Books also broaden out to society, if they move progressively from the personal to the communal—temperance to chastity to friendship—they do so primarily in terms relevant to an interior world. The Proem to Book IV asserts that "all the workes of those wise sages, / And braue exploits which great Heroes wonne, / In loue were either ended or begunne" (Pro. 3). These lines point to motivations which are personal. They express the power of caritas in society, but caritas starts in the individual's heart.[24] In Books II to IV, Spenser is wholly aware that the ordering of normal psychic and sexual activity reflects, as well as reflects upon, society, but he is less interested in Mammon's gold, or in

461

Busyrane's snares, or in Paridell's aggression as elements of a
social landscape than in the inner life, in psychic responses to
these facts, objects, and situations. Society, as it exists in these
central Books, exists primarily within the mind or for the sake
of the mind. The landscape is that of the mind's action, rather
than that of a denoted world-out-there—denoted for its own sake,
external to the beholder.

In contrast, Arthur's quest on behalf of Belge in the latter half
of Book V is to a wholly foreign nation, one quite apart from
Faerie-Britain. The literal landscape of quest—marshes, fens,
actual cities—is more naturalistic (as opposed to mythic) than in
earlier Books. This landscape may reflect Belge's desolation,
but it only reflects it. The landscape is not so highly allegorical
as the Wandering Wood, the Idle Lake, the Gulf of Greediness, the
Rich Strand, or even the Gardens of Adonis. Belge herself, old,
hiding among "marishes, and myrie bogs," with "fearefull ewftes
. . . mongst the croking frogs," suggests anything but the typical
Faerie damsel in distress. She is so far from the stereotype of
regality that she has almost a touch of Glauce about her:

> . . . And you Sir knight
> (Said she) that taken haue this toylesome paine
> For wretched woman, miserable wight,
> May you in heauen immortall guerdon gaine . . .   (x.21)

Even the verse is plain—chiefly straight narrative in this episode,
as it is in Artegall's parallel quest to Irena's land. Actions tend
to lose their figurative signification and have meaning only in a
narrative context. Arthur's compassion—"low dismounting from
his loftie steede, / Gan to recomfort her"—is seldom paralleled
in the poem.[25] Quite to the contrary, dismounting is usually
associated with degradation or with vulnerability. Belge's world
is neither so dominantly psychic and personal as those in Books
II to IV, nor so exclusively abstract and impersonal as that evident in the first two cantos of Book V.

It is to this type of world, actual, objective, and contemporary,
that Artegall returns after leaving Radegone; had he not done so,
Book V would be about some virtue other than justice. Artegall,
after all, has been through a number of the experiences in Book V
before. The half-human figure we first meet in V has much in
common with the "saluage wight," "Saluagesse sans finesse" (IV.
iv.39). This figure is unaware of his humanity; he lacks consciousness of it: "Ne other to himselfe is knowne this day, / But

that he by an Elfe was gotten of a Fay" (III.iii.26); or as Britomart
once observed so truly, "Nor man it is" but only the "shade and
semblant of a knight" (III.ii.38). If Artegall falls into a human context in V, he has already done so in Book IV; he is only catching up
with himself, finding himself, in the later book.[26] In other words,
if Artegall's experiences as a person and Knight in Book IV had
been directly relevant to justice, we might have dispensed with the
first seven cantos of Book V; and if Artegall had been allowed to
remain in a world of inner concerns and inner order, the world
which Britomart reforms and in which she deals "true Iustice,"
then we might have dispensed with the last five cantos. In these
is presented a world more complex and more truly objective than
that of the early cantos, a world which mirrors or corresponds to
Artegall's new and better perception of reality. As we saw at the
end of canto vii, Britomart becomes aware of the relation between
an impersonal quest and Artegall's personal honor, but it is Artegall, not Britomart, who must make this relation actual, who must
realize it in a world external to the psyche.

Though Artegall leaves the inner world after Radegone, it is in
an interior sense still with him. If he crosses over from a person
to a Principle, the fact remains that his principle has itself become
interiorized, indeed, personalized. His justice has been touched by
love, and it now includes a different kind of justice: "Charity never
leaves a [natural] moral virtue as it finds it. There is not a single
moral act which does not through it become another act, as can be
seen by a simple glance at the metamorphosis to which Charity
subjects it."[27] But the virtue of the just man is an inner one, an
inner justice. This kind of justice may enrich the man who acquires it, but it is not continuous with the world around him. Justice with its own end, the good of society, Justice as such, is not
the same thing.[28] Nor is it exercised in the same kind of world
as is an inner justice. It is at the point where the consciousness
of being just and being a man is continuous that Artegall reenters
a social world. Further, it is in the world which follows the Radigund episode that the topical allegory becomes inescapable and
wholly transparent. It exposes the leap from inner to outer world
for what it is. Potentially Artegall now embodies the relation between an abstract and a personal world, but he has to externalize
and thus fulfill this wholeness, and the realities of an actual and
outer world—the facts of Elizabethan history, for one thing—keep
getting in his way.

A truly objective world exerts pressures which are complex
and too often contradictory. Once set moving in a world charac-

terized by men and women and experiences, rather than simply
by objects, abstract essences, and examples, Artegall is plagued
by the very inclusiveness of his identity. If his Justice has been
humanized, it is now inseparable from his identity as a human
being. In his encounter with Burbon, therefore, Artegall must be
susceptible to the demands made on him as a man, a Knight, Britomart's lover. Yet, as we see when Artegall leaves Britomart,
these demands have nothing to do with Justice as such. Before
Radegone, Artegall always seemed of two minds, but he existed
and acted now as the one, now as the other—now as the Justice
who executes Munera, now as the Knight at Marinell's wedding;
now as the Principle who demolishes the Giant, now as the man
who cannot slay Radigund. After Radegone, Artegall is faced with
the need for a unified response to a world which is really complex,
contradictory, and unyielding.

Artegall's dilemma relates to a tension between the concerns of
Artegall himself and those of Justice as such. This tension exists
between "just" in the sense that a circle is just or a man is complete, true; and "just" in the sense that a man is a true justicer or
is Justice. In the first sense, Aristotle explains: "Metaphorically
and in virtue of a certain resemblance there is a justice, not indeed between a man and himself, but between certain parts of him;
yet not every kind of justice but that of master and servant or that
of husband and wife. For these are the ratios in which the part of
the soul that has a rational principle stands to the irrational part;
and it is with a view to these parts that people also think a man
can be unjust to himself."[29] If Aristotle is really talking about
temperance, which both he and Spenser assume as a condition for
the just man, he is talking only metaphorically about Justice. "Like
the other virtues," explains Gilson, "justice must be interiorized if
it is to become Christian. Before being just in the City, we must
be just in our own eyes in order to be just in the eyes of God."
Nonetheless the matter on which justice "is directly exercised is
no longer the passions of the soul . . . It is not up to justice but
to fortitude or temperance to redress these passions [vengeance,
covetousness]. Justice only intervenes to redress the unjust act
as such."[30] In other words, the personal virtues enable the virtuous man to keep the passions "in a just mean in relation to himself." Justice seeks the just mean in a relationship between two
things external to the virtuous man, to his act, and to the person
acted upon: "It is no longer a question, therefore, of someone who
keeps himself in the just mean but of keeping the just mean of
some thing."

As the just—in the sense of virtuous, true—man differs from Justice itself, so he can differ from the Justicer. No man can be judge and party to an action at the same time. The justicer must abstract himself from direct involvement. Thus "the judge is to be a sort of animate justice . . . an intermediate"; he is sought as "one who is the personification of justice"; he is "only the interpreter of justice . . . he is a living justice."[31] As a living Justice, as an animated principle, Artegall, also a Knight and a human being, is bound to get into trouble—to mix himself or his various selves up. Perhaps the simplest example of this necessity can be stated abstractly. "What most frequently destroys justice is respect of persons,"[32] something less than a wholly "abstracted" or a wholly objective point of view.

There would seem to be no place in an idealized history of Justice for actuality and no place in an animate Justice, abstracted from consideration of persons—himself or others—for the personal motivations of chivalry, of knighthood, of romantic love, or of any ideal, any formalized aspiration, that transcends the purely rational.[33] There would certainly seem to be no place in an idealized history for topical allegory or in an animate Justice for the motivations of a human being. Yet in the latter half of V, we find at once the transparent reference to Belge's land and Arthur's single-handed success in stamping out corruption. Comparison with the actual history of British expeditions to the Netherlands,[34] a comparison invited by both the narrative context and the transparent allegory, suggests that Arthur's action is a pretty fiction with a simplistic (or idealistic) relation to actuality. The same applies to Artegall's success in Irena's land.[35] In V, we are also invited to watch the Justicer, Artegall. Yet we hear Sergis in canto xii tell Artegall that Irena is awaiting the appointed time in Ireland: "In which . . . [he] promist, as . . . [he] were a Knight, / To meete her" (xi.39). Oddly enough, it is at once the Knight whose honor motivates him to put down injustice and the Knight who is late because he could not slay Radigund.

Often in Book V, Spenser invokes Hercules and, as Hallett Smith would have it, the choice of Hercules.[36] Actually the changes which Spenser rings on the traditional choice offer a perfect image of Artegall's dilemma. Instead of a clear-cut distinction and choice between pleasure and virtue, justice in this case, we find Artegall first on the side of justice, a choice made by Astraea, rather than by Artegall himself; next wavering between the two sides at Marinell's spousals; then giving in to "pleasure" in his encounter with Radigund; and finally appearing as a truly just man, greatly dependent on Britomart and Arthur for his efficacy. While Britomart and Arthur embody virtue, for Artegall they also embody pleasure, however virtuous—love and friendship or knightly brotherhood. Both are associated with Artegall's personal honor. Apparently Artegall's legend is concerned less with virtue as such or with history as such than with the way virtue is relevant to a real world, with justice as it is actually found in history, with concept and symbol as they really interact with human motivation and human experience.

VI

We have traced Artegall's progress through the Radigund episode and have seen that the problem is only intensified, now that Artegall is both a Justicer and a Knight. After the Radigund episode, the story operates on a constant split between Artegall's two identities, until Artegall separates from Arthur. As long as Artegall and Arthur are together, Artegall can act as a principle, an abstraction, because Arthur acts as a knight. We might say that this is Spenser's way of protecting Artegall, even while he is allowed to be more exclusively a principle than in the early cantos of the Book. A dual identity in terms of the story, an objective dimension, allows Artegall to maintain a unified identity in symbolic and subjective terms. To this degree no reality need be sacrificed: Artegall remains a man by reference to his identity in Radegone and, for that matter, as an aspect of Arthur in the cantos which they share. Since Arthur is there, Artegall does not have to act within the limitations which accrue to a man and a knight. Following his separation from Arthur, however, he is again on his own as both Justice and Knight. Quite understandably, the hags and the Blatant Beast find him an inviting victim.

Artegall's first action after leaving Britomart is thoroughly consonant with his character as a Knight. He joins in the rescue of a Lady whom Arthur is also rescuing from two pagan knights. There is one pagan for Arthur to kill and one for Artegall. The Lady's name happens to be Samient ("sameness" or "likeness"). If these coincidences were not sufficiently obvious to underline a relation between Arthur and Artegall, we might also recall that they are in fact related, according to Merlin's prophecy in Book III.[37]

Yet no sooner have Prince Arthur and Artegall killed their pagans, than the Prince mistakes Artegall for one of the pagan knights, that is, for one of the Prince's opposites. The Prince

and Artegall prepare to fight, but sure enough, Samient stops
them. Then they

> . . . Ventailes reare, each other to behold.
> Tho when as Artegall did Arthure vew,
> So faire a creature, and so wondrous bold,
> He much admired both his heart and hew,
> And touched with intire affection, nigh him drew.
>
> Saying, Sir Knight, of pardon I you pray,
> That all vnweeting haue you wrong'd thus sore,
> Suffring my hand against my heart to stray:
> Which if ye please forgiue, I will therefore
> Yeeld for amends my selfe yours euermore . . .
> To whom the Prince . . .
> . . . I did mistake the liuing for the ded.
>
> (viii.12–13; my italics)

In context these stanzas are romantic and imbued with an affective quality wholly absent from Artegall's character before Radegone; yet they bristle with allegorical implications. Arthur sees
Artegall in the armor of Justice, of the "saluage wight" "sans
finesse," and he mistakes him for the dead, for the inhuman.[38]
More explicitly, he mistakes him for a natural (pagan) moral virtue which has not been transformed by love. He mistakes Artegall for Justice, only to discover when he sees Artegall's face,
when Artegall lifts his visor, that the Champion of Justice is a
human being and a just man. Equally significant is Artegall's human and knightly response, evident especially in his "intire affection" and in the contrast between his hand and his heart. In a
manner of speaking—or of writing allegory—Artegall then gives
himself—("my selfe"), his self—to Arthur in these stanzas. If
Artegall does not give his body to the Prince in a concrete or
literal sense, he nonetheless gives him his human existence, his
personality as a Knight. Immediately after this episode, Artegall
dons the armor of one of the dead pagan knights. Where before he
had to disguise himself to act as a man and a Knight, Artegall
must now disguise himself in order to act as a principle, an abstraction, a Justicer, or in other words, to be these things.
    In cantos viii and ix, there are repeated silhouettes of Arthur
and Artegall together, as one might expect of the personal and
abstract aspects of a single identity, that of the just man. They
appear on either side of Mercilla during the trial, where one re-

sponds with "fancies ruth" and the other by the ruthless letter of
the law; both are seen in front of Malengin's cave; both are opposed to the Suldan and Adicia. In each case, Arthur battles the
manifestation of force and manifests "knightly" principles, while
Artegall is freed to deal with the principle of injustice and to respond as a living Justice, an animate principle, should. Thus
Arthur destroys the Suldan, the embodiment of tyrannic, or lawless, force, while Artegall, "himselfe discouering plaine" (viii.50),
deals with Adicia, the principle of injustice and lawlessness behind
the Suldan. Adicia keeps to her castle while the Suldan goes outside the castle to commit the specific crime; yet she counsels and
indeed provokes him to break all laws and rules of right, and it is
"she her selfe [who] professeth mortall foe / To Iustice" (viii.20).
The Suldan, or what is left of him, Arthur makes into an "eternall
token" of justice, something to show to the world, but before Artegall can destroy or even restrain Adicia permanently, she breaks
from him and metamorphoses into a tiger. She metamorphoses
into a beast, with which Artegall-the-principle, as we know from
canto i, has been quite capable of dealing, and into a myth, in
which the poet can deal with her: "Tygres scath / In crueltie and
outrage she did pas, / To proue her surname true" (viii.49). If
we are to assume that an Artegallian solution is implicit in
Adicia's metamorphosis, this solution exists only as a reference
to the Artegall of canto i, that is, only in symbolic terms. We do
not see Adicia slaughtered.

In the Malengin episode, Arthur stays before the cave waiting
for the shaggy man, but once Malengin turns into a principle,
Guyle, and into a mythic changeling, only Artegall and his iron
man can deal with him. Similarly, at Mercilla's castle, Arthur
responds as any "empassionate" knight would to a damsel in distress, with so "great ruth his courage gan relent." He responds
the way Artegall responded to Radigund, and his response again
reaffirms the validity of Artegall's in the earlier canto. Because
Arthur is there to respond to Duessa, Artegall does not have to.
Instead, "<u>Artegall</u> with constant firme intent, / for zeale of Iustice
was against her bent." His attitude again recalls canto i, when
Artegall "flam'd with zeale of vengeance inwardly."[39] But here
we again see the difference between Artegall as Justice before
Radegone and Artegall as Justice after Radegone. If Adicia is
destroyed only in symbolic terms, so Duessa is condemned by the
firm intent of Justice, rather than by the flames of vengeance.

Cantos viii and ix suggest that for Artegall as Justicer and for
the poet as allegorizer of Justice there are two possibilities, one

in a world of history and knights and one in a world of myth and
abstraction—one Malfont and one Bonfont. The solutions to both
the problem of Adicia and that of Malengin, who must be destroyed
when he returns to "former hew," must be reached in a recognizable or "fixed," static guise. The real problem seems to be that
the principle of injustice is always returning in another guise; injustice, like Guyle, is not only lawless but formless and limitless
or else it would not be unjust. To give injustice form, whether in
poetry or in actual society, is to deal only with an example, a
symptom, or a single manifestation.[40] Equation of one ill with all
ills, or one unjust person with injustice, ignores the distinction
between general and specific, mythic and actual, or even abstract
and personal. It also ignores the dual movement in Book V: one
force tends towards social actuality and topical allegory, towards
other than strictly rational goals, such as honor, and on an artistic
level, towards personality or characterization; the other force
tends towards the woods and the mythic past,[41] towards rational
abstractions, such as justice and injustice, and towards personifications, animated principles, beast fables, and the like. The one
moves towards a world of actuality; the other, towards a world
which is real only if we think about it.

Arthur accomplishes his mission to Belge's land in cantos x
and xi. He kills his tyrant and destroys his beast (the institutions
of tyranny). He establishes peace in a specific instance and place,
by fighting with the embodiment of specific ills. There is a form,
or limit, to Arthur's task. Yet even the mythological detail begins
now to betray the artificiality of Arthur's triumph and the limitations of analogy between a mythic beast and the actual institutions
of tyranny. "Orthrus," the "two headed dogge" associated with
Geryoneo, is, for example, begot of "Typhaon," begetter of unfavorable winds and god of evil (all the storms, tempests, ill
winds in Book V). Typhaon also kills Osiris, god of justice and
associated earlier with Artegall. But Echidna, mother of Orthrus,
is also mother both of the beast that Arthur kills in canto x and of
the Blatant Beast.[42] Still, Hercules "them all did ouercome in
fight" (x.9—10); and Artegall is a type of Hercules, the Justicer.
When even these references are taken together, their cyclical implications and the implications of limitless repetition are obvious.
If it were otherwise, the Blatant Beast would not be so hot at
Artegall's heels.

An interesting structural development follows the "too-neat"
conclusion of Arthur's chivalric task—to help a damsel and to
slay a dragon. This task marks Arthur's first separation from

469

Artegall since canto viii. Yet Arthur conspicuously divides canto xi with Artegall—a division, or sharing, which is infrequent in The Faerie Queene—and it suggests a deliberate paralleling of the two knights in their final adventures, once again a "sameness."

When Arthur is separated from Artegall, the latter is no longer free to act as a living Justice. Both in his answers to Sergis and in his counsel and assistance to Burbon, Artegall practices and speaks in a chivalric context: "Is ought on earth so pretious or deare, / As prayse and honour?" (xi.62). When Artegall fights Grantorto, he fights a tyrannic figure very much like Arthur's tyrant, and he fights, like Arthur, to save a damsel in distress. Artegall wins as a Knight and in a knightly context, but he is not allowèd to fulfill his mission as a living Justice.[43] He wins the battle with Grantorto, but he does not establish his principle; he does not embody Justice in society. This would, indeed, be to render earth ready for the return of the mythic Astraea. In trying to reform the country, Artegall no longer battles with ills crystallized in one beast and one idol. He battles "all hidden crimes," an image no more autonomous with respect to actuality than are the peasants who beset Burbon.

Artegall's last attempt to be a principle proves abortive. His ending is not, like Arthur's, that of all happy stories:

> And all the vulgar did about them throng,
> To see . . . [the Prince], whose euerlasting praise
> They all were bound to all posterities to raise.   (xi.34)

Unlike Isis, Osiris, or even Arthur, Artegall is not allowed to become a myth or a god. At the end the split in his identity is reasserted. He is still both Knight and Justicer, and his mission ends with the barking of the Blatant Beast. In that bark is the dissonance of two realities, the one within and the one without us.

RENAISSANCE CONCEPTS OF JUSTICE AND THE STRUCTURE OF THE FAERIE QUEENE, BOOK V

James E. Phillips

The Legend of Justice, if not the "riot of formlessness" which Book IV has been called, nonetheless presents problems of plan and structure troubling to critical readers. Some, like H. S. V. Jones, find the first three exempla "in no way connected with the objective or subsequent developments of the plot" and the Radigund-Britomart episode "quite independent of what precedes and follows." Others are concerned about what Kathleen Williams, in her recent study of the epic, terms the "irrelevance" of the last six episodes. Almost all are inclined to agree with Leicester Bradner that the book is a patchwork arrangement and hence an artistic failure. Josephine Waters Bennett convincingly suggests how this apparent patchwork arrangement probably evolved, as Spenser tried to adapt older materials to changing plans and purposes, but she too finds the results disappointing in terms of narrative and allegorical consistency and laments what she terms the "structural failure of the poem."[1]

The disappointment with Book V arises perhaps from the fact that most critics have looked for the controlling pattern in a consistent narrative plan that carries with it a consistent, chronologically developed allegorical plan. On this assumption, it is quite true, as Bradner complains, that "allegory and narrative . . . are not well adjusted." But, as Mrs. Bennett suggests and as William Nelson and Paul Alpers seem to agree, the principles which guided Spenser in the selection and arrangement of his various materials may not have been primarily narrative and chronological, but rather analytical and logical. As Nelson says, this book, like the others, is "a carefully considered composition in which theme, rather than fable, is the central structural element." Yet, even on the premise that, as Mrs. Bennett concludes, the structural principle of Book V is "a logical rather than a temporal order,"

Reprinted from Huntington Library Quarterly, Vol. 33 (1970), pp. 103–120, by permission of the author and the publisher. A shorter version of this essay was read before the English 4 section, "Period of Spenser," at the Modern Language Association meeting in New York in December 1966.

she and others find such episodes as the Amazonian interlude and
the historical allegories at the end difficult to fit into even a logical or analytical pattern.[2]

These continuing disappointments suggest that we perhaps have
not clearly or accurately understood the nature of the logical and
analytical principles which governed Spenser's plan for Book V.
Virgil Whitaker, I think, gives us an important clue to the struc-
turing of every book of The Faerie Queene. Speaking of Book I
he argues that "the moral allegory . . . is theological in its
structure and is based upon the arrangement of points customary
in Renaissance confessionals." He then shows that the adventures
of Red Cross Knight are arranged not to trace the temporal progress of a Christian soul from baptism to redemption, but rather
to develop the logical points that were customarily taken up in
theological treatises, from Revelation and Original Sin through
Justification, Election, Grace, the Church, and the Sacraments.[3]

Following Whitaker's lead, I suggest that if we understand how
Renaissance theorists on Justice arranged and developed their
points according to accepted principles of logical analysis, we
can then see that all of Spenser's seemingly miscellaneous narrative materials in Book V have been consistently selected and
arranged to develop analytically the idea of justice as he and his
age understood it. These principles, I believe, rather than those
of narrative consistency and allegorical continuity, guided the
poet in planning the final disposition of the various episodes which
he had written at different times and for different purposes.

The principles of analysis and exposition spelled out by contemporary rhetoricians with whom Spenser was probably familiar
included Invention, or the determination of points to be made in
developing a subject; and Disposition, or the effective arrangement of the points thus determined.[4] To these, Abraham Fraunce,
a Ramist, added what he termed "Method," or "a disposition of
divers coherent axioms, whereby the most general is ever first
placed: and of divers syllogisms . . . in such sort that thereby
all of them may bee more easily perceaved and better remembered." Elsewhere he stressed, as did most rhetoricians, the
usefulness of exempla in developing the points thus arranged. He
exempted poets from strict adherence to his method, but concluded
that even they must "as much as they may, follow and express
generally the methode which I first put downe." And he noted approvingly in this connection that Spenser had followed just such a
"method" in the April Eclogue.[5]

Principles of logical analysis and exposition such as these

seem to have guided Renaissance political theorists in their efforts
to explain the nature of Justice. Treatises on the subject consistently define and expound it in terms of three major topics or
places: namely, Justice, Equity, and Mercy or Clemency—where
Justice is the absolute, measure-for-measure equation of exact
reward and punishment according to the letter of the law, where
Equity is the taking into account of the individual circumstances
in each case, and where Mercy or Clemency is the human and
divine impulse to forgive. Sir Thomas Elyot apparently had these
three elements in mind when he observed that, "He that hastily
punisseth, ofte tymes sone repenteth. And who that over moche
correcteth, observeth none equitie. And if ye aske what mercy is,
it is a temperaunce of the mynde of hym that hath power to be
avenged, and it is called in Latin Clementia."[6] Elyot, apparently
following the prescription of the rhetoricians, develops these
points primarily by means of exempla drawn from classical history and literature. The same three components of Justice are
delineated in Saint German's Dialogues (1528), in Justus Lipsius'
Sixe Bookes of Politickes, translated in 1594, in Arthur Golding's
1595 translation of Jacques Hurault's Politike, Moral and Martiall
Discourses, and in other expositions of the subject current in the
sixteenth century.[7] Specific definitions and expositions differed,
but the three basic points themselves—Justice, Equity, and Mercy—
appear to have been the fixed "method" in considerations of the
subject as a whole.

These same topics or places, I think, rather than the requirements of narrative consistency, determined Spenser's selection
and arrangement in Book V of narrative materials which he wrote
at different times and often with different purposes in mind. He
begins the book, as did most expositors of Justice, with a general
definition of the subject. Hooker, for example, following Aristotle,
defined Justice basically as the rewarding of good and the punishment of evil.[8] Spenser similarly defines it in the Proem as that
virtue which "both to good and bad dealeth right" (St. 10). But almost immediately he suggests, in Canto i, the three aspects of the
subject outlined in contemporary considerations of the whole nature of Justice: that is, Justice Absolute, which weighs "both
right and wrong / In equall balance with due recompence"; second,
"equitie to measure out along, / According to the line of conscience"; and finally, the quality of mercy, when Justice "needs
with rigour to dispence" (i.7). Having thus introduced the three
topics involved in a discussion of the subject, Spenser proceeds,
in the three main sections of Book V that follow, to exemplify each

with carefully chosen narrative exempla which, as Fraunce had prescribed, are "knit together with transitions, telling briefly what is done, and what is to be."[9]

Like most Renaissance expositors, Spenser turns first in his analysis of the subject to what might be called Justice Absolute— that is, the "measure for measure" concept of exact retribution that rigorously applies the letter of the law to every case. Elyot, calling it "a wille perpetuall and constant, whiche gyveth to every man his right," associates this aspect of Justice with Fortitude, and he provides numerous examples demonstrating the operation of this Justice Absolute in social, political, and economic areas of human activity.[10] Saint German, Lipsius, and Hurault, among other theorists, begin their analyses of Justice in the same way.[11]

And so, I would argue, does Spenser. The first six episodes of Book V, from Sir Sanglier through Terpine, seem clearly to have been selected and arranged as exempla illustrating Justice Absolute, the execution of the letter of the law in a variety of areas. As is often his practice, Spenser breaks into the narrative to emphasize his point in general terms when he says in the first stanza of Canto iv:

> Who so upon him selfe will take the skill
>   True Justice unto people to divide,
>   Had neede have mightie hands, for to fulfill
>   That, which he doth with righteous doome decide,
>   And for to maister wrong and puissant pride.
>   For vaine it is to deeme of things aright,
>   And makes wrong doers justice to deride,
>   Unlesse it be perform'd with dreadlesse might.
> For powre is the right hand of Justice truely hight.

The function of Talus in each of these first six episodes, offensive to some readers because of his unrestrained and remorseless execution of the law, rhetorically underlines the same point. As Graham Hough has observed of Talus in these opening cantos, it is "not his business to consider equity or mercy"—the two other qualities essential to a complete exposition of Justice as the Renaissance understood the virtue.[12] Spenser makes the same point himself when he says, with reference to Artegall's punishment of Munera:

> Yet for no pitty would he change the course
>   Of Justice which in Talus hand did lye;
>   Who rudely hayld her forth without remorse. . . . (ii.26)

With similar ruthlessness, unrestrained by Artegall, Talus pushes
the Giant of Canto ii off a cliff to be shattered on the rocks below
and metes out exact humiliation to punish the unjustified pretensions of Braggadochio in Canto iii. Consistently in this first third
of Book V Talus is perhaps the symbol and certainly the instrument of exact retribution and Justice Absolute, "Immoveable, re-
sistlesse, without end" (i.12), in striking contrast, as we shall see,
to his quite different function in the last two sections of the book.

The episodes themselves appear to have been chosen, as Elyot
chose his in The Governour, to illustrate the operation of Justice
Absolute in various areas of human activity.[13] Exact retribution
for criminality involving murder and rape is demonstrated in the
Sanglier episode. Economic injustice, as exemplified by the rob-
ber baron Pollente and his daughter, is righted with similar rigor
of the law:

> All which when Talus throughly had perfourmed,
> Sir Artegall undid the evill fashion,
> And wicked customes of that Bridge refourmed.   (ii.28)

In the area of social order, Talus makes brutally short work of
the Giant, who, against the laws of God and Nature that established the hierarchy of degrees in all things, "all things would
reduce unto equality" (ii.32). The "spousals of faire Florimell"
in Canto iii, wherein also "Braggadochio is uncas'd," is especially
revealing of Spenser's adaptation of older material to the present
purpose of exemplifying Justice Absolute operating in the area of
personal and domestic relationships. Mrs. Bennett has persua-
sively argued that the tournament for Florimell's wedding and the
disgrace of both Braggadochio and the False Florimell are narrative materials which Spenser had prepared even before the
Florimell episodes in Book IV and probably hark back to his
original introduction of the theme in Book III.[14] Her conclusion
that this material "was obviously put into this book because it was
left over from the story of Florimell and because it shows justice
being meted out to both Braggadochio and the false Florimell" is
confirmed by Spenser's own admission that he is here adapting
the story to his analytical purpose. While disclaiming his ability
to describe the pageantry of this chivalric occasion, he nevertheless concludes:

> But for so much as to my lot here lights,
> That with this present treatise doth agree,
> True vertue to advance, shall here recounted bee.   (iii.3)

In a work which the poet himself regards as a "treatise," the episode of the False Florimell is a logically relevant exemplum designed to illustrate the measure-for-measure aspect of Justice. She is literally weighed in the balance and "vanisht into naught" (iii.24), while Talus strips Braggadochio of the symbols of his unjustified chivalry. As Spenser observes, tying the whole exemplum into his theme:

> these counterfeits were thus uncased
> Out of the foreside of their forgerie,
> And in the sight of all men cleane disgraced. . . . (iii.39)

In Canto iv, Artegall's adjudication of the conflicting claims of Amidas and Bracidas, the one for his brother's land brought by the sea and the other for his brother's treasure brought by the same sea, carries the exemplification of exact, letter-of-the-law justice into the area of property rights. As Greenlaw pointed out, the episode possibly refers, historically, to "the right of the Queen to lands, leavings of the sea, which had been discovered by her mariners." But I cannot agree with Jones or Osgood that Spenser is here illustrating the principle of Equity, or at least, the principle of Equity as the poet and his contemporaries understood it.[15] That principle, as we shall see shortly, involves exceptions to the rule of law. Here, however, Artegall makes it quite clear that he is applying the exact letter of the law of God and Nature as he himself had expounded it to the Giant in Canto ii:

> What though the sea with waves continuall
> Doe eate the earth, it is no more at all:
> Ne is the earth the lesse, or loseth ought,
> For whatsoever from one place doth fall,
> Is with the tide unto an other brought:
> For there is nothing lost, that may be found, if sought.
>
> (ii.39)

So Artegall tells both the brothers in Canto iv, in an exact application of this principle,

> Your right is good (sayd he) and so I deeme
> That what the sea unto you sent, your own should seeme.
>
> (iv.17)

Although Talus, the ruthless executioner, has no function here,

the episode nevertheless clearly seems to have been placed by
Spenser at this point as a further exemplum of Justice Absolute,
or the exact application of the letter of the law.

Finally, the episode in which Artegall and Talus release
Terpine from the "crueltie of womenkynd" and, temporarily at
least, defeat the Amazonian Queen Radigund (iv.21–51) was
probably regarded by Spenser as the sixth and last of the exempla
which he chose to illustrate the nature of Justice Absolute.[16]
Here, if we understand the Elizabethan view of the particular law
involved, Talus clearly seems to be carrying out, as before, the
letter of a law concerning government by women which was of
primary interest in a century that produced Mary Tudor, Mary
Stuart, and Elizabeth I. As I have shown elsewhere, Spenser
agreed with many of his contemporaries that government by
women was against the fundamental laws of God and Nature unless God raised up a clear exception to His own law.[17] When a
woman ruler was a Catholic, as were Mary Tudor and Mary
Stuart, Protestant political theorists, such as John Knox in The
First Blast of the Trumpet against the Monstrous Regiment of
Women (1558), regarded such government as an abomination
contrary to all law and order, calling for the full rigor of Justice Absolute. But to accommodate the Protestant Queen Elizabeth, theorists like Bishop John Aylmer, in An Harborowe . . .
agaynst the Late Blowne Blaste (1559), argued, as did Knox himself eventually, that God would sometimes raise up an exception
to the general rule in order to restore true justice by over-
throwing an unjust (i.e., Catholic) woman ruler. Spenser sub-
scribes to the same argument when he observes in Canto v,
stanza 25, "Vertuous women wisely understand, / That they were
borne to base humilitie, / Unlesse the heavens them lift to lawfull
soveraigntie."

In this light, the Terpine episode and the first defeat of Radigund in Canto iv seem to exemplify not the divine exceptions but
rather the fundamental law against female government itself.
Britomart will subsequently be introduced as a divine exception
to the rule, in illustration of the principle of equity, but in the
present episode, significantly, she has no part. Instead, the letter
of the law against the woman ruler is here executed, as in the
preceding episodes, by Talus as the instrument of Justice Absolute. Because Artegall

> himself did shame on womankinde
> His mighty hand to shend, he Talus sent

> To wrecke on them their follies hardyment:
> Who with few sowces of his yron flaile,
> Dispersed all their troupe incontinent. . . .   (iv.24)

And a few stanzas later, in a second encounter with the Amazons, Talus again executes the letter of the law against female government:

> And every while that mighty yron man,
>   With his strange weapon, never wont in warre,
>   Them sorely vext, and courst, and overran,
>   And broke their bowes, and did their shooting marre. . . .
>   (iv.44)

By the end of Canto iv, then, Spenser has adapted or created six narrative episodes designed to illustrate Justice Absolute, the first point or place in a complete exposition of Justice as this virtue was understood and analyzed in the Renaissance. Given the poet's proclivity to arrange his materials schematically, it might be noted here that these six exempla of Justice Absolute exactly balance the six episodes involving Mercy which conclude Book V.

Exact retribution according to the letter of the law was not, however, either for Renaissance theorists or for Spenser, the only aspect of Justice to be considered. Intimately involved with it was the principle of Equity, usually introduced in contemporary literature as the second place or topic in a logical exposition of the whole subject. Elyot touched on Equity, as distinct from Justice and Mercy but joined to both, and so did Lipsius and Hurault. But Saint German gave the clearest definition of the principle when he described it as "an exception of the law of god, or of the law of reason from the general rules of the law of man, when they by reason of their generalty would in any partycular case judge against the law of god, or the law of reason, the which exception is secretly understand [sic] in every general rule of every positive law."[18] René Graziani explains—rightly, I think—that this concept of Equity "was not 'ordained against the Cruelness of the Law,' but against the chance that a good law might prove unfair in the exceptional case that the infinite variety in men's deeds will produce, thus agreeing with Aristotle's distinction between equity and justice."[19]

I suggest that Spenser in selecting and adapting narrative exempla to illustrate the whole nature of Justice turned next, in the

Temple of Isis and the Amazonian episodes that occupy the center
of Book V, to an exposition of Equity as it was understood in his
day.[20] He signals his intention when he remarks that Isis "in her
person cunningly did shade / That part of Justice, which is Equity, /
Whereof I have to treat here presently" (vii.3). Hence, as Graziani
has argued very convincingly, Britomart's visit to Isis' church
must be identified with this aspect of Justice which is "the main
ethical safety valve between rigid application of law and a reactive
sentimental pity."[21] While few commentators have denied that the
Isis passage is concerned with Equity, the majority tend to regard
the subsequent overthrow of Radigund by Britomart as irrelevant
to this concern and, accordingly, another instance of the narrative
and allegorical inconsistency of the book as a whole. Like other
critics, Graziani finds the killing of Radigund and the violent
destruction of the Amazonian order by another woman to be, as
he says, "not notably clement."[22]

Clement perhaps not. But Equity in the Renaissance sense of
the term, not Clemency, appears to be the point of the exemplum
which Spenser introduces here. Once again, reference to the
Elizabethan controversy about the "regiment of women" makes
the overthrow of Radigund as well as the Isis episode highly relevant to the poet's delineation of Equity as an aspect of Justice.
We have already seen that he appeared to agree with many of his
contemporaries that government by women—and by Catholic
women in particular—was a violation of all law and order, meriting the exact retribution which Talus administers according to
the letter of the law in Canto iv. But Spenser also appears to
have agreed with those of his contemporaries who sought to justify, contrary to the letter of the law, the triumphant gynecocracy
of the Protestant Queen Elizabeth. As I have argued elsewhere:

> It is in Britomart, as she overthrows Radigund and the
> Amazonian system of government, that we see most clearly
> how God, by endowing a woman with the virtue of justice,
> singles her out as an exception to the general law of nature
> that forbids female government. Having vanquished Radi-
> gund in battle and entered her stronghold, Britomart re-
> mains for a period,

> > During which space she there as Princess rained,
> > And changing all that forme of common weale,
> > The liberty of women did repeale,
> > Which they had long usurpt; and them restoring
> > To mens subjection, did true Justice deale: . . .

Thus, Spenser's Amazons have "shaken off the shamefast band, / With which wise Nature did them strongly bynd. . . ." But, because she demonstrates her ability to administer justice by forcing women into the "base humilitie" to which they were born under "man's well ruling hand," Britomart clearly identifies herself as one of those exceptional women, instruments of divine justice, whom the heavens "lift to lawful soveraintie."[23]

Here, I think, we have a clear exemplum of that aspect of Justice called Equity, "an Exception of the Law of God, or of the Law of Reason." For true and complete Justice requires, as Spenser insists, subservience of women to men. But if the attainment of this end can be accomplished by no other means, then God will make an equitable exception to his own law and "lift to lawfull soveraintie" a woman like Britomart, endowed with special qualifications, who will "true Justice deale."

In this context, the Dolon episode preceding Britomart's visit to Isis' church and her overthrow of Radigund is not only consistent with the concept of Equity exemplified in these central cantos of Book V, but absolutely essential to it.[24] Most commentators agree with A. B. Gough in reading this episode as historical allegory reflecting the futile efforts of Philip II and the Guises of France to trap Elizabeth before she could execute Mary Queen of Scots in 1587.[25] Such a reading does not preclude the probability that Spenser also saw these events as an exemplum of an essential topic in his exposition of Equity. He makes it clear, as did his contemporaries, that when God raises an exception to the law against government by a woman, he does so by endowing her with capacity to "true Justice deale," the first requirement in any governor. Sir Thomas Craig, for example, argued on scriptural authority that God may grant this special ability to women and thereby qualify them as his chosen representatives.[26] Logically, then, it was essential that Spenser first exemplify the capacity to administer justice, even Justice Absolute, in a woman who will be the exception to the law against the woman ruler. Significantly in this respect, Dolon himself mistakes Britomart for Artegall "chiefly by that yron page he ghest, / Which still was wont with Artegall to remaine" (vi.34). In other words Talus, already identified in preceding episodes as ruthless executioner of Justice Absolute, is here associated with a woman, as "With his rude yron flaile" Dolon's sons and their forces "gan flie." But in the following canto, when Britomart enters the Temple of

Isis and the definition as well as the exemplification of the principle of Equity begins, "Talus mote not be admitted to her part"
(vii.3); moreover, his function as executioner of the Amazons is
restrained by Britomart in a way that Artegall never demonstrated
in the earlier episodes:

> Yet when she saw the heapes, which he did make,
> Of slaughtred carkasses, her heart did quake
> For very ruth, which did it almost rive,
> That she his fury willed him to slake: . . .   (vii.36)

Clearly Spenser here seems to be adapting what Mrs. Bennett
calls older, Ariostan narrative material to exemplify not the nature of Justice Absolute but rather the principle of Equity as
illustrated in a woman qualified to bear governance as an exception to the law against the woman ruler.[27]

But neither Spenser nor Renaissance theorists regarded Justice to be completely analyzed and described if it involved only
the "rigour" of the law and the equitable exception to the rule.
The third and usually the final topic or place developed in expositions of the virtue was Mercy, or Clemency. Elyot called
Mercy "a temperance of the minde of hym that hath power to be
avenged, and it is called in Latin Clementia, and is always joyned
with reason." He contrasts it with "Misericordia," or vain pity,
a sentimentality that he says is ultimately cruel and unjust.[28]
Lipsius, who had discussed Justice and Equity together as the
first and foremost of "the great resplendent lights" necessary for
a prince, similarly turned next to "Clemencie" as the second
"resplendent light," or "the Moon of Empires," defining it as "a
vertue of the mind, which with judgement, enclineth from punishment, or revenge, to lenitie."[29] Hurault agreed that "a prince
ought to be merciful"; but he added, in a characteristic sixteenth-
century view of the quality, that "this mercie consisteth in par-
donning the offences that concern but the prince himselfe, and the
partie that is hurt by them, and not any other mens that are done
against the common-weale." Echoing Elyot's warnings against
"Misericordia" or vain pity, he concluded: "For favour and
mercy granted to naughty-packs, is not else but crueltie towards
good men."[30]

Despite the arguments of Hough and others that the final six
episodes of Book V are not only irrelevant but cruel, I would agree
with Hamilton and Nelson that these exempla "focus on the triumph
of Mercy which fulfills justice."[31] Viewed in the light of contem-

porary ideas on the subject, all of these episodes, without exception, appear to be illustrations of an Elizabethan concept of Mercy selected and arranged by Spenser to complete his exposition of the whole nature of Justice.

Most commentators agree that the last six episodes of Book V allegorize events in Elizabethan history, and I for one am convinced by Mrs. Bennett's argument that each episode specifically allegorizes a historical instance of Elizabeth's punitive actions against the Catholic enemies of Protestantism.[32] Strange as it may seem to Graham Hough and others who regard these actions as harsher than Hitlerism, the same actions were nevertheless repeatedly described at the time as acts of Mercy, while any show of softness toward the Catholic "naughty-packs" was regularly called "misericordia," or that vain pity which is ultimately cruel. For example, a paper presented to Commons in 1572 urging Elizabeth to proceed "with severity" against Mary Queen of Scots concluded:

> Therefore as the Queens Majesty indeed is mercifull, so we most humbly desire her that she will open her Mercy towards Gods People and her good Subjects, in dispatching those Enemies that seek the confusion of God's cause amongst us, and of this noble Realm.
>
> It may also be said that to spare one Person being an Enemy, a Stranger, a professed Member of Antichrist . . . may justly be termed <u>Crudelis misericordia</u>.[33]

A reading of the final episodes of Book V as exempla of Mercy in this Elizabethan sense has previously been suggested for some of the incidents. Graziani, for example, has noted that the trial of Mary Stuart, which every reader since her own son has recognized to be allegorized in Canto ix, was justified by contemporaries on the grounds that Elizabeth on this occasion showed "her Mercy towards Gods People and her good Subjects, in dispatching those enemies that seek the confusion of Gods cause amongst us."[34] Similarly, H. S. V. Jones has pointed out that the Belge episode in Canto x portrays Elizabeth's policy in the Low Countries as merciful because of her sympathy for an oppressed Protestant population.[35] His reading of this episode is supported by Spenser's general statement on the nature of Mercy, which stands at the head of this same canto, balancing the general statements on Justice Absolute at the head of Canto iv and on Equity at the head of Canto vii. Spenser seems to signal his intention in

this final third of Book V quite explicitly when he begins Canto x
by stating:

> Some Clarkes doe doubt in their devicefull art,
> Whether this heavenly thing whereof I treat,
> To weeten Mercie, be of Justice part. . . .   (x.1)

Concluding that Mercy is indeed coequal with Justice Absolute, he
continues:

> For if that Vertue [i.e., Justice Absolute] be of so great
>   might,
> Which from just verdict will for nothing start,
> But to preserve inviolated right,
> Oft spilles the principall, to save the part:
> So much more then is that of powre and art,
> That seekes to save the subject of her skill,
> Yet never doth from doome of right depart:
> As it is greater prayse to save, then spill,
> And better to reforme, then to cut off the ill.   (x.2)

And he ends his general statement by identifying Mercilla with
Elizabeth herself as the embodiment of this uniquely Elizabethan
concept of mercy:

> Those Nations farre thy justice doe adore:
> But thine own people do thy mercy prayse much more. (x.3)

Assuming, as Spenser probably did, that Elizabeth's "own
people," both at home and abroad, were Protestants either threatened or persecuted, then her "mercy" in destroying the Catholic
enemies of Protestantism appears to be clearly exemplified not
only in the Mary Stuart and the Netherlands allegories, as Graziani and Jones have suggested, but also in the other four episodes
in this last section of Book V.

In this context, the Souldan episode in Canto viii, identified by
most commentators as an allegory of the defeat of the Armada,
would seem to be intended by Spenser as an obvious example of
Mercy—God's and the queen's—toward threatened Protestants.
Such, at any rate, was the interpretation of the Spanish defeat
given in innumerable pamphlets and broadsides published in 1588
and 1589 commemorating the English victory.[36] Similarly, the
struggle with Guile in Canto ix, commonly interpreted as an alle-

gory of English efforts to exterminate Catholic Irish rebels, might also be regarded as an exemplum appropriate to the development of this Protestant Elizabethan concept of Mercy. The case is even stronger if we accept Mrs. Bennett's argument that "the Guile episode represents a further phase of the religious struggle—that of the English law with the Jesuits and missionary priests who worked in both England and Ireland."[37] Elizabeth's repressive measures against the Jesuits had already been identified as acts of mercy by William Cecil, Lord Burghley, himself, in the peroration of his pamphlet, The Execution of Justice in England (1583). Defending the queen's harsh laws against this "wicked flock of the seedemen of sedition" he concludes:

> there is no doubt by Gods grace (her Majestie being so much given to mercie and devoted to peace) but al coleur and occasion of shedding the blood of any more of her naturall subjectes of this land, should utterly cease. Against whose malices, if they shall not desist, Almighty God continue her Majestie with his spirit & power long to reigne and live in his feare, and to be able to vanquish them and all Gods enemies, and her rebels & traitors both at home and abroad, and to maintaine and preserve all her naturall good loving subjectes, to the true service of the same Almightie God according to his holy worde and will.[38]

The Bourbon episode in Canto xi, ambiguous and qualified as it is, would probably have been viewed by Spenser and his contemporaries as still another exemplum drawn from current history to illustrate the Elizabethan concept of Mercy. Artegall's rescue of Bourbon, after chiding him for throwing away his shield, and his subsequent reuniting of Bourbon with the lady Flourdelis, has generally been recognized as a transparent allegory of English aid to Henry of Navarre even after that Huguenot prince found Paris worth a Mass and renounced his Protestant faith in 1593.[39] Distressing as this apostasy was to the English, they nevertheless appear to have regarded Henry, a moderate Catholic, as far less a danger to the Protestant cause in general and to England in particular than was the Guise–Spanish Catholic party in France, instigators of the well-remembered St. Bartholomew Massacre; Henry, with English aid, finally broke their power in 1595.[40] Relatively speaking, then, the Bourbon episode thus construed might well have been considered by Spenser as another act of "Mercy towards God's people" suitable for inclusion in this final section of his exposition of Justice.

The climactic episode of Book V—the rescue of Irena from Grantorto—offers perhaps the clearest evidence that Spenser regarded all of these final episodes as exempla of the Mercy towards God's people that fulfills Justice. Whether we accept the traditional identification of Artegall as Lord Grey or agree with Mrs. Bennett that he is Sir John Norris, the fact remains that his actions allegorize an English policy in Ireland which Spenser regarded as truly merciful. In <u>A View of the Present State of Ireland</u> he is explicit on this point of policy. After hearing of the sufferings of the queen's subjects in Ireland, Eudox is made to say:

> But now when all thinges are brought to this passe and all filled with this rufull spectacles of soe manie wretched Carcasses starvinge, goodlie Countries wasted, so huge a desolation and Confusion as even I . . . do greatlie pittye and Comiserate, if it shall happen that the state of this miserye and lamentable image of thinges shalbe tolde and felingelye presented to her sacred majestye beinge by nature full of mercye and Clemencye whoe is moste inclynable to such pittifull Complaintes and will not endure to heare suche tragedies made of her people and pore subjectes as some aboute her maie insinuate, then shee perhaps for verye Compassion of such Calamities will not onelye stopp the streame of suche violence and retorne to her wonted mildnes, but allso con them litle thankes which have bene the Aucthors and Counsellours of suche blodye platformes. So I remember that in the late government of that good Lo. Grey when after longe travell and manye perilous assayes he had broughte thinges allmoste to this passe that yee speake of, that it was even made readie for reformacion and mighte have bene broughte to what her majestie woulde, like Complainte was made againste him that he was a blodye man and regarded not the lief of her subjectes no more than dogges but had wasted and Consumed all, soe as now she had nothinge allmoste lefte but to raigne in theire ashes. Eare was sone lente thearunto, all sodenlye turned topsyde-turvey, He noble Lord eftsones was blamed the / The wretched people pittied and new Councells plotted in which it was Concluded that a generall pardone shoulde be sente over to all that woulde accepte of it. uppon which all former purposes weare blanked, the governour at a baye and not onelye all that greate and longe Chardge which she had before bene at quite loste and Cancelled, but allso all

that hope of good which was even at the dore put backe and Cleane frustrate.[41]

The point made here that a harsh policy with Catholic rebels, which was true mercy to Elizabeth's Protestant subjects, had been frustrated by a vain pity or misericordia that by pardoning the sources of trouble was ultimately destructive and cruel to these same Protestant subjects, was reiterated by Spenser in the direct appeal to the queen which he made in A Brief Note of Ireland. Writing "Out of the ashes of disolacon and wastnes of this your wretched Realme of Ireland," he complains that while she has relieved the "destitute Calamities" in "Countries moste remote" (i.e., the Protestants on the Continent), she "yet upon this miserable land being your owne juste and heritable dominion letteth no one little beame of your large mercie to be shed. . . ."[42] Therefore, as he assures the queen later in the document,

> Whereas your Majestie as you have hitherto made your selfe through all the worlde a gloriouse example of mercie and Clemencye and even unto these vile Catifes (though moste unworthie thereof) So nowe by extending upon them the terror of your wrath in avengement of there continuall disloyalltie and disobedience you shall spreade the honorable fame of your Justice and redeeme both your owne honour and allso the reputacion of your people. . . . But our feare is leste your Majestes wonted mercifull minde should againe be wrought to your wonted milde courses and perswaded by some milde meanes either of pardons or proteccions, this rebelliouse nacion may be againe brought to some good conformacion which wee beseech allmightie god to averte.
>
> (pp. 241–242)

Spenser's insistence in these passages that true mercy for God's people can only be manifest if vain pity for Catholic rebels is rejected explains why he would regard the Artegall-Irena-Grantorto episode as the most appropriate exemplum drawn from current history to demonstrate the nature of that mercy which fulfills justice. With the aid of Talus, symbol of Justice Absolute, Artegall destroys Grantorto, the Catholic cause whether he be identified with Philip II or with the Pope,

> And all such persons, as did late maintayne
> That Tyrants part, with close or open ayde,
> He sorely punished with heavie payne. . . .   (xii.25)

Then, like Lord Grey in The View, who "broughte thinges allmoste to this passe that yee speake of, that it was even made readie for reformacion," so Artegall,

> During which time, that he did there remaine,
>   His studie was true Justice how to deale,
>   And day and night employ'd his busie paine
>   How to reforme that ragged common-weale. . . . (xii.26)

But just as Lord Grey was recalled at the behest of parties who, moved by the "vain pity" which is ultimately cruel, charged that he was "a blodye man" and urged "pardons or proteccions" for all offenders, so Artegall "His course of Justice . . . was forst to stay" and was recalled to be maliciously attacked by the hags Envie and Detraction, who claimed

> that he had with unmanly guile,
>   And foul abusion both his honour blent,
>   And that bright sword, the sword of Justice lent,
>   Had stayned with reprochfull crueltie,
>   In guiltlesse blood of many an innocent. . . .   (xii.40)

Mrs. Bennett has pointed out that Artegall's fate is equally applicable to Lord Grey and Sir John Norris (pp. 191, 195, 201). Regardless of historical identifications, however, Artegall's adventures in the Irena episode clearly defend an English policy in Ireland which Spenser represents not as "reproachfull cruel-tie" but rather as the "mercy and clemency which will not endure to heare such tragedies made of her people." Viewed in this light, as an illustration of the mercy that fulfills justice for God's people, the Irena episode becomes not only the logical but also the inevitable exemplum culminating the tripartite exposition of Justice, Equity, and Mercy which governs the structure and de-velopment of Book V.

OUR NEW POET: SPENSER, "WELL OF ENGLISH UNDEFYLD"

A. C. Hamilton

Allegorical interpretation is the art of telling "stretchers." Accordingly, the case against interpretation of The Faerie Queene is formidable. I have presented it in part in a recent article on modern critical approaches to the poem:

> For a poem which is such an elaborate dance of meanings, it becomes clear very quickly that interpretation is a matter of saying what the poem chooses not to say, and certainly not in the critic's words, or making explicit what the poem poem prefers to keep implicit. It forces a reading which the work obstinately resists or withholds for the moment of its own choosing. . . . All interpretation violates the poem's subtlety, complexity, and wholeness by rationalizing its imaginative statements. It seems designed to protect us from fearful exposure to the work itself. . . . Once criticism has brought an informed reader to the poem, it should leave him alone. As much may be said for any imaginative work, but it needs to be said with special emphasis for allegory whose images depend upon the responses that they awaken in readers, and above all for Spenser's allegory whose end is not understanding but virtuous action. The Faerie Queene is not meant to be understood but to be possessed. We look for moral meaning when we should be attending to released moral energy. [1]

I do not wish to press this case further except to stress, for my immediate purpose in this paper, that interpretation juggles words out of context. It selects its words by examining the poem through opaque filters—usually moral ones that come only in shades of grey—which allow only certain words to pass through, dim and distorted. After these words are associated with some analogous use in selected non-poetic contexts, they are put back into the

Forthcoming in A Theatre for Spenserians, ed. Judith M. Kennedy and James A. Reither, to be published by the University of Toronto Press. First delivered as a lecture at the International Spenser Colloquium held at Fredericton, October 22–24, 1969.

poem; but now they are infected, being drained of poetic vitality and charged with non-poetic meaning.

I cannot recall any interpretation of The Faerie Queene which may not be faulted as a partial and distorted image of the poem. I am not thinking of perverse readings which offer a new view of the poem by turning it upside down but rather of those which all of us would accept as persuasive. For example, when the Red Cross Knight is defeated by Orgoglio, it seems reasonable to infer that he falls through pride. Most certainly he falls: one who was on horseback lies upon the ground, first to rest in the shade and then to lie with Duessa; although he staggers to his feet, he soon falls senseless upon the ground; and finally, he is placed deep underground in the Giant's dungeon. The Giant himself is not "identified" until after the Knight's fall: then he is not named Pride but rather Orgoglio, a very un-English and unpronounceable name. Though he is a proud giant, his pride is only one detail in a very complex description. In his size, descent, features, weapon, gait, and mode of fighting, he is seen as a particular giant: he is not seen as a particular kind of pride. To name him Pride is to select a few words—and not particularly interesting ones—such as "arrogant" and "presumption" out of some twenty-six lines or about two hundred words, and to weight these as pride from their significance in theology. If then we say that the Knight falls through Pride, we interpret the episode perhaps to the satisfaction of most readers but we have left the poetry altogether. While the Knight is guilty of sloth and lust before he falls, he is not proud; in fact, he has just escaped from the house of Pride. At this point the interpreter may be tempted to ignore Orgoglio altogether and say simply that the Knight falls through lust. Then the sin of concupiscence supplies the basis for a religious reading of the episode. Yet Spenser prevents any direct religious reading— he deliberately prevents it—by attributing the Knight's weakness before Orgoglio to his act of drinking, in ignorance, the enfeebling waters issuing from a nymph who, like him, rested in the middle of her quest.

My immediate quarrel with interpretation, however, is not that it remains abstract, generalized and unfocussed, but that it engages too little of the poem too obliquely and always at two removes from its "Idea or fore-conceit." It engages too few words in the poem, and even these it reads out of context.

Interpretation may be controlled and refined by reading the words more carefully in context. The canto that relates the Knight's fall begins:

What man so wise, what earthly wit so ware,
As to descry the crafty cunning traine,
By which deceipt doth maske in visour faire,
And cast her colours dyed deepe in graine,
To seeme like Truth.

Since these lines seem to provide no more than a very general moral comment upon what follows, the reader is tempted to hurry over them. Yet he should pause because some words call attention to themselves within the context of the poem. For example, "traine" signifies "guile" but also the robe in which Duessa, the daughter of Deceit, is disguised, Duessa "cast[s] her colours" in the sense in which that term is used in rhetoric and also in painting: she "arranged her colours." Yet the phrase means also "to lose colour" for Duessa, "clad in scarlot red" (ii 13) appears in Una's "visour faire." Yet her colours are "dyed deepe in graine" both in the general sense, "dyed thoroughly" and in the particular sense, "dyed scarlot." The care and precision with which these words are used should alert the reader to an awareness that each word and action may be significant: the Knight rests, he rests by a fountain, he is disarmed, his armour is rejected as "yron-coted Plate," his steed feeds, he feeds upon the shade—and so throughout the canto.

The significance of the words in the poem is defined by the language of allegory which Spenser employs. That the Knight "feedes upon the cooling shade" and bathes his forehead in the wind which plays through "the trembling leaves" recalls in general terms Jeremiah's denunciation of the sinner who lay down like a harlot under every tree that had green leaves. However, the meaning of these words is defined specifically by the similar setting of Fradubio's story of his fall (ii 28) and later by the Giant's entrance at which "trees did tremble" (vii 7). Further, the act of feeding upon the shade of the tree and of drinking the poisoned water become a prelude to the Knight's defeat by Orgoglio as later his feeding upon the Tree of Life and drinking from the Well of Life become a prelude to his victory over the Dragon. Spenser's language of allegory demands that one read the poem with the same care with which it was written. When its grammar is mastered, more words may be included in our response. For example any reader should be prepared to respond to the careful word-play in the lines that describe the Knight and Duessa as they "bathe in pleasaunce of the joyous shade, / Which shielded them against the boyling heat" (vii 4). The use of that very Spenserian term "pleas

490

aunce" has been restricted to the kind of pleasure that the Knight first took with Duessa when he made "faire seemely pleasaunce" (ii 30) with her under Fradubio's shade, and to the activity in the house of Pride when Lucifera's crew fed "with pleasaunce of the breathing fields" (iv 38). The fact that the shade—"joyous shade" is an oxymoron—now shields him infers the loss of his true shield of faith and so points to his present helplessness before "the destruction that wasteth at noon day" (Psalm xci 6).

In the article quoted earlier, I noted that modern criticism is "moving to the point where each word bears an equal weight of significance." The reviewer in the Times Literary Supplement termed such criticism "a nightmare vision." However, I approve its direction though I would claim that all words are equal in Orwell's sense 'All words are equal but some words are more equal than others.' Ideally one should respond wholly to the poem by responding to it as a whole. In practice, critics short-circuit much of it in order to assert some prose summary of meaning. Unfortunately, The Faerie Queene may be read all too easily on a number of allegorical levels. It remains very difficult to read on its literal level: then one must respond not to what it may be taken generally to mean but to what its words actually say. Most readers, at least most critics, forsake the golden words for drab ideas. In place of that maker who offers "the brightnesse of brave and glorious words,"[2] we have substituted the philosopher /thinker / Church adherent who is the product of the Renaissance and Reformation (that was yesterday) or the "sage and serious teacher" who is a severely Miltonic Spenser (that is today). Spenser as the poet, the skilled craftsman in words, has hardly been understood. He deserves the praise which Jonson threw away on Coryate: "he is a great and bold Carpenter of words, or (to expresse him in one like his owne) a Logodaedale."

In his art of language, Spenser is closer to the fabulous artificer Joyce than he is to the allegorist Dante. He shares Yeats's faith that "Words alone are certain good"; he believes with Wallace Stevens that "the gaiety of language is our seigneur"; and, above all, he practises the craftsmanship of words upheld by Dylan Thomas:

> I am a painstaking, conscientious, involved and devious craftsman in words . . . I use everything and anything to make my poems work and move in the directions I want them to: old tricks, new tricks, puns, portmanteau-words, paradox, allusion, paranomasia, paragram, catachresis,

slang, assonantal rhymes, vowel rhymes, sprung rhythm.
Every device there is in language is there to be used if you
will. Poets have got to enjoy themselves sometimes, and
the twistings and convolutions of words, the inventions and
contrivances, are all part of the joy that is part of the painful, voluntary work.[3]

These verbal devices and many others are exploited by Spenser
with the result that The Faerie Queene illustrates and justifies
Sidney's daring claim that the English language is "indeed capable
of any excellent exercising of it."[4]

In this paper I intend to consider the range and variety of Spenser's verbal craftsmanship: his care and precision in choice of
words, his use of etymology and puns, his use of ambiguity in
syntax and meanings of words, and his word-coinages. Since his
art of language is sophisticated, complex and immensely varied,
I restrict myself to a general survey and cite only representative
examples from the poem. My subject remains largely unexplored
and my remarks are merely suggestive.

The general meaning of a word in its poetic context may be
clarified through spelling or etymology, its place in the line, its
relation to other words in the line and stanza, and its thematic
use in the canto or Book. For most words, one need note only the
care and precision with which they are used to reveal their meanings. For example, after Guyon leaves Phaedria's island and before he meets Mammon, he is compared to a mariner:

> As Pilot well expert in perilous wave,
>   That to a stedfast starre his course hath bent,
>   When foggy mistes, or cloudy tempests have
>   The faithfull light of that faire lampe yblent,
>   And cover'd heaven with hideous dreriment,
>   Upon his card and compas firmes his eye,
>   The maisters of his long experiment,
>   And to them does the steddy helme apply,
> Bidding his winged vessell fairely forward fly:
>
> So Guyon having lost his trusty guide,
>   Late left beyond that Ydle lake, proceedes
>   Yet on his way, of none accompanide;
>   And evermore himselfe with comfort feedes,
>   Of his owne vertues, and prayse-worthy deedes.
>
> (II vii 1–2)

These lines serve usefully enough as filler between two major episodes in Guyon's journey. The simile itself is too traditional to call attention to itself. Only through reading the rest of the poem may the reader appreciate and understand its use here, and recognize, for example, its special relevance to the knight of Temperance whose mastery over the passions is expressed as a victory over water. The phrase, "a stedfast starre," may be taken to refer to "the stedfast starre" (I ii 1) which, as the curious reader may note, is Arcturus, that star associated with Arthur who guides each knight. However, the indefinite article controls any larger inference here. The balanced phrases, "faithfull light" and "faire lampe" express the love of light and horror of darkness which extend throughout the poem, again without any special point here except as Guyon is about to enter the darkness of Mammon's cave. The term "dreriment" would strike any reader as particularly Spenserian: its general meanings, whatever they are, are felt rather than understood, and made sufficiently explicit by the re-enforcing adjective "hideous." The first word that needs any gloss for a modern reader is "card," which refers to the mariner's geographical chart rather than the graduated compass card; and the first phrase that needs any explication is "maisters of his long experiment" which means "instruments of his long experience." Yet for the sixteenth-century reader neither word or phrase would cause any difficulty. Even for the modern reader, the import of the two lines in which they occur is clear: as the mariner must turn from sure, heavenly guidance to his own, less reliable means, so Guyon must turn from the sure, outward guidance of the Palmer to his own inner virtue. In the ninth line, the alliteration of "f" in "fairely forward fly" communicates a sense of speed—a dangerous speed—as it comes at the end of the stanza, but its use here as a verbal device is not obtrusive. In the next stanza, the "comfort" that Guyon finds in his own virtue has a precise sixteenth-century sense, "aid, support" (OED 1); it lacks entirely the modern sense of "moral smugness" (which it seems to arouse in Guyon's modern readers). "In this time, place, and fortune," Sidney's two princes say in a similar moment of crisis, "it is lawful for us to speak gloriously." The entire phrase, "with comfort feedes, / Of his owne vertues," reveals both the self-sufficiency by which Guyon may resist Mammon's temptations and the limitations of his virtue. As he feeds upon his virtues, he confronts Mammon who "feede[s] his eye" (4) upon gold, and is led into a realm where he too "did feed his eyes" (24) upon Mammon's riches. By the end of the temptation, he has consumed his own virtues, faints through lack of food, and lies helpless before his enemies. The fuller import of the simile that opens Canto vii is realized only in Canto viii: heavenly powers must guide the Palmer to Guyon's side, and the Palmer, in turn, guides Arthur to uphold his side in the quarrel with Pyrochles and Cymochles. Only then does Guyon regain that sure, outward guidance which will carry him successfully on his voyage to the Bower of Bliss. In that final voyage the Palmer's staff and the helmsman's stiff oars comment upon the "card and compas"—notoriously unreliable means of navigation in the sixteenth century—to which his virtue may only be compared at the mid-point of his quest. Though these opening lines continually expand in significance through their context, their meaning is sufficiently clear in themselves. In these lines, then, and generally throughout the poem—though a poem of 36,000 lines—words are chosen with scrupulous care for their clarity and precision.

Any word or phrase that is repeated justifies the attention called to it. It does so because the whole poem possesses the harmonious unity of a dance. For example, when Guyon confronts Acrasia in her Bower, he binds her and "their gardins did deface" (II xii 83). To many modern readers it has seemed that Guyon suddenly loses his cool and over-reacts. Yet that painful word, "deface," with its implication of a wanton destruction of beauty, suggests how carefully Spenser articulates the concluding action of Book II. As Arthur had confronted Maleger whose forces almost "deface" (xi 6) the Castle of Alma until he, in response, "fowle Maleger doth deface" (xi Arg.), so Guyon confronts Acrasia whose lover "his nobility [doth] so foul deface" (xii 79) and, imitating Arthur in his response, "their gardins did deface." With larger scope, repetition may be expressed through comparable actions within an episode and beyond it to include a whole book. For example, when Gardante wounds Britomart with his arrow,

> yet was the wound not deepe,
> But lightly rased her soft silken skin,
> That drops of purple bloud thereout did weepe,
> Which did her lilly smock with staines of vermeil steepe.
>
> (III i 65)

Immediately this description suggests Adonis' wound shown in the tapestry of the house of Malecasta: "the gore, / Which staines his snowy skin with hatefull hew" (38). Love's wounding is shown to afflict all characters in the Book. In the next canto the origin of

her wound by Gardante is explained: she has been wounded by
love through the sight of Artegall in Venus' glass (ii 24 ff). At the
end of the Book she receives a similar wound from Busyrane:

> it strooke into her snowie chest,
> That little drops empurpled her faire brest . . .
> Albe the wound were nothing deepe imprest.   (xii 33)

The curious word "imprest," which means imprinted, indicates
that Busyrane marks in her flesh the characters which he writes
with Amoret's blood in order to enchant her. This word in one
of several designed to show how Britomart submits herself to
Amoret's torture. She forces Busyrane to "reherse" (36) the
bloody verses that charm Amoret, that is, say over again what he
had said to her. Upon hearing his verses, "horror gain the virgins hart to perse" (36) just as Amoret's heart had been pierced.
Through her chastity, however, she triumphs. Such repetition
suggests that Amoret embodies Britomart's love for Artegall.
Further, it clarifies Britomart's role in Book III. While the Red
Cross Knight defeats his enemy by force and Guyon his by wit,
she triumphs by submitting herself as a sacrifice. By closely
attending to such a simple device as verbal repetition, the reader
is led to understand the allegory.

Scrupulous care and precision in choice of words mark any
major poet. Among them Spenser is distinguished as a Renaissance poet by his witty use of words; and among Renaissance
poets, he is distinguished by his joy in words. Only Shakespeare
in Love's Labour's Lost matches him. He was sustained to write
the longest major poem in our language because words released
in him enormous creative powers. He seems never to tire. After
the lengthy procession of rivers, which may exhaust the attention
of the most sympathetic reader, he continues:

> O what an endlesse worke have I in hand,
>   To count the seas abundant progeny,
>   Whose fruitfull seede farre passeth those in land,
>   And also those which wonne in th'azure sky?
>   For much more eath to tell the starres on hy,
>   Albe they endlesse seeme in estimation,
>   Then to recount the Seas posterity:
>   So fertile be the flouds in generation,
> So huge their numbers, and so numberlesse their nation.
>   (IV xii 1)

Everywhere the poem displays his ceaseless curiosity about
words: their etymology, history and imagery; their clash of literal and metaphorical meanings; and the rivalry of meanings
which expresses their life. Puns, quibbles and riddles may
emerge anywhere. When words fail him, he invents new ones or
revives obsolete senses. He labours ceaselessly to make each
word contain and express its nature.

Etymology is one major poetic device by which Spenser forces
a word to express its true meanings. The etymology of his names
has been noted in a number of recent studies, and in unpublished
doctoral dissertations by Martha Craig, Alice Blitch, and, thoroughly, by J. Belson.[5] These studies show how a character's
name reveals his nature and function in the allegory. For example, the etymology of the Red Cross Knight's name has been
known since 1758 when Upton noted that Voragine's Golden Legend
was Spenser's source for the life of St. George. According to the
Legend, "George is sayd of geos / Whiche is as moche to saye as
erthe and orge / that is tilyenge / so george is to saye as tilyenge
the erthe / that is his flesshe . . . Or George may be sayd of
gera: that is holy / and of gyon that is a wrasteler / that is an
holy wrasteler. For he wrasteled with the dragon.[6] Spenser
frames the Knight's character and actions through an awareness
of such etymologies. He is found in a ploughman's furrow and
raised in ploughman's state by which he gains his name (x 66); he
is associated with Orgoglio, his fallen form, by a shared etymology—Georgos, Orgo-glio (the latter also linked with a furrow, viii
8); and he is associated with Guyon, his natural form, as both are
wrestlers.[7] Like Adam, he is named after the earth of which he
is made: hence Contemplation names him simply "thou man of
earth" (x 52).

Witty playing upon the complex etymology of names obsessed
Spenser so entirely throughout the poem that one may suspect an
oblique allusion to the Queen's name in the closing lines where he
prays for the time when "all shall rest eternally / With Him that
is the God of Sabbaoth hight / O that great Sabbaoth God, graunt
me that Sabaoths sight." Since Spenser would know that "Sabbath"
signifies "rest," his final prayer at the end of his six days of
labour is for sight of that day of rest: that great Sabbath and
eternal rest. Since Spenser would know also that Elizabeth signifies "Peace of the Lord, or quiet rest of the Lord,"[8] his final
prayer as an exile in war-ravaged Ireland is for sight of the Queen
and the rest which she signifies. It is also Arthur's prayer for the
sight of his Faery Queen. Such speculation suggests that if one

fully understood the poem's names, one would fully understand its allegory.

Interest in etymology leads Spenser to employ etymological spelling and the etymological epithet. Hence Orgoglio is called a "Geant" (I vii 8) because he is the son of Gea, the earth; Duessa's breath "abhominably smeld" (I vii 47) because she is <u>ab homine,</u> from man and hence beastly; Phaedria's lake is named the "Ydle Lake" in the lines cited above because the gnostic Y describes the paths of virtue and vice which Phaedria places before man; and the feminine in opposition to the masculine is spelled "foeminine" at II ix 22 because it is the "foe to man." Where spelling does not work, Spenser uses an epithet. As a general rule an epithet defines; rarely is it simply descriptive. In the catalogue of beasts tamed by Satyrane each is cited in its characteristic strength in order to show his superior power:

> The spotted Panther, and the tusked Bore,
> The Pardale swift, and the Tigre cruell;
> The Antelope, and the Wolfe both fierce and fell.   (I vi 26)

An exception to the rule would seem to be the "spotted Panther" until one learns that the beast was thought to attract its prey by its spotted hide. The best-known example of Spenser's use of the characterizing epithet is found in the catalogue of the rivers at IV xi where he labours to give the rivers "their righte names."[9] More representative of his use is his account of "The Rock of vile <u>Reproch</u>" which Guyon encounters on his voyage to Acrasia's Bower. Since the Rock wrecks those of "lost credite and consumed thrift," it is a "daungerous" place in the obsolete sense of "to be in danger": to be in debt (OED 1). It is attended by "yelling Meawes, with Seagulles hoarse and bace, / And Cormoyrants, with birds of ravenous race" (II xii 8). "Meaws" attend because the word signifies "prison" and they are "yelling" because the echoic verb "mew," which we apply to cats, was applied to sea-birds in the sixteenth century. Gulls are present because the word signifies "trickery" and hence they are called "bace." "Cormoyrant" was a term applied to usurers; and being a sea-raven, it is called "ravenous." These birds watch "on that wastfull clift" because the rock is a fitting punishment for the wasteful. Often the etymological epithet expands into a brief allegory. The jealous Malbecco feeds on dread "That doth with curelesse care consume the hart" (III x 59). "Care" is "curelesse" because the word comes from Latin <u>cura,</u> care; it consumes the heart because of its re-

ceived etymology: <u>cura quod cor edat,</u> which Spenser's phrase
directly translates.

Etymology and associated word-play may initiate the larger
action of a canto as it does in the poem's opening episode. The
Knight's journey through the Wandering Wood to Error's den becomes one extended pun as complex in its way as a chapter of
<u>Finnegans Wake.</u> I shall follow only a few threads through that
labyrinth. The "harbour" or place of retreat which the Knight
and Una seek to protect them from the storm becomes an arbour
or shady retreat. At first they cannot see the wood for the trees;
but once they do, "in diverse doubt they been." "Doubt," with the
added sense "fear" is "diverse" in a sense peculiar to Spenser:
it is distracting, from the etymological sense "turned different
ways." At the centre of the Wandering Wood is Error's den whose
hidden danger "breedes dreadfull doubts." It follows, then, that
the Knight sees Error with her brood. Her half-woman shape embodies the pleasures of the Wandering Wood; her tail, the labyrinth
which entangles the Knight in doubt; and its mortal sting, death
which comes at the end. When she sees him, she rushes from her
den, "hurling her hideous taile / About her cursed head, whose
folds displaid / Were stretcht now forth at length without entraile."
"Hurling," which combines "hurtling" and "whirling" later expresses the violent motion of Lucifera (iv 16), Orgoglio (viii 17)
and the Dragon (xi 23). "Entraile" combines the noun which signifies "intestines" and the verb "entwine": hence it combines
the entwined and entwining paths of the labyrinth and the beast's
entrails which now surround the Knight. When she winds her
"huge traine" or tail about him, the poet adds in the next line,
"God helpe the man so wrapt in <u>Errours</u> endlesse traine." The
duplicated rhyme, "traine," signifies treachery or deceit, thus
linking the literal and allegorical senses of the monster's tail with
the Wandering Wood. Una is sad to see his "sore constraint," i.e.,
his fettered state, the term being used in the etymological sense of
the Latin <u>constringere,</u> "to draw tight." The Knight endures "in
great perplexitie," referring to his mental bewilderment, his physical distress (now an obsolete sense), and literally to his entangled
state (from the Latin <u>perplex</u>). When he strangles the monster,
she spews her filthy "parbreake" upon him: this term for vomit
is used here in its etymological sense, "breaking out," in order
to indicate the monster's violence which is first shown when she
"upstart[s]" upon seeing the Knight.

After the Knight defeats Error, he wrestles with Archimago's
"diverse dreame" (44): again "diverse" suggests its etymological

sense, "turning different ways" because Archimago endeavours
to separate him from Una. Hence it adds the sense of the Italian
diverso, "wicked, perverse." In response to the dream, for fear
"of doing aught amis, / He started up" (49), which is the characteristic action of Error. Afterwards he is left "musing" (55) i.e.,
wandering in a mental maze. In the final stage of his deception
when his sleep is broken by Archimago's news of the false pair,
"All in amaze he suddenly up start" (ii 5): clearly he is now
Error's victim.

The Knight flees from Una leaving them both "divided into
double parts" (ii 9). Here "double" carries an added sense, "divided": he is divided from himself so that now he is first named
when the false Saint George appears as the disguised Archimago,
and divided in himself so that he meets aspects of himself in
Sansfoy, Sansjoy, and finally Orgoglio. Una cannot be divided in
herself, being one; yet she is divided from herself so that she is
first named when the false Una appears (i 45) and again (ii 9)
before the entrance of her double, Duessa. She is "from her
knight divorced in despaire / And her due loves deriv'd to that
vile witches share" (iii 2): here "divorc'd" is used in the explicit sense, "dissolving the marriage contract" for her love is
diverted or drawn away (from divertium, the Latin root of "di-
vorce") when he pledges himself to Duessa "in safe assurance"
(ii 27). Accordingly, when Una meets him again, she says: "welcome now my Lord, in wele or woe" (viii 43), by these words renewing their marriage vow. Here I leave this labyrinth of etymologies: I tire, as you must, though Spenser never does.

I shall leave the subject, too, after illustrating how etymology
may outline the scope of an action that extends through several
books. In his story of Florimell's flight, Spenser pauses at midpoint. Already he has subjected her to the terrors of the land and
is about to subject her to the terrors of the sea until she remains
imprisoned "under a mightie rocke" (III viii 37) because of her
constant love for Marinell. The moment is crucial to her story:
up to this point her flight has not been unusual: it imitates the
flight of heroines of romance, such as Angelica's at the opening
of the Orlando Furioso. From this point, however, her flight involves metamorphosis and "death": it imitates that of Britomartis
of classical legend, to whom, as Britomart, Florimell now acts as
surrogate. The poet laments:

> So oft as I this history record,
>   My hart doth melt with meere compassion,

> To thinke, how causelesse of her owne accord
> This gentle Damzell, whom I write upon,
> Should plonged be in such affliction,
> Without all hope of comfort or reliefe,
> That sure I weene, the hardest hart of stone,
> Would hardly find to aggravate her griefe;
> For misery craves rather mercie, then repriefe. (III viii 1)

In anticipation of the action, "affliction" is used in its etymological sense, "thrown down": literally, she is to be thrown down to the bottom of the sea. "Aggravate" is also used in its etymological sense, "weigh down," "put weight on": literally she is to be held under a rock. I note in passing as examples of word-play that "find" implies "find the means to" but also "devise, invent": despite his pity, the poet intends to aggravate Florimell's grief. Also, "the hardest hart of stone" alludes to Marinell's "stony heart" (IV xii 13) for his rejection of love—taught him by his mother therefore in a "rocky cave" (III iv 20)—brings Florimell's imprisonment in walls of stone.

Spenser's delight in etymology is one part of his enormous pleasure, which he expects his readers to share, in all kinds of witty word-play. Puns spring up everywhere, most frequently in erotic episodes, but they may be found at any place where the pressure of meaning overloads a word's normal range of significance. They range from the simplest play upon double senses— "dismall day," for example, is hardly more than a schoolboy's howler on its root, dies mali—to the most serious conjunction of different senses. Dame Caelia greets Una with an apostrophe to the "happie earth, / Whereon thy innocent feed doe ever tread, / . . . Yet ceasest not thy wearie soles to lead" (I x 9): "soles" refers to men's souls as pilgrims which are in the keeping of the Church. Before the Knight encounters the Dragon, Una warns him: "henceforth be at your keeping well" (I xi 2): she means that if he wishes to triumph, he must be on his guard and also at the Well of Life which will keep him well. At the outset of the battle, the Dragon "made wide shadow under his huge wast" (I xi 8): "wast" refers both to his body and to the vast expanse (Lat. vastus) of land reduced to a waste by this shadow of death. During the battle, his flames "swinged" the Knight's beard—the term means both scorched and whipped—so that "through his armour all his body seard / That he could not endure so cruel cace" (I xi 26). "Seard" means literally "burned by hot iron"; "cace" refers both to the Knight's plight and to the armour which burns him. Such word-play points to the central paradox that the armour which defends him and later slays the Dragon now causes him to fall, but to fall so that he may arise renewed. This paradox is enforced by the jingle of echoing rhymes in the next stanza: "fyrie steele now burnt, that earst him arm'd, / That erst him goodly arm'd, now most of all him harm'd."

Through extended use a pun may become part of the language of allegory. For example, "incontinent" signifies both "intemperate" in the literal sense of not restraining oneself, and "immediately." Throughout the poem, both senses are usually present. In Book I, Arthur gives the Red Cross Knight a "few drops of liquor pure, /. . . That any wound could heale incontinent" (ix 19). In Book II it is said that if man's body is not kept in sober government "It growes a Monster, and incontinent / Doth loose his dignitie and native grace" (ix 7). In Book III, Britomart laments by the seashore at the beginning of her quest: she compares her state to a storm-tossed ship and appeals for "some gentle gale of ease" from the God of Winds "that raignest in the seas, / That raignest also in the Continent" (iv 10), referring to those who are ruled by Love and those who are continent. As she soon discovers, the land is ruled by the continent Marinell. When he is wounded by her, his mother comes from the ocean and "threw her selfe down on the Continent" (iv 30). Here the pun clarifies the nature of Marinell, a creature of the land and sea, and suggests why his marriage to Florimell, a creature of the land held by the sea, should resolve the action of Books III and IV. When this same word-play occurs in the following canto, it hardly constitutes a pun: the separate meanings have merged. Timias slays the lustful Foster "Right as he entring was into the flood": and fittingly "The carkas with the streame was carried downe, / But th'head fell backeward on the Continent" (v 25).

The simplest kind of word-play is repetition of a word. When the "dead" Guyon is defended by Arthur, his body is called a "carcass" four times within a few stanzas. Such repetition enforces the literal sense of that word, "fallen flesh," and clarifies Arthur's redemption of Guyon. In this same episode, Guyon's enemies are repeatedly called "pagans" or "paynim" brothers, terms not used since Book I where they describe the Red Cross Knight's enemies. (With one exception their use is restricted to this episode.) Such repeated use suggests that now God has directly intervened on behalf of Guyon, Guyon's enemies have become his. When a word is repeated in different contexts, it may accumulate meanings so that it becomes a centre of our understanding.[10] One example is the

word-play upon "heart" in the Despair episode. Earlier Duessa
brandished her charmed cup from which "Death and despeyre did
many thereof sup, /. . . Th'eternall bale of heavie wounded harts"
(I viii 14). Though Death is defeated when the Knight is rescued
from the dungeon, Despair remains. When he confronts Trevisan
who flees Despair, he seeks by "bold hartie speach" to embolden
his "bloud-frosen hart" (ix 25). He cannot do so because he and
his companion were overcome by Despair when he "felt our feeble
harts / Embost with bale" (29). This pun on "heart"—a hunted
hart is "embost" when it foams with fatigue—introduces elaborate
play upon the word when the Knight himself confronts Despair. At
the end Despair's speech pierces his heart until Una's speech
persuades him rather not to let "vaine words bewitch [his] manly
hart" (53). Since the poem is an elaborately constructed allegory,
any word in it may become a latent pun.

Word-play may be displayed through ambiguous syntax.[11]
Spenser commonly employs the floating adjective or adverb. When
Guyon confronts Mammon, he

> lightly to him leaping, stayd
> His hand, that trembled, as one terrifyde;
> And though him selfe were at the sight dismayd,
> Yet him perforce restraynd, and to him doubtfull sayd.
>
> (II vii 6)

"To him doubtfull": i.e., to the fearful Mammon. Yet the term
applies equally to Guyon: he is doubtful about Mammon's identity
and fearful—as "dismayd" suggests—of the temptation that confronts him. Pronouns may be used ambiguously, as one would
expect in an allegory where characters are states, and action consists of conflict between projections of a character or aspects of
his state. When Britomart holds her sword over Busyrane to
force him to recite the charms that may free Amoret,

> Anon she gan perceive the house to quake,
>> And all the dores to rattle round about;
>> Yet all that did not her dismaied make,
>> Nor slake her threatfull hand for daungers dout,
>> But still with stedfast eye and courage stout
>> Abode, to weet what end would come of all.
>> At last that mightie chaine, which round about
>> Her tender waste was wound, adowne gan fall,
> And that great brasen pillour broke in peeces small.
>
> (III xii 37)

If we were reading a novel, we would understand immediately that "her tender waste" refers to Amoret. Since we are reading an allegory, the reference remains ambiguous in order to avoid confusion. A similar, brilliant example of ambiguity is found in the concluding words of Book I canto xi. After the Knight has slain the Dragon, Una approaches to praise him:

> Then God she praysd, and thankt her faithfull knight,
> That had atchiev'd so great a conquest by his might.

"By his might" refers both to God and to the Knight; in so doing, it resolves the action of the episode and the Book. Since God's grace is fully manifest in man's might, the Knight is seen in the lineaments of Christ, the Dragon-killer.

In considering Spenser's art of language, I have been singling out examples that are special, though numerous. At any point in the poem, however, a reader is impressed by Spenser's witty play with the meanings of words and their emotive and imaginative impact. Typically Spenserian is the vaguely suggestive word: "dreriment," mentioned earlier, is a representative example. After the Red Cross Knight hears Fradubio's story, he is left "Full of sad feare and ghastly dreriment" (I ii 44). Although the word has not occurred before in the poem, and its formation—adding "-ment" to an adjective—is unusual, its general sense causes no problem. It is glossed "dreery and heavy cheere" by E. K. when it occurs in The Shepheardes Calender November eclogue. "Ghastly dreriment" functions chiefly to give weight to the simple phrase "sad feare." While "ghastly" suggests explicitly the terror evoked by the sight of a ghost, here Fradubio's, "dreriment" remains purposely vague. By remaining vague, it expresses the ominous, nightmarish and unrealized "sad feare" from which the Knight suffers. His inner fear takes shape in outer action only later when he encounters the person of Sansjoy. "Dreriment" belongs to a word-play extended throughout Book I: the Knight enters upon his quest "too solemne sad" (i 2), during it he calls upon death on four occasions, and only by passing through the house of Penaunce does he learn "himselfe to chearish" (x 29).

Another typically Spenserian word is "griesly." When we read that Phaedria's boat drives through "the slouthfull wave of that great griesly lake" (II vi 18), we understand that word at first as though it meant "horrible." Spenser allies the word to "griesy" and by extended use of both seeks their latent, active sense, "producing horror" (from O. F. gris). In the episode above we learn later that

503

> The waves thereof so slow and sluggish were,
> Engrost with mud, which did them foul agrise
> That every weightie thing they did upbeare.   (vi 46)

When these waters, acting contrary to their nature, fail to quench Pyrochles' inner flames, instead rendering him more foul, it becomes clear why they arouse horror, why they are called "griesly."

Throughout his poem Spenser defines the meanings of his words by careful, precise use and by parallel but significantly different use in a variety of contexts. He may begin by exploiting the multiple meanings of words he inherits. Adonis is slain by the boar that "with his cruell tuske him deadly cloyd" (III vi 48). Here "cloyd" signifies "pierced, gored" (cf. OED v. 12); also, since the boar signifies lust and his wound concupiscence, the term includes its modern sense, "the surfeiting of desire." When Cymochles lies in the Bower surrounded by naked maidens, "some bathed kisses, and did soft embrew / The sugred licour through his melting lips" (II v 33). The OED cites the use of "embrew" as unique and accepts Johnson's definition, "pour, emit moisture." From the etymological sense, the meaning is "cause to drink"; however, the entire range of sixteenth-century meanings is implied: steep, thrust, stain and infect. Betrayed by Duessa, the Red Cross Knight is called "dissolute" (I vii 51). The term means debauched, enfeebled, relaxed and careless. Also it implies "dissolved" (OED 1), from the Latin dissolutus, loose: the Knight was betrayed when he lay "pourd out in loosnesse on the grassy grownd" (vii 7). Yet further, one must allow that here, as always, Spenser says what he means and means what he says: the Knight is "dissolute" in the precise sense of being dissolved: by drinking from the fountain, his "chearefull bloud in faintnesse chill did melt" (vii 6), that is, his blood is corrupted to the polluted water which he drinks.

When inherited words could not be adapted to serve his needs, Spenser invented new ones. Fully representative of his usual practice are his coinages[12] in the stanzas which describe Arthur's battle with Cymochles. Arthur thrusts his spear "that through his thigh the mortall steele did gryde" (II viii 36). Obviously Spenser delights in the antique word "gryde" (which E. K. defines as "pierce" in his gloss to the February eclogue) because it conveys the grating sound of the weapon as it tears through flesh with rasping pain. When the spear breaks, the blood flows "that underneath his feet soone made a purple plesh": here alliteration conveys the onomatopoeic origin of "plesh." Arthur strikes twice at Cymochles, "that twise him forst his foot revoke" (39): "revoke" signifies

504

"withdraw," cited by OED as a unique usage. The term may be modelled upon the Latin phrase, revocare pedem, though the general sense of the word, "to call back" sufficiently accounts for its use. In his anger Arthur fights like a lion that "wexeth wood and yond" (40): "yond" has been taken as Spenser's misunderstanding of Chaucer's "egre as is a tygre yond in Inde," but Martha Craig suggests more correctly that "wood and yond" implies "madness and going beyond madness." Arthur fights as a savage bull "when rancour doth with rage him once engore" (42). "Engore" implies the effect of his being goaded: rancour and rage cause him to engore his enemy. He fights "renfierst with wrath" (45): here "renfierst" is a portmanteau word that means both "re-enforced" and "rendered more fierce."

More interesting are those many moments in the poem when the sheer pressure of the allegory forces Spenser to fashion a new word. I offer two examples, only one of which I believe I understand. When Una's parents may at last leave their besieged castle, they go to the field "where that champion stout / After his foes defeasance did remaine" (I xii 12). The sense of "defeasance," defeat, is attributed to Spenser by OED; it is used only here. Yet Spenser does not use the word "defeat" but fashions a new sense by adapting an earlier legal sense, from the French "defesaunce," which means "to render a claim null and void." Spenser uses "defeasance," then, to note that the Dragon usurped Adam's Kingdom: by his defeat, his claim to the land now ends. Una's parents ruled "from East to Westerne shore" (I i 5) until they were expelled by the Dragon, and in their place Duessa's parents now rule only "the wide West" (ii 22). The prior claim of Una's parents to Eden has extended political, religious and ecclesiastical significance which "defeasance," is coined to clarify.

My second example is more interesting though puzzling. After the Red Cross Knight had been rudely attacked by Guyon, he asks him courteously:

> Now mote I weet,
> Sir Guyon, why with so fierce saliaunce,
> And fell intent ye did at earst me meet;
> For sith I know your goodly governaunce. (II i 29)

Apparently from the context, "saliaunce" means "assault, onslaught." Evidently it is coined from saliaunt, salire, to leap, by way of the heraldic term, "salient," which is the posture of leaping. I suspect that the term holds heraldic significance which I fail to understand. This much does seem clear: the term stresses Guyon's hasty violence in attacking the Red Cross Knight without a formal challenge. Later Pyrochles attacks Arthur in the same manner: he gains the reproof and punishment which Guyon here for his intent deserves, and vicariously receives (II viii 31). In this connection it would seem relevant that "sallied," that is, "leapt" is used twice in the poem: it describes Guyon's leaping from Phaedria's boat to continue his journey to the Bower (vi 38) and his leaping from the mariner's boat to enter Acrasia's realm (xii 38).

Through his art of language, Spenser seeks to purify words by restoring them to their true, original meanings. When Adam fell, he lost that natural language in which words contain and reveal the realities they name.[13] Though corrupt, languages remain divinely given and the poet's burden is to purify the language of his own tribe. Words have been "wrested from their true calling": the poet attempts to wrest them back. Spenser "writ no language," as Jonson noted: that is, he avoids a fallen language which would only confirm man in his state of bondage. By his language of allegory, he recreates that natural language in which the word and its reality again merge. Like Adam, he gives names to his creatures which express their natures. He shares Bacon's distrust of language and even his scorn for those who care more for words than matter. His word-play is not an idle game but a sustained and serious effort to plant words as seeds in the reader's imagination. In Jonson's phrase, he "makes their minds like the thing he writes."[14] He shares Bacon's faith that the true end of knowledge is "a restitution and reinvesting (in great part) of man to the sovereignty and power (for whensoever he shall be able to call the creatures by their true names he shall again command them) which he had in his first state of creation."[15] Although his poem remains largely unfinished, he has restored at least those words which are capable of fashioning his reader in virtuous and gentle discipline.

II. THE MINOR POEMS

SPENSER'S PROTHALAMION: AN INTERPRETATION

Harry Berger, Jr.

   Prothalamion is a simple-seeming poem and the particular
problem it poses for interpretation appears to be straightforward:
in a poem of ten stanzas nominally celebrating the double marriage
of 'two Honourable & vertuous/Ladies' to 'two worthie/Gentlemen,'
why are two stanzas devoted to the poet's own life and troubles, and
a third to some patron-seeking praise of Essex? If one appeals to
conventional assumptions about genre, decorum and poetic intention,
does this not make for an indecisive and inconsistent poem? Why is
part of the poem about the speaker and part about the two Ladies,
and what, if any, is the relation between these two themes? I propose to deal with these problems in an indirect manner, through a
running commentary which is guided by a few simple (and perhaps
arbitrary) assumptions about the reading of lyric poetry. These
assumptions are best set forth in advance.
   In reading lyric poems—i.e., poetry in the first person—it is
vitally important to determine whether the speaker is only a narrator or whether he is involved in the experience as an agent and
patient. Even when, as in Prothalamion, the speaker is describing
something that happened in the past, the present tense of utterance
is part of the poem. We ought not to ignore the possibility that the
poem may be an unfolding now as well as a reported then, and we
should also be prepared to view the narration about others at least
partly as an aspect of what happens to the self.[1] If we view Spenser's poem from this perspective, and if we take it as we have it—
stanza by stanza and first stanza first—we are initially directed
not to the two ladies and not merely to the calm day, but to the
speaker in the act of remembering the calm day:

>   Calme was the day, and through the trembling ayre,
>   Sweete breathing Zephyrus did softly play
>   A gentle spirit, that lightly did delay
>   Hot Titans beames, which then did glyster fayre:

Reprinted from Essays in Criticism, Vol. 15 (1965), pp. 363–379, by permission of the author and the publisher, F. W. Bateson.

When I whom sullein care,
Through discontent of my long fruitless stay
In Princess Court, and expectation vayne
Of idle hopes, which still doe fly away,
Like empty shaddowes, did aflict my brayne,
Walkt forth to ease my payne
Along the shoare of silver streaming Themmes,
Whose rutty Bancke, the which his River hemmes,
Way paynted all with variable flowers,
And all the meades adorned with daintie gemmes,
Fit to decke maydens bowres,
And crowne their Paramours,
Against the Brydale day, which is not long:
    Sweete Themmes runne softly, till I end my Song

This is not to be read as a dramatic monologue assigned by a Browningesque poet to a disappointed courtier, for we have before us both the title and Ponsonby's title-page: 'Prothalamion/Or/A Spousall Verse made by/Edm. Spenser.' In cases of this sort it is better to forget the ingenious and often unnecessary distinction between poet and speaker (persona) which modern critics frequently like to make. The disappointed courtier is a poet with a poem to write, an occasion to celebrate.[2] The occasion he describes is itself a celebration, a progress or water-fete in honour of the double betrothal.[3] It is important to note that the poem is formally in honour of the marriage rather than the progress or betrothal. The relation between poet and brides in the remembered event is accidental: <u>happening</u> to do down to the river to console himself, he 'chaunced to espy' the 'Nymphes' and then the brides. This chance meeting is now revived as a remembered image and used within the controlled context of poetic celebration. So much, then, for the plot background. From the standpoint of interpretation it makes no difference whether or not this actually happened to Edmund Spenser, though historical evidence tends to verify or help fill in the implied sequence of events generated in and by the lyric utterance.

The fact that Spenser has transformed the progress to a visionary scene poses a further problem, if we are going to be serious and precise about attending to what happens in the poem: did this visionary transformation take place <u>then</u>, as he watched the progress, or <u>now</u>, as he remembers it? It may be that part of his past consolation consisted in giving play to his fancy, so that the river episode was a kind of busman's holiday. The walk is treated as a pastoral escape from the cares of society to the pleasures of 'nature,' and he may have intensified this escape by his recreative metamorphosis of the actual world into an Ovidian idyll. All this is not so fanciful or irrelevant as it may seem, for it directs us to those relations and phenomena of consciousness which characterise a poem as an embodied moment of experience, a public monument of the inner life. We must ask, then, whether the poet in the present tense of utterance is merely recording his fantasy or revising it, whether he submits to his memory or copes with it, whether he is still in need of consolation, still trying to escape.

The poem offers us a general rule of thumb for dealing with such questions, which may be illustrated by comparing the second and third stanzas. The second is straightforward description of what he saw—some nymphs with 'greenish' hair. This is the only image in the stanza which suggests transformation rather than reporting, even this may be ascribed to costumery rather than fantasy:

> There, in a Meadow, by the Rivers side,
> A Flocke of Nymphes I chaunced to espy,
> All lovely Daughters of the Flood thereby,
> With goodly greenish locks all loose untyde,
> As each had bene a Bryde. . . .

It is mainly the syntactical sweep of the strophe which conveys the sense of an image already possessed or worked out and merely being described, 'musically,' in the present moment. Though most of the lines are end-stopped, the conjunctions, appositions and inversions produce an interlocking effect which directs us toward the unified visual image itself rather than toward the temporal act of describing.

The second stanza is ambiguously poised between actual and imaginary landscapes, a little on this side of the imaginary, and it is not until the opening of the third stanza—'With that, I saw two Swannes'—that two parallel landscapes emerge, making us think, 'Scene here, vision there.' The hesitations, disjunctions and repetitions of this stanza produce a totally different effect: we become aware of the poet struggling now with a problem of decorum, i.e., trying to do justice to the image of the brides. And the chief cause of our awareness is the way Spenser moves from the neutral analogy of Pindus to the more or less loaded analogy of the rape of Leda:

511

With that, I saw two Swannes of goodly hewe,
Come softly swimming downe along the Lee;
Two fairer Birds I yet did never see:
The snow which doth the top of Pindus strew,
Did never whiter shew,
Nor Jove himselfe when he a Swan would be
For love of Leda, whiter did appeare:
Yet Leda was they say as white as he,
Yet not so white as these, nor nothing neare;
So purely white they were,
That even the gentle streame, the which them bare,
Seem'd foule to them, and bad his billowes spare
To wet their silken feathers, least they might
Soyle their fayre plumes with water not so fayre,
And marre their beauties bright,
That shone as heavens light,
Against their Brydale day, which was not long:
    Sweete Themmes runne softly, till I end my Song.

Spenser lingers over the Leda analogy as if, in reaching for an obvious mythic comparison to swans and whiteness, he stumbles on unwanted implications from which he must extricate himself: 'Jove as a bird was no whiter than these swans. Yet Leda was certainly as white as Jove. Though of course she wasn't nearly as white as the prospective brides, "so purely white they were."' The logical inconsistency, the awkward moves from male to female to the final dissociation of the brides, the blurred suggestiveness of purely—these changes seem simultaneously to tone down the allusion and play up the whiteness. Spenser seems to want the touch of malaise as a visible effect—for reasons to be suggested later—and it is just by these shifts that he makes it noticeable.

This distinction between completed and ongoing imaginative action may be conveniently put in terms of scenic and figurative imagery. Acts of comparison—e.g., metaphor and simile—belong to the present tense of utterance, to the experience of the creative will interpreting and perhaps evaluating or revising its data. The scenic quality of the second stanza[4] suggests a more passive response to the data of memory and this allows the past mood—the urge to escape—to impinge on the present. The reason the urge malingers even after Spenser's river-walk, is given in the first stanza, which states that his idle hopes 'still doe fly away,/Like empty shaddowes.' Presumably the river-walk and the chance

512

visionary diversion did not ease his pain for long. Therefore the spousall verse gives him an occasion to revive his feelings and reconstruct the event with the prospect of practical as well as psychological benefit.

The relation of scenic (visual) to figurative (verbal) imagery, of passive recall to active interpretation, reveals an ambiguous frame of mind in the first stanza: the poet still in pain, moved by the impulse to escape yet covertly acknowledging the conditions to be mastered. The periphrases of the opening quatrain suggest the locus amoenus which is an artificial and mental rather than a natural 'place.' They remind us of the formal and occasional limits which the poet actively accepts. But the figures that follow the straightforward idiom of complaint produce a different effect: the escape to nature finds a rhetorical parallel in the move from the actuality of 'Princes Court' to the artificial world of painted flowers and 'meades adorned with daintie gemmes.' This leads to the general subject of marriage and to the specific recollection of the aquatic progress. Thus the poetic act itself seems at the beginning to turn from unhappy self to happy others, from real pain to an idyllic landscape. This raises a question about the poet's control, for he appears to submit to the same escape urge which failed him before.

But although this impulse is most conspicuous, another element of Spenser's consciousness works against it, an element best revealed by exploring the intricacies of the refrain couplet. In the phrase, 'Against the Brydale day,' against may mean in preparation for, looking forward to or in avoidance of, hoping to fend off; 'which is not long' may mean the bridal day is not far off, but also, it is a very short day. The complexity of the final line is iconographic as well as verbal. Hemmed in by its painted banks, the river was the pleasant place to which the poet escaped, also the site of the progress and therefore the stage or vehicle of his vision. But since the previous line refers to what rivers conventionally symbolise, the apostrophe invokes one of poetry's more sought-after powers: its ability to slow down tempus edax and draw out the rare interludes of 'Sweete Time.' Thus the earlier impulse to escape is revived with a greater consciousness of its cause and meaning. The very action of remembering, imagining and verbalising changes the memory: if the first escape had been from a symbolic to a literal river, the present occasion acknowledges this and recovers the symbolic reference. The poet no longer hopes to stop time, merely to make it run more softly. The limits of control are implied by the soft playing of Zephyrus

'That lightly did delay/Hot Titans beames'—elsewhere in Spenser's poetry the hot sun symbolises unpleasant actuality,[5] and so the 'gentle spirit' here suggests the slowing spell of imagination. The poet's mind is its own pleasant place, but gently, and lightly, and only till he ends his song.

If the effects described so far were restricted to the delineation of the poet's sensibility, Spenser might justly be accused of sacrificing the brides and the <u>spousall verse</u> to his lyric self-concern. But this is not the case, for his description of the brides emphasises the same tendencies and implies the same problems. His 'struggle' to do them justice in the third stanza suggests their limits, their own version of the escape impulse, in a curiously pointed way. When we read that their beauties shone 'Against their Brydale day, which was not long,' our first thought is that they are eager to get married and radiant with anticipation, etc. But couldn't they also be anxious to put it off? It will mean the end of courtship, with its parties and water fetes, the end of recreative youth with its independence and freedom from domestic care. Other virgins will replace them as centres of social attention. The bridal day—a threshold, maybe the last Good Time—will be here soon enough, and gone soon enough, and after it their freedom, youth, and beauty. Something of this feeling emerges from the blurred syntax of the phrase, 'the gentle streame . . ./Seem'd foule to them'—foul in comparison, but also foul in their estimation. They sense and enjoy the effects of their Belphoeban splendor on worshippers along the river bank. The womb of time may produce a future 'not so fayre,/And marre their beauties bright,' therefore they too must feel some at least unacknowledged urge to make time run more softly till they end their lark.

To these implications, the Jove-Leda allusion adds overtones of the feminine love psychology which Spenser has elaborately explored in the romance of Britomart, especially in the treatment of Belphoebe and Amoret, in his portrayal of the virgin's natural <u>daunger</u> as well as her natural fear and desire of erotic possession. Belphoebe embodies a woman's inborn reluctance to give herself. Her virginal <u>daunger</u> is a sometimes fiercely instinctive safeguard of her sovereignty and otherness, protecting her free soul from the tyrannies of Venus in whatever form they appear— the generative cycle, domestic care, submission to lordship. Amoret embodies the opposed psychic reflex: the capacity for fixed love, the woman's image of herself as wife, her need for a male protector and husband, for social and domestic fulfillment. The dynamic transition from Belphoebe to Amoret is embodied

in Florimell, Flower-Honey or the lure of the beautiful, whose
appearance marks the vernal season of love in woman's soul.
Florimell's love begins as a desire or wound, inflicted from the
outside, which draws her out into the world toward the one man
she loves. In the wilderness of wood or ocean her desire is
tested, threatened and confirmed. But Amoret is carefully trained
in the seclusion of garden and temple. Her capacity for love is
not shown to spring from an inflicted pain, but to be the product of
education. Her chief concern is the love she has to offer rather
than the particular man to whom she offers it; when Scudamour
approaches her in the Temple of Venus, she is reluctant to exchange the service of love for that of the lover, to give up her
symbolic role as virgin priestess of Venus—as an exemplary
image of true love—for the actuality of wifehood. Where Florimell's love is based on insufficiency of self, on the need of the
other, Amoret requires an other—the Husband (as C. S. Lewis has
aptly termed Scudamour's function), whoever he is. Her love like
Scudamour's is mainly a form of self-love concerned with honour,
decorum, and social value. She is as averse to total possession
as Scudamour is in favour of it.

It is Amoret that Busirane captures by way of fulfilling his
narrative function in Britomart's adventure, which is to dissuade
her from her proper goal—marriage and true love—by showing
her a nightmare vision of that future state. Busirane plays on
Britomart's virgin fear of losing independence and tries to evoke
the 'phantasies/In wavering wemens wit' (III. xii. 26) by presenting
love as absolute subjection to male desire. Among his tapestries
is an image of Leda enjoying the swan: 'She slept, yet twixt her
eyelids closely spyde,/How towards her he rusht, and smiled at
his pryde' (III. xi. 32). Since the divine rape may project both sides
of the threat to feminine self-control—wish-fulfilment as well as
nightmare force—its appearance in Prothalamion, even though
relatively circumspect, disturbs the bland surface of celebration.[6]
Indeed, the ambiguous attitude toward the bridal day may extend to
the moment at the altar, as when Spenser imagines his love acting
daungerously in Epithalamion:

> Why blush ye love to give to me your hand,
> The pledge of all our band? (238–239)

The figure of the swan provides a link between the attitude of
the poet and that which he delineates in the brides. At the outset
it is only a complimentary trope emphasising grace and beauty in

general, more specifically the whiteness denoted in the mythic
comparisons—also a touch of coolness suggested by the snows of
Pindus. Because the swans have silken feathers and are 'softly
swimming' (like the gentle spirit softly playing), the figure is a
metamorphosis rather than a metaphor; what the poet remembers
and reports is his vision rather than the objective landscape which
caused it. Spenser characteristically uses the Ovidian strategy to
denote an escape—or a wish to escape—from a threatening situation; by choice or force, the victim is deprived of humanity and
reduced to a simpler state. The reduction of Bride to Bird may
here project a lovely but imperfect condition, the pride and beauty
and appeal of virgins, a condition which exists in order to be
transcended. Thus the swans represent a 'purity' of mind in
brides and poet, a tendency toward escape from the actual. Functioning as both descriptive interpretation and lyric projection, the
swan-image reconciles the two sides of the poem. More precisely,
the spousall verse gives the poet an occasion to objectify his own
problems in terms of the brides, to establish a bond between himself and others. So far, the bond has been established only under
the aspect of escape. But in the next four stanzas there is a turning of the poet's spirit.

The pace quickens in the fourth stanza, not only because the
nymphs run 'all in haste' but also because of the sharp transition
from the nymph's hypothesis of eternity to the poet's pun on
Somerset/Summer's heat. The pun leads to the statement that
the swans seemed as fresh as day which, like flowers, does not
last long. This makes the mythic supposition look like hyperbole
and locates the genesis of assertions about eternity in the dreamlike urge to abolish time. The poet seems during the course of
this stanza to consign this tendency of his consciousness to the
nymphs and then to identify himself with the realistic 'they say.'
The sense of passage sharpens in the last six lines and begins to
take on the urgency of a carpe diem.

This leads to the shimmering and complicated movement of the
fifth stanza. If in the fourth stanza the symbol of swans had been
complicated by reference to the mythic, historical and natural
orders (the historical order denoted by the place-and family-name),
here the symbol of the river is complicated by a fusion of Peneus
and Thames: the distant, the past and the mythic closes with the
proximate, the present and the actual. If the fourth stanza unfolded
the different orders, here they are infolded. The Peneus rises on
Mt. Pindus—no doubt from the melted snows of the third stanza—
and flows past the place where the river-god's daughter, Daphne,

was transformed because Cupid shot her with the leaden arrow of daunger. 'That they appeare,' in line 81, is a blurred reference— indicating either Thames or Peneus—which blends the two land-scapes. The two extremes of stanza 4—mythic eternity and nature —now merge in a 'river' which seems to project not only temporal but also imaginative flux, the metamorphosis of forms from beauty to beauty. Since time will not slow down, he will mythologise on its terms; now time, change and death lace the fluid landscape of vision. If the river resembles the floor of a bride's chamber, the fragrant and short-lived chamber flore must also be part of the 'river': lilies symbolise virginity and death, cut lilies symbolise marriage as a death to virginity, and from this point of view, mar-riage is merely one of the steps to death.

Thus from the first to the fifth stanza, the poet's dominant or overt attitude has changed from escape to acceptance. His sense of loss, of pain and passage, presses into the bridal vision and into the undulatory line of the long stanzaic period. At the same time he has transcended the options available in the opening stan-zas—escape from Court to river, from actuality to visionary arti-fice, from 'history' to 'nature,' from his own woes to the joys of others. Those options presupposed a despair whose only outlet was surrender to the actual or escape to fantasy, the second being merely a circumvention of the first.

'Idle hopes, which still doe fly away,/Like empty shaddowes': the feeling generates a sympathy for the daunger he perceives in the swanlike virgins. The image of scattered flowers once, like virgins, 'the honour of the field,' poignantly justifies the urge to resist the tide and slow down the progress. If, in his accidental encounter with the water fête, he was consoling himself, now, in his formal celebration of the impending marriage, he consoles the brides. As the first half of the poetic experience comes to an end, he has made his cause theirs and their cause his. Turning away from himself, he finds himself in them. And this, he might well claim in promoting his effort at occasional verse, is one meaning of marriage.

It is the meaning the nymphs articulate in the sixth stanza. Again, Spenser executes a turn on a key phrase. 'Prepar'd against that day,/Against their Brydale day, which was not long,' takes its negative force from the context, and this is augmented by the repe-tition. But what the nymphs actually sing is on behalf of the bridal day. The nymphs, who formerly had eternal thoughts, not utter the poet's persuasion: Go love. If this is phrased in the conventional hyperboles of occasional rhetoric, there is yet a peculiarly urgent

and personal quality to the sentiments which makes the persuasions more decorous as the utterance of nymphs than as the wishes
of a poet and commoner for two noble ladies. And since this is obviously not what the 'nymphs' of the water fête sang, it is clear that
the whole action is being re-cast <u>now</u> within the poet: these are
imaginary figures through which Spenser addresses the brides as
through a mask or mouthpiece. This stanza in isolation would have
been much blander, would in fact have provided the bare bones of
the occasional requirement. But coming where it does, and especially following the movement from the Somers-heat pun through
the fifth stanza, the song dramatically opposes the daunger that
keeps the brides from seizing the day: If they stay locked within
themselves, they will merely wither, like all closed systems;
therefore let them open themselves to the metabolic interchange
of 'loves couplement' which will sustain, repair and amplify them
as they age. Spenser knows the brides need to be persuaded and
he knows that only the 'heart-quelling' force of Cupid can overcome their daunger ('Loves dislike'). Thus looking back through
his own bitter experience, the poet communes with the innocence
of the brides, is moved by its beauty still untouched by time, yet
counsels them to abandon it. The inner mastery he urges is a
mastery he now exercises, perhaps too late for him, but not too
late for them. He is aware that there will be foes to confound, but
he also knows that joys 'redound,/Upon your Brydale day, which
is not long.'

The seventh stanza seems mainly to depict the harmonious
vision which emerges from the previous meditation. In exter-
nalising his care, Spenser has transformed the original event and
vision in such a way that his profound understanding of the brides
—their psychology and human condition—seems to have reordered
his own feeling about the life in time. His concern for them has
eased his own despair and his experience of time and love and
'fortunes wreck' has made him sensitive to their natural diffidence.
From his own standpoint, the progress has served its function and
he can, as it were, break the transference. This he does by describing a cosmic harmony which gives the effect of a happy ending: nymphs, Echo 'from the neighbour ground,' the river and 'all
the foule which in his flood did dwell' are now 'enranged well.'
The comparison to Cynthia and the lesser stars extends the image
to the sky and provides a summary perspective through the goddess
of chastity. 'So forth those joyous Birdes did passe along': the
scene is distanced as he sends them downstream, where they yield
to his own still unresolved predicament:

SPENSER'S 'PROTHALAMION'

> At length they all to mery London came,
> To Mery London, my most kyndly Nurse. . . .

The return to London is contrary to the gesture of escape which opened the poem, and in stanzas 8 and 9 we are much more firmly in the present (and future) tense: the poet now confronts his predicament, sees it as the instance of a more general tendency and tries—here in the poem—to do something about it.[7] It should be noted that London is not merely the literal or actual city: as a kindly nurse, as bricky towers riding on the river or on time, it figures man's historical environment; his social, legal and political concerns are indicated, also the fact that the city outlasts its makers. The objectifications of spirit in culture improve on the brief flowering of natural things—the 'house of auncient fame' is at least rhetorically more durable than Somers heat—but provide no guarantee against the forms of human weakness.

The stanza receives its symbolic generality from the retrospective views extending forty-odd years back to Spenser's birth, almost three centuries to the persecution of the Knights Templar, some eight years to Leicester's lifetime; also from the implication that pride, death and misfortune are all causes of decay. Historical time is more complex than natural time; its relatively stable environment—the human City—allows for positive as well as negative mutability. The 'Templar Knights' may have been more dashing before they became bankers and decayed through pride, but the 'studious Lawyers' represent the wave of the present and future, the development from chivalric force to legal persuasion. This increased organisation makes possible the new type of national hero exemplified by Essex.

Thus by compression and generalisation, by facing the literal image of actuality and focusing it as a symbol of human realities, the poet displays that mastery of fact by imagination, that reorganisation of the inward environment, which is man's peculiar power, and which had failed him at the beginning of the poetic experience. Turning away from self to brides, turning back to self from brides, he comes to an insight into the condition which underlies, explains and unites their separate destinies. The attitude which he had envisaged for them now becomes his own as he opens himself with renewed hope to the future. The hope is embodied in the apparent detour of the ninth stanza: the 'joyes to tell/Against the bridale daye' remind us of his responsibility to the occasion, while the 'Yet therein' suggests a change of direction; he will linger in the 'stately place' in order to give his own joy fuller play.

If this justifies the dramatic function of the ninth stanza, the praise of Essex may still cause uneasiness because it is so conventionally hyperbolic and so blatant a piece of patron-seeking. Indeed, the rhetorical echoes of the nymphs' occasional (stanza 6) are double-edged: it is possible to say that Spenser wants to emphasise the similar quality of both stanzas as references to the good of 'marriage.' Where the nymphs persuade the brides, Spenser tries to persuade Essex of the benefits accruing from a symbolic alliance between hero and poet, and as we know, Essex could have used a persuasive propagandist in 'ages following.' On the other hand, both stanzas differ markedly from the rest of the poem when read out of context because their rhetoric smacks of the professional performance, as if the poet were saying, 'This is the kind of job demanded by the public occasion itself—what a paid poet <u>might</u> sing in honour of brides and heroes, if his relationship to his patrons were strictly financial and practical.' The value of such journey-work lies in the domain of business rather than poetry, of actuality rather than imagination. If this is degrading to a pure poet, still the poet as man must stoop, must compromise his purity and be realistic in order to survive. The kind of concession to fact and need which Spenser makes in stanza 9 is one of the prices the self must pay, one of the ways in which it weathers the life in time. And the nymphs' rhetoric in stanza 6 reveals or conceals the need of a similar concession on the part of the brides. We see once again how his musing on the situation of the brides provides a model for the attitude he subsequently adopts.

In stanza 10, the praise of Essex is superficially justified by his presence at the progress, and the mood of the ninth stanza is momentarily extended in two ways: by the comparison and by the delayed verb (<u>Descended</u>), which makes it seem that the present tense of the preceding stanzas is being sustained. The rhymed participles and especially the envelop words' <u>issuing-ensuing</u> give the effect of a continued action. Essex issues from 'those high Towers' of the 'stately place,' but also, in a figurative sense, from the high towers of Spenser's blazon.

The two mythological similes have a peculiar generalising effect, mainly because they <u>are</u> similes and not outright indications of the time of day—it is not evening on the Thames at the day of the progress. The sense of passing time is powerfully conveyed by the transition from the rising star to the night sky, but it is the time of the mood, of the poem, of the life. Essex brings new hope late in the poet's career, and this hope emerges late in the experience of the poem. The twins of Jove, on the other hand, 'emerge'

from the rape of Leda in stanza 3, so that if one takes a poet's
mythological patterns seriously the twins represent both sons and
lovers—the whole burden of fulfilment by which divine rape and
self-surrender are justified, though only in the fullness of time.
The change in mood is partly caused by the shift in the contexts
of the myths—from the fabulous references of stanzas 3–5 to the
astronomical usage in stanzas 7 and 10. We feel this movement
from fable to actuality to mark a triumphant assertion of the
ordering mind, as it does less subtly, for example, at the end of
Ovid's <u>Metamorphoses</u>. Spenser's assertion is, as always, paradoxical: he moves from an order <u>made</u> to an order <u>named</u>, from
the imaginary toward what he hopes is real and thus beyond the
powers 'we men can fayne.' From the disordered actuality of
first sight, the poem passes through the insight of imagination
toward the ordered actuality of second sight. In this sense too,
all such bright emergences come toward evening. They are consequent rather than prior forms, won only by and through the inward mastery of experience. The lesson the poet learns in his
poem is the lesson the poem will teach the brides.

What the poem does for the poet is evident in the way the verb-
tenses relate the stanza to the rest of the poem. At the end of the
poem the preterite is suddenly extended when the knights

> Received those two faire Brides, their Loves delight,
> Which at th'appointed tyde,
> Each one did make his Bryde,
> Against their Brydale day, which is not long.

Previously the utterance of the poem seemed chronologically to
lie between the completed progress and the prospective wedding.
This was especially the sense gathered from stanzas 8 and 9
where the wedding was related to the speaker's present tense as
a future event. Now, suddenly, the wedding is placed in the past.
At the same time, the bridal day '<u>is</u> not long,' and this strips
away the prolepsis leaving only the maxim, 'it is in general a
very short day.' One possible effect of the change is to emphasise
the sense of time passing, i.e., 'A few moments ago, during my
meditation, it was a future event. Now, already, it seems to have
happened. It is as if the saying of the poem has made me feel
time all the more keenly.'

Yet the true quality of this feeling can only be gauged by comparing it with the first stanza. There too the formula had only
the flavour of a general observation: the meadows along the river

were fit to deck maidens' bowers 'And crowne their Paramours,/ Against the Brydale day, which is not long.' But the generalisation was informed by the pressure of disappointment, the school-of-hard-knocks feeling of the stanza: 'I ought to know how short such happy days are, since I'm so miserable.' There the meaning of Against was relatively limited, but stanza 10 gives the word its full positive range: supported by, towards and into contact with, by the time of, in full view of the bridal day. One may also feel a new negative implication: so significant an event as marriage transpired in spite of the shortness of the bridal day; the main difference between the first and last stanzas, the difference achieved by the poetic experience, is caught in this sense of the phrase. A wedding, like a poem, is 'for short time an endlesse moniment.'

The 'appointed tyde' unites progress and wedding, the literal and the metaphoric rivers. Perhaps one reason the brides themselves are so named only in the last stanza is that they were not brides during the progress; we need not assume Spenser to have meant the term in a vague extended sense. At any moment before the actual wedding they are not brides but only birds, proud and lovely though imperfect until they give themselves. The point or moment of utterance thus becomes, so to speak, the apex of a triangle travelling down to include the past progress and the future wedding as its bases. The progress and the meeting become symbolic, suggesting a new interpretation of the visionary image: the brides moving down the river of life and time, at a certain moment meeting—marrying—the knights, and through this appointed occasion being received beside the high towers of the city, escaping the irreversible current even while opening themselves to the future.

As a symbolic tableau, this stanza describes an external event less than it objectifies the inward mastery achieved in the poem. For time is never literally transcended and the elegiac feeling is of course not extinguished. The refrain line takes on a new meaning at the end of the poem: 'Sweete Themmes runne softly, till I end my Song' in its terminal position emphasises till—'when I end my song you may flow as usual.' The triumph of imagination comprises this acceptance, and the acceptance defines all the more lucidly what it is to do poetry. The poet is now fully aware that poetry cannot abolish actuality and ought not therefore be used as a means of escape. All it can do is change one's spirit, redirect the soul. But this is everything: by imagination—and not of poets alone but also by the imagination of virgins and heroes—experience can be mastered, the self opened to greater organisation in the life-repairing communion of love. As the time between progress and marriage vanishes, as the poem ends, the opposed stresses of the poem merge in tensional embrace. Time may flow as usual because this is the nature of things, and nothing can be done about it, also because the occasion has been used, poetry has done its work and made a symbolic form which infolds all such occasions and manifests their true importance. The very shortness of time enchases the human triumph: the brief occasion is repaid with interest by the moniments of imagination. Thus if, at poem's end, we catch an echo of Eliot's elegiac 'for I sing not loud nor long,' we hear also the present and living joy of the Wife of Bath: 'I have had my world as in my tyme.'

AN APOLOGY FOR SPENSER'S AMORETTI

Waldo F. McNeir

Why do Spenser's sonnets need a formal defense?[1] His poetry
as a whole needs restitution to its rightful place in English literature, and this can come only from re-consideration of "the grave
and diligent Spenser," in Ben Jonson's phrase, free from the pre-
dilections of earlier critics. Neglect by the no longer new New
Critics has been the bane—or blessing—of this poet. Rehabilita-
tion of Spenser has not resulted from John Crow Ransom's argument in The World's Body that sonnet 56 of Amoretti is structurally a perfect example of what the four-part English sonnet should
be, in contrast to the defective structure of most of Shakespeare's
sonnets.[2] This kind of praise is damaging. Even more invidious
was William Van O'Connor's unfavorable comparison of Spenser's
seventy-second sonnet with poems by Herrick and Stevens, and
his judgment that Spenser's poem is a failure on the basis of some
preconceived formula for the lyric.[3] The general neglect is
strange, since Spenser abounds in irony and humor, qualities that
are now much admired.[4] Maurice Evans feels that Spenser's
sonnets have "more humour and maturity than any other [Eliza-
bethan] cycle,"[5] and, surprisingly, Louis L. Martz shares this
opinion in his fine study of Amoretti in the English Institute
Essays of 1961.[6] But such judgments are rare.

If the Amoretti have been largely ignored by the New Critics,
they have been under-valued by the old-line historical scholars.
Sidney Lee, writing before the penetration of Elizabethan England
by the classical doctrine of imitatio was understood, could see in
Spenser's sonnets—as indeed in nearly all Elizabethan sonnets—
nothing but a fashionable vein of artifice, resting inertly on Petrarc
and the poets of the Pléiade.[7] Thomas Seccombe and J. W. Allen
say that Spenser lacked sufficient power of concentration to write
perfect sonnets, and that the form did not offer enough scope for
his "verbal painting,"[8] a stereotyped nineteenth-century view
echoed by A. A. Jack, who feels that the general effect of the

Reprinted from Die Neueren Sprachen, Vol. 14 (1965), pp. 1–9, with corrections by the author, by permission of the author and the publisher.

sequence is "idly spread," or too diffused.[9] The idea that Spenser
is primarily a painter of leisurely pageants was given scholarly
respectability by Émile Legouis; though demonstrably wrong, it
tenaciously lingers. In Legouis's opinion Spenser's sonnets lack
"la brusquerie dramatique et la flamme" of Sidney's.[10] When
W. L. Renwick, after saying that Spenser never wrote an outstanding sonnet to rank with Drayton's masterpiece—"Since there's no
help, come, let us kiss and part"—or Sidney's best, that he lacks
Shakespeare's compression and magical phrasing, Ronsard's
solidity, and Petrarch's subtlety, then goes on to concede that
Spenser "kept a better level than most, and if he never wrote a
great sonnet he never wrote a bad one," he merely damns with
faint praise.[11] Hallett Smith considers Spenser's style "reflective, musical, flowing" in contrast to the athletic qualities of
Sidney's style, and calls his calm tone "reflective rather than
impatient or dramatic."[12] J. W. Lever subjects Spenser's sonnets to the kind of mauling rearrangement that Shakespeare's
have so commonly received, finds Spenser's imagery, diction, and
verse form distinctive but not admirable, and the Amoretti as a
whole undramatic.[13] Finally, C. S. Lewis, a stout champion of
Spenser whose chapter on The Faerie Queene in The Allegory of
Love is one of the great landmarks of historical and evaluative
criticism,[14] nevertheless in English Literature in the Sixteenth
Century Excluding Drama characterizes Spenser as "not one of
the great sonneteers," describes his style as "devout, quiet, harmonious," and dismisses the Amoretti in a paragraph.[15]

These representative judgments of Spenser's sonnets, I submit, do little credit to the critics and less to his achievement.
For, contrary to prevailing opinion, these sonnets are original in
conception, well organized collectively and individually, metrically
dexterous, and dramatic in method.

Their conception is original because the circumstances which
led to their composition are unique in Renaissance sonnet literature. Spenser was not, like Petrarch, anatomizing a life-long love
of another man's wife—both alive and dead; nor was he, like Ronsard, driven in his late twenties to write love poems to a teenage
peasant lass, or in his fifties to frighten with fleshly proposals a
pathologically frigid girl young enough to be his granddaughter—
an early version of the Lolita syndrome. Spenser's case was
spectacularly normal. When he was a widower approaching forty,
he fell in love with a young woman named Elizabeth Boyle, courted
her for a year, and on June 11, 1594, married her. It is useless
to speculate that he may have written certain sonnets of the

Amoretti series earlier or for other occasions. The fact is that he intended it as a record of his courtship of Elizabeth Boyle, and its sequel the Epithalamion, which has rightly been called by Douglas Bush the finest love poem in the language,[16] celebrates the culmination of that courtship in marriage. No other Elizabethan sonnet sequence has such an honorable occasion, much less such an honorable outcome. Consequently, we do not find in these poems the hyperfervid paradoxes of Sidney's conflict of conscience in his belated pursuit of Lady Rich, or the complex ambiguities of Shakespeare's simultaneous relations with a man and a woman friend. In these poems no less than in The Faerie Queene, Spenser's opposition to both the code of courtly love and the Ovidian magnification of sex makes him, as C. S. Lewis has said, "the greatest among the founders of that romantic conception of marriage which is the basis of all our love literature from Shakespeare to Meredith."[17] In all of his poetry he consistently expressed an idealistic conception of love and marriage. The subject of Spenser's sonnets, then, could not have been more novel if he had tried to make it so. It was certainly not preformed by the tradition. His sonnets are sui generis in the love poetry of the sixteenth century. I am not forgetting the sonnets written by Vittoria Colonna to her husband after his death, but that was obviously a different situation.

The structure of the series is that of a chronological narrative. One critic has perceived its similarity to the plan of The Shepheardes Calender, with the passage of time corresponding to the change in the seasons.[18] As in the earlier work, the passage of time also corresponds to the changing prospects of the poet in his love suit and to the changing weather of his mind. When he wrote his Amoretti, Spenser had already showed his skill as a narrative poet in the first three books of The Faerie Queene, published in 1590, and even as he courted Elizabeth Boyle he was pushing ahead with the writing of the following three books of his epic published two years later in 1596. It was as a narrative poet that he excelled, indeed has had few equals; he wrote the sonnets late in his career and at the height of his powers. Guiding and shaping the narrative progress and pattern of the sequence are, first, those sonnets we may call seasonal or calendar poems. Sonnet 4 welcomes the New Year (March 25 in Elizabethan reckoning), "forth looking out of Ianus gate"; sonnet 19 announces "the merry Cuckow, messenger of Spring"; sonnet 22 brings us to Easter; 26 shows that summer flowers are blooming; 60 reviews the past year that Spenser has been in love, "The which doth longer vnto me appeare,/Then al those fourty which my life outwent"; 62 ushers in a second New Year, its "shew of morning mylde" promising a "change of weather" also in "our mynds and former liues"; 68 brings us to a second Easter since the beginning of the cycle; and 70 celebrates the May Day that followed a few weeks later. The elapsed time since the beginning of the court-ship and hence since the beginning of the action recorded in the series is a little over a year. Chronology is thus a linking thread that runs through the sequence and stitches it together. Like the beginning of the experience with a New Year, the climax of the courtship in sonnet 63, with the lady's acceptance of him, comes with symbolic aptness just after the dawn of another New Year.

In addition to these seasonal indications, at once literal and symbolic, other sonnets strengthen the narrative structure by presenting details of events, situations, and incidents that occur in the course of the courtship. Near the beginning these may be conventional, such as the warfare in 11, the ambush in 12, the siege in 14, Love's archers in 16. It may be remarked in passing that the importance of convention to the Elizabethan love poet in establishing an identity or <u>persona</u>, to use the terminology of mod-ern criticism, has been rarely understood by modern critics.[19] In reality, most of Spenser's situational sonnets are circumstantial in their explicit reference to events. Many are anecdotal, after the establishment of the characters of the two chief actors in the dra-ma, such as those which tell of his leaving her house in a rain storm (46), her burning his verses in anger (48), his illness and his conversation with his physician (50), the discouragement of another visit to her in which no progress was made (52), her laugh-ing at him for the way he acts different rôles, Proteus-like, in love's theater (54), the debate between them on the weakness and strength of self-assurance (58 and 59), the first kiss (64), his half-reverent awe at her acceptance of him (67), her embroidery (71), a day at the beach (75), his finishing the first six books of <u>The Faerie Queene</u> (80), slanderers who cause misunderstanding (86), and the temporary separation of the lovers which ends the series in a minor key (87, 88, 89). But that is not the end; the <u>Epithalamion</u> hymns in swelling major chords Spenser's marriage that summer. The point is that at least thirty sonnets in the <u>Amoretti</u> are pre-dominantly narrative, either chronological or situational poems that organize the whole series on a firm basis of events occurring in time. Here, as in nearly everything he wrote, Spenser shows a flair for design.

Together with their aspect of actuality, their personal historicity as a whole, these poems are individually marked by the same con-ceptualizing grasp. In the manipulation of sound, in the reinforce-

ment of meaning by metrical variation, in the cadenced flow of
thought Spenser is one of the great masters. His control of technical means is that of a virtuoso. The rhyme scheme he used
was an innovation: abab bcbc cdcd ee. It is like no other form of
the sonnet. The linked quatrains are distinctive, characteristic
also of the Spenserian stanza, and the chief norm of internal
structure. The interlocking rhymes of the quatrains hold together
unfolding ideas, working in conjunction with syntactical articula-
tion to bind the poem into a single, developing, and dynamic expression. A progressive principle of organization, which we may
call hypotactic, akin to what Aristotle in his Rhetoric (III, ix),
speaking of sentence structure, calls periodic, is used to produce
sequential subordination of the parts to a whole.[20] Sonnet 75 will
illustrate.

> One day I wrote her name vpon the strand,
> But came the waues and washed it away:
> Agayne I wrote it with a second hand,
> But came the tyde, and made my paynes his pray.
> "Vayne man," sayd she, "that doest in vaine assay
> A mortall thing so to immortalize,
> For I my selue shall lyke to this decay,
> And eek my name bee wyped out lykewize."
> "Not so," (quod I) "let baser things deuize
> To dy in dust, but you shall liue by fame:
> My verse your virtues rare shall eternize,
> And in the heauens wryte your glorious name.
> Where whenas death shall all the world subdew,
> Our loue shall liue, and later life renew."

The structure here grows out of the first quatrain, which presents in simple language the timeless situation of a man in love
writing a woman's name in the sand and watching the waves eradicate it. But what Spenser makes of this is unexpected. The second
quatrain suddenly reveals that the woman is with him, and the implicit drama becomes explicit; she speaks, chiding his folly with a
metaphysical reminder of her own mutability. In the third quatrain
the lover replies, capping her mortal objections with a confident
assertion of the immortality of poetry, and this is more emphatically stated in Christian terms in the resounding period of the last
two lines, the Platonic concept of heavenly love expanding and
transcending the physical world of sand and sea in which the lovers
move to give a glimpse of eternity. Each quatrain, then, rises to a

higher sphere of meaning than the preceding one, with the second and third quatrains spiraling up out of the first, and the conclusion rising higher still. The discourse which carries these successive levels of meaning proceeds from narrative through drama and comes to rest in philosophy. It is this kind of sequential development that reveals the <u>Gestalt</u> of many of Spenser's sonnets.[21] The ascent to a universal idea rather than resting in the limitations of a subjective emotional response is a feature of the <u>Amoretti</u> that gives the series one kind of unity. It is, of course, akin to the symbolizing and allegorizing tendency of <u>The Faerie Queene</u>. Spenser's sonnets have neither the symmetrical rise and fall in octave and sestet of the Italian form, nor the graduated climax reaching a crescendo in the final couplet of the English form. The continuity and flow of their own internal logic—in this case, meta-logic—are their chief characteristics.

Let us consider another principle of internal structure and poetic technique, the use of metrical variations from the iambic pentameter norm of the sonnet. His metrical versatility makes Spenser, like Milton, one of the great poetic craftsmen of the Renaissance, an age when artists and artisans practiced kindred skills. Much progress in metrics had been made in England since the unscannable experiments of Wyatt early in the sixteenth century, the regularizing efforts of Surrey which followed, and the attainment of monotonous competence by Gascoigne in the 1570's in his twenty-four sonnets scattered through half a dozen works. Many of the leading sonneteers of the 1590's at the height of the sonnet vogue are still rather unsure metrists with certain conspicuous idiosyncrasies: Fulke Greville in <u>Caelica</u> is over-fond of feminine endings; Samuel Daniel in <u>Delia</u> has heavy caesuras in nearly every line, and very few run-on lines; Henry Constable in <u>Diana</u> is paradoxically afraid of metrical variations while straining for harebrained conceits; nearly a third of Thomas Lodge's lines in <u>Phillis</u> spill over into eleven syllables; Michael Drayton in <u>Idea</u> has an average of four non-pentameter lines in each sonnet; William Percy in <u>Coelia</u> writes with an hysterical emphasis betrayed by too many spondees.[22] Spenser's use of metrical irregularities is more subtly harmonious. His substitutions are made intelligently, neither too conservatively nor too adventurously, there being fourteen percent of substituted or non-iambic feet in his eighty-eight sonnets[23]—Shakespeare has about eleven percent in his one hundred fifty-four sonnets. In Spenser's substitutions, spondees outnumber trochees in a ratio of eight to five, and a negligible number of pyrrhics is used. No other kinds of substituted feet occur.

Spenser's anti-normative metrical feet relate meter to meaning. For example, the largest number of trochees in any of his sonnets is eleven in number 8, each of the last six lines beginning with a trochee. Why this falling rhythm or descending effect in the sestet of this particular sonnet? For good reason—it is accusatory concerning the chastening, depressant effect of the lady's virtue:

> You frame my thoughts and fashion me within,
> You stop my toung, and teach my hart to speake,
> You calme the storme that passion did begin,
> Strong thrugh your cause, but by your vertue weak.
> Dark is the world, where your light shined neuer;
> Well is he borne, that may behold you euer.

The two feminine endings of the couplet ("neuer" and "euer") also contribute to the rhythm of declination and the resigned tone of acceptance of what he can not change. Again, in sonnet 14 occur a large number of spondees, eleven, of which seven are appropriately concentrated near the strong conclusion of an image of love's stern warfare:

> Bring therefore all the forces that ye may,
> And lay incessant battery to her heart,
> Playnts, prayers, vowes, ruth, sorrow, and dismay,
> Those engins can the proudest loue conuert.
> But if those fayle, fall downe and dy before her,
> So dying liue, and liuing do adore her.

A spondaic rhythm impinges twelve times on the iambic pattern of the verse for a strong effect in sonnet 13, as in the line "But that same lofty countenance seemes to scorne"; nine times in sonnet 33, as in the lines "Great wrong I doe, I can it not deny,/To that most sacred Empresse my dear dred"; nine times in sonnet 84, as in the lines "But speak no word to her of these sad plights,/ Which her too constant stiffenesse doth constrayn." Sonnet 67, which comes after the turning point of the sequence, shows a control of rhythmic variation seldom surpassed in English poetry, the lover-huntsman's agitation as he ponders the strange submission of the once-wild deer being conveyed by the artful distribution of seven trochees and thirteen spondees in play against the iambic measure:

Lýke ãs a huntsman aftér weary chace,
Séeiñg the game from him escapt away,
Sĭts dówn to rest hĭm iñ sóme shády place,
With panting hounds beguiled of their pray:
Só áfter long pursuit and vaine assay,
When I áll wéary had the chase forsooke,
The gentle deare returned the self-sáme way,
Thĭnkiñg to quench her thirst át thē néxt bróoke.
Thére she beholding me with mylder looke,
Soúght nót to fly, but fearlesse still did bide:
Tĭll I in hand hér yēt hálfe trémbling tooke,
Ańd wĭth her owne goódwĭll hir fyrmely tyde.
Stránge thĭng me seemd to see a beast so wyld,
Só góodly wonne with her ówne wĭll beguyld.

In addition to the frequent substitution of a non-iambic foot at
the beginning of a line (in all but lines 4, 6, 7, and 11 here), the
counterpoint of trochees and spondees occurring internally and
terminally makes this sonnet a metrical marvel. It is no less
distinguished in its handling of the central image of the "gentle
deare," used also by Petrarch, Horace, Wyatt, della Casa, and
John Hall.[24] Finally, the largest number of pyrrhic substitutions,
five, occurs in sonnet 88, in which the poet has been separated
from his fiancée and meditates in a muted half-whisper on the
heart-ache of absence.

In many other situations Spenser places or clusters his variations from the normative iambic measure in accordance with
theme and tone. The rising iambic inflection is of course dominant. Departures from it are controlled. The falling trochaic
intonation, the drumbeat spondaic stamp, and the toneless pyrrhic
—all are made to serve special purposes as the metrical tension
contracts or relaxes.

One last point and this brief for Spenser's <u>Amoretti</u> has been
entered. His sonnets, like many of Sidney's, have the immediacy
of dramatic method; that is, they are spoken by one person to
another, speech employed in direct address. Thirty of the eighty-
eight poems are wholly dramatic, and ten others partly dramatic.
The person speaking is nearly always Spenser himself, in his own
character, without disguise—whatever the variety of his feelings
—speaking as a particular lover of a particular woman. As in no
other English cyclè, the impression of the poet's own mind and
personality are conveyed. Sidney in his sonnets speaks in the
character of Astrophel, the rôle he assumes.[25] Most of the other

Elizabethan sonneteers speak in a variety of <u>personae</u> to unidenti-
fiable ladies. In many of the sonnets of direct address, Spenser is
talking to Elizabeth, the woman he is courting, the woman he won
and married. But, significantly, he addresses her in only three
sonnets of the first twenty of the series, and then only briefly and
diffidently at the end of each poem. This is a dramatization in the
early part of the sequence of the "lingua sed torpet" theme appearing in poems of Sappho, Theocritus, and Catullus, and re-worked
by later poets from Dante to Donne.[26] As intimacy develops, his
boldness increases; he delivers expostulatory, ironically protesting monologues, veering from honest exasperation to tolerant
laughter at the whole convention even as he uses it and illustrates
every ploy in the game. Elizabeth is fully characterized—so are
many of the women characters in The Faerie Queene—by what he
says about her in frequent and sometimes playfully exaggerated
complaints of her stubborn pride, her tough sense of her own
power and individual worth which prevents her from yielding to
his suit (5, 6, 10, 13, 17, 21, 27, 31, 49, 56)—ten sonnets develop
this theme before she accepts him. Yet he is realistically grateful that he is pursuing no mere push-over, and he rebukes a friend
in sonnet 5 for criticizing her "portliness," or unattainability.
Humanly enough, he can criticize her, but nobody else can. Her
physical effect on him is almost overwhelming; but his idealism
and his ultimate aim, aided by her strength of character, enable
him to control his feelings. The external drama of pursuit and
flight, persuasion and denial, is accompanied by an equally intense
internal drama of the mind portraying the psychological states of
a middle-aged widower who has found a woman he wants to marry.
Thus the poet-lover is as fully characterized as the lady—by every
word he speaks, by every move he makes.[27] Life expectancy in
Elizabethan times being what it was, Spenser at forty was past
what we consider middle age; as a matter of fact, he was to have
only six years of the happiness he found with Elizabeth Boyle. So
he had to overcome or allay—quickly, if he could, and with under-
standable apprehension and a sense of urgency—her misgivings
about the loss of her freedom (65) and about the difference in their
age and station (66), for she was somewhat above him in social
position (82).

Besides the sonnets in which he is exhorting, cajoling, extolling,
bantering, and soothing Elizabeth, in other sonnets of direct address he speaks to the "leaues, lines, and rymes" of his book (1),
his "vnquiet thought" that started it all (2), her "fayre eyes, the
myrror of my mazed hart" (7, 8), his defeated forces on their

repulse (14), the "tradefull Merchants" whose treasure from "both the Indias" is no match for her worth (15), his friend Lodowick Bryskett in answer to the charge of neglecting his work on <u>The Faerie Queene</u> (33), her deceptive, Mona Lisa-like smile (39), the "innocent paper" with a sonnet written on it that she burned in a fit of anger (48), the doctor attending him during a sickness, who has "but little priefe / In deep discouery of the mynds disease" (50), the "fresh spring" told to call forth his love to go a-Maying (70), her breasts (76), and the mischief-makers creating misunderstanding between him and Elizabeth (86). The tone of these is greatly varied—now ringing (2 and 15), now calm (33 and 50); now in earnest (39 and 76), now mock-heroic (14 and 48). Fully three-fourths of Spenser's sonnets are inherently narrative or drama, or both, because of their narrative basis in physical events and their dramatic method of presentation.

This evaluation of the <u>Amoretti</u> goes against the prevailing view of Spenser's sonnets—their purport, artistry, principal features, and general and particular poetic qualities. These sonnets have been misjudged and under-rated—more so, in my opinion, than any other of Spenser's works. No one would disturb Shakespeare's position as the most eminent of the Elizabethan sonnet writers; it is deserved and unchallengeable. Spenser, his peer as a poet in many respects, belongs only a little below him as a maker of sonnets.

THE TRIUMPH OVER HASTY ACCIDENTS: A NOTE ON THE SYMBOLIC MODE OF THE 'EPITHALAMION'

Richard Neuse

Spenser's Epithalamion has recently been shown to be of greater complexity as a poetic artefact than had been suspected. The number symbolism which A. K. Hieatt has, to my mind convincingly, demonstrated for the poem,[1] indicates the care with which Spenser composed his poem, the great importance he apparently attached to it. One of the puzzles raised by Mr. Hieatt's discovery is why Spenser should have done so: what in the nature of the poem warranted this expenditure of energy and ingenuity?

I attempt an answer to this question by dealing first with a part of the poem that has always seemed very puzzling to me: the envoy. No critical account I have seen does justice to the obscurities of the envoy, and the hypothesis which this essay proposes is intended to resolve at least some of these. At the same time it has necessitated another hypothesis, that of a continuity between Amoretti and Epithalamion. In short, I am proposing that the envoy represents the climax of a deliberate progression that moves from the sonnets to the marriage song. And it is in terms of this progression, and the Epithalamion's special place in it, that I think much of its unusual complexity can be understood.

In general terms, the progression is one from romantic to conjugal love and all that this implies; in aesthetic terms it involves the transition from an essentially platonic to a sacramental mode of symbolization. But the word 'progression' is misleading here insofar as it connotes a straightforward linear development. On the surface, indeed, a series of love poems culminating in a marriage song looks straightforward, not to say conventional (even if at Spenser's time it was not). But the envoy itself helps to warn us that the appearances are deceptive: it reminds us that the lovers are not merely (or primarily) figures of literary convention but also actual persons subject to the vicissitudes and discontinuities of actual experience. Finally, it seems to indicate that the

Reprinted from Modern Language Review, Vol. 61 (1966), pp. 161–174, by permission of the author and The Modern Humanities Research Association

Epithalamion is the poet's personal response to such discontinuities: more than a 'mere,' epithalamium, in other words, it must
test and extend the very nature and function of such a poem.

Whereas in the previous stanzas the poet invoked the powers
of heaven and earth to set off his wedding day as special and
auspicious, in the envoy he addresses his poem itself:

> Song made in lieu of many ornaments,
> With which my loue should duly haue bene dect,
> Which cutting off through hasty accidents,
> Ye would not stay your dew time to expect,
> But promist both to recompens,
> Be vnto her a goodly ornament,
> And for short time an endlesse moniment.   (ll. 427–33)

Some of the questions that present themselves here may be stated
as follows. Why is the envoy there at all? What function does it
serve? What are the many ornaments with which his love should
have been decked? What the hasty accidents? What is the due
time? What are the antecedents of 'which' in the third line, and
of 'both' in the fifth?

Obviously, first of all, the envoy functions to state the special
purpose which the poem is intended to serve. By breaking with
the formal rhythm of the preceding stanzas, it pulls the reader up
short and invites him to contemplate the meaning of the ornament-
monument which the poet is presenting to his bride. Further, as
we shall try to show, the envoy serves to place the wedding song
in the context of the personal drama which began with the sonnet
sequence.

That the 'many ornaments' refer to poems[2] is suggested by the
idea of poem-as-ornament in the envoy itself and in the beginning
of the Epithalamion ('Ye learned sisters which haue oftentime/
Beene to me ayding, others to adorne. . . .'). The poet, in that
case, feels he should have adorned his love with many poems, but
that the Epithalamion, 'cutting off' these many, is now to serve as
the single ornament-poem in their stead. For it has 'promist both
to recompens,' that is, to make up for the 'many ornaments' and
the 'hasty accidents.'

The meaning of these ornaments and accidents becomes clearer
if we invoke our second hypothesis, namely that the Amoretti and
Epithalamion, published together in 1595, constitute a unit.[3] Now
one of the striking features of the sonnet sequence is that it stops
abruptly—as if 'through hasty accidents'—with the separation of

the lovers. The 'many ornaments' of the envoy, I therefore suggest, refer to those sonnets that should 'duly' have been written to celebrate the happy reunion of the lovers. These were never, in fact, composed, and in their stead the Epithalamion shaped itself in the poet's imagination.

This idea is reinforced by a major element of continuity between sonnet sequence and wedding song: an overarching time scheme plotted in the Amoretti and leading into the 'dew time' of the Epithalamion. For the due time the latter would not stay to await is, I think, precisely the time which it celebrates: the actual wedding day. In a partly witty but obscure way, therefore, the envoy seems to say that though the poem was written for a special occasion, it is not merely occasional or conventional, but the product of an imperious inner impulse.

The 'incompleteness' of the Amoretti, as well as their continuity with the Epithalamion, is intimated in a number of ways. Thus the love affair follows a well-defined time sequence: New Year (Sonnet 4), Spring (19), one year (60), a second New Year (62), Easter (68), and Spring (70); but with the separation of the lovers the seasonal progression breaks off on a note of wintry desolation:

> Lyke as the Culuer on the bared bough,
> Sits mourning for the absence of her mate:
> and in her songs sends many a wishfull vow,
> for his returne that seemes to linger late.
> So I alone now left disconsolate,
> Mourne to my selfe the absence of my loue.   (Sonnet 89)

The Epithalamion's opening address to the Muses alludes to the conclusion of the Amoretti:

> Helpe me mine owne loues prayses to resound,
> Ne let the same of any be enuide:
> So Orpheus did for his own bride,
> So I vnto my selfe alone will sing,
> The woods shall to me answer and my Eccho ring.
> (ll. 14–18. My italics)

The poem is born of a sense of privation, and the Orpheus simile indicates what is to be its major task: to invoke, by the magic of its music, the presence of the bride. And here we see another way in which the wedding song brings to fulfilment what has been a 'failure' in the sonnet sequence. The image of the beloved that the sonneteer cultivates in his own soul—'Her temple fayre is built within my mind,/in which her glorious image placed is,/on which my thoughts do day and night attend' (22)—reflects in its development his growth in love.[4] But at the point when he needs it most to sustain him, the image fails him. The crisis, foreshadowed in Sonnet 78, comes to a climax in Sonnet 88, where, with the absence of the Lady, the interior image dissolves because it is utterly unconsoling:

> Ne ought I see, though in the clearest day,
> when others gaze vpon theyr shadowes vayne:
> but th'onely image of that heauenly ray,
> whereof some glance doth in mine eie remayne.
> Of which beholding the Idaea playne,
> through contemplation of my purest part:
> with light thereof I doe my selfe sustayne,
> and thereon feed my loue-affamisht hart.
> But with such brightnesse whylest I fill my mind,
> I starue my body and mine eyes doe blynd.

The precise nature of this crisis is and must remain obscure. But we may imagine it as followed by a period during which the lover meditates on the relationship which the sonnets have celebrated and the claims his love will have upon him as a person without the mask of the poet in a world of accidents and impermanent feelings. From the meditation there emerges the Epithalamion; 'promist both to recompens,' it will deal with and make up for the predicament on which the Amoretti had 'foundered.' It will assert an image of the bride that will outlive the night of separation and the vagaries of time. How can it do so when the sonnets have already declared the inadequacy of the image? It will do so by means of a poetic mode especially designed to come to terms with, if not to 'conquer,' Time. On this point above all, I believe, Spenser brought to bear the full resources of his imagination, and the resultant strategy can best be understood in terms of the Pythagorism of sixteenth-century Humanist aesthetics.[5]

Here Mr. Hieatt's discovery of a complex symbolism in the Epithalamion's stanza and line numbers is of capital importance. He has shown that its numbers—corresponding to the hours of the day, the days of the year, and so forth—make the poem into a symbol of all time, 'a Calendar for euery yeare.' Now this framework of an ideal time fits in exactly with a cardinal feature of the Pythagorean aesthetic, namely the hidden or implicit harmony which the artist was supposed to impose upon his work. Thus the numerical-symbolic structure of the Epithalamion serves, in Pythagorean fashion, to express its secret affinity with the mathematical order of the universe and functions as a means of invoking quasi-magical powers.

For combined with its demand for an abstract structure or pattern, Humanist Pythagorism had a conception of artistic production as a kind of magical ars ministra naturae.[6] The artist's imagination must enter into, become identified with Nature's generative course, and produce images as by her agency. This is the same idea as Pico's natural magic which, 'in calling forth into the light as if from their hiding-places the powers scattered and sown in the world by the loving-kindness of God, does not so much work wonders as diligently serve a wonder-working nature.' The magician, says Pico,

> Having more searchingly examined into the harmony of the universe, which the Greeks with greater significance call $\sigma\nu\mu\pi\acute{\alpha}\theta\epsilon\iota\alpha$, and having clearly perceived the reciprocal affinity of natures, . . . brings forth into the open the miracles concealed in the recesses of the world, in the depths of nature, . . . just as if she herself were their maker; and, as the farmer weds his elms to vines, even so does the magus wed earth to heaven, that is, he weds lower things to the endowments and powers of higher things.[7]

The embodiment of this Humanist dream of man's power over nature was the poet-magician Orpheus.[8] To this figure, it will be remembered, Spenser relates himself in the first stanza and it is indeed with an Orphic voice that he sings his epithalamium. He knows that natural magic commands nature by obeying it, that he 'conquers' time by submitting to it (thus fashioning a 'short time's endless monument'). Hence in demanding of the sun 'let this one day be myne' (l. 125) the poet at the same time through the very form of his poem gives the progress of the sun its due, translating the rhythm of nature into the poem's numbers, for these are also the hours through which the sun moves (cf. ll. 278 ff.). The zodiacal motion in the poet's wit is in harmony with that of the heavens.

That time is thus of the essence in the Epithalamion appears not only from the poem's temporal structure but also from the basically temporal nature of its major symbols. Following Mr. Hieatt's lead, we have seen how the sun, and its movement (sol temporis auctor: Macrobius), serves as paradigm for the poem's movement. Night, out of which the sun emerges and to which it returns, plays an analogous though more complex rôle, and may serve as our first and principal example of the Epithalamion's symbolic mode. Much of the imagery, it may be noted in passing, which in the Amoretti served as part of the metaphoric play of the sonnet conceit, is taken up again in the Epithalamion. There it is used, characteristically, to point simultaneously to an external reality in time and to the inward activity of the mind, establishing a sense of mysterious congruence between them.

The Amoretti ended in a metaphoric night, the Epithalamion begins in a literal night: in terms of the day whose progression the poem imitates, it is still night when the poem opens (and night again in its final stanzas). Night is thus, as it were, the source of the day which the poet tries to make his own, but it also comes to be felt as its potential negation. 'I wander as in darknesse of the night,' the poet had said in Sonnet 88, and the associations of this statement linger on in the Epithalamion. They have been well described by Thomas Greene:

> The poem is unconventional in the repeated expression it gives to the ominous elements associated with night, the elements which might potentially destroy the joy of the wedding and even the marriage. The induction refers to mishaps raised by "death or love or fortune's wreck" in the lives of those who have appeared earlier in Spenser's poems. The second stanza refers to the vicissitudes of the courtship dramatized in the Amoretti, the "pains and sorrows past," and the Muses are asked to sing of "solace" as well as of joy to the bride. At nightfall the appearance of Hesperus . . . occasions unconventional praise of the star for its guidance of lovers "through the night's sad dread." This "sad dread" is elaborated two stanzas below in the invocation to night. . . .
>   The ominous associations of darkness are evoked again, . . . in the last stanza, where the stars are described as torches in the temple of heaven
>
>> that to us wretched earthly clods
>> In dreadful darkness lend desired light.
>
> Here it is not only the marriage but the whole of human experience which is menaced by the night's sad dread. Thus the threat of disaster, the irrational fear of vaguely specified

539

suffering, hovers faintly over the poem, lending particular urgency to the concluding prayers. It is perhaps not too fanciful to relate the wolves of the fourth stanza to this cluster of night associations and to find in the decorative invocation to the "lightfoot maids" an added symbolic nuance. . . .[9]

This excellent account of Night in its negative, threatening aspects, needs only to be extended and made more specific in one particular point. The 'fear of vaguely specified suffering' can be linked with the poet's anguish described in the last sonnets of the Amoretti. Remembering the images of night and darkness with which the Amoretti concluded, and the Orpheus image in the first stanza of the Epithalamion, we can add: it is out of this very night that the wedding must be evoked; in the face of its hostile, almost demonic, forces the wedding day's resplendent actuality must be asserted.

A suggestion of this is to be found in the description of the sunrise, with the continued appeal to the Muses, in stanza 2:

> Early before the worlds light giuing lampe,
> His golden beame vpon the hils doth spred,
> Hauing disperst the nights vnchearefull dampe,
> Doe ye awake, and with fresh lusty hed,
> Go to the bowre of my beloued loue,
> My truest turtle doue,
> Bid her awake. . . .   (ll. 19–25)

The sun rising and dispersing the night's dampness is, as the wording seems to imply, a repetition of the first 'Let there be light'; and the poem, an analogous creative act, intends what the Muses are called upon to do: to rouse the bride out of the night of absence and separation.

But the negative is only part of Night's symbolic significance in the poem. It is balanced by a positive rôle such as appears in the sixth stanza, for instance. As parent, with Day, of the Hours, Night is shown to be also an integral element in the creative dynamism at the heart of the poem's design:

> But first come ye fayre houres which were begot
> In loues sweet paradice, of Day and Night,
> Which doe the seasons of the yeare allot,
> And al that euer in this world is fayre
> Doe make and still repayre.   (ll. 98–102)

The Hours are the Horai of Greek mythology, identified variously with the seasons, as givers of fertility, ripeness, and so forth. But they are also the twenty-four segments of the day, and thus point to the conception of time as an essentially generative process. The other, destructive rôle of time is also hinted at, however, in the word repayre. We may conclude that the creative and destructive are here seen as dual aspects of time dialectically related; or that in the temporal process there is a negative element, nothingness, into which things pass but out of which they also come into being.

It is in the latter part of the poem that Night's dual rôle is emphatically restated:

> Now welcome night, thou night so long expected,
> That long daies labour doest at last defray,
> And all my cares, which cruell loue collected,
> Hast sumd in one, and cancelled for aye;
> Spread thy broad wing ouer my loue and me,
> That no man may vs see,
> And in thy sable mantle vs enwrap,
> From feare of perrill and foule horror free,
> Let no false treason seeke vs to entrap, . . .
> But let the night be calme and quietsome,
> Without tempestuous storms or sad afray:
> Lyke as when Ioue with great Alcmena lay,
> When he begot the great Tirynthian groome:
> Or lyke as when he with thy selfe did lie,
> And begot Maiesty.   (ll. 315–31)

Night as the sum of all 'cares' (griefs and fears) embodies the negative rôle of an antagonistic, destructive force. It symbolizes the source of chaos, of hasty accidents wreaking havoc with human existence, of time the destroyer, with which, as we saw, the poet had to come to terms. The Epithalamion was his way of doing so, and the degree to which it has succeeded in its task and wrought a redemption of time, is here symbolically asserted: through this same night all the cares are now 'cancelled for aye.'

The rôle of Jove (embodiment of power and a kind of grace) hinted at in this and the preceding stanza, represents a striking parallel to that of the poet. Thus the bride is compared to Maia, 'when as Ioue her tooke/In Tempe, lying on the flowry gras,/Twixt sleepe and wake' (ll. 307–9, my italics); and as Jove descends and takes Maia, so the poet has conjured the Muses, and through them the bride, out of 'sleep' and awakened her to life in his soul as in his poem.

With Alcmena Jove momentarily made time stand still as he extended one night into three (and made it fruitful). The poet has performed a similar if lesser feat in incorporating the wedding day—his day—in the timely-timeless structure of his poem. Finally, Jove lying with Night and begetting Majesty, quae mundum temperat omnem (Fasti, V, 25), sums up most fully the genesis of the poem.

Majestic is surely the one adjective to apply to bride and poem, both in the traditional and mythic Ovidian sense. But if we understand the mythological imagery in an internal, spiritual sense, then night points to a state like that self-absorption of the soul when, as Dante describes it, the senses are extinguished and it is ready for the grace of inspiration: into the soul's darkness there enters the 'light formed in heaven' (Purgatorio, xvii, 17). So Jove cohabiting with Night would parallel the sunrise (described in stanza 2) seen as the light dawning upon the landscape of the soul. In both cases, it may be thought, the majesty of the visible world of day is engendered.

Aside from encompassing the ambivalence of Time's process, Night accordingly expresses an ecstatic, timeless moment by which the imagination is enabled to divine the creative ground at the source of this process.[10] As such it is perhaps the most complex figure, but its operation can be paralleled by the other major symbols of the poem. In stanza 2, for instance, we are told that

> Hymen is awake,
> And long since ready forth his maske to moue,
> With his bright Tead that flames with many a flake,
> And many a bachelor towaite on him. . . . (ll. 25-8)

The figure of Hymen reflects the image of the sun (at the beginning of this stanza) waiting in the dark to move over the rim of the horizon. It is set in dance-like motion as the performer of the day's ceremonial, and this motion echoes the larger rhythm of the day and of the sun, so that lower things are again wedded to the endowments of higher things.

At the same time Hymen with his masque is none other than the epithalamium, the embodied symbol of the poem itself. The Muses, Nymphs, Graces, and Hours, therefore, come to be seen as participants in this masque, as if sprung from its 'Invention.'

But just as the processional masque of the sixteenth century created its setting by transforming the actual social scene into an
integral part of its symbolic ritual, so the figures of the Epithalamion become more than allegories or symbols: each in turn
and in its way is made to unfold its traditional associations, thus
fashioning a scene for the wedding.

The movement is from convention outward to the establishment
of a natural and social context, and the poetic principle involved
is that of echo. This, as the refrain indicates, is also the poem's
fundamental device, and the Muses' rôle is paradigmatic in this
respect. Traditionally, they can 'teach the woods and waters to
lament' (1. 10), so that the pastoral song finds its resonance from
without: 'The woods shall to you answer and your Eccho ring.'
So as the poet invokes the various figures, they come forth as an
echo to his command or song; he re-discovers them, as it were,
out there, with their multiple associations and functions. The
echo is thus truly incremental: in response to the (initially) single
voice there is created a regular polyphony of voices which, inter-
penetrating, form an expanding context for the rite to be enacted.

By the end of the poem the image of Hymen's torch has undergone enormous expansion to encompass the host of 'other stars':

> And ye high heauens, the temple of the gods,
> In which a thousand torches flaming bright
> Doe burne, that to vs wretched earthly clods,
> In dreadful darkness lend desired light. . . .   (ll. 409–12)

The image of the cosmic temple framing earthly existence here
is itself the culmination of a development that has its antecedents
in the Amoretti. There the temple occurs as part of the meta-
phorics of the sonnet: the Lady's 'temple fayre is built within my
mind. . . .' (Sonnet 22). A similar imagery is applied to the bride
in the Epithalamion, but no longer with merely internal reference:

> . . . all her body like a pallace fayre,
> Ascending vppe with many a stately stayre,
> To honors seat and chastities sweet bowre.   (ll. 178–80)

The ascent from physical to spiritual and moral, into the inner
chamber to see 'that which no eyes can see,/The inward beauty
of her liuely spright' (ll. 185–6), is moreover, directly paralleled
to the entry into the actual temple:

Open the temple gates vnto my loue,
Open them wide that she may enter in, . . .
And all the pillours deck with girlands trim,
For to recyue this Saynt with honour dew,
That commeth in to you.
With trembling steps and humble reuerence,
She commeth in, before th'almighties vew,
Of her ye virgins learn obedience,
When so ye come into these holy places,
To humble your proud faces. . . .   (ll. 204–14)

Palace, royal throne of the mind (l. 194), and temple images fuse into the image of the bride as at once real woman and saint in her own temple, a physical, moral, and spiritual exemplar in one.

The command in the temple: 'all the posts adorne as doth behoue,/And all the pillours deck . . .' (ll. 206–7) is echoed by that after the temple ceremony, at home: 'Sprinkle all the postes and wals with wine . . .' (l. 253). We can say that we have moved from one 'holy place' to another: for Bacchic feast and holy day (stanzas 14 and 15) sanctify even the home. Or else the temple and its ceremony have expanded to include the home and its feast, just as by the end of the poem the temple image has expanded to encompass the cosmos in a hallowing of all space: 'And ye high heauens, the temple of the gods,/In which a thousand torches flaming bright. . . .' (ll. 409–10).

The kind of symbolism that the poem achieves may best be called typological as this term is now used in Dante criticism.[11] At the least, it represents an extension of the typological principle insofar as it combines the visionary with the sense or authority of a literal reality (thought to be) revealed by scripture or similarly sacred tradition. Thus we might speak here of a twofold typological symbolism, of which one is essentially Biblical: the temple imagery, that is, draws upon the Solomonic temple and the pleromatic temple of the New Jerusalem (Revelation, 21), and the architectural (and other) imagery applied to the bride in stanza 10 is based upon the 'epithalamium' of the Song of Songs.[12] The second kind consists of the typology of the day or time and is essentially liturgical, though it might also draw on a text like Ephesians 5:13–16:

For whatsoever is manifest, that same is light. Wherfore he sayth: Awake thou that slepest, and stond vppe from deeth, and Christ shall geve the light.

THE SYMBOLIC MODE OF THE 'EPITHALAMION'

> Take hede therfore that ye walke circumspectly: not
> as foles: but as wyse redemynge the tyme: for the dayes
> are evyll.   (Tyndale's translation, 1534)

Poetically it is achieved through the interpenetration of images,
by which the images of the imagination are wedded to the typical,
the diurnally repeated phenomenon. Thus Hymen, invoked for the
unique occasion of this particular day, comes to participate in
the reality and power of the sun's daily passage from night to
day. In this sense, it is another way of looking upon the event of
dawn.[13]

The concept of typological symbolism was introduced in part
because I think that if we combine it with the poem's ritual, in-
cantatory manner we may be justified in seeing the Epithalamion
as a poetic analogue to the religious sacrament whose signs
'function to transform man and the world on a supernatural
level.'[14] Like the sacrament, the poem may itself be regarded
as a dramatic performance taking place in the poet's soul, in
such a way that 'the meaning of the symbolic words, acts, . . .
are not only brought to mind but are effected, caused, actually
happen' there.[15]

For further illustration let us consider the typology of the
solstitial holy day, which culminates with the boldest stroke of
literal realism. At the homeward procession, the poet exclaims:
'Make feast . . . now all this liue long day,/This day for euer to
me holy is' (ll. 248–9). Next he proclaims it a holiday, calling
for a general cessation from profane labours:

> Ring ye the bels, ye yong men of the towne,
> And leaue your wonted labors for this day:
> This day is holy; doe ye write it down,
> That ye for euer it remember may.   (ll. 261–4)

And finally comes the triumphant assertion that this is literally
a calendrical holiday:

> This day the sunne is in his chiefest hight,
> With Barnaby the bright,
> From whence declining daily by degrees,
> He somewhat loseth of his heat and light,
> When once the Crab behind his back he sees.   (ll. 265–9)

Here the poem has achieved its greatest expansion: its symbols momentarily become transparent, as it were, to the real sun and to real time. This is perhaps the closest the poet can come in his mimesis of the sacrament whose signs 'effect what they signify.'

The day of the solstice itself is, then, the most perfect embodiment or analogue of the poem. It signifies the apex of Time's plenitude, and as a turning point in the annual calendar when the sun (and thus time) seems temporarily to stand still, it represents an ecstatic moment which, to men of earlier societies, afforded an extraordinary perspective on the very rhythm of nature and the eternal pattern or powers controlling its course. As in the poem, therefore, men experienced their existence as participating simultaneously in a timeless, eternal order and in a temporal one. This conjunction may be the essence of the holy; it signified a highly intensified mode of life in which existence was felt to be charged with and taken out of itself by celestial vigour. These feelings found formal expression in the festival, which enacted the cosmic event by participation, as it were. Through ritual release from the profane time of everyday, the celebrants returned to a 'mythical dream-time . . . located simultaneously at the beginning and outside of evolution.'[16] The ritual varied, but had two typical features: Dionysian revelry, excess; and ceremonial gesture, invocation, dance.

The solstitial holiday heightens the festal nature of the wedding and gives it an added dimension. The Dionysian excess in stanza 14, 'Poure out the wine without restraint or stay,/Poure not by cups, but by the belly full . . .' (ll. 250–1) implies release and festive immersion in the beneficent fullness of life corresponding to the 'height' of solar power of the next stanza. And there the singing and dancing about bonfires—a standard feature of Midsummer festivals[17]—points to ritual participation in the plenitude of the sun's energy.

Now, in terms both of the year and day, the sun is 'declining . . . by degrees' from 'his chiefest hight.' And the poet-lover impatiently urges it on its way: 'Hast thee O fayrest Planet to thy home/Within the Westerne fome. . . .' (ll. 282–3). And with nightfall he dissolves the masque which has been his wedding song: 'Now ceasse ye damsels' (merchants' daughters? Muses? Nymphs? All 'these glad many,' l. 294)

> your delights forepast;
> Enough is it, that all the day was youres:
> Now day is doen. . . . (ll. 296–8)

THE SYMBOLIC MODE OF THE 'EPITHALAMION'

The very thing the poet had striven to make his—'this one day'—
he now surrenders as, Prospero-like, he dismisses the revels
and their cast:

> Now it is night ye damsels may be gon,
> And leaue my loue alone,
> And leaue likewise your former lay to sing:
> The woods no more shal answere, nor your echo ring.
>
> (ll. 311–14)

With the return of night we sense again an inward movement
of the imagination, as indicated by the poet's withdrawal from the
damsels and the change to the negative refrain. With significant
variations,[18] the symbolic-reflexive mode of the beginning of the
poem reappears, and it is as though the poem has, in circular
fashion, turned in upon itself. The poet's sacrament, generated
out of the night, having passed through the circling hours of the
day, finds its conclusion where it began, rediscovers its source,
but a source clarified and transformed.

The transformation is signalized by the change of pronoun
from You (as in the dismissal of the damsels: 'your delights
forepast') to We in the final stanzas, where it becomes part of
the refrain to form 'our song.' The poem thus has moved from
the single I of the first refrain to the personal plural. And in the
course of this movement it, or the poet's self, has discovered
that it was never really alone in the radical, singular meaning of
the term. What has been clarified is the nature of the self as
containing the love which is both the subject of the poem and its
generative law. For Spenser this love leads forward as well as
upward, into the future symbolized in the poem by the generations
of a 'large posterity' (l. 417), but also into a realm before which
his art finally abdicates. The envoy deliberately breaks with the
symmetrical structure of the Epithalamion, as the poet offers up
the poem on which he has expended the full resources of his
imagination to the greater reality of his bride to be.

In this realm—outside the poem—his song is to be no more than
ornament for the woman. And yet in this one point art and life do
meet again: the ornamental function of poetry as an enrichment of
existence. More: art is also paying back its debt to life; for it
was through the real woman, his relationship to her, that the poet
found his true self in relation to the 'short time' which in the re-
demptive transformation of the Epithalamion has become the
infinitely precious moment of human existence. The stage at which
he has arrived has a perfect gloss in the thought of Kierkegaard:[19]

Time, where the aesthete gets stranded, is important. The Judge [in Either/Or] asserts this by an aesthetic analogy. He says that the better an art knows how to express its theme in time, the higher it stands. The highest of all arts is the art of living and time is its medium, as it is with music. Marriage belongs to the art of living and therefore time is its medium too. He who recognizes the value of time lives as a Person; i.e. as a persona in a play where God is both Playwright and Prompter. This play has time as its real element. The person in the play has a history. It is the history imparted to him by God and his own reflective will. As Kierkegaard puts it elsewhere, "Time is taken into the service of an ethically existing individual."

Intertwined with the time element, whose invisible arc extends from the Amoretti to the Epithalamion, the poet's personal history has been in the background all along. Thus the consciousness of time is there from the outset: to a limited extent it affects and controls the more or less extravagant play of attitudes and images of the Amoretti. But the latter ended inconclusively, even despairingly, in the face of time's hasty accidents.

In the ensuing crisis the mind resolves its perplexity: still speaking in Kierkegaard's terms, it makes a leap from the aesthetic to the ethical, from romantic to conjugal love. The leap does not mean an abandonment of the aesthetic-romantic ideality and inwardness (or even its theatrical playfulness); instead, these are transfigured in the ethical-sacramental perspective of the Epithalamion, whose magical mode achieved a kind of identity between its aesthetic time and real time by divining the eternal centre in mutability. In the envoy, therefore, the poet's Self can shed all poetic disguises and renew its history on the stage where all are merely players for the short time allotted to them. The part he must play is revealed: his poem is its 'endlesse moniment.'

ALLEGORY AND PASTORAL IN THE SHEPHEARDES CALENDER

Isabel G. MacCaffrey

To read the large-scale masterpieces of Elizabethan literature
with something of the agility they assume and demand is an art
which must be self-consciously cultivated by us today. The Shepheardes Calender, an early, relatively brief essay in a complex
mode, provides exercise for our wit in smaller compass. We
ought, I believe, to bring to it something of the same resources
that we bring to Spenser's larger work. As Ernest de Selincourt
wrote, "It lies along the high-road that leads him to Faery land."[1]
It is the product of the same sensibility, and in it we can discern
the special proclivities of the poet's imagination: the preference
for radical allegory and "iconographical ambiguity";[2] the search
for a form that will contain variety and unify it without violating
its subtle life-patterns; the exploitation of a setting that can also
serve as a complex controlling metaphor. The great invention of
Faerie Land is anticipated by Spenser's evocation of the archetypal hills, valleys, woods, and pastures of the Calender.
Early critics tended to read the work as a kind of anthology, a
series of experiments in various verse-forms; Spenser's themes,
conceived as subordinate to his forms, could be subsumed under
E. K.'s categories, plaintive, moral, and recreative.[3] The poem's
reputation has taken an upward turn in the past few years, accompanied by a critical tendency to stress the unifying power of its
metaphors, and there have been several attempts to reduce its
pattern to a single thematic statement. The reconstruction of the
poem's composition by Paul McLane suggests the difficulties of
determining the history of Spenser's intention; but McLane's conclusion supports the inclination of modern readers to see the
Calender as the product of a unified design, eventually more or
less explicit in the poet's imagination.[4]
While it is, I believe, essential to assume that The Shepheardes
Calender makes sense as a whole, many readings of it, though

Reprinted from English Literary History, Vol. 36 (1969), pp. 88–109, ©
The Johns Hopkins Press, by permission of the author and The Johns
Hopkins Press.

subtly argued, in the end ignore certain of its elements that may not conform to the proposed pattern. A. C. Hamilton's discussion of the poet's "effort to find himself," R. A. Durr's distinction "between the flesh and the spirit, amor carnis and amor spiritus," M. C. Bradbrook's thesis that Spenser deals with "the pursuit of honour, surveyed from what was traditionally the lowest of human occupations"—all of these accounts, and others, offer us valuable perspectives on Spenser's themes.[5] But all underestimate the power of the poet's imagination, its world-making energy, its drive toward comprehensiveness, its urge to include rather than to exclude meanings.

This energy is visible at the start in Spenser's very choice of forms. His "originality" lay in combining a group of eclogues with a calendar framework, that is, variety with unity.[6] It is a typically Spenserian invention: the two forms neutralize each other's disadvantages and cooperate to produce a structure that uniquely combines symbolic range and resonance with the most fundamental ordering pattern in our experience, the life-cycle itself. The etymology of eclogue encourages us to view the separate poems as independent "selections"; the calendar offers the limitation of a circumscribing frame at once linear and cyclical. In consequence, the Calender already exhibits the formal paradoxes that confront us in infinite recombination in The Faerie Queene: discontinuous continuity, multiple reference, analogical relationships that point simultaneously to likeness and to unlikeness.

These paradoxes are set in motion and contained by the pastoral paradigm, which is to some degree implied by both of the poem's formal components, eclogue and calendar. Development of the implications of pastoral in the early Renaissance had brought it to a point of relative sophistication which was exploited and then notably extended in Spenser's poem. It is important to realize that by the 1570's, the paradigm was not confined exclusively to idyllic themes. Originating in the impulse to criticize artificial and corrupt urban civilization, the pastoral "world" itself was soon infected by that corruption and became in turn the object of critical scrutiny. In the eclogues of Mantuan and Barnabe Googe, the pastoral metaphor is microcosmic, and the preoccupations of fallen man, as well as his vision of unfallen bliss, can be accommodated within it. So, in the Calender, Spenser's imagined world includes storms and sunshine, friendly and hostile landscapes, benevolent and ravenous animals, good and bad shepherds, high and low personages. The poet has chosen not to limit himself to the merely idyllic version of pastoral. This choice is reflected in the formal range of the Calender. The decorum of the convention dictated that it move, stylistically, in a temperate zone between the heights of epic and tragedy, and the depths of satirical comedy; the range was wide enough, however, to permit excursions into both these extreme borderlands, as the Maye and October eclogues demonstrate. The twin concepts of the calendar, with its changing seasons and months, and of the eclogue-group, with its changing metrical and tonal patterns, thus combine with the multiple references of sophisticated pastoral to compose a design of rich potentiality. Above all, this complex literary paradigm offers a context hospitable to allegory; as A. C. Hamilton has said, "the most obvious parallel between the Calender and [The Faerie Queene] is that each is radically allegorical."[7]

We have to ask, then, what the nature and concern of the allegory may be; and the answer must resemble the answers we devise in commenting on the much more complex allegory of the later poem. Paul McLane has observed that Colin Clout's career is like that of "the main characters of the Faerie Queene, most of whom lead a double or triple life on the various levels of the poem."[8] Though the metaphor of "levels" is, I believe, one that we ought to discard in speaking of allegory, McLane's point concerning the multiple life of Colin can be extended to all the major images of the Calender. An obvious example is provided by the avatars of Pan, who figures as Henry VIII, as the "God of shepheards all," and as Christ, "the onely and very Pan, then suffering for his flock."[9] These meanings are not equally valid or ultimate, metaphysically, but they are equally potent in the poem, and they imply each other. We lose something by insisting on any single meaning of a Spenserian image, for the reason that all the meanings are related to and shed light on each other. The "statement" incarnate in each thus includes a comment on the relationship of a particular imagining to congruent ones. The Calender, like The Faerie Queene, is encyclopedic in its design, for Spenser's imagination (like Milton's) is most at home when it is working in a context that can include, or at least allude to, the entire cosmic order. The poem's concern is the nature of human life—our life's shape and quality, its form, its content or "feel," and ultimately its relation to the one life outside and beyond it.

It is this effort at comprehensiveness that makes us uneasy with any single formula for the Calender's meaning, whether religious, social, or metaphysical. Boccaccio's defense of the poet's fictions includes the remark that images are used to "make truths

. . . the object of strong intellectual effort and various interpretation."[10] Pope, who thought The Shepheardes Calender "sometimes too allegorical," praised the poem's basic metaphor because it allowed Spenser to expose "to his readers a view of the great and little worlds, and their various changes and aspects."[11] He is speaking of the pastoral which, like the calendar frame, encourages, indeed demands, variety of reference; in Puttenham's famous phrase, it was devised "to insinuate and glaunce at greater matters," which, as W. L. Renwick pointed out in the commentary to his edition, could refer to several kinds of subject. "Since all personal and contemporary affairs were proper subject for Pastoral, the interpretation of the simple allegory is various: the shepherds are poets, scholars, governors, ecclesiastics, by a series of easy allusions."[12] All of these matters, in Spenser's imagination, involved each other; each area of "meaning" overlaps with the others, and each alone can offer only an incomplete statement concerning human life.

Renaissance and medieval ontology provided, of course, a rationale for a literature of multiple significances. In a world of concentric realities, a single metaphor could touch several circumferences in one trajectory; intersecting a number of different but analogous worlds, it could speak of church, of state, of poetry, of the individual soul's destiny, of divine providence as manifested in the cosmic pattern. It is well to remind ourselves of this relationship between the literature and the "world picture" of the Elizabethans, for although it has now become a cliché, it lends point to the choice of allegory as the vehicle for major works by Spenser and others, as well as to the development of a drama with broad symbolic resources. For Spenser, the interlocking complexities of reality could only be rendered accurately in a sequence of metaphors susceptible of simultaneous reference—that is, the continued metaphor of allegory.

The Shepheardes Calender, then, as Spenser's first attempt to devise a "visionary geography,"[13] must be read as an anticipation of his greatest work. The formal differences between the two poems are, of course, obvious. The continuousness of the metaphor in the Calender is not that of narrative; the poem "has a situation but no plot."[14] The ground-metaphor of The Faerie Queene is the chivalric world of Faerie Land, a place where lives unfold and journeys are traced. Time dominates the Calender not as the medium of narrative, but as a geometric pattern which may be described schematically as a circle intersected by linear tracks. The space of the poem is an imagined space whose emblematic features conform to the particular circumstances of each eclogue and are related to those of other eclogues, both adjacent and remote. All of them are drawn from the body of images loosely contained within the pastoral paradigm, but spatial continuity, like narrative line, is not to be insisted upon. The description of the structure by W. W. Greg is still the most comprehensive and objective:

> The architectonic basis of Spenser's design consists of the three Colin eclogues standing respectively at the beginning, in the middle, and at the close of the year. These are symmetrically arranged . . . [and supported] by two subsidiary eclogues, those of April and August, in both of which another shepherd sings one of Colin's lays. . . . It is upon this framework that are woven the various moral, polemical, and idyllic themes which Spenser introduces.[15]

In this geometrical structure, the poem's meaning is figured. As almost every recent critic has said, that meaning somehow concerns man's relation to the cycle of nature.[16] Spenser is considering the degree to which "natural" terms must enter into a definition of what man is; we are made aware of the pattern of human life as biologically cyclical, but also as spiritually transcendent in various directions: hence the design of linear or vertically oriented images intersecting the circular ground-plan. "Man is part of nature, but this world's brief beauty gives him less than he asks, and though he loves it he needs to look beyond it. . . . For us the natural cycle is in itself the way of death, and we will gain life only by looking to the cycle's source."[17] The character whose life is defined by these patterns, as Greg's description properly points out, is Colin Clout. Yet exclusive concentration on Colin may obscure Spenser's purpose; if this hero is a pilgrim, he never attains the Heavenly City, and it is left to other voices to define for us the alternatives to the life within "nature" figured by Colin's career. His life is congruent with the circle's movement toward "experience" and imminent death. He is an anti-hero, his unredeemed existence tracing a movement which defines the failure of man to realize his own nature. Colin recognizes that submission to the seasonal round has led only to death: "So now my yeare drawes to his latter terme" (Dec. 127); his life has passed like a dream, and bidding adieu to the "delightes, that lulled me asleepe" (151), he is left alone in a winter landscape. Colin's uncompleted quest for understanding is expressed in

the poem by a sequence of changes in the relationship between
nature and man, devised with a good deal of subtlety by Spenser
to provide simultaneously a commentary upon and a critique of
the macrocosm / microcosm analogy at the root of the pastoral
paradigm. The Calender begins in January, principally so that
Spenser may stress the circular pattern by framing his poem
with "winter" eclogues.[18] Since Januarye is also the first stage
in Spenser's critique of his analogical base, we must see man
and nature in it as congruent. Hence, when the poem begins, the
protagonist has already suffered disillusionment as the result of
love-longing; "his carefull case" resembles "the sadde season of
the yeare," as the Argument painstakingly indicates. In fact, we
are to see Colin in unwounded innocence only through the reminiscences of other shepherds. The Colin of Januarye, however,
is still a literary innocent; in making his comparison between
careful case and sad season, he uses the metaphor of the mirror,[19] indicating that for him the macrocosm still reflects
accurately the little world of man, offering valid analogies for
his inner state:

> And from mine eyes the drizling teares descend,
> As on your boughes the ysicles depend.   (41–42)

In Iune, however, as Greg points out, Spenser devises "a specific inversion of the 'pathetic fallacy' "[20] in order to express
Colin's literary disillusionment. The insights of experience include the recognition that a naive version of the pastoral metaphor inadequately expresses reality. It is no accident that in Iune
Colin explicitly renounces the "rymes and roundelayes" of his
youth, thus described by Hobbinol:

> Whose Echo made the neyghbour groues to ring,
> And taught the byrds, which in the lower spring
> Did shroude in shady leaues from sonny rayes,
> Frame to thy songe their chereful cheriping.   (52–5)

The relationship of sound to echo, a version of the mirror-image
of Januarye, is shown to be invalid in June when the harmonies of
nature clash with the disharmony of Colin's suffering. He is
exiled from Paradise, and those songs now seem to him "weary
wanton toyes" (48).

In December, Colin reflects on life and death, finally recognizing, and despairingly accepting, the fundamental incongruity

of man and nature. His Muse is "hoarse and weary"; his pipe is
hung up on a tree (140–41).

> And I, that whilome wont to frame my pype,
> Vnto the shifting of the shepheards foote:
> Sike follies nowe haue gathered as too ripe
> And cast hem out, as rotten and vnsoote.   (115–18)

Those aspects of his life which indicate its congruence with nature are unsatisfying or inadequate to the demands made upon
them. The old Colin is wise in nature's ways; he has learned
"the soothe of byrds" and "the power of herbs," yet this knowledge is of no avail in curing his "ranckling wound."

> But ah vnwise and witlesse Colin cloute,
> That kydst the hidden kinds of many a wede:
> Yet kydst not ene to cure thy sore hart roote,
> Whose ranckling wound as yet does rifelye bleede.   (91–4)

The metaphor of unripeness, which Milton was later to develop in
the opening lines of Lycidas, insists that fulfilment for man cannot be looked for within the cycle.

> The flatring fruite is fallen to grownd before,
> And rotted, ere they were halfe mellow ripe.   (106–7)

The life of Colin Clout, then, traces for us the line of human
life as it diverges psychologically from the life of nature, while
remaining physically bound to it. The event which allows this
divergence to manifest itself is a familiar one in pastoral poetry
from Theocritus to Marvell. It is love, the disturber of pastoral
harmony, a metaphor for the troubling of human life which we
call sin—that is, the dominance of passion. It is, as Colin says,
the result of pride: "But ah such pryde at length was ill repayde"
by Cupid (Dec. 49). In consequence the orderly cycle of human
life is turned awry, its promise blasted. This melancholy situation is depicted in Theocritus' eighth Idyll, as rendered by an
anonymous translator of 1588:

> A tempest marreth trees; and drought, a spring:
> Snares unto foules, to beastes, netts are a smarte;
> Love spoiles a man.

Mantuan's Eclogue II (Turberville's translation) describes the
pains of the "unlucky lad" Amyntas:

> Forgetful he of former flocke, and damage done with knaves,
> Was all inraged with this flash; at night he nought but raves.
> The season that for quiet sleepe by nature poynted was,
> In bitter plaintes and cruell cries, this burning Boy did passe.[21]

And Marvell's Mower, in the century after Spenser, complains of
the "unusual Heats" that accompany Juliana:

> This heat the Sun could never raise,
> Nor Dog-star so inflame's the dayes.
> It from an higher Beauty grow'th,
> Which burns the Fields and Mower both:
> Which mads the Dog, and makes the Sun
> Hotter than his own Phaeton.
> Not July causeth these extremes,
> But Juliana's scorching beams.[22]

The interesting feature of all these descriptions of love lies in
their stress on the disruption of macrocosmic harmony. Images
of tempest, drought, insomnia, and withered grass became appropriate figures for man's fallen state, the seasons' difference that
signifies the penalty of Adam. In the Argument to December
Colin's "summer" is meteorologically described: "which he
sayth, was consumed with greate heate and excessiue drouth
caused throughe a Comet or blasinge starre, by which he meaneth
loue, which passion is comenly compared to such flames and immoderate heate." Colin himself repeats the point:

> A comett stird vp that vnkindly heate,
> That reigned (as men sayd) in Venus seate.　　　　　(59–60)

The congruence between man's nature and external nature is violently reestablished in a baleful conjunction of planets and passions; the analogy becomes a kind of parody upon the harmonious
prelapsarian unity.

The pastoral metaphor is further developed in Iulye, in which
Colin does not figure and where Spenser sophisticates the man /
nature relationship with specific reference to the Fall of Man and
the loss of the eternal spring of Paradise. This eclogue, like
Damon the Mower, identifies unusual heats with a higher cause,
but theological rather than amorous. In an astrological passage,

the shepherd Thomalin deplores the weather of the dog days and declines to ascend the hills where he will be exposed to it.

> And now the Sonne hath reared vp
>   his fyrie footed teme.
> Making his way betweene the Cuppe,
>   and golden Diademe:
> The rampant Lyon hunts he fast,
>   with Dogge of noysome breath,
> Whose balefull barking bringes in hast
>   pyne, plagues, and dreery death.
> Agaynst his cruell scortching heate
>   where hast thou couerture?   (17–26)

The hills have been unsafe for man, Spenser goes on to say, ever since "by his foly one did fall," to make us all exiles. Sin thus condemns man to live in an unsheltered world, hostile and uncongenial, characterized by unhappy love, alienation from God, and finally, the despair of December.

Spenser develops the theme of exposure to a hostile environment in several of the eclogues, and in varying tones. In Iune, the outcast Colin "Can nowhere fynd, to shroude my lucklesse pate" (16). In the quaint fable at the end of Iulye, the good Algrin meets the fate of Aeschylus. His "bared scalpe" has been the target for a shellfish dropped by an eagle, and he now "lyes in lingring peyne" (221, 228), a warning against exposure to the rigors of the heights. A different sort of exposure, another kind of hostility, are displayed in the "recreative" mood of March. In this eclogue, the shepherd Thomalin, like Colin when we first meet him, is already love-wounded. Spenser recounts the process by which the wounding occurred, the surprising of Cupid "within an Yuie todde" and the god's mocking revenge for having been hunted. March is playful, even trivial, but it is integrated into the scheme of the Calender, obliquely through the analogue with Colin, and more directly as one of Spenser's presentations of the dangers that attend our lives. Willye's account of his father's adventure with Cupid extends the relevance of the little incident.

> For once I heard my father say,
> How he him caught vpon a day,
>   (Whereof he wilbe wroken)
> Entangled in a fowling net,
> Which he for carrion Crowes had set,
>   That in our Peeretree haunted.   (106–11)

It is an experience that recurs in each generation, indeed in almost every human life. In the spring of all our years, "lustie Loue" awakens and makes sport of us; the paradox of the huntsman ensnared expresses a characteristic experience.[23] No shepherd, "wandring vp and downe the lande" (64), is safe; the darts of love will penetrate his presumption, as the shellfish punished the innocent aspiration of Algrin in Iulye.

The notion of an environment that is hostile to man is, of course, one of the insights of experience, which moves from "soft" to "hard" pastoral. Spenser traces this process in the dialogue between youth and age in Februarie; and it is figuratively reiterated by Colin, looking back over his life:

> Where I was wont to seeke the honey Bee,
> Working her formall rowmes in Wexen frame:
> The grieslie Todestoole growne there mought I see
> And loathed Paddocks lording on the same.
> And where the chaunting birds luld me a sleepe,
> The ghastlie Owle her grieuous ynne doth keepe.
>
> (Dec. 67–72)

The emblem of an orderly nature that offers a model for man gives way to the décor of death. In fact, Nature is a threat to man, who must assume with respect to it an attitude of constant vigilance. The darkest eclogue of The Shepheardes Calender is September where the theme of the watchful shepherd is presented in the fable of Roffyn and the wolf. Diggon Davie anticipates Colin's figure of the sleep of illusion as he points the moral:

> How, but with heede and watchfulnesse,
> Forstallen hem of their wilinesse?
> For thy with shepheard sittes not playe,
> Or sleepe, as some doen, all the long day.   (230–33)

It is a harsher version of the austere message of Piers in Maye. Hobbinol's protesting reply to Diggon conveys, beneath the speaker's hedonism, despair and a sense of inevitable decay.

> Ah Diggon, thilke same rule were too straight,
> All the cold season to wach and waite.
> We bene of fleshe, men as other bee.
> Why should we be bound to such miseree?
> What euer thing lacketh chaungeable rest,
> Mought needes decay, when it is at best.   (236–41)

At the end, in answer to Diggon's question, "what way shall I wend, / My piteous plight and losse to amend?" he can offer only stoic retirement to his cottage until "fayrer Fortune" shall prevail (244–5, 257). Blindfolded, fickle Fortune, Milton's "blind Fury," was the favorite Renaissance emblem for the random, meaningless condition of earthly life. Hobbinol's solution sounds naive, and is meant to; Colin in Iune admired him as a model of pastoral harmony, but September may be read as an ironic commentary on that vision of regained Paradise. Hobbinol could not, then, cure Colin, nor can he now evade the fact that men of flesh are "bound to . . . miseree." Diggon is being punished for his foolhardiness in seeking an "vncouth" fortune outside his pastoral homeland; but this exile is the fate of each of us and should not be construed as merely another critique of "ambition." Diggon is not a "worldes childe" in the sense that Spenser uses that phrase of Palinode in Maye. His comments on life's bleakness are generalized in the fable of September. Roffyn, Colin Clout's master, is clearly a virtuous shepherd, "meeke, wise, and merciable" (174), as well as "Argus eyed" (203); his misfortune, and his vigilance, express the eclogue's theme: "God shield man, he should so ill haue thriue" (226).

Immediately following the nadir of September, the Calender takes an upward turn. If we look at the structure as a whole, not merely at the Colin "plot," we can observe Spenser causing his form to cooperate with his theme. As E. K. observes, October and Nouember are in a higher mood than any of the eclogues that preceded them (with the exception of the Aprill lay). We ought to take seriously his epithet for October, "loftye"; high flight is the motif of both these poems, "vertical" imagery prevails, and both anticipate escape from that wheel of "miseree" to which September saw men bound. Yet both poems belong to "the cold season," and thus mark, structurally, a divergence between the declining seasonal round and the uplifting powers of the human imagination. Though both include laments—for the decay of poetry and the death of Dido—both also show the means of transcendence and escape from these disasters. Within "nature," spring follows the cold season; within human life, there is a movement not identical, but analogous. In Nouember, the pattern is familiar, inevitable in a Christian pastoral elegy: La mort ny mord, death is "the grene path way to lyfe" (p. 463). In October, the solution is secular and less final, but it turns on a similar paradox: love, the source of human distress and a figure for man's fall into sin, is at the same time the pathway to regained Paradise. The design of the two poems is the same—out of suffering springs joy and release—and both are thus "answers" to Diggon's question, "What shall I doe?" in September; both demonstrate that escape from the wheel is possible. The impeccable poetic logic supports E. K.'s description of the Calender as "finely framed, and strongly trussed vp together" (p. 417).

The poem's final movement, then, as Durr has said, "declares that man cannot, like the other creatures, live his life in accordance with the seasonal round."[24] But Spenser's analysis of human life involves neither an ascetic disdain for the pleasures of the temporal world, nor a "rejection" of pastoral. Rather, those pleasures are defined and confirmed with relation to an ultimately religious sanction; and the power of the pastoral paradigm is reaffirmed as having metaphorical validity. Like Milton in Lycidas, Spenser forces upon us the unwilling recognition that we can never regain Paradise literally. Hobbinol's idyll in Iune is threatened by all the hostile forces loose in the poem, including death, which enters Iune itself in the lament for Tityrus. Just so, the singer of Lycidas must recognize that the idyllic world of "Rural ditties" has been lost forever, that the dead shepherd can never return in his old form. But he will undergo a sea-change into "the Genius of the shore." So Dido, in Nouember, lives again, transformed:

> The honor now of highest gods she is,
> That whilome was poore shepheards pryde.   (197–98)

The meaning of both Lycidas and The Shepheardes Calender concerns the need for us to accept a nonliteral, invisible reality[25] as the one most relevant to us as human beings. This reality, in both poems, is defined in the Christian terms conventional for pastoral elegy; in October, it is accessible, as well, to the poetic imagination. Awareness of a nonliteral realm of experience can be made to enlighten our earthly lives. We must follow the permutations of this theme through several eclogues, to demonstrate how, within the paradigm of the pastoral, Spenser creates his interrelated meanings.

Iulye lies at the center of the Calender and in many respects is its pivot. In both Iune and Iulye the Fall of Man is mentioned explicitly; and an awareness of our fallen state is crucial to an understanding of both eclogues. Iulye can also be read as an affirmation of the pastoral life understood in terms of biblical metaphor, rather than in the literal terms of Hobbinol's stanzas in Iune—upon which, in fact, it serves as a commentary. The two Emblems of Iulye clash and cooperate to make Spenser's point. In medio virtus, says Thomalin; In summo felicitas, says

Morrell. The moral seems plain: virtue and happiness are incompatible in this life, since one cannot be in medio and in summo at the same time. Or rather, one cannot unless one is aware
of the figurative ranges of meaning for these terms, which support the Christian paradox of the exaltation of the lowly. Spenser
presents his shepherd and goatherd in a paysage moralisé which
one of them interprets correctly (that is, figuratively) and the
other presumptuously (that is, literally). Morrell supports his
claim that hills are the healthiest habitat for man with references
to saints, to the vision of Endymion, and to Christ on Mount Olivet;
but none of these parallels is relevant to his own condition.
Finally, he insists:

> Hereto, the hills bene nigher heauen,
>   And thence the passage ethe.
> As well can proue the piercing leuin,
>   that seeldome falls bynethe.   (89–92)

His image is a dangerous one; and his method is that of "a lewde
lorrell," as Thomalin scornfully points out, demanding that the
emblems of nature be read with a less literal mind.

> Alsoone may shepheard clymbe to skye,
>   that leades in lowly dales,
> As Goteherd prowd that sitting hye,
>   vpon the Mountaine sayles.   (101–4)

E. K. enforces the point: "Note the shepheards simplenesse,
which supposeth that from the hylls is nearer ways to heauen"
(p. 447). What emerges from Iulye is a definition of two versions
of "shepheards simpleness"—simple-mindedness, and a sophisticated awareness of the true meaning of simplicity. The analogue
adduced by Thomalin is Abel, the first shepherd; we remember
that he was a type of Christ, and the implications are finally elaborated in E. K.'s lengthy gloss of the Emblems. He admits that
Morrell's Emblem is "most true," Thomalin's being obviously
"true" as well; both have the sanction of "olde Philosophers."
They can be reconciled only when we see that for man their truth
must be understood figuratively; they are literally reconciled
only in the Christian godhead where all paradoxes are resolved.
E. K. approves of both interlocutors in his last sentence, the
"great doctour" who offers as a model Christus humillimus, and
the "gentle man" who responds with an allusion to Deus altissimus.
We must follow both, remembering that, at last, they are one.

Leading a retired life in anticipation of the reward achieved by
Dido in Nouember, the good shepherds of Iulye exemplify one way
in which pastoral can provide us with a model. They are early
versions of characters in The Faerie Queene: Heavenly Contemplation who instructs the Red Cross Knight, and the Hermit who
heals Serena and Timias in Book VI. Yet allusion to these characters can help us to see that "religious" solutions to the human
predicament must be augmented by models for virtuous life in the
world. Heavenly Contemplation sends the Knight back to the world
to complete his quest, and the Hermit has himself been a knight,
"proued oft in many perillous fight" (VI. vi. 4). There is no question
but that Spenser in the Calender was recommending to the clerics
of his day the life of lowly retirement that imitates the apostles.
The allusion to the shepherd of Ida in Iulye (145–48), to say nothing
of Piers' overt moralizing in Maye, brings home to us the incompatibility of pastoral virtue and fallen human history.

"But shepheard must walke another way" from children of the
world (Maye, 81); for those in secular life there must be other
solutions. Some of the possibilities for a virtuous life within
society are explored in August, in Aprill, and in the discussion of
imagination in October and its gloss. August and October provide
Spenser's readers with a comprehension of the significance of
"pleasaunt layes" that passes beyond the complaints of Colin
Clout. In Iune, he laments because poetry is not magic. Tityrus'
songs could not save him from the outrage of death; and as the
eclogue ends, Colin is recognizing his own impotence: "I am not,
as I wish I were" (105), that is, capable of piercing Rosalind's
stony heart. Had he inherited Tityrus' powers, he says, "I soone
would learne these woods, to wayle my woe" (95). The argument
ignores the earlier awareness that Tityrus had been unable to
salvage his own "skill" from death's ruin; but in one line, Colin
glances at a source of solace that Spenser will develop later.
Poetic skill is as "passing" as its human possessors, but its
memory survives in the "workes of learned wits," "The fame
whereof doth dayly greater growe" (92). The growth of Colin's
own fame is signified, in the action of the Calender, by the presence of three of his songs, performed by his friends and betoken-
ing the true power of art. It cannot effect literal changes in the
world of nature; but in its imagined worlds, perfect harmony can
reign, to be recreated each time the song is sung for our instruction and delight. The sestina of August, whose power and sophistication contrast notably with the naive rhymes of Perigot and
Willye, is an "answer" to the harsh insights of Iune. It is "a doole-
full verse / Of Rosalend," the record of suffering, of passion, but

here transformed into a fictive action that reproduces the dolorous harmonies envisaged in Iune. There, the literal woods hardheartedly refused to wail; but here, "wild woddes" resound Colin's sorrows, "banefull byrds" accompany his complaint, and a "gastfull groue" offers appropriate décor for the melancholy scene. The poem is a kind of charm, evoking in imagination the correspondence of microcosm and macrocosm, accidentally but temporarily visible in Ianuarye, and unobtainable in the literal "nature" of Iune. The effect of the song on the other shepherds is insisted on; though it is a "heauy laye," Willye eagerly anticipates its performance:

> For neuer thing on earth so pleaseth me,
> As him to heare, or matter of his deede.   (147–8)

At the end, both song and performance are praised.

> O Colin, Colin, the shepheards ioye,
>   How I admire ech turning of thy verse:
> And Cuddie, fresh Cuddie the liefest boye,
>   How dolefully his doole thou didst rehearse.   (190–3)

"Doole" becomes a source of delight as it is transmuted into art; though it cannot "cure" its maker, it can confer on him an immortality of fame, for "monuments of Poetry abide for euer" (p. 467).

These are E. K.'s last words; they are augmented by his gloss for October, where Spenser makes explicit the two aspects of his definition of art, obliquely rendered in August. Poetry is a nonliteral action, and a source of immortality. Though the poet does not make a logical connection between these two ideas, we may see them as related: because poetry's mode of being is outside the world of nature, it can defy natural decay. E. K.'s explication of the Emblem is a definition of imagination which suggests that this relationship was present in Spenser's mind: "Poetry is a diuine instinct and vnnatural rage passing the reache of comen reason" (p. 459). Like the divine furor of love, it can provide a ladder that will take us out of the foul rag-and-bone shop of nature's cycles. Piers' exhortation to Cuddie to summon up his poetic powers uses the same figure to describe love's power:

> Lyft vp thy selfe out of the lowly dust   (38)

>   loue does teach him climbe so hie,
> And lyftes him vp out of the loathsome myre.   (91–2)

MACCAFFREY

As a consequence of this "lifting up," love itself is immortalized, as it was in August; and immortality can be conferred, as well, on others. A familiar Renaissance solace appears in E. K.'s gloss: poets achieve eternity of fame not only for themselves, but for their subjects, whose "worthines and valor shold through theyr famous Posies be commended to all posterities" (p. 459).

The vertical perspectives offered by these two "ladders"— poetic inspiration, and love—are extended and consummated in the elegy sung in Nouember, where a vision of Dido's immortality consoles its lamenting audience:

> Ay francke shepheard, how bene thy verses meint
> With doolful pleasaunce, so as I ne wotte,
> Whether reioyce or weepe for great constrainte?   (203—5)

The paradoxes expressed in these lines are neither exclusively theological, nor exclusively aesthetic; they are both at once, the point being that art is the most exact mirror of ultimate mysteries. As every alert reader of the Calender observes, Nouember provides the source and end for all lesser visions.[26] The transposition of pastoral imagery into a transcendental key, deriving as it ultimately does from Revelation, confers upon this mode of imagining the sanction of the divine artist. "Fayre fieldes and pleasaunt layes there bene" in Heaven (188); as a result, fields and lays are reinvigorated for us as metaphorical anticipations of bliss.

But the elegy is also an object lesson in the limits of poetry's power; it cannot alter things as they are by reviving Dido and reversing the calendar. She was "the fayrest May . . . that euer went" (39), but this is November, and remains November within the literal action. In "the trustlesse state of earthly things" (153), no springtime lasts, and man has only one springtime. Spenser enforces this implied statement of poetry's powers and limits in his allusion to Orpheus in October. Piers is praising Cuddie's songs:

> Soone as thou gynst to sette thy notes in frame
> O how the rurall routes to thee doe cleaue:
> Seemeth thou dost their soule of sence bereaue,
> All as the shepheard, that did fetch his dame
> From Plutoes baleful bowre withouten leaue:
> His musicks might the hellish hound did tame.   (25—30)

In spite of his "musicks might," Orpheus did not succeed, finally, in reversing the course of nature, and Eurydice's ultimate fate would, one imagines, have been present in the minds of Spenser's readers. What is not in question, however, is poetry's power to tame Cerberus and to ravish the sense of its human audience.

What emerges, then, from the climactic eclogues of The Shepheardes Calender is a balance of attitudes held in equilibrium, intensifying the complex point of view visible in the work as a whole. Man must suffer inevitable outrage from the forces released in nature at the Fall, and against these forces there is no remedy within nature itself, or within the power of mere "natural man." Poetry cannot provide a talisman against death, nor heal the wounds of love, nor recreate the state of innocence. Yet the power of imagination in man is a real power, if rightly understood as "an vnnatural rage"; it gives us access to a transnatural realm of being where our ultimate destiny lies.

The lay of Aprill, the third of Colin's songs, is designed, like those in August and Nouember, to confirm Piers' claim in October that love, seconded by imagination, can lift us out of the cycle of death. All three poems offer visions of a world in which reality corresponds to human desires. All are elaborate in form, their higher mood surpassing the reach of ordinary shepherds' wit. In celebrating Eliza, Rosalind, and Dido, Colin must keep decorum with themes that transcend the natural order as he observes it in "reality" in many of the other eclogues. The fox of Maye, the wolf of September, the "Ambitious brere" of Februarye, the lowly pastors of Iulye, the disharmonies of Iune—all these manifest the nature of fallen being. But Aprill and August offer visions of possibility, and Nouember a glimpse of actuality that transcends all human potentiality. Bacon was later to disparage poets for submitting "the shows of things to the desires of the mind," but as both Sidney and Spenser affirm, those desires themselves bear witness to the presence of a realm of being inadequately figured by the shows of things.

All three of Colin Clout's songs are monuments of wit and demonstrations of its capacities; the Aprill lay is, in addition, Spenser's most eloquent depiction of a monument of power, a model that refers to our life on earth. It is a vision of perfection within fallen nature that can be effected by exercising another kind of art. Once our world has become the prey of sin, nature can be restored to something like its original purity only with the aid of civilization, that "nurture" regularly opposed in Elizabethan

debates to unaltered "nature." The arts of government can unite
antagonists and create another Eden, at least a demi-paradise—
the garden of the world, as Elizabeth's poets were fond of calling
her kingdom. This world is presented in Aprill, where the lay's
formal artifice can be taken as a symbol of all the artful patterns
that bring order out of chaos. Aprill speaks of the work of art, be
it a commonwealth, a dance, or a poem; October speaks of the
maker, "the perfect paterne of a Poete" (p. 456). He can create
on earth a mirror, fragile but exact, of the world not as it is but
as it might be. The making of golden worlds is the chief function
assigned to poetry by Sidney; and it lies behind Piers' description
of the poet's heavenly goal in October:

> Then make thee winges of thine aspyring wit,
> And, whence thou camst, flye backe to heaven apace. (83–4)

In Nouember we contemplate the true heavenly garden; in Aprill
we see a fictive version of its earthly counterpart, transient but
potent, created by poet and queen.[27] Colin's art cooperates with
that of "our most gracious souereigne" to produce a golden world
in imagination; and this world is capable, as the Envoy to the
Calender insists, of surviving every catastrophe except the final
one: "It shall continewe till the worlds disolution" (p. 467).

The microcosmic character of the lay of Aprill hardly requires
elaboration. The images create a comprehensive harmony that
extends from the flowers on the green to golden Phoebus and silver Cynthia, removed from their "natural" orbits, like the Sun in
Donne's The Sunne Rising, to circle this little cosmos and do
homage to its sustaining power. Here, as in Eden, spring and
autumn dance hand in hand and flowers of all seasons blossom
together to deck Eliza, whose complexion predictably unites "the
Redde rose medled with the White yfere" (68). Joining classical
and native strains, as later they were to be joined in Epithalamion,
nymphs of Helicon dance beside Ladies of the Lake and "shepheards daughters, that dwell on the greene" (127)—the two latter
groups figuring, it has been suggested, a union of the spirits of
water and land.[28] The "chiefest Nymph" brings the final tribute:
a coronal of olive branches, signifying the surcease of war,
Eliza's establishment of the Peaceable Kingdom, the Golden Age
restored. The Aprill lay, though not composed in the heroic mode
prescribed by Piers in October, speaks of the subjects there rec-
ommended, and is presided over by Calliope (100). The epic poet
is to turn to

those, that weld the awful crowne,
To doubted Knights, whose woundlesse armour rusts,
And helmes vnbruzed wexen dayly browne.   (Oct., 40–42)

Another incarnation of Elizabeth, Mercilla in Faerie Queene V,
is also a peaceable ruler; at her feet is a sword "Whose long rest
rusted the bright steely brand" (V. ix. 30). The sterner style of
epic demands images like those of the rusted armour or sword;
and those images, too, remind us that epic treats of life in a harsh
and threatened fallen world, where the sword may at any moment
be drawn. For the homely yet courtly vision of high pastoral, the
coronal of olive is more decorous. Yet both images project an
ideal that was often referred to by writers on the arts of government. Spenser's version of it in Aprill is a world of possibility
created by poetry; Castiglione celebrates princely virtue in The
Courtier in a congruent allusion:

> That vertue, which perhaps among all the matters that be-
> long unto man is the chiefest and rarest, that is to say, the
> manner and way to rule and to raigne in the right kinde.
> Which alone were sufficient to make men happie, and to
> bring once againe into the world the golden age, which is
> written to have beene when Saturnus raigned in the olde
> time.[29]

Pastoral imagery finds a new sanction in figuring this happy
state, as in Nouember its validity was to be confirmed in another
direction. The more one reads The Shepheardes Calender, the
more one is struck by the force of Hallett Smith's judgment that
"the pastoral idea, in its various ramifications, is the Calender."[30]
The pastoral paradigm, in the service of a potent and resourceful
imagination, proves itself to be a flexible expressive instrument.
The serious use of pastoral in the Renaissance, by Spenser and
others, received, of course, support from its presence in the Bible
and from the central paradox of Christianity where low degree is
exalted. So the humblest genre can figure the highest matters.
This paradox is exploited by Spenser in a secular context in Aprill,
where the greatest personage of the land enters the shepherds'
country world and hallows it. In turn, that world itself provides
emblems supremely apt for figuring the special graces of her
reign. There is a union of estates, a little mirror of Gloriana's
England—appropriately enough, if we recall that on the twenty-
third of the month was celebrated the feast of England's patron
saint.

Having tested for himself the resources of one of the basic metaphors of his tradition, Spenser laid aside his pastoral pipe for a time. Already, the queen of shepherds was being metamorphosed into the queen of faerie. Yet pastoral was not abandoned for good; it is absorbed into Faerie Land itself, making an essential contribution to the vast landscape of The Faerie Queene. And in one of his last poems, Colin Clouts Come Home Againe, Spenser produced a classic example of the pastoral paradigm. Yet in the end, the interest for us of The Shepheardes Calender lies not in the pastoral "matter," but in the mode of its handling. De Selincourt's view of the poem as embodying "a world of Spenser's own" strikes the most relevant note.[31] Formally and thematically, it stands as a characteristic product of this poet's imagination, which from the beginning was a maker of worlds. The Calender is an ambitious, encyclopedic allegory, controlled by a metaphor that is capable of sustaining a complex significatio. Spenser's powers were to develop far beyond the point which they had attained in 1579; particularly in the matter of inventing a narrative, he had much to learn. Yet this early work, especially as it offered an opportunity to explore the imagined landscape of an allegorical country, can be seen as an essential prologue to the bold inventions of The Faerie Queene, where the romantic world of the medieval storytellers is transformed into a visionary geography of unsurpassed flexibility, enchantment, and expressive power.

THE UNIQUENESS OF SPENSER'S <u>EPITHALAMION</u>

Wolfgang Clemen

Spenser's <u>Epithalamion</u> is one of the great poems of English literature. It has maintained its reputation and rank throughout the centuries in spite of the changes in taste and outlook.[1] In reading it today we can still enjoy it with that immediacy of pleasure which also for a closer scholarly investigation forms the best condition. We can still appreciate the beautiful melody of the stanzas, the imaginative richness of the language, the freshness of the poem and its personal tone, the intensity of emotion, the moving union of the sensuous and the spiritual, the striking fusion of many disparate elements; we can still enjoy the dramatic presentation of scene and action, the wealth of visual and oral impressions, the vividness of concrete details.

There are only a few random impressions which the ordinary, unprepared reader might share with us, but despite their value as an indication of the poem's enduring effect, they are too vague and general for a discriminating evaluation. The scholar is constantly faced with the task of penetrating to the core of impressions such as these, and, by tracing each one back to its component aspects, he may transform a mere impression into demonstrable fact. The effect of artistic perfection and emotional intensity, the impression of what we would call high poetic quality, is usually a product of a number of factors co-operating toward a common goal.[2] In reading a poem only once or twice we cannot become aware of this complicated interplay of various elements. It is only by closer examination that we discover how many different things had to come together to make this achievement possible.

Moreover, a poem of great perfection and great beauty often forms a milestone in the history of English poetry. Its freshness and liveliness derive from the fact that certain structural qualities, certain principles of composition and poetic organization, were achieved here for the first time in a successful manner. The poet

From The Poetic Tradition: Essays on Greek, Latin, and English Poetry, ed. Don Cameron Allen and Henry T. Rowell, Baltimore 1968, pp. 81–98. © The Johns Hopkins Press. Reprinted by permission of the author and The Johns Hopkins Press.

who writes a perfect poem that may be regarded as a climax in the poetry of his time has usually succeeded in solving problems for which neither his predecessors nor even he himself in earlier poems had managed to find a satisfactory solution. Poetry, in spite of its claim to inspiration, is an art in which much has to be learned before a masterpiece can be produced. The instruments of versification and diction must be refined to a degree of perfection, devices of composition and organization must have been found, means of poetic expression must have been developed, ways of giving shape to abstract notions must be at the poet's disposal in order that a successful "long poem" of some complexity may be born.

Looking back over the history of English poetry in the sixteenth century, and examining the way in which these arts of poetic composition and expression developed, we would have to admit that the Epithalamion could not have been written in the sixties, seventies or eighties of the sixteenth century. A process of gradual development was necessary for English poetry to reach a stage at which a man of genius like Spenser could find at his disposal an instrument sufficiently refined to enable him to write a great poem. This does not mean that the evolution of a style of poetry over a period of several decades would automatically lead to a masterpiece. However, it was not mere chance that Spenser's achievement with his Epithalamion appeared at the same time as the crowning achievement of Elizabethan lyric poetry, as a consummation of some of the highest potentialities and poetic endeavors of this important phase in English poetry. It is with a view to this twofold quality of Spenser's Epithalamion, as a great representative poem of the English Renaissance and as Spenser's most perfect work of art, that I propose to speak of its "uniqueness."

"Uniqueness" and "perfection," however, are the results of the fortunate co-operation of several basic qualities. I should like therefore to concentrate on the question: What are the distinguishing features which go to constitute the poem's excellence and its uniqueness? It may be appropriate to gauge these qualities first by looking back on works of comparable length and subject matter written before Spenser's poem.

Spenser's Epithalamion is one of these "long poems" which in the literature of the sixteenth century form a class of their own. A "long poem" has always set special problems for its author.[3] It has a tendency to become tedious, so variety, change in tone and color, but also growth and development, are essential. But this again might well impair the poem's unity and consistency.

Thus the special difficulties attributed to the long poem have often been the problems of organization and of unification. And we can easily see that the long poems before Spenser generally fail in this respect.[4] They could just as well go on for another ten stanzas, they have no climax and often no central theme to which all minor details should be related. They are loosely constructed and their method of composition is rather one of stringing together a series of ideas, conventions, and incidents. The Epithalamies[5] by Bartholomew Young and Sir Philip Sidney are particularly suited for such a comparison as they belong to the same literary genre and employ similar conventions to Spenser's <u>Epithalamion</u>. In Young's <u>Epithalamion</u>, for instance, the sequence of the stanzas could even be changed without detriment to the intelligibility of the poem; there is no link between the stanzas and little or no connection between the different motifs which are treated separately in the course of the poem. Spenser's poem, on the other hand, displays unity, order, inner cohesion, and clear organization. In fact, it appears to be the first long poem in the history of English poetry to be composed according to a well-calculated plan. It has its own curve and development, its proper preparation at the beginning leading us leisurely and step by step toward the core of the poem and it has its proper ending. We can even detect an elaborate symmetry, so characteristic of Renaissance art, in the construction of this poem.

After the invocation to the Muses ten stanzas out of twenty-three lead up to the great moment when the bride enters the church, so that the actual marriage ceremony takes place in the exact center of the poem. But this marriage ceremony also coincides with the middle of the day, with the sun reaching its zenith. Two structural patterns thus correspond to each other, and the two halves into which we can divide the poem (if we take the middle of the day with the wedding ceremony as the division line) also bear resemblances to each other and disclose correspondences. Thus, as William Nelson has pointed out in his recent book on Spenser[6] "the opening invocation of the Muses, the Nymphs, the Hours and the Graces is matched by concluding prayers to Cynthia, Juno, Genius, Hebe and the 'high heavens.' The bride is roused from sleep at the beginning and is sung to sleep at the end. The rising sun has its balance in the evening star, the moon, and the 'thousand torches flaming bright.' In the morning the Hours are asked to adorn and array the bride; when the sun sets the attendant damsels disarray her." Another critic, Hieatt, has gone even further and has tried to point out, as regards the use of numbers and recurring motifs,

CLEMEN

subtle correspondences between the stanzas occupying the same
position in both parts.[7]

As Spenser describes the progress of his marriage day from
early morning until late at night, his poem is given a definite
framework of time and experience. But within this running action
each stanza depicts a situation, a moment or a phase which is
complete in itself and forms a unit within the larger composition
of the whole poem. This art of elaborating a situation, presenting
it to us as a living picture but integrating this pictorial mode of
presentation into a steadily progressing action, is evident in
Spenser's Faerie Queene. In the Epithalamion this art reappears
in a more concentrated form combined with a convincing and well-
rounded cyclic pattern. For the natural order of a twenty-four-
hour cycle binds the happenings of the poem close together and
also places the reader in a revolving time scheme which he may
relate to his own daily experience. The order and ritual of the
marriage day in accordance with the custom of the time are carefully observed; the progress of the marriage procession bringing
the bride from her home to the church and taking her back to her
home constitutes a conspicuous groundplan and allows every
minor detail as well as every convention of the epithalamic tradition to fall into its concrete place in time and locality. For when
reading the poem we always know where and in which phase of the
day we find ourselves. Thus we can say that in Spenser's poem
order and organization are closely combined with a constant endeavor to relate all traditional conventions and motifs to the
specific happenings of this marriage day; a process which we
might call "concretization."

However, order and organization in a perfect poem are inevitably linked with the problem of unity. Unity is not uniformity.
For uniformity effected through monotonous versification and
diction, the regular recurrence of certain rhetorical figures or
conventions was what the poets before Spenser had as a rule produced instead of genuine unity. Spenser's poem, however, is a
work of variety, of changing tempo and diction, of surprising transitions between varying levels of style and techniques of description. To give unity to such a poem of many colors and great
diversity, Spenser had to use several means. (Whether the poet
contrived these means consciously or unconsciously is a problem
which we cannot discuss here.) However, we could draw up a long
list of features and devices which contribute toward unifying of
the poem. I can mention here only a few.

In several respects the bride is the center of the poem, the

572

pervading theme to which everything else is related. To begin
with, Spenser succeeds in connecting most of the minor decorative
details, almost all the ornament and imagery, with the bride, who
is referred to in almost every stanza. The nymphs, the graces,
and the village girls are invoked to awaken, to adorn, to dress the
bride; to sing her praise, to help in the preparation of the wedding.
But the same applies to others appearing in the course of the poem
—the "fresh boyes" (112), the minstrels, the damsels in the street,
the virgins, and also the non-human beings—the birds, the woods,
the moon, the evening-star, the night, the "sonnes of Venus." This
unifying effect, if we may put it that way, is enhanced by the fact
that it is the poet himself who calls upon all these beings and people to serve the bride in some way or other, to sing her praise, to
contribute to her happiness and well-being.

The poet is at the same time the bridegroom, who describes
his own marriage day and gives his entire poem as a present to
his bride. But his role is also that of a director of a masque or
pageant, for, like a master of the revels, he arranges everything
and the main initiative always comes from him. He is also the
speaker who in his complex role as poet, bridegroom, and master
of the revels can address his own bride with the same naturalness
as the Muses, Juno, or the "merchants daughters." This continuous presence of the poet himself, acting beside the bride as the
second central figure in the poem and to whose voice we listen,
not only increases the personal meaning and appeal of this poem
but is another important factor in producing its unity. Moreover,
the poem in itself appears as a gift from the poet to his bride, as
an "ornament" that crowns the activity of adorning and praising
referred to in every stanza. The poem's last stanza, the "envoy,"
reads:

> Song made in lieu of many ornaments,
> With which my love should duly have bene dect,

ending

> Be unto her a goodly ornament,
> And for short time an endlesse moniment.[8]

Now we find that this motif of adorning is one of the recurring
leitmotifs. The Muses often helped the poets "others to adorne"
(2). The whole third stanza is about the adorning of the bridal
chambers, and in the fourth stanza it is the bride herself who is

to be adorned. In the sixth stanza the three Graces are called
upon to "adorne my beautifullest bride" (105). I quote the third
stanza to illustrate the manner in which Spenser interweaves this
motif of adorning into the running account of the marriage day:

> Bring with you all the Nymphes that you can heare
> Both of the rivers and the forrests greene:
> And of the sea that neighbours to her neare,
> Al with gay girlands goodly wel beseene.
> And let them also with them bring in hand
> Another gay girland
> For my fayre love of lillyes and of roses,
> Bound truelove wize with a blew silke riband.
> And let them make great store of bridale poses,
> And let them eeke bring store of other flowers
> To deck the bridal bowers.
> And let the ground whereas her foot shall tread,
> For feare the stones her tender foot should wrong
> Be strewed with fragrant flowers all along,
> And diapred lyke the discolored mead.
> Which done, doe at her chamber dore awayt,
> For she will waken strayt,
> The whiles doe ye this song unto her sing,
> The woods shall to you answer and your Eccho ring.

Singing and rejoicing are other often recurring motifs which help
to convey a certain coloring and mood to this poem. Or note the
frequency of words expressing joy: joyance, pleasure, pleasance,
delight, happiness, jollity, cheerful, glad, happy, or the frequency
of other key words like fair, fresh, sweet, goodly, gentle, seemly.
    Such a use of vocabulary may also be found in other Elizabethan
poems. But of a more intricate and subtle effect as a unifying factor is the imagery of light which pervades the whole poem. For it
is derived quite organically from the rising and descending sun,
followed by the rising moon. These metaphors of light, however,
are invariably related to the bride, so that there is a constant
fluctuation and correspondence between the real sun and its symbolic significance. The seventh stanza may illustrate this point:

> Now is my love all ready forth to come,
> Let all the virgins therefore well awayt,
> And ye fresh boyes that tend upon her groome
> Prepare your selves; for he is comming strayt.

> Set all your things in seemely good aray
> Fit for so joyful day,
> The joyfulst day that ever sunne did see.
> Faire Sun, shew forth thy favourable ray,
> And let thy lifull heat not fervent be
> For feare of burning her sunshyny face,
> Her beauty to disgrace.
> O fayrest Phœbus, father of the Muse,
> If ever I did honour thee aright,
> Or sing the thing, that mote thy mind delight,
> Doe not thy servants simple boone refuse,
> But let this day let this one day be myne,
> Let all the rest be thine.
> Then I thy soverayne prayses loud wil sing,
> That all the woods shal answer and theyr eccho ring.

Thus we find that the organization of unity is closely bound up with
the establishing of correspondences and interrelationships. The
course of outward events, the situations visually described, and
the stages of this marriage day are at the same time, as a more
detailed study might show, expressive of inner moods. The outward form of this poem has become "inner form," for the curve
of external happenings on this marriage day coincides with the
curve of inner experience. The day's natural cycle governed by
the rising and setting sun is a perfect image of what the poet
wanted to convey in the sphere of ideas, feelings, and ethical
values.

But unity also means integration of heterogeneous elements.
Let us begin with the integration of the traditional conventions
which belonged to the "epithalamium." The apparatus of epithalamic conventions has been carefully explored by several scholars.[9]
Spenser observes most of these conventions but we are scarcely
aware of their "conventional origin," for he has enlivened and con-
cretized them by relating them closely to the actual events of the
day and by turning them to dramatic account. Even the first invocations to the nymphs and the graces (37, 103) are utilized in this
particular manner. The nymphs, for example, are called upon to
decorate the bridal bowers with flowers and to wait for the bride
at the chamber door, thus resembling the customary bridesmaids
who appear at a wedding (45 ff.). But if we read on we notice that
the "light foot maids" (67) who are addressed as the "Nymphes of
Mulla" are more or less identical with the daughters of the tenants
and farmers in the country round the castle of Kilcolman where

Spenser's marriage actually took place. In other stanzas, too, the mythological figures merge into the familiar people of Spenser's own countryside, just as the ideal scenery and the conventional setting of the <u>Epithalamion</u> constantly blend with the local Irish scenery and the actual circumstances of Spenser's marriage day.[10] Mythology, on the other hand, is fused with folklore and popular custom, so that there is a constant transition between the literary tradition of the "epithalamium" and the actual wedding customs still in use in Spenser's own time. This point may be illustrated by the stanzas VIII (129 ff.) or XV (260 ff.) where we hear of the festivities connected with St. Barnabas Day, or stanza XIX (334 ff.), where there is mention of "Pouke" and "other evill sprights" and "mischivous witches with theyr charmes." The stanza should be quoted in full:

> Let no lamenting cryes, nor dolefull teares,
> Be heard all night within nor yet without:
> Ne let false whispers breeding hidden feares,
> Breake gentle sleepe with misconceived dout.
> Let no deluding dreames, nor dreadful sights
> Make sudden sad affrights;
> Ne let housefyres, nor lightnings helpelesse harmes,
> Ne let the Pouke, nor other evill sprights,
> Ne let mischivous witches with theyr charmes,
> Ne let hob Goblins, names whose sence we see not,
> Fray us with things that be not.
> Let not the shriech Oule, nor the Storke be heard:
> Nor the night Raven that still deadly yels,
> Nor damned ghosts cald up with mighty spels,
> Nor griesly vultures make us once affeard:
> Ne let th'unpleasant Quyre of Frogs still croking
> Make us to wish theyr choking.
> Let none of these theyr drery accents sing;
> Ne let the woods them answer, nor theyr eccho ring.

If we listen to a reading of Spenser's <u>Epithalamion</u> we become particularly aware of the unifying function of the refrain at the end of each stanza. This most musical and perfect refrain not only rounds off each stanza but also evokes the same symbolic background of scenery and echoing music to which the stanza contributes its own particular feature. However, this refrain is more than a recurring leitmotif. For through the slight modification to which each new refrain is submitted we are reminded of the gradual passage of time. Whereas the sixteenth stanza describing the last part of the day ended "That all the woods them answer and their echo ring" the following stanza (the seventeenth) emphasizes the beginning of night with lines like:

> Now day is doen, and night is nighing fast:
> Now bring the Bryde into the brydall boures.
> Now night is come, now soone her disaray . . .

and concludes

> Now it is night, ye damsels may be gon,
> And leave my love alone,
> And leave likewise your former lay to sing:
> The woods no more shal answere, nor your echo ring.

Thus the problem of unity and integration, on which we have so far dwelled, leads us to another important aspect of the poem, its organic growth and its time-consciousness. Looking at comparable longer poems of the period we find that no consistent use is made of the passing of time. Narrative poems of the pastoral kind certainly present an action which moves forward, but we are not really made to feel the lapse of time. Spenser's <u>Epithalamion</u> appears to be composed on another principle, which we might call the principle of organic growth alternating between movement and suspense, progress and immobility, for each stanza gives us a new picture and exploits a new situation which gains life before our eyes. But in almost every stanza we are also reminded that the action has moved forward and that time is passing. The natural sequence of the hours of the day serves as a "clock-time scheme." But within this "clock-time scheme" we have the subjective time experience. Time may pass quickly or it may linger on endlessly. The varying tempo produced within each stanza by versification and diction helps to produce this feeling of passing time. There are stanzas with quick movement where several things happen at once in an almost dramatic simultaneity, and there are stanzas of a lingering mood, in which time seems to stand still. The moods of expectancy and impatience, of happiness and fulfilment are invariably expressed by references to the passing of time. Thus we have the subjective experience of slow-moving time in line 280:

> How slowly do the houres their numbers spend?
> How slowly does sad Time his feathers move?

Spenser's subtle use of time contributes to the over-all effect that something is really happening in the poem, happening at this very moment; that we ourselves are taking part in this day and are watching the progress of an actual experience. Indeed we even believe that we are among the bystanders lining the road while the procession moves forward.

But how does the poet achieve this effect of immediacy and of presence? For this is perhaps the most remarkable feature in a poem handling a classical convention, and it is, moreover, an effect we do not find in the "long poems" of the Elizabethan Age. In analyzing this effect we come upon a number of devices which again no other poet of Spenser's time has used in this subtle manner. For all descriptions of events, of situations, of persons grow out of an act of looking, watching, hearing. They are not given "objectively" but are reflected by someone who watches. This may be the poet-bridegroom himself, or the boys and maidens in the street looking at the bride as she passes by, or it may even be ourselves, the audience. For we are constantly called upon to see, to gaze, to hear, to listen (cf. 64, 129, 167, 185, 223, 372, 377).[11] Even the sun and the moon, as well as the angels, are to take part in this process.[12] Thus Spenser, the painter-poet of the eye, has endowed the figures he puts into his poem with his own gift of gazing. This immediacy and directness are further enhanced by the role assumed by the poet himself, which we have already compared to the role of a producer or "master of the revels." For it is the poet who directly addresses the nymphs, the bridesmaids, and all other groups which turn up in the course of the day, telling them what to do, what to look at, or what to expect. Thus we find, instead of the objective statement or the detached description, the direct address, the imperative, the question. At one point the poet even addresses his own bride, for in the midst of the ceremony in the church he asks her: "Why blush ye love to give to me your hand?" (238).

Thus a dialogic partnership is established throughout the poem. Of some stanzas we can even say that the dramatic mode is employed, for we are given little scenes with the movements, gestures, and doings of various persons or groups of people. This immediacy and directness of presentation also helps to bridge the gap between the conventions—the learned allusions on the one hand and the familiar contemporary world of Spenser's readers on the other hand. For beside the conventions deriving from the epithalamic tradition, there are spread throughout the poem a great many (in fact hundreds) of references to the Bible, to classical,

medieval, and Renaissance authors.[13] Spenser has absorbed and
integrated this mass of learned material from myth and legend,
from the literary tradition and theology to such extraordinary
degree that we scarcely become aware of this background, for it
has been transformed into fresh and actual experience, it has been
welded and integrated into the organic texture of the poem. As
Douglas Bush has shown us, there is in many Elizabethan poems
an amalgam of pagan and Christian deities, of legend and mythology
together with contemporary allusion,[14] but I would suggest that
there is no other longer poem of the sixteenth century in which this
fusion of heterogeneous material, of disparate notions and motifs
has reached the same degree of perfection, at the same time successfully increasing the poem's complexity, richness, and unity.

However, in Spenser's <u>Epithalamion</u> we do not only find the
muses, graces and pagan deities like Bacchus, Hymen, Hebe, and
Juno side by side with the Christian angels, the "temple gates" by
the altar (204, 215), but we also find very different levels of style
and of expression. For the scale of Spenser's language reaches
from everyday idiom up to the most elaborate diction of Elizabethan poetry. Compare, for example, short monosyllabic phrases
like:

> For they can doo it best (258)
> And in her bed her lay (301)
> That no man may us see (320)

with lines like

> Her long loose yellow locks lyke golden wyre,
> Sprinckled with perle, and perling flowres a tweene. (154–55)

And compare again these lines with the colloquial simplicity of:

> Ah my deere love why doe ye sleepe thus long (85)

or

> Enough is it, that all the day was youres. (297)

But Spenser's vocabulary in the poem also includes archaic words,
as had already been used in <u>The Shepherd's Calender</u>, though here
they are applied with more discretion.

This wide range of his linguistic and stylistic resources allows

Spenser to express changes of mood and tempo, to achieve a transition from stylization and formality to a natural and easy manner. Of the many examples which could illustrate this point I should like to draw attention to some contrasting stanzas. Stanza VIII (129 ff.) gives us the bustle and noisy activity in the street with its "confused noyce" and the sound of all the merry music, of pipe and tabor:

> Harke how the Minstrels gin to shrill aloud
> Their merry Musick that resounds from far,
> The pipe, the tabor, and the trembling Croud,
> That well agree withouten breach or jar.
> But most of all the Damzels doe delite,
> When they their tymbrels smyte,
> And thereunto doe daunce and carrol sweet,
> That all the sences they doe ravish quite,
> The whyles the boyes run up and downe the street,
> Crying aloud with strong confused noyce,
> As if it were one voyce.
> Hymen io Hymen, Hymen they do shout,
> That even to the heavens theyr shouting shrill
> Doth reach, and all the firmament doth fill,
> To which the people standing all about,
> As in approvance doe thereto applaud
> And loud advaunce her laud,
> And evermore they Hymen Hymen sing,
> That al the woods them answer and theyr eccho ring.

But the following stanza has quite a different pace. It solemnly announces the appearance of the bride; all stir and movement come to a halt and we are arrested by the gorgeous beauty of the poetry:

> Loe where she comes along with portly pace,
> Lyke Phoebe from her chamber of the East,
> Arysing forth to run her mighty race,
> Clad all in white, that seemes a virgin best.
> So well it her beseemes that ye would weene
> Some angell she had beene.
> Her long loose yellow locks lyke golden wyre,
> Sprinckled with perle, and perling flowres a tweene,
> Doe lyke a golden mantle her attyre,
> And being crowned with a girland greene,
> Seeme lyke some mayden Queene.

> Her modest eyes abashed to behold
> So many gazers, as on her do stare,
> Upon the lowly ground affixed are.
> Ne dare lift up her countenance too bold,
> But blush to heare her prayses sung so loud,
> So farre from being proud.
> Nathlesse doe ye still loud her prayses sing,
> That all the woods may answer and your eccho ring.

The mood of solemn gravity and intimate silence finds its place
in this poem as well as the mood of jolly merriment, and both
are given their appropriate stylistic expression. Thus Spenser
gives us in his <u>Epithalamion</u>, on different levels, "variety within
unity." In emphasizing this aspect, however, we must also consider his versification. For this most elaborate and intricate
stanza of eighteen or nineteen lines which Spenser developed out
of the Italian <u>canzone</u> allows for changes of rhythm and tempo.
Short lines alternate with long ones and the meter is often modified and shifted. A special study would be needed to show how
this flexible manipulation of meter contributes toward the effect
of suspense, of slowing down and speeding up, of heightening tension. And it would also be worth while demonstrating how Spenser
makes use of the rhetorical figures of assonance, anaphora, alliteration, of word-echo, of inverted word order or of certain syntactical patterns to underline or intensify the significance of particular passages. It goes without saying that these "arts of
language" are given masterly treatment by a poet who had gone
through years of intense poetic training. But this refined instrument of poetical expression is not in itself a product of art but
merely a servant. It had to find its thematic counterpart, its
adequate conception and framework, in order to exert its full
power.

I have limited myself to aspects of Spenser's poetic art which
combine to make up the poem's high artistic quality. I have omitted Spenser's handling and modification of the genre to which this
poem belongs, the marriage poem or "epithalamium" which from
antiquity onward up to Spenser undergoes considerable transformation. Such a study, which has already been carried out by other
scholars,[15] would confirm the impression which our reading of
the poem has so far given us: that Spenser is at the same time
traditional and original, typical and personal, private and public,
and that the poet has carefully preserved a great many traditional
motifs out of which he has built a poem of great originality.

Inquiring into the way by which Spenser includes traditional elements of the classic marriage poem makes us even more aware of Spenser's achievement. For he succeeds in combining his personal concern and his own personal experience with the objective requirements and the "super-personal" validity of the wedding poem.

However, there is one aspect related to the poem's subject matter and purpose which I cannot omit, as it is intimately connected with what I have called the poem's uniqueness. This becomes apparent when we read the last three stanzas of the Epithalamion, in which Spenser gives his poem an almost metaphysical or religious turn. Here, too, the poem includes an element that points far beyond the boundaries of the conventional "epithalamium." For the love treated previously in Renaissance poetry had as a rule not been the love between a married couple but mostly love outside marriage. But Spenser, by praising his own bride and dedicating his wedding poem to his own wife, by invoking the blessing of the "high heavens" (409 ff.) for the raising of "a large posterity," gives a new dignity to the institution of marriage. This was a new development in the history of the "epithalamium" in European literature.

The last three or four stanzas may also convey a deeper meaning to all the preceding parts of the poem. For we now realize that the sensuousness and wealth of concrete detail contained in the description of the events of the wedding day and the festivities at night are only a foreground for something else that takes place on the spiritual plane. In fact, sensuality and spirituality are combined in this poem in a unique manner.[16] Spenser gives us a wealth of sensuous impressions to please our ear and eye and to stir our imagination, but he also extends our vision from this worldly level to another plane. We are made to feel that beyond and above this earthly merriment and bustle there is a higher spiritual world. The sequence of stanzas X and XI, where the appraisal of the bride's inward beauty follows on the sensuous description of her physical beauty, is only one case in point. The reference to Spenser's use of neoplatonic concepts[17] is helpful in this connection but cannot fully account for this particular feature in the poem.

Let us sum up: our reading of Spenser's Epithalamion has provided us with a number of characteristics which by virtue of their specific combination contribute toward the poem's excellence. Taken individually, however, none of these characteristic features would be sufficient to produce poetry of a high order. Such poetry is born out of a happy coincidence of several factors, at a climax of a poet's artistic career which coincides with a supreme moment in his own inner experience but which also is a consummation of the lyrical potentialities of a whole period.[18] To conclude our lecture let us look back over the main points we have made in order to decide whether these points may also reveal to us something of a more general significance. We found that Spenser's Epithalamion is a "long poem" carefully planned and organized round a significant center; a poem of order and symmetry in which the outward course of events corresponds to the process of inner experience so that the outward form has become inner form. We emphasized the poem's unity and coherence, produced by several means and on several levels, and we stated that it was a unity in spite of its variety. We also noted the establishing of interrelationships and correspondences between the different parts and thematic levels of the poem. We spoke of the "concretization" of all conventions and motifs which helped to relate every detail to a specific, concrete moment and event during the course of the marriage day. We discussed the assimilation and integration of mythology and learned allusions which were enlivened and brought within the reach of the reader's familiar experience. And we mentioned the art by which Spenser takes up many of the traditional conventions attached to the marriage poem but uses them in such a way that they gain actuality and new life. We noticed the sense of time, the observance of time and locality, and we stressed the effect of immediacy, spontaneity, and presence which was in part produced by a dramatic mode of presentation, and we finally hinted at the metaphysical and spiritual level in the poem. But the most striking quality which emerges from most of these points is the poem's inclusiveness, its "triumphant fusion of many different elements" as C. S. Lewis, in discussing the Epithalamion, has expressed it.[19] For from whatever angle we look at this poem we are struck by this inclusiveness. Spenser's Epithalamion unites the epic and the lyric mode, realism and formalism, high seriousness and jollity, mythology and contemporary custom, objective detachment and personal concern, sensuality and spirituality, and several other such pairs of contrasting qualities.

Thus we may conclude by saying that Spenser's Epithalamion, apart from its loveliness and charm, can also disclose to us the co-operation of some basic principles of poetic art. For terms like order, organic structure, unity in variety, amalgamation of traditional material, observance of time and locality, immediacy and directness of presentation, and especially inclusiveness, designate fundamental processes which had to be attained not only in Spenser's age but in all poetry aiming at greater complexity and higher perfection. Some of these principles can be applied with particular aptness to the poetry of the Renaissance, but others are of a universal validity. The taste of a Renaissance audience was different from ours. There are, to be sure, phrases and images in this poem which may be hard to accept for a modern reader, who may also be disturbed by the amount of stylization, by the mythological invocations, by the idealizing glorification of the poet's own bride. But these are features to be appreciated within the context and against the background of English Renaissance poetry, and they do not detract from the poem's inner consistency and its perfection as a work of art. This exemplary nature of our poem may be another justification for speaking of the uniqueness of Spenser's Epithalamion today.[20]

NOTES

LEWIS, The Faerie Queene (pp. 3–12).
1. F. Q. VI. v, vi.
2. F. Q. II. v. 29.
3. Ibid. xii. 50.
4. F. Q. II. xii. 58.
5. Ibid. xii. 61.
6. Ibid. III. vi. 29.
7. F. Q. III. vi. 34.
8. Ibid. vi. 44.
9. Ibid. II. xii. 44, 45.
10. Ibid. III. vi. 45.
11. v. supra, p. 151. The fact that all the references to Art in the Bower are copied from Tasso does not invalidate my argument: the opposite passages in the Garden are not.
12. F. Q. II. ix. 50, 53. Perhaps Mutabilitie, vi. 8, should also be mentioned as an exception. I do not understand this passage and suspect astronomical or astrological meanings.
13. Ibid. III. i. 34 et seq.
14. Ibid. i. 33.
15. Ibid. xi. 29 et seq.
16. Ibid. IV. x. 6.
17. Ibid. 25–7.
18. Ibid. 42.
19. Ibid. 21, 22.
20. Ibid. 23, 24.
21. Ibid. VI. x. 5.
22. F. Q. I. v. 51.
23. Ibid. II. vii. 15.
24. Ibid. 45, 47.
25. Ibid. III. viii. 5.
26. Ibid. IV, Proem 2.
27. Ibid. III. ix. 28, x. 6, 8.
28. F. Q. III. xi. 28.
29. Ibid. V. iii. 3. Cf. Milton, P. L. ix. 33 et seq.
30. v. Dr. Janet Spens, Spenser's Faerie Queene, p. 62, London, 1934.
31. F. Q. VI. Proem 5, 4.
32. Ibid. VI. ix. 6, cf. Tasso G. L. VII.
33. F. Q. III. vi. 36.
34. Ibid. Mutabilitie, vi. 35, vii. 15.
35. F. Q. II. xii. 63 et seq.; VI. x. II et seq.
36. Ibid. III. vi. 46.
37. Ibid. i. 36.

38. F. Q. II. v. 34.
39. Ibid. III. vi. 41.
40. Ibid. II. xii. 78.
41. Ibid. III. xii (First Version), 43-7.
42. F. Q. I. ix. 9-15.
43. Ibid. II. xii. 1.

NEVO, Spenser's "Bower of Bliss" and a Key Metaphor from Renaissance Poetic (pp. 29-39).
1. (Oxford, 1936), chap. VII, sect. iii.
2. My italics.
3. OED gives as earlier usage, "to hide oneself," "to escape observation," "to be concealed," for lurk, as well as today's "to shuffle along," "to sneak away."
4. See the Introduction to The Arte of English Poesie [London, 1589], ed. Willcock and Walker (Cambridge, 1936).
5. Ib., pp. 305 ff.
6. Ib., p. 160.
7. Ib., pp. 306-7.
8. Ib., p. 154.
9. Directions for Speech and Style [MS ca. 1599], ed. H. H. Hudson, (Princeton, 1935), p. 2.
10. Ib. p. 18 ff.

HANKINS, Spenser and the Revelation of St. John (pp. 40-57).
1. The Evolution of "The Faerie Queene" (Chicago, 1942), ch. ix.
2. For the readers' convenience, I quote textual and numerical references from the Authorised Version (1611), after making sure that the significant phrases were available in earlier versions.
3. These are conveniently listed sub "Apocalypse" in the indexes to J. P. Migne's Patrologia Latina (hereafter referred to as PL), CCXVIII, 667.
4. Op. cit., p. 116.
5. "Spenser's Lucifera and Philotime," MLN, LIX (1944), 413-415.
6. Gregory, Moralium, XXIII, vi; Haymo, PL, CXVI, 791-792; Primasius, PL, LXVIII, 898 D.
7. Vide infra, above note 28.
8. PL, CXVII, 1142 C.
9. PL, XXXV, 2449.
10. PL, CXCVI, 799 D.
11. PL, CLXV, 668 A.
12. Variorum, I, 217-223, 404-416.
13. I state these suggestions tentatively, since scholars are not agreed as to Spenser's knowledge of Dante's work.
14. Cf. Bennett, op. cit., pp. 109, 114.
15. PL, XXXV, 2442.
16. PL, CXCVI, 818 C.

17. See Jan Van Der Noot, The Theatre for Voluptuous Worldlings (1569), fol. 24; also Bennett, op. cit., pp. 110–112.

18. PL, CCIX, 398–399.

19. PL, CXCVI, 853 A.

20. Op. cit., fols. 33–34.

21. See Mat. 24:11, 24. II Pet. 2:1. I John 4:1.

22. The False Prophet will presumably reappear in the reign of Antichrist before the second resurrection. Most commentators agree that Antichrist will reappear, though the Revelation mentions only the return of Satan at that time. Cf. Haymo, PL, CXVII, 1187 C.

23. Op. cit., p. 109.

24. Most commentators assume that here Michael allegorically represents Christ.

25. See Haymo, PL, CXVII, 1081–83; Augustine, PL, XXXV, 2441.

26. Ibid. See also Primasius, PL, LXVIII, 872–874; Martin, PL, CCIX, 365; Bruno, PL, CLXV, 667–670; Anselm, PL, CLXII, 1543–45.

27. Through her identity with the Virgin. See Rupert, PL, CLXVIII, 889; Alanus De Insulis, PL, CCX. 95 B; Paschasius, PL, CXX, 106 D; Bernard, PL, CLXXXIII, 1009 D; Bruno, PL, CLXV, 717 B.

28. PL, CXCVI, 887 B.

29. Variorum, I, 259.

30. Gerusalemme Liberata, vii, 82.

31. De Civitate Dei, XX, vi–vii. The Catholic Encyclopedia, sub "Millennium," gives this view as the present opinion of the church.

32. Variorum, I, 377.

33. Upton notes Job 41:15, "His scales are his pride," as a parallel but fails to observe the other resemblances. For these, read vv. 14–29.

34. Gregory, Moralium, XXXIII, ix; Herveus, PL, CLXXXI S, 165–166.

35. De Principiis, I, V, in Ante-Nicene Fathers (Buffalo, 1886), IV, 259.

36. Ante-Nicene Fathers, VIII, 435–458.

37. Haymo, PL, CXVII, 1085–86; Primasius, PL, LXVIII, 874 D.

38. Alanus De Insulis, PL, CCX, 812–813; Rabanus Maurus, PL, CXII, 1022 A.

39. The 1943 MLA program lists an article on the subject by Mrs. Bennett.

40. Variorum, I, 472.

41. Inferno, iv; Summa Theologica, Pt. III (Supplement), Q. 69, A. 5.

42. Psalms 107:16, 18. See also Origen's Commentary on Matthew, XII, xiii, in Ante-Nicene Fathers, IX, 457.

43. See any concordance which gives readings from both the Authorised and the Revised Versions.

44. "Biblical Echoes in the Final Scene of Dr. Faustus," Studies in English (University of Kansas Press, 1940), p. 7.

45. Several of these pictures are reproduced in Grillot de Givry's Witchcraft, Magic, and Alchemy (London, 1931).

46. Job 41:4 in the Vulgate, corresponding to 41:13 in the Authorised Version, which gives a different reading.

47. PL, XXXV, 2451.

48. Op. cit., fols. 92–93.
49. PL, CXVII, 1139 D.
50. Rom. 16:16, I Cor. 16:20, II Cor. 13:12, I Thess. 5:26, I Pet. 5:14.
51. PL, CLXV, 720–721.
52. "Mist" in the Authorised Version, "fons" in the Vulgate.
53. Anselm, PL, CLXII, 1583 C; Martin, PL, CCIX, 413 B.
54. PL, XXXV, 2459.
55. PL, CXVI, 539 C.
56. Variorum, I, 303.
57. PL, CXVI, 915 A.
58. Augustine, PL, XXXV, 2459–60; Martin, PL, CCIX, 413 C; Haymo, PL, CXVII, 1211 D.
59. Anselm, PL, CLXII, 1583 D; Richard of St. Victor, PL, CXCVI, 876 A.
60. Laws of Ecclesiastical Polity, V, lxviii, 11.
61. Ante-Nicene Fathers, VIII, 436, 449.

WOODHOUSE, Nature and Grace in The Faerie Queene (pp. 58–83).

1. The Argument of Milton's Comus, University of Toronto Quarterly (1941). 46–71.
2. The account of the frame of reference is adapted from my article on Comus.
3. Puritanism and Liberty (London, 1938), introduction, pp. 57–60.
4. F. M. Padelford, The Spiritual Allegory of the Faerie Queene, Book One, Journal of English and Germanic Philology, 22 (1923). 1–17. Cf. P. Siegel, Spenser and the Calvinistic View of Life, Studies in Philology, 41 (1944), 201–22. In effect, though not explicitly, Padelford discriminates between nature and grace. In pursuance of his own principle that "in studying the relationships and inter-connections of man's intellectual history, is well not to be too schematic" (p. 215), Siegel confuses the two orders, finding Puritanism in Guyon's rejection of Mammon's offers of wealth as, "above all, distraction from the pursuit of a righteous life" (p. 203), and talking of Calidore's return, after his pastoral interlude, "to the service of Gloriana and God" (p. 204). Obviously the principle is wrong. What is required is the highest degree of precision (which involves schematism) in the formulation of positions and their consequences, and the ability to determine when an author recognizes these consequences and when he does not.
5. The Ancient Bounds (London, 1645): reprinted in my Puritanism and Liberty (spelling, etc., modernized), pp. 247–8.
6. By Professor Fredson Bowers, at the M.L.A., December, 1948, Group English IV (see multigraphed summary).
7. Thus Padelford in The Allegory of Chastity in the Faerie Queene, Studies in Philology, 21 (1924). 367–81: Variorum Spenser 3.324.
8. Spenser's word in the Letter is, of course, magnificence, but in the poem magnanimity.
9. As cited in n. 4.
10. W. F. DeMoss, Spenser's Twelve Moral Virtues 'according to

Aristotle,' Modern Philology, 26 (1918). 23–8, 245–70; Lilian Winstanley, in introduction to her edition of Book II (Cambridge, 1914).

11. 1. 10.

12. It has not, I think, been noticed that in Spenser's description of Faith the serpent in the chalice (1. 10. 13) bears a double significance, both in the order of grace: besides being the symbol of healing (the emblem of Aescalapius) and of salvation (Moses' serpent on the staff— Numb. 21.9—the type of Christ on the Cross), it is also a symbol of menace, doubtless with reference to 1 Cor. 12.27–9 and its doctrine as repeated in the Book of Common Prayer.

13. Harold Golder, Bunyan and Spenser, P.M.L.A., 45 (1930). 216–37.

14. 1. 3; H. S.V. Jones, Spenser Handbook (N. Y., 1930), 159. The two orders are again brought face to face in the meeting of Una with the satyrs and Sir Satyrane (1. 6), which yields a similar result: the friendship of uncorrupted nature for grace, but the limits, nevertheless, of merely natural perceptions.

15. 1. 4–5; 1. 7

16. 1. 8. 37–9. Another and less significant juxtaposition of the two orders occurs in the encounter with Despair (1. 9): Sir Terwin is reduced to despair and impelled to suicide by a sense of earthly misfortune: it is an offence against nature (and of course against religion, which is not invoked); the Redcross Knight, by a sense of sin and spiritual shipwreck: it is an offence against religion (and of course against nature, which is not invoked).

17. Guyon's encounter with the Redcross Knight (2. 1. 26–34) has for its general significance a further note on the relation of the order of nature to the order of grace: the harmony of natural ethics with religious, so far as the former can go (cf. 1. 3, as explained above, and n. 14) and the recognition of the claims of the higher order by the lower and by reason (cf. 7. 59 as explained below, and n. 54). Guyon is more swift to recognize and bow to the symbol of the cross on St. George's shield than is the latter to recognize Guyon as the worthy representative of one of the natural virtues. The Palmer (reason), coming up later, confirms Guyon's judgment. Guyon's reference to "The sacred badge of my Redeemers death" might seem at first to run counter to our hypothesis that Guyon stands for natural as distinguished from Christian virtue, but the distinction is not between pagan and Christian, but between unconverted (natural) man and converted (regenerate). Though denied by some extreme Calvinists (cf. Prynne, in my Puritanism and Liberty, p. 233), Christ was generally held to have died for all men and so might be referred to, even by the unconverted, as "my Redeemer," though confessedly Spenser momentarily obscures his pattern by the phrase. It is but momentarily, however; for, as I shall argue below, a large part of the significance of Book II turns on the assignment of Guyon to the order of nature, consistently maintained throughout. And to deny it in this early episode would be to rob the episode itself of much of its meaning. Observe that the Palmer recognizes the Redcross Knight for a saint, a being of a different order, but characteristically attributes his reward

to his own merit, which the Redcross Knight, also characteristically, is swift to deny, with gentle reproof, "His be the praise that this achievement wrought." The Palmer speaks of Guyon as having to set out from the point at which the Redcross Knight started, not from the point which he reached (i.e., not with his virtue achieved) as would be demanded by Professor Bowers' hypothesis, and he prays that God may guide him in his task, the God (no doubt) who presides over the order of nature as well as over the order of grace.

18. 2.2.

19. Medina's house is described as "wondrous strong by nature, and by skilful frame" (2.2.12).

20. J. S. Harrison in Variorum Spenser, 2.416.

21. Cf. F. M. Padelford, ibid., 420.

22. 1.10.1.

23. 2.9.1.

24. It is significant that virtually all the instances of "grace" meaning the grace of God in its full extent (i.e., (i) and closely related senses) occur in Book I. For example: "heavenly grace" (which supports) (1.7. 12; 1.8.1); "of grace" (doctrine of grace) (1.10.19); "Where justice growes there grows eke greater grace" (1.9.53); "perfection of all heavenly grace" (state of grace) (1.10.21). In the more extended sense of (ii) and related meanings (God's bounty in bestowing temporal gifts or providential protection, in the natural order), "grace" occurs in all six books. For example: "heavenly grace" (divine protection) (1.5.31); "wondrous grace" (providential intervention) 1.6.argmt.; "God's sole grace . . . To send her succour" (6.4.10); Britomart is saved from disaster "by God's grace and her good heedinesse" (5.6.34); "grace" intervening to check the natural man for his protection, without external instrument (1.9.26), with external instrument (2.11.30); "Providence hevenly passeth living thought, / And doth for wretched mens reliefe make way; / For loe! great grace or fortune thither brought / Comfort to him" (3.5.27) (interesting as suggesting that what is really God's providence is sometimes mistaken for chance by the natural man); "his Creators grace . . . The guifts of soveraine bounty" (2.7.16); "The grace of his Creator [he] doth despise / That will not use his gifts" (4.8.15); "If goodnesse find no grace [divine favour] nor righteousnes no meed" (3. 11.9). The meaning (iii) of natural endowment is not frequent, and in its examples it is probable that the word "grace" actually refers to some natural quality (as goodness of disposition or beauty): 2.9.1 (quoted above); Belphoebe was born with "all the gifts of grace and chastity" (3.6.2); Radigund seemed a "miracle of natures goodly grace" (5.5.12); "deckt with wondrous giftes of natures grace" (6.7.28); "Whether such grace were given her by kynd" (6.6.43). In what is the commonest meaning, (iv) grace of disposition, bearing, manners, or simply beauty, the adjective "heavenly" is sometimes added: thus of Una's "grace" (1.3.4; 1.6.18) where the primary reference is certainly to her beauty; Belphoebe was a "goodly Maide full of divinities / And gifts of heavenly grace" (3.5.34). Our classification is not exhaustive. There are a few

doubtful examples to be noted: Mercy is born in heaven and "thence pour'd down on men in influence of grace" (5.10.1), probably to be classed under (ii); God planted the flower of chastity in Paradise, "to make ensample of his heavenly grace" (3.5.52), and thereafter did it "in stocke of earthly flesh enrace / That mortall men her glory should admyre" (probably to be classed under (iv), but as a disposition which God specially approves); "Nepenthe is a drinck of soverayne grace / Devized by the Gods" (4.3.43): as also in the preceding example, the phrasing appears to be so calculated as to make it available for shadowing forth a religious meaning, which renders it difficult to classify; "grace" would here seem to mean native property (iii), but with the added idea of a divine cause; similar is the remark about fountains, how some have natural properties, and others special properties "by guifte of later grace" (2.2.6).

25. H. S. V. Jones, The Faerie Queene and the Medieval Aristotelian Tradition, Journal of English and Germanic Philology, 25 (1926). 283 ff.; V. B. Hulbert, in Variorum Spenser, 2.424–6.

26. The highminded man (Aristotle, Ethics, 4.8) is apt to appear supercilious, though affable to his inferiors; he is justified in his contempt for ordinary people, whom he is apt to treat with irony. "He is not given to admiration as there is nothing which strikes him as great." He is in the highest degree courageous, of course, when stirred to action, but "there are few things which he values enough to endanger himself for them." He would rather confer than receive benefits; and those received he tries to repay with interest and then forget, "for the recipient is inferior to the benefactor, and the highminded man always aspires to superiority." He is dignified in his movements, with a deep voice and a sedate speech, and is never in a hurry. It seems evident that by a Christian standard he would be condemned as self-sufficient and proud, and by a chivalric, as lacking in generosity and a spirit of adventure.

27. 2.8.23 ff.

28. If one is to interpret correctly the allegories of the Faerie Queene, one must bear this obvious distinction in mind. Some encounters are dramatic projections of an inward struggle in the mind (e.g., the Redcross Knight's meeting with Despair, 1.9); others are conflicts with some outward evil (e.g., his fight with Error, 1.1).

29. The most striking example is the twofold presentation of the principle of generation in the whole natural order, in 3.6., first in the account of the operation of the Genius with matter and forms, then in the myth of Venus and Adonis, which effects the transition to the human level in the myth of Cupid and Psyche.

30. 2.8.1–8.

31. 2.8.1.

32. Legouis (Variorum Spenser, 2.271) complains bitterly of Spenser's thoughtlessness in applying these terms to the virtuous Sir Guyon. It is not the poet who is thoughtless.

33. 2.12.46–9.

34. 2.12.46, 50, 55, 58, 59, 61; C. S. Lewis, The Allegory of Love (London, 1936) pp. 324 ff.

35. 3.6.29–50. I have deliberately refrained in this lecture from going into the details of Spenser's allegory of matter and the forms, since it would carry me too far afield. The rival interpretations are summarized in the Variorum Spenser, 3.340–52. Of these I still prefer, as a basis for further consideration, Dr. Brents Stirling's (ibid., 3.347–52). I have already recorded my reasoned conviction that Spenser's treatment of the myth of Venus and Adonis refers simply to the principle of generation in the natural order, and his treatment of the myth of Cupid and Psyche to the operation of this principle at the human level in the institution of marriage, in other words, that both are in the order of nature (The Argument of Milton's Comus, University of Toronto Quarterly, 11 (1941). 67–9).

36. 3.6.4–11.

37. 3.6.28, 51.

38. 3.2.22 ff.; 3.3.26.

39. It is perhaps unnecessary again to emphasize the fact that the natural does not necessarily connote the pagan. Britomart and Glauce go to church, Britomart thinking only of Artegall, and Glauce only of Britomart, or (as Spenser remarks) "With great devotion, and with little zele" (3.2.48). Glauce's appropriation for Britomart of armour, captured from the pagan Angela, and deposited in a church (3.3.58–9), certainly does not mean that Britomart is clad, like the Redcross Knight, in the armour of the Christian, but perhaps symbolizes the idea that the natural principles (available even to the pagan) on which Britomart proceeds harmonize with, and can be assimilated by, Christianity. This is not Spenser's synthesis of the two orders, but necessary in preparation for any synthesis. It is important that we should be clear on this point. For in her rescue of Amoret, Britomart's shield protects her from the flames, and her sword parts them and makes way for her (3.11.25); but it is not "the shield . . . wherewith ye shall be able to quench all the fiery darts of the wicked," nor "the sword of the Spirit, which is the word of God" (Ephes. 6.16, 17). But this too may prepare for the final synthesis in another way, which I shall suggest at the end of the lecture, by rendering nature eligible as a symbol of grace.

40. F. M. Padelford, The Allegory of Chastity in the Faerie Queene, Studies in Philology, 21 (1925). 367–81; to whose exposition I am deeply indebted.

41. 3.11.19.

42. 5.7.12–16. In addition to the interpretation of the dream (5.7. 22–3), one should observe that four basic facts condition its development and imagery as dream. (i) Britomart's love for Artegall is the dream's directing motive, as appears in its conclusion. (ii) Her memory of her first sight of Artegall in the magic mirror (3.2.17 ff.) and of Merlin's explanation (3.3.21 ff.) have their strong influence. In the latter the child that Britomart is to bear to Artegall is likened to a lion (3.3.30), and again the image of a lion occurs, followed immediately by the image

of a consuming fire (3.3.47–8). In Britomart's dream these images are reproduced in reverse order. (iii) Then there is the whole course of Britomart and Artegall's love story, and especially their fighting against each other (4.6), with Artegall's fierce and impetuous wrath, first stayed, then turned to love, by Britomart's beauty: this too receives symbolic presentment in the dream. (iv) Finally, all is combined with images derived from Britomart's vigil in the temple of Isis. From neophite she herself is transformed to queen or goddess: the moon-shaped mitre, to to a royal crown, and the white vestment to a royal robe of scarlet, blazing with jewels. And here is added the nightmare touch as in a flash the image suggestive of fire becomes the image of fire itself—the fire on the altar of Isis which seems to spread to the temple. But the fire-image has also its place in Merlin's well-remembered prophecy, and so dimly, as it were, and afar off, Artegall is introduced into the dream. Thus when the crocodile, roused from sleep, does battle with the flames, he becomes the symbol of Artegall; for the animal is Osiris, the lover of Isis, and Britomart and Artegall parallel Isis and Osiris. At first, in his pride and impetuosity, the animal seems more like enemy than lover. Here is reflected past experience, when Artegall fought against Britomart; but to this antagonism love had quickly succeeded, as it does when the animal is rebuked by Isis. What follows is prophetic of the consummation of their union and the birth of their child.

43. The pronounced vein of idyllicism in Spenser has been often remarked. It influences his treatment of nature, especially in Book VI, but also at other places, as in 2.7.15–16, where a reference to nature as norm suggests the reflection that "At the well-head the purest streames arise" and leads on to the famous description of the "antique world in his first flowring youth." In a characteristic reference to the unfallen state (1.11.47) the doctrine differs (since one passage bears a reference to nature only, the other to nature and grace), but not the tone: Spenser describes Eden as

> that soile where all good things did grow,
> And freely sprong out of the fruitfull grownd,
> As incorrupted Nature did them sow,
> Till that dred Dragon all did overthrow.

44. 2.12.71, 76.
45. 5.9.32.
46. 5.9.29.
47. 5.10.1.
48. See Variorum Spenser, 2.343.
49. Throughout this episode Prince Arthur retains his role of natural virtue, of magnanimity. Even at the end, it is the water, and not the Prince, that symbolizes grace. The providential intervention which earlier effects the temporary rescue of the Prince is described as an act of grace in the second meaning of the term (see n. 24, above). Its instrument is the Prince's Squire; and, like the treatment of Despair (1.9), the

allegory adds to the firm handling of a proposition genuine psychological insight. The Prince is almost borne down by his subtle inward foes, when the Squire appears, and it is his example that recalls the Prince to himself and to the pursuit of virtue and honour which is the mark of the magnanimous man:

> The whiles the Prince, prickt with reprochful shame,
> As one awakte out of long slombring shade,
> Reviving thought of glory and of fame,
> United all his powers to purge him selfe from blame.　(2.11.31)

And Spenser's comment makes it clear that the Squire's arrival is the effect of Providence, which can on occasion use the weak to save the strong:

> So greatest and most glorious thing on ground
> May often need the helpe of weaker hand;
> So feeble is mans state, and life unsound,
> That in assurance it may never stand,
> Till it dissolved be from earthly band:
> Proofe be thou, Prince, the prowest man alyve, . . .
> That, had not grace thee blest, thou shouldest not survive.
>
> (2.11.30)

50. 1.5.20–3; 4.2.47; 1.1.37.
51. 7.7.58.
52. 3.6.31–3.
53. 7.7.59.
54. 7.8.2. I adopt the correction Sabbaths for Sabaoths; but see D. C. Allen "On the Closing Lines of the Faerie Queene," M. L. N., 64 (1949). 93–4.
55. J. W. Bennett, The Evolution of the Faerie Queene (Chicago, 1942), p. 134.
56. Because the action of Book I (as of the other books) takes place in the material world, the order of nature, while its allegorical content is experience in the order of grace, the lower order stands to the higher throughout the book in the relation of shadow to substance. In his "Spenser and the Enchanted Glass" (Johns Hopkins Alumni Magazine 19 (1930.23–8 Variorum Spenser 1.442–5) Professor C. G. Osgood has shown how penetrating and consistent is the psychology of Spenser's story on the literal (i.e., the natural) level.
57. In his Anglican days Newman had developed this idea (with, of course, no thought of Spenser) as a corollary of Bishop Butler's concept of analogy, read in the light of Keble (see Newman, Apologia pro Vita Sua, Everyman edn., p. 42). The quoted phrase is not Newman's, but from the Book of Common Prayer, added thereto after Spenser's death, but from Nowell's Catechism (1570). Apart from Book I (see n. 56), we can, in the unfinished state of the poem, have only scattered hints of this last relation

between the two orders which I have suggested. They would be best gathered by a close reading of the other books in relation to Book I, as we saw in considering the parallel between the Britomart-Artegall and Una-Redcross Knight stories. That the parallel may extend to some of the details we observed in noting the similarity in the description of Britomart's natural equipment to the Christian's armour (see n. 39).

HOOPES, "God Guide Thee, Guyon": Nature and Grace Reconciled in The Faerie Queene, Book II (pp. 84–95).
    1. E. L. H., xvi (1949), 58–83.
    2. University of Toronto Quarterly, xi (1941–2), 46–71.
    3. 'The Cantos of Mutability: Spenser's Last Testament of Faith,' University of Toronto Quarterly, xxi (1952), 149.
    4. My own feeling is that with these two characters Spenser simply failed to do what he tried to do. Arthur's encounter with them occurs at the same point in Book II as his battle with Orgoglio in Book I, and the rescue of the hero in each instance seems designed to represent a dramatic and climactic step in the development of the total moral allegory. In Book I we grasp that fact artistically, in great part because Orgoglio's dimensions are what they are. Like God and Satan in Paradise Lost, Arthur and the evil giant are fit antagonists for one another. In Book II, when all is said and done, the champion of the world seems forced into a street brawl with a couple of juvenile delinquents.
    5. 'The Faerie Queene, Book II, and the Nicomachean Ethics,' M. P., xlix (1951), 73–100.
    6. 'Milton Revises The Faerie Queene,' M. P., xlviii (1950), 92.
    7. Ibid., p. 90.
    8. He would have agreed with Hooker that although 'nature hath need of grace,' it is equally true 'that grace hath use of nature.' Of the Laws of Ecclesiastical Polity, III. viii. 6. Early in his article Professor Wood-house quotes the passage (to which I have already referred) distinguishing between man as microcosmus and man as microchristus from an anonymous work entitled The Ancient Bounds (London, 1645), as an example of the view of the relation between nature and grace present in Spenser's mind. As another and earlier example, more relevant, I think, to Book II in particular, I offer the following passage in defence of the author's argument, from George Wither's preface to his translation of Bishop Nemesius's treatise on The Nature of Man (London, 1636)—a statement that might well serve as a prefatory 'Argument' to Book II of The Faerie Queene: 'Let no man, therefore, despise this meanes of Instruction, nor prejudicately conceive (because it may have some expressions unsuitable to their opinions) that NATURE is here magnified above GRACE, or in any measure equalled thereunto: or, that any power is thereto ascribed, derogating from the free mercy of God . . . There is not . . . one syllable in this Tract, which tendeth not to the glorifying of GOD'S Grace to Man-kinde. For, whatsoever is ascribed to man, as being primarily in him by nature, is acknowledged to be the gracious gift of GOD: That which is af-firmed to be left in him, since the fall, is confessed to have been justly

forfeited, and yet preserved in him, by the free Grace of the same GOD: The good effects of all those Faculties, which are affirmed in mans power, were not (in my understanding) so much as thought, by this Author, (nor are they so conceived by me) to be wrought at any time without the continuall assistance of the holy Spirit: neither is the naturall power of man, or the excellency of his nature, here set forth for mans owne glory, or that he should arrogate anything to himself.' (Sig. A5ᵛ—A6.)

9. See Articles of Religion, No. X; and Edgar C. S. Gibson, The Thirty-Nine Articles of the Church of England, 2nd ed. (London, 1898), pp. 378–87.

10. Virgil K. Whitaker, The Religious Basis of Spenser's Thought (Stanford, California, 1950), pp. 45–46. See also, by the same author, 'The Theological Structure of the Faerie Queene, Book I,' E. L. H., xix (1952), 151–64. Had it not been for these two studies, the second of which I was privileged to read in manuscript, this article could hardly have been written. Professor Woodhouse indicates his acceptance of the profound influence of Calvin upon Spenser's religious thought by his reference to the work of F. M. Padelford (p. 196, n. 4). My own conviction is that, whatever Spenser's sympathies toward institutional reform and the rooting out of clerical abuse and corruption, he remained theologically high church throughout his life. The Thirty-Nine Articles, with all their ambiguity and fence-sitting, invariably accommodate Spenser's religious ideas (as accurately as we can distil those ideas from their poetic and dramatic contexts) more easily than the rigorous and uncompromising dogmas of Calvin's Institutes.

11. It is almost superfluous to point out that if Spenser had not believed this, The Faerie Queene would have concluded with the sanctification of the Redcross Knight at the end of Book I. See Articles of Religion, No. IX ('Of Original or Birth-sin'): 'And this infection of nature doth remain, yea in them that are regenerated . . .'

12. 'The Argument of Milton's Comus,' p. 61.

13. See Merritt Y. Hughes, 'The Christ of Paradise Regained and the Renaissance Heroic Tradition,' S. P., xxxv (1938), 254–77.

14. See Douglas Bush, English Literature in the Earlier Seventeenth Century (Oxford, 1945), p. 391.

15. The Spirit of Medieval Philosophy, tr. A. H. C. Downes (New York, 1940), p. 12.

WHITAKER, The Theological Structure of The Faerie Queene, Book I (pp. 101–112).

1. Cf. T. W. Baldwin, William Shakspere's Petty School (Urbana: University of Illinois Press, 1943), pp. 65–6, 89, etc.; William Shakspere' Small Latine and Lesse Greeke (Urbana: University of Illinois Press, 1944), I, 181, 311, etc. Alexander Nowell, A Catechism Written in Latin, etc. ed. G. E. Corie (Parker Society 32; Cambridge: University Press, 1853).

2. Cf. The Works of Edmund Spenser: A Variorum Edition, The Faerie Queene, Book II (Baltimore: The Johns Hopkins Press, 1933), p. 467.

3. Ibid., pp. 411, 416.

4. Cf. Virgil K. Whitaker, The Religious Basis of Spenser's Thought (Stanford: Stanford University Press, 1950), pp. 34–35.

5. Ibid., pp. 44–47, etc.

6. Cf. Edwin Greenlaw, Studies in Spenser's Historical Allegory (Baltimore: Johns Hopkins Press, 1932), pp. 91–96.

7. Variorum Spenser: The Faerie Queene, Book I (Baltimore: Johns Hopkins Press, 1932), p. 169.

8. Ibid., p. 184.

9. Confessions, VIII, v, 12.

10. Summa Theologica, Ia–IIae, Q. 113, A. 6.

11. Cf. "The Second Part of the Sermon of Salvation," Certain Sermons or Homilies Appointed to be Read in Churches in the Time of Queen Elizabeth (London: Society for Promoting Christian Knowledge, 1914), p. 27.

12. Walter Clyde Curry, Shakespeare's Philosophical Patterns (Baton Rouge: Louisiana State University Press, 1937), pp. 103–19.

13. Paradise Lost, IX, 351–63, 703–09, 955–59, 997–99.

14. Summa Theologica, Ia–IIae, Q. 76–Q. 78; Richard Hooker, Laws of Ecclesiastical Polity, I, vii.

15. Summa Theologica, Ia–IIae, Q. 80, A. 2.

16. Summa Theologica, Ia–IIae, Q. 77, A. 5.

17. Cf. Richard Hooker: "There is not that good which concerneth us, but it hath evidence enough for itself, if Reason were diligent to search it out. Through neglect thereof, abused we are with the show of that which is not; sometimes the subtility of Satan inveigling us as it did Eve, sometimes the hastiness of our Wills preventing the more considerate advice of sound Reason . . ." Laws of Ecclesiastical Polity, I, vii, 7.

18. So J. E. Whitney calls him "braggart, carnal, or physical pride" but F. M. Padelford, "spiritual pride" (Variorum Spenser: The Faerie Queene, Book I, pp. 428, 438).

19. Irish Articles No. 38, translated from Lambeth Articles No. V; in Charles Hardwick, A History of the Articles of Religion (London: George Bell, 1888), pp. 363, 378. This was one of the five points reaffirmed by the Synod of Dort in 1619.

20. R. E. Neil Dodge, "The Well of Life and the Tree of Life," Modern Philology, VI (1908), 191–96.

DURLING, The Bower of Bliss and Armida's Palace (pp. 113–124).

1. E. Koeppel, "Die englischen Tasso-Übersetzungen des 16. Jahrhunderts," Anglia, XI (1889), 341–352.

2. See, e.g., Koeppel, p. 343: ". . . man wird im vergleich mit dem original Spensers schilderung etwas uberladen finden."

3. The Poetical Works of Edmund Spenser, ed. J. C. Smith and E. de Selincourt (Oxford, 1912), pp. xlii–xliii. All citations of Spenser are to this edition.

4. Alberto Castelli, La Gerusalemme liberata nella Inghilterra di Spenser (Milan, 1936), p. 26 and passim.

5. C. S. Lewis, The Allegory of Love (Oxford, 1936), pp. 324 ff.

6. For lists of parallel passages, see Koeppel's article and H. H. Blanchard, "Imitations of Tasso in the Faerie Queene," (SP, XXII (1925), 208–209. Spenser also knew, of course, Ariosto's account of Alcina's palace in Orlando furioso, vi–viii and x, and the Bower is closer to it in some respects than to Armida's palace. Acrasia and Alcina are true Circes, while Armida remains virtuous until she falls in love with Rinaldo. Alcina's lovers are transformed into plants, streams, or beasts, and Acrasia's into beasts; but Armida has no lover but Rinaldo, and the beasts outside her palace seem to have no connection with the knights she turns into fish in G. L., x, 65–66. Acrasia is similar to Armida, however, in not owing her beauty to enchantment, as does Alcina. R. E. N. Dodge, in "Spenser's Imitations from Ariosto," PMLA, XII (1897), 200, lists only one verbal parallel from Ariosto in the Bower (O. F., x, 39–40; F. Q., II, xii, 56) and H. H. Blanchard, in his unpublished dissertation, "Italian Influence on the Faerie Queene" (Harvard, 1921), pp. 105 f., has only one doubtful parallel to add (O. F., vii, 28: F. Q., II, xii, 77). With the possible exceptions of the name Acrasia-Acratia, which is a natural and possibly independent formation from the Greek, and the fact that the enchantress is in both cases captured (unlike Alcina or Armida), none of the similarities between the Bower and the palace of Acratia in Trissino's L'Italia liberata dai Goti, iv–v, are to my mind so exact or extensive as to warrant the assertion that Spenser was influenced by Trissino (cf. C. W. Lemmi, "The Influence of Trissino on the Faerie Queene," PQ, VII, 1928, 220–223). Spenser's only important debt in the Bower, then, is to Tasso, and I shall refer to other treatments of the theme only incidentally.

6a. Spenser apparently thought of the difficulties of the voyage to the Bower (F. Q., II, xii, 2–37) as directed specifically at Guyon and the Palmer, since Mordant, Atin, and Cymochles enter and leave the Bower freely by some other unspecified route (F. Q., II, i, 51, 55; v, 25–28; v, 37–vi, 2).

7. All citations of the Gerusalemme liberata are to the edition by Luigi Bonfigli (Bari, 1930).

8. We should recall the difference in the mythological scenes carved in the gates of the two gardens. Tasso shows Hercules' servitude to Iole and Antony's defeat at Actium (G. L., xvi, 1–7), both traditional exempla illustrating the incompatibility of love and the life of honor. Spenser shows "the famous history / Of Iason and Medea" (F. Q., II, xii, 44–45), an example which draws attention rather to the atrocious acts to which sensuality can lead.

9. All italics are added.

10. Prose diverse, ed. Cesare Guasti (Florence, 1875), I, 303 f.

11. "Apologia in difesa della Gerusalemme liberata," Prose diverse, I, 354.

12. G. L., xvi, 65 ff. Cf. Aristotle, Ethica Nich., VII, 3 (1147^{a}): "It is plain, then, that incontinent people must be said to be in a similar condi-

tion to men asleep, mad, or drunk" (trans. W. D. Ross, in The Basic Works of Aristotle, ed. Richard McKeon, New York, 1941).

13. Both Ariosto (O. F., vii) and Tasso describe the cure of incontinence in terms of magic. Tasso's knights flash before Rinaldo's eyes the magic mirror, in which he sees how his sensuality has degraded him (G. L., xvi, 30). Reason and will, overcome by appetite but fundamentally uncorrupted, apparently need only knowledge in order to overcome incontinence (cf. O. F., x, 59–60; G. L., xiv, 77). The weight of evidence seems to favor the notion that Rinaldo is brought to self-knowledge by purely natural means, especially the fact that the white magic of the hermit (G. L., xiv, 41–42) is a clear allegory of natural truth, originally acquired by the natural reason of the pagans, and now employed by Christians who are guided by providence. If this is so, the mirror must represent the power of rational persuasion.

14. Lettere, ed. Guasti (Naples, 1857), I, 179, 186–189.

15. Rinaldo has, for instance, a curiously chivalrous attitude toward his temptress even after his reason is restored to control. He says to her at parting:

"Errasti, è vero, e trapassasti i modi
ora gli amori essercitando, or gli odì:

ma che? son colpe umane, e colpe usate:
scuso la natía legge, il sesso, e gli anni . . .
Fra le care memorie ed onorate
mi sarai ne le gioie e ne gli affanni:
sarò tuo cavalier, quanto concede
la guerra d'Asia e con l'onor la fede."   (G. L., xvi, 53–54)

16. See note 12 above.

17. The Book of the Courtier, trans. Hoby, Everyman's Library (London, 1928), pp. 269 ff.

18. H. S. V. Jones, in The Faerie Queene and the Medieval Aristotelian Tradition," JEGP, XXV (1926), 283 ff., suggests that Spenser is indebted for certain aspects of his Aristotelianism to the Protestant Thomist Melanchthon.

19. "Nature and Grace in The Faerie Queene," ELH, XVI (1949), 221–222.

20. Summa theol., trans. Fathers of the English Dominican Province (New York, 1921), II, ii. Q. 155, Art. 4.

21. Allegory of Love, p. 332.

22. Summa theol., ibid.

23. Ibid.

24. Other considerations support this interpretation. Spenser tells us (F. Q., II, xii, 41) that the Palmer's staff is made of the same wood as Mercury's caduceus. Natalis Comes interprets Mercury as he appears in Homer and Ovid as the power either of human reason or of divine wisdom (Mythologiae, siue Explicationum fabularum libri decem, Paris, 1583, I,

447). The Palmer's staff has an obvious similarity to the herb moly, which Hermes gives to Odysseus to protect him against Circe's spells; Comes takes the moly to signify the aid of grace which strengthens men against sensuality (Mythologiae, II, 509).

25. Spenser probably knew and may have been influenced by Sidney's distinction between the two kinds of art: "For I will not deny, but that man's wit may make poetry, which should be εἰκαστική, which some learned have defined, figuring forth good things to be φανταστική, which does contrariwise infect the fancy with unworthy objects" (The Defence of Poesy, ed. A. S. Cook, Boston, 1890, p. 37). Spenser may also have known Plato's discussion in the Sophist, where the distinction is made that, while εἰκαστική produces true "likeness," φαυταστική produces deceptive "semblances" (F. M. Cornford, Plato's Theory of Knowledge, London, 1935, pp. 170f., 323–329)—a distinction which may have suggested the deceptiveness of the art of the Bower and the "guileful semblaunts" of F.Q., II, xii, 48.

HENINGER, The Orgoglio Episode in The Faerie Queene (pp. 125–138).

1. Philadelphus, or A Defence of Brutes, and the Brutans History (London, 1593), G3. The titlepage of Matthew of Westminster's Flores historiarum (London, 1570) quotes the well-known dictum of Cicero: "Historia testis temporum, lux veritatis, vita memoriæ, magistra vitæ, et vetustatis nuntia" (De oratore, II. 36)

2. Giovanni Florio, A worlde of Wordes, or dictionarie in Italian and English (London, 1598), p. 248.

3. Three proper, and wittie, familiar Letters (London, 1580), B4ᵛ.

4. Liturgies and Occasional Forms of Prayer Set Forth in the Reign of Queen Elizabeth (Parker Society, 1847), p. 464.

5. Abraham Fleming, A Bright Burning Beacon (London, 1580), E1–E1ᵛ.

6. I quote from the translation of Arthur Golding (1567) reprinted as Shakespeare's Ovid, ed. W. H. D. Rouse (London, 1904), p. 91, line 461.

7. Ibid., p. 91, lines 477–478.

8. P. 3, lines 113–116.

9. See particularly Josephine W. Bennett, The Evolution of "The Faerie Queene" (Univ. of Chicago Press, 1942), pp. 109–119; and John E. Hankins, "Spenser and the Revelation of St. John," PMLA, LX (1945), 364–381.

10. A hundred sermons vpon the Apocalipse (2nd ed.; London, 1573), A6ᵛ–A7. See also Franciscus Junius, The apocalyps . . . With a briefe and methodical exposition (Cambridge, 1596), p. 76; and The Bible (London, 1603), with comm. of Junius on Revelation [STC 2190], fol. 113.

11. This allegory is explicated in the introductory stanza of Canto X (I. x. 1. 1–5).

12. Many details of Cantos VII and VIII identify Orgoglio with the Antichrist as conceived by Protestants. He dresses Duessa in the gold and purple of the Babylonian Whore (i. vii. 16. 3), he sets the triple crown of the hated Papacy upon her head (I. vii. 16. 4), and he provides her with

the seven-headed scarlet-colored Beast (I. vii. 16. 6–9 ff.). The gorgeous trappings of his palace (I. viii. 35. 1–4) suggest the decadent splendor of Babylon and Rome. The floor is covered "with bloud of guiltlesse babes, and innocents trew" (I. viii. 35. 6); and the souls of martyrs are discovered beneath a sacrificial altar (I. viii. 36. 1–9). These evidently are the same victims of Antichrist revealed beneath the fifth seal in the Book of Revelation (vi. 9–11). See Hankins, "Spenser and Revelation of St. John," pp. 365, 378.

13. Hundred Sermons, B1ᵛ.

14. Theogony, 113 ff., 183 ff., 617 ff.

15. Metamorphoses, tr. Golding, p. 24, lines 171 ff. [I. 151 ff.].

16. Spenser makes numerous references to "the Titans, that whylome rebelled/Gainst highest heauen" (V. i. 9. 6–7), and he presents many of his vicious and villainous characters in this form: Lucifera (I. iv. 8. 5 ff.), Disdaine (II. vii. 41. 6–8, VI. vii. 41. 1 ff.), Argante (III. vii. 47. 2 ff.) and Ollyphant (III. xi. 3. 3 ff.), Care (IV. v. 37. 1–2), Geryoneo (V. x. 8. 6 ff.), Grantorto (V. xii. 15. 1–9), and Change (VII. vi. 2. 5 ff.).

17. "The Symbolism of the Classical Episodes in The Faerie Queene," PQ, VIII (1929), 275–276. See Natalis Comes, Mythologiae (Padua, 1616), p. 344 [VI. xxi].

18. Gilbertus Cognatus, Adagiorum συλλογή, printed with Erasmus, Adagia (Frankfurt, 1656), p. 196 [many earlier eds.]. See Isabel E. Rathborne, The Meaning of Spenser's Fairyland (Columbia Univ. Press, 1937), pp. 146–148.

19. Ed. C. de Beor, Verhandelingen der Koninklijke Akademie van Wetenschappen, Afdeeling Letterkunde, nieuwe reeks XV (1915).

20. For example, Matthew of Westminster, Flores historiarum, p. 50— where, incidentally, Nimrod is called gigas famosissimus. The lexicographer Pierre Danet summarizes the Scriptural commentary: "L'Ecriture dit que Nembrod fut le premier Géant, puisqu'il fut le chef de la révolte des Géants posterieurs au Déluge, & liguez pour la construction de la Tour de Babel" (Dictionarium Antiquitatum Romanarum et Graecarum [Paris, 1698], p. 428). When Nimrod appears in the dungeon beneath Lucifera's palace, Spenser takes note of his role as the original Giant: "great Nimrod" was the "first [who] the world with sword and fire warrayd" (I. v. 48. 1–2).

21. Aduersus Valentini, et similium Gnosticorum Haereses, Libri quinque (Paris, 1576), p. 371 [V. xxx].

22. Bale, The Image of Both Churches in Works (Parker Society, 1849), p. 448; and Napier, Plaine discouery of Reuelation, pp. 69–70. See also "Irenaeus" in General Index to the Publications of the Parker Society (1855).

23. See Hesiod, Theogony, 820 ff.; and Natalis Comes, Mythologiae, pp. 344–349 [VI. xxii].

24. See Hesiod, Theogony, 836 ff.; and Vergil, Georgics, I. 277 ff.

25. Diodorus Siculus also had recorded the Isis-Osiris legends (Book I. xi passim). Rathborne (Spenser's Fairyland, pp. 79 ff.) discusses the Osiris mythology as presented in the spurious chronicle of "Berosus the

Chaldean," first published late in the fifteenth century. There Cham, the wicked son of Noah who had received Africa as his heritage after the Flood, is depicted as "the universal enemy of God and man, the very type of tyranny and usurpation" (p. 87). Cham had three children: the good Isis and Osiris, who inherited the throne of Egypt, and Typhon, "inheritor of the sins of Cham" (p. 88), who killed Osiris and was in turn killed by Hercules and Isis. Nimrod (see p. 182, above) was the grandson of Cham (Genesis, x. 6–9).

26. Plutarch, The morals, tr. P. Holland (London, 1603), p. 1292.

27. Theogony, 831–832.

28. Ibid., 306 ff.

29. See Hesiod, Theogony, 308 ff.; and Hyginus, Fabulae (Basle, 1570), pp. 2 [prologue] and 35 [cli].

30. Tr. from Natalis Comes, Mythologiae, p. 349 [VI. xxii]. Spenser recalls Typhon's story for this same moral lesson in VII. vi. 29. 1–9. In a discussion of the Herculean antecedents for Prince Arthur, Merritt Y. Hughes suggests the need of a Typhon-like malefactor for Hercules-Arthur to overcome ("The Arthurs of The Faerie Queene," Etudes anglaises, VI [1953], 208).

31. Alexander Ross, Mystagogus Poeticus, or The Muses Interpreter (2nd ed.; London, 1648), pp. 404–405.

FOWLER, The Image of Mortality: The Faerie Queene, II. i–ii (pp. 139–152.

1. All Faerie Queene references, unless noted otherwise, are to The Works of Edmund Spenser: A Variorum Edition, ed. Edwin Greenlaw et al. (Baltimore, 1932–49).

2. A. C. Hamilton, "A Theological Reading of The Faerie Queene, Book II," ELH, XXV (1958), 155 ff. Hamilton does not, however, extend his inquiry to the death of Mordant and Amavia or to the Faunus myth. In his article "The Faerie Queene, Book II: Mordant, Ruddymane, and the Nymph's Well," English Studies in Honor of James Southall Wilson, ed. Fredson Bowers (Charlottesville, Va., 1951), p. 243, Bowers believes Spenser to be touching on the "doctrine of retribution" both in Mordant's death and in the indelible bloodstains. In the nymph's well he sees a "sacramental reference," probably to Holy Communion (p. 249). Spenser, he conjectures, held a sacramental theory of the direct mingling of the divine absolute with the mortal recipient, so that Mordant died because of the contact between his sinful body and the divine absolute in the pure water. Interesting though they are, Bowers' suggestions are too imprecise and speculative to take us very far.

3. II. i. 49. The form Mordant is preferred on the basis of II. ii. 45 and the Argument to Canto i.

4. The reiterated floral imagery ("freshest flowre of lustie hed," "rosy," "blossome of his age") conveys the transience of the flesh—flowers being a standard symbol of human frailty; see Pierio Valeriano, Hieroglyphicorum collectanea (Lyons, 1610), Bk. LV, Ch. i, p. 581D, "Imbecillitas humana."

5. Cf. the tree of I. ii. 30–44, also composed of two human elements: Fradubio (the doubting mind) and Fraelissa (human frailty).

6. See Joseph A. Robinson, The Body: A Study in Pauline Theology, Stud. in Bib. Theology, No. 5 (London, 1952), pp. 18–21.

7. The same obvious metaphor for the captivity of sin is used by Tasso in Gerusalemme liberata, Canto vii, etc., whose Armida—explicitly identified as concupiscence—captivates Goffredo's knights.

8. Rom. vii. 7–13. Elizabethan spelling is not retained in biblical quotations, which are from the Matthew Version of the Geneva Bible unless otherwise stated; cf. Rom. iv. 15 and v. 20. See Robinson, pp. 34–37; and, for a Reformation discussion, John Calvin, Institutio christianae religionis (Basel, 1536), Bk. II, Ch. vii, Sec. 7. At this point I am heavily indebted to T. M. Gang, who noticed the Pauline context and correctly interpreted Mordant's death in a paper yet unpublished.

9. For a history of the term, see Norman P. Williams, The Ideas of the Fall and of Original Sin (London, 1927), pp. 243 f., 458, etc. Elizabethan biblical commentaries show a predominance of the narrower interpretation; even Andrew Willet's comprehensive discussion in Hexapla: . . . A Sixfold Commentarie (n.p., 1611), pp. 320–323, eventually settles on the meaning lust. See also n. 7 above.

10. See, for example, Valeriano, Bk. XXXVIII, Ch. xix, p. 405; and Sir John Harington's notes on Bk. VI of his translation of Ariosto's Orlando Furioso (London, 1634). Harington follows Simone Fornari, La spositione sopra l'Orlando Furioso (Florence, 1549), IV, 49 f., for whom the symbolism is e modo usitato.

11. Enarrationes in psalmos, xlii. 1.

12. Morale reductorium super totam Bibliam ([Nuremberg], 1517), Bk. VIII, Ch. iii, Sec. 4.

13. Ibid., Bk. VIII, Ch. iii, Sec. 33, using Solinus, "Sicilia," Polyhistor (Venice, 1473), Ch. xi. Since John Upton's edition of The Faerie Queene in 1758, the source of the charm has been regarded as Heliodorus, Aethiopica, V, a passage that—as Charles W. Lemmi recognizes in his "The Influence of Trissino on The Faerie Queene," Philological Quarterly, VII (1928), 220–223—may have suggested Spenser's wording but can throw no light on his symbolism.

14. (Antwerp, 1624), Emblem I. viii. For the motif, a popular one in 17th-century devotional literature, see Mario Praz, Studies in Seventeenth-Century Imagery, I (London, 1939), 148 and 133; Praz's comment on Hugo's choice of biblical texts with sensuous metaphors would apply equally to Spenser. [For figure references see original publication.]

15. See, for example, Hugo, Emblem III. xli, "Quemadmodum desiderat cervus ad fontes aquarum," where a winged Christ-Eros stands with outstretched arms above a laver. The similarity to Emblem I. viii shows how closely the Fountain of Repentance was related to the Fountain of Life; it is easy to see how Spenser could fuse the two motifs to signify incorporation in Christ by baptism. Bersuire, "De Jordane," Morale reductorium . . . , Bk. VIII, Ch. iv, Sec. 1, says that the two heads of the river of baptism are "the fountain of contrition on the part of the penitent sinner and the fountain

of pity and compassion on the part of the remitter of sins." The same writer, in his Commentary on Isaiah, i, attaches to one river all the meanings we have assigned to Spenser's well. Other Old Testament streams and wells were traditionally interpreted as figures of baptism: those of Zech. xiii. 1, Isa. xii. 3, etc.

16. For the origins of the motif, see P. A. Underwood, "The Fountain of Life in Manuscripts of the Gospels," Dumbarton Oaks Papers, V (1950), 43–138. Patristic elaborations of the fountain symbolism were revived in the late medieval period: the Breviary Office of the Precious Blood, for example, has a hymn on the Fountain of Life. The iconography of the theme in this period is studied in E. Mâle, L'Art religieux de la fin du moyen âge en France (Paris, 1925), pp. 109–118. Usually the fountain purified by washing, as when the crucifixion was represented above a stone bath—the balnea salutatis—into which the living fountain fell. In a window of the Church of the Trinity in Vendôme (Mâle's Fig. 59), Adam and Eve stand up to their waists in the bath that cleanses original sin. Occasionally, however, the Johannine idea of drinking living water is also introduced. Thus Emblem III (our Fig. 2) in Georgette de Montenay's Emblemes, ou devises chrestiennes (Lyons, 1571)—which is probably the first appearance of the motif in emblem literature—the crippled and deformed come, not to bathe, but to drink from the laver. In the accompanying Latin epigram in a later (1584) edition, Christ says: "Are you looking for water from the living fountain of righteousness? Come here, drink here from a full cup the liquor you have desired, here where the living fountain of the waters of righteousness flow."

17. Isa. i. 15–18; cf. Ps. li, which is also a context of the allegory.

18. Hamilton and Bowers are quite justified in relating the nymph's well to the well of life in Book I. Just as the trunk of Fradubio and Fraelissa had to be bathed in that well for their deliverance, so in this a "braunch" (II. ii. 2) is bathed. Bowers is wrong, however, when he treats the symbolism of the wells as predominantly eucharistic. The Eucharist is obviously involved, in that it reaffirms the incorporation in Christ established by baptism and confirmation. But it cannot be the main subject of Spenser's allegory; as Mâle shows, the iconography of representations of the Eucharist was quite different.

19. Rom. vi. 3–6; and see Robinson, pp. 43 ff.

20. A Child by a river was a traditional symbol for the new man: a symbol based, as Bersuire notes, on allegorization of the finding of Moses in the Nile (Exo. ii). The whole of Bersuire's discussion of the new man in terms of growth (growth of a child, growth of a river) is interesting: see Morale reductorium . . . , Bk. VIII, Ch. iii ("De fluviis"), especially Sec. 8; Ch. iv ("De Jordane"); Ch. v ("De Nilo"); and Ch. vi ("De rivo").

21. The Faerie Queene: Book II, ed. Lillian Winstanley (Cambridge, Eng., 1919), p. 243.

22. Cf. Gilbert Burnet's definition of flesh as "the natural state of mankind." In An Exposition of the Thirty-Nine Articles, ed. James R. Page (London, 1837), p. 143.

23. Hamilton, 158 f. The failure of baptism to clear Ruddymane of the

effects of original sin upsets Virgil Whitaker's contention (The Religious Basis of Spenser's Thought [Stanford, 1950], p. 50) that Spenser's view of baptism was contrary to Calvin's. According to Whitaker, the Anglicans (and Spenser) held that baptism exempted the believer from original sin. In actual fact, the Anglican and Calvinist views were far from being so directly opposed in Spenser's time: Calvin, indeed, held precisely the view of baptismal regeneration formulated in the 1604 Anglican Catechism and said by Whitaker to contradict him (see, for example, Calvin, Institutio . . . , Bk. IV, Ch. xv, Sec. 10). But, if anything, Spenser here inclines toward the Calvinist view, rather than toward the Arminian position Whitaker seems to be thinking of.

24. This rare word, which in the F. Q. appears only in Bk. II (ii. 30 and vii. 19), would be associated very specifically with one context: Coverdale's and Matthew's versions of the penitential psalm: "Deliver me from blood guiltiness, O God" (Ps. li. 14). This psalm provided countless commentators, from Augustine to Calvin, and from Calvin to Hildersham and Smith, with an occasion to discuss the doctrine of original sin, a proof text of which was its fifth verse: "I was born in wickedness, in sin hath my mother conceived me."

25. See Williams, pp. 265 ff.

26. Ruddymane is a witnesse who is to attest his mother's innocence from blemish criminall (II. i. 37), as she bequeathd in her last testament (ii. ii. 10); while her cause (case) is reserved until the eternal judgment (II. i. 58–59).

27. Hamilton interestingly cites here a passage from Calvin's Institutio . . ., "'haereditaria naturae nostrae pravitas et corruptio in omnes animae partes diffusa, quae primum facit reos irae Dei'"; but we need not share his conclusion that the special Calvinist doctrine of total depravity is implied by Spenser. The stanza might have been illustrated just as aptly from Aquinas. For the idea that original sin alters the blood, see Burnet, p. 144; for the contagion image, p. 143; and for original sin as a slow-acting poison, p. 141.

28. The Allegorical Temper (New Haven, 1957), p. 46.

29. In the Renaissance the satyr was a common symbol of concupiscence in the sense of lust: see, for example, Andrea Alciati, Emblemata (Lyons, 1600), p. 273, Emblem LXXII; Cesare, Ripa, Iconologia (Padua, 1611), p. 315, for Faunus as lust. Eusebius, however, had lent authority to a wider interpretation by explaining the satyrs as "the foul and licentious passions of mankind." In Evangelica praeparatio, Bk. III, Ch. iiiC. Lilio G. Giraldi, in his Operum quae extant omnium (Basel, 1580), I, 426, l. 21, quotes Phornutus to the effect that the satyr is a symbol of "ekstaseōs, id est mentis excessus."

30. As he is in Henrik Goltzius' engraving "Satisfactio Christi" (B.67 ["B" refers to Adam Bartsch, Le peintre graveur, III (Vienna, 1803), 29]: our Fig. 3). There Faunus-Satan stands under the crucified Christ, from whom fountains of blood fall into a human heart, opened and containing the tablets of the Law. Overflowing, the blood spills into a chalice, which is being weighed by Justitia against the guilt-laden heart in the scales.

Identification of Faunus with Satan may have been assisted by the scholiast Porphyry's comment on Horace's "Faune, Nympharum fugentium amator" (Carminum, Bk, III, No. xviii, l. 1): Faunus, he says, was "a hellish and pestilential god." The source of this idea is Vergil's account—Aeneid, Bk. VII, ll. 89–91—of the oracle of Faunus, where the priest had speech with "Acheron and the deepest tract of hell." This passage retains the older Roman view of Faunus as a prophet. There was also a tradition—see Publilius Syris, n. 110—that fauni were incubi, imaginations attacking the mind of a sleeper.

31. The Faunus myth in Bk. VII is again a Fall myth, though there the cosmic, rather than the individual, implications are considered. For the virgin symbol see Bersuire, Dictionarium (Venice, 1583), s.v. "Virgo," where the meaning mentis integritas is given.

32. Giovanni Giorgio Trissino (Rome, 1547). Trissino's fountain also has a similar function to Spenser's in the larger ordering of the poem, as I try to show in my paper, "Emblems of Temperance in The Faerie Queene, Book II," Review of English Studies, N. S., XI (1960), 143–149.

33. De religione christiana (Paris, 1559), fol. 105^V.

34. II Cor. v. 4: cf. Rom. viii. 23. Armor was a common image for human nature: cf., for example, William Langland, Piers the Plowman, ed. Walter W. Skeat (Oxford, 1886), I, Text B, Passus XVIII, l. 23, where Christ assumes human nature by putting on Pier's armor; he jousts "In his helme and in his haberioun humana natura."

35. The similarity is pointed up with verbal echoes, noted by Miss Winstanley (pp. 241, 242): cf. II. i. 36 with I. ix. 38; cf. II. i. 47–48 with I. ix. 40.

36. Our Fig. 4. In the 1619 Frankfurt edition an English epigram is included: "To kill thy selfe, and so depart, / Out of this world, it is no art; / But to rise, and live again? / Thou art not able it is certain; / Of thy self, but must like a stone / Lye, til Jesus Christ Gods sonne, / Comes. For none but he can cure thine wound / Or make thee rise from the ground."

37. See Calvin, Institutio . . . , Bk. II, Ch. i, Sec. 6; Samuel Smith, Davids Repentance (London, 1614), pp. 219f. Henry Bullinger, "The Third Decade," in The Decades, trans. H. I., ed. T. Harding, Parker Soc. (Cambridge, Eng., 1850), pp. 362ff.

38. The conviction that sin is accidental to the natural order is central enough to affect the whole conduct of the narrative, including even the syntax, which (as Harry Berger rightly observes on p. 46) often implies contingency—Faunus chanced to meet the nymph; an occasion strange befell her. I would not agree with Berger's inference that this diction is intended to show the large part played by chance in the natural order.

39. Aquinas, Quaestiones disputatae, IV: de malo; Calvin, Institutio . . . , Bk. II, Ch. i, Secs. 6 and 10. The best-known expression of the idea is probably: "Earth felt the wound." In John Milton, " Paradise Lost," Poetical Works, ed. Helen Darbishire, (Oxford, 1952), Bk. IX, l. 782.

40. Cf. Calvin, Institutio . . . , Bk. IV, Ch. xv, Secs. 10–11, on the persistence of concupiscence throughout this life.

41. Page 240. Berger seems to regard the inconclusiveness as a result of the limitations of temperance rather than those of all Christian life in this world.

42. A. S. P. Woodhouse, "Nature and Grace in The Faerie Queene," ELH, XVI (1949), 205, n. 17, and cf. 198–199.

43. "Nature and Grace in The Faerie Queene: The Problem Reviewed," ELH, XXVI (1959), 1 ff. Cf. also Robert Hoopes, " 'God Guide Thee, Guyon': Nature and Grace Reconciled in The Faerie Queene, Book II," RES, N.S., V (1954), 14 ff.

44. For Spenser's conception of Guyon as a river bringing water of regeneration, see my note "The River Guyon," Modern Language Notes, LXXV (1960), 289–292; also my "Emblems of Temperance in The Faerie Queene, Book II."

45. See N. S. Brooke, "C. S. Lewis and Spenser: Nature, Art and the Bower of Bliss," Cambridge Journal, II (1949), 420–434, for the idea that the Bower is an allegorical representation of the intemperate body.

46. F. Q. II. xii. 1. Frame not only means "building" but also "human nature"; cf. Burnet, p. 145: "Adam, by corrupting his own frame, corrupted the frame of his whole posterity."

FRYE, The Structure of Imagery in The Faerie Queene (pp. 153–170).

1. In what follows the debt is obvious to A. S. P. Woodhouse, "Nature and Grace in The Faerie Queene," ELH (Sept. 1949), but there are some differences of emphasis owing to the fact that I am looking for a structure of images rather than of concepts. Rep. 58–83 above.

2. Cf. George Macdonald's romance Phantastes, the title of which is said to come from Phineas Fletcher rather than Spenser.

3. This detail is not in The Faerie Queene: see Colin Clouts Come Home Againe, 800 ff.

MAC LURE, Nature and Art in The Faerie Queene (pp. 171–188).

1. Cf. N. S. Brooke, "C. S. Lewis and Spenser: Nature, Art and the Bower of Bliss," Cambridge Journal, II (1948–49), 425; Rosemond Tuve, Elizabethan and Metaphysical Imagery (Chicago, 1947), p. 52.

2. The Allegory of Love (Oxford, 1936), pp. 326–7, and see Brooke, passim.

3. A. S. P. Woodhouse, "Nature and Grace in The Faerie Queene," ELH, XVI (1949), 212–3.

4. Cf. CCCHA, ll. 835–86.

5. Laws of Ecclesiastical Polity, I, ix, 1.

6. So Danaeus, Wonderful Workmanship of the World, trans. T. T. (1578), quoted in Theodore Spencer, Shakespeare and the Nature of Man (New York, 1943), p. 25.

7. Cf. Puttenham, Arte of English Poesie, in Elizabethan Critical Essays, ed. Gregory Smith (Oxford, 1904), II, 187: "In some cases we

say arte is an ayde and coadiutor to nature, and a furtherer of her actions to good effect, or peradventure a meane to supply her wants."

8. Politics, VII, 1334 b.

9. Cf. the characterization of the "English style" in the Tudor period by John Gloag, The English Tradition in Design (Penguin Books, 1947), pp. 8–9.

10. Elizabethan and Metaphysical Imagery, p. 51.

11. The Winter's Tale, V, ii. 105–12.

12. See E. Curtius, European Literature and the Latin Middle Ages (London, 1953), app. xix, "The Ape as Metaphor"; cf. Puttenham, comparing art as counterfeitor to "the Marmoset."

13. Harry Berger, Jr., The Allegorical Temper (New Haven, 1957), p. 228.

14. Lewis, Allegory of Love, p. 340.

15. See J. Huizinga, The Waning of the Middle Ages (Anchor Books, 1954), ch. X and authorities there cited.

16. The definitive study is by Richard Bernheimer, Wild Men in the Middle Ages (Cambridge, Mass., 1952).

17. Sir Daniel Wilson, Caliban, The Missing Link (London, 1873); Frank Kermode, in his introduction to the New Arden The Tempest (London, 1954), discusses Caliban in relation to the wild man tradition.

18. Bernheimer, pp. 101–2, 262.

19. Cf. Edward Phillips' description of "that Melior natura which the Poet speaks of, with which whoever is amply indued, take that Man from his Infancy, throw him into the Desarts of Arabia, there let him converse some years with Tygers and Leopards, and at last bring him where civil society and conversation abides, and ye shall see how on a sudden, the scales and dross of his barbarity purging off by degrees, he will start up a Prince or Legislator, or some such illustrious Person." Theatrum Poetarum (1675), quoted in Kermode, p. xiv.

20. Nennio, or A Treatise of Nobility (1595), Book I. (Spenser wrote a commendatory sonnet for this volume, as did Chapman and Daniel.)

21. The Book of the Courtier (Everyman, n. d.), p. 32.

22. That is, if we assume a consistency between the proem to Book V and VII, vii, 49–56.

23. Reproduced by a number of authorities, e.g. by E. J. Holmyard, Alchemy (Penguin Books, 1957), pl. 34.

24. On the iconography of the Graces see E. Wind, Pagan Mysteries of the Renaissance (London, 1958), especially pp. 33–4, 37–8, 104–5.

ROCHE, The Challenge to Chastity: Britomart at the House of Busyrane (pp. 189–198).

1. Chaucer, The Romaunt of the Rose, Fragment A, ll. 531–584, Works, ed. F. N. Robinson (Cambridge, Mass. 1957).

2. Beaumont and Fletcher, A Wife for a Moneth, Works, ed. A. R. Waller, 10 vols. (Cambridge, 1907), V, 25–26.

3. C. S. Lewis, The Allegory of Love, pp. 364–366.

4. See Variorum, I, 441; III, 303, 320, 326, 354, 373; VIII, 446.

5. Variorum, III, 287.

6. See Wallis Budge, Osiris and the Egyptian Resurrection, 2 vols. (London, 1911). Chapter i gives a summary of the ancient writers who deal with this story, including Plutarch, Diodorus Siculus, Apollodorus, Isocrates, Herodotus, and Ovid. See also Heywood's dumbshow in The Brazen Age, Dramatic Works, ed. Pearson, 6 vols. (London, 1874), III, 183; Ralegh, The History of the World (London, 1614), p. 204; Paradise Lost, I.307, and Isabel Rathborne, The Meaning of Spenser's Fairyland, pp. 86–90.

7. Ovid, Ars Amatoria, trans. J. H. Mozley (Loeb, 1947), p. 57 (Book I, ll. 643–658).

HIEATT, Scudamour's Practice of Maistrye Upon Amoret (pp. 199–201).

1. Roman matrons invoked Concordia as the mistress of conjugal affection at the festival of Caristia or Cara Cognatio. She was also invoked along with Venus and Fortuna virilis on April 1. See Ovid, Fasti 2. 617, 631; Valerius Maximus, 2. 1. 6; Ch. Daremberg and Edm. Saglio, Dictionnaire des Antiquités . . . (Paris, 1887), "Concordia."

WILLIAMS, Venus and Diana: Some Uses of Myth in The Faerie Queene (pp. 202–219).

1. Similar conclusions as to the probable connection of Busyrane with the Ars Amatoria have been reached by Mr. Thomas P. Roche, in a paper, "The Challenge to Chastity: Britomart at the House of Busyrane," delivered at the conference of the Modern Language Association in December 1959. Reprinted pp. 189–198.

NELLIST, The Allegory of Guyon's Voyage: An Interpretation (pp. 238–252).

1. Gerusalemme Liberata XV.
2. Elizabethan Poetry, Harvard 1952, p. 293.
3. Works, ed. A. Grosart, 1885, vol. I, p. 272.
4. See Tasso's account of the allegory appended to the poem.
5. "The allegory driven through the whole Odysseys," Homer's Odysseys, ed. W. H. D. Rouse, 1897, vol. II, p. 274.
6. Metamorphoses, 1640, B1^v.
7. Emblemata, Padua 1620, p. 828; J. Masenius, Speculum Imaginum, Cologne 1650 p. 353.
8. Ger. Lib. XV. 9.
9. Learned Sermon, 1581, C2^v.
10. E. H. Fellowes, English Madrigal Verse, Oxford 1920, p. 45.
11. D. Price, The Marchant, Oxford 1608, C3.
12. Ascribed to Hugh of St. Victor in Patrologia Latina, CLXXVII. 907.
13. H. Rahner, Griechische Mythen in christlicher Deutung, Zurich 1945, p. 430.
14. Op. cit., Patrologia Graeca, LXIV. 21.
15. Phaedrus, 247 c.
16. Quoted in Alardus Aemstelredamus, Selectae Aliquot Similitudines, Cologne 1539, 202.
17. M. P. Tilley, Dictionary of Proverbs, Michigan 1950, S. 174.

18. Epist. LXXXV. 33.
19. Humphrey Gifford, Complete Poems, ed. A. Grosart, 1875, p. 144.
20. Poetical Rhapsody, ed. H. Rollins, Harvard 1931, vol. I, p. 171.
21. J. Davies of Hereford, Works, ed. A. Grosart, 1878, vol. II "Micro-cosmos," p. 39.
22. FQ. II. xii. 3 and 11.
23. Sundry Sonnets, 1593, I. 81.
24. G. Owst, Literature and Pulpit, Cambridge 1933, p. 71; Anthony of Padua, Opera Omnia, Paris 1641, p. 120.
25. John Bradford, Sermons etc., ed. A. Townsend, Parker Soc. 1848, p. 336.
26. Complete Poems, 1875, p. 148.
27. Serm. Suppos. lxxii, PL. XXXIX. 1885.
28. Scala Paradisi, PG. LXXXVIII. 1015; P. Valeriano, op. cit., Bale 1575, 214^v—15.
29. John of Howden, Poems, ed. F. J. E. Raby, Surtees Soc. 1939, p. 77.
30. FQ. II. xii. 5.
31. Progresse of Piety, Parker Soc. 1847, p. 108.
32. E. H. Fellowes, Madrigal Verse, p. 45.
33. FQ. II. xii. 8.
34. Ibid. xii. 10.
35. Ibid. xii. 15.
36. Ibid. xii. 11.
37. Ibid. xii. 17.
38. Ep. xiv, PL. XXII. 351—2.
39. Erasmus, Adagia, Frankfurt 1643, p. 493.
40. Works, ed. Spedding, Ellis and Heath, vol. VI, 1878, p. 755.
41. Mythologia, Padua 1637, p. 456.
42. Reductorium Morale, Venice 1583, VIII. xi. 18, R3^v.
43. Nocturnall Lucubrations, 1638, E1.
44. H. Platt, Manuale, 1594, d4.
45. Pilgrimage of Life, tr. Lydgate, EETS es 1899—1904, p. 523.
46. FQ. II. xii. 21.
47. For the Old Testament image of the sea, see P. Reymond, L'Eau dans l' Ancien Testament, Leyden 1958, chap. 5 passim.
48. Suasoriae of Seneca, ed. W. A. Edward, Cambridge 1928, p. 85.
49. Ps. 104. 25.
50. Joannes Gorus (San Geminianus), Summa de Exemplis, Antwerp 1609, f. 97 gives an allegory in seven distinctions on the wave of pride.
51. Ennaratio in Ps. CIII, PL. XXXVII. 1380.
52. Poems, ed. F. J. E. Raby, 1939, p. 79.
53. Enn. in Ps., PL. XXXVII. 1380.
54. Variorum Spenser, vol. II, Johns Hopkins 1933, p. 370.
55. FQ. II. xii. 25.
56. Augustines Praiers, tr. T. Rogers, 1581, E5.
57. FQ. II. xii. 26.
58. Ibid. xii. 27.
59. Malory, Works, ed. Vinaver, Oxford 1954, p. 676.

60. FQ. II. xii. 29.
61. Ibid. II. xii. 31.
62. Ibid. II. xii. 32.
63. Epist. PL. LXI. 232.
64. Purgatorio, XIX. 19; cf. Horace, Sat. II. iii, Loeb ed. p. 152.
65. G. Sandys Metamorphoses, 1640, P4ᵛ.
66. Erasmus, Opera Omnia, Leyden 1703, vol. I, c. 603 and 613;
Alciati, Emblemata, Padua 1620, p. 487.
67. Metamorphoses, 1640, Q1.
68. Fulgentius, Mythographi Latini II, Amsterdam 1681, p. 84.
69. FQ. II. xii. 34.
70. Hugh of St. Victor, de Sacramentis I. i. 27, PL. CLXXVI. 203;
Richard of St. Victor, Allegoriae, PL. CLXXV. 637 and 638; Alan of Lille
tells us that the birds of the air of Ps. 8. 8 signify the proud (i.e. the
spiritual sin) and in Christ's parable of the sower the birds that eat up
the seed are types of the devil, Distinctiones, PL. CCX. 716; cf. Eucherius,
Formulae, PL. L. 749.
71. Joannes Gorus, Summa de Exemplis, Antwerp 1609, f. 65 explains
how the sea is the source of the fog of error.
72. Apol. David Altera, PL. XIV. 934.
73. FQ. II. xii. 37.
74. Ibid. xii. 38.
75. Divine and Moral Speculations, 1654, M2ᵛ.

BLISSETT, Spenser's Mutabilitie (pp. 253–266).
1. All quotations from Spenser are taken from the Variorum edition
edited by Edwin Greenlaw and others (Baltimore, 1932–57). Evidence for
the date of the "Cantos" and their relation to The Faerie Queene may be
found in Variorum VI, 433 ff. See also Northrop Frye, "The Structure of
Imagery in The Faerie Queene," UTQ, XXX (1961), 111–112.
2. To the commentators in the Variorum should be added Kathleen
Williams, "Eterne in Mutabilitie," ELH, XIX (1952), 115–130; Judah L.
Stampfer, "The Cantos of Mutabilitie: Spenser's Last Testament of
Faith," UTQ, XXI (1952), 140–6; and Sherman Hawkins, "Mutabilitie
and the Cycle of the Months," in William Nelson, ed., Form and Convention in the Poetry of Edmund Spenser (New York, 1961), 76–102.
3. C. S. Lewis, English Literature in the Sixteenth Century (Oxford,
1954), 392.
4. Jean Seznec, The Survival of the Pagan Gods, tr. Barbara F.
Sessions (New York, 1953), pt. I.
5. For the morality and politics of the "malcontent" type, see
Lawrence Babb, The Elizabethan Malady (University of Michigan Press,
1951), ch. IV and bibliography; for the background of the suggested physical allegory, see Victor Harris, All Coherence Gone (Chicago, 1949),
esp. 86–128, and bibliography. Hyperbole and bold presumption combine
in the Elizabethan word chosen by Harry Levin as title for his book on
Marlowe, The Overreacher (Cambridge, Mass., 1952). The quotation
from St. Paul is central to C. S. Lewis's discussion of the "Cantos" in

The Allegory of Love (Oxford, 1936), 353–7. John Norden in Vicissitudo Rerum (1600; facsimile, Oxford, 1931) teaches the physical lesson of mutability without fable—or poetry. Albert Camus seems to have regarded the period before 1789 as pre-history; but much of what he says about "metaphysical rebellion" applies in our context of thought. See L'homme révolté (Paris: Gallimard, 1951), pt. 2.

6. The reader will recall the Giant in F.Q., V, ii, 30 ff., whom Artegall is allowed to out-argue easily and punish with capital severity. Jove and the Giants appear in Ruines of Rome, ll. 4, 11, and 12. Jove himself, however, is accused of "doome unjust" and favouritism in Teares of the Muses, ll. 69–70.

7. E. C. Wilson, England's Eliza (Cambridge, Mass., 1939), 317–18; for other references to the Queen's constancy in the face of time, see 46, 258, 355, 408 n. 16.

8. Erwin Panofsky, Albrecht Dürer (Princeton, 1948), I, 156–71. Babb, 77, quotes the earliest English reference to the picture (Burton's Anatomy, ed. Shillitoe, I, 451): the malcontent is "not affable in speech, dull, sad, austere, cogitabundi still, very intent, and, as Albertus Durer paints Melancholy like a sad woman leaning on her arm with fixed looks, neglect habit, &c. held therefore by some proud, soft, sottish, or half mad . . . and yet of a deep reach, excellent apprehension, judicious, wise, & witty." Melancholia and Mutabilitie strikingly figure the related opposites of resentment and rebellion as discussed by Camus (following Scheler) and of acedia and furious activity as discussed by Josef Pieper, Leisure the Basis of Culture (London, 1952), 49.

9. "Titan" for Spenser, as for Shakespeare, is normally metonymy for the sun. "Titans" are mentioned (III, vii, 47) as parents of Argante, elsewhere a "giantesse," and (V, i, 9) as adversaries of Jove subdued by Artegall's sword. The word "titaness" is reserved for Mutabilitie, who is only once (VII, vi, 13) called a "giantess." H. G. Lotspeich points out that Spenser, following classical precedent, conflates the Titans, who are gods supplanted by the superior force or guile of the Olympians, with the Giants, who are in a sense a second appearance of the Titans but are earthborn and in rebellion against established authority. See Classical Mythology in the Poetry of Edmund Spenser (Princeton, 1932) under Giants, Titans, and Mutabilitie. Nevertheless, in our context, much of the original distinction survives, for Mutabilitie is no crude heaper-up of mountains, but a skilled pleader, and belongs by birthright in the company of Atlas and Prometheus and whatever is nobly titanic from Milton to Beethoven.

10. Thomas Dekker, Dramatic Works, ed. Fredson Bowers (Cambridge, 1953), I, 113–14. Gloriana and Belphoebe are clear allusions to types of Queen Elizabeth in The Faerie Queene, and Astraea is a possible further Spenserian allusion. Following Ralegh, Spenser speaks of the Queen under the name of Cynthia in Colin Clout, and in The Teares of the Muses (578–80) he exclaims:

The true Pandora of all heauenly graces,
Divine Elisa, sacred Emperesse:
Live she for ever . . .

11. John Nichols, The Progresses and Public Processions of Queen Elizabeth (London, 1823), I, 48.

12. Willard M. Wallace, Sir Walter Raleigh (Princeton, 1959), 206: we are reminded that the day of Ralegh's trial in 1603, November 17, was Queen Elizabeth's accession day, now for the first time in over forty years not kept as a holiday.

13. Roy C. Strong, Portraits of Queen Elizabeth I (Oxford, 1963), 153-4.

14. John Norden, Vicissitudo Rerum, stanza 157.

15. H. H. Hudson, ed. and tr., The Praise of Folly (Princeton, 1941), esp. 14, 39, 51, passages in which Folly exposes the pretentions of Stoic apathy as Mutabilitie is to expose those of Stoic constancy. Spenser's figure is closer to Erasmus's than to any of the varieties of fool described by Enid Welsford, The Fool (London, 1935).

16. Compare the digression in Marlowe's Hero and Leander. See M. Marjorie Crump, The Epyllion from Theocritus to Ovid (Oxford, 1931), 23; see also 228-9 for a discussion of the set speech of formal appeal as a convention of the epyllion.

17. The figure of Nature is most fully discussed in a series of articles by E. C. Knowlton: "The Goddess Natura in Early Periods," JEGP, XIX (1920), 224-253; "Nature in Middle English," JEGP, XX (1921), 186-207; "Nature in Old French," MP, XX (1923), 309-329; "Spenser and Nature," JEGP, XXXIV (1935), 366-376. See also E. R. Curtius, European Literature and the Latin Middle Ages, tr. Willard R. Trask (New York, 1953), ch. 6; J. A. W. Bennett, The Parlement of Foules (Oxford, 1957), 108, 112; Edgar Wind, Pagan Mysteries in the Renaissance (London, 1958), ch. 14.

18. This is more than the locus amoenus described by Curtius, 195 ff.: it is also the "centre" as understood by Mircea Eliade in The Myth of the Eternal Return (New York, 1955), 12 ff.

19. The prime literary source is Book XV of Ovid's Metamorphoses, as was demonstrated by William P. Cumming, SP, XXVII (1931), 241-256. The passage (ll. 75-478) is elevated and emphatic: it is a description (not a pageant) of change working in all things, its argument being omnia mutantur, nihil interit (165); but the speaker uses his arts in the interest of mild government and vegetarianism, and his voice is less living and urgent than Mutabilitie's.

20. The O. E. D. traces the development in Old French of "revel" through the senses of rebellion, tumult, disturbance, noisy mirth before its appearance in English. See Enid Welsford, The Court Masque (London, 1927), 359. The double senses of "rout" as tumult and as succession, order, retinue; and of "brawl" (separately derived) as noisy turbulent quarrel and pace or movement in dance—both current in sixteenth-

century England—likewise provide corroboration in the details of language for the psychological phenomenon of which Mutabilitie is an expression.

21. Cf. Enid Welsford, The Court Masque, 304, who likens the pageant to a masque; C. S. Lewis, The Allegory of Love, 356, who speaks of the "grotesque antimasque of Faunus"; Sherman Hawkins (see n. 2), who observes (88): "The entrance of the months and seasons resembles the climax of a masque: we have had the allegorical débat and the comic antimasque: now in glorious procession the masquers march before us."

22. There is a fine passage in Janet Spens, Spenser's Faerie Queene (London, 1934), 47: "All the figures in the masque—the Seasons, Months, Hours, Night and Day and Life—are, like Death itself, mere creations of our minds. The details of the pictures—winter's breath frozen on his beard, October 'tottie of the must'—are concretely vivid, but the seasons and months themselves are abstractions—ideas or names round which our constructive thought groups these pungent but fleeting impressions and by this grouping gives them 'a local habitation and a name.'"

23. Mutabilitie's euhemerism is her own, but her astronomy resembles that of the proem to Book V. In both passages, I am convinced, the physical decay of the cosmos is essentially a metaphor of the Fall. See Millar MacLure, "Nature and Art in The Faerie Queene," ELH, XXVIII (1961), 17.

24. See E. C. Knowlton, "Spenser and Nature," 370. Compare also the figure of Nature at the beginning and the end of John Lyly's The Woman in the Moon (registered 1595, published 1597), in Complete Works, ed. R. Warwick Bond (Oxford, 1902), III. The play opens thus:

NATURE

Nature descends from farre aboue the spheeres,
To frolicke heere in fayre Vtopia,
Where my chiefe workes do florish in their prime,
And wanton in their first simplicitie. . . .
But what meanes Discord so to knit the browes,
With sorrowes clowde ecclipsing our delights?

DISCORD

It grieues my hart, that still in euery worke
My fellow Concorde frustrates my desire,
When I to perfect vp some wondrous deed,
Do bring forth good and bad, or light and darke
Pleasant and sad, moouing and fixed things,
Fraile and immortall, or like contraries:
She with her hand vnites them all in one,
And so makes voide the end of mine attempt.

NATURE

I tell thee Discord while you twaine attend
On Natures traine, your worke must prooue but one:

And in your selues though you be different,
Yet in my seruice must you well agree.
For Nature workes her will from contraries,—
But see where our Vtopian Shepheardes come.

The Utopian Shepherds come to beg Pandora of Nature, and from that request arises the action of the play, the inconstancy and folly of Pandora
being preyed upon by the envious gods. At the end Pandora makes this
speech of submission to Nature as judge:

Fayre Nature let thy hand mayd dwell with her,
For know that change is my felicity,
And fickleness Pandoraes proper forme.
Thou madst me sullen first, and then Ioue, proud;
Thou bloody minded; he a Puritan:
Thou Venus madst me loue all that I saw,
And Hermes to deceiue all that I loue;
But Cynthia made me idle, mutable,
Forgetfull, foolish, fickle, franticke, madde;
These be the humors that content me best,
And therefore I will stay with Cynthia.

25. Gabriel Harvey, Letter Book, ed. E. J. L. Scott (Camden Society,
1884), 87.

26. Milton Miller, "Nature in the Faerie Queene," ELH, XVIII (1951),
199: "She tries to prove that the heavens are, in fact, mutable, and yet
is attempting to extend her sway over them. But obviously if the heavens
are mutable, she does already reign in them; if they are not, she is
merely overreaching herself, as both Jove and Nature maintain."

27. See A. S. P. Woodhouse, "Nature and Grace in The Faerie Queene,"
ELH, XVI (1949), 194-228.

28. For medieval retractations (or retractions) see F. N. Robinson's
note in his Complete Works of Geoffrey Chaucer (Cambridge, Mass.,
1933), 880-1. Sidney speaks of "certaine verses, which . . . she would
haue adioyned as a retraction to the other"; Arcadia, ed. A. Feuillerat
(Cambridge, 1912), 173. This is the word; "leave me, o love" is the
thing.

29. T. S. Eliot, Four Quartets (London, 1944), 39.

KERMODE, The Faerie Queene, I and V (pp. 267-288).

1. See A. D. S. Fowler, "Oxford and London Marginalia to The Faerie
Queene," Notes and Queries, ccvi (1961), 416-19.

2. Robert Ellrodt, Neoplatonism in Spenser (1961)—a book which
argues admirably for a Spenser simplified philosophically by the elimina-
tion of Renaissance Neoplatonism from The Faerie Queene—opens with an
account of this development.

3. The Allegory of Love (1936; references to edition of 1958). "Popular, homely, patriotic" (p. 311) is Lewis's description of the allegory of

Book I. "We have long looked," he says, "for the origins of The Faerie Queene in Renaissance palaces and Platonic Academies, and forgotten that it has humbler origins in the Lord Mayor's Show, the chap-book, the bedtime story, the family Bible, and the village church" (p. 312). "Churchwardenly," "honest," "domestic," belong to a provocative list of epithets on p. 321.

4. This apocalyptic strain persisted into the next reign in the post-humous portraits of Elizabeth; see Roy C. Strong, Portraits of Queen Elizabeth I (1963). And see T. Brightman, The Revelation of S. John Illustrated (1616), pp. 490f.

5. A. C. Hamilton, The Structure of Allegory in The Faerie Queene (1961), pp. 5, 7, 10, 11, 17.

6. "Nature and Grace in The Faerie Queene," E.L.H., xvi (1949), 216, n. 42.

7. Graham Hough, A Preface to The Faerie Queene (1926), p. 107.

8. Spenser and the Allegorists (1963).

9. John Jewel, Works (Parker Society, 1848), iii. 79.

10. John Napier, A Plaine Discovery of the Whole Revelation (1593), p. 36.

11. "The Popular Celebration of the Accession Day of Queen Elizabeth I," Journal of the Warburg and Courtauld Institutes, xxi (1958), 86–103.

12. M. Augustine Marlorat, A catholike exposition upon the Revelation of Saint John (1574), p. 167 verso.

13. Strong, "Accession Day," 101.

14. See E. Kantorowicz, The King's Two Bodies (1957), p. 346.

15. E. Greenlaw, Studies in Spenser's Historical Allegory (1932), cap. I.

16. Thus the queen is shown in portraits not only as wearing the imperial diadem and trampling on the Pope (so revenging the indignity of Frederick Barbarossa) but also as the woman clothed with the sun, or True Church. See Roy C. Strong (p. 26, n. 1 supra).

17. See The Works of Spenser: a Variorum Edition, ed. E. Greenlaw, C. G. Osgood, F. M. Padelford, and R. Heffner, i (1932), 450.

18. "Queen Elizabeth as Astraea," Journal of the Warburg and Courtauld Institutes, x (1948), 68.

19. Jewel, Works, iii, 76, 85–86.

20. John Bale, The Image of Both Churches, Select Works, ed. Christmas (Parker Society, 1849) pp. 322ff.

21. Acts and Monuments of the Church, ed. M. H. Seymour (1838), p. 221.

22. Bale, Image of Both Churches, p. 352.

23. Marlorat, op. cit., p. 199 recto.

24. Napier, Plaine Discovery, Appendix (unpaginated). See also Jewel, Works, ii. 85.

25. Acts and Monuments, p. 112.

26. Ibid. p. 663.

27. Acts and Monuments, p. 112.

28. Works, iii. 75, 76, 99, 116.

29. Acts and Monuments, p. 391. Foxe does not name Sergius, but see Wyclif, De pontificium Romanorum Schismate, Select Works, ed. Arnold (1869-71), iii. 245, and E. L. Tuveson, Millennium and Utopia (1949), p. 23.

30. Works, iii. 104.

31. F. Q., II. ii. 23.

32. "Spenser's Kirkrapine and the Elizabethans," Studies in Philology, i (1953), 457-75.

33. Sermons, ed. John Ayre (Parker Society, 1842), p. 122.

34. Preface to the Revelation of Saint John, 1545; in Works (1932), vi. 479-88.

35. Prose Works (Bohn edition, 1895), ed. J. A. St. John, ii. 415.

36. See Paul E. Maclane, Spenser's Shepheardes Calender (1961), p. 127.

37. Sermons, p. 64.

38. It must be admitted that Spenser himself, like the queen, felt some distaste for married priests, at any rate in the Shepheardes Calender.

39. Quoted in Foxe, Acts and Monuments, p. 227.

40. Variorum.

41. See J. W. Bennett, "Britain among the Fortunate Isles," Studies in Philology, liii (1956), 114 ff.

42. Acts and Monuments, p. 998.

43. F. A. Yates, "Queen Elizabeth as Astraea," see note 2, p. 133, supra; and "Fêtes et Cérémonies au temps de Charles Quint," Les Fêtes de la Renaissance, n.d., pp. 57-97.

44. For Astraea as Justice (in a temple) see the lines addressed by Sir Robert Whittington to Sir Thomas More: they allude to Astraeae criticae mystica chrismata / et Aeris fixa tholo verba minantia. See R. S. Sylvester's transcription of the lines in Huntington Library Quarterly, xxvi (1963), 147 ff.

45. Variorum, v. 216.

46. As in Bartolomeo Delbene, Civitas Veri 1609 (written in the fifteen-eighties). There are Temples of Justice and of Injustice in this book, which was dedicated to Henry III and reflects the mode of the philosophical discussions held in the Palace Academy (see F. A. Yates, The French Academies of the Sixteenth Century (1947), pp. 111 ff.)

47. See E. Kantorowicz, "ΣΥΝΘΡΟΝΟΣΔΙΚΗΙ," American Journal of Archaeology, lvii (1953), 65 ff.

48. H. Kantorowicz, Studies in Glossators of the Roman Law (1938), pp. 183 ff.

49. W. Ullmann, The Medieval Idea of Law (1946), p. 43, quoting de Penna: Ius simpliciter sumptum est aequitas.

50. Ullmann, Medieval Idea of Law, pp. 183 ff.

51. Civitas Veri, pp. 168 and 174 (illustration).

52. Ullmann, p. 50.

53. This large suggestion I make in the hope that someone may pursue it. It was put to me by Professor Gordon Rupp after my lecture. It does

not seem improbable that Luther should apply to theology doctrine associated with the emperor.

54. E. Kantorowicz, The King's Two Bodies, cap. IV.

55. F. W. Maitland, "English Law and the Renaissance," in Historical Essays (1957), p. 140.

56. See G. B. Harrison, Robert Devereux, Earl of Essex (1937), pp. 263–4.

57. W. S. Holdsworth, A History of English Law (1924), i. 505.

58. Evidence for this in Holdsworth, i. 508–9, and in George Spence, The Equitable Jurisdiction of the Court of Chancery (1846), i. Part 2, Book i. For a useful recent summary see John W. Dickinson, "Renaissance Equity and Measure for Measure," Shakespeare Quarterly, xiii (1962), 287–97.

59. Holdsworth, i. 500.

60. Maitland, p. 147.

61. Maitland, p. 134. Works of Francis Bacon, ed. Spedding, Ellis and Heath (1861), xiv. 292.

62. Quoted by C. H. McIlwain, The High Court of Parliament (1910), p. 330.

63. McIlwain, p. 294.

64. Ullmann, p. 43.

65. Ullmann, p. 53.

66. E. Kantorowicz, King's Two Bodies, p. 111, n. 70.

67. De Iside et Osiride, in Moralia, ed. Babbitt (1936), v. 11.

68. See F. A. Yates, "The Religious Policy of Giordano Bruno," Journal of the Warburg Institute, iii (1939–40), 183–4. The Egyptian goddess could conceivably also suggest the ancient Church of England, which Bruno called "Egyptian."

69. Variorum, v. 214–15.

70. Moralia, v. 133.

71. See George Rowley, Ambrogio Lorenzetti (1958); N. Rubenstein, "Political Ideas in Sienese Art," Journal of the Warburg and Courtauld Institutes, xxi (1958), 179ff; E. Kantorowicz, The King's Two Bodies, pp. 112–13. For Iustitia and the emperor represented as equally enthroned—as might be said of Isis and Mercilla—see the article of E. Kantorowicz cited in n. 3, p. 141.

72. H. Kantorowicz compares Placentinus' Iustitia with a Renaissance maestà (Glossators, p. 186); but E. Kantorowicz contests this (King's Two Bodies, p. 112, n. 76). For elements of Mariolatry in the Elizabeth cult see Yates, "Queen Elizabeth as Astraea," pp. 76ff.

73. Yates, "Queen Elizabeth as Astraea," p. 62.

74. Ullmann, p. 170.

75. Strong, "Accession Day," p. 99.

76. E. L. H. (1949), p. 216, n. 42.

RINGLER, The Faunus Episode (pp. 289–298).

1. This paper is a revision of chapter V of my Ph.D. thesis, "Spenser's Mutability Cantos" (Harvard, 1961).

2. All Spenser quotations in this paper are from the Variorum.

3. A Preface to "The Faerie Queene" (London, 1962), p. 214.

4. Mythology and the Renaissance Tradition in English Poetry (Minneapolis, 1932), pp. 119–20.

5. "A Lost Poem by Edmund Spenser," Macmillan's Magazine, XLII (1880), 147.

6. "The Mutability Cantos and the Succession," PMLA, LIX (1944), 999–1000.

7. "The Cantos of Mutability: Spenser's Last Testament of Faith," University of Toronto Quarterly, XXI (1951–52), 153.

8. In the first thirty-five stanzas of the Mutability Cantos, Mutability is called "bold" or "hardy" fourteen times (a highly significant repetition) and "foolish" twice. In his eighteen stanzas, Faunus is called "foolish" four times and "foole-hardy" once. Clearly, these designations are to some degree reciprocal. Mutability is "bold" because of her descent from the Titans-Giants (those archetypes of violent boldness); Faunus is foolish because (as William Nelson has pointed out) "Vergil's annotator Servius derives Faunus and Fatuus, the Foolish One, from the same root" (The Poetry of Edmund Spenser [New York, 1963], p. 300).

9. Sir Frederick Pollock and Frederic William Maitland, The History of English Law before the Time of Edward I, (2 vols.; 2d ed.; Cambridge, 1899), II, 503.

10. Ibid.

11. I hope to treat the legal aspects of the Mutability Cantos on a future occasion. In the meantime, a brief glance through them will serve to convince the reader of the extent and accuracy of their legal terminology.

12. The paronomasia here was probably suggested to Spenser by suppositious Elizabethan etymologizing; cf. Turberville's account of the hobby:

"These kind of hawkes are used of such as go with nets, and spaniels: The order of which game is this.

"The doggs they range the field to spring the fowle, and the Hobbies they accustome to flee aloft ouer them, soaring in the ayre, whome the silly birdes espying at that aduantage, & fearing this conspiracy (as it were) betwixt the dogs and hawkes, for their undoing and confusion, dare in no wise commit themselues to their wings, but do lie as close and flat on the ground as they possible [sic] may do, & so are taken in the nets, which with us in England is called Daring, a sport of all other most proper to the Hobbie." (George Turberville, The Booke of Falconrie or Hawking [London, 1611], pp. 56–57; the first italics are mine, the second Turberville's.)

Dryden in The Conquest of Granada uses the same paronomasia. Almanzor is speaking:

Then, to my rage left naked and alone,
Thy too much freedome thou shouldst soon bemoan:
Dar'd, like a Lark, that on the open plain,
Pursu'd and cuff'd, seeks shelter now in vain:
So on the ground would'st thou expecting lye,
Not daring to afford me victory

(Montague Summers (ed.), Dryden: The Dramatic Works [6 vols.; London, 1931–32], III, 149; my italics).

13. "Charge, custody, jurisdiction, power" (NED).

14. Pollock and Maitland, op. cit., 490.

15. For this assertion Spenser had the authority of Boccaccio, who entitles a chapter of his mythological treatise "De Fauno Pyci filio, qui genuit Faunos, Satyros, Panes et Silvanos . . ." (Genealogie deorum gentilium libri, ed. Vincenzo Romano [2 vols.; Bari, 1951], I, 407).

16. Pollock and Maitland, op. cit., 509.

17. Herbert J. C. Grierson (ed.), The Poems of John Donne (2 vols.; Oxford, 1912), I, 262.

18. See William P. Cumming, "The Influence of Ovid's Metamorphoses on Spenser's 'Mutabilitie' Cantos," SP, XXVIII (1931), 245–46. These three episodes and the incident in the Fasti are Spenser's "sources." The grotesque contretemps of Faunus and Diana in the thirteenth-century prose Merlin does not seem to have affected Spenser. The similarities are suggestive but clearly accidental. See Gaston Paris and Jacob Ulrich (eds.), Merlin: Roman en prose du XIIIᵉ siècle (2 vols.; Paris, 1886), II, 145–49.

19. Cumming, loc. cit., p. 246.

20. All classical quotations in this paper are from the Loeb editions.

21. It is true, of course, that Faunus represents luxuria in Alciati's Emblematum liber and is in Spenser "true to the character given him by Horace, Odes 3. 18. 1, 'Faune, Nympharum fugientum amator' " (see Henry Gibbons Lotspeich, Classical Mythology in the Poetry of Edmund Spenser [Princeton, N. J., 1932], p. 60).

22. Incidentally, this passage in the Fasti may have contributed to Spenser's account of Malecasta's midnight assault upon Britomart (FQ, III, i, 58–62). There is a similarity in the details, and something of Ovid's humor shines fitfully through the chinks in Spenser's high seriousness.

23. Marcellus Palingenius, The Zodiake of Life, trans. Barnabe Googe, ed. Rosemond Tuve (New York, 1947), p. 137.

24. Lotspeich, op. cit., p. 32.

25. Natalis Comes, Mythologæ, sive explicationis fabvlarvm, libri decem (Frankfurt, 1596).

26. It is not enough to locate the variant myth in Comes and stop there; Spenser's adoption of a variant implies choice, and choice implies purpose.

27. Loeb translation.

28. Lotspeich, op. cit., p. 9.
29. P. W. Joyce, "Spenser's Irish Rivers," Fraser's Magazine, XCVII (1878), 329.
30. Rudolph B. Gottfried, "Spenser and the Italian Myth of Locality," SP, XXXIV (1937), 108.
31. Ibid., p. 110.
32. I.e., the Florentine and Neapolitan practitioners of the "Italian myth of locality," an Ovidian tradition to which Gottfried feels the Faunus episode belongs. Unfortunately, none of the works cited by Gottfried bears any specific resemblance to the episode, and everything in Spenser has sufficient authority in Ovid. The Italians are probably superfluous.
33. Gottfried, p. 125.
34. It is tempting to press this metaphor too far. The antimasque apparently has affiliations with the satyr play, and Faunus is certainly related to the satyrs (see n. 15, above). Unfortunately, the relationship of masque and antimasque was not articulated by Jonson until 1609 in the preface to The Masqve of Qveenes. There he speaks of the antimasque as "a spectacle of strangenesse, producing multiplicity of Gesture, and not vnaptly sorting wth the current, and whole fall of the Deuise" (C. H. Herford, Percy Simpson, and Evelyn Simpson (eds.), Ben Jonson, VII [Oxford, 1941], 282). This seems a strangely apropos description of the Faunus episode vis-à-vis its context. Equally interesting and suggestive are Miss Bradbrook's observations on the meaningful relationship of plot and subplot in Elizabethan tragedy (M. C. Bradbrook, Themes and Conventions of Elizabethan Tragedy [Cambridge, 1952], pp. 46, 48–49, 221).
35. Nelson's remarks on the relationship of Faunus and Mutability (The Poetry of Edmund Spenser [New York, 1963]) suggest two further nexuses between the two stories: (1) "Like the tale of Mutabilitie's assault upon heaven, this episode is not a borrowing from the Metamorphoses but a kind of parody of it" (p. 300); (2) the stable worlds that are assaulted by Mutability and Faunus are identical, as is the anarchy that results in both cases. There is an implicit equation of the "cosmos before Mutabilitie's foolish exchange of wrong for right and death for life, and Arlo Hill before Faunus' fatuous pursuit of forbidden knowledge. . . . The folly of Mutabilitie has fouled the pure world with sin and death, that of Faunus with wolves and robbers" (p. 302). "The folly of Faunus and of Mutabilitie is . . . an allusion to Adam's error" (p. 310).
36. Lotspeich, op. cit., p. 12.
37. C. S. Lewis, The Allegory of Love (Oxford, 1936), p. 356.

MILLER, A Secular Reading of The Faerie Queene, Book II (pp. 299–312).
1. Quotations from Spenser in my text are from The Works of Edmund Spenser, A Variorum Edition, ed. Edwin Greenlaw, C. G. Osgood, F. M. Padelford (Baltimore, 1933), II.
2. For example, see M. Pauline Parker, The Allegory of the Faerie Queene (Oxford, 1960), p. 132; Frank Kermode, "The Cave of Mammon," Stratford-upon-Avon Studies 2, Elizabethan Poetry, 151–173.

3. A. S. P. Woodhouse, in spite of his important distinctions between the realms of nature and grace ("Nature and Grace in The Faerie Queene," ELH, XVI [1949], 194–228), does acknowledge the workings of grace in Book II to aid and sustain the limitations of nature and reason. See below p. 306.

4. Hamilton, ELH, XXV (1958), 156.

5. A. D. S. Fowler, "The Image of Mortality: The Faerie Queene, II. i–ii," HLQ, XXIV (1961), 108. For another theological discussion of this episode, see Fredson Bowers, "The Faerie Queene, Book II: Mordant, Ruddymane and the Nymph's Well" English Studies in Honor of James Southall Wilson, ed. Fredson Bowers (Charlottesville, 1951), pp. 243–253.

6. A. C. Hamilton sees in the closing lines of the stanza a suggestion of "the Calvinist doctrine of man's total depravity" (p. 158; see above n. 4); in his full-length study, The Structure of Allegory in The Faerie Queene (Oxford, 1961), Mr. Hamilton mistakenly asserts that "the blood upon the Babe's hands . . . is interpreted by the Palmer as a token of man's 'bloudguiltinesse,' " p. 95. It is not the Palmer, but Sir Guyon who offers the theological interpretation.

7. Having listened to the Palmer's secular explanation, Guyon "hearkned to his reason" (ii, 11).

8. See above, n. 5.

9. See my "Phaedria, Mammon, and Sir Guyon's Education by Error," JEGP, LXIII (1964), 33–44, where Guyon's adventure in cantos vi and vii is described as a vicious swing from one Aristotelian extreme to another, from the excess of licentiousness to the deficiency of insensibility. Mordant's death and Guyon's swoon can be viewed as reactions to the same psychic imbalance.

10. The Nymphe in Book II, canto ii, is not reprehensible for the act of fleeing from Faunus but for the icy attitudes exhibited in her flight and in the attributes of the fountain into which she is transformed. Although Belphoebe finally flees from Braggadocchio, she does so without fear and shame. (When Faunus peers with lascivious eyes at Diana bathing with her nymphs [VII, vi. 45–47], no fearful flight ensues; the nymphs "drew him by the hornes and shook.")

11. That Ruddymane's hands cannot be cleansed by such water indicates that Mordant and Amavia cannot be avenged (the blood on Ruddymane's hands is a "Symbole . . . to minde reuengement"), the enchantress Acrasia cannot be destroyed, through the channels of shame and fear.

12. That radical movement from one extreme to another which is so fatal to Sir Mordant will emerge again, this time jeopardizing the life of the hero of Book II; see above, n. 9.

13. The Allegorical Temper: Vision and Reality in Book II of Spenser's Faerie Queene (New Haven, 1957), p. 42.

14. Berger, p. 44.

15. The Structure of Allegory, p. 102 (my emphasis); the view that Temperance is "upheld by divine grace" in the second half of Book II is typical.

16. In cantos vi and vii, Guyon acts without the aid of his Palmer; i.e. he acts without his reason.

17. The lines which follow these—"Yet will I not forgoe, ne yet forget The care thereof my selfe vnto the end, / But euermore him succour, and defend / Against his foe and mine," suggest that Guyon and his reason are not sufficiently strong in defending themselves from foes which may (and do) appear. But the angel which "vanisht quite away" never again appears. And the possibility that Prince Arthur arrives in the capacity of God's grace is, as I shall show, a most unlikely interpretation.

18. Pp. 211-212; see above n. 3.

19. M. Pauline Parker also feels impelled to view the Arthur of Book II as a part both of the classical and the Christian cosmology: Arthur is "the . . . perfect gift which comes down from the Father of Light at the providential moment, the grace of the occasion," and then, as if an afterthought, "but always taking the form of the virtue immediately concerned" (The Allegory of The Faerie Queene, p. 136). Mr. Berger is careful not to employ the term "grace," but his consideration of Arthur implies as much—for him, Arthur is an "instrument" of Providence (The Allegorical Temper, p. 100).

20. The Structure of Allegory, p. 99.

21. The Structure of Allegory, p. 101.

22. The Structure of Allegory, p. 113.

23. The Structure of Allegory, p. 119.

24. One will think immediately of Artegall and Braggadocchio in Book V, canto iii. But the shield transfer there is reciprocal and of little allegorical significance, as the boaster is ultimately exposed for what he is.

25. Hamilton, though one of the few critics who attend to the weapon transfer at all, ignores the peculiar significance of this action: "That Pyrochles wields Guyon's shield and Arthur's sword shows that man's natural powers both resist and oppose overthrow" (The Structure of Allegory, p. 112).

26. It is also significant, in viewing Arthur's fight with Pyrochles as an inversion of Pyrochles's fight with Guyon, that Pyrochles in canto v, like Arthur in canto viii, pays homage (although it is "vnwilling worship") to the portrait upon Guyon's shield (II, v, 11, and II, viii, 43).

27. Hamilton rightly calls this a "wound of concupiscence"; but not wishing to see any imperfections in Arthur, Hamilton goes on to qualify: "the wound of concupiscence, or more correctly, of love to which he is subject, even in his consenting to be Guyon's 'dayes-man' " (The Structure of Allegory, p. 113).

28. M. Pauline Parker is right to say of Arthur here that his "character of perfect Temperance is well illustrated by stanzas 47-48 where his coolness and self-command are contrasted with the frantic fury of Pyrochles" (The Allegory of The Faerie Queene, p. 136). However, Sister Parker sees in Arthur an ideal Temperance throughout Book II. In respect to Arthur's fight with Pyrochles and Cymochles, Robert Hoopes believes that "the claims of theological and moral allegory yield to the claims of romance as Spenser allows the battle to see-saw in fa-

miliar fashion until right finally triumphs" (" 'God Guide Thee, Guyon': Nature and Grace Reconciled in The Faerie Queen, Book II," RES, V [1954], 18). We have found, on the contrary, that in Arthur's encounter with Pyrochles and Cymochles the claims of chivalry and romance yield to the claims of Spenser's moral allegory.

29. I have suggested elsewhere that Prince Arthur, in his victory over Maleger, finally overcomes his limitations; I have further argued that the standing lake into which Maleger is cast is not filled with holy waters (II, xi). See "Arthur, Maleger, and History in the Allegorical Context," UTQ, XXXV (1966), 176–187.

30. The Structure of Allegory, p. 115.

31. Pico della Mirandola, "Oration on the Dignity of Man," in The Renaissance Philosophy of Man, ed. Ernst Cassirer, P. O. Kristeller, J. H. Randall, Jr. (Chicago, 1950), p. 225.

CRAIG, The Secret Wit Of Spenser's Language (pp. 313–333).

1. B. E. C. Davis, Edmund Spenser: A Critical Study (Cambridge, 1933), p. 155. "His diction is decorative rather than composite or associative, differing from Milton's as the music of Schubert from that of Bach, appealing through spontaneity and inherent suggestiveness, independent of source or application. It is the surface lustre that has made Spenser the poet's poet."

2. C. S. Lewis, "Edmund Spenser, 1552–99," Studies in Medieval and Renaissance Literature (Cambridge, 1966), p. 143.

3. W. L. Renwick, Edmund Spenser, An Essay on Renaissance Poetry, (London, 1925). The book was preceded by two articles, "The Critical Origins of Spenser's Diction," MLR, XVII (1922), 1–16; "Mulcaster and DuBellay," MLR, XVII (1922), 282–7.

4. Bruce R. McElderry, Jr., "Archaism and Innovation in Spenser's Poetic Diction," PMLA, XLVII (1932), 144–70, concludes that the number of archaisms and innovations in Spenser's poetry has been greatly over-estimated. Yet the list according to McElderry's criteria, in turn, tends to be too inclusive: he regards "keen" in the sense of "sharp" as an archaism, for example (p. 151). What strikes the reader most vividly about McElderry's list is the number of terms that seem to be simple substitutions for terms current in Spenser's day: "allege" for "allay," "blend" for "blind," "eath" for "easy," "forthy" for "therefore." Other terms, like "yfere" for "together," are more formally distinct, yet they still do not seem needed to fill a gap in the Elizabethan vocabulary. There are very few archaisms and innovations with sufficiently distinctive connotation to "enrich the language" as the modern reader understands that phrase.

5. Richard Mulcaster, Spenser's master at the Merchant Taylors' School, cites the Cratylus in the peroration to the first part of his Elementarie, 1582, proving the existence and importance of "right names" (ed. E. T. Campagnac, Oxford, 1925, p. 188), and Richard Wills, commonly regarded as the Willye of Spenser's Shepheardes Calendar, in his De Re Poetica, 1573, gives a nearly verbatim rendering of a passage

from Marsilio Ficino's introduction to the dialogue for his Latin edition
of Plato (De Re Poetica, ed. A. D. S. Fowler, Oxford, Luttrell Society,
1958, p. 73). Interest in the Cratylus during the Renaissance seems to
have been spurred by Peter Ramus (Pierre de la Ramée). He first cites
the Cratylus in his Dialecticae Institutiones (Paris, 1543). The reference
is dropped from the text of the famous Dialecticae Libri Duo (Paris, 1556)
but returns and is greatly elaborated in the commentaries of Ramus' editors, in the edition of Beurhusius, for example, printed at London in 1581,
or in Abraham Fraunce, Lawier's Logike (London, 1588).

6. Marsilio Ficino, "In Cratylum," Opera Omnia (Torino, 1959, a reproduction of the Opera Omnia, Basilea, 1576), II, i, p. 1311, translated by
the author. Compare Richard Wills, p. 73:

> So Plato, when he inquires in Cratylus who are learned in the true
> names of things, with good reason ridicules the sophists, and judges
> it necessary to go to the poets—not indiscriminately to all of them,
> but to such as are divine; as if they had learned the true names of
> things from the gods.

7. Abraham Fraunce, for example, makes this clear in Lawier's
Logike, I, i, p. 4.

> Whatsoever it bee, nay whatsoever thou canst imagine to bee, al-
> though it bee not, never was, nor never shall bee, yet by reason it
> is invented, taught, ordered, confirmed: as the description of fame
> in Virgil, of famine in Ovid, of Elysian fields, of Styx, of Acheron,
> of the golden apples, and a thousand such poeticall imaginations.
> And therefore Logike hath beene of a loong time untollerably
> abused by those miserable Sorbonists, & dunsicall Quidditaries,
> who thought there was no reasoning without Arguitur quod sic;
> Probatur quod non: no part of Logike without Ergo and Igitur.
> Whereas indeede the true use of Logike is as well apparent in sim-
> ple playne, and easie explication, as in subtile, strict, and concised
> probation. Reade Homer, reade Demosthenes, reade Virgill, read
> Cicero, reade Bartas, reade Torquato Tasso, reade that most
> worthie ornament of our English tongue, the Countesse of Pem-
> brooke's Arcadia, and therein see the true effectes of natural
> logike which is the ground of artificiall, farre different from this
> rude and barbarous kind of outworne sophistrie: which if it had
> anie use at all, yet this was all, to feede the vaine humors of some
> curious heades in obscure schooles, whereas the Art of reasoning
> hath somewhat to doe in everiething, and nothyng is anything without
> this one thing. Some Artes are appliable onely to some certayne
> subject, but Logike is scientia scientiarum, as I sayd before, not
> tyed to one thing, but apt for aniething, free from all, yet fit for all,
> framing orderly, proving strongely, expounding playnly, perswading
> forcibly, any Arte, any cause, any question, any man whatsoever.

Present day commentators (for example, W. S. Howell, Logic and Rhetoric in England, 1500-1700, Princeton, 1956) tend to confuse the Ramists' division between logic and rhetoric for purposes of exposition and instruction with a division in practice and in fact, or at least they so stress the former that the fundamental identification of logic and rhetoric is lost sight of.

8. In P. Rami, Dialecticae Libros Duos, ed. Fredericus Beurhusius (London: Henricus Bynneman, 1581), I, xxiv, p. 110, "Notatio est nominis interpretatio: nomina siquidem sunt notae rerum, nominumque vel derivatorum, vel compositorum, si vera notatione fiant, ratio reddi potest ex aliquo argumento primo: ut, homo ab humo Ovid. 6. Fast."

9. Fraunce, I, xii, p. 57.

10. Fraunce, I, xii, p. 51. "Grammatica notatio exponit vocū adsignificationē; Logica vero causam explicat, cur hoc nomen huic rei sit impositū." "Nomina sunt argumenta, non quatenus ad rem significandam referuntur, sed quatenus referuntur vel inter se mutuo, ut coniugata: vel ad suae originis interpretationem, quae Notatio dicitur. Sed sic non considerantur ut nomina, id est symbola, sed ut res quędam, seu onta quędam. Piscator."

11. Ficino, "Inter haec ostendit Homeri poesim allegoricam esse, etiam ubi historiam narrare videtur, quemadmodum in nominibus allegorice fictis apparet. Refert autem multa apud Homerum heroum nomina certa allegoriae ratione composita."

12. Socrates points out that in the old form of the Greek language the terms for "spirits" and for "wise" or "knowing" were the same (Cratylus, 398 B). Spenser invokes this etymology in his use of "Daemogorgon" in Book I: Night was begot in "Daemogorgons hall" where she "sawst the secrets of the world unmade" (I. v. 22). Spenser sees another etymological connection, however, to Greek demein, to build, which is also present here and elsewhere. In IV. ii. 47 Agape, to discover the secret of her sons' fate, descends into the "fatall sisters house" where "Demogorgon in dull darkness pent, / Farre from the view of Gods and heavens bliss, / The hideous Chaos keepes, their dreadfull dwelling is."

13. It requires the whole of Book VI to reveal all the implications of "Calidore," derived from Greek kalos, beauty and dōron, gift. The most important aspect of Spenser's meaning is symbolized by the Graces on Mount Acidale who present their gift of beauty to the poet Colin Clout not when he wills but as they will, graciously. Courtesy like grace is a gift which the receiver in turn gives.

14. A Latin translation of Plato's epistles with commentary was brought out by Peter Ramus at Paris in 1549. The Seventh Epistle seems to contradict the Cratylus because in it words are considered arbitrary and conventional; Plato's authorship has even been questioned specifically on these grounds. (Cf. Glenn R. Morrow, Studies in the Platonic Epistles, University of Illinois Studies in Language and Literature, XXXII, No. xliii (1935) 69.) But the Seventh Epistle describes language as it is, not the ideal which the Renaissance Platonist found in the Cratylus.

15. The "heroicke" spirit is an erotic one, Amor and Mars natural

companions, as the ambiguity of "courage" and "heart" in the poem confirms. This idea is first suggested in the proem to Book I but is most explicitly elaborated in the defense of love in the proem to Book IV.

> Which who so list looke backe to former ages,
> And call to count the things that then were donne,
> Shall find, that all the workes of those wise sages,
> And brave exploits which great Heroes wonne,
> In love were either ended or begunne:
> Witnesse the father of Philosophie,
> Which to his Critias, shaded oft from sunne,
> Of love full manie lessons did apply,
> The which these Stoicke censours cannot well deny. IV. Proem. iii

The appearance of "Critias" suggests a comparable ambiguity. He is Socrates' chosen, a critic who is not a censour like the Stoics but a discerner, one for whom "philosophie" is the love of wisdom and the wisdom of love, the erotic heroism of the mind.

16. Fraunce, I, xii, p. 57, derives "Hypocrisis, of hypo," (for hyper, it seems) "which is over, and chrysos, gold, because hypocrites bee cloaked with a golden shew overcast." He regards this as a "monkish" and ignorant definition, however, and gives the proper one as hypokrinomai, to dissemble.

17. Randle Cotgrave, A Dictionarie of the French and English Tongues, (London, 1611).

18. This word play on deus or dieu, god, and mundus or monde, earth, as an explanation for Spenser's deviation from his Ariostan source seems much more satisfactory than D. C. Allen's explanation in terms of the Christian symbolism of stones, "Arthur's Diamond Shield in The Faerie Queene," JEGP, XXXVI (1937), 234–43. Allen's explanation for the change from carbuncle to diamond requires that Arthur be seen as a symbol not of grace but reverence, which hardly corresponds to the suggestions of the text.

19. John Florio, Queen Anna's New World of Words (London, 1611). (Not included in A Worlde of Wordes, 1598.)

20. Greene ends with a very practical moral: "Then blest are they that like the toyling Ant, /Provide in time gainst winters wofull want," Groats-worth of Witte, Bought with a Million of Repentance, (1592), the end.

21. R. H. Super, "Spenser's Faerie Queene II. i. 490–492," The Explicator XI (1953), 30.

22. Bollakar, English Expositor (1616), quoted in the NED. The idea is traditional from Aristotle, History of Animals, 519. 19.

23. As quoted in E. W. Bligh, Sir Kenelm Digby and His Venetia (London, 1932), p. 279.

ALPERS, How To Read The Faerie Queene (pp. 334–346).
1. Cf. Shakespeare, sonnet 104, which imitates Horace, Epodes 11.6,

which in turn imitates Virgil, Georgics 2.404. In the Latin poets the word is honor.

2. Like Milton's 'branching elm star-proof' (Arcades 89), this line adapts Statius's description of Sleep's grove as nulli penetrabilis astro (Thebaid 10.85).

CARSCALLEN, The Goodly Frame of Temperance: The Metaphor of Cosmos in The Faerie Queene, Book II (pp. 347–365).

All quotations from Spenser are taken from the Works, ed. E. Greenlaw et al., 11 vols., Johns Hopkins, 1932–57, referred to below as Variorum.

1. See A. D. S. Fowler, "Emblems of Temperance in The Faerie Queene, Book II," RES, N.S. XI (1960), 143–9.

2. Peter de la Primaudaye, The French Academie (London, 1618), 74.

3. See Rosemond Tuve, "A Mediaeval Commonplace in Spenser's Cosmology," SP, XXX (1933), 133–47. Spenser treats this concept explicitly in FQ, IV, x, 31–47; CCCHA, 835ff.; HL, 57–91. It is common in other English writings in the Renaissance, and for the structure of FQ, II, certain dramatic works are especially interesting: Henry Medwall's morality interlude Nature (c. 1515) and such masques as Jonson's Hymenae and Thomas Nabbes' Microcosmus (1637), in which the antimasque-figures are the elements or their counterparts. For the conception of the discordia concors, see Edgar Wind, Pagan Mysteries in the Renaissance (Yale, 1958), 81–88; Earl Wasserman, The Subtler Language (Johns Hopkins, 1959) especially pp. 53–4; Leo Spitzer, Classical and Christian Ideas of World Harmony (Johns Hopkins, 1963), passim.

4. In studies of FQ, II, this conception has perhaps been most clearly stated by M. Y. Hughes ("Burton on Spenser," PMLA, XLI [1926], 545–67; excerpted in Variorum, II, 459). See also Harry Berger, Jr., The Allegorical Temper (Yale, 1957), 65–7, for a discussion of krasis or mixture as the basis of temperance.

5. Among discussions of FQ, II, relating it to Aristotle, Ernest Sirluck's "The Faerie Queene, Book II, and the Nicomachean Ethics" (MP, XLIX [1951], 73–100) is especially important. For the Seven Deadly Sins see J. Holloway, "The Seven Deadly Sins in The Faerie Queene, Book II," RES, N.S. III (1952), 13–18; R. C. Fox, "Temperance and the Seven Deadly Sins, in The Faerie Queene, Book II," RES, N.S. XII (1961), 1–6.

6. Both words go back to furere, "to rage, be mad." For their association with the elements, see OED s.v. "fury," sense 3. In King Lear the fury of Poor Tom (III, iv, 136) is closely linked to that of the storm (III, i, 9). Cf. Tempest, I, ii, 391–2. See also Cicero, Tusc. Disp., III, v, for an important source.

7. See Variorum, II, 231–3.

8. The most important classical sources are Timaeus, 22–3; Seneca, Quaest. Nat., III, xxix; Macrobius, In Somn. Scip., II, x, 12–13. Fire and water are important in traditions of initiation, as can be seen in The Magic Flute, and Paolo Beni in his commentary on the Poetics (Venice, 1622) discusses purgations of both macrocosm and microcosm by these two ele-

mcnts (166–7). Spenser pairs them elsewhere (Mutabilitie, vii, 25; CCCHA, 837–8; HL, 83), and on a larger scale uses the fire of love and the ocean of flux as organizing images in FQ, III and IV. Thus they can be principles of life as well: the marriage of fire and water can be found in Jonson's Hymenaei, 176–9, where Jonson is following Plutarch, Roman Questions, I, and Varro, De Ling. Lat., V, 61. In all these authors fire is the male and water the female, and we can imagine the union of Heaven and Earth either in this way or with Heaven as a lady showering grace on her earthly votary. The brotherhood of Cymochles and Pyrochles is rather the deadly union of "water with fire / In ruin reconcil'd" (Paradise Regained, IV, 412–3).

9. This is the view of Holloway (17), who also associates sloth with Phaedria. I know of no accounts in which the phlegmatic man is lustful or changeable, but by Spenser's day a slothful person did not have to be at all dull or averse to a good time. Spenser's own figure of Idleness is given to "lawlesse riotise" (FQ, I, iv, 20), although like Cymochles he illustrates the sluggishness of idleness more than its frivolity. Phaedria, on the other hand, is all frivolity, yet she dwells on the sluggish Idle Lake and lulls Cymochles to sleep.

10. See Lemnius, Touchstone of Complexions, tr. T. Newton (London, 1581), 101ᵛ; J. B. Bamborough, The Little World of Man (London, 1952), 93 ff. We should remember that the sanguine temperament was associated, like Phaedria, with youth and spring (Raymond Klibansky et al., Saturn and Melancholy [London, 1964], 10). Phaedria's "immodest mirth" is also the perturbation usually called by similar names, Cicero's "immoderata laetitia" (Tusc. Disp., III, x); and it may be related to Aristotle's intemperance (in the strict sense) and buffoonery (see Sirluck, 85–7).

11. Klibansky, 60.

12. As far as I am aware, no one attempted to make one-to-one correspondences of all the individual perturbations with appropriate complexions, but the perturbations are regularly discussed in association with the complexions (e.g., by T. Bright, Treatise of Melancholie, ed. H. Craig [New York, 1940], chaps. XV–XVI; Burton, Anatomy of Melancholy, I, ii, 3), and have much the same symbolism.

13. A similar passage is Guyon's advice to Pyrochles (v, 16).

14. William Nelson, The Poetry of Edmund Spenser: a Study (Columbia, 1963), 182–90. Donald Cheney's recent discussion of Spenser's "soft" and "hard" versions of nature (Spenser's Image of Nature [Yale, 1966], 11–14) is, I think, concerned with the same distinction.

15. Complete Poems, ed. P. Henderson (London, 1931), 206–7.

16. See Wind, 81–8.

17. See Burton, I, ii, 1, 2, especially the section on the elemental spirits. One difficulty in associating Phaedria with air lies in the fact that she is much more like a water-spirit than an air-spirit. But even though Phaedria keeps to the air, she is really the creature of the Idle Lake—the material world, though in its slothful rather than careful aspect—and appears as a kind of iridescence on its surface, like her flowers that wave in the air but are rooted in the earth.

18. Thomas Wilson, Discourse upon Usury, ed. R. H. Tawney (London, 1962), 228.

19. In this general sense my interpretation of Mammon's temptation agrees with that of Frank Kermode in "The Cave of Mammon" in Elizabethan Poetry, ed. Brown and Harris (London, 1960), 151–73.

20. For the argument that Guyon puts himself in the wrong by entering the Cave, see among others Berger, Pt. I; Maurice Evans, "The fall of Guyon," ELH, XXVIII (1961), 215–24; L. H. Miller, Jr., "Phaedria, Mammon, and Sir Guyon's Education by Error," JEGP, LXIII (1964), 33–44.

21. See A. C. Hamilton's comments on the elements as they appear in the sea journey (ELH, XXVI [1959], 343).

22. A. S. P. Woodhouse in his great study "Nature and Grace in The Faerie Queene" (ELH, XVI [1949], 194–228) argues that the lake is the water of baptism, which would certainly heal man of all that Maleger represents. In relation to Maleger himself, on the other hand, it seems to be the water of death, and I think that this accounts for the word "standing" (xi, 46), which in Spenser's time had associations, not only of motionlessness (a lake, not a stream), but of stagnation: this water is a corruption beyond the ebb and flow of time. See Burton, I, ii, 2, 1.

23. See E. W. Tayler, Nature and Art in Renaissance Literature (Columbia, 1964) for a general discussion of this subject. For Spenser's treatment of art and nature see M. MacLure, "Nature and Art in The Faerie Queene," ELH, XXVIII (1961), 1–20, and the writings referred to by MacLure; also H. Guth, "Allegorical implications of artifice in Spenser's Faerie Queene," PMLA, LXXVI (1961), 474–9.

24. See Spitzer, 108 ff.

25. See the entries under "Fortune" and "Occasion" in Guy Tervarent, Attributs et Symboles (Geneva, 1958); also S. Chew, The Pilgrimage of Life (Yale, 1962), 26–30; M. Y. Hughes, "Spenser's Acrasia and the Circe of the Renaissance," JHI, IV (1943), 381–99. A. C. Hamilton (ELH, XXVI [1959], 345–6) associates Acrasia with Venus, and Verdant with Adonis. Acrasia and Verdant are also Venus and Mars, trapped in Vulcan's net. These parents of Harmony (Wind, 81) have a cosmogonic function, but the cosmos of the Bower of Bliss is a false and sterile one, which must be exposed and rejected.

26. See Nelson, 179.

27. Without attempting to review the very difficult question of the orders of nature and grace in Spenser, I should state briefly the assumptions beneath my own argument. I feel that, while Guyon's ends are natural ones, to be reached without Christian conversion, and while the grace that assists him can be called "God's bounty to all His creatures" and not the special "working of divine grace upon the heart of the believer" (Woodhouse, RES, N.S. VI [1955], 286), nevertheless Spenser's knights always act in deliberate allegiance to patrons and counsellors, and a supernatural counsellor must be present and recognized when the task of natural virtue requires it to look beyond Nature. If it failed to do so, the Castle of Alma would not be a faithful analogy of the New Jerusalem, but a blasphemous parody, like the Bower of Bliss. Rosemond Tuve, in her illuminating recent study Allegorical Imagery (Princeton, 1966), has emphasized that natural virtue

became closely linked with the workings of grace; and Spenser had ample precedent for a Palmer who represents reason, certainly, but reason the "divine counsellor . . . mindful of his origin" (Erasmus, Enchiridion, tr. R. Himelick [Indiana U. P., 1963], 67).

28. See B. Nellist, "The Allegory of Guyon's Voyage: An Interpretation," ELH, XXX (1963), 89–106.

NEUSE, Book VI As Conclusion To The Faerie Queene (pp. 366–388).

1. A parallel might also be seen between the Retractation and the Mutability Cantos. On the analogy of the Retractation one is tempted to take "canto vnperfite" as Spenser's own superscription and to see in the concluding prayer an acknowledgment that every design of the poet's must remain "vnperfite" here in this realm which itself awaits the "perfection" or completion of God's eternal realm.

2. Northrop Frye, "The Structure of Imagery in The Faerie Queene," Fables of Identity: Studies in Poetic Mythology (New York, 1963), p. 70.

3. Ibid.

4. The Allegory of Love: A Study in Medieval Tradition (Galaxy Books, New York, 1958), p. 351. Cf. the fine comments by Kathleen Williams, "Courtesy and Pastoral in The Faerie Queene, Book VI," RES, 13 (1962), 342–3.

5. The ultimate source of this image is probably the philosophic allegory in Platonic Epistle II, 312e: "Upon the king of all do all things turn; he is the end and the cause of all good." Plato's Epistles, tr. with Critical Essays and Notes, Glenn R. Morrow (Indianapolis; New York, 1962), p. 196; for the subsequent history of this passage see ibid., p. 116 and e.g., Ficino, Comm. in Conv., Oratio Secunda, Cap. IV (R. Marcel, ed. and tr., Commentaire sur la Banquet de Platon [Paris, 1956], p. 150); also More's Utopia (ed. Surtz [New Haven, 1964], p. 17) for a less purely idealizing use of the image.

6. John Lyly: The Humanist as Courtier (Cambridge, Mass., 1962), p. 15; and see the whole chapter "Humanism and Courtship."

7. For a contemporary discussion of how such a problem should be handled, see Jean Bodin, Les six Livres de la Republique, IV, ch. vii (The Six Bookes of a Commonweale: A Facsimile repr. of the English trans. of 1606 . . . ed. with an introd. by K. D. McRae [Cambridge, Mass., 1962], p. 531).

8. Cf. W. V. Nestrick, "The Virtuous and Gentle Discipline of Gentlemen and Poets," ELH, 29 (1962), 357–71, esp. 359f. Of the two emblematic figures of withdrawal in the book only the knight-become-hermit represents an authentic solution—to the failure of chivalry, not, of course, to the dilemmas of society. Meliboe, the retired gardener, seems to be a low-life parody of the idea of withdrawing to a pastoral idyll.

9. The Republic, tr. F. M. Cornford (Oxford, 1941), p. 196. Bodin, following Plato, speaks of a many-headed beast (The Six Bookes, ed. McRae, p. 531), as does Elyot in reference to Athenian democracy: The Boke Named the Governour (Everyman's Library ed.), p. 7.

10. We recall the poet's tongue nailed to a post in Mercilla's castle

(5.9.25–6). Was this poet bad? Or was it that he dared to write about political matters? The problem of the poet's place in society is much on Spenser's mind in these final books. Whether the poet with the severed tongue is harmless victim or justly punished evildoer, finally, he seems an ironic anticipation of the many-tongued beast of slander in Book VI.

11. Rep., tr. Cornford, pp. 309, 310.

12. Sartor Resartus, ed. C. E. Harrold (New York, 1937), p. 238.

13. As the realm of Night to which Duessa descends (1.5.31 ff.); the Cave of Mammon (2.7); the Cave of Morpheus (1.1); or the "Chaos" at the base of the Garden of Adonis, which has all the associations of a nightmarish demon-empire (3.6.36, 37).

14. Cf. M. Stauffer, Der Wald: Zur Darstellung und Deutung der Natur im Mittelalter (Bern, 1959).

15. For the etymological connection—Lat. silva, It. selva and selvaggio, selvatico—see R. Bernheimer's indispensable Wild Men in the Middle Ages: A Study in Art, Sentiment, and Demonology (Cambridge, Mass., 1952), p. 20.

16. For a parallel in the iconography of the wild man from the fourteenth century, see Bernheimer, pp. 143–5.

17. 1.6.23–30. For Satyrane as wild man, see Bernheimer, esp. pp. 11, 18–19. Note also the satyrs, called "a saluage nation" (1.6.11) and "saluage people" (1.6.19).

18. Dominating the book is the figure of Hercules, a classical avatar of the wild man: see Bernheimer, pp. 101 ff.

19. Cf. Stefano Guazzo's definition of the perfect gentleman in The Civile Conversation, cited by J. L. Lievsay, Stefano Guazzo and the English Renaissance (Chapel Hill, 1961), p. 23 f.

20. The Consolation of Philosophy, III, metr. 6, tr. H. F. Stewart and E. K. Rand (Loeb Class. Libr. ed.), pp. 249–51.

21. The description of Blandina entertaining Arthur with "courteous glee" (6.41–3) contains suggestive parallels with this stanza.

22. The abuse of the term courtesy recalls the earlier narrative by the anonymous knight's lady describing another scene of interrupted lovemaking in terms of courtesy (2.16). Here is an ethos in which "courtesies" and service de dames are reduced to barest essentials: "Vnarm'd all was the knight, as then more meete / For Ladies seruice, and for loues delight" (2.18).

23. D. Cheney, Spenser's Image of Nature: Wild Man and Shepherd in The Faerie Queene (New Haven, 1966), p. 194.

24. J. S. White, Renaissance Cavalier (New York, 1959), p. 8.

25. Ibid., pp. 12, 13.

26. This is the implied conclusion of Cheney's argument, p. 195 f.

27. Image and idea are ultimately derived from I Corinthians 3.16–17, but the formulation is taken from Sartor Resartus, ed. Harrold, p. 238.

28. Cf. O. B. Hardison, Jr., The Enduring Monument: A Study of the Idea of Praise in Renaissance Literary Theory and Practice (Chapel Hill, 1962).

29. J. W. Kleinstück, Chaucers Stellung in der Mittelalterlichen Literatur (Hamburg, 1956), p. 15.

30. Ll. 752–68. And compare the courtier-poets listed in Colin Clout as well as the whole satire of the court there, which accords well with the view of the court implied, as I have argued, in Book VI (see esp. ll. 700–10).

31. White, p. 10.

32. The mythological confusion, therefore, in stanza 13, is perhaps rather a deliberate conflation: i.e., though the "bloudy fray" took place at the wedding of Pirithous and Hippodamia and not at Theseus' with Ariadne, Theseus was known as having fought the Centaurs (cf. Variorum, Books 6 and 7, p. 251). At 4.1.23 Hercules is correctly named as the dispatcher of "So many Centaures drunken soules to hell" at "the bloodie feast," but his action is more ambiguous in that his "furie" seems to partake of the spirit of Ate and he is not, like Theseus (in the Acidale simile), setting his own house in order.

33. Harry Berger, Jr., "A Secret Discipline, The Faerie Queene, Book VI," in Form and Convention in the Poetry of Edmund Spenser, ed. W. Nelson (New York, 1961), p. 43. (My indebtedness to this most stimulating article will be apparent to the reader.)

34. Though it does not consistently differentiate the terms in this way, the poem does imply such a distinction: cf. 10.23.

BAYBAK, DELANY, and HIEATT, Placement "In The Middest" In The Faerie Queene (pp. 389–394).

1. See William Nelson, The Poetry of Edmund Spenser (New York, 1963), p. 209, and additional citations in his corresponding n. 4.

2. For our interpretation of changes in the edition of 1596, see n. 20 below.

3. The Book of the Courtier, transl. Thomas Hoby, ed. W. H. D. Rouse (London, New York, 1959), pp. 308–09.

4. "Loves Progress" (Elegy XVIII), ll. 33–36, John Donne: The Elegies and The Songs and Sonnets, ed. Helen Gardner (Oxford, 1965).

5. Less often it was the navel. See Alastair Fowler, Spenser and the Numbers of Time (London, 1964), pp. 260–68, for contemporary references to this figure.

6. Cf. Adonis' reproductive function: "For him the Father of all formes they call; / Therefore needs mote he liue, that liuing giues to all" (III. vii. 47).

7. This count and those for Books I and II below include only the twelve cantos of each book, not its proem and not the four-line "arguments" prefaced to each canto. Furthermore, in Book III the changes at the end in the 1596 text move the center point one stanza back. See n. 20 below.

8. Spenser is quoted from The Works . . . A Variorum Edition, ed. Greenlaw et al. (Baltimore, 1932–57).

9. The Structure of Allegory in the Faerie Queene (Oxford, 1961), Ch. IV.

10. These are the six knights led by Gardante in Canto i, and Busirane alone in Canto xii. Verbal parallels between the two episodes are close. Compare i. 65–66 with xii. 33–34.

11. Our suggestion implies, of course, that Book III can be taken by itself as an aesthetically satisfying unit; it was after all published six years before Book IV, and with a more emphatic conclusion than the one substituted in 1596.

12. Fowler (p. 72) already considers the arithmetically central point of Book I significant, but his location of it at I. vii. 5 is not precisely correct by any count.

13. E. g., Hamilton, pp. 71 ff.; Robert Kellogg and Oliver Steele eds., Books I and II of The Faerie Queene . . . (New York, 1965), p. 30.

14. P. 152, n.

15. Leaving out, as we did with Book III, the four prefatory stanzas. See n. 7 above. The addition of I. xi. 3 in the 1596 text again throws the pattern off.

16. Stanza 54 is the middle one of Book II, omitting the prefatory stanzas. We think that this stanza should be taken with the stanza preceding and the one following as a single unit of description. In any case, Stanza 54 describes the apples which offer the culminating temptation.

We may note here that the phrase "in the midst" or "in the middest" is fairly often used by Spenser—some eighteen times in FQ—and not only at or near the middle points of Books. It occurs seven times in one episode, the dance of the Graces on Mount Acidale (VI. x), where Spenser's preoccupation with the central position in a symmetrical design is manifest, especially in Stanza 12:

> All they without were raunged in a ring,
> And danced round; but in the midst of them
> Three other Ladies did both daunce and sing,
> The whilest the rest them round about did hemme,
> And like a girlond did in compasse stemme:
> And in the middest of those same three, was placed
> Another Damzell, as a precious gemme,
> Amidst a ring most richly well enchaced,
> That with her goodly presence all the rest much graced.

17. A further resemblance between the conditions of the heroes at the midpoints of Books I and II may be pointed out as Red Cross, lolling on the greensward with Duessa, is weakened by drinking from the fountain, so Guyon is also weakened by his temptation. But because Guyon resists, Providence helps him more directly than it does Red Cross, with an angelic intervention.

18. "The Cave of Mammon," in Stratford-upon-Avon Studies 2: Elizabethan Poetry (London, 1960), p. 158.

19. See the famous passage on Spenser in Areopagitica (Complete Poems and Major Prose, ed. M. Y. Hughes [New York, 1957], pp. 728–29). The temptation of Guyon may lead toward overweening infringement upon the divine ("sicut dii") rather than mental intemperance ("scientes bonum et malum"). Guyon, it is true, refuses to sit on the seat or pluck the apples; and he abuses Tantalus, who strives vainly to reach the fruit, as

"ensample . . . of mind intemperate" (vii. 60). But an interpretation of somewhat different emphasis from Kermode's is made possible by a point which he neglects concerning the two named sufferers, Tantalus and Pilate, steeped in the black flood around the Garden. Pelops, the victim—indeed substance—of the ambitious feast which Tantalus had given for "high Ioue" (II. vii. 59) and for the other gods, is reborn; so is the Divine, eucharistic victim delivered over by hand-washing Pilate (vii. 61—62). In the one case, Tantalus aspires toward the condition of the gods; in the other, man dares to punish God. In both the one and the other case, there is a vindicatory apotheosis. Cf. Kellogg and Steele, p. 315, n.

20. The evidence of the text of 1596 suggests that Spenser was not preoccupied with the symmetry involved in numerical center-points of Books when he came to put together in final form Books IV, V, and VI; at least we find in them no significant central point except, possibly, for one noted by Fowler (p. 220): in Book V, the stanza about the like race run in equal justice by Isis and Osiris (the sun and the moon) (V. vii. 4) is the 294th out of 588. But this count includes the proem and the arguments. Whatever Spenser's inconsistencies may have been, and however attractive this citation may be, we do not here invite skeptics to trust inconsistent ways of counting stanzas. We have counted only canto-stanzas.

Notes 7 and 15 already have indicated further evidence for Spenser's lack of preoccupation with such symmetry in the 1596 edition: his changes in Books I and III move the center-points to insignificant stanzas. But for the less skeptical there is one further consideration, in addition to Fowler's. The Mutability Cantos were printed in 1609 as Cantos vi and vii of Book VII. As we have seen, presumably significant central points in Books I and II fall in seventh cantos. Is the figure of Nature, throned in her locus amoenus on a central mound in the plateau on Arlo Hill in VII. vii. 3—13, the planned center of yet another book? Spenser might have so conceived it earlier in his career. The gods are ranged around her, but the catchword "in the middest" does not appear.

KASKE, The Dragon's Spark And Sting And The Structure Of Red Cross's Dragon-Fight: The Faerie Queene, I. xi—xii (pp. 425—446).
1. See, for example, A. C. Hamilton, "The Vision of Piers Plowman and The Faerie Queene," in Form and Convention in the Poetry of Edmund Spenser, ed. William Nelson, English Institute Essays (New York, 1961), p. 18; for more detail, see his "Spenser and Langland," SP, LV (1958), 546.
2. Courthope, Works, Variorum ed. (Baltimore, 1932—58): The battle is slow-paced, nor is it allegorical enough to be interesting on a higher level, I, 377. M. P. Parker, The Allegory of 'The Faerie Queene' (Oxford, 1960): the battle external, p. 99; the outcome foreseen, p. 104. See also Linwood E. Orange, "Spenser's Old Dragon," MLN, LXXIV (1959): the dragon must represent something external such as Death (an interpretation which will be refuted below), since a further battle with sin would be "anticlimactic," p. 680. William Nelson, The Poetry of Edmund

Spenser (New York, 1963): presupposing an interior dimension to the battle, Red Cross's setbacks are indeed anticlimactic, more of the same
backsliding into sin evinced in previous episodes, showing the idea of virtue in this book to be so Calvinistic as to admit of no real progress in this
life, p. 174. The only attempt I know of to assign a specific meaning to
the incidents is that of R. Kellogg and O. Steele, edd., Spenser, Books I
and II of 'The Faerie Queene'. . . (New York, 1965), p. 211, treating them
not as setbacks but as the sufferings of Christ at his Passion and thus ignoring any impression of anticlimax. How my interpretation differs from
theirs will I trust become apparent as we proceed.

    3. Luther, A commentarie of M. Dr. Martin Luther upon the Epistle
to the Galathians, trans. by several hands, all anonymous (London, 1575),
fol. 88^v on Gal. 3. 1. Latin, Werke (Weimar, 1883–1957), XL. i, 312–3;
Luther's commentary comes to us in two Latin versions of equal authority, both printed here.

    4. The proverb is Prov. 6. 27; Peter Martyr Vermigli, The Common
Places . . . trans. Anthony Marten (London, 1583), hereafter cited as CP,
Part 2, p. 273b. The entire passage, beginning on p. 272b, is a good con-
temporary example of the definition of concupiscence and its breakdown
into fomes and first motions. Peter Martyr's importance is attested by
the many references, passim, in Philip Hughes, The Reformation in England, rev. ed. (New York, 1963); for example, the instance in which an
Anglican bishop "set" Martyr's Common Places along with Calvin's
Institutes as required reading for his clergy, III, 141, n. 1. Martyr, like
Melanchthon, is of that Christianized Aristotelian tradition known to have
played a large part in Spenser's thought; and the translation of the Common Places makes it one of the very few exegetical works of any scope
available to Spenser in English. Allegoriae simul et tropologiae in locos
utriusque testamenti . . . ed. Gottfried Tilmann, 2nd ed. (Paris, 1574),
"Super Matthaeum," fol. 384 f. Cf. Martyr, "Wherefore, setting aside
sinne against the holie Ghost, other sins are divided into three degrees.
In the first is coveting or lust, which is ingraffed in us; secondlie, out of
it dooth spring continuallie the first motions and impulsions unto divers
sorts of wickednesse; thirdlie commeth a consent of the will, and breaketh
forth into act," etc., CP 2, 272b–273a; see also his Most learned and
fruitfull Commentaries of D. Peter Martir Vermilius . . . upon . . .
Romanes . . . trans., H[einrich?] B[ullinger?] (London, 1568), fol. 109^v
on Rom. 5. 12 and fol. 150^{r-v} on Rom. 6. 12. For the scholastics and
Luther on the fomes, which corresponds to Martyr's first degree in all
but name, see Peter Lombard, Sentences, Lib. II, Dist. xxx, sections 7
and 8, PL 192, col. 722; Aquinas, ST, I–IIae 74, 3 ad 2; Luther, Werke,
LVI, 69; 70 adding the word fomes to his source, see n. on lives 12–13;
313; 353; and Hugh of St. Cher with seven degrees of sin, Opera (Lyon,
1645), VII, 44. 3—all on Rom. 7. See in general Odon Lottin, Psychologie
et morale aux XIIe–XIIIe siècles (Louvain and Gembloux, 1942–60), II. i,
particularly p. 522 and n. 1; p. 525 on William of Auxerre; and pp. 526–7
on Hugh of St. Cher.

    5. In Spenser, FQ II.xii.39.3; III.viii.25.2; IV.ii.5.5; SC, Dec., 21. The

scorpion is the wicked woman in Ecclus. 26. 7. For the scorpion associa-
ted with sexual lust generally in the Renaissance, see Piero Valeriano,
Hieroglyphica (Lyon, 1595), "Serpens," III, i.e., Lib. XVI, p. 150; Cesare
Ripa, Iconologia (Siena, 1613), "Libidine," Part II, p. 10; Natalis Comes,
Mythologia (Frankfurt, 1588), VIII. xiii, "De Orione," pp. 884–6. For the
scorpion as sexual lust in medieval portrayals of virtues and vices, see
Morton W. Bloomfield, The Seven Deadly Sins (East Lansing, Mich., 1952),
pp. 136, 149, 249, citing mainly the Ancrene Riwle, (ed. Mabel Day, EETS,
OS 225, London, 1952, pp. 90–92). In Spenser's avowed master Chaucer,
the Parson employs the biblical scorpion for woman as the embodiment of
sexual lust; so also does the Merchant, according to George B. Pace,
"The Scorpion in Chaucer's Merchant's Tale," MLQ, XXVI (1965), 369–74.
Pace traces the astronomical tradition, represented above by Ripa and
Valeriano, to Manilius's Astronomicon.

 6. Ambrosius Calepinus, Dictionarium (Lyon, 1634, octolingual ed.),
"Stimulus. . . . ANGL. A prik or sting. . . . Per translationem dicitur
omne illud a quo vexamur. . . . Hinc stimulum carnis . . . dicimus," II,
sig. Pp1^r. Stimulus, while corresponding to "thorn" in II Cor. 12. 7 and
"pricke" in the Geneva gloss on it quoted below, does correspond to
"sting" in the famous verses, "O death, where is thy sting? . . . The
sting of death is sinne" (I Cor. 15. 55a–56a, Geneva version, which will be
used for all Biblical quotations in English unless otherwise noted). More
important, Spenser himself uses "sting" in phrases and contexts echoing
Latin uses of stimulus cited in Renaissance dictionaries, cf. for example,
"Venus sting," II. xii. 39. 3, with "Veneris stimuli," Lucretius, De rerum
natura, IV. 245; the sting of Envy's serpent, I. iv. 31. 5 with "Invidiae
stimulo," Silius Italicus, Punica, VII. 103; and the several "stings of lust"
with the repeated "stimuli amoris," most strikingly, "Heate of heedlesse
lust me so did sting," SC, Dec., 21, with "stimulos caeci amoris," Vergil,
Georgics, III. 42, all cited in R. Stephanus's Thesaurus and/or Thos.
Cooper's Thesaurus Linguae Romanae & Britannicae.

 7. Spenser quotations are from Works, Variorum ed., I. Certain non-
functional spelling variations such as the interchange of i and j have been
normalized; quotations from older prose have occasionally been repunctu-
ated for clarity; translations are my own.

 8. On the stimulus carnis as concupiscence, see also, for example,
the sixteenth-century compendium of Hieronymus Lauretus, Sylva alle-
goriarum totius Sacrae Scripturae (Lyon, 1622), p. 721. A literary treatment of concupiscence as the last and insurmountable hurdle of one sort
of education in virtue, similar in many respects to that which I am about
to propose for Spenser, is found in Inferno I, where, according to John
Freccero, "Dante's Firm Foot and the Journey Without a Guide," Harvard
Theological Review, LII (1959), 277–280, concupiscence is the she-wolf,
the last and unconquerable beast barring Dante's ascent of the mountain
of virtue.

 9. On the scorpion, Sermo CLI, PL 38, 818 on Rom. 7. 18. On Rom.
7. 8, Opus Imp. Contra Jul., PL 45, 1607, see also 1605–6.

 10. Martyr emphasizes that reason too is subject to sinful "first

motions" or impulses, CP 2, 220b, 570b; Melanchthon cites as virtual constituents of concupiscence such sins against faith as "illa ingens dubitatio, quae in omnium animis haeret," "indignatio adversus Deum," "desperatio," and "natura . . . confidens non Dei auxilio," Opera, ed. C. G. Brettschneider, Corpus Reformatorum (Halle, 1834–60), XV, cols. 643–4, 651.

11. Bersuire, Reductorium morale, VI. vii, Petri Berchorii . . . opera omnia (Cologne, 1730–31), II, 141. J. E. Hankins, "Spenser and the Revelation of St. John," PMLA, LX (1945): "The burning eyes, smoking mouth and nostrils, close-fitting scales, invulnerability to wounds, enormous size and overwhelming power are reminiscent of the Leviathan," p. 373, see also 376. Lauretus, "Exhalare," p. 309, citing Gregory, Mor. in Job, XXXIII, xlv [sic, for xxxviii–xxxix], 67–8 on Job. 41. 12, PL 76, 716–8. A burning wind also signifies the devil's suggestio, ibid., "Accendere," p. 30.

12. The stages are suggestio, delectatio, and consensus. The most relevant example is found in a work having its own interest for Spenser, Bede's Historia ecclesiastica, III. ix, PL 95, cols. 66–8, quoting an otherwise unknown letter of Gregory. This patristic analysis originated apparently with Augustine, see De Sermo Domini in Monte, I. xii. 33–6, PL 34, cols. 1246–7 on Mt. 5. 27–8, repeated throughout his works, e.g., De Trinitate, XII. xii, PL 42, cols. 1007–8. Other references in Gregory, with additional stages not applicable to Spenser, Mor. in Job, IV. xxvii, 49 on Job 3. 11–2, PL 75, col. 661; Expositio de Septem Psalmos Poenitentiales, PL 79, col. 608 on Ps. 101. 6 (Vulg.); Regula pastoralis, III. xxix, PL 77, col. 109. Later examples will be cited as we proceed; for still others, see D. W. Robertson, A Preface to Chaucer (Princeton, 1962), p. 73, nn. 37, 38, and for a similar breakdown with no relevance to our incident beyond the distinction between concupiscence and consent, Martyr, CP 2, 363b.

13. Ancrene Riwle, pp. 129–30. Bernard, "Ponamus, itaque velut quandam animae cutem cogitationem, carnem affectionem, ut consequenter os eius intentionem possimus accipere. Decoloratur cutis, cum videlicet inutilis cogitatio in corde versatur. Nonnunquam vero etiam caro vulneratur, quando scilicet ad hoc usque cogitatio perniciosa procedit, ut delectatione corrumpatur affectio. . . . Peccati cogitatio decolorat, affectio vulnerat; sic consensus omnino animam necat. Caveamus ergo, dilectissimi, cogitationes inutiles, ut animarum facies decora maneat," De cute, carne, et ossibus animae, sermo, Opera in duos tomos distincta . . . (Venice, 1575), fol. 162ʳ.

14. I quote the passage in full: "Omnis qui viderit mulierem ad concupiscendum eam. Quia videre absolute non est malum, sed inquantum ex eo sequitur concupiscentia interior. Et ista concupiscentia sic procedit: quia primo ex aspectu mulieris causatur concupiscentia in appetitu sensitivo qui dicitur sensualitas et praevenit actum rationis, et sic non est peccatum nec veniale nec mortale. Cuius ratio est: quia talis motus sensualitatis non est in potestate hominis, et per consequens non est peccatum. Sed retentio huius concupiscentiae postquam percepta est bene est

peccatum. Unde dicit Augustinus, 'Non est in potestate nostra quibus visis tangamur, sed est in potestate nostra ea respuere vel acceptare.' Et sic patet quod praedictus motus sensualitatis non est peccatum, sed materia exercendae virtutis si ei resistatur per rationem. Si autem teneatur per delectationem morosam absque consensu tamen, tunc est peccatum, sed veniale. Si autem sequatur consensus in animo, tunc est peccatum mortale etiam antequam exprimatur facto vel signo. Et ideo de tali concupiscentia quae est consensus dicit Salvator: 'Iam moechatus est eam in corde suo,' " Biblia cum glosis ordinarijs et interlinearibus . . . cum expositione Nicolai de lyra . . . (Venice, 1495), hereafter cited as Glossa, fols. 1026ᵛ–1027ʳ on Mt. 5. 27–8. See also the stages according to Bonaventura: cognitio, delectatio, deliberatio, electio, Dom. III in Quadrag., Sermo II, Opera omnia (Quaracchi, 1882–1902), IX, 225.

15. Augustine, Sermo in Scripturis CLIII, PL 38, 831 on Rom. 7. 8, 11. Spenser alludes to Rom. 7 elsewhere in an important and pervasive way, in FQ, II. i. 54–6, as A. D. S. Fowler has noted, "The Image of Mortality," HLQ, XXIV (1961), 93–4, hereafter cited as "Fowler." Undocumented generalizations about interpretations of Rom. 7 are to be taken as based on a majority of the following commentaries on Romans: the sermon of Augustine cited above and the one following it, CLIV (PL numbering, Ren. ed. De Verbis Apostoli IV and V); Origen, PG 14; Ambrosiaster, PL 17; Glossa, quotation from Augustine, fol. 1200ʳ on 7. 11; Hugh of St. Cher, Opera, VII; Aquinas, Opera omnia (Parma, 1852–73), XIII: Ficino, Opera (Paris, 1641), I; Colet, An Exposition of St. Paul's Epistle to the Romans, delivered as lectures at Oxford, c. 1497, first ed. and trans. J. H. Lupton (London, 1873); Luther, Werke, LVI; Calvin, Romans and Thessalonians, trans. R. Mackenzie, Calvin's New Testament Commentaries, VIII (Grand Rapids, Mich. 1961); Melanchthon, Opera, XV; Martyr, Most learned and fruitful Commentaries . . . upon Romanes; the glosses of the Geneva Bible; the glosses of the Junius-Tremellius-Beza Bible, the main Protestant Latin version; Augustin Marlorat, Novi Testamenti catholica expositio (Paris, 1561); Guilelmus Estius (1542–1613), Absolutissima in omnes . . . Epistolas commentaria (Paris, 1666), I; Cornelius a Lapide (c. 1566–1637), Commentaria (Antwerp, 1616–53); John Diodati, Pious and Learned Annotations . . . trans. R. G. (London, 1664).

16. Martyr, "Out of our contaminate and corrupt nature, when it was provoked by the Law, sprang all maner of sinnes . . . ," Most learned . . . Commentaries, fol. 167ʳ on Rom. 7. 8; "our lust being irritated by the Lawe, committeth more haynouser wicked facts . . . ," fol. 168ᵛ and for a fuller explanation, on Rom. 5. 20, fols. 135ᵛ–136ʳ; see also fol. 109ᵛ on Rom. 5. 12. Glossa, "Exteriorem [hominem] vero [dicit] contra interiorem et contra legem repugnare. . . . Revixit [peccatum]: Coepit apparere et rebellare," fol. 1200ʳ on Rom. 7. 9; "Quod concupiscitur, fit dulcius dum vetatur et sic fallit peccatum per mandatum. Ex prohibitione, namque ubi charitas deficit, desiderium mali crescit: quo aucto, dulcius fit quod prohibetur," ibid., on 7. 11; Nicolas of Lyra, "Occasione autem . . . homo appetit liberatem et frequenter in hoc decipitur credens esse libertatem agere quicquid vult sine freno legis, quod tamen est destructio libertatis

secundum Philosophum. Et ideo <u>homo nititur in vetitum</u>, propter quod per legem concupiscentiam prohibentem concupiscentia fuit in contrarium excitate," <u>ibid.</u>, on 7. 8. Calvin, "[<u>And the commandment which was unto life,</u>] this I found to be unto death . . . None of us, however, obeys the law, rather, we plunge head over heels into that course of life from which the law recalls us," pp. 144–5 on Rom. 7. 10.

17. <u>CP</u> 1, 184a–185b; see also the anonymous <u>Allegoriae</u>, passage quoted in part above, fol. 384 f., and Aquinas, <u>ST</u> I–IIae, <u>Qq.</u> 75–81.

18. "Suasio delectationis ad peccandum vehementior est, cum adest prohibitio," <u>De diversis quaest.</u> 83, q. 66, <u>PL</u> 40, 63. Augustine, <u>De Sermo Domini</u>, I. xii. 36, <u>PL</u> 34, col. 1247; Gregory-Bede, <u>Historia</u>, III. ix, <u>PL</u> 95, col. 68; Aquinas, <u>ST</u> I–IIae Q. 74, 8.

19. Petrus Berchorius, <u>Metamorphosis Ouidiana moraliter a Magistro Thoma Walleys Anglico . . . explanata</u> (Paris, 1509), fols. lxvii^v–lxviii^r; for an interpretation of Hercules' mode of death as a punishment for concupiscence in its ordinary sexual sense, see Alexander Ross, <u>Mystagogus Poeticus</u> . . . 6th ed. rev. (London, 1675), p. 169; and Natalis Comes, VII. 1, p. 709.

20. The fire cremated Hercules in vices according to Bersuire, quoted above. Luther, interlinear gloss, "fuit <u>mihi mortem</u> anime scilicet et corporis <u>ut fiat supra modum peccans</u> peccator per actualia <u>peccatum</u> fomes ipse," <u>Werke</u>, LVI, 69 on Rom. 7. 13; Calvin, quoted in n. 16, above; Hugh of St. Cher, "Et etiam fomes <u>seduxit</u> [supply "per"] illam delectationem quae est in peccato apponendo. <u>Et per illud occidit</u>, per perpetrationem peccati," <u>Opera</u>, VII, 42. 3 on Rom. 7. 11.

21. The early Augustine followed on Rom. 7 by the <u>Glossa</u> and the scholastics worries that Paul's pessimistic verses throughout Romans seem to condemn the law and to deny free will: "itaque, quatuor istos gradus hominis distinguamus, ante legem, sub lege, in gratia, in pace," in only one of which is good will altogether driven to will evil: "Ante legem, sequimur concupiscentiam carnis, sub lege, trahimur ab ea"; again, under law, although "utique nolumus facere" (<u>Expositio . . . Propositionum . . . Rom.</u>, <u>PL</u> 35, 2065), still "concupiscentia carnis [mentem] in consensionem peccati captivam ducit [Rom. 7. 23]," <u>Ep. Gal. Expos.</u>, <u>PL</u> 35, 2139. The sins of the persona in Rom. 7. 8, therefore, are those not of the regenerate Paul but of an adopted persona of someone still under law (<u>Sermo CLIV</u>, <u>PL</u> 38, 830). Augustine's widely accepted explanation of Paul's setbacks in Rom. 7 as those of an inferior grade of mankind will serve to reconcile Red Cross's similar setbacks with his Christlike victory. See also <u>Glossa</u>, fol. 1200^v at v. 9 (Vulg.) on the persona and at vv. 11, 13 on mortal sin; Hugh, VII. 42. 4, "Expositio Glossae" on the persona; 42. 3 at 7. 11; 42. 4–43. 1, "Expositio Glossae" at 7. 9 on mortal or actual sin; Nicolas, referring them to actual sin; "<u>Ego autem carnalis</u>, id est sequens carnis, seu sensualitatis impulsum. Et loquitur Apostolus . . . in persona generis humani lapsi," at 7. 14, see also at 7. 11, in <u>Glossa</u>, fol. 1200^v; Luther (who vacillates, however, regarding Paul's persona) "In Justis autem, qui diligunt legem Dei, [lex] non operatur concupiscentiam nec dat occasionem nec accipitur a peccato, quia non est ibi," 67, n. at 7. 8;

cf. 69, gloss, at 7. 12; contra 68, n. 2 at 7. 10; Martyr, asserting the converse, that if the persona is regenerate, the sin he confesses to in Rom. 7. 8 cannot have been the "actuall sinne" it seems to be, but only concupiscence, fol. 167ʳ at 7. 8.

22. Whitaker, "The Theological Structure of The Faerie Queene, Book I," ELH, XIX (1952), 151-64, views the sequence of events such as Red Cross's baptism as following no realistic chronology but rather the order of topics in systematic theologies; M. P. Parker asserts that, since Red Cross is already a Christian, the well cannot be baptism, Allegory of 'The Faerie Queene,' p. 102. For the Christological details mentioned below, see Hankins, "Spenser and the Revelation," pp. 374-5; Hamilton, "Spenser and Langland," p. 546.

23. The day begins with some hints of the Resurrection (an event to which the Harrowing of Hell is attached both in time and in theme). A warrior arises on the third day of his battle, healed by a power that "could . . . reare again / The senselesse corse appointed for the grave" (48. 7-8). As will be explained below, a crucifixion, if only a vicarious one, is behind him. The elaborate description of dawn (51), though part of an ornamental pattern of epic descriptions of dawn and dusk (31. 1-4; 33. 1-5; 49. 5-9), also recalls the mention of dawn in the accounts both of the resurrection in the gospels (Mt. 28. 1; Mk. 16. 2; Lk. 23. 1; Jn. 20. 1) and of the Harrowing of Hell in Piers Plowman (B-text Passus XVIII, 67; 123-24; 178-79; 424) and Vida's Christiad (in connection with the Resurrection, VI, 314-17—with the souls liberated from Hell, paralleling Spenser's second description of this same dawn in xii. 2, VI, 288-95). The dragon's fears because of past experience (52. 8) recall the popular motif of Satan's similar worries on Christ's entrance into Hell ("Gospel of Nicodemus," in The Apocryphal New Testament, ed. M. R. James [Oxford, 1950], Latin B, III [xix], pp. 125-26; Latin A, IV [xx], pp. 131-32). The watchman on the tower or wall expecting (xi. 3. 2-7) and announcing (xii. 2. 6) the victory represents the Old Testament prophets who are often pictured both in accounts of the Harrowing of Hell as announcing Christ's entry (Gos. Nic. Latin A, II [xviii], pp. 124, 125; Greek, II [xviii], pp. 124-25; Cursor mundi, ed. Richard Morris, EETS OS, 62 [London, 1874-93], ll. 18098-18102; and The York Plays, ed. Lucy Toulmin Smith [Oxford, 1885], Play XXXVII, 49-60) and in the Bible generally as watchmen, sometimes specifically on towers and "wayting" (Isa. 21. 5-11; 52. 4-8; 61. 6; Jer. 6. 17; 31. 6; Ezek. 3. 17; 33. 2-7; Hos. 9. 8; Hab. 2. 1) for "tydings glad," i.e., the gospel (see Lk. 1. 19; 8-1; Acts 13. 32; and especially Rom. 10. 14-5). The "Peres" would correspond to the "patriarchs" and the other citizens to the "other saintes all" in Harrowing of Hell accounts.

24. Allegorical Imagery: Some Mediaeval Books and Their Posterity (Princeton, 1966), pp. 110-1. Future reference will be to pp. 110-2, where she repudiates almost the entire Christological and sacramental interpretations.

25. Commentarie . . . Galathians, fol. 159ʳ on 3. 23.

26. Sermo in Scripturis CLIV on Rom. 7, PL 38, 831; Enarratio in Ps. 33, PL 36, 302; Enarratio in Ps. 143, PL 37, 1855-6; Lauretus, "Arma," p. 102; see also Lapide, In Lib. Hist., pp. 311-3 on I Reg. 17.

27. For the image of one wounded foot, see Freccero, "Dante's Firm Foot," pp. 251–68. For a winged person with one foot weighted, see Daniel Cramer, Emblemata moralia nova (Frankfurt a.M., 1630), "Velle non posse, dolendum est," p. 289, allegorizing Rom. 7.
28. Spenser's World of Glass (Berkeley, 1966), p. 31 and n. 22.
29. "Figura," in Scenes from the Drama of European Literature, trans. Ralph Mannheim (New York, 1959), pp. 11–76. I would add to his definition that naturalistic parallelism tends to be heightened by magic or coincidence as in our episode.
30. Events and Their Afterlife: The Dialectics of Christian Typology in the Bible and Dante (Cambridge, 1966), pp. 8, 158–69, et passim. On Arthur and Orgoglio, see Hamilton, Structure of Allegory, p. 78 and Vern Torczon, "Spenser's Orgoglio and Despaire," TSLL III (1961).

ANDERSON, "Nor Man It Is": The Knight Of Justice In Book V Of Spenser's Faerie Queene (pp. 447–470).
1. See Aristotle and Aquinas, n. 4, below; Richard Hooker, "A Learned Sermon of the Nature of Pride," Works, 7th ed. (Oxford, 1888), III, 616–617; Cicero, De Officiis, trans. W. Miller, 3rd ed., Loeb (New York, 1928), Bk. I. xliii. 153–155; Sir Thomas Elyot, The Boke named The Gouernor, ed. H. S. Croft (London, 1883), II, 187; Rosemond Tuve, Allegorical Imagery: Some Medieval Books and Their Posterity (Princeton, N. J., 1966), p. 66; Edmund Spenser, Spenser's Faerie Queene, ed. J. C. Smith, 2nd ed., 2 vols. (Oxford, 1961), II, Bk. V. Pro. x. 1–2. All references to The Faerie Queene are to this edition.
2. See A. C. Hamilton, The Structure of Allegory in "The Faerie Queene" (Oxford, 1961), pp. 152, 189–190; Frances A. Yates, "Queen Elizabeth as Astraea," JWCI, x (1947), 30, 63; Plutarch, "De Iside et Osiride" in Plutarch's Moralia, trans. F. C. Babbitt, Loeb (Cambridge, Mass., 1936), p. 151: 377A.
3. Etienne Gilson, The Christian Philosophy of St. Thomas Aquinas, trans. L. K. Shook (New York, 1956), pp. 306–307.
4. Aristotle, "Nicomachean Ethics," Introduction to Aristotle, ed. Richard McKeon (New York, 1947); Nic. Eth. v. i. 1130a 1–15. Cf. St. Thomas Aquinas, Summa Theologica, trans. Dominican Province (New York, 1947), II–II, q. 58, a. 2, 12.
5. Allan H. Gilbert, ed., Literary Criticism: Plato to Dryden (New York, 1940), pp. 482–483, 488, 490–491, 306, 367–370; Joel E. Spingarn, A History of Literary Criticism in the Renaissance (London, 1889), pp. 120–121; Spenser's Letter to Raleigh in Spenser's Faerie Queene, II, 485: "I chose the historye of king Arthure, as . . . furthest from the daunger of enuy, and suspition of present time."
6. Hamilton, p. 152; Kathleen Williams, Spenser's Faerie Queene: The World of Glass (London, 1966), p. 188; Janet Spens, Spenser's Faerie Queene: An Interpretation (London, 1934), p. 85; Edgar Wind, Pagan Mysteries in the Renaissance (New Haven, 1958), p. 81; Thomas P. Roche, Jr., The Kindly Flame: A Study of the Third and Fourth Books of Spenser's "Faerie Queene" (Princeton, 1964), p. 193.

7. Hamilton and Alastair Fowler emphasize the possibility of apocalypse in V: Spenser and the Numbers of Time (London, 1964), p. 43 n. Donald Cheney suggests that the inclusiveness of V constitutes an "imaginative failure": Spenser's Image of Nature: Wild Man and Shepherd in "The Faerie Queene" (New Haven, 1966), p. 168. Cf. also T. K. Dunseath, Spenser's Allegory of Justice in Book Five of "The Faerie Queene" (Princeton, 1968), a helpful study which has unfortunately appeared too late to bear on the present article.

8. F.Q. V.xi.46, 52 [my italics], 56.

9. F.Q. V.xiii.2. Cf. Williams, p. 152.

10. Cf. Tuve, pp. 302, 309–310, 424: Miss Tuve makes a number of relevant points, though she erects too impenetrable a wall between tenor and vehicle (or content and form).

11. Gilson, p. 309. Cf. Aquinas, S. T. II-II, q. 58, a. 10.

12. Harry Berger, Jr., "The Prospect of Imagination: Spenser and the Limits of Poetry," SEL, I (1961), 100–101. Suggestions advanced by Berger in this article have been seminal here, as elsewhere in these pages.

13. The Works of Edmund Spenser (A Variorum Edition), "The Faerie Queene," Bk. V, special ed., Ray Heffner (Baltimore, 1936), pp. 165–166.

14. See, e.g., William Nelson, The Poetry of Edmund Spenser (New York, 1963), p. 264; Williams, pp. 70, 180. In A View of the Present State of Ireland (ed. W. L. Renwick, London, 1934, p. 124) Spenser makes the distinction between evil and an evil person: "cuttinge of those evills which I before blamed, and not of the people which are evill, for evill people by good ordynance and gouernment, maye bee made good."

15. E.g., see F.Q. V.v.39–40.

16. F.Q. V.v.7–8. On the traditional symbolism of the anvil, see Tuve, pp. 270 ff.

17. H. S. V. Jones, A Spenser Handbook, 2nd ed. (New York, 1958), p. 257. Cf. Elyot, pp. 73, 80, 86; Cicero, Bk. I.xv.46; Bk. III.xi.46–47.

18. Hamilton, p. 183.

19. Cicero, Bk. I.vii.23; xiii.39; Elyot, pp. 246 ff., 260; and n. 31, below. In Artegall's waiting for Britomart we can also see Justice's waiting for Mercy; and fallen man's, for Love.

20. See Berger, "Prospects," pp. 98–99.

21. Cf. Una in I.vii.20–27; also W. B. C. Watkins, Shakespeare and Spenser (Princeton, 1950), pp. 139–143; E. M. W. Tillyard, The English Epic and Its Background (London, 1954), p. 271.

22. Kathleen Williams suggests that these echoes of Christ's passion remind us that "perfect justice is also love, perpetually betrayed by the wickedness or weakness of man" (p. 162), but this suggestion fails to account for the tone of the stanzas involved or for the quality of Britomart's experiences. A notable gap lies between Britomart's passion at this point and Christ's, even though a relation can be seen between the two. (Given Britomart's state of mind in canto vi, it is worth noting that the cock is also a "conventional symbol of jealous wakefulness" and hence of self-interest: see John M. Steadman, "Spenser's House of Care: A Reinterpretation," SRen, VII, 1960, 223–224.)

23. See Berger, "Prospect," p. 100; Hamilton, p. 180; Graham Hough, A Preface to "The Faerie Queene" (New York, 1963), p. 200; Plutarch, pp. 121, 129–131: 371B, 372E–F; Edwin Greenlaw, "Some Old Religious Cults in Spenser," SP, XX (1923), 239–240; Angus Fletcher, Allegory: The Theory of a Symbolic Mode (Ithaca, N. Y., 1964), pp. 321–322.

24. Cf. F. Q. IV. Pro. 4–5. See Northrop Frye, "The Structure of Imagery in The Faerie Queene," Fables of Identity (New York, 1963), pp. 75, 77; Roche, p. 200.

25. F. Q. V.x.22, 23. Cf. Hamilton, pp. 173–174. Paul J. Alpers starts with similar observations; his conclusions suggest that rhetorical criticism does not by itself offer an adequate approach to Book V: The Poetry of "The Faerie Queene" (Princeton, 1967), pp. 299–303.

26. Traditionally Justice is associated with Time (the Litae in canto ix, or Horus, the son of Isis/Osiris; or Artegall's deadline in Ireland); see Samuel Chew, The Virtues Reconciled (Toronto, 1947), p. 90; Plutarch, pp. 131: 373A; 139: 374D–F; Fowler, p. 216. Given the history of Artegall in Bks. III–V, the association of Justice with Time suggests another dimension: "according to Plotinus, awareness of self is the foundation of memory." G. J. Whitrow, The Natural Philosophy of Time (London, 1961), p. 111; Plotinus, The Six-Enneads, trans. Stephen MacKenna and B. S. Page (Chicago, 1952), En. IV.iv.2; IV.iii.24–32; IV.iv.1–8.

27. Gilson, p. 349. Perhaps more to the point, Romans xiii.10; I Cor. xiii. Cf. Aquinas, S. T. II–II, q. 23, a. 7–8; I–II, q. 65, a. 2–3; q. 63, a. 1–4; q. 66, a. 6. Cf. Tuve, pp. 49, 66–68.

28. Gilson, p. 308.

29. Aristotle, Nic. Eth. V.xi.1138b 5–10. Cf. Aquinas, S. T. II–II, q. 58, a. 2.

30. Gilson, pp. 308–309. Cf. Aquinas, S. T. II–II, q. 58, a. 10; q. 60, a. 1.

31. Aristotle, Nic. Eth. V.iv.1132a 22–26; Aquinas, S. T. II–II, q. 60, a. 1; Gilson, p. 316.

32. Gilson, p. 312. Cf. Aquinas, S. T. II–II, q. 63, a. 1; and Chew, p. 92.

33. Cf. J. Huizinga, The Waning of the Middle Ages (London, 1924), p. 58; Edwin B. Benjamin, "Fame, Poetry, and the Order of History in the Literature of the English Renaissance," SRen, VI (1959), 70, 80–81.

34. M. Pauline Parker, The Allegory of the "Faerie Queene," 2nd ed. (Oxford, 1962), p. 317; but conversely, Viola Blackburn Hulbert, "The Belge Episode in the Faerie Queene," SP, XXXVI (1939), 124–146; and Josephine Waters Bennett, The Evolution of "The Faerie Queene" (Chicago, 1942), pp. 190–191. Whatever the precise historical referents of the Belge episode, it is obvious in canto x that Belge's emissary first seeks aid from Mercilla-Elizabeth and Arthur goes to Belge's assistance. At the very least, then, time is telescoped (Bennett, p. 190) and unhappy events—the death of Sidney, for example (Hulbert, p. 140)—are simply overlooked. Surely the Belge episode is a simplification (or idealization), even though it is possible to argue that Leicester's campaign is neither precisely nor exclusively intended.

35. Parker, pp. 317ff.; and Spenser, View, pp. 137–139 (on Grey) and pp. 283, n–285, n.

36. Elizabethan Poetry (Cambridge, Mass., 1952), pp. 293–303.

37. On Artegall's name (Art equal or Arthur's equal) and relation to Arthur, see Roche, pp. 48–49; and Nelson, p. 257.

38. See F. Q. V.vii.41; v.21. It may simply be the fact that Arthur sees Artegall in armor, rather than in Artegall's old armor. The point is that Artegall's real self, or at least his inner self, is disguised to Arthur's view; Arthur sees him as inhuman, hard, cruel, pagan, "ded."

39. F. Q. V.ix.46, 49; i.14.

40. This statement is indebted to Berger, "Prospect," p. 101.

41. Cf. Kathleen Williams, "'Eterne in Mutabilitie,': The Unified World of The Faerie Queene," That Soueraine Light, ed. William R. Mueller and Don Cameron Allen (Baltimore, 1952), p. 42; and Cheney, p. 165.

42. See Natalis Comitis, Mythologiae sive Explicationis Fabvlarvm, Libri decem (Genevae, 1651), Bk. VII.i, p. 679; Henry Gibbons Lotspeich, Classical Mythology in the Poetry of Edmund Spenser, 2nd ed. (New York, 1965), pp. 113, 63, 56.

43. Even in this battle, an ironic tone (reminiscent of early cantos) creeps in: V.xii.23, vs. 9.

PHILLIPS, Renaissance Concepts Of Justice And The Structure Of The Faerie Queene, Book V (pp. 471–487).

1. H. S. V. Jones, A Spenser Handbook (New York, 1947), pp. 249–250; Kathleen Williams, Spenser's World of Glass: A Reading of "The Faerie Queene" (Berkeley and Los Angeles, 1966), p. 152; Leicester Bradner, Edmund Spenser and the "Faerie Queene" (Chicago, 1948), p. 94; Josephine W. Bennett, The Evolution of "The Faerie Queene" (Chicago, 1942), p. 250; cf. also p. 185, where she finds Cantos viii–xii "distinct from the rest of the book."

2. Bradner, p. 101; Bennett, pp. 183, 189, 247; William Nelson, The Poetry of Edmund Spenser (New York, 1963), pp. 116, 143, 145; cf. also p. 135: "Nor does The Faerie Queene become more coherent if the reader seeks for a continuing moral tale of which the literal one is a metaphor"; Paul J. Alpers, "Narrative and Rhetoric in the Faerie Queene," SEL, II (1962), 27–46; A. C. Hamilton, The Structure of Allegory in "The Faerie Queene" (Oxford, 1961), pp. 178ff. In Spenser's Allegory of Justice in Book Five of "The Faerie Queene" (Princeton, 1968), T. K. Dunseath attempts to solve the problem by arguing for the development of the main persons in the book as consistent characters in a consistent poetic narrative.

3. Virgil K. Whitaker, "The Theological Structure of the 'Faerie Queene' Book I," That Soueraine Light: Essays in Honor of Edmund Spenser 1552–1952 (Baltimore, 1952), pp. 71ff. Cf. also Whitaker, The Religious Basis of Spenser's Thought (Stanford, 1950), where his thesis is convincingly documented.

4. Cf. especially, e.g., Leonard Cox, The Arte or Crafte of Rhethoryke (1552), where the principles of Invention and Disposition are illustrated by examples drawn from an exposition of Justice.

5. Abraham Fraunce, The Lawyers Logike (1588), foll. 113–118.

6. Sir Thomas Elyot, The Boke Named The Governour, Everyman's Library ed. (London, 1937), p. 145. Cf. also p. 195, where Elyot associates the three aspects of Justice with Fortitude, Prudence, and Temperance, respectively.

7. Christopher Saint German, Dialogus de Fundamentis Legum Anglie et de Conscientia (1528): see STC 21559 et seq. for the numerous editions, translations, and amplifications of this work; subsequent references are to The Dialogues in English, between a Doctor of Divinity and a Student in the Lawes of England (London, 1580: STC 21574); Justus Lipsius, Politicorum, sive, Civilis Doctrinae Libri Sex (1589); references here are to Sixe Bookes of Politickes or Civil Doctrine . . . Done into English by William Jones, Gentleman (London, 1594: STC 15701); Jacques Hurault, Politike, Moral and Martial Discourses (1588), translated by Arthur Golding (London, 1595: STC 14000). Cf., also, Leonard Cox, The Arte or Crafte of Rhethoryke (1552); Thomas Pritchard, The Schoole of Honest and Vertuouse Lyfe (1579); Simon Harward, Encheiridion Morale (1596).

8. Richard Hooker, Of the Laws of Ecclesiastical Polity, Everyman's Library ed. (London, 1907), I, 192–193.

9. The Lawyers Logike, fol. 113^V. Mrs. Bennett (pp. 178–179) recognizes three distinct narrative and compositional sections in Bk. V which, for different reasons, closely approximate those which I shall describe.

10. The Governour, pp. 195 ff.

11. Cf. n. 7, above, and Saint German, Chs. v–xi, and especially fol. 27^r; Lipsius, pp. 27–30; Hurault, pp. 170 ff.

12. A Preface to "The Faerie Queene" (New York, 1962), p. 196. Cf. Nelson's similar view in The Poetry of Edmund Spenser, p. 264.

13. Cf. The Governour, pp. 196 ff.

14. Bennett, pp. 180–183. Cf. also Nelson, p. 263, who sees the episode in a similar light.

15. E. A. Greenlaw, "Spenser and British Imperialism," quoted in The Works of Edmund Spenser: A Variorum Edition: "The Faerie Queene," Book V (Baltimore, 1936), pp. 303–304; C. G. Osgood, ibid., p. 195; Jones, Spenser Handbook, p. 256.

16. Mrs. Bennett (pp. 183–184) would cut off the first section of Bk. V at St. 21 of Canto iv, considering the Terpine-Radigund-Artegall episode that concludes the canto to belong properly to the second, central section of the book. Strictly in terms of the narrative, she is probably right in arguing that the adventures of Artegall and Britomart among the Amazons are older material, written in imitation of Ariosto for quite different purposes, which Spenser subsequently "adapted to, rather than created for, Book V." But on the assumption that in adapting older material the poet was guided less by principles of narrative consistency than by those of logical analysis and exposition of his subject, I suggest that he reworked the Terpine-Radigund episode as an exemplum of the first point or place in his exposition of Justice, i.e., Justice Absolute, before adapting the rest of this Ariostan material to his second major point or place, the

principle of Equity, in the central section of Bk. V. The function of Talus in the Terpine episode, in contrast to what Mrs. Bennett herself acknowledges to be his quite different and more restrained function after Canto iv, argues for the logical association of this exemplum with the exposition of Justice Absolute.

17. James E. Phillips, "The Background of Spenser's Attitude toward Women Rulers" and "The Woman Ruler in Spenser's Faerie Queene," HLQ, V (1941–42), 5–32; 211–234.

18. The Governour, p. 195; Lipsius, Six Bookes of Politickes, pp. 28, 33; Hurault, Politike . . . Discourses, pp. 184, 211; Saint German, The Dialoges, foll. 27ᵛ–28ʳ, who continues: "And so it appeareth that equity taketh not away ye very right but only that, yt seemeth to be right by the general words of ye law, nor it is not ordeined against the cruelness of the law, for the law in such case generally taken, is good in himself but equity followeth ye law in al particuler cases where right & justice requireth, notwithstanding that general rule of ye law be to ye contrary: wherfore it appereth yt if any law were made by a man without any such exception expressed or implied it were manifestly unreasonable, & were not to be suffered: for such cases might come yt he that would observe ye law should breake both the law of God & the lawe of reason."

19. "Elizabeth at Isis Church," PMLA, LXXIX (1964), 378. In Icons of Justice: Iconography and Thematic Imagery in Book V of "The Faerie Queene" (New York, 1969), Ch. vi, Jane Aptekar similarly identifies Britomart with Equity.

20. Cf. Bennett, p. 184.

21. Graziani, p. 376.

22. Graziani, loc. cit.

23. Phillips, pp. 233–234.

24. Cf. Bennett, pp. 183–184, esp. p. 183, n. 8, where she notes that the Dolon episode, like the rest of the narrative material in Cantos v–viii in which Britomart supplants Artegall as the protagonist, appears to be early material written in imitation of Ariosto that was subsequently adapted to different purposes when the poet came to compile Bk. V.

25. Alfred B. Gough, ed., The Faerie Queene, Book V (Oxford, 1918), quoted in the Variorum Spenser, Bk. V, p. 211. Cf. Jones, p. 261, and Graziani, p. 387.

26. Concerning the Right of Succession to the Kingdom of England (London, 1703), p. 83. Craig died in 1603.

27. Mrs. Bennett (p. 184) notes that Talus is an addition to the earlier Ariostan material, a further indication that Spenser was deliberately seeking to adapt older narrative material to a newer expository purpose.

28. The Governour, p. 145.

29. Sixe Bookes of Politickes, p. 31.

30. Politike, Moral, and Martial Discourses, pp. 191–192. Lipsius (p. 32) also makes the distinction between true mercy and harmful or cruel vain pity; he writes: "But he ought (as I sayd) practice this vertue not inconsiderately, but with judgement: for without discretion it should be too much effeminateness and lenitie, and vice rather than vertue."

31. Hough, pp. 196–197; Hamilton, p. 178; Nelson, pp. 266 ff.; Jones, p. 264.

32. Bennett, pp. 187–188.

33. Quoted in Graziani, p. 380.

34. Ibid., pp. 378–381.

35. Jones, p. 264.

36. Cf. Variorum Spenser, Bk. V, App. II.

37. Pages 188–189. Mrs. Bennett notes that the arrangement of episodes in this section "is a logical rather than a temporal order, presenting a sequence of growing strength" of the Protestant cause.

38. Ed. F. L. Baumer, Scholars' Facsimiles and Reprints (New York, 1938), sig. [Eiv^V].

39. Cf. especially Ray Heffner, "Essex and Book Five of the Faerie Queene" (Variorum Spenser, Bk. V, pp. 324 ff.); Bennett, pp. 191 ff.; and Jones, p. 268. Whether Artegall be identified with Essex, Grey, or Sir John Norris is immaterial if the episode is read as an example of Elizabethan policy against Spanish-Catholicism in France, the Low Countries, and Ireland.

40. Conyers Read, Lord Burghley and Queen Elizabeth (New York, 1960), p. 412, quotes a letter from Burghley to the marshal of France (Oct. 2, 1592) clearly indicating that in view of Henry's impending apostasy, Elizabeth's chief minister was prepared to concede "the necessity of toleration for the French Roman Catholics."

41. Variorum Spenser, The Prose Works, pp. 159–160.

42. Ibid., p. 236.

HAMILTON, Our New Poet: Spenser, "Well Of English Undefyld" (pp. 488–506).

1. Critical approaches to six major English works, ed. R. M. Lumiansky and Herschel Baker (Philadelphia 1968), pp. 160–1.

2. E. K.'s praise of The Shepheardes Calender in his Dedicatory epistle.

3. Constantine Fitzgibbon, The life of Dylan Thomas (London 1965), p. 371.

4. An apology for poetry, ed. G. Shepherd (London 1965), p. 140.

5. Martha Craig, "Language and concept in The Faerie Queene," DD Yale 1959, and see her "The secret wit of Spenser's language" in Elizabethan poetry, Modern essays in criticism, ed. Paul J. Alpers (New York 1967), 447–72; Alice Blitch, "Etymon and image in The Faerie Queene," DD Columbia, Michigan State; J. Belson, "The names in The Faerie Queene," DD Columbia 1964. See also the important general article, K. K. Ruthven, "The poet as etymologist," Critical Quarterly, II (1969), 9–37.

6. The lyfe of Saynt George, reprinted from Caxton's translation of The Golden Legend (Wynken de Worde, 1512) in Alexander Barclay's The Life of St. George (EETS O. S. 230, 1955), p. 112. See William Nelson, The poetry of Edmund Spenser (New York 1963), p. 151.

7. See Susan Snyder, "Guyon the wrestler, Renaissance News, 14 (1961) 249—52.

8. William Camden, Remains concerning Britain (first printed 1605; London 1870), p. 102.

9. From Spenser's account of his Epithalamion Thamesis, in Three proper wittie familiar letters in Poetical Works, ed. J. C. Smith and E. de Selincourt (Oxford 1912), p. 612.

10. A. W. Satterthwaite observes that "Spenser's words are heavily fraught with the meanings they acquire through their repeated use in certain contexts in his whole work. They become as 'loaded' as any words a poet ever used" (Spenser, Ronsard, and Du Bellay: A Renaissance comparison (Princeton 1960), p. 154 n. 21). Cf. Kathleen Williams' penetrating comment on the phrase "they that love do live" (III iv 37): "The words themselves—life, death, love—are flat through long use and misuse, and any writer must recharge them if we are to be convinced that he is dealing not in paltry effects of verbal jugglery but in a felt paradox. Spenser does recharge them; they are the explosive point of an accumulated force coming from the finely structured narrative and its images" (Spenser's Faerie Queene: the world of glass (London 1966), p. 142.

11. Paul J. Alpers has some illuminating comments on this topic in The Poetry of The Faerie Queene (Princeton 1967), pp. 77—95.

12. I use the term loosely: properly speaking, coinages are only those words coined by Spenser which are unhistorical in development or uncertain in origin. See Bruce R. McElderry, "Archaism and innovation in Spenser's poetic diction," PMLA 47 (1932), 161.

13. See Arnold Williams, The common expositor (Chapel Hill 1948), pp. 228—32.

14. Discoveries, in Works, ed. Herford, Simpson (Oxford 1947), VIII 588.

15. Valerius Terminus, in Philosophical Works, ed. J. M. Robertson (London 1905), p. 188. On the Elizabethan attitude towards language see M. M. Mahood, Shakespeare's wordplay (London 1957), pp. 169—75. See Christopher Ricks' account of Milton's effort to "re-create something of the prelapsarian state of language" (Milton's grand style (Oxford 1963), p. 110 ff.)

BERGER, Spenser's Prothalamion: An Interpretation (pp. 509—523).

1. Various forms of this view of lyric have governed a number of recent studies of seventeenth-century poetry. Cf. Louis Martz, The Poetry of Meditation, New Haven 1962 (second edition); Lowry Nelson, Baroque Lyric Poetry, New Haven 1961; Frank Warnke, European Metaphysical Poetry, New Haven & London 1961. For an attempt to apply this view to Spenser, see my 'Spenser's Gardens of Adonis: Force and Form in the Renaissance Imagination,' UTQ, XXX, No. 2 (January 1961), 128—150.

2. See the Variorum edition of the Minor Poems, Volume II, Baltimore 1947, 662—666. As Renwick points out, it is unclear whether Spenser

was commissioned to write the poem or wrote it on his own initiative. For our purposes the distinction is irrelevant. All we need to know is that the imaginary experience includes the fact of a poet making a poem to celebrate an occasion.

3. See especially Manly, Var. 2.665.

4. As we have seen, even the nymph passage may be descriptive rather than figurative. The exceptions are minor: the fifth line ('as each had bene a Bryde'), which is a dubious case, and the observation that the daisy 'at evening closes.' This remark is more conspicuous than the other modifiers mainly because it is longer, but also because of its relevance to the mutability theme.

5. See, for example, F.Q. I. ii. 28–29, vii. 2–5; II. xii. 51, 63, 71 ff.; III. v. 39–40, 51, vi. 6 ff., 42–44; VI. ix. 22–23. See also Shepherd's Calendar, June and July eclogues; Virgils Gnat, ll. 65–252 passim.

6. A similar complexity informs the Divine Philanderer comparisons in Epithalamion 307–310 and 328–331.

7. The shift of interest from brides to self is revealed by the fact that the preterit 'There when they came . . .' is left incomplete. Though this is no doubt an oversight, it suggests the psychological continuity as the poet, having in effect mastered the vision, moves beyond it to the still unmastered actuality which gave rise to the poem.

MCNEIR, An Apology For Spenser's Amoretti (pp. 524–533).

1. In slightly shorter form, this paper was read at the meeting of the Pacific Northwest Renaissance Conference at Western Washington State College in 1963. It has been documented.

2. (New York, 1938), pp. 273–275.

3. "Tension and Structure of Poetry," Sewanee Review, LI (1943), 556–561. For a specific rebuttal and a general defense of Spenser's poetic craftsmanship, while calling the Amoretti "of all Spenser's mature poems the least exciting," see W. B. C. Watkins, Shakespeare and Spenser (Princeton, 1950), pp. 259–292.

4. His humor has been ponderously noted but not done justice by Allan Gilbert, "Spenserian Comedy," Tennessee Studies in English, II (1957), 95–104; Robert O. Evans, "Spenserian Humor: Faerie Queene III and IV," Neuphilologische Mitteilungen, LX (1959), 288–299; and A. C. Hamilton, The Structure of Allegory in "The Faerie Queene" (Oxford, 1961), pp. 70–71, 74–75, 157, 161, 209–210.

5. English Poetry in the Sixteenth Century (London, 1955), pp. 101–103.

6. "The Amoretti: 'Most Goodly Temperature,'" Form and Convention in the Poetry of Edmund Spenser, ed. William Nelson (New York, 1961), pp. 146–168.

7. Elizabethan Sonnets (London, 1904), I, xcii–xcix.

8. The Age of Shakespeare (1579–1631) (London, 1903), I, 22–24.

9. A Commentary on the Poetry of Chaucer and Spenser (Glasgow, 1920), p. 250.

10. Edmund Spenser (Paris, 1923), p. 172.

11. Ed., Daphnaida and Other Poems (London, 1929), pp. 195-196.

12. Elizabethan Poetry (Cambridge, Mass., 1952), pp. 163-171.

13. The Elizabethan Love Sonnet (London, 1956), pp. 92-138.

14. Rev. ed. (London, 1948), pp. 297-360.

15. (Oxford, 1954), p. 372.

16. Classical Influences in Renaissance Literature (Cambridge, Mass., 1952), pp. 35-47.

17. The Allegory of Love, p. 360.

18. Hallett Smith, pp. 165-166.

19. For a striking exception, see Theodore Spencer, "The Poetry of Sir Philip Sidney," ELH, XII (1949), 251-278.

20. Elias L. Rivers shows in his illuminating study, "Certain Formal Characteristics of the Primitive Love Sonnet," Speculum, XXXIII (1958), 42-55, especially 49-52, that a periodic structure appears in some of the sonnets of Giacomo da Lentino.

21. Fairly often the periodic structure produces a circular rather than a progressive movement, as in 1, 18, 19, 30, 37, 56, 64, 71, 74, and 86.

22. All of these except Greville's sequence are reprinted by Sidney Lee in vol. II of Elizabethan Sonnets; Caelica has been edited by Una M. Ellis-Fermor (London, 1936). Giles Fletcher in Licia, 1593, has better control of meter than most of his contemporaries. At the other extreme is the anonymous Zepheria, 1594, in which the scansion is uncertain because of awkward construction and crude rhythm.

23. Although the sonnets are numbered 1-89, number 35 occurs again as number 83.

24. For an excellent comparison of these poets, but with no mention of Spenser's poem, see H. M. Richmond, The School of Love: The Evolution of the Stuart Love Lyric (Princeton, N. J., 1964), pp. 251-259.

25. On the "rôle" of Astrophel, see Richard B. Young "English Petrarke: A Study of Sidney's Astrophel and Stella," in Three Studies in the Renaissance, Yale Studies in English, vol. 138 (New Haven, 1958), pp. 40-88.

26. See Richmond's discussion, pp. 37-49, with his slighting reference to Spenser's sonnet 3 (p. 45).

27. I agree with Hallett Smith, p. 166, that Spenser's lady "is more elaborately presented, both physically and spiritually, than any of the Delias, Dianas, Phillises, Lauras, or even Stellas of the time," but I think he is mistaken when he says "in Spenser it is not the lover who is portrayed most fully; it is the lady." They are both fully portrayed.

NEUSE, The Triumph Over Hasty Accidents: A Note On The Symbolic Mode Of The 'Epithalamion' (pp. 534-548).

1. See Short Time's Endless Monument: The symbolism of the numbers in Edmund Spenser's Epithalamion (New York, 1960). Cf. the same author's 'The Daughters of Horus: Order in the stanzas of Epithalamion,' in Form and Convention in the Poetry of Edmund Spenser, edited by W. Nelson (New York, 1961), pp. 103-21. Spenser citations are from Spenser's Minor Poems, edited by E. de Selincourt (Oxford, 1910).

2. See A. C. Judson, The Life of Edmund Spenser (Baltimore, 1945), p. 172.

3. The intervening anacreontics may serve as a way of marking the break between Amoretti and Epithalamion, on which see below.

4. Cf. Ficino: 'amans amati figuram suo sculpit in animo. Fit itaque amantis animus speculum in quo amati relucet imago.' Commentarium in Convivium, in Opera Omnia (Facsimile edition, Turin, 1959), Vol. II, Tomus I, 1329. Also A. Chastel, Marsile Ficin et l'Art (Geneva and Lille, 1954), p. 119. Other sonnets involving the inner image are numbers 8, 45, 51, and 61.

5. See R. Klein, 'La Forme et l'Intelligible,' in Umanesimo et Simbolismo, edited by E. Castelli (Padua, 1958), pp. 102–21; also A. Chastel, Art et Humanisme à Florence au Temps de Laurent le Magnifique (Paris, 1959), pp. 99 ff. For the manipulation of time in Renaissance poetry, see L. Nelson, Baroque Lyric Poetry (New Haven, 1961).

6. See Klein, esp. pp. 104 f., 111.

7. Giovanni Pico della Mirandola, Oration on the Dignity of Man, translated by E. L. Forbes, in The Renaissance Philosophy of Man, edited by E. Cassirer et al. (Chicago, 1959), pp. 248–9. For the poet's imitation of Nature in her inner drive (natura naturans) see further H. S. Wilson, 'Some Meanings of "Nature" in Renaissance Literary Theory,' Journal of the History of Ideas, 2 (1941), 434 ff.; and compare the use of energeia by Puttenham (Elizabethan Critical Essays, edited by G. G. Smith, II, 148, and n., 419); Scaliger's efficacia is echoed by Sidney (Eliz. Crit. Ess., I, 157 and n., 386).

8. See A. Chastel, Art et Humanisme, p. 272, and the same author's Marsile Ficin et l'Art, 'Prométhée et Orphée,' esp. pp. 175–6; 'Connaissance Orphique et Magie,' pp. 71 ff., 94 f.

9. 'Spenser and the Epithalamic Convention,' Comparative Literature, 9 (1957), 226–7.

10. For the 'intuition of becoming' see G. Poulet, Studies in Human Time, translated by E. Coleman (New York, 1959), pp. 31–3. Also, Augustine's discussion of Time, Confessions, XI, xxvii ff.; J. F. Callahan, Four Views of Time in Ancient Philosophy (Cambridge, Mass., 1948), Chapter 4, esp. pp. 177 ff.; and Plotinus, Enneads, III, vii, 13. There is a multiplicity of sources from Hesiod's Theogony and the Orphic Hymn to Night to Chapman's The Shadow of Night (1594) for Night as an ambivalent figure at once demonic and a creative source. For Chapman's association of Night with 'rapture,' see M. C. Bradbrook, The School of Night: A study of the literary Relationships of Sir Walter Raleigh (Cambridge, 1936), pp. 134, 136.

11. Cf. J. Chydenius, The Typological Problem in Dante: A study in the history of Medieval ideas (Copenhagen, 1958). Another term would be 'figural': cf. E. Auerbach, 'Figura,' Scenes from the Drama of European Literature (New York, 1959), pp. 11–76. Spenser employed this kind of symbolism earlier in Book I of the Faerie Queene.

12. See Israel Baroway, 'The Imagery of Spenser and the Song of Songs' J.E.G.P., 33 (1934), 23–45. For the sacramental and typological importance

of Canticles, see Jean Daniélou, The Bible and the Liturgy (Notre Dame, Indiana, 1956), pp. 193 ff.

13. Both kinds of symbolism, Biblical and diurnal, are combined in the bride, who rises in a gradual birth out of darkness: ll. 93 ff., 148 ff. As type of rising evening star, moon, sun (ll. 151, 154 ff.) she partici- pates in the celestial masque of Hymen. At the same time, the bride's existence as real woman is established by the realistic social context projected: ll. 159 ff.

14. Sister M. Laurentia Digges, C. S. J., Transfigured World: Design, Theme and Symbol in Worship (New York, 1957), p. 25. Cf. J. Daniélou, The Bible and the Liturgy, p. 3; and Hooker's Anglican view of the Sacra- ments, Of the Laws of Ecclesiastical Polity, V, lvii (Everyman edition, II, 236). Spenser was familiar with and made poetic use of traditional medieval (Catholic) sacramentalism, as Beatrice Ricks shows: 'Catholic Sacramentals and Symbolism in Spenser's Faerie Queene,' J.E.G.P., 52 (1953), 322–31.

15. Digges, p. 26. Cf. The ancient Greek concept of mousiké and the comments on the poem as 'performance' in Nelson, Baroque Lyric Poetry, pp. 71 ff.

16. R. Caillois, Man and the Sacred, translated by M. Barash (Glencoe, Illinois, 1959), p. 103. For the importance of seasonal festivals in Eliza- bethan literature, see G. L. Barber, Shakespeare's Festive Comedy: A study of dramatic form and its relation to social custom (Princeton, 1959). For his key terms, 'release' and 'clarification,' see Chapter 1, 'The Saturnalian Pattern.'

17. This custom appears to be the chief Midsummer ceremony. See Thomas Naogeorgus (Kirchmaier), 'Popular and Popish Superstitions and Customs on Saints-Days and Holy-Days . . . being the Fourth Booke of The Popish Kingdome . . . englyshed by Barnabe Googe . . . 1570,' in Phillip Stubbes's Anatomy of the Abuses in England, edited by F. J. Furni- vall (London, 1877–82), Part I, p. 339, ll. 769 ff. An unresolved problem is the customary dating of Midsummer on John the Baptist's Day, June 24; however, many ceremonies were associated with more than one day, and according to one tradition Barnabas's had a broad designation: 'The author of the Festa Anglo Romana says, p. 72, "This Barnaby-day, or thereabout, is the summer solstice . . . being the longest day of the year, about the 11th or 12th of June; it is taken for the whole time, when the days appear not for fourteen days together either to lengthen or shorten."' (John Brand, Observations on the Popular Antiquities of Great Britain, enlarged by Sir Henry Ellis, London, 1890, I, 294.) In other words, Spen- ser's day might be one in and for a number of days, like Jove's three nights in one with Alcmena.

Despite its obvious importance, I pass over the possible liturgical organization of the Epithalamion. (e.g., the poem might be seen as the wedding framed by Matins and Vespers—the 'reformed' Hours of the Book of Common Prayer.) See H. C. White, The Tudor Books of Private Devotion (Madison, Wisconsin, 1951).

18. Cf. L. W. Hyman, 'Structure and Meaning in Spenser's Epithalamion,' Tennessee Studies in Literature, 3 (1958), 40, 41.

19. T. H. Croxall, Kierkegaard Commentary (New York, 1956), p. 118. See also Kierkegaard's Either/Or for the aesthetic-ethical distinction mentioned below.

MACCAFFREY, Allegory And Pastoral In The Shepheardes Calender (pp. 549–568).

1. "Introduction," The Poetical Works of Edmund Spenser, ed. J. C. Smith and E. de Selincourt (Oxford Standard Authors, London, 1961), p. xx.

2. C. S. Lewis's useful term for the Renaissance way of reading images, Studies in Medieval and Renaissance Literature (Cambridge, 1966) p. 160.

3. See comments in the Variorum (The Minor Poems, Vol. I, ed. C. G. Osgood and H. G. Lotspeich, Baltimore, 1943) by Herford (p. 581) and Mackail (pp. 584–85); and W. L. Renwick's suggestions on the composition of the poem in his edition, The Shepherd's Calendar (London, 1930), p. 167.

4. Spenser's Shepheardes Calender: A Study in Elizabethan Allegory (Notre Dame, 1961), p. 326.

5. Essays cited are, seriatim: A. C. Hamilton, "The Argument of Spenser's Shepheardes Calender," ELH, XXIII (1956), 171–82; R. A. Durr, "Spenser's Calendar of Christian Time," ELH, XXIV (1957), 269–95; M. C. Bradbrook, "No Room at the Top: Spenser's Pursuit of Fame," Elizabethan Poetry, ed. J. R. Brown and Bernard Harris (London, 1960), pp. 91–109.

6. The generic traditions are outlined by S. K. Heninger, Jr., "The Implications of Form for The Shepheardes Calender," SR, IX (1962), 309–21.

7. The Structure of Allegory in The Faerie Queene (Oxford, 1961), p. 47.

8. Spenser's Shepheardes Calender, p. 322.

9. The text of The Shepheardes Calender quoted in this essay is that of the Oxford one-volume edition, cited in Note 1. Citations will be to line numbers for the poem, page numbers for prose and gloss. References to Pan are in Aprill, p. 434; December, 7; Maye, p. 439.

10. Boccaccio on Poetry, ed. C. G. Osgood (Library of Liberal Arts, New York, 1956), p. 60.

11. Discourse on Pastoral Poetry; Variorum, p. 574.

12. The Shepheardes Calender, pp. 164–65.

13. C. S. Lewis, The Allegory of Love (Oxford, 1948), p. 260. Lewis points out the necessity of an imagined "world" for fully developed allegory.

14. Durr, "Spenser's Calendar of Christian Time," p. 284.

15. Pastoral Poetry and Pastoral Drama (London, 1906), p. 91.

16. See Durr, "Spenser's Calendar," pp. 290–99; and Hamilton's discussion of the theme of "the dedicated life where man does not live according to Nature but seeks escape out of Nature," "The Argument," pp. 175–76.

17. Kathleen Williams, Spenser's World of Glass (Berkeley & Los Angeles, 1966), p. 203. Miss Williams' succinct pages on the Calender in this book outline a view of the poem close to the one I am arguing in many respects.

18. Heninger discusses this aspect of the structure, "a pattern repeated endlessly throughout eternity," in "The Implications of Form," p. 317.

19. For an excellent analysis of these stanzas of Januarye, see Hallett Smith, Elizabethan Poetry (Cambridge, Mass., 1952), p. 35.

20. Pastoral Poetry, p. 93.

21. The quotations are from the texts printed in Frank Kermode, ed., English Pastoral Poetry (London, 1952), pp. 63, 77.

22. "Damon the Mower," ll. 17–24, The Poems of Andrew Marvell, ed. Hugh Macdonald (The Muses' Library, London, 1956), p. 44.

23. D. C. Allen's analysis of this eclogue relates its theme to the rest of the Calender: "The sensitive shepherd has learned a great deal about the nature of love, and what he has learned is both a poetic explanation of the malady of Colin-Spenser and an apologia for his cold Decemberish rejection of love." Image and Meaning: Metaphoric Traditions in Renaissance Poetry (Baltimore, 1960), p. 19.

24. "Spenser's Calendar," p. 290.

25. I prefer these terms, vaguer but more comprehensive, to Durr's exclusively religious vocabulary which reduces too radically, in my opinion, the implications of Spenser's metaphors.

26. E.g., Kathleen Williams: "For us the natural cycle is in itself the way to death, and we will gain life only by looking to the cycle's source." Spenser's World of Glass, p. 203.

27. "Colin's two songs in the Calender, the praise of Elisa and the lament for Dido, come between them the whole situation." Williams, idem.

28. W. F. Staton, Jr., "Spenser's 'April' Lay as a Dramatic Chorus," SP, LIX (1962), 115. Warton was the first to note the similarity between Aprill and the royal entertainments; Variorum, pp. 284–85.

29. The Book of the Courtier, tr. Thomas Hoby (Everyman's Library, London, 1948), p. 273.

30. Elizabethan Poetry, p. 46.

31. "Introduction," p. xx.

CLEMEN, The Uniqueness Of Spenser's Epithalamion (pp. 569–584).

1. For assessments see The Works of Edmund Spenser. A Variorum Edition, The Minor Poems, II (Baltimore, 1947).

2. Cf. René Wellek, Concepts of Criticism (New Haven, 1963).

3. On this aspect, in view of Spenser's achievement, see W. H. Stevenson, "The Spaciousness of Spenser's 'Epithalamion,' " R.E.L., 5 (1964): 61–69.

4. E. G. Daniel's "The Complaint of Rosamond," Ralegh's "Cynthia," Barnfield's "The Affectionate Shepheard."

5. Reprinted in Robert H. Case, English Epithalamies (London, 1896).

6. William Nelson, The Poetry of Edmund Spenser (New York, 1963), p. 95.

7. A. Kent Hieatt, Short Time's Endless Monument. The Symbolism of the Numbers in Edmund Spenser's Epithalamion (New York, 1960).

8. The text used is that of the Variorum Edition of The Works of Edmund Spenser (Baltimore, 1947). The letters u-v, and i-j have, however, been modernized.

9. Thomas M. Greene, "Spenser and the Epithalamic Convention," Comparative Literature, 9 (1957): 215–28. Hallett Smith, "The Use of Conventions in Spenser's Minor Poems," Form and Convention in the Poetry of Edmund Spenser, English Institute Essays (New York, 1961), pp. 122–45.

10. Thus in the fourth stanza Spenser evokes the scenery round his castle in referring to the "silver scaly trouts" on which Renwick (in his edition of the Epithalamion) remarks: "There are good trout in Awbeg still." (Daphnaïda and other Poems, ed. by W. L. Renwick [London, 1929], p. 205.)

11. Some of the stanzas actually begin with this request as, e.g.,

VIII (129) Harke how the Minstrels gin to shrill aloud
X   (167) Tell me ye merchants daughters did ye see
XIII (223) Behold whiles she before the altar stands.

12. E.g.

That even th'Angels which continually,
About the sacred Altare doe remaine,
Forget their service and about her fly,
Ofte peeping in her face that seemes more fayre,
The more they on it stare (229–33).

13. See the commentary by Cortlandt van Winkle (New York, 1926).

14. Douglas Bush, Mythology and the Renaissance Tradition in English Poetry (New York, 1957).

15. See note 2 above.

16. This aspect has been particularly stressed by Lawrence W. Hyman, "Structure and Meaning in Spenser's Epithalamion," Tennessee Studies in Literature, 3 (1958): 37–42.

17. R. Ellrodt, Neoplatonism in the Poetry of Spenser (Geneva, 1960).

18. Cf. W. L. Renwick in his comments on the poem (Daphnaïda and other Poems [London, 1929]).

19. C. S. Lewis, English Literature in the Sixteenth Century (Oxford, 1954), p. 373.

20. For this lecture I have used some of the material contained in my German study of Spenser's poem: Spensers Epithalamion. Zum Problem der künstlerischen Wertmaßstäbe. Sitzungsberichte der Bayerischen Akademie der Wissenschaften, Philosophisch-Historische Klasse (München, 1964, Heft 8).

NOTE: The author is under obligation for help and advice to W. L. Renwick, Robert Birley, Hans-Jürgen Diller, and Wolfgang Weiss.